Lecture Notes in Computer Science 12546

Formal Methods

Subline of Lectures Notes in Computer Science

More information about this series at http://www.springer.com/series/7408

Brijesh Dongol · Elena Troubitsyna (Eds.)

Integrated Formal Methods

16th International Conference, IFM 2020
Lugano, Switzerland, November 16–20, 2020
Proceedings

 Springer

Editors
Brijesh Dongol 🆔
University of Surrey
Guildford, UK

Elena Troubitsyna
Royal Institute of Technology - KTH
Stockholm, Sweden

ISSN 0302-9743   ISSN 1611-3349   (electronic)
Lecture Notes in Computer Science
ISBN 978-3-030-63460-5   ISBN 978-3-030-63461-2   (eBook)
https://doi.org/10.1007/978-3-030-63461-2

LNCS Sublibrary: SL2 – Programming and Software Engineering

This Springer imprint is published by the registered company Springer Nature Switzerland AG
The registered company address is: Gewerbestrasse 11, 6330 Cham, Switzerland

Preface

In recent years, we have witnessed a proliferation of approaches that integrate several modeling, verification, and simulation techniques, facilitating more versatile and efficient analysis of computation-intensive systems. These approaches provide powerful support for the analysis of different functional and non-functional properties of the systems, different hardware and software components, and their interaction, as well as design and validation of diverse aspects of system behavior.

This volume contains the papers presented at the 16th International Conference on integrated Formal Methods (iFM 2020), which has taken place virtually due to the COVID-19 pandemic. The iFM conference series is a forum for discussing recent research advances in the development of integrated approaches to formal modeling and analysis. The conference covers all aspects of the design of integrated techniques, including language design, system verification and validation, automated tool support, and the use of such techniques in practice. We are also seeing increasing interest in the integration of fields such as machine learning and program synthesis with traditional formal approaches.

iFM 2020 solicited high-quality papers reporting novel research results as well as tool papers and experience reports. The Program Committee (PC) received 63 submissions and selected 24 for the publication, of which 2 are short papers. The acceptance rate is 38% (which also includes short papers). Each paper received three reviews. The PC members thoroughly discussed the merits of each paper before making the final decisions.

The program of iFM 2020 also includes keynote talks given by three prominent researchers:

- Edward A. Lee from the University of California, Berkeley, USA
- David Parker from the University of Birmingham, UK
- Hongseok Yang from the School of Computing, KAIST, South Korea

We would like to thank the invited speakers for accepting our invitation and agreeing to share their research results and aspirations with the iFM 2020 audience.

The PC co-chairs would like to thank the PC members for their active work in advertising iFM 2020, contributing to the program and reviewing submissions. We also thank all our subreviewers for providing expert guidance and contributing to the PC discussions. Despite the pandemic, the PC members and subreviewers stayed active throughout the entire review and discussion processes. We are especially grateful to the general chair Carlo A. Furia from Università della Svizzera italiana, Switzerland, for organizing the conference, and Springer for sponsoring iFM 2020. Finally, we would like to thank all the authors, who despite hard pandemic times, prepared submissions and helped us to build a strong and interesting iFM 2020 program.

We hope you enjoyed the conference!

November 2020

Brijesh Dongol
Elena Troubitsyna

Organization

Program Committee

Erika Abraham	RWTH Aachen University, Germany
Wolfgang Ahrendt	Chalmers University of Technology, Sweden
Yamine Ait Ameur	IRIT, INPT-ENSEEIHT, France
Étienne André	Université de Lorraine, CNRS, Inria, LORIA, France
Richard Banach	The University of Manchester, UK
Pierre-Evariste Dagand	LIP6, CNRS, France
Ferruccio Damiani	Universitá degli Studi di Torino, Italy
John Derrick	The University of Sheffield, UK
Brijesh Dongol	University of Surrey, UK
Marc Frappier	Université de Sherbrooke, Canada
Carlo A. Furia	Università della Svizzera italiana, Switzerland
Marieke Huisman	University of Twente, The Netherlands
Fuyuki Ishikawa	National Institute of Informatics, Japan
Einar Broch Johnsen	University of Oslo, Norway
Stephan Merz	Inria, France
Paritosh Pandya	TIFR, India
Patrizio Pelliccione	Chalmers University of Technology, Sweden
Luigia Petre	Åbo Akademi University, Finland
R. Ramanujam	Institute of Mathematical Sciences, Chennai, India
Steve Schneider	University of Surrey, UK
Emil Sekerinski	McMaster University, Canada
Silvia Lizeth Tapia Tarifa	University of Oslo, Norway
Maurice H. ter Beek	ISTI-CNR, Italy
Stefano Tonetta	FBK-irst, Italy
Elena Troubitsyna	KTH, Sweden
Juri Vain	Tallinn University of Technology, Estonia
Tomáš Vojnar	Brno University of Technology, Czech Republic
Farn Wang	National Taiwan University, Taiwan
Heike Wehrheim	Paderborn University, Germany
Kirsten Winter	The University of Queensland, Australia
Naijun Zhan	Institute of Software, Chinese Academy of Sciences, China

Additional Reviewers

An, Jie
Armborst, Lukas
Audrito, Giorgio
Bai, Yunjun
Baldan, Paolo
Bettini, Lorenzo
Bubel, Richard
Bussi, Laura
Casadei, Roberto
Coughlin, Nicholas
D'Souza, Deepak
Din, Crystal Chang
Fava, Daniel
Fiedor, Jan
Guha, Shibashis
Haltermann, Jan
Havlena, Vojtěch
Kamburjan, Eduard
Keiren, Jeroen J. A.
Kirsten, Michael
Kobayashi, Tsutomu
Konnov, Igor
König, Jürgen
Lengal, Ondrej
Lin, Shang-Wei

Lööw, Andreas
Maarand, Hendrik
Monti, Raúl E.
Owe, Olaf
Pauck, Felix
Petrocchi, Marinella
Pianini, Danilo
Pun, Violet Ka I.
Richter, Cedric
Saivasan, Prakash
Schiffl, Jonas
Schlatte, Rudolf
Sharma, Arnab
Srivathsan, B.
Steffen, Martin
Stolz, Volker
Sundararajan, Vaishnavi
Suresh, S. P.
Torta, Gianluca
Turin, Gianluca
Tveito, Lars
Wang, Qiuye
Yan, Rongjie
Zhan, Bohua
Zuleger, Florian

Contents

Algebraic Techniques

Integrating Machine Learning and Formal Modelling

Formal Policy Synthesis for Continuous-State Systems via Reinforcement Learning

Milad Kazemi[✉] and Sadegh Soudjani[✉]

School of Computing, Newcastle University, Newcastle upon Tyne, UK
{M.Kazemi2,Sadegh.Soudjani}@newcastle.ac.uk

Abstract. This paper studies satisfaction of temporal properties on unknown stochastic processes that have continuous state spaces. We show how reinforcement learning (RL) can be applied for computing policies that are finite-memory and deterministic using only the paths of the stochastic process. We address properties expressed in linear temporal logic (LTL) and use their automaton representation to give a path-dependent reward function maximised via the RL algorithm. We develop the required assumptions and theories for the convergence of the learned policy to the optimal policy in the continuous state space. To improve the performance of the learning on the constructed sparse reward function, we propose a sequential learning procedure based on a sequence of labelling functions obtained from the positive normal form of the LTL specification. We use this procedure to guide the RL algorithm towards a policy that converges to an optimal policy under suitable assumptions on the process. We demonstrate the approach on a 4-dim cart-pole system and 6-dim boat driving problem.

Keywords: Continuous-state stochastic systems · Linear temporal logic · Model-free policy synthesis · Reinforcement learning

1 Introduction

Motivations. Omega-regular languages provide a rich formalism to unambiguously express desired properties of the system. Linear temporal logic (LTL), as a class of omega-regular languages, is widely used for task specification such as safety, liveness, and repeated reachability. Synthesising policies formally for a system to satisfy a specification requires the knowledge of a model of the system. Extensive techniques are developed in the literature for different classes of models including finite-space models [1] and continuous-state or hybrid models [10, 21, 24, 25]. Reinforcement learning (RL) is a promising paradigm for sequential decision making when a model of the system is not available or is very hard to construct and analyse. The objective of an RL algorithm is to find suitable action policies in order to maximise the collected rewards that depend on the

© Springer Nature Switzerland AG 2020
B. Dongol and E. Troubitsyna (Eds.): IFM 2020, LNCS 12546, pp. 3–21, 2020.
https://doi.org/10.1007/978-3-030-63461-2_1

states and actions taken at those states. The RL algorithms are in particular useful when the total collected reward has an additive structure.

Many objectives including satisfaction of omega-regular properties on stochastic systems do not admit an equivalent additive reward structure. A natural approach used in the literature (e.g., [22]), is to use heuristics for assigning additive rewards and then apply RL algorithms to obtain a policy. Unfortunately, there is no unique procedure for constructing these rewards and the learning does not necessarily converge to the optimal policy. Due to all of these limitations, there is a need to provide data-driven algorithms that do not require any heuristics and have suitable convergence guarantees to policies that are optimal for satisfaction of temporal properties.

Related Works. In the last few years, researchers have started developing RL-based policy synthesis techniques in order to satisfy temporal properties. There is a large body of literature in safe reinforcement learning (see e.g. [9,28]). The problem of learning a policy to maximise the satisfaction probability of a temporal property was first introduced in 2014 [4,8,29]. The work [4] provides a heuristic-driven partial exploration of the model to find bounds for reachability probability. The work [8] uses model-based RL in order to maximise the satisfaction probability of the property expressed as deterministic Rabin automaton (DRA). Given a Markov decision process (MDP) with unknown transition probabilities as the model of the system, the algorithms build a probably approximately correct MDP, which is then composed with the DRA for policy synthesis. The work [29] is limited to policies that generate traces satisfying the specification with probability one. The provided algorithm needs to compute all the transitions probabilities which in result requires a large memory usage. This issue is partially addressed in [32] by introducing an actor-critic algorithm that obtains transition probabilities only when needed in an approximate dynamic programming framework.

Satisfaction of LTL formulas can be checked on a class of automata called *Limit-Deterministic Büchi Automata* (LDBA) [5,11,30]. An implementation of a wide range of algorithms for translating LTL specifications to various types of automata is also available [20]. The equivalent LDBA of [30] is used in [13,15] to constrain the learning algorithm and is applied to an unknown finite MDP. The work [12] provides an RL-based policy synthesis for finite MDPs with unknown transition probabilities. It transforms the specification to an LDBA using [11], and then constructs a parameterised augmented MDP. It shows that the optimal policy obtained by RL for the reachability probability on the augmented MDP gives a policy for the MDP with a suitable convergence guarantee. In [3], the authors utilise the LDBA representation, provide a path-dependent discounting mechanism for the RL algorithm, and prove convergence of their approach on finite MDPs when the discounting factor goes to one.

The literature on learning algorithms for formal synthesis on *continuous-state* models is very limited. To the best of our knowledge, the only works developed for continuous-state stochastic models are [14,16,21]. The work [21] provides formal error bounds by discretising the space of the model, thus is only applicable to *finite-horizon* properties. The works [14,16] use respectively neural fitted Q-iteration and deep deterministic policy gradient(DDPG) approach without providing a proper formal convergence guarantee. Our approach extends [21] to all LTL properties instead of finite-horizon properties and does not require any discretisation or knowledge of the continuity properties of the system. Our approach is closely related to [12] that discusses only *finite-state* MDPs. We utilise the same technique and provide an example that shows the convergence guarantees of [12] do not hold for all continuous-state MDPs but require an additional assumption on the model. Our proofs are for general state spaces and do not rely on the properties of the bottom strongly-connected components of the MDP, thus simplify the ones in [12]. Due to the space restrictions, these proofs are included in the extended version [19].

Main Contributions. We apply RL algorithms to *continuous-state* stochastic systems using only paths of the system to find optimal policies satisfying an LTL specification. We show that if a suitable assumption on the system holds, the formulated optimal average reward converges linearly to the true optimal satisfaction probability. We use negation of the specification and learn a lower bound on this satisfaction probability. To improve the performance of the learning on the constructed sparse reward function, we show how to construct a sequence of labelling functions based on the positive normal form of the LTL specification and use them for guiding the RL algorithm in learning the policy and its associated value function. This sequential learning is able to find policies for our case studies in less than 1.5 h but direct learning does not converge in 24 h.

Organisation. Section 2 recalls definition of controlled Markov processes (CMPs) as the unknown model. We also give linear temporal logic, limit-deterministic automata, and the problem statement in the same section. Section 3 gives construction of the augmented CMP and the product CMP. It establishes the relation between the reachability on the augmented CMP and the LTL satisfaction on the original CMP. Section 4 gives the reward function for reachability on the augmented CMP that can be used by RL algorithms. It also gives a procedure for guiding the learning task via a sequence of labelling functions. Finally, Sect. 5 illustrates our approach on two case studies, a 4-dim cart-pole system and 6-dim boat driving problem.

2   Preliminaries and Problem Statement

We consider a probability space $(\Omega, \mathcal{F}_\Omega, P_\Omega)$, where Ω is the sample space, $\mathcal{F}_\Omega$ is a sigma-algebra on Ω comprising subsets of Ω as events, and P_Ω is a probability measure that assigns probabilities to events. We assume that random variables introduced in this article are measurable functions of the form $X : (\Omega, \mathcal{F}_\Omega) \to (S_X, \mathcal{F}_X)$ from the measurable space $(\Omega, \mathcal{F}_\Omega)$ to a measurable space $(S_X, \mathcal{F}_X)$. Any random variable X induces a probability measure on its space $(S_X, \mathcal{F}_X)$ as $Prob\{A\} = P_\Omega\{X^{-1}(A)\}$ for any $A \in \mathcal{F}_X$. We often directly discuss the probability measure on $(S_X, \mathcal{F}_X)$ without explicitly mentioning the underlying sample space and the function X itself.

A topological space S is called a Borel space if it is homeomorphic to a Borel subset of a Polish space (i.e., a separable and completely metrisable space). Examples of a Borel space are the Euclidean spaces $\mathbb{R}^n$, its Borel subsets endowed with a subspace topology, as well as hybrid spaces of the form $Q \times \mathbb{R}^n$ with Q being a finite set. Any Borel space S is assumed to be endowed with a Borel sigma-algebra, which is denoted by $\mathcal{B}(S)$. We say that a map $f : S \to Y$ is measurable whenever it is Borel measurable. We denote the set of non-negative integers by $\mathbb{N} := \{0, 1, 2, \ldots\}$ and the empty set by $\emptyset$.

2.1   Controlled Markov Processes

Controlled Markov processes (CMPs) are a natural choice for physical systems that have three main features: an uncountable state space that can be continuous or hybrid, control inputs to be designed, and inputs in the form of disturbance which have certain probabilistic behaviour [6].

We consider CMPs in discrete time defined over a general state space, characterised by the tuple $\mathfrak{S} = (\mathcal{S}, \mathcal{U}, \{\mathcal{U}(s)|s \in \mathcal{S}\}, T_{\mathfrak{s}})$, where $\mathcal{S}$ is a Borel space as the state space of the CMP. We denote by $(\mathcal{S}, \mathcal{B}(\mathcal{S}))$ the measurable space with $\mathcal{B}(\mathcal{S})$ being the Borel sigma-algebra on the state space. $\mathcal{U}$ is a Borel space as the input space of the CMP. The set $\{\mathcal{U}(s)|s \in \mathcal{S}\}$ is a family of non-empty measurable subsets of $\mathcal{U}$ with the property that $\mathcal{K} := \{(s, u) : s \in \mathcal{S}, u \in \mathcal{U}(s)\}$ is measurable in $\mathcal{S} \times \mathcal{U}$. Intuitively, $\mathcal{U}(s)$ is the set of inputs that are feasible at state $s \in \mathcal{S}$. $T_{\mathfrak{s}} : \mathcal{B}(\mathcal{S}) \times \mathcal{S} \times \mathcal{U} \to [0, 1]$, is a conditional stochastic kernel that assigns to any $s \in \mathcal{S}$ and $u \in \mathcal{U}(s)$ a probability measure $T_{\mathfrak{s}}(\cdot|s, u)$ on the measurable space $(\mathcal{S}, \mathcal{B}(\mathcal{S}))$ so that for any set $A \in \mathcal{B}(\mathcal{S}), P_{s,u}(A) = \int_A T_s(ds|s, u)$, where $P_{s,u}$ denotes the conditional probability $P(\cdot|s, u)$.

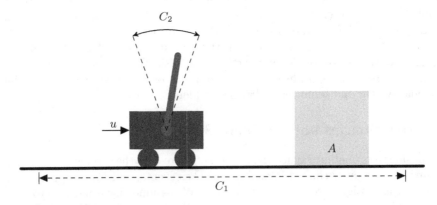

Fig. 1. Cart-pole system with a 4-dim state space. It should stay within the limits specified by C_1, always keep the pole upright in the range C_2, and reach the region A.

Example 1. Consider the cart-pole in Fig. 1. The cart moves along a line in either direction. The states are position s^1, velocity s^2, pole's angle s^3, and the angular velocity s^4. The input u_n is the force applied to the cart at time step n. Its dynamics in discrete time are according to the following 4-dim difference equation:

$$
\begin{cases}
s^1_{n+1} = s^1_n + \Delta s^2_n \\
s^2_{n+1} = s^2_n + \Delta a_3 \\
s^3_{n+1} = s^3_n + \Delta s^2_n \\
s^4_{n+1} = s^4_n + \Delta a_2 + \eta_n,
\end{cases}
\text{with}
\begin{cases}
a_3 := a_1 - \dfrac{l a_2 \cos(s^3_n)}{(M+m)} \\
a_2 := \dfrac{g \sin(s^3_n) - \cos(s^3_n) a_1}{l(\frac{4}{3} - m(\cos(s^3_n))^2/(M+m))} \\
a_1 := \dfrac{u_n + l(s^4_n)^2 \sin(s^3_n)}{M+m}.
\end{cases}
\tag{1}
$$

Δ is the sampling time, M is the mass of the cart, m is the mass of the pole, l is the half length of the pole, and η_n models the disturbance. The cart has discrete input and can be either pushed to the left or right with a fixed value, $\mathcal{U} = \{-F_{max}, F_{max}\}$. This input u_n appears in a_1 that affects both a_2 and a_3. Assuming that the disturbances are all independent with normal distribution $\mathcal{N}(\cdot\,; 0, \sigma^2)$, this system is a CMP with $\mathcal{S} = \mathbb{R}^4$, $\mathcal{U}(s) = \mathcal{U}$ for all $s \in \mathcal{S}$, and kernel

$$
T_s(d\bar{s} \mid s, u) = \mathcal{N}(d\bar{s}^4\,;\, s^4_n + \Delta a_2,\, \sigma^2)\delta(d\bar{s}^1\,;\, s^1_n + \Delta s^2_n)
$$
$$
\times \delta(d\bar{s}^2\,;\, s^2_n + \Delta a_3)\delta(d\bar{s}^3\,;\, s^3_n + \Delta s^2_n),
$$

where $\delta(\cdot\,; a)$ is the Dirac delta measure centred at a and $\mathcal{N}(\cdot\,; m, \sigma^2)$ is the normal probability measure with mean m and variance σ^2.

2.2   Semantics of Controlled Markov Processes

The semantics of a CMP is characterised by its *paths* or executions, which reflect both the history of previous states of the system and of implemented control inputs. Paths are used to measure the performance of the system.

Definition 1. *A finite path of* $\mathfrak{G}$ *is a sequence* $w_n = (s_0, u_0, \ldots, s_{n-1}, u_{n-1}, s_n)$, $n \in \mathbb{N}$, *where* $s_i \in \mathcal{S}$ *are state coordinates and* $u_i \in \mathcal{U}(s_i)$ *are control input coordinates of the path. The space of all paths of length n is denoted by* $\mathsf{PATH}_n :=$ $\mathcal{K}^n \times \mathcal{S}$. *Further, we denote projections by* $w_n[i] := s_i$ *and* $w_n(i) := u_i$. *An infinite path of the CMP* $\mathfrak{G}$ *is the sequence* $w = (s_0, u_0, s_1, u_1, \ldots)$, *where* $s_i \in \mathcal{S}$ *and* $u_i \in \mathcal{U}(s_i)$ *for all* $i \in \mathbb{N}$. *As above, let us introduce* $w[i] := s_i$ *and* $w(i) := u_i$. *The space of all infinite paths is denoted by* $\mathsf{PATH}_\infty := \mathcal{K}^\infty$.

Given an infinite path w or a finite path w_n, we assume below that s_i and u_i are their state and control coordinates respectively, unless otherwise stated. For any infinite path $w \in \mathsf{PATH}_\infty$, its n-prefix (ending in a state) w_n is a finite path of length n, which we also call n-*history*. We are now ready to introduce the notion of control policy.

Definition 2. *A policy is a sequence* $\rho = (\rho_0, \rho_1, \rho_2, \ldots)$ *of universally measurable stochastic kernels* ρ_n *[2], each defined on the input space* $\mathcal{U}$ *given* PATH_n *and such that for all* $w_n \in \mathsf{PATH}_n$ *with* $n \in \mathbb{N}$, $\rho_n(\mathcal{U}(s_n)|w_n) = 1$. *The set of all policies is denoted by* Π.

Given a policy $\rho \in \Pi$ and a finite path $w_n \in \mathsf{PATH}_n$, the distribution of the next control input u_n is given by $\rho_n(\cdot|w_n)$ and is supported on $\mathcal{U}(s_n)$ (i.e., the chance of selecting an invalid input at s_n is zero). For a CMP $\mathfrak{S}$, any policy $\rho \in \Pi$ together with an initial probability measure $\alpha : \mathcal{B}(\mathcal{S}) \to [0,1]$ of the CMP induce a unique probability measure on the canonical sample space of paths [17] denoted by P_α^ρ with the expectation $\mathbb{E}_\alpha^\rho$. When the initial probability measure is supported on a single point, i.e., $\alpha(s) = 1$, we write P_s^ρ and $\mathbb{E}_s^\rho$ in place of P_α^ρ and $\mathbb{E}_\alpha^\rho$, respectively. We denote the set of probability measures on $(\mathcal{S}, \mathcal{B}(\mathcal{S}))$ by $\mathfrak{D}$. Implementation of a general policy requires an infinite memory. In this work, we restrict our attention to the class of policies that depend on the paths via a *finite memory*.

Definition 3. *A finite-memory policy for* $\mathfrak{S}$ *is a tuple* $\rho_f := (\hat{\mathcal{S}}, \hat{s}_0, T_\mathfrak{p}, T_\mathfrak{o})$, *where* $\hat{\mathcal{S}}$ *is the state space of the policy,* $\hat{s}_0 \in \hat{\mathcal{S}}$ *is the initial state,* $T_\mathfrak{p} : \hat{\mathcal{S}} \times \mathcal{S} \times \mathcal{B}(\hat{\mathcal{S}}) \to [0,1]$ *is the stochastic kernel for updating the state of the policy, and* $T_\mathfrak{o} : \hat{\mathcal{S}} \times \mathcal{S} \times \mathcal{B}(\mathcal{U}) \to [0,1]$ *is the output kernel such that* $T_\mathfrak{o}(\mathcal{U}(s) \,|\, \hat{s}, s) = 1$ *for all* $\hat{s} \in \hat{\mathcal{S}}$ *and* $s \in \mathcal{S}$. *We denote the set of such policies by* $\Pi_f \subset \Pi$.

Note that the state space $\hat{\mathcal{S}}$ could in general be any continuous or hybrid space. The policy has access to the current state s_n of $\mathfrak{S}$ and updates its own state $\hat{s}_n$ according to $\hat{s}_{n+1} \sim T_\mathfrak{p}(\cdot \,|\, \hat{s}_n, s_n)$. As we will see later in Lemma 1, a finite $\hat{\mathcal{S}}$ is sufficient for optimal satisfaction of LTL specifications.

There is a special class of policies called *positional* that do not need a memory state as defined next.

Definition 4. *A policy* ρ *is* positional *if there is a stochastic kernel* $C : \mathcal{S} \times \mathcal{B}(\mathcal{U}) \to [0,1]$ *such that at any time* $n \in \mathbb{N}$, *the input* u_n *is taken from the probability measure* $C(\cdot|s_n)$. *Namely, the output kernel* $T_\mathfrak{o}(\cdot|\hat{s}, s)$ *in Definition 3 is independent of* $\hat{s}$. *We denote the class of positional policies by* $\Pi_p \subset \Pi_f$ *and a positional policy just by the kernel* $C \in \Pi_p$.

Designing optimal finite-memory policies to satisfy a specification on $\mathfrak{S}$ can be reduced to finding an optimal positional policy for satisfying a specification on an extended model $\mathfrak{S}'$. This is formally proved in Sect. 3. Next we define the class of specifications used in this paper.

2.3 Linear Temporal Logic

Linear temporal logic (LTL) provides a high-level language for describing the desired behaviour of a process. Formulas in this logic are constructed inductively by using a set of atomic propositions and combining them via Boolean operators. Consider a finite set of atomic propositions AP that defines the alphabet

$\Sigma := 2^{\mathsf{AP}}$. Thus, each letter of this alphabet evaluates a subset of the atomic propositions as true. Composed as an infinite string, these letters form infinite words defined as $\boldsymbol{\omega} = \omega_0, \omega_1, \omega_2, \ldots \in \Sigma^{\mathbb{N}}$. These words are connected to paths of CMP $\mathfrak{S}$ via a measurable labelling function $\mathsf{L} : \mathcal{S} \to \Sigma$ that assigns letters $\alpha = \mathsf{L}(s)$ to state $s \in \mathcal{S}$. That is, infinite paths $w = (s_0, u_0, s_1, u_1, \ldots)$ are mapped to the set of infinite words $\Sigma^{\mathbb{N}}$, as $\boldsymbol{\omega} = \mathsf{L}(w) := (\mathsf{L}(s_0), \mathsf{L}(s_1), \mathsf{L}(s_2), \ldots)$.

Definition 5. *An LTL formula over a set of atomic propositions* AP *is constructed inductively as*

$$\psi ::= \textit{true} \,|\, \textit{false} \,|\, p \,|\, \neg p \,|\, \psi_1 \wedge \psi_2 \,|\, \psi_1 \vee \psi_2 \,|\, \bigcirc \psi \,|\, \psi_1 \,\mathsf{U}\, \psi_2 \,|\, \psi_1 \,\mathsf{R}\, \psi_2, \quad p \in \mathsf{AP}, \quad (2)$$

with ψ_1, ψ_2, ψ *being LTL formulas.*

Let $\boldsymbol{\omega}_n = (\omega_n, \omega_{n+1}, \omega_{n+2}, \ldots)$ be a postfix of $\boldsymbol{\omega}$. The satisfaction relation is denoted by $\boldsymbol{\omega} \vDash \psi$ (or equivalently $\boldsymbol{\omega}_0 \vDash \psi$) and is defined recursively as follows

- $\boldsymbol{\omega}_n \vDash \textit{true}$ always hold and $\boldsymbol{\omega}_n \vDash \textit{false}$ does not hold.
- An atomic proposition, $\boldsymbol{\omega}_n \vDash p$ for $p \in \mathsf{AP}$ holds if $p \in \omega_n$.
- A negation, $\boldsymbol{\omega}_n \vDash \neg p$, holds if $\boldsymbol{\omega}_n \nvDash p$.
- A logical conjunction, $\boldsymbol{\omega}_n \vDash \psi_1 \wedge \psi_2$, holds if $\boldsymbol{\omega}_n \vDash \psi_1$ and $\boldsymbol{\omega}_n \vDash \psi_2$.
- A logical disjunction, $\boldsymbol{\omega}_n \vDash \psi_1 \vee \psi_2$, holds if $\boldsymbol{\omega}_n \vDash \psi_1$ or $\boldsymbol{\omega}_n \vDash \psi_2$.
- A temporal next operator, $\boldsymbol{\omega}_n \vDash \bigcirc \psi$, holds if $\boldsymbol{\omega}_{n+1} \vDash \psi$.
- A temporal until operator, $\boldsymbol{\omega}_n \vDash \psi_1 \,\mathsf{U}\, \psi_2$, holds if there exists an $i \in \mathbb{N}$ such that $\boldsymbol{\omega}_{n+i} \vDash \psi_2$, and for all $j \in \mathbb{N}$, $0 \le j < i$, we have $\boldsymbol{\omega}_{n+j} \vDash \psi_1$.
- A temporal release operator is dual of the until operator and is defied as $\boldsymbol{\omega}_n \vDash \psi_1 \,\mathsf{R}\, \psi_2$ if $\boldsymbol{\omega}_n \nvDash \neg \psi_1 \,\mathsf{U}\, \neg \psi_2$.

In addition to the aforementioned operators, we can also use *eventually* $\Diamond$, and *always* $\square$ operators as $\Diamond \psi := (\textsf{true} \,\mathsf{U}\, \psi)$ and $\square \psi := \textsf{false} \,\mathsf{R}\, \psi$.

Remark 1. The above definition is the canonical form of LTL and is called *positive normal form* (PNF), in which negations only occur adjacent to atomic propositions. If this is not the case, it is possible to construct an equivalent formula [1, Theorem 5.24] in the canonical form in polynomial time as a function of the length of the formula. We utilise the canonical form in Sect. 4.1 to construct a sequence of learning procedures that guides the optimal policy learning problem.

Example 1 (Continued). The cart in Fig. 1 should stay within the limits specified by C_1, always keep the pole upright in the range C_2, and reach the region A. We can express this requirement as the LTL specification

$$\psi = \Diamond a \wedge \square(c_1 \wedge c_2) \quad (3)$$

with $\mathsf{AP} = \{a, c_1, c_2\}$ and the labelling function L with $a \in \mathsf{L}(s)$ if the cart is inside A, $c_1 \in \mathsf{L}(s)$ if the cart is inside C_1, and $c_2 \in \mathsf{L}(s)$ if the pole angle is inside the specified range of C_2.

2.4 Problem Statement

We are interested in the probability that an LTL specification ψ can be satisfied by paths of a CMP $\mathfrak{S}$ under different policies. Suppose a CMP $\mathfrak{S} = (\mathcal{S}, \mathcal{U}, \{\mathcal{U}(s) | s \in \mathcal{S}\}, T_s)$, an LTL specification ψ over the alphabet Σ, and a labelling function $\mathsf{L} : \mathcal{S} \to \Sigma$ are given. An infinite path $w = (s_0, u_0, s_1, u_1, \ldots)$ of $\mathfrak{S}$ satisfies ψ if the infinite word $\omega = \mathsf{L}(w) \in \Sigma^{\mathbb{N}}$ satisfies ψ. We denote such an event by $\mathfrak{S} \models \psi$ and will study the probability of the event.

Remark 2. In general, one should use the notation $\mathfrak{S} \models_{\mathsf{L}} \psi$ to emphasise the role of labelling function L in the satisfaction of ψ by paths of $\mathfrak{S}$. We eliminate the subscript L with the understanding that it is clear from the context. We add the labelling function in Sect. 4.1 when discussing multiple labelling functions for evaluation of $\mathfrak{S} \models \psi$.

Given a policy $\rho \in \varPi_f$ and initial state $s \in \mathcal{S}$, we define the satisfaction probability as $f(s, \rho) := P_s^\rho(\mathfrak{S} \models \psi)$, and the supremum satisfaction probability $f^*(s) := \sup_{\rho \in \varPi_f} P_s^\rho(\mathfrak{S} \models \psi)$.

Problem 1 (Synthesis for LTL). Given CMP $\mathfrak{S}$, LTL specification ψ, and labelling function L, find an optimal policy $\rho^* \in \varPi_f$ along with $f^*(s)$ s.t. $P_s^{\rho^*}(\mathfrak{S} \models \psi) = f^*(s)$.

Measurability of the set $\{\mathfrak{S} \models \psi\}$ in the canonical sample space of paths under the probability measure P_s^ρ is proved in [31]. The function $f^*(s)$ is studied in [31] with an approximation procedure presented in [24]. These works are for fully known $\mathfrak{S}$ and only for *Büchi conditions* where the system should visit a set $B \subset \mathcal{S}$ infinitely often. This condition is denoted by $\psi = \square\lozenge B$.

Problem 2 (Synthesis for Büchi Conditions). Given $\mathfrak{S}$, a set of accepting states $B \in \mathcal{B}(\mathcal{S})$, find an optimal positional policy $\rho^* \in \varPi_p$ along with $f^*(s)$ s.t. $P_s^{\rho^*}(\mathfrak{S} \models \square\lozenge B) = f^*(s)$.

Remark 3 We have restricted our attention to finite-memory policies in Problem 1. This is due to the fact that proving existence of an optimal policy $\rho^* \in \varPi$ is an open problem. We note that existence of ϵ-optimal policies is already proved [7,23]. We prove in Sect. 3 that Problems 1 and 2 are closely related: in order to find a solution for Problem 1, we can find a solution for Problems 2 on another CMP with an extended state space.

2.5 Limit-Deterministic Büchi Automata

Satisfaction of LTL formulas can be checked on a class of automata called *Limit-Deterministic Büchi Automata* (LDBA) [5,11,12,30]. Similar to [12], we use the translation of the specification to an LDBA that has one set of accepting transitions and is presented next. This translation is provided by [11]. An implementation of a wide range of algorithms for translating LTL to various types of automata is also available [20].

Definition 6 (LDBA). *An LDBA is a tuple $\mathcal{A} = (Q, \Sigma, \delta, q_0, \mathsf{Acc})$, where Q is a finite set of states, Σ is a finite alphabet, $\delta : Q \times (\Sigma \cup \{\epsilon\}) \to 2^Q$ is a partial transition function, $q_0 \in Q$ is an initial state, and $\mathsf{Acc} \subset Q \times \Sigma \times Q$ is a set of accepting transitions. The transition function δ is such that it is total for all $(q, \omega) \in Q \times \Sigma$, i.e., $|\delta(q, \omega)| \leq 1$ for all $\omega \neq \epsilon$ and $q \in Q$. Moreover, there is a partition $\{Q_N, Q_D\}$ for Q such that*

- *$\delta(q, \epsilon) = \emptyset$ for all $q \in Q_D$, i.e., the ϵ-transitions can only occur in Q_N.*
- *$\delta(q, \omega) \subset Q_D$ for all $q \in Q_D$ and $\omega \in \Sigma$, i.e., the transitions starting in Q_D remain in Q_D.*
- *$\mathsf{Acc} \subset Q_D \times \Sigma \times Q_D$, the accepting transitions start only in Q_D.*

We can associate to an infinite word $\boldsymbol{\omega} = (\omega_0, \omega_1, \omega_2, \ldots) \in (\Sigma \cup \{\epsilon\})^{\mathbb{N}}$, a path $r = (q_0, \omega_0, q_1, \omega_1, q_2, \ldots)$ to $\mathcal{A}$ such that q_0 is the initial state of $\mathcal{A}$ and $q_{n+1} \in \delta(q_n, \omega_n)$ for all $n \in \mathbb{N}$. Such a path always exists when $\boldsymbol{\omega} \in \Sigma^{\mathbb{N}}$. Let us denote by $inf(r)$ as the set of transitions (q, ω, q') appearing in r infinitely often. We say the word $\boldsymbol{\omega}$ is accepted by $\mathcal{A}$ if it has a path r with $inf(r) \cap \mathsf{Acc} \neq \emptyset$. The *accepting language* of $\mathcal{A}$ is the set of words accepted by $\mathcal{A}$ and is denoted by $\mathcal{L}(\mathcal{A})$.

3   Augmented CMP with Reachability Specification

In this section we discuss approximating solutions of Problems 1 and 2 using reachability specifications. This section contains one of the main contributions of the paper that is formulating Assumption 1 and proving Theorems 1-3 and Lemma 1 for continuous-state CMPs.

3.1   The Augmented CMP

Given $\mathfrak{S} = (\mathcal{S}, \mathcal{U}, \{\mathcal{U}(s) | s \in \mathcal{S}\}, T_{\mathfrak{s}})$ and a set of accepting states $B \subset \mathcal{S}$, we construct an augmented CMP $\mathfrak{S}_\zeta = \left(\mathcal{S}_\zeta, \mathcal{U}, \{\mathcal{U}_\zeta(s) | s \in \mathcal{S}_\zeta\}, T_{\mathfrak{s}}^\zeta\right)$ that has an additional dummy state ϕ, $\mathcal{S}_\zeta := \mathcal{S} \cup \{\phi\}$ and the same input space $\mathcal{U}$. The set of valid inputs $\mathcal{U}_\zeta(s)$ is the same as $\mathcal{U}(s)$ for all $s \in \mathcal{S}$ and $\mathcal{U}_\zeta(\phi) = \mathcal{U}$. The stochastic kernel of $\mathfrak{S}_\zeta$ is a modified version of $T_{\mathfrak{s}}$ as $T_{\mathfrak{s}}^\zeta(A | s, u) = [1 - (1 - \zeta)\mathbf{1}_B(s)]T_{\mathfrak{s}}(A | s, u)$, $T_{\mathfrak{s}}^\zeta(\phi | s, u) = (1 - \zeta)\mathbf{1}_B(s)$, and $T_{\mathfrak{s}}(\phi | \phi, u) = 1$, for all $A \in \mathcal{B}(\mathcal{S})$, $s \in \mathcal{S}$ and $u \in \mathcal{U}_\zeta(s)$. In words, $T_{\mathfrak{s}}^\zeta$ takes the same $T_{\mathfrak{s}}$, adds a sink state ϕ, and for any accepting state $s \in B$, the process will jump to ϕ with probability $(1 - \zeta)$. It also normalises the outgoing transition probabilities of accepting ones with ζ. We establish a relation between $\mathfrak{S}$ and $\mathfrak{S}_\zeta$ regarding satisfaction of Büchi conditions under the following assumption.

Assumption 1. *For $\mathfrak{S}$ and a set B, define the random variable τ_B as the number of times the set B is visited in paths of $\mathfrak{S}$ conditioned on having it as a finite number. The quantity $\tau_B^* := \sup_\rho \mathbb{E}_s^\rho(\tau_B)$ is bounded for any $s \in \mathcal{S}$.*

Theorem 1. *Given $\mathfrak{S}$ satisfying Assumption 1 and for any positional policy ρ on $\mathfrak{S}$, there is a positional policy $\bar\rho$ on $\mathfrak{S}_\zeta$ such that*

$$P_s^{\bar\rho}(\mathfrak{S}_\zeta \models \Diamond\phi) - (1-\zeta)\mathbb{E}_s^\rho(\tau_B) \leq P_s^\rho(\mathfrak{S} \models \Box\Diamond B) \leq P_s^{\bar\rho}(\mathfrak{S}_\zeta \models \Diamond\phi). \quad (4)$$

For any $\bar\rho$ on $\mathfrak{S}_\zeta$, there is ρ on $\mathfrak{S}$ such that the same inequality holds.

The above theorem shows that the probability of satisfying a Büchi condition with accepting set $B \subset \mathcal{S}$ by $\mathfrak{S}$ is upper bounded by the probability of reaching ϕ in $\mathfrak{S}_\zeta$. It also establishes a lower bound but requires knowing $\mathbb{E}_s^\rho(\tau_B)$.

Inequalities of Theorem 1 can be extended to optimal satisfaction probabilities as stated in the next theorem.

Theorem 2. *For any $\mathfrak{S}$ satisfying Assumption 1, we have*

$$\sup_{\bar\rho} P_s^{\bar\rho}(\mathfrak{S}_\zeta \models \Diamond\phi) - (1-\zeta)\tau_B^* \leq \sup_\rho P_s^\rho(\mathfrak{S} \models \Box\Diamond B) \leq \sup_{\bar\rho} P_s^{\bar\rho}(\mathfrak{S}_\zeta \models \Diamond\phi). \quad (5)$$

Corollary 1. *Under Assumption 1, the optimal value $\sup_{\bar\rho} P_s^{\bar\rho}(\mathfrak{S}_\zeta \models \Diamond\phi)$ converges to $\sup_\rho P_s^\rho(\mathfrak{S} \models \Box\Diamond B)$ from above when ζ converges to one from below, and the rate of convergence is at least linear with $(1-\zeta)$.*

Next example highlights the need for Assumption 1 on $\mathfrak{S}$ to get the linear convergence. Such an assumption holds for all $\mathfrak{S}$ with finite state spaces as used in [3,12] but it may not hold for $\mathfrak{S}$ with infinite state spaces.

Example 2. Consider the $\mathfrak{S}$ presented in Fig. 2, which has a countable state space $\{1, 2, 3, \dots\}$ and the input space is singleton. $\mathfrak{S}$ starts at state $s = 2$. The state 1 is absorbing. From any other state n, it jumps to state 1 with probability $\frac{1}{n}$ and to state $(n+1)$ with probability $\frac{n-1}{n}$. Take the set of accepting states $B = \{3, 4, 5, \dots\}$. $\mathbb{E}_s^\rho(\tau_B)$ is unbounded for $\mathfrak{S}$:

$$\mathbb{E}_s^\rho(\tau_B) = \sum_{n=1}^\infty n \times \frac{1}{2} \times \frac{2}{3} \times \frac{3}{4} \times \cdots \frac{n}{n+1} \times \frac{1}{n+2} = \sum_{n=1}^\infty \frac{n}{(n+1)(n+2)} = \infty.$$

It can be easily verified that

$$P_s^\rho(\mathfrak{S} \models \Box\Diamond B) = \frac{1}{2} \times \frac{2}{3} \times \frac{3}{4} \times \frac{4}{5} \times \cdots = 0$$

$$P_s^{\bar\rho}(\mathfrak{S}_\zeta \models \Diamond\phi) = (1-\zeta)\left[1 + \frac{1}{2}\zeta + \frac{1}{3}\zeta^2 + \frac{1}{4}\zeta^3 + \dots\right] = \frac{-(1-\zeta)\ln(1-\zeta)}{\zeta}.$$

The left-hand side of inequality (5) is still technically true for this $\mathfrak{S}$ despite $\mathbb{E}_s^\rho(\tau_B) = \infty$, but the provided lower bound is trivial and does not give linear convergence mentioned in Corollary 1.

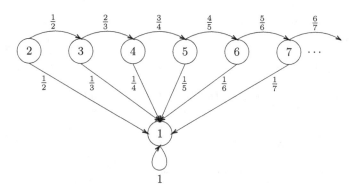

Fig. 2. A CMP with space $\{1, 2, 3, \ldots\}$, a single input and accepting states $B = \{3, 4, 5, \ldots\}$. Its augmented CMP $\mathfrak{G}_\zeta$ does not show convergence with a linear rate.

Remark 4. The lower bound in (5) is useful for showing linear convergence when $\zeta \to 1^-$, but it is not beneficial for learning purposes since the computation of τ_B^* requires knowing the structure of the underlying unknown transition kernel T_s. In the next subsection, we utilise Theorem 2 to give a lower bound independent of τ_B^*. We also demonstrate convergence experimentally in the case study section.

3.2   The Product CMP

The product of a CMP and an LDBA is used in the literature, e.g., [3,12,15] for finite state spaces. We provide this construction for continuous-state CMPs.

Definition 7. *The product CMP* $\mathfrak{G}^\otimes = (\mathcal{S}^\otimes, \mathcal{U}^\otimes, \{\mathcal{U}^\otimes(x) | x \in \mathcal{S}^\otimes\}, T_x^\otimes)$ *of an CMP* $(\mathcal{S}, \mathcal{U}, \{\mathcal{U}(s) | s \in \mathcal{S}\}, T_s)$ *and an LDBA* $\mathcal{A} = (Q, \Sigma, \delta, q_0, \mathsf{Acc})$ *is defined as follows:* $\mathcal{S}^\otimes := S \times Q$ *is the set of states,* $\mathcal{U}^\otimes := \mathcal{U} \cup A^\epsilon$ *with* $A^\epsilon := \{\epsilon_q | q \in Q\}$ *is the set of actions. The valid input sets are* $\mathcal{U}^\otimes(s, q) = \mathcal{U}(s)$ *if* $\delta(q, \epsilon) = \emptyset$ *and* $\mathcal{U}^\otimes(s, q) = \epsilon_{q'}$ *if* $q' \in \delta(q, \epsilon)$. *The stochastic kernel is defined as*

$$T_x^\otimes(A \times \{q'\} | s, q, u) := \begin{cases} T_s(A | s, u) & \text{if } q' = \delta(q, L(s)) \text{ and } u \in \mathcal{U}(s) \\ \mathbf{1}_A(s) & \text{if } q' = \delta(q, \epsilon) \text{ and } u = \epsilon_{q'} \\ 0, & \text{otherwise,} \end{cases}$$

where $\mathbf{1}_A(s)$ *is the indicator function of the set* A.

Any distribution $\alpha : \mathcal{B}(\mathcal{S}) \to [0, 1]$ for the initial state of $\mathfrak{G}$ induces an initial distribution $\alpha^\otimes : \mathcal{B}(\hat{\mathcal{S}}) \to [0, 1]$ with $\alpha^\otimes(A \times \{q\}) := \alpha(A)$ for any $A \in \mathcal{B}(\mathcal{S})$ and $q = q_0$, and zero otherwise. The set of accepting states in the product CMP $\mathfrak{G}^\otimes$ is

$$\mathsf{Acc}^\otimes = \{(s, q) \mid (q, L(s), q') \in \mathsf{Acc}, q' = \delta(q, L(s))\}. \tag{6}$$

We say the path $w^\otimes$ of $\mathfrak{G}^\otimes$ satisfies the Büchi condition ψ_B if the number of states in $\mathsf{Acc}^\otimes$ visited by the path is not finite (the set is visited infinitely often).

Lemma 1. *Any positional policy on $\mathfrak{S}^{\otimes}$ can be translated into a finite-memory policy for $\mathfrak{S}$ that has a finite state space equal to the space of the LDBA $\mathcal{A}$. Moreover, the class of finite-memory policies are sufficient for solving Problem 1 if an optimal policy exists.*

Due to Lemma 1, we focus in the next section on finding positional policies for the product CMP using reinforcement learning. Next theorem is one of the main contributions of the paper that formalises a lower bound on the optimal satisfaction probability.

Theorem 3. *For any $\mathfrak{S}$, specification ψ, labelling function L, and any $s \in \mathcal{S}$,*

$$1 - \inf_{\bar{\rho}} P^{\bar{\rho}}_{s,q_0}(\mathfrak{S}^{\otimes}_{1\zeta} \models \Diamond\phi) \leq \sup_{\rho} P^{\rho}_s(\mathfrak{S} \models \psi) \leq \sup_{\bar{\rho}} P^{\bar{\rho}}_{s,q_0}(\mathfrak{S}^{\otimes}_{2\zeta} \models \Diamond\phi), \qquad (7)$$

where $\mathfrak{S}^{\otimes}_{1\zeta}$ and $\mathfrak{S}^{\otimes}_{2\zeta}$ are the augmented CMPs constructed for the products of $\mathfrak{S}$ with $\mathcal{A}_{\neg\psi}$ and $\mathcal{A}_{\psi}$, respectively.

In the next section, we focus on the computation of the right-hand side of (7) using RL. The left-hand side is computed similarly.

4   Reinforcement Learning for Policy Synthesis

This section contains another main contributions of the paper that is using relaxed versions of the LTL specification in learning a policy. We have shown that Problem 1 can be reduced to Problem 2 on a product CMP, which then can be approximated using reachability objectives as shown in (7). The reachability probability is an average reward criterion

$$P^{\bar{\rho}}_s(\mathfrak{S}_\zeta \models \Diamond\phi) = \lim_{N \to \infty} \frac{1}{N+1} \mathbb{E}^{\bar{\rho}}_s \sum_{n=0}^{N} R(s_n), \qquad (8)$$

with the reward function $R : \mathcal{S}_\zeta \to \mathbb{R}$ defined as $R(s) = 1$ for $s = \phi$ and $R(s) = 0$ otherwise. It can alternatively be written with a total (undiscounted) additive reward criterion by assigning reward one to the first visit of the ϕ and zero otherwise. Both cases can be computed by RL algorithms whenever the model of the CMP is not known or is hard to analyse. Any off-the-shelf RL algorithm for continuous systems can be used to learn a policy. Note that for a general LTL specification, the reward function R is state dependent on the product CMP, but it becomes path dependent when interpreted over the original CMP through the LDBA of the specification.

Advantage Actor-Critic RL. RL algorithms are either value based or policy based. In value-based RL, the algorithm tries to maximise a value function that is a mapping between a state-input pair and a value. Policy-based RL tries to find the optimal policy without using a value function. The policy-based RL has better convergence and effectiveness on high dimensions or continuous state spaces, while value-based RL is more sample efficient and steady. The intersection between these two categories is the actor-critic RL, where the goal is to optimise the policy and the value function together. It optimises the policy and value function as a function of state. We use in this paper the *Advantage Actor-Critic RL* (A2C) [26] that takes the value function as a baseline. It makes the cumulative reward smaller by subtracting it with the baseline, thus have smaller gradients and more stable updates. It works better in comparison with other actor-critic RL in terms of the stability of the learning process and lower variance. An implementation of A2C is available in MATLAB. We have taken this implementation and adapted it to be applicable to the augmented CMP $\mathfrak{S}_\zeta^\otimes$. A pseudo algorithm of our approach based on the A2C is provided in the extended version [19].

4.1   Specification-Guided Learning

The reward function R used in (8) is sparse and it slows down the learning. To improve the learning performance, we give an algorithm that sequentially trains the Actor and Critic networks and guides the learning process by a sequence of labelling functions defining satisfaction of the specification with different relaxation degrees. This sequential training has a similar spirit as the approach of [22]. The novelty of our algorithm is in constructing a sequence of labelling functions that automatically encode the satisfaction relaxation, thus requires Actor and Critic networks with fixed structures.

Relaxed Labelling Functions. We denote the elements of the alphabet by $\Sigma = \{\Sigma_1, \ldots, \Sigma_m\}$. The labelling function $\mathsf{L} : \mathcal{S} \to \Sigma$ induces a partition of the state space $\{S_1, S_2, \ldots, S_m\}$ such that $S_i := \mathsf{L}^{-1}(\Sigma_i)$, $\mathcal{S} = \cup_{i=1}^n S_i$, and $S_i \cap S_j = \emptyset$ for all $i \neq j$. Define the *r-expanded* version of a set $S \subset \mathcal{S}$ by

$$S^{+r} := \{s \in \mathcal{S} \mid \exists s' \in S \text{ with } \|s - s'\|_\infty \leq r\}, \tag{9}$$

for any $r \geq 0$, where $\| \cdot \|_\infty$ is the infinity norm. Define the *r-relaxed* labelling function $\mathsf{L}_r : \mathcal{S} \to 2^\Sigma$ with

$$\mathsf{L}_r(s) := \{\Sigma_i \mid \mathsf{L}(S_i) = \Sigma_i \text{ and } s \in S_i^{+r}\}, \qquad \text{for all } s \in \mathcal{S}. \tag{10}$$

Theorem 4. *The relaxed labelling functions L_r are monotonic with respect to r, i.e., for any $0 \leq r \leq r'$ and L, we have $\{\mathsf{L}(s)\} = \mathsf{L}_0(s) \subset \mathsf{L}_r(s) \subset \mathsf{L}_{r'}(s)$.*

Specification interpreted over Σ. We interpret the specification ψ over the letters in Σ instead of the atomic propositions in AP. For this, we take the PNF form of ψ and replace an atomic proposition p by $\vee_i\{\Sigma_i \mid p \in \Sigma_i\}$. We also replace $\neg p$ by $\vee_i\{\Sigma_i \mid p \notin \Sigma_i\}$. Let us denote this specification in PNF with the letters $\{\Sigma_1, \ldots, \Sigma_m\}$ treated as atomic propositions $\bar{\psi}$. We can construct its associated LDBA $\bar{\mathcal{A}}_\psi$ as discussed in Sect. 2.5,

$$\bar{\mathcal{A}}_\psi := (\bar{Q}, 2^\Sigma, \bar{\delta}, \bar{q}_0, \overline{\mathsf{Acc}}). \tag{11}$$

Algorithm 1: Specification-Guided Learning

---

    input : CMP $\mathfrak{S}$ as a black box, specification ψ, labelling function $\mathsf{L} : \mathcal{S} \to \Sigma$

    output: Actor network $\mu(s, q | \theta^\mu)$ and Critic network $\mathcal{Q}(s, q | \theta^\mathcal{Q})$

1 Select **hyper-parameters** $r_m > r_{m-1} > \ldots r_1 > r_0 = 0$

2 Compute *r-relaxed* labelling functions $\mathsf{L}_{r_i} : \mathcal{S} \to 2^\Sigma$ according to (10)

3 Compute LDBA $\bar{\mathcal{A}}_\psi$ as discussed for (11)

4 Run the Actor-Critic RL with $(\mathfrak{S}, \bar{\mathcal{A}}_\psi, \mathsf{L}_{r_m})$ to get Actor and Critic networks $\mu(s, q | \theta^\mu)$ and $\mathcal{Q}(s, q | \theta^\mathcal{Q})$

5 **for** $i = m$ **to** 1 **do**

6   Fix parameters θ^μ of the Actor network by setting its learning rate to zero

7   Run Actor-Critic RL with $\mathsf{L}_{r_{i-1}}$ to train only the Critic network

8   Change the learning rate of Actor back to normal

9   Run Actor-Critic RL with $\mathsf{L}_{r_{i-1}}$ and initial parameters obtained in Steps 6 and 7

10 **end**

Theorem 5. *For any $0 \leq r \leq r'$ and L, we have*

$$\{\mathfrak{S} \models_{\mathsf{L}} \psi\} = \{\mathfrak{S} \models_{\mathsf{L}_0} \bar{\psi}\} \subset \{\mathfrak{S} \models_{\mathsf{L}_r} \bar{\psi}\} \subset \{\mathfrak{S} \models_{\mathsf{L}_{r'}} \bar{\psi}\}, \tag{12}$$

where L_r is the r-relaxed labelling function defined in (10), and $\bar{\psi}$ is the specification ψ in PNF and interpreted over Σ.

A pseudo algorithm for the specification-guided learning is provided in Algorithm 1 that is based on repeatedly applying an RL algorithm to $\mathfrak{S}$ using a sequence of r-relaxed labelling functions. The algorithm starts by applying Actor-Critic RL to the most relaxed labelling function L_{r_m}. Then it repeatedly fixes the actor network (the policy) by setting its learning rate to zero (Step 6), runs Actor-Critic RL on the next most relaxed labelling function to update the Critic network that gives the total reward (Step 7), and uses these two networks as initialisation for running Actor-Critic RL to optimise both Actor and Critic networks (Step 9).

Remark 5. The main feature of Algorithm 1 is that the structure of the LDBA $\bar{\mathcal{A}}_\psi$ is fixed through the entire algorithm and only the labelling function (thus the reward function) is changed in each iteration.

We presented Algorithm 1 for the computation of the right-hand side of (7). The lower bound in (7) is computed similarly. The only difference is that the LDBA is constructed using $\neg \psi$. The reward function should assign zero to ϕ and one to all other states. The r-relaxed labelling functions in (10) can be used for guiding the computation of the lower bound.

5   Case Studies

To demonstrate our model-free policy synthesis method, we first apply it to the cart-pole system of Example 1 and then discuss the results on a 6-dim boat driving problem. Note that it is not possible to compare our approach with [21] that only handles finite-horizon specifications. Also, the approach of [14,16] maximises the frequency of visiting a sequence of sets of accepting transitions and does not come with formal convergence or lower-bound guarantees.

Our algorithms are implemented in MATLAB R2019a on a 64-bit machine with an Intel Core(TM) i7 CPU at 3.2 GHz and 16 GB RAM.

5.1   Cart-Pole System

We use negation of the specification (3) to learn a lower bound on the optimal satisfaction probability. We set the safe interval $C_2 = [-12°, 12°]$ for the angle, safe range $C_1 = [-1, 1]$ and reach set $A = [0.4, 1]$ in meters for the location. We first directly apply A2C RL to the specification (3) and set the timeout of 24 hours. The RL does not converge to a policy within this time frame. Note that it is a very challenging task to keep the pole upright and at the same time move the cart to reach the desired location.

We then apply Algorithm 1 by using the expanded sets $A^{+i} = [\alpha_i, 1]$ with $\alpha_i \in \{-1, 0.01, 0.4\}$ for defining the relaxed labelling functions L_i. We select the Actor network to have 7 inputs (4 real states and 3 discrete states of the automaton) and 2 outputs. It also has two fully-connected hidden layers each with 7 nodes. The Critic network has the same number of inputs as Actor network, one output, and one fully-connected layer with 7 nodes. We also set $\zeta = 0.999$, learning rate 8×10^{-4}, and episode horizon $N = 500$.

Our sequential learning procedure successfully learns the policy within 44 minutes and gives the lower bound 0.9526 for satisfaction probability (according to Theorem 3). Figure 3 shows cart's position (left) and pole's angle (right) for 50,000 trajectories under the learned policy. The grey area is an envelop for these trajectories, their mean is indicated by the solid line and the standard deviation around mean is indicated by dashed lines. Only 515 trajectories (1.03%) go outside of the safe location $[-1, 1]$ or drop the pole outside of the angle interval $[-12°, 12°]$. All trajectories reach the location $[0.4, 1]$. The histogram of the first time the trajectories reach this interval is presented in Fig. 4, which shows majority of the trajectories reach this interval within 150 time steps.

Using Hoeffding's inequality,[1] we get that the true satisfaction probability under the learned policy is in the interval $[0.975, 1]$ with confidence $1 - 4 \times 10^{-10}$. This is in line with the lower bound 0.9526 computed by the RL.

---

[1] Hoeffding's inequality asserts that the tail of the binomial distribution is exponentially decaying: $Prob(H \geq (p + \varepsilon)N) \leq exp(-2\varepsilon^2 N)$ for all $\varepsilon > 0$ with the number of trials N, the success probability p, and the observed number of successes H.

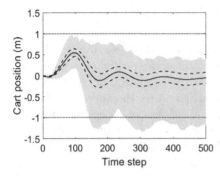
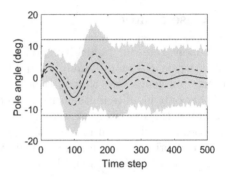

Fig. 3. Cart-pole system. Cart's position (left) and pole's angle (right) for $50,000$ trajectories under the learned policy. The grey area is an envelop for these trajectories, their mean is indicated by the solid line and the standard deviation around mean is indicated by dashed lines. Only 515 trajectories (1.03%) go outside of the safe location $[-1, 1]$ or drop the pole outside of the angle interval $[-12°, 12°]$.

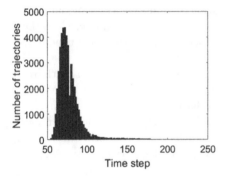
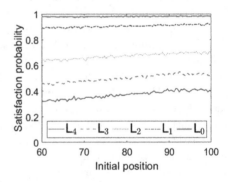

Fig. 4. Cart-pole system. Histogram of the first time the trajectories reach the interval $[0.4, 1]$. A majority of the trajectories reach this interval within 150 time steps.

Fig. 5. Boat driving problem. The satisfaction probability as a function of the initial position y_0 for the policies learned with labelling functions L_i, $i \in \{0, 1, 2, 3, 4\}$.

5.2 Boat Driving Problem

The objective in the boat driving problem is to design a policy for driving a boat from the left bank to the right bank quay in a river with strong nonlinear current. Variations of this problem have been used in the literature (see e.g. [27]). We use a more general version presented in [18] with the dynamics reported in [19]. The model has six continuous states including x and y coordinates for the location both in the interval $[0, 200]$. The boat starts its journey from the left bank of the river $x_0 = 0$ and $y_0 \in [60, 100]$ and should reach the right bank of the river $x_n = 200$ and $y_n \in [95, 105]$ for some n. There is an unknown nonlinear stochastic current affecting the location of the boat.

Direct application of A2C RL does not converge to a policy within 24 hours. We then apply Algorithm 1 with labelling functions L_4, L_3, L_2, L_1, L_0 respectively with the target range $[50, 150]$, $[80, 120]$, $[85, 115]$, $[90, 110]$, and $[95, 105]$. We also adaptively increase the value of ζ to get better lower bounds on the satisfaction probability: $\zeta_4 = 0.9950$, $\zeta_3 = 0.9965$, $\zeta_2 = 0.9980$, $\zeta_1 = 0.9995$, and $\zeta_0 = 0.9999$. The results of this sequential learning procedure are presented in Fig. 5 as a function of the initial position of the boat. The learning rate is set to 8×10^{-4} and the computational time is 70 minutes. The results show that the lower bound on satisfaction probability is monotonically increasing for all initial positions of the boat when ζ increases, which shows also convergence as a function of ζ.

In order to validate the computed bound, we took the initial position $(x_0, y_0) = (0, 80)$ and obtained 50,000 trajectories. All trajectories reach the target location. Based on Hoeffding's inequality, the true probability is in $[0.99, 1]$ with confidence 5×10^{-5}, which confirms the lower bound 0.9810 computed by RL.

6 Future Work

We presented an approach for applying reinforcement learning (RL) to unknown continuous-state stochastic systems with the goal of satisfying a linear temporal logic specification. We formulated an optimal average reward criterion that converges linearly to the true optimal satisfaction probability under suitable assumptions. We used RL to learn a lower bound on this optimal value and improved the performance of the learning by a sequential algorithm using relaxed versions of the specification. In future, we plan to study the relation with discounting reward functions [3], formal connections with maximising frequency of visits, and providing guidance in adapting the network architecture in the RL to the structure of the specification.

References

1. Baier, C., Katoen, J.P.: Principles of Model Checking. MIT Press, Cambridge (2008)
2. Bertsekas, D., Shreve, S.: Stochastic Optimal Control: The Discrete-Time Case. Athena Scientific, Nashua (1996)
3. Bozkurt, A.K., Wang, Y., Zavlanos, M.M., Pajic, M.: Control synthesis from linear temporal logic specifications using model-free reinforcement learning. In: 2020 IEEE International Conference on Robotics and Automation (ICRA), pp. 10349–10355. IEEE (2020)
4. Brázdil, T., et al.: Verification of Markov decision processes using learning algorithms. In: Cassez, F., Raskin, J.-F. (eds.) ATVA 2014. LNCS, vol. 8837, pp. 98–114. Springer, Cham (2014). https://doi.org/10.1007/978-3-319-11936-6_8
5. Courcoubetis, C., Yannakakis, M.: The complexity of probabilistic verification. J. ACM (JACM) 42(4), 857–907 (1995)
6. Dynkin, E.B., Yushkevich, A.A.: Controlled Markov Processes, vol. 235. Springer, New York (1979)

7. Flesch, J., Predtetchinski, A., Sudderth, W.: Simplifying optimal strategies in lim-sup and liminf stochastic games. Discret. Appl. Math. **251**, 40–56 (2018)

8. Fu, J., Topcu, U.: Probably approximately correct MDP learning and control with temporal logic constraints. In: Proceedings of Robotics: Science and Systems (2014)

9. Garcıa, J., Fernández, F.: A comprehensive survey on safe reinforcement learning. J. Mach. Learn. Res. **16**(1), 1437–1480 (2015)

10. Haesaert, S., Soudjani, S.: Robust dynamic programming for temporal logic control of stochastic systems. IEEE Trans. Autom. Control (2020)

11. Hahn, E.M., Li, G., Schewe, S., Turrini, A., Zhang, L.: Lazy probabilistic model checking without determinisation. In: International Conference on Concurrency Theory (CONCUR), pp. 354–367 (2015)

12. Hahn, E.M., Perez, M., Schewe, S., Somenzi, F., Trivedi, A., Wojtczak, D.: Omega-regular objectives in model-free reinforcement learning. In: Vojnar, T., Zhang, L. (eds.) TACAS 2019. LNCS, vol. 11427, pp. 395–412. Springer, Cham (2019). https://doi.org/10.1007/978-3-030-17462-0_27

13. Hasanbeig, M., Abate, A., Kröning, D.: Logically-constrained reinforcement learning. arXiv preprint arXiv:1801.08099 (2018)

14. Hasanbeig, M., Abate, A., Kröning, D.: Logically-constrained neural fitted Q-iteration. In: Proceedings of the 18th International Conference on Autonomous Agents and MultiAgent Systems (AAMS), pp. 2012–2014 (2019)

15. Hasanbeig, M., Kantaros, Y., Abate, A., Kroening, D., Pappas, G.J., Lee, I.: Reinforcement learning for temporal logic control synthesis with probabilistic satisfaction guarantees. In: IEEE Conference on Decision and Control (CDC), pp. 5338–5343. IEEE (2019)

16. Hasanbeig, M., Kroening, D., Abate, A.: Deep reinforcement learning with temporal logics. In: Formal Modeling and Analysis of Timed Systems, pp. 1–22 (2020)

17. Hernández-Lerma, O., Lasserre, J.B.: Discrete-Time Markov Control Processes: Basic Optimality Criteria. Stochastic Modelling and Applied Probability, vol. 30. Springer, New York (1996)

18. Jouffe, L.: Fuzzy inference system learning by reinforcement methods. IEEE Trans. Syst. Man Cybern. **28**(3), 338–355 (1998)

19. Kazemi, M., Soudjani, S.: Formal policy synthesis for continuous-space systems via reinforcement learning. arXiv:2005.01319 (2020)

20. Křetínský, J., Meggendorfer, T., Sickert, S.: Owl: a library for ω-words, automata, and LTL. In: Lahiri, S.K., Wang, C. (eds.) ATVA 2018. LNCS, vol. 11138, pp. 543–550. Springer, Cham (2018). https://doi.org/10.1007/978-3-030-01090-4_34

21. Lavaei, A., Somenzi, F., Soudjani, S., Trivedi, A., Zamani, M.: Formal controller synthesis for continuous-space MDPs via model-free reinforcement learning. In: International Conference on Cyber-Physical Systems (ICCPS), pp. 98–107 (2020)

22. Lazaric, A., Restelli, M., Bonarini, A.: Reinforcement learning in continuous action spaces through sequential Monte Carlo methods. In: Advances in Neural Information Processing Systems, pp. 833–840 (2008)

23. Maitra, A., Sudderth, W.: Borel stochastic games with lim sup payoff. Ann. Probab. **21**(2), 861–885 (1993)

24. Majumdar, R., Mallik, K., Soudjani, S.: Symbolic controller synthesis for Büchi specifications on stochastic systems. In: International Conference on Hybrid Systems: Computation and Control (HSCC). ACM, New York (2020)

25. Mallik, K., Soudjani, S., Schmuck, A.K., Majumdar, R.: Compositional construction of finite state abstractions for stochastic control systems. In: Conference on Decision and Control (CDC), pp. 550–557. IEEE (2017)

26. Mnih, V., et al.: Asynchronous methods for deep reinforcement learning. In: International Conference on Machine Learning, vol. 48, pp. 1928–1937 (2016)
27. Piche, S.W.: Steepest descent algorithms for neural network controllers and filters. IEEE Trans. Neural Netw. **5**(2), 198–212 (1994)
28. Recht, B.: A tour of reinforcement learning: the view from continuous control. Ann. Rev. Control Robot. Auton. Syst. **2**, 253–279 (2018)
29. Sadigh, D., Kim, E.S., Coogan, S., Sastry, S.S., Seshia, S.A.: A learning based approach to control synthesis of Markov decision processes for linear temporal logic specifications. In: Conference on Decision and Control, pp. 1091–1096 (2014)
30. Sickert, S., Esparza, J., Jaax, S., Křetínský, J.: Limit-deterministic Büchi automata for linear temporal logic. In: Chaudhuri, S., Farzan, A. (eds.) CAV 2016. LNCS, vol. 9780, pp. 312–332. Springer, Cham (2016). https://doi.org/10.1007/978-3-319-41540-6_17
31. Tkachev, I., Mereacre, A., Katoen, J.P., Abate, A.: Quantitative model-checking of controlled discrete-time Markov processes. Inf. Comput. **253**, 1–35 (2017)
32. Wang, J., Ding, X., Lahijanian, M., Paschalidis, I.C., Belta, C.A.: Temporal logic motion control using actor-critic methods. Int. J. Robot. Res. **34**(10), 1329–1344 (2015)

Grey-Box Learning of Register Automata

Bharat Garhewal[1]([✉]), Frits Vaandrager[1], Falk Howar[2], Timo Schrijvers[1],
Toon Lenaerts[1], and Rob Smits[1]

[1] Radboud University, Nijmegen, The Netherlands
{bharat.garhewal,frits.vaandrager}@ru.nl
[2] Dortmund University of Technology, Dortmund, Germany

Abstract. Model learning (a.k.a. active automata learning) is a highly effective technique for obtaining black-box finite state models of software components. We show how one can boost the performance of model learning techniques for register automata by extracting the constraints on input and output parameters from a run, and making this grey-box information available to the learner. More specifically, we provide new implementations of the tree oracle and equivalence oracle from the RALib tool, which use the derived constraints. We extract the constraints from runs of Python programs using an existing tainting library for Python, and compare our grey-box version of RALib with the existing black-box version on several benchmarks, including some data structures from Python's standard library. Our proof-of-principle implementation results in almost two orders of magnitude improvement in terms of numbers of inputs sent to the software system. Our approach, which can be generalized to richer model classes, also enables RALib to learn models that are out of reach of black-box techniques, such as combination locks.

Keywords: Model learning · Active automata learning · Register automata · RALib · Grey-box · Tainting

1 Introduction

Model learning, also known as active automata learning, is a black-box technique for constructing state machine models of software and hardware components from information obtained through testing (i.e., providing inputs and observing the resulting outputs). Model learning has been successfully used in numerous applications, for instance for generating conformance test suites of software components [13], finding mistakes in implementations of security-critical protocols [8–10], learning interfaces of classes in software libraries [14], and checking that a legacy component and a refactored implementation have the same behaviour [19]. We refer to [17,20] for surveys and further references.

In many applications it is crucial for models to describe *control flow*, i.e., states of a component, *data flow*, i.e., constraints on data parameters that are

B. Garhewal—Supported by NWO TOP project 612.001.852 "Grey-box learning of Interfaces for Refactoring Legacy Software (GIRLS)".

B. Dongol and E. Troubitsyna (Eds.): IFM 2020, LNCS 12546, pp. 22–40, 2020.
https://doi.org/10.1007/978-3-030-63461-2_2

passed when the component interacts with its environment, as well as the mutual influence between control flow and data flow. Such models often take the form of *extended finite state machines* (EFSMs). Recently, various techniques have been employed to extend automata learning to a specific class of EFSMs called *register automata*, which combine control flow with guards and assignments to data variables [1,2,6].

While these works demonstrate that it is theoretically possible to infer such richer models, the presented approaches do not scale well and are not yet satisfactorily developed for richer classes of models (c.f. [16]): Existing techniques either rely on manually constructed mappers that abstract the data aspects of input and output symbols into a finite alphabet, or otherwise infer guards and assignments from black-box observations of test outputs. The latter can be costly, especially for models where control flow depends on test on data parameters in input: in this case, learning an exact guard that separates two control flow branches may require a large number of queries.

One promising strategy for addressing the challenge of identifying data-flow constraints is to augment learning algorithms with white-box information extraction methods, which are able to obtain information about the System Under Test (SUT) at lower cost than black-box techniques. Several researchers have explored this idea. Giannakopoulou et al. [11] develop an active learning algorithm that infers safe interfaces of software components with guarded actions. In their model, the teacher is implemented using concolic execution for the identification of guards. Cho et al. [7] present MACE an approach for concolic exploration of protocol behaviour. The approach uses active automata learning for discovering so-called deep states in the protocol behaviour. From these states, concolic execution is employed in order to discover vulnerabilities. Similarly, Botinčan and Babć [4] present a learning algorithm for inferring models of stream transducers that integrates active automata learning with symbolic execution and counterexample-guided abstraction refinement. They show how the models can be used to verify properties of input sanitizers in Web applications. Finally, Howar et al. [15] extend the work of [11] and integrate knowledge obtained through static code analysis about the potential effects of component method invocations on a component's state to improve the performance during symbolic queries. So far, however, white-box techniques have never been integrated with learning algorithms for register automata.

In this article, we present the first active learning algorithm for a general class of register automata that uses white-box techniques. More specifically, we show how dynamic taint analysis can be used to efficiently extract constraints on input and output parameters from a test, and how these constraints can be used to improve the performance of the SL^* algorithm of Cassel et al. [6]. The SL^* algorithm generalizes the classical L^* algorithm of Angluin [3] and has been used successfully to learn register automaton models, for instance of Linux and Windows implementations of TCP [9]. We have implemented the presented method on top of RALib [5], a library that provides an implementation of the SL^* algorithm.

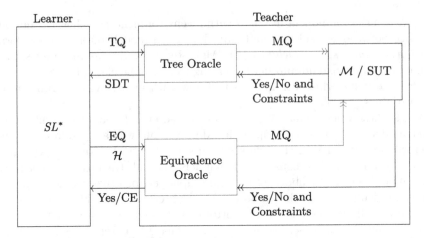

Fig. 1. MAT Framework (Our addition—tainting—in red): Double arrows indicate possible multiple instances of a query made by an oracle for a single query by the learner. (Color figure online)

The integration of the two techniques (dynamic taint analysis and learning of register automata models) can be explained most easily with reference to the architecture of RALib, shown in Fig. 1, which is a variation of the *Minimally Adequate Teacher* (MAT) framework of [3]: In the MAT framework, learning is viewed as a game in which a *learner* has to infer the behaviour of an unknown register automaton M by asking queries to a *teacher*. We postulate M models the behaviour of a *System Under Test (SUT)*. In the learning phase, the learner (that is, SL^*) is allowed to ask questions to the teacher in the form of *tree queries* (TQs) and the teacher responds with *symbolic decision trees* (SDTs). In order to construct these SDTs, the teacher uses a *tree oracle*, which queries the SUT with *membership queries* (MQs) and receives a yes/no reply to each. Typically, the tree oracle asks multiple MQs to answer a single tree query in order to infer causal impact and flow of data values. Based on the answers on a number of tree queries, the learner constructs a *hypothesis* in the form of a register automaton H. The learner submits H as an *equivalence query (EQ)* to the teacher, asking whether H is equivalent to the SUT model M. The teacher uses an *equivalence oracle* to answer equivalence queries. Typically, the equivalence oracle asks multiple MQs to answer a single equivalence query. If, for all membership queries, the output produced by the SUT is consistent with hypothesis H, the answer to the equivalence query is 'Yes' (indicating learning is complete). Otherwise, the answer 'No' is provided, together with a *counterexample* (CE) that indicates a difference between H and M. Based on this CE, learning continues. In this extended MAT framework, we have constructed new implementations of the tree oracle and equivalence oracle that leverage the constraints on input and output parameters that are imposed by a program run: dynamic tainting is used to extract the constraints on parameters that are encountered during a run of a program. Our implementation learns models of Python programs, using

an existing tainting library for Python [12]. Effectively, the combination of the
SL^* with our new tree and equivalence oracles constitutes a *grey-box* learning
algorithm, since we only give the learner partial information about the internal
structure of the SUT.

We compare our grey-box tree and equivalence oracles with the existing
black-box versions of these oracles on several benchmarks, including Python's
queue and set modules. Our proof-of-concept implementation[1] results in almost
two orders of magnitude improvement in terms of numbers of inputs sent to the
software system. Our approach, which generalises to richer model classes, also
enables RALib to learn models that are completely out of reach for black-box
techniques, such as combination locks. The full version of this article (with proofs
for correctness) is available online[2].

Outline: Section 2 contains preliminaries; Section 3 discusses tainting in our
Python SUTs; Section 4 contains the algorithms we use to answer TQs using
tainting and the definition for the tainted equivalence oracle needed to learn
combination lock automata; Section 5 contains the experimental evaluation of
our technique; and Sect. 6 concludes.

2   Preliminary Definitions and Constructions

This section contains the definitions and constructions necessary to understand
active automata learning for models with dataflow. We first define the concept
of a *structure*, followed by *guards, data languages, register automata*, and finally
symbolic decision trees.

Definition 1 (Structure). *A structure $S = \langle R, D, R \rangle$ is a triple where R is
a set of relation symbols, each equipped with an arity, D is an infinite domain
of data values, and R contains a distinguished n-ary relation $r^R \subseteq D^n$ for each
n-ary relation symbol $r \in R$.*

In the remainder of this article, we fix a structure $S = \langle R, D, R \rangle$, where R
contains a binary relation symbol $=$ and unary relation symbols $= c$, for each c
contained in a finite set C of constant symbols, D equals the set $\mathbb{N}$ of natural
numbers, $=^R$ is interpreted as the equality predicate on $\mathbb{N}$, and to each symbol
$c \in C$ a natural number n_c is associated such that $(= c)^R = \{n_c\}$.

Guards are a restricted type of Boolean formulas that may contain relation
symbols from R.

Definition 2 (Guards). *We postulate a countably infinite set $V = \{v_1, v_2, \ldots\}$
of variables. In addition, there is a variable $p \notin V$ that will play a special role
as formal parameter of input symbols; we write $V^+ = V \cup \{p\}$. A guard is
a conjunction of relation symbols and negated relation symbols over variables.
Formally, the set of guards is inductively defined as follows:*

---

[1] Available at https://bitbucket.org/toonlenaerts/taintralib/src/basic.
[2] See https://arxiv.org/abs/2009.09975.

- If $r \in R$ is an n-ary relation symbol and $x_1, \ldots, x_n$ are variables from $\mathcal{V}^+$, then $r(x_1, \ldots, x_n)$ and $\neg r(x_1, \ldots, x_n)$ are guards.
- If g_1 and g_2 are guards then $g_1 \wedge g_2$ is a guard.

Let $X \subset \mathcal{V}^+$. We say that g is a guard over X if all variables that occur in g are contained in X. A variable renaming is a function $\sigma : X \to \mathcal{V}^+$. If g is a guard over X then $g[\sigma]$ is the guard obtained by replacing each variable x in g by $\sigma(x)$.

Next, we define the notion of a *data language*. For this, we fix a finite set of *actions* Σ. A *data symbol* $\alpha(d)$ is a pair consisting of an action $\alpha \in \Sigma$ and a data value $d \in \mathcal{D}$. While relations may have arbitrary arity, we will assume that all actions have an arity of one to ease notation and simplify the text. A *data word* is a finite sequence of data symbols, and a *data language* is a set of data words. We denote concatenation of data words w and w' by $w \cdot w'$, where w is the *prefix* and w' is the *suffix*. $Acts(w)$ denotes the sequence of actions $\alpha_1 \alpha_2 \ldots \alpha_n$ in w, and $Vals(w)$ denotes the sequence of data values $d_1 d_2 \ldots d_n$ in w. We refer to a sequence of actions in Σ^* as a *symbolic suffix*. If w is a symbolic suffix then we write $[\![w]\!]$ for the set of data words u with $Acts(u) = w$.

Data languages may be represented by *register automaton*, defined below.

Definition 3 (Register Automaton). *A Register Automaton (RA) is a tuple* $\mathcal{M} = (L, l_0, \mathcal{X}, \Gamma, \lambda)$ *where*

- L *is a finite set of locations, with l_0 as the initial location;*
- $\mathcal{X}$ *maps each location $l \in L$ to a finite set of registers $\mathcal{X}(l)$;*
- Γ *is a finite set of transitions, each of the form $\langle l, \alpha(p), g, \pi, l' \rangle$, where*
  - l, l' *are source and target locations respectively,*
  - $\alpha(p)$ *is a parametrised action,*
  - g *is a guard over $\mathcal{X}(l) \cup \{p\}$, and*
  - π *is an assignment mapping from $\mathcal{X}(l')$ to $\mathcal{X}(l) \cup \{p\}$; and*
- λ *maps each location in L to either accepting $(+)$ or rejecting $(-)$.*

We require that $\mathcal{M}$ is deterministic in the sense that for each location $l \in L$ and input symbol $\alpha \in \Sigma$, the conjunction of the guards of any pair of distinct α-transitions with source l is not satisfiable. $\mathcal{M}$ is completely specified if for all α-transitions out of a location, the disjunction of the guards of the α-transitions is a tautology. $\mathcal{M}$ is said to be simple if there are no registers in the initial location, i.e., $\mathcal{X}(l_0) = \varnothing$. In this text, all RAs are assumed to be completely specified and simple, unless explicitly stated otherwise. Locations $l \in L$ with $\lambda(l) = +$ are called accepting, and locations with $\lambda(l) = -$ rejecting.

Example 1 (FIFO-buffer). The register automaton displayed in Fig. 2 models a FIFO-buffer with capacity 2. It has three accepting locations l_0, l_1 and l_2 (denoted by a double circle), and one rejecting "sink" location l_3 (denoted by a single circle). Function $\mathcal{X}$ assigns the empty set of registers to locations l_0 and l_3, singleton set $\{x\}$ to location l_1, and set $\{x, y\}$ to l_2.

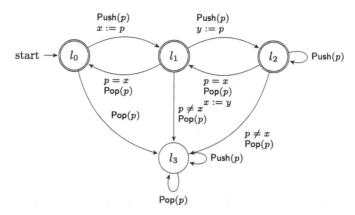

Fig. 2. FIFO-buffer with a capacity of 2 modeled as a register automaton.

2.1   Semantics of a RA

We now formalise the semantics of an RA. A *valuation* of a set of variables X is a function $\nu : X \to \mathcal{D}$ that assigns data values to variables in X. If ν is a valuation of X and g is a guard over X then $\nu \models g$ is defined inductively by:

- $\nu \models r(x_1, \ldots, x_n)$ iff $(\nu(x_1), \ldots, \nu(x_n)) \in r^{\mathcal{R}}$
- $\nu \models \neg r(x_1, \ldots, x_n)$ iff $(\nu(x_1), \ldots, \nu(x_n)) \notin r^{\mathcal{R}}$
- $\nu \models g_1 \wedge g_2$ iff $\nu \models g_1$ and $\nu \models g_2$

A *state* of a RA $\mathcal{M} = (L, l_0, \mathcal{X}, \Gamma, \lambda)$ is a pair $\langle l, \nu \rangle$, where $l \in L$ is a location and $\nu : \mathcal{X}(l) \to \mathcal{D}$ is a valuation of the set of registers at location l. A *run* of $\mathcal{M}$ over data word $w = \alpha_1(d_1) \ldots \alpha_n(d_n)$ is a sequence

$$\langle l_0, \nu_0 \rangle \xrightarrow{\alpha_1(d_1), g_1, \pi_1} \langle l_1, \nu_1 \rangle \ldots \langle l_{n-1}, \nu_{n-1} \rangle \xrightarrow{\alpha_n(d_n), g_n, \pi_n} \langle l_n, \nu_n \rangle,$$

where

- for each $0 \leq i \leq n$, $\langle l_i, \nu_i \rangle$ is a state (with l_0 the initial location),
- for each $0 < i \leq n$, $\langle l_{i-1}, \alpha_i(p), g_i, \pi_i, l_i \rangle \in \Gamma$ such that $\iota_i \models g_i$ and $\nu_i = \iota_i \circ \pi_i$, where $\iota_i = \nu_{i-1} \cup \{[p \mapsto d_i]\}$ extends ν_{i-1} by mapping p to d_i.

A run is *accepting* if $\lambda(l_n) = +$, else *rejecting*. The language of $\mathcal{M}$, notation $L(\mathcal{M})$, is the set of words w such that $\mathcal{M}$ has an accepting run over w. Word w is *accepted (rejected) under* valuation ν_0 if $\mathcal{M}$ has an accepting (rejecting) run that starts in state $\langle l_0, \nu_o \rangle$.

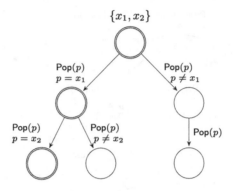

Fig. 3. SDT for prefix Push(5) Push(7) and (symbolic) suffix Pop Pop.

Example 2. Consider the FIFO-buffer example from Fig. 2. This RA has a run

$$\langle l_0, \nu_0 = [] \rangle \xrightarrow{\text{Push}(7), g_1 \equiv \top, \pi_1 = [x \mapsto p]} \langle l_1, \nu_1 = [x \mapsto 7] \rangle$$
$$\xrightarrow{\text{Push}(7), g_2 \equiv \top, \pi_2 = [x \mapsto x, y \mapsto p]} \langle l_2, \nu_2 = [x \mapsto 7, y \mapsto 7] \rangle$$
$$\xrightarrow{\text{Pop}(7), g_3 \equiv p = x, \pi_3 = [x \mapsto y]} \langle l_1, \nu_3 = [x \mapsto 7] \rangle$$
$$\xrightarrow{\text{Push}(5), g_4 \equiv \top, \pi_4 = [x \mapsto x, y \mapsto p]} \langle l_2, \nu_4 = [x \mapsto 7, y \mapsto 5] \rangle$$
$$\xrightarrow{\text{Pop}(7), g_5 \equiv p = x, \pi_5 = [x \mapsto y]} \langle l_1, \nu_5 = [x \mapsto 5] \rangle$$
$$\xrightarrow{\text{Pop}(5), g_6 \equiv p = x, \pi_6 = []} \langle l_0, \nu_6 = [] \rangle$$

and thus the trace is Push(7) Push(7) Pop(7) Push(5) Pop(7) Pop(5).   ⌐

2.2   Symbolic Decision Tree

The SL^* algorithm uses *tree queries* in place of membership queries. The arguments of a tree query are a prefix data word u and a symbolic suffix w, i.e., a data word with uninstantiated data parameters. The response to a tree query is a so called *symbolic decision tree* (SDT), which has the form of tree-shaped register automaton that accepts/rejects suffixes obtained by instantiating data parameters in one of the symbolic suffixes. Let us illustrate this on the FIFO-buffer example from Fig. 2 for the prefix Push(5) Push(7) and the symbolic suffix Pop Pop. The acceptance/rejection of suffixes obtained by instantiating data parameters after Push(5) Push(7) can be represented by the SDT in Fig. 3. In the initial location, values 5 and 7 from the prefix are stored in registers x_1 and x_2, respectively. Thus, SDTs will generally not be simple RAs. Moreover, since the leaves of an SDT have no outgoing transitions, they are also not completely specified. We use the convention that register x_i stores the ith data value. Thus, initially, register x_1 contains value 5 and register x_2 contains value 7. The initial transitions in the SDT contain an update $x_3 := p$, and the final transitions an update $x_4 := p$. For readability, these updates are not displayed in the diagram. The SDT accepts suffixes of form $\mathsf{Pop}(d_1)\,\mathsf{Pop}(d_2)$ iff d_1 equals the value stored in register x_1, and d_2 equals the data value stored in register x_2. For a more detailed discussion of SDTs we refer to [6].

3 Tainting

We postulate that the behaviour of the SUT (in our case: a Python program) can be modeled by a register automaton $\mathcal{M}$. In a black-box setting, observations on the SUT will then correspond to words from the data language of $\mathcal{M}$. In this section, we will describe the additional observations that a learner can make in a grey-box setting, where the constraints on the data parameters that are imposed within a run become visible. In this setting, observations of the learner will correspond to what we call tainted words of $\mathcal{M}$. Tainting semantics is an extension of the standard semantics in which each input value is "tainted" with a unique marker from $\mathcal{V}$. In a data word $w = \alpha_1(d_1)\alpha_2(d_2)\ldots\alpha_n(d_n)$, the first data value d_1 is tainted with marker v_1, the second data value d_2 with v_2, etc. While the same data value may occur repeatedly in a data word, all the markers are different.

3.1 Semantics of Tainting

A *tainted state* of a RA $\mathcal{M} = (L, l_0, \mathcal{X}, \Gamma, \lambda)$ is a triple $\langle l, \nu, \zeta \rangle$, where $l \in L$ is a location, $\nu : \mathcal{X}(l) \to \mathcal{D}$ is a valuation, and $\zeta : \mathcal{X}(l) \to \mathcal{V}$ is a function that assigns a marker to each register of l. A *tainted run* of $\mathcal{M}$ over data word $w = \alpha_1(d_1)\ldots\alpha_n(d_n)$ is a sequence

$$\tau = \langle l_0, \nu_0, \zeta_0 \rangle \xrightarrow{\alpha_1(d_1),g_1,\pi_1} \langle l_1, \nu_1, \zeta_1 \rangle \ldots \langle l_{n-1}, \nu_{n-1}, \zeta_{n-1} \rangle \xrightarrow{\alpha_n(d_n),g_n,\pi_n} \langle l_n, \nu_n, \zeta_n \rangle,$$

where

- $\langle l_0, \nu_0 \rangle \xrightarrow{\alpha_1(d_1),g_1,\pi_1} \langle l_1, \nu_1 \rangle \ldots \langle l_{n-1}, \nu_{n-1} \rangle \xrightarrow{\alpha_n(d_n),g_n,\pi_n} \langle l_n, \nu_n \rangle$ is a run of $\mathcal{M}$,
- for each $0 \le i \le n$, $\langle l_i, \nu_i, \zeta_i \rangle$ is a tainted state,
- for each $0 < i \le n$, $\zeta_i = \kappa_i \circ \pi_i$, where $\kappa_i = \zeta_{i-1} \cup \{(p, v_i)\}$.

The tainted word of τ is the sequence $w = \alpha_1(d_1)G_1\alpha_2(d_2)G_2 \cdots \alpha_n(d_n)G_n$, where $G_i = g_i[\kappa_i]$, for $0 < i \le n$. We define $constraints_{\mathcal{M}}(\tau) = [G_1, \ldots, G_n]$.

Let $w = \alpha_1(d_1)\ldots\alpha_n(d_n)$ be a data word. Since register automata are deterministic, there is a unique tainted run τ over w. We define $constraints_{\mathcal{M}}(w) = constraints_{\mathcal{M}}(\tau)$, that is, the constraints associated to a data word are the constraints of the unique tainted run that corresponds to it. In the untainted setting a membership query for data word w leads to a response "yes" if $w \in L(\mathcal{M})$, and a response "no" otherwise, but in a tainted setting the predicates $constraints_{\mathcal{M}}(w)$ are also included in the response, and provide additional information that the learner may use.

Example 3. Consider the FIFO-buffer example from Fig. 2. This RA has a tainted run

$$\langle l_0, [], [] \rangle \xrightarrow{\text{Push}(7)} \langle l_1, [x \mapsto 7], [x \mapsto v_1] \rangle \xrightarrow{\text{Push}(7)} \langle l_2, [x \mapsto 7, y \mapsto 7], [x \mapsto v_1, y \mapsto v_2] \rangle$$
$$\xrightarrow{\text{Pop}(7)} \langle l_1, [x \mapsto 7], [x \mapsto v_2] \rangle \xrightarrow{\text{Push}(5)} \langle l_2, [x \mapsto 7, y \mapsto 5], [x \mapsto v_2, y \mapsto v_4] \rangle$$
$$\xrightarrow{\text{Pop}(7)} \langle l_1, [x \mapsto 5], [y \mapsto v_4] \rangle \xrightarrow{\text{Pop}(5)} \langle l_0, [], [] \rangle$$

(For readability, guards g_i and assignments π_i have been left out.) The constraints in the corresponding tainted trace can be computed as follows:

$$\kappa_1 = [p \mapsto v_1] \qquad\qquad G_1 \equiv \top[\kappa_1] \equiv \top$$
$$\kappa_2 = [x \mapsto v_1, p \mapsto v_2] \qquad\qquad G_2 \equiv \top[\kappa_2] \equiv \top$$
$$\kappa_3 = [x \mapsto v_1, y \mapsto v_2, p \mapsto v_3] \qquad\qquad G_3 \equiv (p = x)[\kappa_3] \equiv v_3 = v_1$$
$$\kappa_4 = [x \mapsto v_2, p \mapsto v_4] \qquad\qquad G_4 \equiv \top[\kappa_4] \equiv \top$$
$$\kappa_5 = [x \mapsto v_2, y \mapsto v_4, p \mapsto v_5] \qquad\qquad G_5 \equiv (p = x)[\kappa_5] \equiv v_5 = v_2$$
$$\kappa_6 = [x \mapsto v_4, p \mapsto v_6] \qquad\qquad G_6 \equiv (p = x)[\kappa_6] \equiv v_6 = v_4$$

and thus the tainted word is:

$$\text{Push}(7) \top \text{Push}(7) \top \text{Pop}(7)\ v_3 = v_1\ \text{Push}(5) \top \text{Pop}(7)\ v_5 = v_2\ \text{Pop}(5)\ v_6 = v_4,$$

and the corresponding list of constraints is $[\top, \top, v_3 = v_1, \top, v_5 = v_2, v_6 = v_4]$. ⌐

Various techniques can be used to observe tainted traces, for instance symbolic and concolic execution. In this work, we have used a library called "taintedstr" to achieve tainting in Python and make tainted traces available to the learner.

3.2 Tainting in Python

Tainting in Python is achieved by using a library called "taintedstr"[3], which implements a "tstr" (*tainted string*) class. We do not discuss the entire implementation in detail, but only introduce the portions relevant to our work. The "tstr" class works by *operator overloading*: each operator is overloaded to record its own invocation. The tstr class overloads the implementation of the "__eq__" (equality) method in Python's str class, amongst others. In this text, we only consider the equality method. A tstr object x can be considered as a triple $\langle o, t, cs \rangle$, where o is the (base) string object, t is the taint value associated with string o, and cs is a set of comparisons made by x with other objects, where each comparison $c \in cs$ is a triple $\langle f, a, b \rangle$ with f the name of the binary method invoked on x, a a copy of x, and b the argument supplied to f.

---

[3] See [12] and https://github.com/vrthra/taintedstr.

Each a method f in the `tstr` class is an overloaded implementation of the relevant (base) method f as follows:

```
1  def f(self, other):
2      self.cs.add((m._name_, self, other))
3      return self.o.f(other) # 'o' is the base string
```

We present a short example of how such an overloaded method would work below:

Example 4 (`tstr` tainting). Consider two `tstr` objects: $x_1 = \langle \text{"1"}, 1, \emptyset \rangle$ and $x_2 = \langle \text{"1"}, 2, \emptyset \rangle$. Calling $x_1 == x_2$ returns **True** as $x_1.o = x_2.o$. As a side-effect of f, the set of comparisons $x_1.cs$ is updated with the triple $c = \langle \text{"\_\_eq\_\_"}, x_1, x_2 \rangle$. We may then confirm that x_1 is compared to x_2 by checking the taint values of the variables in comparison c: $x_1.t = 1$ and $x_2.t = 2$.

Note, our approach to tainting limits the recorded information to operations performed on a `tstr` object. Consider the following snippet, where x_1, x_2, x_3 are `tstr` objects with $1, 2, 3$ as taint values respectively:

```
1  if not (x_1 == x_2 or (x_2 != x_3)):
2      # do something
```

If the base values of x_1 and x_2 are equal, the Python interpreter will "short-circuit" the if-statement and the second condition, $x_2 \neq x_3$, will not be evaluated. Thus, we only obtain one comparison: $x_1 = x_2$. On the other hand, if the base values of x_1 and x_2 are not equal, the interpreter will not short-circuit, and both comparisons will be recorded as $\{x_2 = x_3, x_1 \neq x_2\}$. However, the external negation operation will not be recorded by any of the `tstr` objects: the negation was not performed on the `tstr` objects. ⌋

4   Learning Register Automata Using Tainting

Given an SUT and a tree query, we generate an SDT in the following steps: *(i)* construct a *characteristic predicate* of the tree query (Algorithm 1) using membership and guard queries, *(ii)* transform the characteristic predicate into an SDT (Algorithm 2), and *(iii)* minimise the obtained SDT (Algorithm 3).

4.1   Tainted Tree Oracle

Construction of Characteristic Predicate. For $u = \alpha(d_1) \cdots \alpha_k(d_k)$ a data word, ν_u denotes the valuation of $\{x_1, \ldots, x_k\}$ with $\nu_u(x_i) = d_i$, for $1 \leq i \leq k$. Suppose u is a prefix and $w = \alpha_{k+1} \cdots \alpha_{k+n}$ is a symbolic suffix. Then H is a *characteristic predicate* for u and w in $\mathcal{M}$ if, for each valuation ν of $\{x_1, \ldots, x_{k+n}\}$ that extends ν_u,

$$\nu \models H \iff \alpha_1(\nu(x_1)) \cdots \alpha_{k+n}(\nu(x_{k+n})) \in L(\mathcal{M}),$$

that is, H characterizes the data words u' with $Acts(u') = w$ such that $u \cdot u'$ is accepted by $\mathcal{M}$. In the case of the FIFO-buffer example from Fig. 2, a

---

Algorithm 1: ComputeCharacteristicPredicate

Data: A tree query consisting of prefix $u = \alpha_1(d_1) \cdots \alpha_k(d_k)$ and symbolic
     suffix $w = \alpha_{k+1} \cdots \alpha_{k+n}$

Result: A characteristic predicate for u and w in $\mathcal{M}$

1   $G := \top,\ H := \bot,\ V := \{x_1, \ldots, x_{k+n}\}$
2 **while** $\exists$ *valuation ν for V that extends ν_u such that $\nu \models G$* **do**
3     $\nu :=$ valuation for V that extends ν_u such that $\nu \models G$
4     $z := \alpha_1(\nu(x_1)) \cdots \alpha_{k+n}(\nu(x_{k+n}))$ `// Construct membership query`
5     $I := \bigwedge_{i=k+1}^{k+n} constraints_{\mathcal{M}}(z)[i]$ `// Constraints resulting from query`
6   **if** $z \in L(\mathcal{M})$ **then**   `// Result query ''yes'' or ''no''`
7        $H := H \vee I$
8     $G := G \wedge \neg I$
9 **end**
10 **return** H

---

characteristic predicate for prefix Push(5) Push(7) and symbolic suffix Pop Pop
is $x_3 = x_1 \wedge x_4 = x_2$. A characteristic predicate for the empty prefix and symbolic
suffix Pop is $\bot$, since this trace will inevitably lead to the sink location l_3 and
there are no accepting words.

Algorithm 1 shows how a characteristic predicate may be computed by systematically exploring all the (finitely many) paths of $\mathcal{M}$ with prefix u and suffix
w using tainted membership queries. During the execution of Algorithm 1, predicate G describes the part of the parameter space that still needs to be explored,
whereas H is the characteristic predicate for the part of the parameter space that
has been covered. We use the notation $H \equiv T$ to indicate syntactic equivalence,
and $H = T$ to indicate logical equivalence. Note, if there exists no parameter
space to be explored (i.e., w is empty) and $u \in L(\mathcal{M})$, the algorithm returns
$H \equiv \bot \vee \top$ (as the empty conjunction equals $\top$).

Example 5 (Algorithm 1). Consider the FIFO-buffer example and the tree query
with prefix Push(5) Push(7) and symbolic suffix Pop Pop. After the prefix location
l_2 is reached. From there, three paths are possible with actions Pop Pop: $l_2 l_3 l_3$,
$l_2 l_1 l_3$ and $l_2 l_1 l_0$. We consider an example run of Algorithm 1.

Initially, $G_0 \equiv \top$ and $H_0 \equiv \bot$. Let $\nu_1 = [x_1 \mapsto 5, x_2 \mapsto 7, x_3 \mapsto 1, x_4 \mapsto 1]$.
Then ν_1 extends ν_u and $\nu_1 \models G_0$. The resulting tainted run corresponds to path
$l_2 l_3 l_3$ and so the tainted query gives path constraint $I_1 \equiv x_3 \neq x_1 \wedge \top$. Since the
tainted run is rejecting, $H_1 \equiv \bot$ and $G_1 \equiv \top \wedge \neg I_1$.

In the next iteration, we set $\nu_2 = [x_1 \mapsto 5, x_2 \mapsto 7, x_3 \mapsto 5, x_4 \mapsto 1]$. Then ν_2
extends ν_u and $\nu_2 \models G_1$. The resulting tainted run corresponds to path $l_2 l_1 l_3$
and so the tainted query gives path constraint $I_2 \equiv x_3 = x_1 \wedge x_4 \neq x_2$. Since
the tainted run is rejecting, $H_2 \equiv \bot$ and $G_2 \equiv \top \wedge \neg I_1 \wedge \neg I_2$.

In the final iteration, we set $\nu_3 = [x_1 \mapsto 5, x_2 \mapsto 7, x_3 \mapsto 5, x_4 \mapsto 7]$. Then ν_3
extends ν_u and $\nu_3 \models G_2$. The resulting tainted run corresponds to path $l_2 l_1 l_0$
and the tainted query gives path constraint $I_3 \equiv x_3 = x_1 \wedge x_4 = x_2$. Now the

tainted run is accepting, so $H_3 \equiv \perp \vee I_3$ and $G_3 = \top \wedge \neg I_1 \wedge \neg I_2 \wedge \neg I_3$. As G_3 is unsatisfiable, the algorithm terminates and returns characteristic predicate H_3.

Construction of a Non-minimal SDT. For each tree query with prefix u and symbolic suffix w, the corresponding characteristic predicate H is sufficient to construct an SDT using Algorithm 2.

Algorithm 2: SDTConstructor

Data: Characteristic predicate H, index $n = k + 1$,
Number of suffix parameters N
Result: Non-minimal SDT $\mathcal{T}$

```
 1 if n = k + N + 1 then
 2 |   l_0 := SDT node
 3 |   z := if H ⟺ ⊥ then − else +        // Value λ for leaf node of the SDT
 4 |   return ⟨{l_0}, l_0, [l_0 ↦ ∅], ∅, [l_0 ↦ z]⟩        // RA with single location
 5 else
 6 |   T := SDT node
 7 |   I_t := {i | x_n ⊙ x_i ∈ H, n > i}  // x_i may be a parameter or a constant
 8 |   if I_t is ∅ then
 9 |   |   t := SDTConstructor(H, n + 1, N)              // No guards present
10 |   |   Add t with guard ⊤ to T
11 |   else
12 |   |   g := ⋀_{i∈I_t} x_n ≠ x_i                    // Disequality guard case
13 |   |   H' := ⋁_{f∈H} f ∧ g if f ∧ g is satisfiable else ⊥   // f is a disjunct
14 |   |   t' := SDTConstructor(H', n + 1, N)
15 |   |   Add t' with guard g to T
16 |   |   for i ∈ I_t do
17 |   |   |   g := x_n = x_i                          // Equality guard case
18 |   |   |   H' := ⋁_{f∈H} f ∧ g if f ∧ g is satisfiable else ⊥
19 |   |   |   t' := SDTConstructor(H', n + 1, N)
20 |   |   |   Add t' with guard g to T
21 |   |   end
22 |   return T
```

We construct the SDT recursively while processing each action in the symbolic suffix $w = \alpha_{k+1} \cdots \alpha_{k+m}$ in order. The valuation ν is unnecessary, as there are no guards defined over the prefix parameters. During the execution of Algorithm 2, for a suffix action $\alpha(x_n)$, the *potential set* I_t contains the set of parameters to which x_n is compared to in H. Each element in I_t can be either a formal parameter in the tree query or a constant. For each parameter $x_i \in I_t$ we construct an *equality* sub-tree where $x_n = x_i$. We also construct a *disequality* sub-tree where x_n is not equal to any of the parameters in I_t. The base case (i.e., $w = \epsilon$) return an accepting or rejecting leaf node according to the characteristic predicate at the base case: if $H \iff \perp$ then rejecting, else accepting. Example 6 provides a short explanation of Algorithm 2.

Example 6 (Algorithm 2). Consider a characteristic predicate $H \equiv I_1 \vee I_2 \vee I_3 \vee I_4$, where $I_1 \equiv x_2 \neq x_1 \wedge x_3 \neq x_1$, $I_2 \equiv x_2 = x_1 \wedge x_3 \neq x_1$, $I_3 \equiv x_2 \neq x_1 \wedge x_3 = x_1$, $I_4 \equiv x_2 = x_1 \wedge x_3 = x_1$. We discuss only the construction of the sub-tree rooted at node s_{21} for the SDT visualised in Fig. 4a; the construction of the remainder is similar.

Initially, $x_n = x_{k+1} = x_2$. Potential set I_t for x_2 is $\{x_1\}$ as H contains the literals $x_2 = x_1$ and $x_2 \neq x_1$. Consider the construction of the equality guard $g := x_2 = x_1$. The new characteristic predicate is $H' \equiv (I_2 \wedge g) \vee (I_4 \wedge g)$, as I_1 and I_3 are unsatisfiable when conjugated with g.

For the next call, with $n = 3$, the current variable is x_3, with predicate $H = H'$ (from the parent instance). We obtain the potential set for x_3 as $\{x_1\}$. The equality guard is $g' := x_3 = x_1$ with the new characteristic predicate $H'' \equiv I_4 \wedge g \wedge g'$, i.e., $H'' \iff x_2 = x_1 \wedge x_3 = x_1$ (note, $I_2 \wedge g \wedge g'$ is unsatisfiable). In the next call, we have $n = 4$, thus we compute a leaf. As H'' is not $\bot$, we return an accepting leaf t. The disequality guard is $g'' := x_3 \neq x_1$ with characteristic predicate $H''' \iff x_2 = x_1 \wedge x_3 = x_1 \wedge x_3 \neq x_1 \iff \bot$. In the next call, we have $n = 4$, and we return a non-accepting leaf t'. The two trees t and t' are added as sub-trees with their respective guards g' and g'' to a new tree rooted at node s_{21} (see Fig. 4a).   ⌋

SDT Minimisation. Example 6 showed a characteristic predicate H containing redundant comparisons, resulting in the non-minimal SDT in Fig. 4a. We use Algorithm 3 to minimise the SDT in Fig. 4a to the SDT in Fig. 4b.

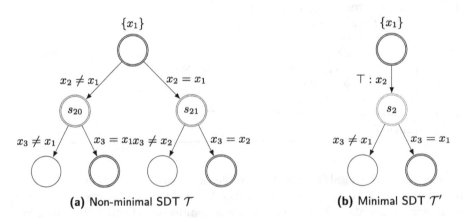

(a) Non-minimal SDT $\mathcal{T}$ (b) Minimal SDT $\mathcal{T}'$

Fig. 4. SDT Minimisation: Redundant nodes (in red, left SDT) are merged together (in green, right SDT). (Color figure online)

We present an example of the application of Algorithm 3, shown for the SDT of Fig. 4a. Figure 4a visualises a non-minimal SDT $\mathcal{T}$, where s_{20} and s_{21} (in red) are essentially "duplicates" of each other: the sub-tree for node s_{20} is isomorphic to the sub-tree for node s_{21} under the relabelling "$x_2 = x_1$". We indicate this

---

Algorithm 3: MinimiseSDT

Data: Non-minimal SDT $\mathcal{T}$, current index n
Result: Minimal SDT $\mathcal{T}'$

1 **if** $\mathcal{T}$ *is a leaf* **then** // Base case
2 | return $\mathcal{T}$
3 **else**
4 | $\mathcal{T}' :=$ SDT node
   | // Minimise the lower levels
5 | **for** *guard g with associated sub-tree t in $\mathcal{T}$* **do**
6 | | Add guard g with associated sub-tree MinimiseSDT($t, n+1$) to $\mathcal{T}'$
7 | **end**
   | // Minimise the current level
8 | $I :=$ Potential set of root node of $\mathcal{T}$
9 | $t' :=$ disequality sub-tree of $\mathcal{T}$ with guard $\bigwedge_{i \in I} x_n \neq x_i$
10 | $I' := \varnothing$
11 | **for** $i \in I$ **do**
12 | | $t :=$ sub-tree of $\mathcal{T}$ with guard $x_n = x_i$
13 | | **if** $t'\langle x_i, x_n \rangle \not\simeq t$ *or* $t'\langle x_i, x_n \rangle$ *is undefined* **then**
14 | | | $I' := I' \cup \{x_i\}$
15 | | | Add guard $x_n = x_i$ with corresponding sub-tree t to $\mathcal{T}'$
16 | **end**
17 | Add guard $\bigwedge_{i \in I'} x_n \neq x_i$ with corresponding sub-tree t' to $\mathcal{T}'$
18 | return $\mathcal{T}'$

---

relabelling using the notation $\mathcal{T}[s_{20}]\langle x_1, x_2 \rangle$ and the isomorphism relation under the relabelling as $\mathcal{T}[s_{20}]\langle x_1, x_2 \rangle \simeq \mathcal{T}[s_{21}]$. Algorithm 3 accepts the non-minimal SDT of Fig. 4a and produces the equivalent minimal SDT in Fig. 4b. Nodes s_{20} and s_{21} are merged into one node, s_2, marked in green. We can observe that both SDTs still encode the same decision tree. With Algorithm 3, we have completed our tainted tree oracle, and can now proceed to the tainted equivalence oracle.

4.2   Tainted Equivalence Oracle

The *tainted equivalence oracle* (TEO), similar to its non-tainted counterpart, accepts a hypothesis $\mathcal{H}$ and verifies whether $\mathcal{H}$ is equivalent to register automaton $\mathcal{M}$ that models the SUT. If $\mathcal{H}$ and $\mathcal{M}$ are equivalent, the oracle replies "yes", otherwise it returns "no" together with a CE. The RandomWalk Equivalence Oracle in RALib constructs random traces in order to find a CE.

Definition 4 (Tainted Equivalence Oracle). *For a given hypothesis $\mathcal{H}$, maximum word length n, and an SUT $\mathcal{S}$, a tainted equivalence oracle is a function $\mathcal{O}_{\mathcal{E}}(\mathcal{H}, n, \mathcal{S})$ for all tainted traces w of $\mathcal{S}$ where $|w| \leq n$, $\mathcal{O}_{\mathcal{E}}(\mathcal{H}, n, \mathcal{S})$ returns w if $w \in \mathcal{L}(\mathcal{H}) \iff w \in \mathcal{L}(\mathcal{S})$ is false, and 'Yes' otherwise.*

The TEO is similar to the construction of the characteristic predicate to find a CE: we randomly generate a symbolic suffix of specified length n (with an empty

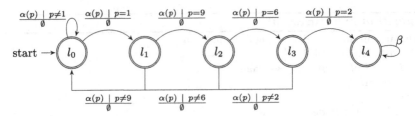

Fig. 5. Combination Lock $\mathcal{C}$: Sequence $\alpha(1)\alpha(9)\alpha(6)\alpha(2)$ *unlocks* the automaton. Error transitions (from $l_3 - l_1$ to l_0) have been 'merged' for conciseness. The sink state has not been drawn.

prefix), and construct a predicate H for the query. For each trace w satisfying a guard in H, we confirm whether $w \in \mathcal{L}(\mathcal{H}) \iff w \in \mathcal{L}(\mathcal{M})$. If false, w is a CE. If no w is false, then we randomly generate another symbolic suffix. In practise, we bound the number of symbolic suffixes to generate. Example 7 presents a scenario of a combination lock automaton that can be learned (relatively easily) using a TEO but cannot be handled by normal oracles.

Example 7 (Combination Lock RA). A combination lock is a type of RA which requires a *sequence* of specific inputs to 'unlock'. Figure 5 presents an RA $\mathcal{C}$ with a '4-digit' combination lock that can be unlocked by the sequence $w = \alpha(c_0)\alpha(c_1)\alpha(c_2)\alpha(c_3)$, where $\{c_0, c_1, c_2, c_3\}$ are constants. Consider a case where a hypothesis $\mathcal{H}$ is being checked for equivalence against the RA $\mathcal{C}$ with $w \notin \mathcal{L}(\mathcal{H})$. While it would be difficult for a normal equivalence oracle to generate the word w randomly; the tainted equivalence oracle will record at every location the comparison of input data value p with some constant c_i and explore all corresponding guards at the location, eventually constructing the word w.

For the combination lock automaton, we may note that as the 'depth' of the lock increases, the possibility of randomly finding a CE decreases.   ⌐

5   Experimental Evaluation

We have used stubbed versions of the Python FIFO-Queue and Set modules[4] for learning the FIFO and Set models, while the Combination Lock automata were constructed manually. Source code for all other models was obtained by translating existing benchmarks from [18] (see also automata.cs.ru.nl) to Python code. We also utilise a 'reset' operation: A 'reset' operation brings an SUT back to its initial state, and is counted as an 'input' for our purposes. Furthermore, each experiment was repeated 30 times with different random seeds. Each experiment was bounded according to the following constraints: learning phase: 10^9 inputs and 5×10^7 resets; testing phase: 10^9 inputs and 5×10^4 resets; length of the longest word during testing: 50; and a ten-minute timeout for the learner to respond.

---

[4] From Python's **queue** module and standard library, respectively.

Figure 6 gives an overview of our experimental results. We use the notation 'TTO' to represent 'Tainted Tree Oracle' (with similar labels for the other oracles). In the figure, we can see that as the size of the container increases, the difference between the fully tainted version (TTO+TEO, in blue) and the completely untainted version (NTO+NEO, in red) increases. In the case where only a tainted tree oracle is used (TTO+NEO, in green), we see that it is following the fully tainted version closely (for the FIFO models) and is slightly better in the case of the SET models.

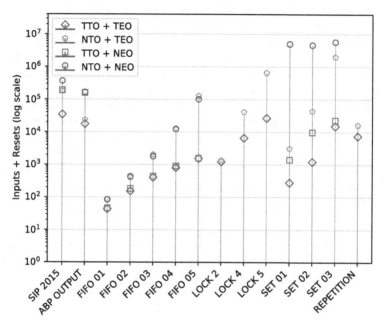

Fig. 6. Benchmark plots: Number of symbols used with tainted oracles (blue and green) are generally *lower* than with normal oracles (red and orange). Note that the y-axis is log-scaled. Additionally, normal oracles are unable to learn the Combination Lock and Repetition automata and are hence not plotted. (Color figure online)

The addition of the TEO gives a conclusive advantage for the Combination Lock and Repetition benchmarks. The addition of the TTO by itself results in significantly fewer number of symbols, even without the tainted equivalence oracle (TTO v/s NTO, compare the green and red lines). With the exception of the Combination Lock and Repetition benchmarks, the TTO+TEO combination does not provide vastly better results in comparison to the TTO+NEO results, however, it is still (slightly) better. We note that—as expected—the NEO does not manage to provide CEs for the Repetition and Combination Lock automata. The TEO is therefore much more useful for finding CEs in SUTs which utilise constants.

6   Conclusions and Future Work

In this article, we have presented an integration of dynamic taint analysis, a white-box technique for tracing data flow, and register automata learning, a black-box technique for inferring behavioral models of components. The combination of the two methods improves upon the state-of-the-art in terms of the class of systems for which models can be generated and in terms of performance: Tainting makes it possible to infer data-flow constraints even in instances with a high intrinsic complexity (e.g., in the case of so-called combination locks). Our implementation outperforms pure black-box learning by two orders of magnitude with a growing impact in the presence of multiple data parameters and registers. Both improvements are important steps towards the applicability of model learning in practice as they will help scaling to industrial use cases.

At the same time our evaluation shows the need for further improvements: Currently, the SL^* algorithm uses symbolic decision trees and tree queries globally, a well-understood weakness of learning algorithms that are based on observation tables. It also uses individual tree oracles each type of operation and relies on syntactic equivalence of decision trees. A more advanced learning algorithm for extended finite state machines will be able to consume fewer tree queries, leverage semantic equivalence of decision trees. Deeper integration with white-box techniques could enable the analysis of many (and more involved) operations on data values.

Acknowledgement. We are grateful to Andreas Zeller for explaining the use of tainting for dynamic tracking of constraints, and to Rahul Gopinath for helping us with his library for tainting Python programs. We also thank the anonymous reviewers for their suggestions.

References

1. Aarts, F., Heidarian, F., Kuppens, H., Olsen, P., Vaandrager, F.: Automata learning through counterexample guided abstraction refinement. In: Giannakopoulou, D., Méry, D. (eds.) FM 2012. LNCS, vol. 7436, pp. 10–27. Springer, Heidelberg (2012). https://doi.org/10.1007/978-3-642-32759-9_4
2. Aarts, F., Jonsson, B., Uijen, J., Vaandrager, F.: Generating models of infinite-state communication protocols using regular inference with abstraction. Formal Meth. Syst. Des. **46**(1), 1–41 (2015). https://doi.org/10.1007/s10703-014-0216-x
3. Angluin, D.: Learning regular sets from queries and counterexamples. Inf. Comput. **75**(2), 87–106 (1987)
4. Botinčan, M., Babić, D.: Sigma*: symbolic learning of input-output specifications. In: POPL 2013, pp. 443–456. ACM, New York (2013)

5. Cassel, S., Howar, F., Jonsson, B., Steffen, B.: Learning extended finite state machines. In: Giannakopoulou, D., Salaün, G. (eds.) SEFM 2014. LNCS, vol. 8702, pp. 250–264. Springer, Cham (2014). https://doi.org/10.1007/978-3-319-10431-7_18

6. Cassel, S., Howar, F., Jonsson, B., Steffen, B.: Active learning for extended finite state machines. Formal Aspects Comput. **28**(2), 233–263 (2016). https://doi.org/10.1007/s00165-016-0355-5

7. Cho, C.Y., Babić, D., Poosankam, P., Chen, K.Z., Wu, E.X., Song, D.: MACE: model-inference-assisted concolic exploration for protocol and vulnerability discovery. In: SEC 2011, p. 10. USENIX, Berkeley, USA (2011)

8. Fiterău-Broştean, P., Janssen, R., Vaandrager, F.: Combining model learning and model checking to analyze TCP implementations. In: Chaudhuri, S., Farzan, A. (eds.) CAV 2016. LNCS, vol. 9780, pp. 454–471. Springer, Cham (2016). https://doi.org/10.1007/978-3-319-41540-6_25

9. Fiterău-Broştean, P., Howar, F.: Learning-based testing the sliding window behavior of TCP implementations. In: Petrucci, L., Seceleanu, C., Cavalcanti, A. (eds.) FMICS/AVoCS - 2017. LNCS, vol. 10471, pp. 185–200. Springer, Cham (2017). https://doi.org/10.1007/978-3-319-67113-0_12

10. Fiterău-Broştean, P., Lenaerts, T., Poll, E., de Ruiter, J., Vaandrager, F., Verleg, P.: Model learning and model checking of SSH implementations. In: SPIN 2017, pp. 142–151. ACM, New York (2017)

11. Giannakopoulou, D., Rakamarić, Z., Raman, V.: Symbolic learning of component interfaces. In: Miné, A., Schmidt, D. (eds.) SAS 2012. LNCS, vol. 7460, pp. 248–264. Springer, Heidelberg (2012). https://doi.org/10.1007/978-3-642-33125-1_18

12. Gopinath, R., Mathis, B., Höschele, M., Kampmann, A., Zeller, A.: Sample-free learning of input grammars for comprehensive software fuzzing. CoRR abs/1810.08289 (2018)

13. Hagerer, A., Margaria, T., Niese, O., Steffen, B., Brune, G., Ide, H.D.: Efficient regression testing of CTI-systems: testing a complex call-center solution. Ann. Rev. Commun. IEC **55**, 1033–1040 (2001)

14. Howar, F., Isberner, M., Steffen, B., Bauer, O., Jonsson, B.: Inferring semantic interfaces of data structures. In: Margaria, T., Steffen, B. (eds.) ISoLA 2012. LNCS, vol. 7609, pp. 554–571. Springer, Heidelberg (2012). https://doi.org/10.1007/978-3-642-34026-0_41

15. Howar, F., Giannakopoulou, D., Rakamarić, Z.: Hybrid learning: interface generation through static, dynamic, and symbolic analysis. In: ISSTA 2013, pp. 268–279. ACM, New York (2013)

16. Howar, F., Jonsson, B., Vaandrager, F.: Combining black-box and white-box techniques for learning register automata. In: Steffen, B., Woeginger, G. (eds.) Computing and Software Science. LNCS, vol. 10000, pp. 563–588. Springer, Cham (2019). https://doi.org/10.1007/978-3-319-91908-9_26

17. Howar, F., Steffen, B.: Active automata learning in practice. In: Bennaceur, A., Hähnle, R., Meinke, K. (eds.) Machine Learning for Dynamic Software Analysis: Potentials and Limits. LNCS, vol. 11026, pp. 123–148. Springer, Cham (2018). https://doi.org/10.1007/978-3-319-96562-8_5

18. Neider, D., Smetsers, R., Vaandrager, F., Kuppens, H.: Benchmarks for automata learning and conformance testing. In: Margaria, T., Graf, S., Larsen, K.G. (eds.) Models, Mindsets, Meta: The What, the How, and the Why Not?. LNCS, vol. 11200, pp. 390–416. Springer, Cham (2019). https://doi.org/10.1007/978-3-030-22348-9_23
19. Schuts, M., Hooman, J., Vaandrager, F.: Refactoring of legacy software using model learning and equivalence checking: an industrial experience report. In: Ábrahám, E., Huisman, M. (eds.) IFM 2016. LNCS, vol. 9681, pp. 311–325. Springer, Cham (2016). https://doi.org/10.1007/978-3-319-33693-0_20
20. Vaandrager, F.: Model learning. Commun. ACM **60**(2), 86–95 (2017)

Clustering-Guided SMT($\mathcal{LRA}$) Learning

Tim Meywerk[1]([⊠]) [iD], Marcel Walter[1] [iD], Daniel Große[2,3] [iD],
and Rolf Drechsler[1,3] [iD]

[1] Research Group of Computer Architecture,
University of Bremen, Bremen, Germany
{tmeywerk,m_walter,drechsler}@uni-bremen.de

[2] Chair of Complex Systems, Johannes Kepler University Linz, Linz, Austria
daniel.grosse@jku.at

[3] Research Department for Cyber-Physical Systems, DFKI GmbH, Bremen, Germany

Abstract. In the SMT($\mathcal{LRA}$) learning problem, the goal is to learn
SMT($\mathcal{LRA}$) constraints from real-world data. To improve the scalability of SMT($\mathcal{LRA}$) learning, we present a novel approach called *SHREC*
which uses hierarchical clustering to guide the search, thus reducing runtime. A designer can choose between higher quality (*SHREC1*) and lower
runtime (*SHREC2*) according to their needs. Our experiments show a
significant scalability improvement and only a negligible loss of accuracy
compared to the current state-of-the-art.

Keywords: Satisfiability modulo theories · Clustering · Machine
learning

1 Introduction

Since the invention of effective solving procedures for the *Boolean Satisfiability* (SAT) problem [20], many formalisms for problem modeling have been introduced over the decades, including but not limited to *Linear Programming* (LP),
Quantified Boolean Formulas (QBF), and *Satisfiability Modulo Theories* (SMT)
(cf. [5] for an overview). With the progressive development of highly specialized
solving engines for these domains [7,8], it has become possible to tackle critical
problems like verification [11]. Also, exact logic synthesis [10], optimal planning,
and other optimization problems [9] could be approached in a more effective
manner (again, cf. [5] for an overview).

A trade-off between SAT's efficient solvers and SMT's expressive power is *Satisfiability Modulo Linear Real Arithmetic* (SMT($\mathcal{LRA}$)) [5]. It combines propositional logic over Boolean variables and linear arithmetic over real-valued variables. SMT($\mathcal{LRA}$) has a wide variety of applications, including formal verification [2,6], AI planning and scheduling [21], and computational biology [24].

The research reported in this paper has been supported by the German Research Foundation DFG, as part of Collaborative Research Center (Sonderforschungsbereich) 1320
EASE – Everyday Activity Science and Engineering, University of Bremen (http://
www.ease-crc.org/). The research was conducted in sub-project P04.

B. Dongol and E. Troubitsyna (Eds.): IFM 2020, LNCS 12546, pp. 41–59, 2020.
https://doi.org/10.1007/978-3-030-63461-2_3

Generating SMT($\mathcal{LRA}$) models[1] by hand is both time-consuming and error-prone and requires detailed domain-specific knowledge. Nevertheless, in many cases, both satisfying and unsatisfying examples of model configurations can be extracted from measurements of the modeling domain. In these cases, the actual modeling task can be automated by an approach called *concept learning*. Concept learning has a long history in artificial intelligence, with *Probably Approximately Correct* (PAC) learning [23], *inductive logic programming* [16], and *constraint programming* [4]. These approaches usually focus on pure Boolean descriptions, i. e. SAT formulae. More recently, [13] introduced SMT($\mathcal{LRA}$) learning, which is the task of learning an SMT($\mathcal{LRA}$) formula from a set of satisfying and unsatisfying examples.

Alternatively, SMT($\mathcal{LRA}$) learning can also be formulated as a variation on the *programming by example* problem known from the *Syntax-Guided Synthesis* (SyGuS) framework. Most solvers in this area (e. g. [1,3,18,22]) are based on enumeration of possible solutions to be able to tackle a wide variety of syntactic constraints. This does, however, lead to overly complicated and inconvenient reasoning on continuous search spaces such as SMT($\mathcal{LRA}$). Apart from that, the problems have further subtle differences, e. g. accuracy of the solutions has higher significance in the concept learning setting.

On top of defining the SMT($\mathcal{LRA}$) learning problem, [13] also introduced an exact algorithm called *INCAL*. As the first of its kind, INCAL naturally comes with certain drawbacks in terms of runtime and is therefore not applicable to learn large models, which are required by most real-world concept learning applications (e. g. [12,15]).

Our contribution in this work is a novel approach for SMT($\mathcal{LRA}$) learning which uses *Hierarchical Clustering* on the examples to guide the search and thus speed up the model generation process. We call our general approach SHREC (SMT($\mathcal{LRA}$) learner with hierarchical example clustering) and introduce two algorithms SHREC1 and SHREC2 based on this idea. SHREC1 aims at a higher accuracy of the solution and therefore requires more runtime than SHREC2. SHREC2 instead follows a very fast and scalable method with minor losses of accuracy. Therefore, we provide the users, i. e. the model designers, with the possibility to choose between maximizing the accuracy of the learned model or improving runtime of the generation process so that also larger models can be learned in a reasonable time frame.

The remainder of this paper is structured as follows: To keep this paper self-contained, Sect. 2 gives an overview of related work and preliminaries in the area of SMT($\mathcal{LRA}$) learning as well as hierarchical clustering. Section 3 and Sect. 4 propose our main ideas, i. e. novel approaches for SMT($\mathcal{LRA}$) learning to tackle larger and more complex models using methods from machine learning. In Sect. 5 we conduct an experimental evaluation where we compare our results to the state-of-the-art. Section 6 concludes the paper.

---

[1] The term *model* is often used to refer to a satisfying assignment to some logical formula. In the context of this paper however, *model* refers to a logical formula that describes a system in the real world.

2 Related Work and Preliminaries

In this section, we give an overview of relevant related work and introduce concepts that we utilize in the remainder of this work.

2.1 SMT($\mathcal{LRA}$) Learning

The problem of SMT($\mathcal{LRA}$) learning has first been introduced in [13]. The goal is to find an SMT($\mathcal{LRA}$) formula which describes some system in the real world. However, no formal representation of the system is available. Instead, a set of measurements is given. In the following, these measurements are called examples. It is further assumed, that there exists an SMT($\mathcal{LRA}$) formula ϕ^* that accurately describes the system. The problem of SMT($\mathcal{LRA}$) learning is now defined as follows:

Definition 1. *Given a finite set of Boolean variables $B := \{b_1, \ldots, b_n\}$ and a finite set of real-valued variables $R := \{r_1, \ldots, r_m\}$ together with a finite set of examples E. Each example $e \in E = (a_e, \phi^*(a_e))$ is a pair of an assignment and a label. An assignment $a_e : B \cup R \mapsto \{\top, \bot\} \cup \mathbb{R}$ maps Boolean variables to true ($\top$) or false ($\bot$), and real-valued variables to real-valued numbers. The label $\phi^*(a_e)$ is the truth value obtained by applying a_e to ϕ^*. We call an example positive if $\phi^*(a_e) = \top$ and negative otherwise. We denote the sets of positive and negative examples by $E^\top$ and $E^\bot$, respectively.*

The task of SMT($\mathcal{LRA}$) learning is to find an SMT($\mathcal{LRA}$) formula ϕ which satisfies all elements in $E^\top$, but does not satisfy any element in $E^\bot$, which can be written as $\forall e \in E : \phi(a_e) = \phi^*(a_e)$.

Example 1. Consider the SMT($\mathcal{LRA}$) formula

$$\phi^*(b_1, r_1) = (\neg b_1 \vee (-0.5 \cdot r_1 \leq -1)) \wedge (b_1 \vee (1 \cdot r_1 \leq 0))$$

A possible set of examples would be

$$E = \{(\{b_1 \mapsto \top, r_1 \mapsto 0\}, \bot), (\{b_1 \mapsto \top, r_1 \mapsto 2.5\}, \top),$$
$$(\{b_1 \mapsto \bot, r_1 \mapsto 2\}, \bot), (\{b_1 \mapsto \bot, r_1 \mapsto -0.6\}, \top)\}$$

We call an algorithm that tackles the task of finding an unknown SMT($\mathcal{LRA}$) formula to a given set of examples, i.e. finding a solution to an instance of the aforementioned problem, *learner*.

Each learner must operate on a given set of possible target formulae, called the *hypothesis space* Φ. Similar to [13], we focus on *CNF* formulae as our hypothesis space.

Definition 2. *A CNF formula over a set of variables $B \cup R$ is a conjunction of clauses, a clause is a disjunction of literals and a literal can be a Boolean variable $b \in B$, its negation, or a linear constraint over the real variables. Linear constraints (also called halfspaces) have the form $a_1 \cdot r_1 + \cdots + a_m \cdot r_m \leq d$ with real constants a_i and d and real variables $r_i \in R$.*

Additionally, we define the cost c of a CNF formula with a given number of clauses k and (not necessarily unique) halfspaces h as $c = w_k \cdot k + w_h \cdot h$, where w_k and w_h are weights associated with clauses and halfspaces, respectively. The cost is a measure for the size and complexity of a formula and can be tuned to focus more on clauses or halfspaces.

A learner tries to find an SMT($\mathcal{LRA}$) formula $\phi \in \Phi$. We say that an example e satisfies a formula ϕ iff $\phi(a_e) = \top$ and is consistent with ϕ iff $\phi(a_e) = \phi^*(a_e)$. Using these definitions, the goal of SMT($\mathcal{LRA}$) learning is to find a formula ϕ that is consistent with all examples, i. e. as mentioned before, one that is satisfied by all positive examples and unsatisfied by all negative ones.

Example 2. Consider the example set E from Example 1 again. A possible CNF solution to those examples would be

$$\phi = (b_1 \vee (0.5 \cdot r_1 \leq -0.25)) \wedge (\neg b_1 \vee (-1 \cdot r_1 \leq -2.1))$$

Obviously, ϕ^* is also a feasible solution, but might not be found by the learner which only knows about the example set E.

Since ϕ^* is not known to the learner and the example set E is usually non-exhaustive, it can not be expected that the learner finds a model equivalent to ϕ^*. It should, however, be as close as possible. This leads to the measure of *accuracy*.

Definition 3. *Given two example sets E_{train} and E_{test} which were independently sampled from the (unknown) SMT($\mathcal{LRA}$) formula ϕ^*, the accuracy of a formula ϕ, which was learned from E_{train}, is the ratio of correctly classified examples in E_{test}.*

Generally, finding any formula for a given example set is not a hard problem. One could construct a simple CNF that explicitly forbids one negative example in each clause and allows all other possible assignments. However, such a formula would have numerous clauses and would not generalize well to new examples, yielding a low accuracy. To avoid such cases of overfitting, a smaller target formula, i. e. one with lower cost, should generally be preferred over a larger i. e. more expensive one.

2.2   INCAL

In addition to introducing the problem of SMT($\mathcal{LRA}$) learning, [13] also presented the first algorithm to tackle it, called *INCAL*. INCAL addresses the SMT($\mathcal{LRA}$) learning problem by fixing the number of clauses k and the number of halfspaces h and then encodes the existence of a feasible CNF with those parameters in SMT($\mathcal{LRA}$). If no such formula exists, different values for k and h need to be used. The order in which to try values for k and h can be guided by the cost function $w_k \cdot k + w_h \cdot h$.

INCAL's SMT encoding uses Boolean variables to encode which clauses contain which literals, real variables for the coefficients and offset of all halfspaces, and Boolean auxiliary variables encoding which halfspace and clause are satisfied by which example. It consists of the definition of those auxiliary variables and a constraint enforcing the consistency of examples with the learned formula. To cope with a high number of examples, INCAL uses an iterative approach and starts the encoding with only a small fraction of all variables. After a solution consistent with this subset has been found, additional conflicting examples are added.

The complexity of the learning problem does however not exclusively stem from the size of the input. Another, arguably even more influential factor is the complexity of the learned formula. If an example set requires numerous clauses or halfspaces, it will be much harder for INCAL to solve.

So far, we have discussed the state-of-the-art related work in SMT($\mathcal{LRA}$) learning. In this work, we present a new SMT($\mathcal{LRA}$) learner which incorporates a *hierarchical clustering* technique. To keep this paper self-contained, we give some preliminaries about clustering in the following section.

2.3   Hierarchical Clustering

In machine learning, the problem of clustering is to group a set of objects into several clusters, such that all objects inside the same cluster are closely related, while all objects from different clusters are as diverse as possible (cf. [14] for an overview). To describe the similarity between objects, a *distance metric* is needed.

Often, objects are described by the means of a vector $(v_1, \ldots, v_n)$ of real values. Typical distance metrics of two vectors v, w are (1) the *Manhattan distance* (L_1 norm) $dist(v, w) = \sum_{i=1}^{n} |v_i - w_i|$, (2) the *Euclidean distance* (L_2 norm) $dist(v, w) = \sqrt{\sum_{i=1}^{n}(v_i - w_i)^2}$, or (3) the L_∞ norm $dist(v, w) = max(|v_i - w_i|)$.

A common approach to clustering is *hierarchical clustering* [19]. The main idea of hierarchical clustering is to build a hierarchical structure of clusters called a *dendrogram*. A dendrogram is a binary tree annotated with distance information. Each node in the dendrogram represents a cluster. Each inner node thereby refers to the union of clusters of its two children; with leaf nodes representing clusters that contain exactly one vector. This way, the number of contained vectors per node increases in root direction with the root node itself containing all vectors given to the clustering algorithm. Each inner node is also annotated with the distance between its two children. In graphical representations of dendrograms, this is usually visualized by the height of these nodes.

Example 3. An example dendrogram can be seen in Fig. 1. The dashed and dotted lines may be ignored for now. The dendrogram shows a clustering over six input vectors, labeled A to F. The distance between nodes can be seen on the y-axis. For instance, the distance between vectors $\{B\}$ and $\{C\}$ is 1, while the distance between their combined cluster $\{B, C\}$ and vector $\{A\}$ is 2.

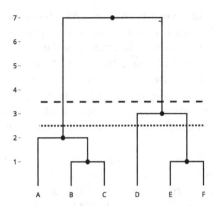

Fig. 1. A simple dendrogram

In this paper, we will focus on *agglomerative hierarchical clustering* [19], which builds the dendrogram by assigning each vector to its own cluster and then combines the two closest clusters until a full dendrogram has been built.

To combine the two closest clusters, it is necessary to not only measure the distance between two vectors but also between larger clusters. To this end, a *linkage criterion* is needed. Given two clusters c and d, some established linkage criteria are (1) the *single linkage* criterion, which picks the minimum distance between two vectors from c and d, (2) the *complete linkage* criterion, which picks the maximum distance between two vectors from c and d, or (3) the *average linkage* criterion, which takes the average of all distances between vectors from c and d.

Most combinations of distance measure and linkage criterion can be applied to a given hierarchical clustering problem. The results may, however, vary heavily depending on the application.

To obtain a concrete clustering from a dendrogram, one fixes a *distance threshold*. The final clustering is then made up of the nodes whose distances lie just below the distance threshold and whose parent nodes are already above it. In graphical representations, the distance threshold can be indicated by a horizontal line, making the clusters easily visible.

Example 4. The dashed line in Fig. 1 represents a distance threshold of 3.5. Following this threshold, the dendrogram would be split into the two clusters $\{A, B, C\}$ and $\{D, E, F\}$. Using a smaller distance threshold of 2.5, indicated by the dotted line, would result in the three clusters $\{A, B, C\}$, $\{D\}$, and $\{E, F\}$.

The following section shows how we utilize hierarchical clustering in our novel SMT($\mathcal{LRA}$) learner.

3   Using Dendrograms for SMT($\mathcal{LRA}$) Learning

In this section, we introduce our novel SMT($\mathcal{LRA}$) learner. We describe how the hierarchical clustering is used to guide its search and discuss the resulting algorithm which we call SHREC1. We start with the general idea in Sect. 3.1, followed by the algorithm in Sect. 3.2 and finally optimizations in Sect. 3.3. In Sect. 4 we present the algorithm SHREC2 to trade-off some accuracy for a further increase of scalability.

3.1   Main Idea

The main scalability problem of exact approaches for SMT($\mathcal{LRA}$) learning lies in the large combined encoding that is needed to describe a full CNF. This encoding quickly becomes hard to solve for SMT solvers when the number of clauses and halfspaces is increased. We, therefore, propose to not learn the target CNF as a whole, but rather to learn single clauses and then combine them into the target formula.

When looking at the structure of CNF formulas, it becomes apparent that positive examples need to satisfy all individual clauses, while negative ones only need to unsatisfy a single one. If one had a perfect prediction, which negative examples belong to which clause, one could simply learn each clause on its own, using a simpler encoding, and still obtain an exact solution. But even an imperfect prediction, which needs some additional clauses, would yield a correct and relatively small solution.

We propose a novel heuristic that produces such a prediction using agglomerative hierarchical clustering. The clustering algorithm partitions the negative examples into groups of closely related examples given their values in the assignment a_e. This is due to the intuition that it is easier to find a single clause for a set of closely related examples as opposed to an arbitrary one. The reason to use hierarchical clustering as opposed to other clustering algorithms is the ability to seamlessly adjust the number of clusters and thus the number of clauses in the target formula.

To obtain a suitable clustering vector, we normalize the examples. For Boolean variables, the values of $\top$ and $\bot$ are replaced with 1 and 0, respectively. The values $a_e(r)$ of real variables r are translated into the form $\frac{a_e(r) - r_{min}}{r_{max} - r_{min}}$, where r_{min} and r_{max} are the smallest and highest possible values for variable r, respectively. If those values are not known beforehand, they can simply be estimated from the existing data. This normalization ensures that all feature values lie in the interval $[0, 1]$, which results in each variable having a similar influence on the clustering outcome.

3.2   Algorithm SHREC1

The full algorithm SHREC1 is described in Algorithm 1. The algorithm receives as input a set of examples E and returns a formula ϕ consistent with E. The first

---

Algorithm 1. Algorithm SHREC1

Input: Example set E
Output: SMT($\mathcal{LRA}$) formula ϕ

1: **function** LEARN-MODEL(E)
2:     $N_0 \leftarrow$ BUILD-DENDROGRAM($E^\perp$)
3:     $cost \leftarrow w_k$
4:     **loop**
5:         $k \leftarrow 1$
6:         **while** $w_k \cdot k \leq cost$ **do**
7:             $\phi \leftarrow \top$
8:             $nodes \leftarrow$ SELECT-NODES(N_0, k)
9:             $h \leftarrow 0$
10:            $valid \leftarrow \top$
11:            **for all** $N_i \in nodes$ **do**
12:                $cost\text{-}bound \leftarrow cost - w_k \cdot k - w_h \cdot h$
13:                $h', \psi \leftarrow$ SEARCH-CLAUSE($N_i, cost\text{-}bound$)
14:                **if** $\psi = \emptyset$ **then**
15:                    $valid \leftarrow \perp$
16:                    **break**
17:                **else**
18:                    $\phi \leftarrow \phi \wedge \psi$
19:                    $h \leftarrow h + h'$
20:            **if** $valid$ **then**
21:                **return** ϕ
22:            **else**
23:                $k \leftarrow k + 1$
24:         $cost \leftarrow$ NEXT-COST($cost$)

25: **function** SEARCH-CLAUSE($N_i, cost\text{-}bound$)
26:     $h \leftarrow 0$
27:     **while** $w_h \cdot h \leq cost\text{-}bound$ **do**
28:         $\omega \leftarrow$ ENCODE-CLAUSE($E^\top \cup N_i, h$)
29:         $\psi \leftarrow$ SOLVE(ω)
30:         **if** $\psi \neq \emptyset$ **then**
31:             **return** h, ψ
32:         $h \leftarrow h + 1$
33:     **return** $h, \emptyset$

---

step of the algorithm is the function BUILD-DENDROGRAM, which uses agglomerative hierarchical clustering to build a dendrogram from the negative examples. The function uses the normalization procedure described in the previous section. Please note that BUILD-DENDROGRAM is agnostic to specific distance metrics and linkage criteria.

The resulting dendrogram is referred to by its root node N_0. Each subsequent node N_i has a unique, positive index i. As we do not need to distinguish between a node and the set of examples covered by it, we use N_i to refer to both the node N_i and its example set.

The algorithm is composed of several nested loops. The outermost loop (Lines 2–24) searches for a solution with increasing cost. Similar to INCAL, the cost is determined using a linear cost function $w_k \cdot k + w_h \cdot h$. The algorithm starts with the cost value set to w_k in the first iteration, allowing a solution with exactly one clause and no halfspaces. After each iteration, the cost is incremented, increasing the search space.

Since for each cost value multiple combinations of k and h are possible, the next loop (Lines 6–23) starts with $k = 1$ and keeps increasing the number of clauses k in each iteration. This, in turn, decreases the number of possible halfspaces. In each iteration, k nodes are selected from the dendrogram through an appropriate distance threshold and stored in the variable *nodes*. The algorithm then tries to find a clause consistent with each node N_i using as few halfspaces as possible. This is done in the function SEARCH-CLAUSE. If clauses for all nodes could be found within the cost bound, they are combined (Line 18) and the resulting CNF formula is returned. Since each clause satisfies all positive examples and each negative example is unsatisfied by at least one clause, this trivial combination yields a consistent CNF.

The function SEARCH-CLAUSE constitutes the innermost loop of the algorithm. Given a node N_i and the remaining cost left for halfspaces, the function tries to find a clause that is consistent with all positive examples and the negative examples in N_i. To keep the cost as low as possible, an incremental approach is used again, starting the search with 0 halfspaces and increasing the number of possible halfspaces h with each iteration. To find a clause for a fixed set of examples and a fixed number of halfspaces, an SMT encoding is used in Line 28. This encoding is a simplified version of the encoding from INCAL and uses the following variables: l_b and $\hat{l}_b$ with $b \in B$ encode whether the clause contains b or its negation, respectively; a_{jr} and d_j with $r \in R$ and $1 \leq j \leq h$ describe the coefficients and offset of halfspace j, respectively; s_{ej} with $e \in E$ and $1 \leq j \leq h$ is an auxiliary variable encoding whether example e satisfies halfspace j.

The overall encoding for a single example e can now be formulated with only two parts, i.e., (1) the definition of s_{ej}, which is identical to INCAL's

$$\bigwedge_{j=1}^{h} s_{ej} \iff \sum_{r \in R} a_{jr} \cdot a_e(r) \leq d_j,$$

and (2) the constraint which enforces consistency of e with the learned clause

$$\bigvee_{j=1}^{h} s_{ej} \vee \bigvee_{b \in B} \left((l_b \wedge a_e(b)) \vee \left(\hat{l}_b \wedge \neg a_e(b) \right) \right), \quad \text{if } \phi^*(a_e)$$

$$\bigwedge_{j=1}^{h} \neg s_{ej} \vee \bigwedge_{b \in B} \left((\neg l_b \vee \neg a_e(b)) \wedge \left(\neg \hat{l}_b \vee a_e(b) \right) \right), \quad \text{otherwise.}$$

The full encoding is the conjunction of the encodings for all examples in $E^\top \cup N_i$. Like INCAL, SHREC1 also uses an incremental approach. First, we only generate the above encoding for a few examples and then iteratively add more conflicting examples.

The function SOLVE in Line 29 takes an encoding, passes it to an SMT solver, and if a solution to the encoding is found, it is translated back into an SMT($\mathcal{LRA}$) clause. Otherwise, SOLVE returns $\emptyset$.

If a clause could be found within the cost bound (Line 30), it is returned together with the number of halfspaces used. Otherwise, $\emptyset$ is returned together with the highest attempted number of halfspaces.

This basic algorithm can be further improved in terms of runtime and cost by two optimizations described in the next section.

3.3   Result Caching and Dendrogram Reordering

The algorithm SHREC1 as described above suffers from two problems, namely (A) repeated computations and (B) an inflexible search, which we will both discuss and fix in this section.

First, we address issue (A), that SHREC1 re-computes certain results multiple times. When a node is passed to the function SEARCH-CLAUSE together with some *cost-bound*, a consistent clause is searched using up to $\frac{cost\text{-}bound}{w_k}$ halfspaces. In later iterations of the algorithm's main loop, SEARCH-CLAUSE is called again with the same node and higher *cost-bound*. This leads to the same SMT encoding being built and solved again. To avoid these repeated computations, each node caches the results of its computations and uses them to avoid unnecessary re-computation in the future.

Second, SHREC1 never modifies the initial dendrogram during the search, making the approach inflexible. We address this issue (B) in the following. If the initial clustering assigns only a single data point to an unfavorable cluster, this might lead to a much larger number of clauses needed to find a consistent formula. This, in turn, leads to a lower accuracy on new examples as well as a higher runtime. To counteract this problem, we apply a novel technique, which we call *dendrogram reordering*: whenever a clause ψ has been found for a given node N_i and some number of halfspaces h, it might be that ψ is also consistent with additional examples, which are not part of N_i, but instead of some other node N_j. To find such nodes N_j, a breadth-first search is conducted on the dendrogram. If some node N_j has been found such that $\forall e \in N_j : \psi(a_e) = \phi^*(a_e)$, the dendrogram is reordered to add N_j to the sub-tree under N_i. This does not increase the cost of N_i, because the new examples are already consistent with ψ, but might reduce the cost of N_j's (transitive) parent node(s).

Figure 2 illustrates the reordering procedure, which consists of the following steps: (1) Generate a new node N_k and insert it between N_i and its parent. Consequently, N_k's first child node is N_i and its parent node is N_i's former parent node. Set N_k's cached clause to ψ. (2) Remove N_j and its whole sub-tree from its original place in the dendrogram and move it under N_k as N_k's second child node. (3) To preserve the binary structure of the dendrogram, N_j's former parent node must now be removed. The former sibling node of N_j takes its place in the dendrogram.

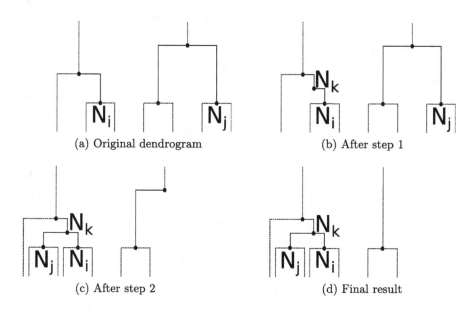

(a) Original dendrogram   (b) After step 1

(c) After step 2   (d) Final result

Fig. 2. Dendrogram reordering

This way, additional examples can be assigned to an already computed clause, reducing the complexity in other parts of the dendrogram, too, inherently. Consequently, the reordering can only decrease the overall cost of the dendrogram and never increase it. Therefore, dendrogram reordering can handle imperfect initial clusterings by dynamically improving them.

4 Improving Runtime Using Nested Dendrograms

In the previous section, we introduced a novel SMT($\mathcal{LRA}$) learner with improved runtime compared to INCAL (as we will demonstrate by an experimental evaluation in Sect. 5) without a significant impact on the quality, i.e. the accuracy of the resulting formulae. In real-world applications, however, an even faster and more scalable algorithm might be preferred, even with minor losses of accuracy. In this section, we propose a technique for *nested hierarchical clustering* to realize this trade-off. We call this algorithm SHREC2.

4.1 Main Idea

While SHREC1 is already expected to reduce the runtime of the SMT($\mathcal{LRA}$) learner, it still has to solve relatively complex SMT constraints to find a consistent clause. To further improve runtime, we again reduce the complexity of these SMT solver calls. The algorithm SHREC2 starts just like SHREC1 by clustering the negative examples and then searching for clauses consistent with the different clusters. However, instead of searching for consistent clauses through an SMT encoding, SHREC2 also clusters the positive examples, ultimately leaving only the learning of single halfspaces to the solver. This is realized through a simpler encoding, shifting the algorithm's overall complexity from exponential to polynomial runtime.

When searching for a single clause, negative examples must not satisfy any literal of the clause, while positive examples only have to satisfy a single literal each. This fact can now be used to learn literals one by one. To this end, *nested dendrograms* are introduced.

We, therefore, extend our definition of dendrograms from the previous sections. A dendrogram that clusters negative examples like the one used in SHREC1 is called a *negative dendrogram* from now on. Its nodes are called *negative nodes* denoted as $N_i^\perp$. In SHREC2, we also use *positive dendrograms*, which analogously cluster the positive examples. Each node $N_i^\perp$ of the negative dendrogram is assigned a new positive dendrogram $N_{i,0}^\top$. Each positive node $N_{i,j}^\top$ holds a set of positive examples from $E^\top$ which again are being clustered just like their negative counterparts.

Given a negative node $N_i^\perp$ and some halfspaces h, SHREC2 first finds all Boolean literals that are consistent with the examples in $N_i^\perp$. Because the cost function is only dependent on the number of clauses and halfspaces, these Boolean literals can be part of the clause without increasing the cost. Then, all positive examples that are inconsistent with any of the Boolean literals are determined. These examples constitute $N_{i,0}^\top$. The positive dendrogram under $N_{i,0}^\top$ is built in the same manner as the negative dendrogram, using the same normalization scheme. Values of Boolean variables are however left out of the clustering.

To find a set of halfspaces that are consistent with the remaining positive examples as well as the negative examples in $N_i^\perp$, an encoding is generated for each of the top h nodes from $N_{i,0}^\top$ matching them with individual halfspaces.

4.2 Algorithm SHREC2

Algorithm 2 describes the algorithm SHREC2. The main function (LEARN-MODEL) is identical to the one in Algorithm 1. The difference here can be found

---

Algorithm 2. Algorithm SHREC2

Input: Example set E
Output: SMT($\mathcal{LRA}$) formula ϕ

1: **function** LEARN-MODEL(E)
2: | $\ldots$ ▷ identical to SHREC1

3: **function** SEARCH-CLAUSE($N_i^\perp$, *cost-bound*)
4: | $L \leftarrow \{b \in B \mid \forall e \in N_i^\perp : a_e(b) = \perp\} \cup$
   | $\qquad \{\neg b \mid b \in B, \forall e \in N_i^\perp : a_e(b) = \top\}$
5: | $\psi \leftarrow \bigvee_{l \in L} l$
6: | $\psi' \leftarrow \psi$
7: | $E' \leftarrow \{e \in E^\top \mid \psi(a_e) = \perp\}$
8: | **if** $E' = \emptyset$ **then**
9: | | **return** $0, \psi$
10: | $N_{i,0}^\top \leftarrow$ BUILD-DENDROGRAM(E')
11: | $h \leftarrow 1$
12: | **while** $w_h \cdot h \leq$ *cost-bound* **do**
13: | | $\psi \leftarrow \psi'$
14: | | $nodes \leftarrow$ SELECT-NODES($N_{i,0}^\top, h$)
15: | | $valid \leftarrow true$
16: | | **for all** $N_{i,j}^\top \in nodes$ **do**
17: | | | $\omega \leftarrow$ ENCODE-HALFSPACE($N_i^\perp \cup N_{i,j}^\top$)
18: | | | $\theta \leftarrow$ SOLVE(ω)
19: | | | **if** $\theta = \emptyset$ **then**
20: | | | | $valid \leftarrow false$
21: | | | | **break**
22: | | | **else**
23: | | | | $\psi \leftarrow \psi \vee \theta$
24: | | **if** $valid$ **then**
25: | | | **return** h, ψ
26: | | **else**
27: | | | $h \leftarrow h + 1$
28: | **return** $h, \emptyset$

---

in the function SEARCH-CLAUSE, which tries to learn a clause given a set of negative examples and a cost bound.

The function starts by computing the set L of all literals that are consistent with all negative examples in $N_i^\perp$ (Line 4). It then computes the subset E' of all positive examples not consistent with any literal in L (Line 7). These remaining examples need further literals to be consistent with the clause. Consequently, if E' is already empty at this point, the disjunction of the literals in L is already a consistent clause and can be returned.

Otherwise, additional literals are needed. Because any further Boolean literals would be inconsistent with the negative examples, halfspaces are needed. To find a reasonable assignment of examples in E' to halfspaces, hierarchical clustering is used again. Instead of clustering the negative examples, the algorithm clusters the positive ones in E'. Since Boolean values have no influence on the halfspaces, they are not used in this clustering.

The remainder of the algorithm is now very similar to the process in the main function. The algorithm increases the number of halfspaces in each iteration, starting at 1, until a solution has been found or the cost bound has been reached. In each iteration, the top h nodes from the positive dendrogram are selected. For each node $N_{i,j}^{\top}$, the algorithm tries to find a halfspace for the examples in $N_i^{\perp}$ and $N_{i,j}^{\top}$ via an encoding. If no such halfspace exists, the algorithm retries with an increased h. If halfspaces could be found for all nodes, a disjunction of those halfspaces and the literals in L is returned as a consistent clause.

The encoding for a single example $e \in E$ is a simplified version of the one used in SHREC1, which uses variables a_r and d, describing the coefficients and offset of the halfspace, respectively. The encoding now only consists of a single constraint per example:

$$\sum_{r \in R} a_r \cdot a_e(r) \bowtie d$$

where $\bowtie$ is $\leq$ if $\phi^*(a_e) = \top$ and $>$ otherwise. The full encoding is again the conjunction of the encodings for all examples. Like in INCAL and SHREC1, examples are also added iteratively. Please note that the encoding of SHREC2 is only a linear program instead of a more complex SMT($\mathcal{LRA}$) encoding, making it solvable in polynomial time.

SHREC2 also uses result caching and dendrogram reordering in both levels of dendrograms. Besides, the positive dendrograms are computed only once for each negative node $N_i^{\perp}$ and are immediately cached for faster access.

5   Experiments

In this section, we evaluate the capabilities and applicability of the proposed algorithms SHREC1 and SHREC2. We have implemented them in Python using the SMT solver *Z3* [7] version 4.8.6 64 Bit and the *scikit-learn* package [17] version 1.3.1 for the hierarchical clustering. To this end, we conducted case studies and compared the results in terms of accuracy and runtime to INCAL. We ran all evaluations on an Intel Xeon E3-1240 v2 machine with 3.40 GHz (up to 3.80 GHz boost) and 32 GB of main memory running Fedora 26. In the following, we give detailed insight into the experimental setup in Sect. 5.1. We present the comparison of our approaches to INCAL in Sect. 5.2.

5.1   Experimental Setup

Due to the poor scalability of current approaches, no suitable real-world benchmarks for SMT($\mathcal{LRA}$) learning exist yet. In addition, benchmarks for SMT solving like the SMT-LIB collection are usually either unsatisfiable or only satisfied by few assignments, meaning they do not produce adequately balanced example sets. Therefore, experiments have to be conducted on randomly generated benchmarks. To this end, we use an approach similar to [13]: Given a set of parameters consisting of the number of clauses (k) and halfspaces per clause (h), we generate a CNF formula fitting these parameters. The generation procedure is also given a set of 1000 randomly generated assignments from variables to their respective values. The formula is then generated in such a way, that at least 30% and at most 70% of those assignments satisfy it. To ensure that the formula does not become trivial, it is also required that each clause is satisfied by at least $\frac{30}{k}$% of assignments that did not satisfy any previous clause. This ensures, that each clause has a significant influence on the formula and cannot be trivially simplified.

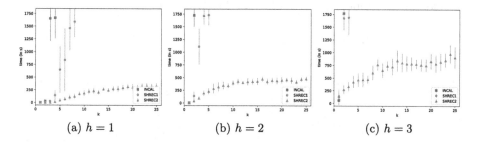

(a) $h = 1$ (b) $h = 2$ (c) $h = 3$

Fig. 3. Runtime comparison for different values of h

Since the main focus of SHREC is the improved scalability on larger formulae, we (similar to [13]) generated benchmarks with increasing k and h and fixed all other parameters to constant values. All generated formulae have 4 Boolean variables, 4 real variables, and 3 literals per clause. The benchmarks have between 1 and 25 clauses and between 1 and 3 halfspaces per clause, resulting in 75 different parameter configurations. We expect a higher number of clauses or halfspaces per clause to generally result in a harder benchmark. Since we cannot precisely control the difficulty, however, some smaller formulae might turn out to be more difficult than other larger ones. To mitigate these random fluctuations, we generated 10 formulae for each configuration, resulting in a total of 750 benchmarks.

For each benchmark, 1000 examples were randomly drawn. Boolean variables had an equal probability to be assigned to $\top$ or $\bot$. Real values were uniformly distributed in the interval $[0, 1)$.[2]

We used INCAL, SHREC1, and SHREC2 to find a CNF formula consistent with all examples. All three algorithms used a cost function with equal weights for clauses and halfspaces ($w_k = w_h = 1$). For each run, we measured the runtime and the accuracy on another independent set of 1000 examples. We set

---

[2] Please note that the choice of the interval does not influence the hardness of the learning problem because smaller values do not make the SMT solving process easier.

a timeout of 30 minutes for each run. This timeout is substantially longer than the one used in [13] and allows us to adequately observe the effect of the different configurations.

In the following section, the results are presented and discussed.

5.2 Comparison to INCAL

As mentioned in Sect. 3, SHREC1 and SHREC2 are able to use various distance metrics and linkage criteria in their clustering routine. To determine the most effective combination, we ran some preliminary experiments on a subset of the generated benchmarks. We evaluated the Manhattan distance, Euclidean distance, and the L_∞ norm as possible distance metrics and the single, complete and average linkage criteria. Out of the nine possible combinations, the Manhattan distance together with the average linkage criterion performed best. Therefore, this combination is used in the following comparison with INCAL.

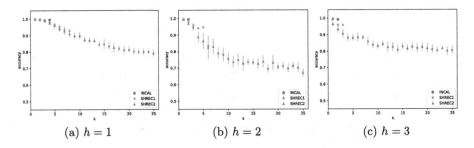

(a) $h = 1$ (b) $h = 2$ (c) $h = 3$

Fig. 4. Accuracy comparison for different values of h

Figure 3 shows the runtime for 1, 2 and 3 halfspaces per clause, respectively. On the x-axis, the number of clauses from $k = 1$ to $k = 25$ is shown. The y-axis shows the runtime in seconds. Each data point covers the runs on the 10 different benchmarks for the respective configuration. The squares, circles, and triangles mark the mean of all 10 runtimes, while the vertical error bars show the standard deviation. Runs that timed out were included in the calculation of mean and standard deviation as if they needed exactly 1800 s. If all runs of one configuration timed out, no data point is shown.

As expected, the number of clauses and halfspaces increases the runtime of all three algorithms. However, we can observe that the increase in runtime becomes smaller at a higher number of clauses. INCAL already times out at $k \geq 5$ for benchmarks with a single halfspace per clause and even at $k \geq 3$ for benchmarks with 2 or 3 halfspaces per clause. SHREC1 is able to handle larger benchmarks better, but still times out at $k \geq 8$, $k \geq 6$ and $k \geq 4$ for $h = 1$, $h = 2$, and $h = 3$, respectively. On instances where neither INCAL nor SHREC1 time out, SHREC1 is consistently considerably faster. SHREC2 is a lot more robust for increasing k and h and does not time out for any benchmark. SHREC2's runtime stays far below that of INCAL and SHREC1 for almost all of the benchmarks. This indicates SHREC2's superior scalability in terms of runtime, outperforming INCAL and SHREC1 by a large margin.

Naturally, we expect this success to come with a trade-off in the form of lower accuracy. Figure 4 shows the accuracy for 1, 2 and 3 halfspaces per clause, respectively. As before, each data point shows the mean and standard deviation of 10 benchmarks. Timeouts were not considered in the calculation this time. Configurations with 10 timeouts again have no data point displayed. As expected, the accuracy of all three algorithms is lower for larger problems. This is because a more complicated CNF needs to be found with the same number of examples. One can also observe, that SHREC1 and especially SHREC2 suffer more from this decrease in accuracy than INCAL. However, as Fig. 4a shows, SHREC1's accuracy still stays above 95% even for benchmarks with up to 7 clauses.

The decrease of accuracy is only crucial for larger values of k and h, which were not solved by INCAL at all. If given enough time, we can also expect INCAL to show a lower accuracy for these harder benchmarks. For the benchmarks which were solved by INCAL, SHREC1 and SHREC2 stay very close to 100% accuracy, as well. If one wants to compensate for the lower accuracy in other ways, the improved scalability of SHREC1 and SHREC2 could also be utilized to simply incorporate more training examples that can be handled due to better scalability.

Overall, the experimental results clearly show that SHREC is superior to the state-of-the-art exact approach INCAL in terms of scalability. SHREC1 needs considerably less runtime to learn formulae with only a slight loss of accuracy, while SHREC2 was several magnitudes faster and still kept the accuracy at a reasonable level.

6   Conclusion

In this work, we proposed a novel approach for SMT($\mathcal{LRA}$) learning. Our approach, SHREC, incorporates hierarchical clustering to speed up the learning process. Additionally, we presented two specific algorithms exploiting our findings with different objectives: SHREC1 aims for high accuracy of the learned model while SHREC2 trades-off accuracy for runtime, yielding a scalable approach to tackle even harder problems.

Our conducted experimental evaluation supports these claims. When compared to the state-of-the-art algorithm INCAL, our results clearly show that SHREC1 outperforms INCAL in terms of runtime with almost no loss of accuracy. SHREC2 on the other hand can handle benchmarks for which INCAL and SHREC1 timeout.

The better scalability permits our approach to handling interesting real-world problems on a larger scale. This opens up new possibilities on a variety of applications and enables future research in the domain.

References

1. Alur, R., Radhakrishna, A., Udupa, A.: Scaling enumerative program synthesis via divide and conquer. In: Legay, A., Margaria, T. (eds.) TACAS 2017. LNCS, vol. 10205, pp. 319–336. Springer, Heidelberg (2017). https://doi.org/10.1007/978-3-662-54577-5_18

2. Baldoni, R., Coppa, E., D'Elia, D.C., Demetrescu, C., Finocchi, I.: A survey of symbolic execution techniques. ACM Comput. Surv. **51**(3), 1–39 (2018)

3. Barbosa, H., Reynolds, A., Larraz, D., Tinelli, C.: Extending enumerative function synthesis via SMT-driven classification. In: Formal Methods in Computer Aided Design (FMCAD), pp. 212–220 (2019)

4. Bessiere, C., Coletta, R., Koriche, F., O'Sullivan, B.: A SAT-based version space algorithm for acquiring constraint satisfaction problems. In: Gama, J., Camacho, R., Brazdil, P.B., Jorge, A.M., Torgo, L. (eds.) ECML 2005. LNCS (LNAI), vol. 3720, pp. 23–34. Springer, Heidelberg (2005). https://doi.org/10.1007/11564096_8

5. Biere, A., Heule, M., van Maaren, H.: Handbook of Satisfiability, vol. 185. IOS press (2009)

6. Cordeiro, L., Fischer, B.: Verifying multi-threaded software using smt-based context-bounded model checking. In: 2011 33rd International Conference on Software Engineering (ICSE). IEEE (2011)

7. de Moura, L., Bjørner, N.: Z3: an efficient SMT solver. In: Ramakrishnan, C.R., Rehof, J. (eds.) TACAS 2008. LNCS, vol. 4963, pp. 337–340. Springer, Heidelberg (2008). https://doi.org/10.1007/978-3-540-78800-3_24

8. Eén, N., Sörensson, N.: An extensible SAT-solver. In: Giunchiglia, E., Tacchella, A. (eds.) SAT 2003. LNCS, vol. 2919, pp. 502–518. Springer, Heidelberg (2004). https://doi.org/10.1007/978-3-540-24605-3_37

9. Green, C.: Application of theorem proving to problem solving. In: Readings in Artificial Intelligence, pp. 202–222. Elsevier (1981)

10. Haaswijk, W., Mishchenko, A., Soeken, M., De Micheli, G.: SAT based exact synthesis using DAG topology families. In: Proceedings of the 55th Annual Design Automation Conference, p. 53. ACM (2018)

11. King, J.C.: Symbolic Execution and Program Testing. Commun. ACM **19**(7), 385–394 (1976)

12. Kolb, S., Paramonov, S., Guns, T., De Raedt, L.: Learning constraints in spreadsheets and tabular data. Mach. Learn. 1441–1468 (2017). https://doi.org/10.1007/s10994-017-5640-x

13. Kolb, S., Teso, S., Passerini, A., De Raedt, L.: Learning SMT(LRA) constraints using SMT solvers. In: Proceedings of the 27th International Joint Conference on Artificial Intelligence, IJCAI 2018, pp. 2333–2340. (2018)

14. Maimon, O., Rokach, L.: Data Mining and Knowledge Discovery Handbook, 2nd edn. Springer, Boston (2010). https://doi.org/10.1007/978-0-387-09823-4

15. Michalowski, M., Knoblock, C.A., Bayer, K., Choueiry, B.Y.: Exploiting automatically inferred constraint-models for building identification in satellite imagery. In: Proceedings of the 15th International Symposium on Advances in Geographic Information Systems (2007)

16. Muggleton, S., de Raedt, L.: Inductive logic programming: theory and methods. J. Logic Program. **19–20**, 629–679 (1994)

17. Pedregosa, F., Varoquaux, G., Gramfort, A., Michel, V., Thirion, B., Grisel, O., Blondel, M., Prettenhofer, P., Weiss, R., Dubourg, V., Vanderplas, J., Passos, A., Cournapeau, D., Brucher, M., Perrot, M., Duchesnay, E.: Scikit-learn: machine learning in python. J. Mach. Learn. Res. **12**, 2825–2830 (2011)

18. Reynolds, A., Barbosa, H., Nötzli, A., Barrett, C., Tinelli, C.: cvc4sy: smart and fast term enumeration for syntax-guided synthesis. In: Computer Aided Verification. pp. 74–83 (2019)
19. Sibson, R.: SLINK: an optimally efficient algorithm for the single-link cluster method. Comput. J. **16**(1), 30–34 (1973)
20. Silva, J.P.M., Sakallah, K.A.: GRASP-a new search algorithm for satisfiability. In: Proceedings of the International Conference on Computer-Aided Design, pp. 220–227 (1996)
21. Steiner, W.: An evaluation of SMT-based schedule synthesis for time-triggered multi-hop networks. In: Proceedings - Real-Time Systems Symposium, pp. 375–384 (2010)
22. Udupa, A., Raghavan, A., Deshmukh, J., Mador-Haim, S., Martin, M., Alur, R.: Transit: specifying protocols with concolic snippets. ACM SIGPLAN Not. **48**, 287 (2013)
23. Valiant, L.G.: A theory of the learnable. Commun. ACM **27**(11), 1134–1142 (1984)
24. Yordanov, B., Wintersteiger, C.M., Hamadi, Y., Kugler, H.: SMT-based analysis of biological computation. In: Brat, G., Rungta, N., Venet, A. (eds.) NFM 2013. LNCS, vol. 7871, pp. 78–92. Springer, Heidelberg (2013). https://doi.org/10.1007/978-3-642-38088-4_6

Modelling and Verification in B and Event-B

Fast and Effective Well-Definedness Checking

Michael Leuschel$^{(\boxtimes)}$ (iD)

Institut für Informatik, Universität Düsseldorf Universitätsstr. 1,
40225 Düsseldorf, Germany
michael.leuschel@hhu.de

Abstract. Well-Definedness is important for many formal methods. In B and Event-B it ensures that certain kinds of errors (e.g., division by 0) cannot appear and that proof rules based on two-valued logic are sound. For validation tools such as PROB, well-definedness is important for constraint solving. B and Event-B establish well-definedness by generating dedicated proof obligations (POs). Unfortunately, the standard provers are not always very good at discharging them. In this paper, we present a new integrated technique to simultaneously generate and discharge well-definedness POs. The implementation contains a dedicated rule-based prover written in Prolog supporting B, Event-B and extensions thereof for data validation. We show that the generation and discharging is significantly faster than existing implementations in RODIN and ATELIER-B and that a large number of POs are automatically discharged. The POs are fine-grained enough to provide precise source code feedback, and allow inspection of problematic POs within various editors.

1 Introduction and Motivation

Well-definedness is an important issue in formal methods. Various approaches exist to dealing with ill-defined expressions such as a division by zero or a function applied outside of its domain.

Three-valued logic is one such approach, but is rarely used in practice. Indeed, some important proof rules or techniques (e.g., proof by contradiction) are not sound in three-valued logic. This famous quote by the mathematician Hilbert is also relevant for automated provers: *"Taking the principle of excluded middle from the mathematician would be the same, say, as proscribing the telescope to the astronomer or to the boxer the use of his fists. To prohibit existence statements and the principle of excluded middle is tantamount to relinquishing the science of mathematics altogether.".* [1]

Another approach is to only allow total functions (over the underlying argument types), but preclude any knowledge about the function's value for problematic inputs. E.g., in the case of division the expression 1/0 would denote a

---

[1] Taken from https://en.wikipedia.org/wiki/Brouwer?Hilbert_controversy.

© Springer Nature Switzerland AG 2020
B. Dongol and E. Troubitsyna (Eds.): IFM 2020, LNCS 12546, pp. 63–81, 2020.
https://doi.org/10.1007/978-3-030-63461-2_4

number, but one has no knowledge about its value within a proof. In this approach we thus can neither prove $1/0 = 0$ nor $1/0 \neq 0$, but we can prove the predicates $1/0 = 1/0$ or $\exists y.y = 1/0$. This approach is convenient for constraint solving or model finding and is typically used by SMTLib or Why3 [20]. Its main drawback is that problematic expressions such as $1/0$ may lurk within a formal model without a user realising it.

The approach of the B-method is to generate well-definedness (WD) proof obligations (POs) [5] for all formulas under consideration. These POs can be generated by the RODIN platform [3] or by ATELIER-B (where they are called WD-lemmas). If they are discharged we know that the corresponding formulas are well-defined and that we can apply two-valued logic. This approach is good for automated proving, enabling to apply effective provers based on two-valued logic. Also, for users it is good to obtain feedback about ill-defined expressions, rather than silently giving them an arbitrary value.

There are unfortunately a few outstanding practical issues:

– Discharging the WD proof obligations themselves is often quite time consuming, and the built-in provers of RODIN or ATELIER-B are not very good at discharging certain types of relevant goals (e.g., finiteness proof obligations or boundedness proof obligations for *min* and *max*).
– The POs generated by RODIN or ATELIER-B apply to entire formulas (e.g., invariants or guards), and it would be useful to be able to more precisely pinpoint problematic expressions and operators in the formal models. This is useful for user feedback, e.g., in an editor. Also, for constraint solving, ill-defined expressions pose a particular threat. Here a precise annotation can help the constraint solver in knowing, e.g., which division is susceptible to divide by zero. We return to this in Sect. 6 below.
– For data validation [23], well-definedness is also an important issue. However, RODIN is missing some datatypes such as strings and sequences (the latter can be added via the theory plugin; but automated proof support is very limited). While ATELIER-B supports sequences and strings, its automated proof support for sequences is not very good. Furthermore, extensions to B are used for data validation (see [16]) which are not (yet) supported by ATELIER-B.

Contributions. In this article we present a new combined well-definedness PO generator and prover, which has been integrated into the PROB validation tool, and which

– is based on a fast algorithm to generate WD proof obligations and discharge them at the same time,
– deals with Event-B, classical B and PROB's extensions for data validation (or with any other formalisms which PROB translates internally to B, namely TLA+, Alloy and Z),
– provides proof support for the B sequence datatype and its many operators,
– produces precise error feedback, either in PROB's own editor, Atom or VSCode to the end user,

– and can provide precise annotation of those operator nodes in the abstract syntax tree of a formal model which are susceptible to well-definedness errors.

Our prover can be seen as a specialized successor to the ML (mono-lemma) rule-based prover from ATELIER-B, dedicated to discharging WD POs.

2   Well-Definedness Proof-Obligations

We first recall the essential aspects of the well-definedness proof-obligations, as described in [5]. We suppose some familiarity with the B method. By *formula* we here mean either an expression (e.g, $x + 1$), a predicate (e.g., $x > 1$) or a substitution (e.g., $x := 1$). We denote logical equivalence of predicates by $\equiv$.

With each formula f we associate a well-definedness predicate $WD(f)$. This predicate is defined inductively over the structure of f and can be seen as a syntactic operator: it maps a formula f to a predicate. For Event-B the rules can be found in Sect. 5 of [26] in the RODIN handbook or partially in Sect. 5.2.12 of [2]. Here are two such rules for division and function application, where the type of f is $\mathbb{P}(D_f \times R_f)$:

$$WD(a \div b) \equiv WD(a) \wedge WD(b) \wedge b \neq 0$$

$$WD(f(a)) \equiv WD(f) \wedge WD(a) \wedge a \in dom(f) \wedge f \in D_f \twoheadrightarrow R_f$$

An integer literal or a variable has no well-definedness condition:

$$WD(x) \equiv \top \quad \text{for integer literals or variables x}$$

We thus have for example $WD(10 \div (x \div y)) \equiv y \neq 0 \wedge x \div y \neq 0$.
$\mathcal{L}$ *and* $\mathcal{D}$ *and Connectives.* An important aspect arises in the treatment of the logical connectives. There are in fact two approaches [5,8] to computing WD:

– the left-to-right approach $\mathcal{L}$ which requires that well-definedness of a formula must be established by predicates on its left,
– and the more flexible $\mathcal{D}$ approach, which does not impose a strict left-to-right examination of the predicates.

RODIN uses the $\mathcal{L}$ approach, meaning that:

$$WD(P \wedge Q) \equiv WD(P) \wedge (P \Rightarrow WD(Q))$$

In other words, Q need not be well-defined if P is false. Similarly,

$$WD(P \vee Q) \equiv WD(P) \wedge (P \vee WD(Q))$$

Note that the RODIN handbook uses $\mathcal{L}(.)$ to denote this left-to-right WD-condition. In [8] the notation Δ_P^{MC} is used instead, where MC stands for Mc Carthy (see also [9] for CVC-lite).

The more flexible $\mathcal{D}$ approach [5] uses the following rule

$$\mathcal{D}(P \wedge Q) \equiv (\mathcal{D}(P) \wedge \mathcal{D}(Q)) \vee (\mathcal{D}(P) \wedge \neg P) \vee (\mathcal{D}(Q) \wedge \neg Q)$$

In [8] this operator is written as Δ_P^K instead, where K stands for Kleene.

Given $P = (x > 0 \wedge 100/x < 50)$ and $P' = (100/x < 50 \wedge x > 0)$ we have that $WD(P) \equiv \top$ and $WD(P') \equiv (x \neq 0) \not\equiv \top$ but $\mathcal{D}(P) \equiv \mathcal{D}(P') \equiv \top$. The $\mathcal{D}$ approach is more powerful, and is commutative wrt $\wedge$ and $\vee$ but suffers from an exponential blowup of the size of the WD proof obligations. It is not used in practice.[2] We will use the $\mathcal{L}$ approach in the remainder of this article.

B vs Event-B. For classical B the conditions are associated with each operator in [1] or the Atelier-B handbook [11]. The treatment of substitutions is handled in [8]. There are some subtle differences in the WD conditions of B and Event-B. E.g., exponentiation is less permissive in Event-B than inclassical B: $(-2)^3$ is allowed in classical B, but not well-defined in Event-B (cf. page 43, Table 5.2 in [26]).[3]

There is, however, no fundamental difference in the derivation of the WD proof obligations for predicates and expressions (but classical B has many more substitutions, see Sect. 3). Our implementation has a flag indicating the language mode (B, Event-B, Z, Alloy or TLA+), to appropriately adapt the POs.

There is, however, one fundamental difference between Rodin and Atelier-B. Rodin adds the goals of WD proof obligations as hypotheses to subsequent proof obligations. The motivation is to avoid having to re-prove the same goal multiple times. This technique is not described in [2,26], but can be found in [25]. In Atelier-B this technique is not applied.

In the example below, the WD PO for axiom **axm2** in Rodin is $f \in \mathbb{Z} \leftrightarrow \mathbb{Z} \Rightarrow f \in \mathbb{Z} \rightarrow \mathbb{Z} \wedge 2 \in dom(f)$. This PO cannot be proven (and the model contains a WD error), but its goals $f \in \mathbb{Z} \rightarrow \mathbb{Z}$ and $2 \in dom(f)$ are added by Rodin to the hypotheses of the PO for the theorem **thm1**, meaning that it can be trivially proven with the **hyp** rule (which checks if a hypothesis is on the stack).

```
1  context Test_WD_Hyp
2  constants f
3  axioms
4     @axm1 f : INT <-> INT // f is a relation
5     @axm2 f(2) = 3         // this can give rise to a WD error
6     theorem @thm1 f : INT +-> INT // can be proven with hyp in Rodin
7     theorem @thm2 f(2) = 4
8  end
```

Listing 2.1. WD Event-B Rodin Example

---

[2] [12] discusses combining power of $\mathcal{D}$ with the efficiency of $\mathcal{L}$, but is not used in practice as far as we know. It seems to require one to establish the truth or falsity of individual formulas, which may not be easily feasible in practice.

[3] For modulo $-3 \bmod 2 = -1$ is well-defined and true in Event-B, but is not well-defined in classical B. But this is not due to a difference in the WD condition, but due to the fact that $-3 \bmod 2$ is parsed as $-(3 \bmod 2)$ in Rodin and $(-3) \bmod 2$ in Atelier-B. The Rodin handbook requires modulo arguments to be non-negative, which is correct; [26] is in error.

This optimisation also means that discharging all *WD* POs is very important in RODIN: one simple error like using f(2) can be used to prove arbitrary goals (e.g., above one can easily prove a theorem 22=33 by contradiction).

In our algorithm we do not use this optimisation of RODIN. As we will see, our algorithm is fast enough without it, and we also want to establish well-definedness for each program point in isolation and detect all sub-expressions which are potentially ill-defined, not just the first one. For example, in RODIN the well-definedness PO of theorem thm2 is proven. This is particularly relevant when we want to use the information for a constraint solver: it has to know for every program point whether it is guaranteed to be well-defined or not.

3   Fine-Grained WD Proof Obligations

Below we define our more fine grained way of computing well-definedness proof obligations. Rather than computing one proof obligation for an entire formula (such as an invariant or axiom), we will derive *multiple* proof obligations for individual operators within each formula. Our formalization thus uses a relation rather than a function taking a formula and producing a single PO. Our formalization also manages explicitly a single hypothesis environment, rather than putting hypotheses piecemeal into the formulas. The reasons will become apparent later: our formalisation manages the hypotheses like a *stack* and will correspond to an efficient implementation in Prolog.

Our PO generation uses the ternary relation $H \otimes F \twoheadrightarrow P$ meaning that given the current hypotheses H, the formula F gives rise to a proof obligation P. P will always be a predicate of the form *Hypotheses* $\Rightarrow$ *Goal*.

For example, we will have that:

- $H \otimes (10 \div b) \div c \twoheadrightarrow H \Rightarrow b \neq 0$ and
- $H \otimes (10 \div b) \div c \twoheadrightarrow H \Rightarrow c \neq 0$.

We will first provide a generic rule for all binary operators which always requires *both* arguments to be well-defined without additional hypotheses (e.g., $\div, +, \cup$). These operators are sometimes called *strict*. We define the direct well-definedness condition *WDC* for every such operator, ignoring *WD* conditions of arguments. Here are a few rules, where the type of f is $\mathbb{P}(D_f \times R_f)$:

$$WDC(a \div b) \equiv b \neq 0$$

$$WDC(a + b) \equiv \top$$

$$WDC(f(a)) \equiv a \in dom(f) \wedge f \in D_f \twoheadrightarrow R_f$$

$$WDC(first(f)) \equiv f \in seq(R_f) \wedge f \neq \varnothing$$

$$WDC(inter(a)) \equiv a \neq \varnothing$$

In the B language $dom(f)$ denotes the domain of f, $A \twoheadrightarrow B$ denotes the set of partial functions from A to B, $seq(A)$ the set of all sequences over A, $first(f)$ the first element of a sequence f and $inter(a)$ denotes the union of a set of sets a. We can now provide three generic inference rules for all those binary operators BOP where no hypotheses are added or removed for discharging the well-definedness of its arguments:

$$\frac{}{H \otimes a \circ b \ \twoheadrightarrow \ H \Rightarrow WDC(a \circ b)} \ \circ \in BOP$$

$$\frac{H \otimes a \ \twoheadrightarrow \ PO}{H \otimes a \circ b \ \twoheadrightarrow \ PO} \ \circ \in BOP \qquad \frac{H \otimes b \ \twoheadrightarrow \ PO}{H \otimes a \circ b \ \twoheadrightarrow \ PO} \ \circ \in BOP$$

For unary operators UOP such as $-$, union, inter, conc we have the following rules:

$$\frac{}{H \otimes \circ a \ \twoheadrightarrow \ H \Rightarrow WDC(\circ a)} \ \circ \in UOP$$

$$\frac{H \otimes a \ \twoheadrightarrow \ PO}{H \otimes \circ a \ \twoheadrightarrow \ PO} \ \circ \in UOP$$

Logical Connectives. The equivalence $\Leftrightarrow$ can simply be treated by the BOP inference rules with $WDC(P \Leftrightarrow Q) = \top$. Similarly, negation can be treated as a unary operator with $WDC(\neg P) = \top$. For the conjunction the first argument P is pushed onto the hypotheses H for the second argument Q:

$$\frac{H \otimes P \ \twoheadrightarrow \ PO}{H \otimes P \wedge Q \ \twoheadrightarrow \ PO} \qquad \frac{H \wedge P \otimes Q \ \twoheadrightarrow \ PO}{H \otimes P \wedge Q \ \twoheadrightarrow \ PO}$$

The implication has exactly the same inference rules:

$$\frac{H \otimes P \ \twoheadrightarrow \ PO}{H \otimes P \Rightarrow Q \ \twoheadrightarrow \ PO} \qquad \frac{H \wedge P \otimes Q \ \twoheadrightarrow \ PO}{H \otimes P \Rightarrow Q \ \twoheadrightarrow \ PO}$$

For disjunction the negation of P is pushed onto the hypotheses for Q:

$$\frac{H \otimes P \ \twoheadrightarrow \ PO}{H \otimes P \vee Q \ \twoheadrightarrow \ PO} \qquad \frac{H \wedge \neg P \otimes Q \ \twoheadrightarrow \ PO}{H \otimes P \vee Q \ \twoheadrightarrow \ PO}$$

Here we clearly see the difference with the classical formalization of the WD operator in the literature, which inserts a hypothesis into a disjunction of the resulting PO formula: $WD(P \vee Q) \equiv WD(P) \wedge (P \vee WD(Q))$.

The treatment of quantifiers requires the renaming operator $\rho_V(H)$ which renames all variables in the hypotheses which clash with variable in V to fresh new variables. With this operator we can produce the rules for existential and universal quantification:

$$\frac{\rho_V(H) \otimes P \ \twoheadrightarrow \ PO}{H \otimes \exists V.P \ \twoheadrightarrow \ PO} \qquad \frac{\rho_V(H) \otimes P \ \twoheadrightarrow \ PO}{H \otimes \forall V.P \ \twoheadrightarrow \ PO}$$

We have similar rules for other quantified operators, such as $\bigcup$ or $\bigcap$.

Proof Obligations for Substitutions. The ATELIER-B handbook does not detail how well-definedness is established for substitutions, and this aspect is not relevant in RODIN. For our tool we first developed our own *WD* proof rules and then discovered that [8] contains *WD* rules for substitutions, which seem mostly to have been taken over in ATELIER-B. Some constructs like parallel composition or CHOICE are simply "transparent" for *WD* computation and can be treated in the same way as the binary operators above. This means that in a parallel construct $P \parallel Q$ each branch must be well-defined on its own: one cannot make use of guards in P to prove $WD(Q)$ or vice-versa. Some examples in Sect. 5.3 incorrectly rely on the guards in P to establish well-definedness in Q.

Some constructs like IF-THEN-ELSE or SELECT are similar to conjunction in that hypotheses are added for certain subgoals. This is the rule for simple assignments:

$$\frac{H \otimes E \;\rightarrowtail\; PO}{H \otimes x := E \;\rightarrowtail\; PO} \; x \text{ is a simple variable}$$

For the assignment, B also allows to assign to functions and nested functions and to records and nested records. Here are the rules for these cases.

$$\frac{H \otimes E \;\rightarrowtail\; PO}{H \otimes r(x) := E \;\rightarrowtail\; PO} \quad \frac{H \otimes r \;\rightarrowtail\; PO}{H \otimes r(x) := E \;\rightarrowtail\; PO} \quad \frac{H \otimes x \;\rightarrowtail\; PO}{H \otimes r(x) := E \;\rightarrowtail\; PO}$$

$$\frac{H \otimes E \;\rightarrowtail\; PO}{H \otimes r'f := E \;\rightarrowtail\; PO} \quad \frac{H \otimes r \;\rightarrowtail\; PO}{H \otimes r'f := E \;\rightarrowtail\; PO}$$

The above rule also treats nested functions calls. E.g., for the assignment $g(y)(x) := E$ the above rule applies with $r = g(y)$ and we thus require that E and x are well-defined and that $y \in dom(g)$ and that g is a partial function.

For the WHILE substitution we adapted the proof rule from [8]. A tricky aspect is the sequential composition. [8] contains a few specific rules and was trying to avoid having to apply the weakest-precondition computations in full.[4] We have adapted a few of the rules from [8], the most used one being $WD(x := E \; ; \; Q\;) = WD(E) \wedge WD([x := E]Q))$ where $[x := E](P) = P[E/x]$. Note that the default rule for sequential composition treats the assigned variables as fresh variables without hypotheses, and does generate POs for the sub-formulas. Note that [8] also contains a rule for parallel composition followed by sequential composition which is wrong. There is also a special rule for a WHILE loop in the LHS of a sequential composition which we have not implemented. The rules implemented thus far proved sufficient for many applications.

4   Fast Integrated POG and Prover

One can notice that in the above proof rules for $H \otimes F \;\rightarrowtail\; P$ the hypotheses H are passed through to subarguments of F and sometimes a new hypothesis is added. This means that a lot of proof obligations will share common hypotheses.

---

[4] ATELIER-B now uses full WP calculus (private communication from Lilian Burdy).

When using external provers in RODIN, each well-definedness PO is discharged on its own and a new prover instance is launched for every PO. This is not very efficient, especially when the number of hypotheses becomes large (cf. Sect. 5). In ATELIER-B the hypotheses can be numbered and shared amongst proof obligations, which is useful when discharging multiple proof obligations in one tool run. However, for every PO the hypotheses must still be assembled.

One key idea of this paper is to discharge the POs in the same order they are generated by our POG rules and to treat the hypotheses as a *stack*. E.g., when one enters the right-hand side of a conjunction we *push* the left-hand side as a hypothesis onto the stack, when leaving the conjunction we *pop* this hypothesis again. The pushing of a new hypothesis can also conduct a few proof-related tasks, like normalization and indexing.

Another insight of this paper is that in the Prolog programming language the popping can be done very efficiently upon backtracking: the Prolog virtual machine is optimised for these kinds of operations and does them in a memory and time efficient way.

Below we show our implementation of the above POG rule for the conjunction. The Prolog predicate compute_wd encodes our relation $Hypotheses \otimes A \wedge B \twoheadrightarrow PO$ with some additional arguments (for source code locations, typing and options). You can see that there is a call to push A onto the hypothesis stack, but no pop operation, which is performed upon backtracking.

```
1  compute_wd_aux(conjunct(A,B),_,_,_,_,Hypotheses,Options,PO) :- !,
2    (compute_wd(A,Hypotheses,Options,PO)
3    ;
4    push_hyp(Hypotheses,A,Options,NewHyp),
5    compute_wd(B,NewHyp,Options,PO)).
```

Listing 4.1. Prolog clause for processing the conjunction

The push_hyp predicate will also filter useless hypotheses and normalise the useful ones. It also performs indexing to ensure that subsequent proving steps can be performed efficiently. For commutative operators this may mean to store a hypothesis twice. Our technique will ensure that this overhead is only incurred once for all proof obligations having that particular hypothesis on the stack. The proving is performed when an actual PO is generated (in this case, no PO is directly created by the conjunction itself).

For quantifiers we need to provide the renaming mechanism $\rho_V(H)$. To avoid traversing all hypotheses upon every clash, our implementation of $\rho_V(H)$ actually stores a list of variable clashes and renamings. The renamings are not applied to the existing hypotheses, only to new hypotheses and the final goal of the PO.

In essence, the main ideas for obtaining a fast and effective proof obligation generator and prover are:

- use Prolog pattern matching on the syntax tree to implement the POG generation,
- combine proof-obligation generation and proving in a single traversal, discharging POs in the same order they are generated,

- organize the hypothesis as a stack, use Prolog backtracking for popping from the stack,
- pre-compile the hypotheses to enable logarithmic lookup of hypotheses,
- use a rule-based prover in Prolog which only uses such logarithmic lookups in hypotheses, performs rewrite steps using Prolog unification and limiting non-determinism as much as possible.

Normalization and Lookup of Hypotheses. Normalization is employed by many provers, e.g., it is used in ATELIER-B to minimize the number of proof rules that have to be implemented (see Chap. 3 of Interactive Prover manual of [11]).

Our rules are different from the ones in [11], as we are also concerned with ensuring logarithmic lookup of hypotheses. Our hypotheses are stored as an AVL tree using the normalised Prolog term as key. AVL trees are self-balancing binary search trees with logarithmic lookup, insertion and deletion (see, e.g., Sect. 6.2.3 of [19]). We have used the AVL library of SICStus Prolog 4, and implemented a new predicate to enable logarithmic lookup if the first argument of the top-level operator is known, but the second argument may be unknown (making use of lexicographic ordering of Prolog terms).

Table 1. A few normalization rules and the generation of additional hypotheses

Predicate	Normalization	Additional Hypotheses	Conditions
$x > n$	$x \geq n + 1$		if n is a number
$n > x$	$x \leq n - 1$		if n is a number
$x > y$	$x \geq y \wedge x \neq y$	$y \leq x$	otherwise
$x < n$	$x \leq n - 1$		if n is a number
$n < x$	$x \geq n + 1$		if n is a number
$x < y$	$x \leq y \wedge x \neq y$	$y \geq x$	otherwise
$A \subset B$	$A \subseteq B \wedge A \neq B$	$B \supseteq A$	

All hypothesis lookups in our prover are logarithmic (in the number of hypotheses); no lookup requires a linear traversal. Some hypotheses are stored multiple times to enable this logarithmic lookup based on first argument: the predicate $a = b$ is also stored in the form $b = a$ if the term b is susceptible to be looked up. The predicate $a < b$ may result in three hypotheses being added: $a \leq b, b \geq a, a \neq b$. $a \neq b$ is only stored once, as upon lookup time both arguments are known. The Table 1 shows some of our normalization rules.

Table 2 shows the lookups that are made by our prover in the hypothesis stack. As mentioned, the first argument A is always known. All other hypotheses not occuring in Table 2 are not pushed onto the stack (in proving mode), as they would never be used anyway.

Table 2. Lookups made in the Hypothesis Stack (A is always known, B known for $\neq$)

Patterns for Lookups	
$finite(A)$	$A \in B$
$A = B$	$A \neq B$
$A \leq B$	$A \geq B$
$A \subseteq B$	$A \supseteq B$

Predicates Supported by the Prover. The rule-based prover contains various Prolog predicates for proving a few core B predicates, namely those listed in Table 3. The following Prolog clauses contain a small part of the check_finite predicate responsible for proving the B *finite* predicate. The first argument is the B expression which is the argument to the *finite* operator, the second argument is the hypothesis stack while the third argument is a proof tree constructed by the prover (for subsequent inspection or validation). These clauses encode the axioms *finite(BOOL)* and *finite(∅)* as well as the proof rules that *finite(A ∩ B)* holds if either *finite(A)* or *finite(B)* and that *finite(A \ B)* or *finite(ran(A))* hold if *finite(A)*.

```
1  check_finite(bool_set,_,bool_set) :- !.
2  check_finite(empty_set,_,empty_set) :- !.
3  check_finite(intersection(A,B),Hyps,intersection(D,PT)) :- !,
4     (  D=left, check_finite(A,Hyps,PT) -> true
5     ;  D=right, check_finite(B,Hyps,PT)).
6  check_finite(set_subtraction(A,_),Hyps,set_subtraction(PT)) :- !,
7     check_finite(A,Hyps,PT).
8  check_finite(range(A),Hyp,ran(PT)) :- !, check_finite(A,Hyp,PT).
```

Listing 4.2. Some Prolog clauses for checking the finite B predicate

The proof rules and derived Prolog clauses are written such that matching of B predicates (like **intersection** or **set_subtraction** above) always occur at the top-level of the formulas. This ensures that we can use efficient and simple Prolog unification for the proof rules and that Prolog's argument indexing often results in constant time lookup of possible matching proof rules.

Ensuring Termination. To avoid useless rewrites, our prover contains local loop checks within the predicates of Table 3. Some rewrites are also guarded by an occurs check, to prevent rewriting x to something like $rev(rev(x))$. Finally, a depth bound limits the number of equality and subset rewrites applicable within a particular proof. Currently the bound is set to allow 5 rewrites; increasing this bound only minimally increases the number of POs discharged in Sect. 5.3.

Implementation within PROB. The prover has been integrated into the PROB validation tool. On the one hand, this has eased the implementation, as part of PROB's infrastructure (parser, typechecker, static rewriter) could be re-used. For the rules concerning substitutions (Sect. 3), we also reused the code for computing written variables. On the other hand, we also plan to use the output of the prover for PROB's constraint solver; see Sect. 6. Finally, this also enabled to make

Table 3. Prolog prover predicates, where T and T' are maximal type sets

B Predicates handled by the Prover	
$A \subseteq B$	$A \in B$
$A \leq B$	$A \neq B$
$A \in T \nrightarrow T'$	(functional)
$A^{-1} \in T \nrightarrow T'$	(injective)
$A \in seq(T)$	(is sequence)
$finite(T)$	
$dom(A) = D$	$dom(A) \subseteq D'$
$ran(A) = R$	$ran(A) \subseteq R'$

the prover available within RODIN, as part of the PROB-Disprover plugin. This is particularly useful for discharging POs which pose problems to other provers (e.g., for *min, max* and *card*). Existing integrations with editors, such as Atom and VSCode could also be easily extended to highlight potential WD issues.

5 Benchmarks

Below we provide a variety of benchmarks. Section 5.1 contains artificial benchmarks to measure scalability compared with ATELIER-B and RODIN. In Sect. 5.2 we examine a few specific POs extracted as regression tests, while in Sect. 5.3 we perform a more exhaustive evaluation on over 6000 models from the PROB examples repository. All experiments were run on a MacBook Pro 2.8 GHz i7 processor, 16GB of RAM and running macOS 10.14.6. For the experiments we have used version `1.10.0-beta2` of the command-line version `probcli` with the flags `-wd-check -silent`, which runs our PO generator and prover on the provided model and prints a summary information (the `-silent` flag prevents the output of source locations for the undischarged POs) available at:

https://www3.hhu.de/stups/downloads/prob/tcltk/releases/1.10.0-beta2/.

5.1 Artificial Benchmarks

We next present the following artificial benchmark model template, where Nr is a parameter which we have instantiated to various values between 100 and 8000. ATELIER-B generates $3Nr$ proof obligations, while our implementation generates $6Nr$, as we check separately for every function application that ff is a function and that the argument is in the domain of ff.

```
1   MACHINE FunNrWD
2   CONSTANTS ff
3   PROPERTIES
4       /* axm0 */ ff : 1 .. Nr --> 1 .. 90
5     & /* axm1 */ ff(1) < 100
6     & /* axm2 */ ff(2) < 100
7     ...
8     & /* axmNr */ ff(Nr) < 100
9     & /* axm_nest_1 */ ff(ff(1)) < 100
10    ...
11    & /* axm_nest_Nr */ ff(ff(Nr)) < 100
12  INITIALISATION skip
13  END
```

Listing 5.1. Artificial Benchmark Template

AtelierB. We have loaded the above model into the 64-bit version 4.6.0-rc4 of ATELIER-B for macOS. The timings for ATELIER-B were obtained using a stopwatch, after the models had been loaded and typechecked. The timings of our implementation were taken within PROB, using walltime for the total time needed to generate and discharge the POs. The time needed to parse and load and typecheck the machine was *not* measured for either tool.

Table 4. Artificial WD Benchmark FunNrWD (classical B)

Nr	ATELIER-B			PROB WD	
	POG	Proof F0	Discharged	POG + Proof	Discharged
100	4 s	13 s	100%	0.035 s	100%
200	40 s	62 s	100%	0.041 s	100%
500	error	–	0%	0.058 s	100%
1000	error	–	0%	0.083 s	100%
2000	error	–	0%	0.139 s	100%
4000	error	–	0%	0.252 s	100%
8000	error	–	0%	0.478 s	100%

For $Nr = 100$ and $Nr = 200$ our implementation is a few orders of magnitude faster. ATELIER-B ran into a "memory overflow (max expansion reached)" in default settings for $Nr = 200$. After increasing the "m" parameter by a factor of 100 we managed to generate the proof obligations for $Nr = 200$. But for $Nr = 500$ we were not successful (4.25 GB memory were used; error generated after about 90 s, we tried to increase the memory allowance as much as the UI would let us). Note that the first run of the WD prover within PROB is always a bit slower (probably due to JIT startup time) than subsequent runs (e.g., 18 ms for $Nr = 200$). This is relevant when checking many POs (such as in Sect. 5.3) or when PROB is left open while working on a model (Table 4).

Rodin. We encoded the above B machines in Event-B and used RODIN version 3.4. We used a stop watch to measure the POG (building) time and the auto prover time ("Retry Auto Provers" command).

Table 5. Artificial WD Benchmark FunNrWD (Event-B)

Nr	RODIN			PROB WD	
	POG	Auto Prover	Discharged	POG + Proof	Discharged
100	3 s	2 min 28 s	49.5%	0.036 s	100%
200	8.5 s	6 min 05 s	24.5%	0.044 s	100%
500	47 s	17 min 10 s	9.7%	0.063 s	100%
1000	1 min 25 s	+/− 45 min	5.2 %	0.121 s	100%

As Table 5 shows, RODIN is initially slower than ATELIER-B, but is able to process larger models. However, the proving time is quite large, as every proof obligation is sent to a new instance of the provers. For Nr = 100 it is about an order of magnitude slower than ATELIER-B and three orders of magnitude slower than our technique, and discharges only half of the POs. For Nr = 1000 RODIN is about 23,000 times slower than our technique. We did try to prove some of the POs in RODIN by hand. For axm110 the PP prover needs to be interrupted, but ML and Z3 can be used to prove it. For axm_nest_999 the ML prover fails, Z3, veriT, and CVC4 run into timeouts and PP needs to be interrupted.

5.2   A Few Selected POs

The regression test 2018 of PROB contains 189 well-defined formulas which were collected from existing models, leading to 413 POs. Of course this test is biased, as it contains the regression tests for our prover. However, these regression tests were usually extracted from existing models, and were written to cover a large class of typical *WD* situations arising in practice. Here we wish to show that our prover does treat some naturally occurring WD POs better than the standard provers mono-lemma ML and the predicate prover PP in their default settings.

For the experiments we used PROB's atelierb_provers_interface module which calls KRT with the options -a m1500000 -p rmcomm. The results are summarised in Table 6. Our prover discharges all 413 POs in 47 ms, with a maximum walltime of 5 ms per PO. The maximum walltime of ML was about 18 s for the PO

   f : 1,3,5,7,9 --> 1,3,5,7,9 => 5 : dom(f).

If we deduct the minimum walltime of 0.26 s of ML (which is probably due to the overhead of starting a new ML for each PO) we obtain a runtime of around 45 s for all POs.

For PP some POs seemed to run into an infinite loop and we interrupted the prover on 18 occasions, e.g., for the PO:

```
10 / f(a) = 10 / a & a : NATURAL1 & b : NATURAL &
f : NATURAL1 --> NATURAL1
    => b + 1 : dom(f).
```

The longest successful run of PP was around 49 s for the PO:

```
x' : 2 .. 8 => %x.(x : 2 .. 8|10 / x) : (INTEGER) +-> (INTEGER).
```

PP was not able to prove e.g. these two POs:

```
s : perm(1 .. 10) => s : (INTEGER) +-> (INTEGER)
x : POW(1 .. 2) => finite(x).
```

We have also tried to use Z3 4.8.8 via the translation [22] available in PROB. This translation does not support sequences and all B operators, and also unfortunately terminated after 23 POs (with an uncaught "datatype is not well-founded" exception). We tried to selectively skip over some POs, without success. In the future it would be good to try the translation to SMTLib from [13] (but which would not support sequences either).

Table 6. POs Extracted from PROB Regression Tests

Prover	Proved	Unproved	Ctrl-C	Min	Max	Total	w/o Min
PROB-WD	413	0	0	0.000 s	0.006 s	0.047 s	0.047 s
ML	190	223	0	0.260 s	18.725 s	152.633 s	45.253 s
PP	230	165		0.092 s	49.144 s	222.940 s	186.600 s
			18			1017.406 s	−
Z3	9	14	0	0.007 s	2.520 s	crash	−

5.3 Benchmarks from ProB Examples

The PROB source code is accompanied by a large selection of models, which are used for regression tests. In a recent effort, the public part of these models have been made available for reproducible benchmark efforts and other research uses at: https://github.com/hhu-stups/specifications

For this article we have extracted the parseable and type-correct B and Event-B specifications to evaluate our tool. The scripts to run our tool are available in the folder benchmarks/well-definedness of the above repository. The summary is in Table 7; the detailed results for the 2579 B and 760 Event-B models can be found in the above repository. We also ran the experiments on the private B machines (.mch files) and Event-B files in the PROB examples. These are summarised in Table 8.

Table 7. PROB WD on Public Benchmarks using PROB Examples

Formalism	Files	Total POs	Discharged	Perc	Runtime	Avg. per File
B	2579	106784	90357	84.62%	4.46 s	1.7 ms
Event-B	760	42824	38847	90.71%	1.10 s	1.4 ms

Table 8. PROB WD on Private Benchmarks from PROB Examples

Formalism	Files	Total POs	Discharged	Perc	Runtime	Avg. per File
B	3370	354769	288968	81.45%	38.67 s	11.5 ms
Event-B	145	32647	27202	83.32%	1.01 s	7.0 ms

The performance exceeded our initial hopes and one could run this analysis as part of the PROB loading process without users noticing a delay: 82.9% of the more than half a million POs from 6000 models were discharged in less than 50 s. For the public Event-B models the tool managed to discharge over 30000 POs per second. The maximum runtime was 0.310 s for one file (a formal model of the Z80 processor with many equalities in the invariants). With a newer version 1.10.0-beta4 of PROB 87% of these POs are now discharged in almost the same time.

The precision of the analysis is also very satisfactory. For many models 100% of the POs are discharged, e.g. all 114 for a Paxos model by Abrial or all 118 for MovingParticles, an encoding [24] of an ASM machine in Event-B (whose WD POs which are tedious to discharge in RODIN). The analysis has also uncovered a considerable number of real well-definedness issues in existing models. In terms of the true POs, the discharge percentage of our tool should be noticeably higher. Indeed, we checked the unproven POs of the public Event-B models with ML; it managed to discharge only 7% of them (i.e., an additional 0.55% overall).

6   Discussions and Outlook

Explanations for Performance. What can explain the big performance difference of our tool compared to ATELIER-B and RODIN? Some reasons have already been mentioned earlier:

- the combined PO generation and proving in one go definitely reduces some overhead,
- no overhead of calling an external prover (relevant compared to RODIN),
- no need to transmit or load hypotheses for a PO, all hypotheses are pre-compiled on the stack,
- efficient popping of hypotheses using Prolog's backtracking,
- only logarithmic hypotheses lookups are performed in the prover and useless hypotheses are not stored.

Part of the performance also comes from the special nature of WD POs. Indeed, one could try to implement our proof rules as custom proof rules for ML, which would probably boost its benchmark results. Indeed, ATELIER-B uses the *theory language* to express proof rules, which can be viewed as domain specific logic "programming language" tailored to B and proof. While ATELIER-B comes with a custom developed compiler — the *Logic Solver* — it seems like it cannot compete with state-of-the-art Prolog compilers. A small experiment consisted in summing the numbers from 1..500000 in the theory language (written by Thierry Lecomte) and in Prolog. Using krt in ATELIER-B 4.3.1 this task runs in over 6 s, while SICStus Prolog perform the same task in 0.001 s. Thus some of the performance is certainly due to implementing our proof rules in Prolog. The drawback of Prolog is that it has more limited matching (i.e., unification), namely only at the top-level of a Prolog term. This meant that we had to repeat some rewriting rules multiple times (for each predicate in Table 3).

RODIN uses external provers such as ML, PP or Z3 [13], and also the TOM rewriting library[6]. RODIN's internal sequent prover, however, seems to have been developed using hand-written matching, which is probably much less efficient than in Prolog or a dedicated term rewriting system. The hand-written solution can be very verbose: the equivalent of the last line 8 of our Prolog prover in Listing 4.2 is a file FiniteRan.java[5] with 82 lines of code (9 lines are copyright notice). The Prolog code is also very flexible (e.g., it can be used for finding proofs but also for re-playing or checking proofs if the proof tree argument is provided).

We are not the first to use Prolog to implement a prover [7,14,28]. An open question is whether using term rewriting [18] would be an even better approach. As mentioned above, Prolog unification is more limited, but very efficient.[6] Within a term rewriting system we could simplify our prover code, possibly use AC unification and avoid duplication of rewrite rules. An interesting topic for future research would be to port our prover to such a term rewriting system (like Maude) in the hope of not losing too much performance.

WD and Constraint Solving. Well-definedness is important for constraint solving in PROB's kernel. Indeed, constraint propagation can be much more effective if one assumes well-definedness. Take for example the predicate $x \in 1..10 \wedge y \geq 0 \wedge z = x \div y \wedge z > 10$. If we assume well-definedness of $x \div y$, we can infer that $z \in 1..10$ and hence realise that the constraint has no solution. If on the other hand, we wish to detect WD errors, the constraint solver has to delay until it knows whether y is 0 or not. In case $y = 0$ one can produce an error message, and if $y > 0$ the constraint is unsatisfiable. The detection of well-definedness errors is made more complicated by the fact that a solver does not necessarily treat predicates from left-to-right.

This is the reason many constraint solvers ignore well-definedness errors (see also [15]). E.g., in SMTLib or the finite domain constraint library CLP(FD) of SICStus Prolog, a division by zero simply results in an unsatisfiable predicate (and not in an error). This is not the approach used by PROB: it tries to detect well-definedness errors, but unfortunately is not guaranteed to detect all WD errors, because some of the checks would be prohibitively expensive at solving

---

[5] See FiniteRan.java in `org.eventb.internal.core.seqprover.eventbExtensions` at https://sourceforge.net/p/rodin-b-sharp/rodincore. A lot of other proof rules are more compact, though.

[6] The missing occurs check in Prolog is not an issue, because we use the ground representation for the B formulas, and hence any variable in a proof rule is always instantiated to a ground term.

time. Particularly, within nested set comprehensions such well-definedness issues can cause unexpected results. The techniques of this article will allow us to implement a much better approach in the future:

- if all WD POs are discharged, we know that no WD errors can arise. We can then perform stronger constraint propagations in the PROB kernel.
- if not all WD POs are discharged, we can resort to full WD checking at runtime for those places where the POs have not been discharged.

Outlook. Concerning our proof obligation generator we plan to extend it as needed to cover substitutions in classical B more precisely. Full coverage will, however, also require a full implementation of the weakest-precondition computation. The generator is currently tailored for use within PROB; for usage outside of PROB, we will need to allow to preserve the interleaved exact order of theorems and invariants for RODIN models or the order of included invariants in B. It would also be benefical to extract the proof status information from RODIN and ATELIER-B; this will further improve performance and precision and give users a fallback solution in case our prover is not powerful enough.

The prover itself can be further improved, in particular cycle detection can be made more efficient. We also plan to provide a "strength" option to enable more non-deterministic proof rules, at the cost of runtime. The quantifier instantiations and treatment of implications can also be extended.

It would be useful to visualize the proof tree constructed by our tool, and display the useful hypotheses for a particular PO. The proof tree could also be checked by a second tool, for validation purposes. Similar to what was done for ML, we could also attempt to prove all our rewrite rules using another prover.

About 10 years ago Abrial proposed [4] an outline for a new improved prover P3 for the B method. The results of this paper could be an encouragement to try and develop this successor to ML and PP using Prolog, possibly incorporating ideas from SMT solvers into the Prolog prover as shown in [17,27]. Maybe our approach could also be used to provide an easily extensible, yet efficient, prover for RODIN's theory plugin [10].

Summary. In summary, we have developed a new fast and effective integrated proof obligation generator and prover for well-definedness. It can deal with B sequences and with various extensions of the B language. It has been integrated into the PROB validation tool, and is able to analyse formal models effectively and quickly, with average runtimes below 0.01 s for over 6000 benchmark models. Our technique is orders of magnitude faster than existing implementations in ATELIER-B and RODIN. The output of our tool can be inspected either within PROB or within the Atom and VSCode editors, which proved to be useful to detect a considerable number of errors in existing models. The prover is also available in RODIN via PROB's Disprover [21] plugin. In the future, the output of the prover will be used by PROB's constraint solver to improve performance and to better detect well-definedness errors at solving time.

Acknowledgements. Big thanks go to Philipp Körner for scripts for extracting benchmark specification list, Thierry Lecomte for writing the sum Logic Solver example, Sebastian Stock for the VSCode integration and David Geleßus for the ProB2-UI integration. I wish to thank Jean-Raymond Abrial, Lilian Burdy, Michael Butler, Stefan Hallerstede and Laurent Voisin for useful feedback, ATELIER-B and RODIN implementation details and pointers to related research. In particular Laurent Voisin provided many useful hints and corrections. Finally, the anonymous referees of iFM provided very useful feedback.

References

1. Abrial, J.-R.: The B-Book. Cambridge University Press, Cambridge (1996)
2. Abrial, J.-R.: Modeling in Event-B: System and Software Engineering. Cambridge University Press, Cambridge (2010)
3. Abrial, J.-R., Butler, M., Hallerstede, S., Voisin, L.: An open extensible tool environment for Event-B. In: Liu, Z., He, J. (eds.) ICFEM 2006. LNCS, vol. 4260, pp. 588–605. Springer, Heidelberg (2006). https://doi.org/10.1007/11901433_32
4. Abrial, J.-R., Cansell, D., Métayer, C.: Specification of the automatic prover P3. In Proceedings AVoCS 2010 and the Rodin User and Developer Workshop, September 2010. https://wiki.event-b.org/images/Rodin2010-sld-abrial.pdf
5. Abrial, J.-R., Mussat, L.: On using conditional definitions in formal theories. In: Bert, D., Bowen, J.P., Henson, M.C., Robinson, K. (eds.) ZB 2002. LNCS, vol. 2272, pp. 242–269. Springer, Heidelberg (2002). https://doi.org/10.1007/3-540-45648-1_13
6. Balland, E., Brauner, P., Kopetz, R., Moreau, P.-E., Reilles, A.: Tom: piggybacking rewriting on Java. In: Baader, F. (ed.) RTA 2007. LNCS, vol. 4533, pp. 36–47. Springer, Heidelberg (2007). https://doi.org/10.1007/978-3-540-73449-9_5
7. Beckert, B., Posegga, J.: leanTAP: Lean tableau-based deduction. J. Autom. Reasoning **15**(3), 339–358 (1995)
8. Behm, P., Burdy, L., Meynadier, J.-M.: Well defined B. In: Bert, D. (ed.) B 1998. LNCS, vol. 1393, pp. 29–45. Springer, Heidelberg (1998). https://doi.org/10.1007/BFb0053354
9. Berezin, S., Barrett, C., Shikanian, I., Chechik, M., Gurfinkel, A., Dill, D.L.: A practical approach to partial functions in CVC lite. Electron. Notes Theor. Comput. Sci. **125**(3), 13–23 (2005)
10. Butler, M., Maamria, I.: Practical theory extension in Event-B. In: Liu, Z., Woodcock, J., Zhu, H. (eds.) Theories of Programming and Formal Methods. LNCS, vol. 8051, pp. 67–81. Springer, Heidelberg (2013). https://doi.org/10.1007/978-3-642-39698-4_5
11. ClearSy. Atelier, B.: User and Reference Manuals. Aix-en-Provence, France, 2009. http://www.atelierb.eu/
12. Darvas, Á., Mehta, F., Rudich, A.: Efficient well-definedness checking. In: Armando, A., Baumgartner, P., Dowek, G. (eds.) IJCAR 2008. LNCS (LNAI), vol. 5195, pp. 100–115. Springer, Heidelberg (2008). https://doi.org/10.1007/978-3-540-71070-7_8
13. Déharbe, D., Fontaine, P., Guyot, Y., Voisin, L.: Integrating SMT solvers in Rodin. Sci. Comput. Program. **94**, 130–143 (2014)
14. Fitting, M.: leanTAP revisited. J. Log. Comput. **8**(1), 33–47 (1998)

15. Frisch, A.M., Stuckey, P.J.: The proper treatment of undefinedness in constraint languages. In: Gent, I.P. (ed.) CP 2009. LNCS, vol. 5732, pp. 367–382. Springer, Heidelberg (2009). https://doi.org/10.1007/978-3-642-04244-7_30
16. Hansen, D., Schneider, D., Leuschel, M.: Using B and ProB for data validation projects. In: Butler, M., Schewe, K.-D., Mashkoor, A., Biro, M. (eds.) ABZ 2016. LNCS, vol. 9675, pp. 167–182. Springer, Cham (2016). https://doi.org/10.1007/978-3-319-33600-8_10
17. Howe, J.M., King, A.: A pearl on SAT and SMT solving in Prolog. Theor. Comput. Sci. **435**, 43–55 (2012)
18. Hsiang, J., Kirchner, H., Lescanne, P., Rusinowitch, M.: The term rewriting approach to automated theorem proving. J. Log. Program. **14**(1&2), 71–99 (1992)
19. Knuth, D.: The Art of Computer Programming, vol. 3. Addison-Wesley, Boston (1983)
20. Kosmatov, N., Marché, C., Moy, Y., Signoles, J.: Static versus dynamic verification in Why3, Frama-C and SPARK 2014. In: Margaria, T., Steffen, B. (eds.) ISoLA 2016. LNCS, vol. 9952, pp. 461–478. Springer, Cham (2016). https://doi.org/10.1007/978-3-319-47166-2_32
21. Krings, S., Bendisposto, J., Leuschel, M.: From failure to proof: the PROB disprover for B and Event-B. In: Calinescu, R., Rumpe, B. (eds.) SEFM 2015. LNCS, vol. 9276, pp. 199–214. Springer, Cham (2015). https://doi.org/10.1007/978-3-319-22969-0_15
22. Krings, S., Leuschel, M.: SMT solvers for validation of B and Event-B models. In: Ábrahám, E., Huisman, M. (eds.) IFM 2016. LNCS, vol. 9681, pp. 361–375. Springer, Cham (2016). https://doi.org/10.1007/978-3-319-33693-0_23
23. Lecomte, T., Burdy, L., Leuschel, M.: Formally checking large data sets in the railways. Proceedings of DS-Event-B 2012, Kyoto. CoRR, abs/1210.6815 (2012)
24. Leuschel, M., Börger, E.: A compact encoding of sequential ASMs in Event-B. In: Butler, M., Schewe, K.-D., Mashkoor, A., Biro, M. (eds.) ABZ 2016. LNCS, vol. 9675, pp. 119–134. Springer, Cham (2016). https://doi.org/10.1007/978-3-319-33600-8_7
25. Mehta, F.: A practical approach to partiality – a proof based approach. In: Liu, S., Maibaum, T., Araki, K. (eds.) ICFEM 2008. LNCS, vol. 5256, pp. 238–257. Springer, Heidelberg (2008). https://doi.org/10.1007/978-3-540-88194-0_16
26. Métayer, C., Voisin, L.: The Event-B Mathematical Language (2009). http://wiki.event-b.org/index.php/Event-B_Mathematical_Language
27. Robbins, E., Howe, J.M., King, A.: Theory propagation and reification. Sci. Comput. Program. **111**, 3–22 (2015)
28. Stärk, R.F.: The theoretical foundations of LPTP (a logic program theorem prover). J. Logic Program. **36**(3), 241–269 (1998)

An Event-B Based Generic Framework for Hybrid Systems Formal Modelling

Guillaume Dupont[✉], Yamine Aït-Ameur, Marc Pantel, and Neeraj K. Singh

INPT-ENSEEIHT/IRIT, University of Toulouse, Toulouse, France
{guillaume.dupont,yamine,marc.pantel,nsingh}@enseeiht.fr

Abstract. Designing hybrid systems requires the handling of discrete and continuous behaviours. The formal verification of such systems revolves around the use of heavy mathematical features, and related proofs. This paper presents a generic and reusable framework with different patterns, aimed at easing the design and verification of hybrid systems. It relies on refinement and proofs using Event-B, and defines an easily extensible set of generic patterns in the form of theories and models that are proved once and for all. The model of any specific hybrid system is then produced by instantiating the corresponding patterns. The paper illustrates the use of this framework by proposing to realise a well-known case study of the inverted pendulum, which design uses the approximation pattern formally defined and verified in Event-B.

1 Introduction

Formal modelling of hybrid systems requires means to describe both continuous and discrete behaviours in a single setting. Several approaches have been proposed to address this specificity, in general via the integration of theories of continuous functions and differential equations on the one hand, and logic-based reasoning on state-transitions systems on the other hand. The most common methods use hybrid automata [3] to model such systems and hybrid model checking [4,14,15,18] to verify their properties. In addition, some other approaches such as hybrid CSP [9,19], hybrid programs [20,21], continuous action systems [5], refinement and proof based methods with Event-B [11–13,22] and Hybrid Event-B [6], have been developed as well.

In previous work, we extended Event-B modelling language via the development of various theories to design hybrid systems using a correct-by-construction approach [11–13,22]. Theories for continuous mathematics, an approximate refinement relation for approximation following the retrenchment principle [7] and different hybrid systems architectures have been formally modelled.

The *objective of this paper* is two-fold. First, it presents a generic and reusable framework, relying on Event-B, to support and ease the design of hybrid systems. It is built from the generalisation of the models we defined in our previous work and on their instantiation to model specific hybrid systems. This framework defines a set of formalised and reusable patterns, verified once and for all.

B. Dongol and E. Troubitsyna (Eds.): IFM 2020, LNCS 12546, pp. 82–102, 2020.
https://doi.org/10.1007/978-3-030-63461-2_5

Second, it demonstrates the application of this framework, and in particular the approximation pattern, with the development of the inverted pendulum case study, where approximate refinement is used to linearise non-linear dynamics.

The *organisation of this paper* is as follows. Next section presents the designed generic framework. Section 3 describes the case study of the inverted pendulum and Sect. 4 gives an overview of Event-B. Section 5 presents the generic models and theories composing the framework and Sect. 6 is dedicated to the development of the case study. Finally, Sect. 7 concludes the paper.

2 The Designed Framework

The generic framework for formal modelling and verification of hybrid systems relies on the various developments we have conducted to model and verify different types of hybrid systems [10–13]. These developments revealed several reusable building blocks seen as formal development patterns formalised in Event-B. Figure 1 depicts the framework and its different components, split in two categories: *reusable* and *specific*.

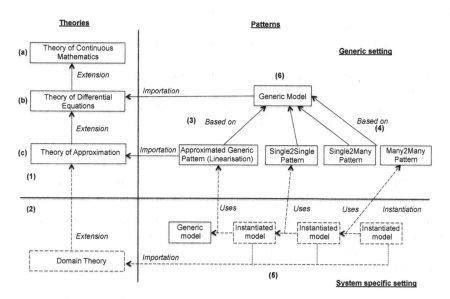

Fig. 1. Our framework: the big picture

2.1 Reusable Components

These components are the theories and the Event-B generic model and patterns to be instantiated for specific hybrid systems.

Relevant Theories (1 on Fig. 1). Event-B is based on set theory and first order logic; this low mathematical level is very expressive, but makes it difficult to handle continuous features, essential in hybrid system modelling. These required mathematical concepts, not available in core Event-B, are defined within mathematical theories, referenced by the models. They make available reals, continuous functions, differential equations and associated properties. In addition, they also formalise approximation and define an approximate refinement operator, which is not available in native Event-B. These theories are defined incrementally, as denoted by the *Extends* operator.

Generic Model and Patterns for Hybrid Systems (3 and 4 on Fig. 1). They are parameterised Event-B models *proved once and for all.*

Generic Model (6 on Fig. 1). It formalises the generic pattern of Fig. 6. It is the root model from which all the other models are derived, using Event-B refinement. Plant and controller behaviours, together with sensing and actuation actions are meddled at a higher abstract level.

Architecture Patterns (4 on Fig. 1). These specific patterns introduce either centralised or distributed control and one or many controlled plants. Three Event-B models refining the generic model define three architecture patterns as *Single-ToSingle* [12], *SingleToMany* [11] and *ManyToMany* [13].

Approximation Pattern (3 on Fig. 1). It consists of another Event-B model, refining the generic model and formalising a commonly used approximation operation realised by designers. In Event-B, this pattern encodes an approximate refinement operation following the principle of retrenchment. Linearisation is an example of such an approximation: a non-linear differential equation is approximately refined by a linear one.

The above introduced components represent a library of patterns deployed to model specific hybrid systems. They are proved once and for all.

2.2 Specific Components

These components are both theories and models developed for particular hybrid systems. They are obtained either by theories extensions or pattern instantiation.

Domain Theories (2 on Fig. 1). These specific theories describe the characteristics of the plant involved in the developed hybrid system, e.g.: kinematics of a car, robot motion, inverted pendulum, etc. In many cases, more than one theory may be needed, in particular when it involves different domains (signal processing, kinematics, etc.).

Instantiation Models (5 on Fig. 1). They are formal models for specific hybrid systems. They are obtained by applying the different patterns sequentially, starting with the generic model. Event-B refinement is used to instantiate those patterns, and witnesses are provided for the parameters of the generic model and patterns. These models refer to the domain theories to access the relevant characteristics of the considered system.

In the remainder of this paper, we show how the defined approximation pattern is deployed. It encodes an Event-B approximate refinement relationship. The case of the inverted pendulum is considered.

3   Case Study: The Inverted Pendulum

We consider the well-known case study of the inverted pendulum. This problem is particularly relevant as it imposes the use of *linearisation* in order to be correctly implemented. The case study is then realised in the Event-B based defined framework using Rodin.

3.1   Description

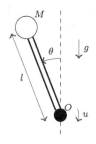

Fig. 2. Inverted pendulum

An object M is attached to a rigid rod of length l, that is itself attached to a step motor at point O. This point is also the origin of the coordinate system. The angle between the rod and the vertical axis is denoted θ, and the motor is capable of providing a torque, denoted u. The system is subject to standard G-force, of intensity g. The goal of the controller is to stabilise the rod in its vertical position by instrumenting the motor (and its torque u). From physics laws, we obtain the system's equation in θ (Fig. 2):

$$\ddot{\theta} - \frac{g}{l}\sin(\theta) = u\cos(\theta) \tag{1}$$

Equation 2 is derived from Eq. 1, as an ODE $\dot{\eta} = f_{NonLin}(\eta, u)$ where $\eta = [\theta\ \dot{\theta}]^\top$ and u is some control command:

$$f_{NonLin}((x_1, x_2), u) = (x_2, u\cos(x_1) + \frac{g}{l}) \tag{2}$$

The factor $\omega_0^2 = \frac{g}{l}$ is generally constant and ω_0 is the angular frequency (pulsatance) of the system, linked to the period of the pendulum's oscillations. This system is controllable when $\theta < \theta_{max}$, where θ_{max} is fixed by ω_0.

Due to the terms $\sin(\theta)$ and $\cos(\theta)$, the system's ODE is non-linear, meaning that it does not have an explicit solution, and the reachability is undecidable. However, when θ is small enough, it is possible to approximate $\sin(\theta)$ and $\cos(\theta)$; more precisely, given θ_{bound}, there exists δ such that, for any θ with $|\theta| < \theta_{bound}$, then $|\sin(\theta) - \theta| < \delta$ and $|1 - \cos(\theta)| < \delta$.

Assuming this condition holds, it is possible to approximate Eq. 1 to a simpler form, so-called *linearised*:

$$\ddot{\theta} - \frac{g}{l}\theta = v, \tag{3}$$

with v an adequate linear control command linked to u after linearisation. It can be expressed as the ODE $\dot{\eta} = f_{Lin}(\eta, v)$ where:

$$f_{Lin}((x_1, x_2), v) = (x_2, v + \frac{g}{l}x_1). \tag{4}$$

This ODE is linear, making it much easier to handle.

3.2   Requirements

The requirements of the system can be summarised as follows:

FUN1 The controller senses the angle (θ) of the pendulum (`:sense_angle`)

FUN2 If the value of the sensed angle is not 0, the controller sends a command to stabilise the pendulum at $\theta = 0$ (`:calculate_control`)

SAF1 For $|\theta| < \theta_{max}$, the system is always controllable

ENV1 The system is subject to perturbations that may cause its angle to vary

ENV2 There exists θ_{bound} such that $|\theta| < \theta_{bound}$; therefore, the non-linear system and the linearised system are always close up to $\delta > 0$

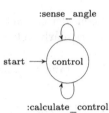

Fig. 3. System mode automaton

4   Event-B

Event-B [1] is a *correct-by-construction* method based on set theory and first order logic. It relies on a powerful state-based modelling language where a set of events allows for state changes[1] (see Table 1). A set of proof obligations (see Tables 2a and 2b) is automatically generated for each model. Event-B is associated with a proof system which contains a set of proof rules for formal reasoning. The design process of the system model consists of an abstract model leading to the final concrete model. Each refinement gradually introduces additional system design decisions.

Context (Table 1.a). A `Context` component describes the static properties. It introduces all the definitions, axioms and theorems needed to describe the required concepts using elementary components such as *Carrier sets s, constants c, axioms A* and *theorems T_{ctx}*.

Machines (Table 1.b). `Machine` describes the model behaviour as a transition system. A set of guarded events is used to modify a set of states using Before-After Predicates (BAP) to record variable changes. They use *variables x, invariants $I(x)$, theorems $T_{mch}(x)$, variants $V(x)$* and *events evt* (possibly guarded by G and/or parameterized by α) as core elementary components.

Refinements (Table 1c). Refinement introduces different characteristics such as functionality, safety, reachability at different abstraction levels. It decomposes a *machine*, a state-transition system, into a less abstract one, with more design decisions (refined states and events) moving from an abstract level to a less abstract one (simulation relationship). Gluing invariants relating to abstract and concrete variables ensures property preservation.

---

[1] **Notation.** The superscripts ^{A} and ^{C} denote abstract and concrete features.

Table 1. Model structure

Context	Machine	Refinement
CONTEXT Ctx	MACHINEM^A	MACHINEM^C
SETSs	SEES Ctx	REFINESM^A
CONSTANTSc	VARIABLESx^A	VARIABLESx^C
AXIOMSA	INVARIANTS$I^A(x^A)$	INVARIANTS$J(x^A, x^C) \wedge I^C(x^C)$
THEOREMST_{ctx}	THEOREMS$T_{mch}(x^A)$	...
END	VARIANT$V(x^A)$	EVENTS
	EVENTS	EVENTevt^C
	EVENTevt^A	REFINESevt^A
	ANYα^A	ANYα^C
	WHERE$G^A(x^A, \alpha^A)$	WHERE$G^C(x^C, \alpha^C)$
	THEN	WITH
	$x^A :\mid BAP^A(\alpha^A, x^A, x^{A\prime})$	$x^{A\prime}, \alpha^A{:}W(\alpha^A, \alpha^C, x^A, x^{A\prime}, x^C, x^{C\prime})$
	END	THEN
	...	$x^C :\mid BAP^C(\alpha^C, x^C, x^{C\prime})$
		END
		...
(a)	(b)	(c)

Table 2. Proof Obligations

(a) Machine Proof obligations

(1) Theorems	$A \Rightarrow T_{ctx}$ $A \wedge I^A(x^A) \Rightarrow T_{mac}(x^A)$
(2) Invariant preservation (INV)	$A \wedge I_A(x^A) \wedge G_A(x^A, \alpha^A)$ $\wedge BAP^A(x^A, \alpha^A, x^{A\prime})$ $\Rightarrow I^A(x^{A\prime})$
(3) Event feasibility (FIS)	$A \wedge I_A(x^A) \wedge G^A(x^A, \alpha^A)$ $\Rightarrow \exists \alpha^A \cdot BAP^A(x^A, \alpha^A, x^{A\prime})$
(4) Variant progress	$A \wedge I^A(x^A) \wedge G^A(x^A, \alpha^A)$ $\wedge BAP^A(x^A, \alpha^A, x^{A\prime})$ $\Rightarrow V(x^{A\prime}) < V(x^A)$

(b) Refinement Proof obligations

(5) Event Simulation (SIM)	$A \wedge I^A(x^A) \wedge J(x^A, x^C)$ $\wedge G^C(x^C, \alpha^C)$ $\wedge W(\alpha^A, \alpha^C, x^A, x^{A\prime}, x^C, x^{C\prime})$ $\wedge BAP^C(x^C, \alpha^C, x^{C\prime})$ $\Rightarrow BAP^A(x_A, \alpha^A, x^{A\prime})$
(6) Guard Strengthening (GS)	$A \wedge I^A(x^A) \wedge J(x^A, x^C)$ $\wedge W(\alpha^A, \alpha^C, x^A, x^{A\prime}, x^C, x^{C\prime})$ $\wedge G^C(x^C, \alpha^C) \Rightarrow G_A(x^A, \alpha^A)$
(7) Invariant preservation (INV)	$A \wedge I^A(x^A)$ $\wedge G^C(x^C, \alpha^C)$ $\wedge W(\alpha^A, \alpha^C, x^A, x^{A\prime}, x^C, x^{C\prime})$ $\wedge BAP^C(x^C, \alpha^C, x^{C\prime})$ $\wedge J(x^A, x^C) \Rightarrow J(x^{A\prime}, x^{C\prime})$

Proof Obligations (PO) and Property Verification. Tables 2a and 2b provide a set of proof obligations to guarantee Event-B model consistency, including refinements. These PO are automatically generated. They must be proven in order to establish the correctness of the defined model.

Extensions with Mathematical Theories. An extension of Event-B is defined [2] to support externally defined mathematical theories. It offers the introduction of new data types by defining new types, sets operators, theorems and associated rewrite and inference rules, all bundled in so-called *theories*.

Rodin. It is an Eclipse based IDE for Event-B project management, model edition, refinement and proof, automatic PO generation, model checking, model animation and code generation. It is equipped with standard provers, including support for external provers such as SMT solvers. A plug-in [8] is also available to support the development of mathematical theories.

5   Modelling the Generic Model and Patterns in Event-B

Modelling hybrid systems requires to handle continuous behaviours. We thus need to access specific mathematical objects and properties, which are not natively available in Event-B. These concepts such as differential equations and their associated properties have been modelled through an intensive use of Event-B theories and have been used to model various case studies found in [10–12].

This section describes the generic resources used by the defined framework. They correspond to the upper parts (1), (3), (4) and (6) of Fig. 1.

5.1   Theories for Continuous Mathematics and Differential Equations (1a and 1b on Fig. 1)

In order to deal with continuous objects, theories have been defined for continuous functions, (ordinary) differential equations as well as for their properties. They are used throughout the defined models. Their complete definitions are available at https://irit.fr/~Guillaume.Dupont/models.php. Some of these concepts as they are used in this paper are recalled below.

Hybrid Modelling Features. Modelling hybrid systems requires to introduce multiple basic operators and primitives defined below.

```
THEORY
  TYPE PARAMETERS E , S
  DATA TYPES
    DE(S)
    CONSTRUCTORS
      ode(f : P(ℝ × S × S) , η₀ : S , t₀ : ℝ)
  OPERATORS
    solutionOf <predicate> (D_R :  P(ℝ),
      η :  ℝ⁺ ⇸ S , eq :  DE(S))
    Feasible <predicate> (x_s :  STATES,
      η :  ℝ⁺ ⇸ S , D_R :  P(ℝ) , P :
      (ℝ⁺ ⇸ S) × (ℝ⁺ ⇸ S) , I :  P(S))
    Solvable <predicate> (D_R :  P(ℝ) , eq :
      DE(S) , I :  P(S))
    ...
END
```

Fig. 4. Differential equation theory snippet

– **DE**(S) type for differential equations which solutions evolve over set S

– **ode**(f, η_0, t_0) is the ODE (Ordinary Differential Equation) $\dot{\eta}(t) = f(\eta(t), t)$ with initial condition $\eta(t_0) = \eta_0$

– **solutionOf**$(D, \eta, \mathcal{E})$ is the predicate stating that function η is a solution of equation $\mathcal{E}$ on subset D

– **Solvable**$(D, \mathcal{E}, \mathcal{I})$ predicate states that equation $\mathcal{E}$ has a solution defined on subset D that satisfies the constraint $\mathcal{I}$

– **Feasible**$(x_s, x_p, D, \mathcal{P}, \mathcal{I})$, the feasible predicate states that, given x_s and x_p, there exists $x'_p \in D \to S$ such that $\mathcal{P}(x_s, x_p, x'_p)$ holds and $\forall t^* \in D, x'_p(t^*) \in \mathcal{I}$. In state x_s, the predicate

$\mathcal{P}$ holds for x_p and its next value x'_p on time interval D fulfils the constraint $\mathcal{I}$. It defines the feasibility condition of a continuous variable (e.g. a state in a model) change. This operator is used to define the continuous before-after predicate (CBAP).

These features are encoded in a theory from which we show a snippet on Fig. 4 (the theory accumulates more than 150 operators and 350 properties).

5.2   A Theory of Approximation (1c on Fig. 1)

In addition to the continuous mathematical objects of Sect. 5.1, a theory of approximation is required to implement approximate refinement in Event-B. In the following, we introduce the necessary concepts and operators related to approximation and used throughout this paper. Let us assume (E, d) to be a metric space with distance d.

Approximation $(\approx^\delta)$. Let $x, y \in E$ and $\delta \in \mathbb{R}^+$. We say that x approximately equals to y by δ (or x is a δ-approximation of y) iff $x \approx^\delta y \equiv d(x, y) \leq \delta$.

δ-expansion. Let $S \subseteq E$ and $\delta \in \mathbb{R}^+$. The δ-expansion of S, noted $\mathcal{E}_\delta(S)$, is defined as $\mathcal{E}_\delta(S) = \{y \in E \mid \exists x \in S, x \approx^\delta y\} = \{y \in E \mid \exists x \in S, d(x, y) \leq \delta\}$.

δ-membership $(\in^\delta)$. Let $\delta \in \mathbb{R}^+$, $S \subseteq E$ and $x \in E$. x belongs to S up to δ, denoted $x \in^\delta S$, iff x belongs to the δ-expansion of S. We write $x \in^\delta S \equiv x \in \mathcal{E}_\delta(S) \equiv \exists y \in S, d(x, y) \leq \delta$.

Extended δ-membership Operators. δ-membership is extended as follows.

- Let $f \in F \to E$ and $X \subseteq F$, then $f \in_X^\delta S \equiv \forall x \in X, f(x) \in^\delta S$
- Let $\Sigma \in F \to \mathbb{P}(E)$ (multivalued function), then $f \in_X^\delta \Sigma \equiv \forall x \in X, f(x) \in^\delta \Sigma(x)$

When X is omitted, the operator is applied on the function's domain of definition (i.e., $X = \mathrm{dom}(f)$).

```
THEORY ApproximationBase          THEORY Approximation
TYPE PARAMETERS F                 IMPORT THEORY ApproximationBase
...                               TYPE PARAMETERS E , F
AXIOMATIC OPERATORS               OPERATORS
  DeltaApproximation <predicate>  --- Definition of f≈δ_{D_E} g
    (δ: R⁺, a: F, b: F)           FDeltaApproximation <predicate>
AXIOMS --- commutativity,           (D_E: P(E), δ: R⁺, f: E ⇸ F, g: E ⇸ F)
    reflexivity, ...                well−definedness condition
                                    D_E ⊆ dom(f), D_E ⊆ dom(g)
                                  ∀x · x ∈ D_E ⇒ DeltaApproximation(δ, f(x), g(x))
                                    ...
```

Fig. 5. Approximation theory excerpt

Note: δ-approximation $(\approx^\delta)$ (resp. δ-membership $(\in^\delta)$) is a weak version of equality (resp. set membership). Indeed, when $\delta = 0$, by the separation property of distance d, we obtain $x \approx^0 y \equiv d(x,y) \leq 0 \equiv x = y$. It follows that for any $S \subseteq E$, $\mathcal{E}_0(S) = S$ and thus $x \in^0 S \equiv x \in S$.

Implementation Using Theories. The above defined operators and concepts have been implemented in two Event-B theories (*ApproximationBase* and *Approximation*) from which an excerpt is given in Fig. 5. Typically, approximation ($\approx^\delta$) is expressed algebraically through the *DeltaApproximation* operator, while its extension to functions is implemented as the *FDeltaApproximation* operator.

5.3   The Generic Model (6 on Fig. 1)

As mentioned previously, the core Event-B does not support continuous behaviours. To handle such behaviours, we have introduced a generic model, acting as a meta-model encoding a hybrid automaton corresponding to the generic hybrid system structure depicted in Fig. 6. The notions of time, continuous states, continuous gluing invariants, continuous assignment and continuous events are introduced. The obtained model interleaves continuous events (with duration) and discrete events (instantaneous) as defined in [10–13].

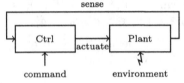

Fig. 6. Generic hybrid system pattern

The generic model is the entry point of the framework on which every pattern is based. It takes the form of an Event-B model that summarises and abstracts any hybrid system conforming to Fig. 6. Refinement is then used to derive any specific hybrid system from it.

Time. A notion of time is needed to define continuous behaviours. We thus introduce dense time $t \in \mathbb{R}^+$, modelled as a continuously evolving variable.

System State. According to the architecture of hybrid systems, we have identified two types of states:

- **Discrete state** $x_s \in STATES$ is a variable that represents the controller's internal state. It evolves in a point-wise manner with instantaneous changes.
- **Continuous state** $x_p \in \mathbb{R}^+ \to S$ represents the plant's state and evolves continuously. It is modelled as a function of time with values in space S.
  In the following, we use x to denote the union of discrete and continuous state variables.

Continuous Assignment. Continuous variables are essentially functions of time and are at least defined on $[0,t]$ (where t is the current time). Updating such variables, thus, requires to (1) make the time progress from t to $t' > t$, and (2) to append to the already existing function a new piece corresponding to its extended behaviour (on $[t,t']$) while ensuring its"past" (i.e. whatever happened on $[0,t]$) remains unchanged.

Similarly to the classic Event-B's before-after predicate (BAP), we define a *continuous before-after predicate* ($CBAP$) operator, denoted $:|_{t \to t'}$, as follows[2]:

$$x_p :|_{t \to t'} \mathcal{P}(x_s, x_p, x_p') \,\&\, \mathcal{I} \equiv [0, t] \lhd x' = [0, t] \lhd x \qquad (PP)$$

$$\wedge \, \mathcal{P}(x_s, [t, t'] \lhd x_p, [t, t'] \lhd x_p') \qquad (PR)$$

$$\wedge \, \forall t^* \in [t, t'], x_p'(t^*) \in \mathcal{I} \qquad (LI)$$

The operator consists of three parts: past preservation and coherence at assignment point (PP), before-after predicate on the added section (PR), and local invariant preservation (LI). The discrete state variables x_s do not change in the interval $[t, t']$ but the predicate $\mathcal{P}$ may use it for control purposes. We note $CBAP(x_s, x_p, x_p') \equiv PP(x_p, x_p') \wedge PR(x_s, x_p, x_p') \wedge LI(x_p, x_p')$.
From the above definition, shortcuts are introduced for readability purposes:

– Continuous assignment: $x :=_{t \to t'} f \,\&\, \mathcal{I} \equiv x :|_{t \to t'} x' = f \,\&\, \mathcal{I}$
– Continuous evolution along a solvable differential equation $\mathcal{E} \in \mathbf{DE}(S)$:
  $x :\sim_{t \to t'} \mathcal{E} \,\&\, \mathcal{I} \equiv x :|_{t \to t'} \mathbf{solutionOf}([t, t'], x', \mathcal{E}) \,\&\, \mathcal{I}$

The Generic Model in Event-B. Once all the features have been defined, we can describe the Event-B model.

```
MACHINE Generic SEES GenericCtx          INITIALISATION
VARIABLES t, x_p, x_s                     WHERE
INVARIANTS                                   act1: t := 0
   inv1: t ∈ ℝ⁺                             act2: x_p :∈ O → S
   inv2: x_p ∈ ℝ⁺ ⇸ S                       act3: x_s :∈ STATES
   inv3: [0, t] ⊆ dom(x_p)                END
   inv4: x_s ∈ STATES
```

Fig. 7. Generic model Event-B machine header

The model handles three variables, time t, the continuous state x_p and the discrete state x_s constrained using invariants (inv1-4). They are initialised with 0 for t and using non-deterministic assignment for x_p and x_s. Further refinements provide more detailed value(s) (Fig. 7).

The events of the generic model follow the arrows of Fig. 6. Figure 8 shows the Transition and the Sense events modelling discrete state changes. Such change can arise following the detection of a change in the plant (sensing) or can be induced by the controller itself (Transition) after a calculation, at the end of a timer, and so on. This difference is captured by guards 2 and 3 of Sense, referencing the continuous state. Transition and Sense are so-called *discrete* events: they are timeless and instantaneous.

Figure 9 shows the other two types of events Behave and Actuate to model a change in the plant, induced either by a change in the controller (actuation) or by

---

[2] The $\lhd$ operator denotes the domain restriction operator.

Transition	Sense

ANY s
 WHERE
    grd1 : $s \in \mathbb{P}1(\text{STATES})$
 THEN
    act1 : $x_s :\in s$
 END
	ANY s , p
	 WHERE
	    grd1−2 : $s \in \mathbb{P}1(\text{STATES})$, $p \in \mathbb{P}(\text{STATES} \times \mathbb{R} \times S)$
	    grd3 : $(x_s \mapsto t \mapsto x_p(t)) \in p$
	 THEN
	    act1 : $x_s :\in s$
	 END

Fig. 8. Transition and sense events

Behave	Actuate

ANY eq , t'
 WHERE
    grd0 : $t' \in \mathbb{R}^+ \wedge t' > t$
    grd1 : $eq \in DE(S)$
    grd2 : $\textbf{Solvable}([t, t'], eq, \top)$
 THEN
    act1 : $t, x_p :\sim_{t \to t'} eq \,\&\, \top$
 END
	ANY eq , s , H , t'
	 WHERE
	    grd0 : $t' \in \mathbb{R}^+ \wedge t' > t$
	    grd1−2 : $eq \in DE(S)$, $\textbf{Solvable}([t, t'], eq, H)$
	    grd3−4 : $s \subseteq \text{STATES}, x_s \in s$
	    grd5−6 : $H \subseteq S, x_p(t) \in H$
	 THEN
	    act1 : $t, x_p :\sim_{t \to t'} eq \,\&\, H$
	 END

Fig. 9. Transition and sense events

the environment (behave). Both events rely on a continuous assignment operator described above. The link between the controller and actuation is modelled by grd3-4 in `Actuate` (absent from `Behave`). Also, the behaviour set in actuation is constrained by an evolution domain (grd5-6).

`Behave` and `Actuate` are *continuous* events: unlike discrete events, they have a duration. *Discrete* events are instantaneous and they preempt *continuous* ones.

Continuous Gluing Invariant. It is defined with the generic form $x_p^A \in \mathcal{O} \circ x_p^C$ where $\mathcal{O} \in S^C \leftrightarrow S^A$ is a relation linking abstract and continuous state-spaces. This invariant glues the abstract x_p^A and concrete x_p^C continuous variables. It is qualified as *exact* since it maps concrete values in S^C to abstract values in S^A using the $\in$ operator. Definition of an approximate gluing invariant, extending exact one, using the $\in^\delta$ operator is presented in next section.

5.4 The Approximation Pattern (3 on Fig. 1)

As mentioned in Sect. 2, we have chosen to illustrate the application of the generic framework using the approximation pattern. The choice of this pattern is motivated by the fact that 1) it uses an externally defined theory (see Sect. 5.2) not available in native Event-B and 2) it requires a specific refinement relationship, weakening classical refinement following the principle of retrenchment [7], and formalising the approximation of a continuous behaviour by another one. We particularly study the case of linearisation, when moving from a behaviour characterised by a non-linear differential equation to a behaviour characterised by a linear differential equation. The definition of this approximate refinement operation follows the approach of [16,17] where approximation is embedded in a simulation relationship. In addition, our definition offers an inductive process.

In this section, we present the approximation pattern as a refinement between an abstract machine (which elements are super-scripted with A) and a concrete machine (with superscript C). Figure 10 shows the respective headers of the machines. Approximation deals with continuous variables $(x_p^{A/C})$.

MACHINE M_A	MACHINE M_C REFINES M_A
VARIABLES t, x_s^A, x_p^A	VARIABLES t, x_s^C, x_p^C
INVARIANTS	INVARIANTS
inv1: $t \in \mathbb{R}^+$	inv2: $x_s^C \in STATES^C$
inv2: $x_s^A \in STATES$	inv3: $x_p^C \in \mathbb{R} \nrightarrow S^C$
inv3: $x_p^A \in \mathbb{R} \nrightarrow S^A$	inv4: $[0,t] \subseteq \mathrm{dom}(x_p^C)$
inv4: $[0,t] \subseteq \mathrm{dom}(x_p^A)$	inv5: $\forall t^* \cdot t^* \in [0,t] \Rightarrow x_p^C(t^*) \in \mathcal{I}^C$
inv5: $\forall t^* \cdot t^* \in [0,t] \Rightarrow x_p^A(t^*) \in \mathcal{I}^A$	inv6: $x_p^A \in^\delta \mathcal{O} \circ x_p^C$
	inv7: $J_s(x_s^C, x_s^A)$

Fig. 10. Machine header

The approximation pattern is applied at the refinement level using *approximated* relations instead, and built using the operators defined in Sect. 5.2, e.g. $\approx^\delta$ or $\in^\delta$ (see Fig. 10). It is formalised by inv6 whee the $\in$ operator is replaced by its approximated version ($\in^\delta$).

EVENT Sense$_A$
WHEN grd1: $x_p^A(t) \in \mathcal{G}^A$
THEN act1: $x_s^A :\in STATES$
END

EVENT Sense$_C$ REFINES Sense$_A$
WHEN grd1: $x_p^C(t) \in \mathcal{G}^C$
THEN act1: $x_s^C :\in STATES$
END

Fig. 11. Sense event

Sensing events (Fig. 11) remain relatively unchanged compared to normal refinement. Guard $\mathcal{G}^C$ must be defined carefully: $\mathcal{G}^C$ shall be stronger than $\mathcal{G}^A$, *taking into account the error* allowed by approximate refinement (guard strengthening PO).

Actuation (Fig. 12) is almost unchanged. The provided *witness* (WITH clause) shall ensure preservation of approximation after occurrence of the Actuate event. This witness leads to a feasibility proof obligation to guarantee that the property $x_p^{A\prime} \in^\delta \mathcal{O} \circ x_p^{C\prime}$ holds (i.e. approximation holds).

EVENT Actuate$_A$	EVENT Actuate$_C$ REFINES Actuate$_A$
ANY t_p	ANY t_p
WHEN	WHEN
grd1: $t_p \in \mathbb{R} \wedge t_p > t$	grd1: $t_p \in \mathbb{R} \wedge t_p > t$
grd2: $x_s = State$	grd2: $x_s = State$
grd3: $\mathbf{Feasible}(x_p^A, [t, t_p], \mathcal{P}^A, \mathcal{I}^A)$	grd3: $\mathbf{Feasible}(x_p^C, [t, t_p], \mathcal{P}^C, \mathcal{I}^C)$
grd4: $x_p^A(t) \in \mathcal{I}^A$	grd4: $x_p^C(t) \in \mathcal{I}^C$
	WITH $x_p^{A\prime} \in^\delta \mathcal{O} \circ x_p^{C\prime}$
THEN	THEN
act1: $x_p^A :|_{t \rightarrow t'} \mathcal{P}^A(x_s^A, x_p^A, x_p^{A\prime}) \& \mathcal{I}^A$	act1: $x_p^C :|_{t \rightarrow t'} \mathcal{P}^C(x_s^C, x_p^C, x_p^{C\prime}) \& \mathcal{I}^C$
END	END

Fig. 12. Actuate event

Table 3. Refinement POs for the generic model: case of approximate refinement

(5) Event Simulation (SIM)	$A \wedge x_p^A \in \mathbb{R} \nrightarrow S^A \wedge [0,t] \subseteq \text{dom}(x_p^A) \wedge x_p^C \in \mathbb{R} \nrightarrow S^C \wedge [0,t] \subseteq \text{dom}(x_p^C)$ $\wedge x_p^A \in \mathcal{I}^A \wedge x_p^C \in \mathcal{I}^C \wedge x_p^C(t) \in \mathcal{G}^C$ $\wedge \boldsymbol{x_p^A \in^\delta \mathcal{O} \circ x_p^C \wedge x_p^{A'} \in^\delta \mathcal{O} \circ x_p^{C'}}$ $\wedge PP(x^C, x^{C'}) \wedge PR(x^C, x^{C'}) \wedge LI(x^C, x^{C'})$ $\Rightarrow PR(x^A, x^{A'}) \wedge LI(x^A, x^{A'})$
(6) Guard Strengthening (GS)	$A \wedge x_p^A \in \mathbb{R} \nrightarrow S^A \wedge [0,t] \subseteq \text{dom}(x_p^A) \wedge x_p^C \in \mathbb{R} \nrightarrow S^C \wedge [0,t] \subseteq \text{dom}(x_p^C)$ $\wedge x_p^A \in \mathcal{I}^A \wedge x_p^C \in \mathcal{I}^C$ $\wedge \boldsymbol{x_p^A \in^\delta \mathcal{O} \circ x_p^C \wedge x_p^{A'} \in^\delta \mathcal{O} \circ x_p^{C'}}$ $\wedge x_p^C(t) \in \mathcal{G}^C \Rightarrow x_p^A(t) \in \mathcal{G}^A$
(7) Invariant Preservation (INV)	$A \wedge x_p^A \in \mathbb{R} \nrightarrow S^A \wedge [0,t] \subseteq \text{dom}(x_p^A) \wedge x_p^C \in \mathbb{R} \nrightarrow S^C \wedge [0,t] \subseteq \text{dom}(x_p^C)$ $\wedge x_p^A \in \mathcal{I}^A \wedge x_p^C \in \mathcal{I}^C \wedge x_p^C(t) \in \mathcal{G}^C \wedge \boldsymbol{x_p^A \in^\delta \mathcal{O} \circ x_p^C}$ $\wedge PP(x^C, x^{C'}) \wedge PR(x^C, x^{C'}) \wedge LI(x^C, x^{C'})$ $\Rightarrow \boldsymbol{x_p^{C'} \in \mathbb{R} \nrightarrow S^C \wedge [0,t'] \subseteq \text{dom}(x_p^{C'}) \wedge x_p^{C'} \in \mathcal{I}^C \wedge x_p^{A'} \in^\delta \mathcal{O} \circ x_p^{C'}}$

Revisited Proof Obligations. Approximation, similar to the *concedes* relation of retrenchment, extends the standard refinement operation which proof obligations are given in Table 2b. The use of well-definedness and witnesses in approximate refinement leads to an updated set of proof obligations (highlighted in bold) in Table 3.

Exact Refinement as a Particular Case of Approximate Refinement. We note that, when $\delta = 0$ in the operators defined in Sect. 5.1, we actually find back standard exact operators: $\approx^0 \; \equiv=$, $\in^0 \; \equiv\in$, etc. By restriction/strengthening, this means that, for $\delta = 0$, defined approximate refinement looks like exact refinement.

5.5   The Architecture Patterns (4 on Fig. 1)

Architecture patterns have been introduced in order to model the different types of structures hybrid systems may have: one controller controlling one plant (simple control, *Single2Single*), one controller and several plants (centralised control, *Single2Many*) and several controllers with several plants (distributed control, *Many2Many*). These patterns have been thoroughly studied, formalised and implemented in [11–13] respectively.

6   Modelling Hybrid Systems

Modelling specific hybrid systems follows the bottom part of Fig. 1. Two steps are identified: the first step introduces definitions relevant to the system (Fig. 1(2)), completing the generic theories of Fig. 1(1) with the relevant types, axioms and theorems for modelling the specific features of the system to design. The second step (Fig. 1(5)) is performed by refining and instantiating patterns to obtain the desired system (used patterns of Fig. 1). This process is exemplified below with the inverted pendulum case study.

6.1   Application to the Case Study

Our framework is used to address the case study introduced in Sect. 3. The exact use of the framework is depicted on Fig. 13, and follows the two steps discussed before: first, a theory for the physics of the inverted pendulum is defined (Fig. 13 (2)); second, the *Single2Single* pattern is applied to the generic model in order to derive a non-linear pendulum model. Finally, the approximation pattern is used to derive a linearised pendulum model from the non-linear one.

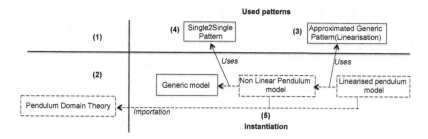

Fig. 13. Framework application to the case study

Step 1: A Theory for Simple Inverted Pendulums (2 in Fig. 13). Before modelling the actual system, we need to develop a domain theory of pendulums, that holds every important concepts needed to model this kind of system: differential equations (both non-linear and linearised) and adequate controls for the systems, as well as various physical and mathematical properties that will help in establishing the system's correctness. The definitions of such a theory correspond to (2) in Fig. 13.

```
THEORY InvertedPendulum IMPORTS Approximation
OPERATORS
    PendulumFun_NonLin <expression> (ω₀: ℝ)
        direct definition
            (λt ↦ (x₁ ↦ x₂) ↦ u · t ∈ ℝ⁺ ∧ (x₁ ↦ x₂) ∈ ℝ² ∧ u ∈ ℝ| x₂ ↦ (u cos(x₁) + ω₀² sin(x₁)) )
    Pendulum_NonLin <expression> (ω₀: ℝ, x₀: ℝ², t₀: ℝ)
        direct definition code(PendulumFun_NonLin(ω₀), x₀, t₀)
    PendulumFun_Lin <expression> (ω₀: ℝ)
        direct definition
            (λt ↦ (x₁ ↦ x₂) ↦ u · t ∈ ℝ⁺ ∧ (x₁ ↦ x₂) ∈ ℝ² ∧ u ∈ ℝ| x₂ ↦ (u + ω₀²x₁) )
    Pendulum_Lin <expression> (ω₀: ℝ, x₀: ℝ², t₀: ℝ)
        direct definition code(PendulumFun_Lin(ω₀), x₀, t₀)
AXIOMATIC DEFINITIONS
    OPERATORS
        theta_max <expression> (ω₀: ℝ) : ℝ
        PendulumControl_NonLin <expression> (ω₀: ℝ, (θ₀, θ̇₀): ℝ², t₀: ℝ⁺) : ℝ ⇸ ℝ
        PendulumControl_Lin <expression> (ω₀: ℝ, (θ₀, θ̇₀): ℝ², t₀: ℝ⁺) : ℝ ⇸ ℝ
        . . .
```

Fig. 14. Pendulum theory excerpt

Listing of Fig. 14 gives an extract of the pendulum defined domain theory. It mainly defines the differential equations associated with both the non-linear ($Pendulum_{NonLin}$) and linearised ($Pendulum_{Lin}$) pendulum systems. It also proposes control functions for both systems ($PendulumControl_{NonLin}$ and $PendulumControl_{Lin}$ resp.) which are algebraically defined together with useful properties used in proofs.

Step 2: Non-Linear Inverted Pendulum Model (5 in Fig. 13). The *Single2Single* architecture pattern is used to derive, by refinement of the generic model, a first model of the inverted pendulum, which features the non-linear differential equation. This step correspond to (4) in Fig. 13.

The context for this model defines the system's pulsatance (ω_0 in axm1-2) and its associated maximum controllable angle (θ_{max} in axm3-5). Last, the only state of the system's mode automaton is declared in *control* (axm6).

```
CONTEXT PendulumCtx EXTENDS GenericCtx
CONSTANTS  ω₀ , θ_max , θ₀ ,  control
AXIOMS
    axm1-2:  ω₀ ∈ ℝ , ω₀ ≠ 0
    axm3-5:  θ_max = theta_max(ω₀) , θ₀ ∈ ℝ , |θ₀| < θ_max
    axm6:  partition(STATES, {control})
END
```

```
MACHINE Pendulum REFINES Generic
SEES PendulumCtx
VARIABLES
    t, θ, θ̇, t^sense, θ^sense, θ̇^sense,
        control_fun
INVARIANTS
    inv1-4:  θ ∈ ℝ ⇸ ℝ , θ̇ ∈ ℝ ⇸ ℝ ,
        [0, t] ⊆ dom(θ) , [0, t] ⊆ dom(θ̇)
    inv5:  x_p = [θ θ̇]^⊤
    inv6:  ∀t* · t* ∈ [0, t] ⇒ |θ(t*)| < θ_max
    inv7:  x_s = control
    inv8-10:  t^sense ∈ ℝ⁺ , θ^sense ∈ ℝ , θ̇^sense ∈ ℝ
    inv11-12:  control_fun ∈ ℝ ⇸ ℝ ,
        [t^sense, +∞[ ⊆ dom(control_fun)
    inv13:  |θ^sense| ≤ θ_max
```

```
INITIALISATION
WITH
    x_p′ :  x_p′ = {0 ↦ (θ₀ ↦ 0)}
    x_s′ :  x_s′ = control
THEN
    act1:  t := 0
    act2:  θ := {0 ↦ θ₀}
    act3:  θ̇ := {0 ↦ 0}
    act4:  t^sense := 0
    act5:  θ^sense, θ̇^sense := θ₀, 0
    act6:  control_fun :=
        PendulumControl_NonLin(ω₀, (θ₀ ↦ 0), 0)
END
```

Fig. 15. Machine header and initialisation

Listings of Fig. 15 give the machine header and the initialisation of the system. The continuous state is the vector $[\dot\theta \, \theta]^\top$ defined in inv1-4. inv5 glues this continuous state to the generic one (x_p). It is constrained by inv6. The mode automaton of the system defines the *control* (inv7) state and the discrete state of the machine comprises variables to store the observation of the system when sensing (*sense* variables super-scripted of inv8-10). At initialisation θ is set to an arbitrary value θ_0 and the control function *control_fun* (inv11-12) is assigned to the non-linear differential equation modelling the behaviour of the pendulum borrowed from the InvertedPendulum theory.

---

sense_angle REFINES *Sense*
WHERE
  grd1: $|\theta(t)| > 0$
WITH
  x_s': $x_s' = control$
  s: $s = \{control\}$
  p: $p = \{control\} \times \mathbb{R} \times$
    $\{\theta^*, \dot{\theta}^* \mid |\theta^*| \geq \theta_{max}\}$
THEN
  act1: $t^{sense}, \theta^{sense}, \dot{\theta}^{sense} := t, \theta(t), \dot{\theta}(t)$
END

---

transition_calculate_control
  REFINES *Transition*
WITH
  x_s': $x_s' = control$
  s: $s = \{control\}$
THEN
  act1: $control\_fun :=$
  $PendulumControl_{NonLin}(\omega_0, \theta^{sense}, \dot{\theta}^{sense}, t^{sense})$
END

Fig. 16. Sensing and transition

---

actuate_balance REFINES *Actuate*
ANY t'
WHERE
  grd1: $t' \in \mathbb{R}^+ \wedge t < t'$
  grd2: **SolvableWith**$([t, t'], Pendulum_{NonLin}(\omega_0, (\theta(t) \mapsto \dot{\theta}(t)), t), control\_fun)$
  grd3: $\theta(t) < \theta_{max}$
WITH
  e: $e = $ **withControl**$([t, t'], Pendulum_{NonLin}(\omega_0, (\theta(t) \mapsto \dot{\theta}(t)), t), control\_fun)$
  H: $H = \{\theta^*, \dot{\theta}^* \mid |\theta^*| < \theta_{max}|\}$
  x_p': $x_p' = \begin{bmatrix} \theta' & \dot{\theta}' \end{bmatrix}^\top$
  s: $s = \{control\}$
THEN
  act1: $t, \theta, \dot{\theta} :\sim_{t \rightarrow t'}$ **withControl**$([t, t'], Pendulum_{NonLin}(\omega_0, (\theta(t) \mapsto \dot{\theta}(t)), t), control\_fun)$
    $\&\{\theta^*, \dot{\theta}^* \mid |\theta^*| < \theta_{max}\}$
END

Fig. 17. System actuation

Following the hybrid automaton of Fig. 3, the system defines two discrete events: the sensing event **sense_angle** reads and stores the continuous state in the *sense* variables, and the transition event **transition_calculate_control** uses the stored continuous state to set up an adequate control function, stored in *control_fun*. An actuation event updates the plant's behaviour with the $Pendulum_{NonLin}$ differential equation, associated with *control_fun*'s new value (Fig. 17).

Step 3: Linearised Inverted Pendulum Model (5 in Fig. 13). The approximation pattern ((3) in Fig. 13) is used to refine the non-linear pendulum model into a linearised one. The theory of approximation of Sect. 5.2 as well as the domain theory of pendulums given in Sect. 6.1 allow us to set up an approximate refinement relationship between the two linear and non-linear models.

CONTEXT PendulumLinCtx **EXTENDS**
   PendulumCtx
CONSTANTS δ , δ_{ctrl} , θ_{bound}
AXIOMS
  axm1–2: $\delta \in \mathbb{R}, 0 < \delta$
  axm3: $\delta_{ctrl} = PendulumControlDelta(\omega_0, \delta)$
  axm4–7: $\theta_{bound} \in \mathbb{R}, 0 < \theta_{bound}$,
         $\theta_{bound} < \theta_{max}, \delta < \theta_{bound}$
END

The context of this system extends the one for the non-linear pendulum. It introduces a fixed δ (axm1-2), to model the maximum difference between the state of both system models as well as a stricter bound for θ (θ_{bound} in axm4-7). Using the pendulum theory, it is possible to synthesise δ_{ctrl}, the maximum difference between the controls of each system model (axm3) (Fig. 18).

MACHINE PendulumLin **REFINES** Pendulum
SEES PendulumLinCtx
VARIABLES t, t^{sense} , $control\_fun\_lin$,
  θ_{Lin} , $\dot{\theta}_{Lin}$, θ_{Lin}^{sense} , $\dot{\theta}_{Lin}^{sense}$
INVARIANTS
  inv1–4: $\theta_{Lin} \in \mathbb{R} \nrightarrow \mathbb{R}, \dot{\theta}_{Lin} \in \mathbb{R} \nrightarrow \mathbb{R}$,
    $[0, t] \subseteq \mathrm{dom}(\theta_{Lin}), [0, t] \subseteq \mathrm{dom}(\dot{\theta}_{Lin})$
  inv5: $[\theta_{Lin}\ \dot{\theta}_{Lin}]^\top \approx_{[0,t]}^{\delta} [\theta\ \dot{\theta}]^\top$
  inv6: $\forall t^* \cdot t^* \in [0, t] \Rightarrow$
    $|\theta(t^*)| < \theta_{bound} \wedge |\theta_{Lin}(t^*)| < \theta_{bound} - \delta$
  inv7: $control\_fun\_lin \in \mathbb{R} \nrightarrow \mathbb{R}$
  inv8:
    $control\_fun\_lin \approx_{[t^{sense}, +\infty[}^{\delta_{ctrl}} control\_fun$

  inv9–10: $\theta_{Lin}^{sense} \in \mathbb{R}$, $\dot{\theta}_{Lin}^{sense} \in \mathbb{R}$
  inv11: $|\theta_{Lin}^{sense}| \le \theta_{bound} - \delta$
  inv12: $[\theta^{sense}\ \dot{\theta}^{sense}]^\top \approx^{\delta} [\theta_{Lin}^{sense}\ \dot{\theta}_{Lin}^{sense}]^\top$

INITIALISATION
WITH
  θ'; $\theta' = \theta_0$, $\dot{\theta}'$: $\dot{\theta}' = 0$
  $\theta^{sense\prime}$: $\theta^{sense\prime} = \theta_0$, $\dot{\theta}^{sense\prime}$: $\dot{\theta}^{sense\prime} = 0$
  $control\_fun'$: $control\_fun' =$
  $PendulumControl_{NonLin}(\omega_0, (\theta_0 \mapsto 0), 0)$
THEN
  act1: $t := 0$
  act2: $t^{sense} := 0$
  act3: $\theta_{Lin} := \{0 \mapsto \theta_0\}$
  act4: $\dot{\theta}_{Lin} := \{0 \mapsto 0\}$
  act5: $control\_fun\_lin :=$
    $PendulumControl_{Lin}(\omega_0, (\theta_0 \mapsto 0), 0)$
  act6: $\theta_{Lin}^{sense}, \dot{\theta}_{Lin}^{sense} := \theta_0, 0$
END

Fig. 18. Machine header and initialisation

The machine header, presented in Fig. 18 is close to the abstract non-linear model with a new state $[\theta_{Lin}\ \dot{\theta}_{Lin}]$ (inv1-4). It is glued with the non-linear abstract state via the **approximate gluing invariant**, inv5. Both abstract and concrete states have strengthened constraints (inv6) to ensure the existence of the approximation relationship. The control function $control\_fun$ is refined by $control\_lin\_fun$ (inv7). It is linked to the abstract control using the approximated refinement gluing invariant of inv8. Refined versions of the sensing variables are introduced. θ_{Lin}^{sense} and $\dot{\theta}_{Lin}^{sense}$ are defined in inv9-10 and constrained in inv11. They are linked to the abstract sensing variables using inv12 gluing invariant. Last, **Initialisation** on the right-hand side of Fig. 18 updates the state variables. Simple witnesses (**WITH** clause) are provided for the refined (disappearing) variables.

```
sense_angle REFINES sense_angle
WHERE
    grd1:  |θ_{Lin}(t)| > 0
WITH
    θ^{sense'}, θ̇^{sense'} :
    [θ^{sense'} θ̇^{sense'}]^⊤ ≈^δ [θ_{Lin}^{sense'} θ̇_{Lin}^{sense'}]^⊤
THEN
    act1:  t^{sense}, θ_{Lin}^{sense}, θ̇_{Lin}^{sense} :=
           t, θ_{Lin}(t), θ̇_{Lin}(t)
END
```

```
transition_calculate_control REFINES
           transition_calculate_control
WITH
    control_fun' :
       control_fun' ≈^δ_{[t^{sense},+∞[} control_fun_lin'
THEN
    act1:  control_fun_lin :=
       PendulumControl_{Lin}(ω_0, θ_{Lin}^{sense}, θ̇_{Lin}^{sense}, t^{sense})
END
```

Fig. 19. Linear refined sense and transition with approximation

The sense and transition events (Fig. 19) update system variables. Witnesses are provided to link the state variables of the abstract and refined models.

```
actuate_balance REFINES actuate_balance
ANY  t'
WHERE
    grd1:  t' ∈ ℝ^+ ∧ t < t'
    grd2:  SolvableWith([t, t'], Pendulum_{Lin}(ω_0, (θ_{Lin}(t) ↦ θ̇_{Lin}(t)), t), control_fun_lin)
    grd3:  |θ_{Lin}(t)| < θ_{bound} - δ
WITH
    θ, θ̇ :  [θ' θ̇'] ≈^δ_{[0,t']} [θ'_{Lin} θ̇'_{Lin}]
THEN
    act1:  t, θ_{Lin}, θ̇_{Lin} :∼_{t→t'}
       withControl([t, t'], Pendulum_{Lin}(ω_0, (θ_{Lin}(t) ↦ θ̇_{Lin}(t)), t), control_fun_lin)
       &{θ^*, θ̇^* | |θ^*| < θ_{bound} - δ}
END
```

Fig. 20. Linear refined actuation with approximation

Last, the actuation event of Fig. 20 updates the state variables by providing a witness using the WITH clause for the abstract continuous state using the defined approximation. It is central to maintain the approximated gluing invariant.

6.2   Assessment

The main advantage of the defined framework is proof reuse. Indeed, proofs are realised at the generic level and do not need to be discharged again. The only remaining proofs relate to the instantiation of the pattern (under the form of refinement POs) and the specific features of the model, namely invariants.

The first refinement generated 100 POs. 34% of them relate to refinement, while the vast majority of the others are about well-definedness (33%) of the operators and invariants (37%), most of which are typing invariants. The second one generated 63 POs. 19% of them come from refinement, and more specifically when using the approximation pattern. Again, a significant number of POs relate to well-definedness (33%) and invariants (44%) are mainly typing invariants. The interactive proofs have been carried out using rewriting rules, deductive rules application, and external automatic provers calls, combined in tactics.

The theory plug-in is still in the early stage of development, it hinders proof automation. For this reason and because our models extensively rely on it, proofs had to be done interactively. All the models shown in this paper can be accessed at https://irit.fr/~Guillaume.Dupont/models.php.

7   Conclusion

The definition of the proposed framework results from the different experiments and models that we defined in previous work. Some of the patterns are identified from our Event-B developments for a simple controlled system [10, 12], centralised control of many plants [11] and distributed control of many controllers [13].

In this paper, we have shown how the defined framework of Fig. 1 is put into practice to model the inverted pendulum case study. First, we applied the *Single2Single* architecture pattern and then the *Approximation* pattern as depicted in Fig. 13 to obtain a verified linearised model of the inverted pendulum.

The Event-B method together with its IDE Rodin proved powerful to support the formalisation of such generic patterns as parameterised Event-B models. These patterns and the necessary theories are proved to be correct once and for all. Specific hybrid systems models are obtained by instantiation i.e. by providing witnesses for the parameters of the generic models satisfying the properties (invariants) expressed at the generic models level. Only this instantiation step requires to be checked, the other proofs are reused, they are not re-proved again.

The defined framework is open and can be enriched, at the generic level, with new patterns and other theories. The added patterns may be connected through refinement to existing ones or may use new other theories. Each time a pattern is added, it needs to be formally verified. Examples of patterns that can be added are: discretisation pattern, PID[3] controller pattern, introduction of theories for partial differential equations or delayed differential equations, etc. In addition, other theories axiomatising different domains from physics should be defined in order to broaden the use of the defined framework.

References

1. Abrial, J.R.: Modeling in Event-B: System and Software Engineering. Cambridge University Press, Cambridge (2010)
2. Abrial, J.R., Butler, M., Hallerstede, S., Leuschel, M., Schmalz, M., Voisin, L.: Proposals for mathematical extensions for Event-B. Technical report (2009). http://deploy-eprints.ecs.soton.ac.uk/216/
3. Alur, R., Courcoubetis, C., Henzinger, T.A., Ho, P.-H.: Hybrid automata: an algorithmic approach to the specification and verification of hybrid systems. In: Grossman, R.L., Nerode, A., Ravn, A.P., Rischel, H. (eds.) HS 1991-1992. LNCS, vol. 736, pp. 209–229. Springer, Heidelberg (1993). https://doi.org/10.1007/3-540-57318-6_30

---

[3] Proportional, Integral, and Derivative.

4. Asarin, E., Dang, T., Maler, O.: The d/dt tool for verification of hybrid systems. In: Brinksma, E., Larsen, K.G. (eds.) CAV 2002. LNCS, vol. 2404, pp. 365–370. Springer, Heidelberg (2002). https://doi.org/10.1007/3-540-45657-0_30
5. Back, R.-J., Petre, L., Porres, I.: Generalizing action systems to hybrid systems. In: Joseph, M. (ed.) FTRTFT 2000. LNCS, vol. 1926, pp. 202–213. Springer, Heidelberg (2000). https://doi.org/10.1007/3-540-45352-0_17
6. Banach, R., Butler, M., Qin, S., Verma, N., Zhu, H.: Core hybrid Event-B I: single hybrid Event-B machines. Sci. Comput. Program. **105**, 92–123 (2015)
7. Banach, R., Poppleton, M., Jeske, C., Stepney, S.: Engineering and theoretical underpinnings of retrenchment. Sci. Comput. Program. **67**(2–3), 301–329 (2007)
8. Butler, M., Maamria, I.: Practical theory extension in Event-B. In: Liu, Z., Woodcock, J., Zhu, H. (eds.) Theories of Programming and Formal Methods. Lecture Notes in Computer Science, vol. 8051, pp. 67–81. Springer, Heidelberg (2013). https://doi.org/10.1007/978-3-642-39698-4_5. Essays Dedicated to Jifeng He on the Occasion of his 70th Birthday
9. Chaochen, Z., Ji, W., Ravn, A.P.: A formal description of hybrid systems. In: Alur, R., Henzinger, T.A., Sontag, E.D. (eds.) HS 1995. LNCS, vol. 1066, pp. 511–530. Springer, Heidelberg (1996). https://doi.org/10.1007/BFb0020972
10. Dupont, G., Aït-Ameur, Y., Pantel, M., Singh, N.K.: Hybrid systems and Event-B: a formal approach to signalised left-turn assist. In: Abdelwahed, E.H., et al. (eds.) MEDI 2018. CCIS, vol. 929, pp. 153–158. Springer, Cham (2018). https://doi.org/10.1007/978-3-030-02852-7_14
11. Dupont, G., Aït-Ameur, Y., Pantel, M., Singh, N.K.: Handling refinement of continuous behaviors: a refinement and proof based approach with Event-B. In: 13th International Symposium TASE, pp. 9–16. IEEE Computer Society Press (2019)
12. Dupont, G., Aït-Ameur, Y., Pantel, M., Singh, N.K.: Proof-based approach to hybrid systems development: dynamic logic and Event-B. In: Butler, M., Raschke, A., Hoang, T.S., Reichl, K. (eds.) ABZ 2018. LNCS, vol. 10817, pp. 155–170. Springer, Cham (2018). https://doi.org/10.1007/978-3-319-91271-4_11
13. Dupont, G., Aït-Ameur, Y., Pantel, M., Singh, N.K.: Formally verified architecture patterns of hybrid systems using proof and refinement with Event-B. In: Raschke, A., Méry, D., Houdek, F. (eds.) ABZ 2020. LNCS, vol. 12071, pp. 169–185. Springer, Cham (2020). https://doi.org/10.1007/978-3-030-48077-6_12
14. Frehse, G.: PHAVer: algorithmic verification of hybrid systems past HyTech. Int. J. Softw. Tools Technol. Transf. **10**(3), 263–279 (2008)
15. Frehse, G., et al.: SpaceEx: scalable verification of hybrid systems. In: Gopalakrishnan, G., Qadeer, S. (eds.) CAV 2011. LNCS, vol. 6806, pp. 379–395. Springer, Heidelberg (2011). https://doi.org/10.1007/978-3-642-22110-1_30
16. Girard, A., Pappas, G.J.: Approximate bisimulation relations for constrained linear systems. Automatica **43**(8), 1307–1317 (2007)
17. Girard, A., Pappas, G.J.: Approximation metrics for discrete and continuous systems. IEEE Trans. Automat. Contr. **52**(5), 782–798 (2007)
18. Henzinger, T.A.: The theory of hybrid automata. In: Inan, M.K., Kurshan, R.P. (eds.) Verification of Digital and Hybrid Systems. NATO ASI Series, vol. 170, pp. 265–292. Springer, Heidelberg (2000). https://doi.org/10.1007/978-3-642-59615-5_13
19. Jifeng, H.: From CSP to hybrid systems. In: Roscoe, A.W. (ed.) A Classical Mind, pp. 171–189. Prentice Hall International (UK) Ltd. (1994)
20. Platzer, A.: Differential dynamic logic for hybrid systems. J. Autom. Reas. **41**(2), 143–189 (2008)

21. Platzer, A., Quesel, J.-D.: KeYmaera: a hybrid theorem prover for hybrid systems (system description). In: Armando, A., Baumgartner, P., Dowek, G. (eds.) IJCAR 2008. LNCS (LNAI), vol. 5195, pp. 171–178. Springer, Heidelberg (2008). https://doi.org/10.1007/978-3-540-71070-7_15
22. Su, W., Abrial, J.R., Zhu, H.: Formalizing hybrid systems with Event-B and the Rodin platform. Sci. Comput. Program. **94**, 164–202 (2014)

Towards Generating SPARK from Event-B Models

Sanjeevan Sritharan and Thai Son Hoang[(✉)]

ECS, University of Southampton, Southampton, UK
{ss6n17,t.s.hoang}@soton.ac.uk

Abstract. This paper presents an approach to generate SPARK code from Event-B models. System models in Event-B are translated into SPARK packages including proof annotations. Properties of the Event-B models such as axioms and invariants are also translated and embedded in the resulting models as pre- and post-conditions. This helps with generating SPARK proof annotations automatically hence ensuring the correct behaviour of the resulting code. A prototype plug-in for the Rodin has been developed and the approach is evaluated on different examples. We also discuss the possible extensions including to generate scheduled code and data structures such as records.

Keywords: Event-B · SPARK · Code generation · Rodin platform

1 Introduction

Ensuring properties of safety- and security-critical systems is paramount. Event-B [1] is a formal modelling method which enables the design of systems, using mathematical proofs ensuring the conformity of the system to declared safety requirements. SPARK [4] is a programming language making use of static analysis tools which verify written code correctly implements the properties of the system as specified in the form of written proof annotations (e.g., pre- and post-conditions). SPARK has been used in many industry-scale projects to implement safety-critical software. However, manually writing SPARK proof annotations can be time-consuming and tedious.

Our motivation is to develop a tool-supported approach to translate an Event-B model into a SPARK package, including proof annotations and other structures, from which manually written SPARK code can be verified, hence ensuring the correct behaviour of the software. Event-B supports development via refinement, allowing details to be consistently introduced into the models. Properties of the systems such as invariances therefore are easier to be discovered compare to SPARK. One aim for our approach is to cover as much as possible the Event-B mathematical language that can be translated into SPARK.

Thai Son Hoang is supported by the HiClass project (113213), which is part of the ATI Programme, a joint Government and industry investment to maintain and grow the UK's competitive position in civil aerospace design and manufacture.

B. Dongol and E. Troubitsyna (Eds.): IFM 2020, LNCS 12546, pp. 103–120, 2020.
https://doi.org/10.1007/978-3-030-63461-2_6

Our contribution is an approach where Event-B sets and relations are translated as SPARK Boolean arrays. A library is built to support the translation. Furthermore, properties of the systems such as axioms and invariants are translated and embedded in SPARK as pre- and post-conditions. These properties, in particular invariance properties, are often global system properties ensuring the safety and consistency of the overall system, and are often difficult to be discovered. Using these conceptual translation rules, a plug-in was created for the Rodin platform [2] and was evaluated with several Event-B models. From the evaluation, we discuss different possible extensions including to generate scheduled code and records data structure.

The rest of the paper is structured as follows. Section 2 gives some background information for the paper. This includes an overview of Event-B, SPARK, and our running example. Our main contribution is presented in Sect. 3. We discuss limitation and possible extensions of the approach in Sect. 4. Section 5 reviews the related work. Finally, we summary and discuss future research direction in Sect. 6.

2   Background

2.1   Event-B

Event-B [1] is a formal method used to design and model software systems, of which certain properties must hold, such as safety properties. This method is useful in modelling safety-critical systems, using mathematical proofs to show consistency of models in adhering to its specification. Models consist of constructs known as machines and contexts. A *context* is the static part of a model, such as *carrier sets* (which are conceptually similar to types), *constants*, and *axioms*. Axioms are properties of carrier sets and constants which always hold. *Machines* describe the dynamic part of the model, that is, how the state of the model changes. The state is represented by the current values of the *variables*, which may change values as the state changes. *Invariants* are declared in the machine, stating properties of variables which should always be true, regardless of the state. *Events* in the machine describe state changes. Events can have *parameters* and *guards* (predicates on variables and event parameters); the guard must hold true for event execution. Each event has a set of *actions* which happen simultaneously, changing the values of the variables, and hence the state. Every machine has an initialisation event which sets initial variable values. An important set of proof obligations are invariant preservation. They are generated and required to be discharged to show that no event can potentially change the state to one which breaks any invariant, a potentially unsafe state.

An essential feature of Event-B, stepwise refinement, is not used within the scope of this project, which focuses on Event-B's modelling of a single abstraction level model. Further details on refinement can be found in [1,10]. In Sect. 2.3 we present the our running example including the Event-B model.

2.2 SPARK

SPARK [4] is a programming language used for systems with high safety standards. It includes tools performing static verification on programs written in the language. SPARK is a subset of another programming language, Ada [5], which is also used for safety-critical software. SPARK removes several major constructs from Ada, allowing feasible and correct static analysis.

SPARK includes a language of annotations, which are specifications for a SPARK program, clarifying what the program should do [13]. While program annotations focus on the flow analysis part of static analysis, focusing on things such as data dependencies, proof annotations support "assertion based formal verification". In particular, a specification for a SPARK procedure has the following aspects:

- Pre aspect: pre-conditions which are required to hold true on calling a subprogram, without which the subprogram has no obligation to work correctly.
- Post: post-conditions which should be achieved by the actions of a subprogram, provided the pre-conditions held initially
- Global aspect: specifying which global variables are involved in this subprogram, and how they are used.
- Depends aspect: which variables or parameters affect the new value of the modified variables

Proof annotations also involve loop invariants, which are conditions which hold true in every iteration of a loop.

This mix of proof and program annotations ensure that any implementation written in SPARK adheres to its specification, producing reliable, safe software.

2.3 A Running Example

To illustrate our approach, we use an adapted version of the example of a building access system from [6]. We only present a part of the model here. The full model and the translation to SPARK is available in [17].

The context declares the sets of PEOPLE and BUILDING with a constant maxsize to indicate the maximum number of registered users. Note that we have introduced axioms to constrain the size of our carrier sets and fix the value of the constant as it is necessary for our generated SPARK code. Normally, Event-B models are often more abstract, e.g., there are no constraints on the size of the carrier sets.

```
context c0
sets PEOPLE BUILDING
constants maxsize
axioms
  @finite−PEOPLE: finite(PEOPLE)
  @card−PEOPLE: card(PEOPLE) = 10
  @finite−BUILDING: finite(BUILDING)
```

@card−BUILDING: card(BUILDING) = 4
@def−maxsize: maxsize=3
end

The machine models the set of register users, their location and their permission for accessing buildings.

machine m0
variables register size location permission
invariants
  @inv1: register $\subseteq$ PEOPLE
  @inv2: size $\leq$ maxsize
  @inv3: location $\in$ register $\nrightarrow$ BUILDING
  @inv4: permission $\in$ register $\leftrightarrow$ BUILDING
  @inv5: location $\subseteq$ permission
events
  ...
end

Invariant @inv5 specifies the access control policy: a register user can only be in a building where they are allowed.

Initially, there are no users in the system, hence all the variables are assigned the empty set.

event INITIALISATION
begin
  @init−register: register := $\varnothing$
  @init−size: size := 0
  @init−location: location := $\varnothing$
  @init−permission: permission := $\varnothing$
end

We also consider two events RegisterUser and Enter. Event RegisterUser models the situation where a new user p registers with the system. Guard @grd2 ensures that the maximum number of registered users will not exceed the limit maxsize.

event RegisterUser
any p where
  @grd1: p $\in$ PERSON \ register
  @grd2: size $\neq$ maxsize
then
  @act1: register := register $\cup$ {p}
  @act2: size := size + 1
end

Event Enter models the situation where a user p enters a building b given that they have the necessary permission.

```
event Enter
any p b where
  @grd1: p ∈ register
  @grd2: b ∈ building
  @grd3: p ∉ dom(location)
  @grd4: p ↦ b ∈ permission
then
  @act1: location(p) := b
end
```

In Sect. 3.2, we will use this example to illustrate our approach to translate Event-B models to SPARK.

3   Contributions

In this section, we first discuss about the translation of the Event-B mathematical language into SPARK, then present the translation of the Event-B models.

3.1   Translation of the Mathematical Language

In term of the translation of the Event-B mathematical language into corresponding constructs in SPARK, our aim is to cover as much as possible the Event-B mathematical language. Due to the abstractness of the Event-B mathematical language, we focus on the collection of often-used constructs, including sets and relations.

Translation of Types. The built-in types in Event-B, i.e., $\mathbb{Z}$ and BOOL, are directly represented as Integer and Boolean in SPARK. Note that there is already a mismatch as Integer in SPARK are finite and bounded while $\mathbb{Z}$ is mathematical set of integers (infinite). However, any range check, i.e., to ensure that integer value are within the range from Min_Int and Max_Int, will be done in SPARK. Other basic types in Event-B are user-defined carrier sets and they will be translated as enumerated type or sub-type of Integer (see Sect. 3.2).

Translation of Sets. With the exception of BOOL and enumeration, Event-B types are often represented as sub-types of Integer in SPARK. As a result, we can represent Event-B sets as SPARK arrays of Boolean value, indexed by the Integer range.

type set **is array** (Integer **range** <>) **of** Boolean;

As a result, a set S containing elements of type T can be declared as

S : set(T);

Subsequently, membership in Event-B, e.g., $e \in S$ can be translated as $S(e) = True$ in SPARK.

Translation of Relations. Similar to translation of sets, we use two-dimensional SPARK arrays of Boolean values to represent relations. The two dimensional arrays are indexed by two Integer ranges corresponding to the type of the domain and range of the relations.

type relation **is array** (Integer **range** <>, Integer **range** <>) **of** Boolean;

Hence, a relation $r \in S \leftrightarrow T$ (where S and T are types) can be declared as

r : relation(S, T)

For a tuple $e \mapsto f$, membership of a relation r, i.e., $e \mapsto f \in r$ will be translated as $r(e, f) = True$ in SPARK.

With this approach to represent sets and relations, these Event-B constructs can thus only have carrier sets (but not enumeration) or Integer type elements, not BOOL. In the future, we will add different translation construct involving enumerations and BOOL.

Translation of Predicates. For propositional operators, such as $\neg$, $\wedge$, $\vee$, $\Rightarrow$ and $\Leftrightarrow$, the translation to SPARK is as expected. In the following, for each formula F in Event-B, let EB2SPARK(F) be the translation of F in SPARK.

- $\neg P$ is translated as not EB2SPARK(P).
- $P1 \wedge P2$ is translated as EB2SPARK(P1) **and then** EB2SPARK(P2)
- $P1 \vee P2$ is translated as EB2SPARK(P1) **or else** EB2SPARK(P2)
- $P1 \Rightarrow P2$ is translated as **if** EB2SPARK(P1) **then** EB2SPARK(P2)
- $P1 \Leftrightarrow P2$ is translated as
  if EB2SPARK(P1) **then** EB2SPARK(P2) **else** (not EB2SPARK(P2))

For quantifiers, i.e., $\forall$ and $\exists$, we need to extract the type of the bound variable accordingly, i.e.,

- $\forall z \cdot P$ is translated as **for all** z **in** z_type = > EB2SPARK(P)
- $\exists z \cdot P$ is translated as **for some** z **in** z_type = > EB2SPARK(P)

Translation of Relational Operators. For relational operators such as $\subseteq$, $\subset$, etc., there are no direct corresponding construct in SPARK. We can translate according to their mathematical definition. For example $S \subseteq T$ can be translated as

for all x **in** S'**Range** = > (**if** S(x) **then** x **in** T'**Range and then** T(x))

(Note that S and T are translated as Boolean arrays in SPARK). To improve the translation process, we define a utility function isSubset as follows.

function isSubset (s1 : set; s2 : set) **return** Boolean **is**
    (**for all** x **in** s1'**Range** => (**if** (s1(x)) **then** x **in** s2'**Range and then** s2(x))));

With this function $S \subseteq T$ can be simply translated as isSubset(S, T). Other relational operators are translated similarly.

The supporting definitions, e.g., definitions for sets and relations, and utility functions, are collected in a supporting SPARK package, namely sr.ads, that will be included in every generated files. The translation is described in details in [17].

3.2   Translation of Event-B Models

Each Event-B model (including the contexts and the machine) will correspond to a SPARK Ada package. We focus at the moment on the package specification. The package body, i.e., the implementation, can be generated similarly and is our future work.

> **with** sr; **use** sr;
> **package** m0 **with** SPARK_Mode **is**
> $--$ *code generated for m0 (including seen contexts)*
> **end** m0;

In particular, each Event-B event corresponds to a procedure where the guard contributes to the precondition and the action contributes to the post-condition. In the following, we describe in details the translation of the different modelling elements.

Translation of Carrier Sets. Carrier sets are types in Event-B and can be enumerated sets or deferred sets. An enumerated set S containing elements E1, ..., En in Event-B is defined as follows.

> sets S
> constants E1 , ... , En
> axioms
>   @def$-$S : partition (S, {E1}, ... , {En})

It is straightforward to represent the enumeration in SPARK as follows.

> **type** S **is** (E1, ..., En);

A deferred set in Event-B will be represented as an Integer subtype in SPARK. As a result, we require that the deferred set in Event-B to be finite and with a specified cardinality. That is, it is declared in Event-B as follows, where n is a literal.

> sets S
> axioms
>   @finite$-$S : finite (S)
>   @card$-$S : card (S) $=$ n

In fact, a carrier set in Event-B provides two concept: a user-defined type and a set containing all elements of that type. As a result, there are two different SPARK elements that are generated:

- A type declaration S_type.
- A variable S corresponding to the set which a Boolean array containing True indicating that set contains all elements of S_type.

> **subtype** S_type **is** Integer **range** 1 .. n;
> S : set(S_type) := (**others** => True);

Example 1 (Translation of Carrier Sets). The carrier sets PEOPLE and BUILDING in the example from Sect. 2.3 are translated as follows.

> **subtype** PEOPLE_type **is** integer **range** 1 .. 10;
> PEOPLE : set (PEOPLE_type) := (**others** => True);
> **subtype** BUILDING_type **is** integer **range** 1 .. 4;
> BUILDING : set (BUILDING_type) := (**others** => True);

Translation of Constants. Event-B constants are translated constant variables in SPARK. Since constant variable declarations in SPARK require that the variable be defined with a value, an axiom defining the value of the constant is also required. As a result, only constants with axioms specifying their values are translated. For example, the following constant C is specified in Event-B as follows, where n is a integer literal.

> constants C
> axioms
>   @def−C: C = n

The specification is translated into SPARK as follows.

> C : **constant** Integer := n;

Example 2 (Translation of Constants). The constant maxsize in the example from Sect. 2.3 is translated as follows.

> maxsize : **constant** Integer := 3;

Translation of Axioms. For each Event-B axiom, an expression function is generated. The name of the function is the axiom label and the predicate is translated according to Sect. 3.1. At the moment, we do not generate SPARK function for axioms about finiteness: all variables in SPARK are finite. We also do not generate SPARK function for axioms about cardinality: they are non-trivial to specify and reason about with arrays. For convenience, we also generate an expression function represent all axioms of the model; we call this expression function **Axioms**. We also include in this **Axioms** constraints about carrier sets, that is they contain all elements of the types.

Example 3. Translation of Axioms. The translation of axioms for the example in Sect. 2.3 is as follows

> **function** def_maxsize **return** Boolean **is** (maxsize = 3);
> **function** Axioms **return** Boolean **is** (
> isFullSet(PEOPLE) **and then**
> isFullSet(BUILDING) **and then**
> def_maxsize);

Here isFullSet is a function defined in sr.ads, ensuring that PEOPLE and BUILDING are arrays containing only True.

Translation of Variables. Each variable in Event-B corresponds to a variable in SPARK. For the variable declaration in SPARK, we need to extract the type of the Event-B variable. At the moment, we support variable types of either basic types (T), set of basic types ($\mathbb{P}(T)$), and relations between basic types ($\mathbb{P}(T1 \times T2)$).

Example 4. Translation of Variables The translation of the variables for the example in Sect. 2.3 is as follows.

> register : set (PEOPLE_type);
> size : Integer;
> location : relation (PEOPLE_type, BUILDING_type);
> permission: relation (PEOPLE_type, BUILDING_type);

Translation of Invariants. Each invariant corresponds to an expression function (similar to axioms) and these invariant functions are used as pre- and post-conditions of every procedures. For convenience, we define an expression function, namely **Invariants** as the conjunction of all invariants.

Example 5 (Translation of Invariants). The translation of the invariants of the example in Sect. 2.3 is as follows.

> **function** inv1 **return** Boolean **is** (isSubset(register, PEOPLE));

> **function** inv2 **return** Boolean **is** (size <= maxsize);

> **function** inv3 **return** Boolean **is**
> isPartialFunction(location, register, BUILDING);

```
function inv4 return Boolean
is isRelation(permission, register, BUILDING);
```

```
function inv5 return Boolean is isSubset(location, permission);
```

```
function Invariants return Boolean is (
inv1 and then
inv2 and then
inv3 and then
inv4 and then
inv5
)
```

Translation of Events. For each Event-B event, a procedure of the same name is generated. The Event-B event parameters corresponding to the SPARK procedure input parameters. The other aspects of the specification, i.e., Global, Depends, Pre and Post are computed accordingly. The following Event-B event

```
event e
any p where
   ...
then
   ...
end
```

is translated into a SPARK procedure with the following structure.

```
procedure e(p : in p_type) with
Pre => Axioms and then Invariants and then event guards
Post => Axioms and then Invariants and then event actions
Global => Computed from the event actions,
Depends => Computed from the event actions,
```

First of all, the Pre and the Post aspects contain both the axioms and invariants. Since SPARK does not provide notation for invariants, we just make the assertions in the pre- and post-conditions of all procedures (except for the one corresponding to the INITIALISATION, where assertions only appear in the post-condition). The translation of guards are the translation of the individual guard predicate as described in Sect. 3.1. For each action the corresponding SPARK post-condition is generated as follows.

- $v := E(p, v)$ is translated as $v = E(p, v'\text{Old})$
- $v :\in E(p, v)$ is translated as $\text{isMember}(v, E(p, v'\text{Old}))$
- $v :| E(p, v, v')$ is translated as $E(p, v'\text{Old}, v)$

Global aspect specifies the access to the global variables and it could be In (for variables that are read), Out (variables that are updated but not read), In_Out (for variables that are both read and updated) or Proof_In (variables that only used in Precondition, i.e., for proving). We generate variables In, Out or In_Out based on how they are used in the event actions. Any other variables will be Proof_In as the preconditions references all variables (since they include all axioms and invariants).

Depends aspect specifies the dependency between the Output variables and the Input variables. We generate the Depends aspects by inspecting individual assignment. Each individual assignment corresponds to an Depends aspects clause, where the left-hand side of the clause is the variable on the left-hand size of the assignment, and the right-hand size of the clause are all variables on the right-hand size of the assignment.

Example 6 (Translation of the INITIALISATION event). The INITIALISATION event in the example from Sect. 2.3 is translated as follows.

```
procedure INITIALISATION with
 Pre => Axioms,
 Post =>
  Axioms and then
  Invariants and then
  isEmpty(register) and then
  size = 0 and then
  isEmpty(location) and then
  isEmpty(permission),
 Global => (
 Out => (register, size, location, permission),
 Proof_In => (PEOPLE, BUILDING, maxsize)
 )
 Depends => (
 register => null,
 size => null,
 location => null,
 permission => null
 )
end INITIALISATION;
```

Example 7 (Translation of the Enter event). The Enter event in the example from Sect. 2.3 is translated as follows.

```
procedure Enter(p : in PEOPLE_type, b : in BUILDING_type) with
 Pre =>
  Axioms and then
  Invariants and then
  register(p) and then
```

```
      BUILDING(b) and then
      not (inDomain(p, location)) and then
      permission(p, b),
   Post =>
      Axioms and then
      Invariants and then
      (for all x in location'Range(1) =>
        if x /= p then (for all y in location'Range(2) =>
                 location(x, y) = location'Old(x,y))
        else (for all y in location'Range(2) =>
                 if y /= b then not location(x, y)
                 else location(x, y))
      ),
   Global => (
      In_Out => (location),
      Proof_In => (PEOPLE, BUILDING, maxsize, register, size, permission)
   )
   Depends => (
      location => (location, p, b),
   )
   end Enter;
```

Here the effect of updating a function is specified using universal quantifiers to ensure that only the location of person p is updated to be b.

4   Discussion

A prototype plug-in was developed for the Rodin platform [2]. The plug-in provide a context menu for Event-B machine to translate the machine to SPARK specification package. Since the Event-B to SPARK translator requires information such as types of variables, etc., the plug-in looks at the statically checked version of the machine then generate the SPARK specification according to the translation described in Sect. 3.

Beside the example of building access control system, we also generate SPARK code from other models, such as a room booking system, a club management system [10], controlling car on a bridge [1]. Note that the plug-in only generate the specification of the package at the moment. We have manually written the package body according to the Event-B model and prove that the model is consistent. More details about these examples can be found in [17].

4.1   Code Scheduling

At the moment, we only generate the SPARK code corresponding to individual events. Combination of these events according to some scheduling rules, such as [13] or some user-defined schedule, such as [8] will be our future work. To investigate the possibility, we also applied our approach to generate SPARK code for developing a lift system (the example used in [16]) and manually wrote the scheduled code in SPARK. The code corresponds to the Event-B model including events for controlling the door of the lift, controlling the lift motor, and changing the direction of travel. Some events relevant for our scheduling example are as follows.

- DoorClosed2Half_Up: to open the door from Closed to Half-closed while the lift travel upwards,
- MotorWinds: to wind the lift motor,
- ChangeDirectionDown_CurrentFloor: to change the lift travel direction to downward due to a request at the current floor to go down.
- ChangeDirectionDown_BelowFloor: to change the lift travel direction to downward due to a request below the current floor.

Our manually written scheduled code are as follows

```
if motor = STOPPED then
  case door is
    when CLOSED =>
      if direction = UP then
        if hasRequest_Up
        then
          DoorClosed2Half_Up;
        else
          if
            floorRequestAbove or
            upRequestAbove or
            downRequestAbove
          then
            MotorWinds;
          else
            if floor /= 0 and then down_buttons_array(floor) = TRUE then
              ChangesDirectionDown_CurrentFloor;
            elsif
              floorRequestBelow or
              upRequestBelow or
              downRequestBelow
            then
              ChangesDirectionDown_BelowFloor;
            end if;
          end if;
        end if;
      else -- direction = Down
        ...
      end if;
    when OPEN => ...
```

```
    when HALF => ...
  end case;
else -- motor /= STOPPED
  ...
end if;
```

In the above, hasRequest_Up, floorRequestAbove, upRequestAbove, etc. are local variables capturing the different requests for the lift. The manually written code invokes the different procedures generated from the Event-B model, e.g., MotorWinds, DoorClosed2Half_Up, ChangesDirectionDown_CurrentFloor, and ChangesDirectionDown_BelowFloor. SPARK generates verification conditions to ensure the correctness of our schedule, e.g., the preconditions of the procedures are met when the they are invoked. We plan to utilise the framework from [8] to allow users to specify the schedule and generate the SPARK scheduling code accordingly. The elevator model and the manually written SPARK code are available from https://doi.org/10.5258/SOTON/D1554.

4.2   Record Data Structures

At the moment, our main data structures for the generated SPARK code is Boolean arrays (one-dimensional arrays for sets and two-dimensional arrays for relations). Some modelling elements are better grouped and represented as record data structures in the code. To investigate the idea, we extend the lift example to a MULTI-lift system. The example is inspired by an actual lift system [18]. The systems allows multiple cabins running on a single shaft system vertically and horizontally. In our formal model, we have variables modelling the status of the different cabins in the lift system, e.g., the floor position (cabins_floor), the cabin motor status (cabins_motor), the door status (cabins_door), the current shaft of the cabin (cabins_shaft), and the cabin floor buttons (cabins_floor_buttons). The types of the variables are as follows.

invariants

@typeof−cabins_floor: cabins_floor $\in$ CABIN $\rightarrow$ 0 .. TOP_FLOOR
@typeof−cabins_motor: cabins_motor $\in$ CABIN $\rightarrow$ MOTOR
@typeof−cabins_door: cabins_door $\in$ CABIN $\rightarrow$ DOOR
@typeof−cabins_shaft: cabins_shaft $\in$ cabins $\rightarrow$ SHAFT
@typeof−floor_buttons: floor_buttons $\in$ cabins $\rightarrow$ $\mathbb{P}(0 ..$ TOP_FLOOR$)$

With our current approach, the variables will be translated individually as Boolean arrays. It is more natural to use a SPARK record to represent the cabin status. For example, the following CABIN_Type record can be used to capture the different attributes of a cabin.

type CABIN_Type **is record**
   floor : Integer; -- *The current floor of the cabin*
   motor : MOTOR_Type; -- *The current status of the cabin motor*
   door : DOOR_Type; -- *The current status of the door*

shaft : SHAFT_Type; —— *The current shaft of the cabin*

—— *The current floor buttons status inside the cabin*
floor_buttons : **array** (Integer **range** 0 .. TOP_FLOOR) **of** Boolean;
end record;

Recognising the record data structures from the Event-B model is one of our future research directions.

5 Related Work

Generating SPARK code from Event-B models has been considered in [13]. Their approach involves not only generating pre- and post-conditions, along with loop invariants, but also generates implementing SPARK code from Event-B models, using the merging rules described by [1], which describe how to generate *sequential programs from Event-B models*. However, the model used in [13] is fairly concrete, in particular in terms of the data structure used in the model. We aim to derive proof annotations from models where mathematically abstract concepts such as sets and relations are used. Given this, the merging rules used in [13] may not be applicable to very abstract models, as such an algorithm may not be represented or derivable. Furthermore, merging rules [1] can only be applied to model with a certain structure where the scheduling is implicitly encoded in the event guards. In our paper, we focus on the translation of the data structure. Furthermore, the translation rules from Event-B to SPARK assertions shown in [13] are limited, particularly in terms of set-theoretical constructs. This is an issue to address given Event-B is a set-theory-focused modelling tool.

Generating proof annotations from Event-B models has been investigated in [8]. Their work explores the mapping between Event-B and Dafny [12] constructs. This paper claims that a "direct mapping between the two is not straight forward". Due to the increased richness of the Event-B notation compared to Dafny, only a subset of Event-B constructs can be translated. Similar to [13], the authors of [8] suggest that a particular level of refinement must be achieved by the Event-B model, to reduce "the syntactic gap between Event-B and Dafny". However, the level of refinement required is needed to have a model containing only those mathematical constructs which have a counterpart in Dafny, not to obtain a model with a clear algorithmic structure present in its events. As such, this approach can still translate fairly abstract models. Their paper states the assumption that the "machine that is being translated is a data refinement of the abstract machine and none of the abstract variables are present in the refined machine". Their approach uses Hoare logic [11], by transforming events into Hoare triples, and deriving the relevant pre- and post-conditions.

Translation of Event-B models into Dafny is also the scope of [7]. The Dafny code generated is then verified using the verification tools available to Dafny. The translation is done so that Dafny code is "correct if and only if the Event-B refinement-based proof obligations hold". In other words, their approach allows users to verify the correctness of their models using a powerful verification tool. Specifically, their paper focuses on refinement proof obligations, showing that the concrete model is a correct refinement of the abstract model. While this is outside of the scope of our paper, it nevertheless introduces some translation rules which are relevant for us. For example, their paper demonstrates how invariants may be translated into Dafny and used in pre-conditions. It also shows an example of how relations in Event-B may be modelled in Dafny.

Another approach explored is the translation of Event-B to JML-annotated Java programs [14], which provides a translation "through syntactic rules". JML provides specifications which Java programs must adhere to, and so it is similar to contracts. Their approach generates Java code as well as JML specifications. Unlike the previous approaches, instead of grouping similar events, every single event is translated independently. This is perhaps not as efficient, as grouping similar events and using specific case guards in the post-conditions to differentiate between the expected outcomes can give an insight into how these events interact. Additionally, event grouping also saves space in the generated code by having fewer methods. This is only foreseen to be a problem when the translated model is concrete, and has several events representing different situational implementations of a single abstract event. Their paper demonstrates translation rules of machines and events to JML-annotated programs. The approach of deriving the JML specifications can possibly be adapted for our purpose, and can perhaps be considered an alternative approach to the one by [8]. However, an interesting point to note from their paper is that the approach given has the ability to generate code even from abstract models. The translation rules given can generate code from variables and assignments to variables in actions, in any level of abstraction or refinement. Hence, this approach of generating code can possibly be adapted for the generation of SPARK code.

6   Conclusion

In summary, we present in this paper an approach to generate SPARK code from Event-B models. We focus on covering as much as possible the Event-B mathematical language by representing sets and relations as Boolean arrays in SPARK. Each Event-B event is translated into a SPARK procedure with pre- and post-conditions, and aspects for flow analysis (i.e., Global and Depends aspects). Axiom and invariance properties of the models are translated into SPARK expression functions and are asserted as both pre- and post-conditions for the generated SPARK procedures. A prototype plug-in for the Rodin platform is developed and evaluated on different examples. We discuss the possible improvement of the approach including generating code corresponding to some schedule and using record data structure.

In term of translating sets and relations, we have also considered different approaches including using *functional sets* and *formal ordered sets* [3]. Our experiment shows that these representations have limited support for set and relational operators and did not work well with the SPARK provers.

For future work, we plan to include the generation of the procedure body with our prototype. The generation will base on the representation of sets and relations by Boolean arrays. We expect that this extension will be straightforward. As mentioned earlier, generating SPARK record data structures from Event-B models is another research direction. The challenge here is to recognise the elements in the Event-B models corresponding to records. With the introduction of records in Event-B [9], the mapping from Event-B elements to record data structures will become straightforward. Furthermore, we aim to develop a development process that starts from modelling at the system level using Event-B, gradually develop the system via refinement and generate SPARK code including event scheduling and data structure such as records.

During system development by refinement in Event-B, abstract variables can be replaced (data refined) by concrete variables. This allows (mathematically) abstract concepts to be replaced by concrete implementation details. Often, systems properties are expressed using abstract variables and are maintained by refinement. In this sense, abstract variables are similar to ghost variables in SPARK. We plan to investigate the translation of abstract variables in Event-B as ghost variables in SPARK.

Models in Event-B are typically system models, that is they contain not only the details about the software system but also the model of the environment where the software system operates. Using decomposition [15], the part of the model corresponding to the software systems can be extracted. Nevertheless, having a "logical" model of the environment will also be useful and it can be represented again using ghost code in SPARK.

Acknowledgements. Supporting material for this study is openly available from the University of Southampton repository at https://doi.org/10.5258/SOTON/D1554.

References

1. Abrial, J.-R.: Modeling in Event-B: System and Software Engineering. Cambridge University Press, Cambridge (2010)
2. Abrial, J.-R., Butler, M., Hallerstede, S., Hoang, T.S., Mehta, F., Voisin, L.: Rodin: an open toolset for modelling and reasoning in Event-B. Softw. Tools Technol. Transf. **12**(6), 447–466 (2010)
3. AdaCore. GNAT Reference Manual, 21.0w edition, July 2020. http://docs.adacore.com/live/wave/gnat_rm/html/gnat_rm/gnat_rm.html
4. Barnes, J.: High Integrity Software: The SPARK Approach to Safety and Security. Addison Wesley, Boston (2003)
5. Booch, G., Bryan, D.: Software Engineering with ADA, 3rd edn. Addison-Wesley, Boston (1993)
6. Butler, M.: Reasoned modelling with Event-B. In: Bowen, J., Liu, Z., Zhang, Z. (eds.) SETSS 2016. LNCS, vol. 10215, pp. 51–109. Springer, Cham (2017). https://doi.org/10.1007/978-3-319-56841-6_3
7. Cataño, N., Leino, K.R.M., Rivera, V.: The EventB2Dafny rodin plug-in. In: Garbervetsky, D., Kim, S. (eds.) Proceedings of the 2nd International Workshop on Developing Tools as Plug-Ins, TOPI 2012, Zurich, Switzerland, 3 June 2012, pp. 49–54. IEEE Computer Society (2012)

8. Dalvandi, M., Butler, M., Rezazadeh, A., Salehi Fathabadi, A.: Verifiable code generation from scheduled Event-B models. In: Butler, M., Raschke, A., Hoang, T.S., Reichl, K. (eds.) ABZ 2018. LNCS, vol. 10817, pp. 234–248. Springer, Cham (2018). https://doi.org/10.1007/978-3-319-91271-4_16

9. Fathabadi, A.S., Snook, C., Hoang, T.S., Dghaym, D., Butler, M.: Extensible data structures in Event-B (submitted to iFM2020)

10. Hoang, T.: Appendix A: an introduction to the Event-B modelling method. In: Romanovsky, A., Thomas, M. (eds.) Industrial Deployment of System Engineering Methods, pp. 211–236. Springer, Heidelberg (2013). https://doi.org/10.1007/978-3-642-33170-1_1

11. Hoare, C.A.R.: An axiomatic basis for computer programming. Commun. ACM **12**(10), 576–580 (1969)

12. Rustan, K., Leino, M.: Developing verified programs with Dafny. In: Joshi, R., Müller, P., Podelski, A. (eds.) VSTTE 2012. LNCS, vol. 7152, p. 82. Springer, Heidelberg (2012). https://doi.org/10.1007/978-3-642-27705-4_7

13. Murali, R., Ireland, A.: E-SPARK: automated generation of provably correct code from formally verified designs. Electron. Commun. EASST **53**, 1–15 (2012)

14. Rivera, V., Cataño, N.: Translating Event-B to JML-specified Java programs. In: Cho, Y., Shin, S.Y., Kim, S.-W., Hung, C.-C., Hong, J. (eds.) Symposium on Applied Computing, SAC 2014, Gyeongju, Republic of Korea, 24–28 March 2014, pp. 1264–1271. ACM (2014)

15. Silva, R., Pascal, C., Hoang, T.S., Butler, M.J.: Decomposition tool for Event-B. Softw. Pract. Exp. **41**(2), 199–208 (2011)

16. Snook, C., et al.: Behaviour-driven formal model development. In: Sun, J., Sun, M. (eds.) ICFEM 2018. LNCS, vol. 11232, pp. 21–36. Springer, Cham (2018). https://doi.org/10.1007/978-3-030-02450-5_2

17. Sritharan, S.: Automated translation of Event-B models to SPARK proof annotations. Technical report, University of Southampton (2020). https://eprints.soton.ac.uk/444034/

18. thyssenkrupp: MULTI - a new era of mobility in buildings. https://www.thyssenkrupp-elevator.com/uk/products/multi/. Accessed July 2020

Program Analysis and Testing

Jaint: A Framework for User-Defined Dynamic Taint-Analyses Based on Dynamic Symbolic Execution of Java Programs

Malte Mues(✉) , Till Schallau , and Falk Howar

Dortmund University of Technology, Dortmund, Germany
malte.mues@tu-dortmund.de

Abstract. We present JAINT, a generic security analysis for JAVA Web-applications that combines concolic execution and dynamic taint analysis in a modular way. JAINT executes user-defined taint analyses that are formally specified in a domain-specific language for expressing taint-flow analyses. We demonstrate how dynamic taint analysis can be integrated into JDART, a dynamic symbolic execution engine for the JAVA virtual machine in JAVA PathFinder. The integration of the two methods is modular in the sense that it traces taint independently of symbolic annotations. Therefore, JAINT is capable of sanitizing taint information (if specified by a taint analysis) and using multi-colored taint for running multiple taint analyses in parallel. We design a domain-specific language that enables users to define specific taint-based security analyses for JAVA Web-applications. Specifications in this domain-specific language serve as a basis for the automated generation of corresponding taint injectors, sanitization points and taint-flow monitors that implement taint analyses in JAINT. We demonstrate the generality and effectiveness of the approach by analyzing the OWASP benchmark set, using generated taint analyses for all 11 classes of CVEs in the benchmark set.

1 Introduction

Web-based enterprise applications are ubiquitous today and many of these applications are developed in JVM-based languages. The Tiobe index tracks the relevance of programming languages. JAVA leads this ranking consistently (with short periods of being ranked second) for the past 15 years[1]. Moreover, Apache Tomcat is running Web-applications for over 5, 000 international companies with a yearly revenue greater than one billion US Dollar each, according to data collected by HG Insights[2]. Therefore, security of Java Web-applications is of critical importance and attacks on them are reported every single day[3]. Though there

---

[1] https://www.tiobe.com/tiobe-index/.
[2] https://discovery.hgdata.com/product/apache-tomcat.
[3] https://www.cvedetails.com/vulnerabilities-by-types.php.

© Springer Nature Switzerland AG 2020
B. Dongol and E. Troubitsyna (Eds.): IFM 2020, LNCS 12546, pp. 123–140, 2020.
https://doi.org/10.1007/978-3-030-63461-2_7

is no publicly available data on the exact distribution of breaches across different programming languages. Based on the market share of JAVA in the realm of enterprise applications, one can assume that a significant fraction of the reported breaches exploits vulnerabilities of JVM-based Web-applications.

Many of the vulnerabilities tracked in the Common Vulnerability and Exposures (CVE)[4] list pertain to the flow of information through a program from a (potentially) malicious *source* to a protected *sink*. In modern Web-applications, such flows almost universally exist as these applications receive inputs from (untrusted) users and, e.g., store these inputs in (protected) databases. These inputs should pass *sanitizing* methods, e.g., for escaping of specific characters in a textual input or prepared and safe statements. Otherwise, attackers might use these inputs maliciously to inject commands into SQL statements in an attack.

Taint analysis is a well-established technique for analyzing the data flow through applications: Inputs are tainted and taint is then propagated along the data flow. Critical sinks (i.e. databases) are monitored by taint guards ensuring that no tainted data values reach the sink (c.f. [1,3,14,23–25]). Otherwise a security vulnerability is detected. Classically, taint analysis is either implemented as a static analysis, over-approximating flow of taint (c.f. [27]), or as a dynamic analysis, under-approximating taint flow by observing concrete program executions (c.f. [12]). The literature distinguishes data-flow taint, i.e., taint that propagates from right to left sides of assignments, and control-flow taint, i.e., taint is propagated through branching conditions to assignments in executed branches (c.f. [24]). One can observe a close similarity to symbolic execution [25]: (Data-flow) taint propagates like symbolic values, and (control-flow) taint captures path constraints of execution paths. However, this close similarity has not yet been fully leveraged as the basis for an integrated analysis for JAVA.

In this paper, we present JAINT, a framework for finding security weaknesses in JAVA Web-applications. The framework combines dynamic symbolic execution and dynamic taint analysis into a powerful analysis engine. This analysis engine is paired with a domain-specific language (DSL) that describes the concrete taint analysis tasks, JAINT executes during one analysis run. It is the first framework exploiting concolic execution for the dynamic but exhaustive exploration of execution paths in JAVA Web-servlets while maintaining explicit multi color taint marks on data values. This multi color taint allows the specification of multiple taint analyses run in parallel tracking data flow from malicious sources to protected sinks and monitoring potential security vulnerabilities. Moreover, as taint marks and symbolic values are separate annotations, the framework supports sanitization definitions on a taint color base making it more precise than previous work using symbolic annotations as taint marks [11]. The combination of dynamic symbolic execution and dynamic taint analysis results in greater precision than can be achieved with classic static taint analysis methods that are insensitive to most conditions on control flow. Moreover, for many of the identified vulnerabilities, our analysis can produce request parameters that exhibit a found vulnerability in a servlet. In contrast to purely dynamic taint

---

[4] https://cve.mitre.org.

analysis techniques, our approach is exhaustive given that dynamic symbolic execution terminates [18]: it generates a set of request parameters for every feasible execution path.

We have implemented JAINT as an extension of JDART [18], a dynamic symbolic execution engine for JAVA, and on top of JAVA PATHFINDER [13], a software model checker for JAVA that is based on a custom implementation of the JAVA virtual machine (JPF-VM). JAINT's DSL for defining concrete taint analyses (i.e., sources, sanitization methods and sinks) is designed on the basis of the Meta Programming System (MPS). JAINT's implementation is publicly available [20]. We evaluate JAINT on the OWASP benchmark suite[5], the current industrial standard for comparing analysis approaches for JAVA Web-applications. All 11 CWEs in the OWASP benchmark suite can be specified in our domain-specific language and JAINT analyzes the OWASP benchmark suite with a false negative rate of 0% and a false positive rate of 0%, identifying all security vulnerabilities.

Related Work. Schwartz et al. [25] describe a formal theory for dynamic taint propagation and discuss challenges in the implementation of an analysis combining dynamic symbolic execution and dynamic taint analysis. Their focus is mostly on memory representation problems for running the symbolic analysis in a programming language that allows pointer arithmetic. Due to the design of the JAVA virtual machine, these concerns are not relevant when analyzing JAVA byte code. The formalization of taint analysis by Schoepe et al. [24] stresses the importance of a clear division of data-flow and control-flow based taint propagation. From our point of view, this observation supports a separation of analysis methods: dynamic taint analysis and dynamic symbolic execution: Dynamic tainting tracks information following the data flow path, e.g., through instrumentation (c.f. [7,8,12,16,17,21,26,28]). Dynamic symbolic execution can be used for controlling the program execution path with external inputs ensuring exhaustive exploration of all paths.

Haldar et al. [12] presented a dynamic tainting mechanism for JAVA propagating the dynamic taint along a single path. JAINT's advantage over the approach of Haldar, is the integration of single path propagation with dynamic symbolic execution [2,6] for exhaustive path enumeration.

For C programs, Corin and Manzano [10] describe the integration of taint analysis into KLEE [5]. Their work is limited to propagation of single color taint and do not show, how different analyses can be run on top of the taint propagation, while we demonstrate how multi color taint can be used to analyze the OWASP benchmark. It seems some work has been started on KLEE-TAINT[6] for a more sophisticated taint analysis in KLEE combining symbolic execution with taint, but the approach requires to rewrite the C program to inject taint assigning methods and taint checks for the analysis. JAINT integrates the taint analysis without any modifications of the bytecode as taint injection and taint monitoring is computed in the virtual machine and not as part of the binary. Both approaches require a driver for the dynamic symbolic execution part.

---

[5] https://github.com/OWASP/Benchmark.
[6] https://github.com/feliam/klee-taint.

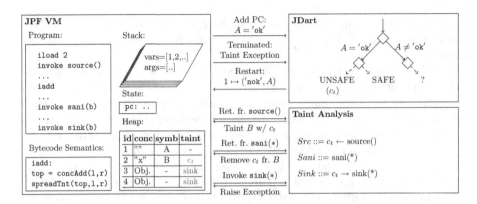

Fig. 1. Software Architecture of the implemented Vulnerability Analysis.

Several strategies for the implementation of taint models and taint propagation have been proposed: They range from integrating the taint check into the interpreter [22] to a complete taint propagation DSL integrating the taint analysis into the program [9]. In between are the flavors of integrating the taint check into the compiler [16,28] or into an execution environment [3,7,8,15,21]. We consider binary instrumentation as part of execution environment modification. The advantage of a DSL integrated into the program is that the execution environment and tool chain stay untouched. JAINT mixes two of those proposals. For the taint propagation, we modified the program interpreter, in our case the JPF-VM. In addition, we defined a DSL that allows to describe in which places taint should be injected, sanitized and checked during execution. As a consequence, the concrete taint injection does not require a modification of the program. Our DSL only describes the analysis and not the taint propagation. Hence, it is a different style of DSL than the one proposed by Conti and Russo [9].

Outline. The paper is structured as follows: We present our analysis framework JAINT in Sect. 2 and discuss the proposed domain-specific language for expressing concrete taint analyses in Sect. 3. Section 4 details results from the evaluation of the integrated analysis on the OWASP benchmark suite. We present conclusions and discuss directions for future research in Sect. 5.

2   Taint Analysis with Jaint

JAINT integrates dynamic symbolic execution and dynamic tainting in a single analysis framework. It is built on top of the JPF-VM. Figure 1 illustrates the interplay between the dynamic symbolic execution handled by JDART [18], the taint analysis and the JPF-VM.

The virtual machine of JAVA PATHFINDER provides several extension mechanisms that JAINT uses for the implementation of the analysis: *VM events, bytecodes, peers*, and *heap annotations. Heap annotations* are a mechanism for annotating objects on the heap with meta-information. *VM events* are hooks an analysis can use to collect or modify meta-information during execution. The JPF-VM allows to replace *bytecode instructions* or extend them to collect information or trace meta-information during symbolic execution. *Peers* can replace implementations of (native) library functions.

The dynamic symbolic execution uses *bytecode semantics* and *peers* for recording symbolic path constraints as shown on the top-most arrow from the JPF-VM box to the JDART box in Fig. 1. Bytecode semantics for symbolic execution and taint analysis are similar: while in the one case the result of operations is computed and maintained symbolically based on the symbolic annotations on operands, in the other case operations propagate existing taint annotations on operands to results of operations. E.g., the implementation of the `iadd` bytecode pops two integers including potential symbolic and taint annotations from the stack, performs a concrete addition, computes a symbolic term representing the result (only in case one of the integers was annotated symbolically), propagates taint from the integers to the result, and pushes the result and annotations back onto the stack. Symbolic values are used in path constraints (recorded on branching bytecode instructions) that accumulate in the constraints tree (upper right corner of the figure). The JDART concolic execution engine interacts with the virtual machine by placing concolic values (concrete values with symbolic annotations as shown in the heap table of the JPF-VM in Fig. 1) on the heap to drive execution down previously unexplored paths in the constraints tree. In the current version of JAINT, bytecode implementations do not remove symbolic annotations or taint (e.g., on multiplication with constant 0). Such behavior could, however, be implemented easily. JDART has the same limitations that symbolic execution has in general: recursion and loops are only analyzed up to a (configurable) fixed number of invocations (iterations, respectively).

The dynamic taint analysis is built around *VM events*. Listening on VM events (returns from methods), the taint analysis injects or removes taint from objects on the heap. E.g., a sanitization interaction between the analysis and the heap is shown in the lower part of Fig. 1. The method exit event for the SANI method interacts with the taint analysis and removes the c_t taint mark from the heap object with id 2 in this analysis. The interaction is represented by the RET. FR. SANI(*) arrow. In addition, the taint analysis will check taint annotations on heap objects and primitive values before entering methods. Those checks are used for monitoring tainting of protected sinks. In combination with the taint propagation in the *bytecodes*, the *VM events* implement the complete multi-colored taint analysis. In the remainder of this section, we discuss the central ideas of the interplay of the internal components of the implementation along a small example and provide a high-level overview of the analysis.

2.1 Integration of Symbolic Execution and Taint Analysis

Let us assume, we want to analyze method `foo(String a, String b)` from the code snippet shown in Listing 1.1. In particular, we want to check that no data flows from malicious method call `source()` to the protected method `sink()`

```
1   static void foo(String a,
         String b){
2     if (a.equals("ok"))
3       b = sani(b);
4     sink(b);}
5   public static void main
6       (...){
7     String a =
8       Verifier.
9         symbString("","A");
10    String b = source();
11    foo(a,b);}
12  public String source(){
13    return Verifier.
14      symbString("x","B");}
```

Listing 1.1. Code Example: Parameter b of method **foo** is only sanitized if parameter a has value "ok".

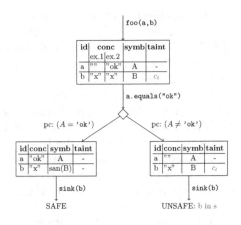

Fig. 2. Tree of concolic executions of method **foo**. Nodes show snapshots of the heap with annotations of taint and symbolic values.

unless the data is sanitized by passing through method **sani()**. This specifies the taint property denoted with taint color c_t in this example and confirms the configurable part we have to write down in JAINT's taint DSL. It is visualized in the lower right part of Fig. 1. We will first describe how dynamic symbolic execution is applied to the example followed by the taint integration.

Dynamic Symbolic Execution. Dynamic symbolic execution (DSE) is a dynamic analysis technique in which a program is executed with concrete data values while constraints that are imposed on these values along a single execution are recorded as path constraints. Recorded symbolic constraints can then be used as a basis for finding new concrete values that drive execution along previously unexplored program paths. The program execution is restarted with the new concrete values. This is represented in the top right corner of Fig. 1.

As DSE is a dynamic technique, a driver for the method under analysis is required. For our example, this can be seen in Listing 1.1. The **main(...)** method is used as a test driver for analyzing method **foo(...)**: in the listing, we create two variables of type String with values "" and "x" and instruct the analysis to annotate these Strings with symbolic values A and B. These annotations are tracked, modified, and propagated by the symbolic part of the underlying execution engine. The state of the analysis is visualized in Fig. 2: the tree represents executions of **foo(...)** with different sets of concrete values. The nodes of the tree visualize the state of the heap, including annotations to heap cells that keep track of symbolic values and taint.

Let us first focus on symbolic values. Initially, variables a and b are marked symbolically and contain the original concrete values (column *ex.1* in the root node of Fig. 2). Execution with these values proceeds down the right path in the tree as a does not equal "ok". Path constraint $A \neq \; 'ok'$ is recorded. After execution terminates, the analysis uses the recorded constraint for generating a new value for a ("ok" in this case) that drives execution down the unexplored path, represented by the left leaf of the execution tree. On this path, statement b=sani(b) is executed and the symbolic value of b is updated accordingly to symbolic value $san(B)$. After execution of the path the tree is complete, i.e., all feasible method paths through foo(...) have been explored and concolic execution halts. Next, we will briefly discuss, how we integrate the taint analysis along the paths discovered by dynamic symbolic execution.

Dynamic Taint Analysis. We check if the defined property is violated on some execution path by tainting relevant data values and tracking propagation of taint (visualized in the last column of the tables that represent the state of the heap in Fig. 2). The taint specification interacts with the JPF-VM using JPF's listener concept for VM events. The taint analysis subscribes to VM events, such as method invocations and method exits. If such an event is triggered, e.g., a method invocation, the generated listener checks whether the invoked method is part of the taint specification. If this is the case, code for injecting taint, removing taint or checking taint gets integrated into the execution. The JPF-VM allows to extend objects with annotations directly on the heap. This is used for adding the taint marks to the objects on the heap. The JPF-VM takes care to track those annotations. If JAVA bytecodes operates on none heap objects as primitive data types, the implemented *bytecode semantics* for symbolic execution get extended with taint propagation semantics.

As the main method used as a driver for running foo only initializes b with a call of source, only b will be tainted as *malicious source* with the c_t taint color. As there is no call to source in any of the assignments to a, a never becomes marked with the c_t taint color. Object s gets annotated as a *protected sink*. During the first execution (along the right path in the tree), the taint marker on b is not removed and a connection from source to sink is established upon invocation of sink(b). The analysis reports that on this path the property that "no data is allowed to flow from the malicious source to the protected sink" is violated. Those taint exceptions directly abort the DSE along a path and trigger the start of the next path. The second execution of foo(...) proceeds along the left path in the figure. In this case, statement b=sani(b) is executed and the taint marker is removed from b. The analysis concludes that the path is safe to execute and exits without any error along this path. After the combined taint analysis and DSE terminates, akin to other dynamic analysis methods, we can produce a concrete witness that exhibits the security vulnerability on the first execution path and triggers our taint monitor. At the same time, we are confident that all feasible program paths (within the cone of influence of the symbolic variables) were analyzed.

In the context of taint analysis, control-flow dependent taint is often discussed as a problem for precise taint analysis. In the scope of the method foo, both parameters are external parameters, but only b becomes tainted. In contrast a is the parameter influencing the control-flow in line 2 of Listing 1.1. As both are external parameters, we model both of them symbolically, and as the parameter a influences the if condition, this example further demonstrates, how

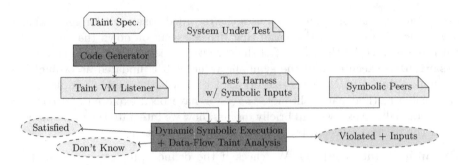

Fig. 3. JAINT combines user-defined dynamic taint-analyses with dynamic symbolic execution of Java programs. Taint DSL Specification (hexagon) and source code artifacts (documents) are compiled and analyzed (rectangles); verdicts shown as ellipses. (Color figure online)

symbolic execution ensures the control-flow dependent value propagation even if the parameter influencing the control-flow is not part of the taint specification. In contrast to pure dynamic tainting approaches, JAINT does this without any over-approximation. Due to the DSE, the analysis keeps track of the different branches and reports precisely which branches eventually violate a property and on which branches the property holds. This way, JAINT integrates DSE and dynamic taint analysis in a single framework splitting the tasks of data-flow tainting and control-flow tainting between the symbolic model in the DSE and the dynamic taint analysis. An appropriate symbolic model takes care of eventual effects from external parameters on the control-flow. The dynamic taint analysis only propagates the different taint colors along the current execution path, checks monitors and eventually removes taint marks wherever required. We will summarize this workflow below.

2.2 User-Defined Taint Analyses with Jaint

As shown in the previous subsection, the JAINT framework combines dynamic taint analysis with DSE. Figure 3 shows the analysis workflow. The cyan boxes are tools built to establish the JAINT workflow. In the center of the lower part is the analysis engine running dynamic symbolic execution and the data-flow taint analysis. An analysis will lead to one of three verdicts: no exploitable vulnerability exists (*Satisfied*, green ellipse), a vulnerability and an exploit are found (*Violated + Inputs*, red ellipse), the instance is undecidable due to an intractable symbolic constraint or due to exhausted resources (*Don't Know*, orange ellipse). In the upper half, the required inputs are represented: For some system under test, a test harness that defines the scope of symbolic analysis, and a set of symbolic peers are provided for the dynamic symbolic execution from the center to the right side. On the left, the required taint inputs are represented. The user provides a taint specification in JAINT's taint DSL. The DSL code generator part of the framework generates the required VM listeners for the taint analysis, which are passed along to the main tool.

JAINT describes taint flow properties in its own domain specific language (DSL), which is described in detail in Sect. 3. The DSL allows to specify different taint analyses which are all executed in parallel during the execution of the program as long as they all use a different taint color. The DSL is built on top of MPS and JAINT runs a code generator (the upper left cyan box) to synthesize the required VM listeners working as taint monitors for each of the specified taint analyses.

A test harness defines the symbolic parts of the system under test and therefore the analysis scope. In the test harness certain inputs are modeled symbolically, while others might remain concrete values. For analyzing JAVA Web-applications, we constructed symbolic String values as part of JDART along with a symbolic peer for String operations as an example for such peers. The symbolic peer models String operations on the basis of symbolic byte arrays. Those byte arrays are logical encoded in the bit-vector theory for constraint solving. The String model is robust enough for the evaluation of the OWASP benchmark and performed well in the Java track of SV-Comp 2020 (c.f. [19]). We released it open source as part of the JDART version[7] used for SV-Comp. Balancing symbolic and concrete parts of the system state space is the key factor for analysis performance. Unnecessary large state spaces waste resources, while a too small state space might harm the analysis verdict by cutting away relevant paths.

The analysis environment can be modeled using symbolic peers in JDART. Apart from the symbolic peer modeling the symbolic operations of Strings, we can use such peers as well to mock the behavior of an interface or model symbolically the execution of an external resource. As an example, in the case of SQL injection analyses, a model for `java.sql.Statement` is required to describe the taint flow appropriate. Similar, we defined symbolic peers for other system resources as the file system or the LDAP API. This allows us to analyze the OWASP benchmark. In the same way, a test harness might skip relevant parts of the execution, a symbolic peer might threat the analysis, if the environment model is an under approximation.

JAINT allows to split the task of establishing an effective security analysis in two domains. A program analysis engineer might model the relevant resources for dynamic symbolic execution, while a security engineer can define the security properties. Next, we will explain the DSL JAINT offers for the security engineer.

3   A DSL for Defining Taint Analyses

In JAINT, concrete taint analyses are specified by means of a domain-specific language (DSL). Taint generators, sanitizers, and monitors are generated from specifications. While code generation is currently tailored towards JPF/JDART, it could easily be adapted to generate code for other verification frameworks. The triggers and conditions for generating and removing taint as well as for raising alarms that can be specified in the language are generic (for JAVA programs). Concrete analyses are however particular to the libraries and frameworks used by a program under analysis: these libraries have APIs and methods in these APIs

---

[7] https://github.com/tudo-aqua/jdart.

may be sources or sinks for taint flow. In this section we present this domain-specific language along with some examples of concrete taint analyses motivated by CWEs in the OWASP benchmark suite.

Specification of Taint Analyses. Our DSL enables the definition of custom taint analyses. An analysis is specified by a tuple $\langle Src, Sani, Sink \rangle$, consisting of malicious sources (Src), sanitization methods $(Sani)$, and protected sinks $(Sink)$. Each of these elements specifies signatures of methods that, upon invocation or return, should trigger either marking a return attribute, removing the mark from an object, or checking for marked parameters, respectively. The syntax of the DSL is defined in (1) as BNF. Constant syntax elements are highlighted with gray boxes.

$$
\begin{aligned}
Generation &::= Analysis(,\ Analysis)^* \\
Analysis &::= (Src)^*, (Sani)^*, Sink \\
Src &::= \boxed{\texttt{Src::=}}\ (\mathbf{id}|\mathbf{id}^+) \leftarrow Signatures \\
Sani &::= \boxed{\texttt{Sani::=}}\ Signatures \\
Sink &::= \boxed{\texttt{Sink::=}}\ (\mathbf{id}|\mathbf{id}^+) \rightarrow Signatures \\
Signatures &::= ExtSignature\ (,\ ExtSignature)^* \\
ExtSignature &::= Signature\ (\boxed{\texttt{.<class>}}Method(Parameter)\boxed{\texttt{)}})^* \qquad (1) \\
Signature &::= \boxed{\texttt{(\_:class)}}.Method(Parameter) \\
Method &::= (\mathbf{method}|\mathbf{<init>}) \\
Parameter &::= (\mathbf{param}|\mathbf{param}^+|ValueCheckExp) \\
ValueCheckExp &::= (ValueCheck\ ((\boxed{\texttt{and}}|\boxed{\texttt{or}})\ ValueCheck)^*) \\
ValueCheck &::= (ParamValue\ \boxed{\texttt{has}}\ (\boxed{\texttt{not}})^*\ \boxed{\texttt{value}}\ \mathbf{value}) \\
ParamValue &::= (\mathbf{type\ param}|\mathbf{class\ id}\ \boxed{\texttt{:}}\ \mathbf{id}\ \boxed{\texttt{.}}\ (Method()|\mathbf{param}))
\end{aligned}
$$

To allow multiple parallel taint analyses the top-level *Generation* allows the containment of multiple *Analysis* elements. Each analysis is based on the tuple $\langle Src, Sani, Sink \rangle$ of which the first two are optional. For some weaknesses sanitization methods are not available and therefore neglectable. Taint analyses which depend on specific argument values of protected sinks and not on taint flow (c.f. example in (5)), do not contain source definitions. Each weakness has its unique identifier (or color) declared by **id** in the *Src* and *Sink* declaration. We use $\mathbf{id}^+$ in *Src* to indicate that fields and nested objects of the returned object are tainted additionally. With the usage of $\mathbf{id}^+$ in *Sink* we indicate that not only immediate taint of some parameter value has to be checked when invoking a sink but also taint of reachable objects from the parameter. The expression **class** matches fully qualified class names and **method** is an expression for matching method names. We allow $*$ as a wildcard for an arbitrary sequence of symbols. With **<init>** we restrict the method check to only consider constructors of the declared class. The expression **param** matches names of parameters. We use the empty String for methods without parameters and $*$ for arbitrary parameters. With **param**$^+$ we define that, instead of the return attribute, the declared parameter will be tainted. To also conveniently describe trigger conditions on the concrete values passed into sink methods: **param** may contain expressions like (int p has value 5) for specific parameter values or (Object o : o.var has value 5) for field accesses. It indicates that a taint alarm should be raised in case of a method invocation with a field value of 5 for the field var of parameter o which is of type Object. For building complex expressions we allow composite boolean expressions with the keywords and and or e.g., (param has value a) or (param has not value b).

To express a sequence of method calls that constitute a protected sink, additional information has to be provided (c.f. *ExtSignature*). For that, **<class>** specifies the type of the returned variable on which taint should be checked.

Example. To clarify this behavior and give an example, we further describe parts of the *Cross Site Scripting* weakness analysis with a code snippet in Listing 1.2 and corresponding DSL snippet in (2). Cross site scripting (CWE 79[8]) occurs when data (e.g., JavaScript code) from an untrusted source is added to the Web-page and served to other users without proper sanitization.

$$Src ::= xss^+ \leftarrow (\_ : *\texttt{HttpServletRequest}).\texttt{get}*(*)$$
$$Sani ::= (\_ : \texttt{org.apache.commons.lang.StringEscapeUtils})$$
$$\texttt{.escapeHtml}(*),$$
$$(\_ : \texttt{org.owasp.esapi.ESAPI}).\texttt{encodeForHTML}(*),$$
$$(\_ : \texttt{org.springframework.web.util.HtmlUtils}) \quad (2)$$
$$\texttt{.htmlEscape}(*)$$
$$Sink ::= xss^+ \rightarrow (\_ : \texttt{javax.servlet.http.HttpServletResponse})$$
$$\texttt{.getWriter().<java.io.PrintWriter>}*(*)$$

```
1  public void doPost(HttpServletRequest request,
2  HttpServletResponse response) {
3      ...
4      String param = "";
5      java.util.Enumeration<String> headers = request.
           getHeaders("Referer");
6      if(headers != null && headers.hasMoreElements()){
7          param = headers.nextElement();
8      }
9      ...
10     response.getWriter().format(..., param, ...);}
```

Listing 1.2. Code Example: Cross side scripting vulnerability in servlet **BenchmarkTest00013** of the OWASP benchmark suite (omissions for improved readability).

---

[8] https://cwe.mitre.org/data/definitions/79.html.

In line 5 data is read from the `HttpServletRequest` object. According to the specification in (2) this classifies as reading from a malicious source. Therefore, the returned value is annotated with a taint marker of type xss during concolic execution. At the same time, all elements contained in the returned `Enumeration<String>` are tainted as well, as the non-immediate taint flag is set (c.f. xss^+ in Src of (2)). This is necessary as the `param` variable is set by getting the next element with the `nextElement()` method in line 7. Without implicit taint propagation the taint information would be lost at this point. From line 7 code is executed that eventually manifests a protected sink for taint of type xss: In line 10 the condition for the protected source is matched. The `PrintWriter` object returned by the `getWriter()` method is flagged to signalize possible future taint violations (c.f. xss^+ in $Sink$ of (2)). Calling the `format(...)` method in the same line first checks the called object if it is flagged. Here, this is the case, so the real taint check on the parameter `param` can be executed. Since the variable is marked as xss-tainted, the analysis will correctly raise an alarm.

4   Evaluation

We evaluate JAINT by applying the framework on the OWASP benchmark. The OWASP benchmark suite (version 1.2) consists of 2,740 servlets that are categorized into 11 CWE classes. We aim to answer the following three research questions during the evaluation:

RQ1: Is JAINT's Taint-DSL expressive enough for specifying security analyses? We approach this question by specifying analyses for the 11 CWEs in the OWASP benchmark and by discussing briefly comparing the expressiveness to the specifications provided by other tools.

RQ2: Does the combination of dynamic symbolic execution and dynamic tainting improve precision over the state of the art in security analysis? We approach this question by comparing JAINT's precision to industrial tools.

RQ3: How expensive is the application of JAINT, especially compared to existing tools? We approach this question by analyzing JAINT's runtime.

We begin by detailing some taint analyses (**RQ1**), before presenting results from a series of experiments (**RQ2** and **RQ3**).

4.1   Taint Analyses for OWASP CWEs

The CWEs included in the OWASP benchmark suite, broadly fall into two classes of properties: *Source-to-Sink-Flow* and *Condition-on-Sink* properties. The first class is the main domain of taint analysis and requires the flow of taint marks from a source to a sink. The second group checks a concrete value for a concrete assignment at a certain point of time in the execution flow. While this is not. the typical strength of dynamic tainting, we can still check those properties easily with JAINT, using only sink conditions. The *Source-to-Sink-Flow* group comprises 8 CWEs: Path Traversal Injection (CWE 22), Cross Site Scripting (CWE 79), SQL Injection (CWE 89), Command Injection (CWE 78), LDAP Injection (CWE 90), Weak Randomness (CWE 330), Trust Bound Violation (CWE 501) and XPath Injection (CWE 643). The *Condition-on-Sink* group comprises 3 CWEs: Weak Crypto (CWE 327), Weak Hashing (CWE 330) and Secure Cookie (CWE 614). In the remainder of this subsection, we detail the specifications for three of the CWEs.

SQL Injection. The structured query language (SQL) is a fourth-generation language and SQL queries are constructed as Strings in JAVA programs. When this is done manually in a servlet, parameters of the HTTP request are typically integrated into the SQL query through String concatenation. Without proper String sanitization before the concatenation, this allows for a so-called SQL injection (CWE 89[9]), i.e., the resulting SQL query can be manipulated by injecting additional SQL statements into the query String.

It is well known that proper sanitization of parameters is hard and SQL injection vulnerabilities are best prevented by using prepared statements instead of building queries manually. Consequently, the OWASP benchmark assumes that there are no adequate sanitization methods for this weakness. The specification of the corresponding taint analysis is shown in (3). We consider the sql parameter of any method as a protected sink in some of the interfaces from the java.sql and org.springframework.jdbc packages.

$$
\begin{aligned}
Src ::= \ & sqli \leftarrow (\_ : *\texttt{HttpServletRequest}).\texttt{get}*() \\
Sink ::= \ & sqli \rightarrow (\_ : \texttt{java.sql.Statement}).*(\texttt{sql}), \\
& (\_ : \texttt{java.sql.Connection}).*(\texttt{sql}), \\
& (\_ : \texttt{org.springframework.jdbc.core.JdbcTemplate}).*(\texttt{sql})
\end{aligned}
\tag{3}
$$

Command Injection. Command injection (CWE 78[10]) attacks are similar to the injection attacks discussed above. However, instead of injecting statements into some query language, these attacks aim at injecting commands into a shell, i.e., into a command that is executed as a new process. (4) specifies the corresponding taint analysis. Methods that match patterns Runtime.exec(*) and ProcessBuilder.*(command) are considered protected sinks.

$$
\begin{aligned}
Src ::= \ & cmdi^+ \leftarrow (\_ : *\texttt{HttpServletRequest}).\texttt{get}*() \\
Sink ::= \ & cmdi \ \rightarrow (\_ : \texttt{java.lang.Runtime}).\texttt{exec}(*), \\
& (\_ : \texttt{java.lang.ProcessBuilder}).*(\texttt{command})
\end{aligned}
\tag{4}
$$

Secure Cookie Flag. A secure cookie flag (CWE 614[11]) weakness exists in a servlet when a cookie with sensitive data is added to the response object without setting the secure cookie flag (setting the flag forces Web-containers to use HTTPS communication). The corresponding taint analysis is specified in

---

[9] https://cwe.mitre.org/data/definitions/89.html.
[10] https://cwe.mitre.org/data/definitions/78.html.
[11] https://cwe.mitre.org/data/definitions/614.html.

(5). When a cookie is added to the request, the analysis checks that the secure flag is set.

$$Sink ::= * \rightarrow (\_ : \texttt{javax.servlet.http.Response}) \tag{5}$$
$$\texttt{.addCookie(cookie} \quad \texttt{c} \; : \; \texttt{c.getSecure() has value false)}$$

Please note that the specification of the trigger condition in (5) is more complex as in the case of SQL injection as we have to express a condition on a field of an object.

Summarizing, the expressiveness of JAINT's taint DSL was sufficient for expressing the CWEs in the OWASP benchmarks.

Comparing the expressiveness to other tools that provide performance data for the OWASP benchmark suite, at least `SBwFindSecBugs` (cf. next subsection) uses an approach similar to JAINT: Method signatures and parameter positions are used for specifying taint sources and sinks. JAINT's taint DSL is more precise and more expressive than `SBwFindSecBugs` by allowing custom sources and sinks per analysis, by allowing to express that an object obtained from a sink becomes a sink as well, and by allowing to specify constraints on parameter values.

Together, these two results provide some confidence in the expressiveness of JAINT's taint DSL (**RQ1**). Of course, there is effort associated with specifying custom sources and sinks for analyses and for analyzed APIs but developers of tools have to spent effort on definition of taint sources and sinks anyway and (in the long run) all tools can profit from more detailed specifications.

4.2   Experimental Performance Analysis

In this subsection we describe the setup used to evaluate our framework on the OWASP benchmark and compare JAINT with the other tools based on precision (**RQ2**). We will show that JAINT successfully beats existing research approaches in precision and discusses JAINT's runtime performance compared with other noncommercial tools (**RQ3**).

Setup. JAINT's taint DSL and a corresponding code generator are implemented in the Meta Programming System (MPS)[12]. We used the implementation to generate monitors and taint injectors together with sanitization points for the 11 CWEs in the OWASP benchmark. We have written a generic *HttpServlet* driver for executing each of the servlets. For the DSE, we modeled all data read from a request object symbolically as it is the untrusted input read from the web. This ensures that we explore all paths across a *HttpServlet* that might be influenced through a request by a malicious attacker, as the OWASP benchmark does not contain another untrusted source. In addition, we provided suitable symbolic peers for the used libraries that require environment interaction. For example, the analysis of a test case related to a potential SQL injection weakness (CWE 89) requires a suitable abstraction for the database interaction involved in the test case. In the same way, we provided abstractions for file system access,

---

[12] https://www.jetbrains.com/mps/.

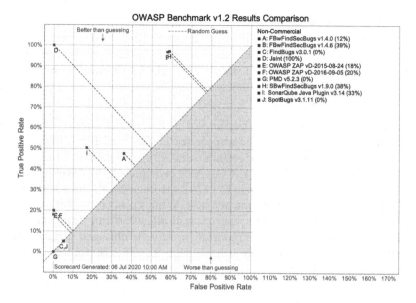

Fig. 4. Comparing our results of the generated DSL specification with results from related work. The percentage is computed as follows: $TruePositiveRate - FalsePositiveRate$.

LDAP related implementations and XPath libraries. Those libraries are required to enable the DSE to process the OWASP benchmark and are not related to the taint analysis. Using the mentioned driver together with the peers, we analyzed every servlet with JAINT and 11 taint colors enabled. All experiments were conducted on an Intel(R) Core(TM) i9-7960X machine with 128 GB RAM and an SSD hard drive, running Ubuntu with kernel 5.4.0-33 (x86_64).

Precision. Over all categories of CWEs, JAINT achieves the maximum possible precision of 100% true verdicts and 0% false verdicts, i.e., it finds all vulnerabilities in the benchmarks and does not raise a single false alarm. It outperforms the other tools for which performance is reported to OWASP by a big margin: the scorecard[13] that is provided by the OWASP benchmark suite is shown in Fig. 4 (JAINT is marked D). The other tools in the card that perform better than random guessing fall into three groups: over-approximating tools with (close to) no false negatives but a high rate of false positives (B, H), under-approximating tools with no false positives but high numbers of false negatives (E, F), and a third group (A, I) with high rates of false positives and false negatives.

For some commercial tools, performance data is not included in the OWASP scorecard, and hence not included in our evaluation, but can be found in promotional statements on the web pages of tool vendors. Most notably, Hdiv's and Contrast's IAST tools also report 100% true verdicts and 0% false positives on the OWASP benchmark suite. It seems, however, that IAST is a dynamic analy-

---

[13] Score computation: https://owasp.org/www-project-benchmark/#div-scoring.

sis and—in contrast to JAINT—cannot guarantee complete exploration. Julia, a commercial static analyzer using abstract interpretation, is reported to achieve a 90% score in the benchmark, which is a very good score but still includes 116 false positive results [4]. So far, JAINT is the only tool that can provide completeness guarantees (within the limits of symbolic execution), while performing precise security analysis (**RQ2**).

Performance. We compare the runtime of JAINT to the static code analysis FindSecBugs (*H*) as performance data for the commercial IAST tools and for Juliet could not be obtained. FindSecBugs needs 62 s (average over 3 runs with no significant variance) for analyzing the OWASP benchmark suite, averaging 23 ms per task. JAINT, in comparison, needs 1 879 s (average over 3 runs with 5 s std. deviation), i.e., an average of 686 ms per task. While this constitutes a thirtyfold increase in runtime, the absolute runtime still allows to run JAINT as part of a CI pipeline, especially since the reported runtime is obtained through single-threaded and sequential task processing, leaving space for runtime optimization through parallelization (**RQ3**).

5   Conclusion

In this paper, we have presented JAINT, a framework for analyzing JAVA Web-Applications. JAINT is the first working proof-of-concept for combining dynamic symbolic execution and dynamic multi-colored taint analysis in JAVA. Our approach strictly separates symbolic annotations and colored taint markers used for a security analysis. This enables analysis of arbitrary sanitization operations while dynamic symbolic execution is still capable of exploring the symbolic state space. JAINT uses JDART and the JPF-VM, as the dynamic symbolic execution engine of JAVA byte code.

We extended JDART with environment models that represent parts of the JAVA standard library and provide symbolic summaries and model taint propagation for some of the interfaces in the JAVA library, e.g., classes from the *java.sql* package. For the specification of security properties that JAINT should check, we provide a domain-specific language (DSL) based on the Meta Programming System (MPS). Custom components for checking of specified properties are generated from specifications (i.e., VM event listeners that can be plugged into the JPF-VM for taint injection, taint sanitization, and taint monitoring).

The evaluation of the approach on the OWASP benchmark shows promising results: the implementation achieves a 100% score and 0% false positive results, outperforming all other research tools for which performance data on the OWASP benchmark suite is available. Basis for the evaluation was the specification of taint analyses for the 11 classes of CWEs in the OWASP benchmark suite using the proposed taint DSL. Specifications were derived by researching CWEs and by inspection of the code of the OWASP benchmark suite and the JAVA class library. As these taint analyses are specified using our DSL we could demonstrate successfully, that our domain-specific language is expressive enough for specifying taint analyses for a relevant set of CWEs.

Being based on the synthetic OWASP benchmark suite, the conducted experiments only provide initial insights into the applicability and challenges of combining dynamic symbolic execution and taint analysis for the analysis of Web-Applications. The scalability of JAINT depends on the performance of the underlying dynamic symbolic execution engine. Here, the manually developed environment models may hamper application in industrial contexts. One direction of future work is thus the automation of environment modeling, e.g., using domain-specific languages.

References

1. Allen, J.: Perl version 5.8.8 documentation - perlsec (May 2016). http://perldoc.perl.org/5.8.8/perlsec.pdf
2. Baldoni, R., Coppa, E., D'elia, D.C., Demetrescu, C., Finocchi, I.: A survey of symbolic execution techniques. ACM Comput. Surv. (CSUR) **51**(3), 50 (2018)
3. Bekrar, S., Bekrar, C., Groz, R., Mounier, L.: A taint based approach for smart fuzzing. In: 2012 IEEE 5th International Conference on Software Testing, Verification and Validation, pp. 818–825. IEEE (2012)
4. Burato, E., Ferrara, P., Spoto, F.: Security analysis of the OWASP benchmark with Julia. In: 2017 Proceedings of ITASEC (2017)
5. Cadar, C., Dunbar, D., Engler, D.R., et al.: KLEE: unassisted and automatic generation of high-coverage tests for complex systems programs. In: OSDI, vol. 8, pp. 209–224 (2008)
6. Cadar, C., Sen, K.: Symbolic execution for software testing: three decades later. Commun. ACM **56**(2), 82–90 (2013). https://doi.org/10.1145/2408776.2408795
7. Cheng, W., Zhao, Q., Yu, B., Hiroshige, S.: TaintTrace: efficient flow tracing with dynamic binary rewriting. In: 11th IEEE Symposium on Computers and Communications, ISCC 2006, pp. 749–754. IEEE (2006)
8. Clause, J., Li, W., Orso, A.: Dytan: a generic dynamic taint analysis framework. In: Proceedings of the 2007 International Symposium on Software Testing and Analysis, pp. 196–206. ACM (2007)
9. Conti, J.J., Russo, A.: A taint mode for Python via a library. In: Aura, T., Järvinen, K., Nyberg, K. (eds.) NordSec 2010. LNCS, vol. 7127, pp. 210–222. Springer, Heidelberg (2012). https://doi.org/10.1007/978-3-642-27937-9_15
10. Corin, R., Manzano, F.A.: Taint analysis of security code in the KLEE symbolic execution engine. In: Chim, T.W., Yuen, T.H. (eds.) ICICS 2012. LNCS, vol. 7618, pp. 264–275. Springer, Heidelberg (2012). https://doi.org/10.1007/978-3-642-34129-8_23
11. Edalat, E., Sadeghiyan, B., Ghassemi, F.: ConsiDroid: A concolic-based tool for detecting SQL injection vulnerability in android apps. CoRR, abs/1811.10448, arXiv arXiv:1811.10448 (2018)
12. Haldar, V., Chandra, D., Franz, M.: Dynamic taint propagation for Java. In: 21st Annual Computer Security Applications Conference, ACSAC 2005, p. 9. IEEE (2005)
13. Havelund, K., Pressburger, T.: Model checking Java programs using Java PathFinder. Int. J. Softw. Tools Technol. Transf. **2**(4), 366–381 (2000)
14. Jee, K., Portokalidis, G., Kemerlis, V.P., Ghosh, S., August, D.I., Keromytis, A.D.: A general approach for efficiently accelerating software-based dynamic data flow tracking on commodity hardware. In: NDSS (2012)

15. Kang, M.G., McCamant, S., Poosankam, P., Song, D.: DTA++: dynamic taint analysis with targeted control-flow propagation. In: Proceedings of the Network and Distributed System Security Symposium, NDSS 2011, San Diego, California, USA, 6–9 February 2011 (2011). http://www.isoc.org/isoc/conferences/ndss/11/pdf/5_4.pdf

16. Lam, L.C., Chiueh, T.: A general dynamic information flow tracking framework for security applications. In: 2006 22nd Annual Computer Security Applications Conference, ACSAC 2006, pp. 463–472. IEEE (2006)

17. Livshits, V.B., Lam, M.S.: Finding security vulnerabilities in Java applications with static analysis. In: USENIX Security Symposium, vol. 14, p. 18 (2005)

18. Luckow, K., et al.: JDART: a dynamic symbolic analysis framework. In: Chechik, M., Raskin, J.-F. (eds.) TACAS 2016. LNCS, vol. 9636, pp. 442–459. Springer, Heidelberg (2016). https://doi.org/10.1007/978-3-662-49674-9_26

19. Mues, M., Howar, F.: JDART: dynamic symbolic execution for JAVA bytecode (competition contribution). In: Biere, A., Parker, D. (eds.) TACAS 2020. LNCS, vol. 12079, pp. 398–402. Springer, Cham (2020). https://doi.org/10.1007/978-3-030-45237-7_28

20. Mues, M., Schallau, T., Howar, F.: Artifact for 'Jaint: A Framework for User-Defined Dynamic Taint-Analyses based on Dynamic Symbolic Execution of Java Programs', September 2020. https://doi.org/10.5281/zenodo.4060244

21. Newsome, J., Song, D.X.: Dynamic taint analysis for automatic detection, analysis, and signature generation of exploits on commodity software. In: NDSS, vol. 5, pp. 3–4. Citeseer (2005)

22. Nguyen-Tuong, A., Guarnieri, S., Greene, D., Shirley, J., Evans, D.: Automatically hardening web applications using precise tainting. In: Sasaki, R., Qing, S., Okamoto, E., Yoshiura, H. (eds.) SEC 2005. IAICT, vol. 181, pp. 295–307. Springer, Boston, MA (2005). https://doi.org/10.1007/0-387-25660-1_20

23. Sabelfeld, A., Myers, A.C.: Language-based information-flow security. IEEE J. Sel. Areas Commun. **21**(1), 5–19 (2003)

24. Schoepe, D., Balliu, M., Pierce, B.C., Sabelfeld, A.: Explicit secrecy: a policy for taint tracking. In: 2016 IEEE European Symposium on Security and Privacy (EuroS&P), pp. 15–30. IEEE (2016)

25. Schwartz, E.J., Avgerinos, T., Brumley, D.: All you ever wanted to know about dynamic taint analysis and forward symbolic execution (but might have been afraid to ask). In: 2010 IEEE Symposium on Security and Privacy, pp. 317–331. IEEE (2010)

26. Song, D., et al.: BitBlaze: a new approach to computer security via binary analysis. In: Sekar, R., Pujari, A.K. (eds.) ICISS 2008. LNCS, vol. 5352, pp. 1–25. Springer, Heidelberg (2008). https://doi.org/10.1007/978-3-540-89862-7_1

27. Spoto, F.: The Julia static analyzer for Java. In: Rival, X. (ed.) SAS 2016. LNCS, vol. 9837, pp. 39–57. Springer, Heidelberg (2016). https://doi.org/10.1007/978-3-662-53413-7_3

28. Xu, W., Bhatkar, S., Sekar, R.: Taint-enhanced policy enforcement: a practical approach to defeat a wide range of attacks. In: USENIX Security Symposium, pp. 121–136 (2006)

Automatic Generation of Guard-Stable Floating-Point Code

Laura Titolo[1]([⊠]), Mariano Moscato[1], Marco A. Feliu[1], and César A. Muñoz[2]

[1] National Institute of Aerospace, Hampton, USA
{laura.titolo,mariano.moscato,marco.feliu}@nianet.org
[2] NASA Langley Research Center, Hampton, USA
cesar.a.munoz@nasa.gov

Abstract. In floating-point programs, guard instability occurs when the control flow of a conditional statement diverges from its ideal execution under real arithmetic. This phenomenon is caused by the presence of round-off errors in floating-point computations. Writing programs that correctly handle guard instability often requires expertise on finite precision arithmetic. This paper presents a fully automatic toolchain that generates and formally verifies a guard-stable floating-point C program from its functional specification in real arithmetic. The generated program is instrumented to soundly detect when unstable guards may occur and, in these cases, to issue a warning. The proposed approach combines the PRECiSA floating-point static analyzer, the Frama-C software verification suite, and the PVS theorem prover.

1 Introduction

The development of floating-point software is particularly challenging due to the presence of round-off errors, which originate from the difference between real numbers and their finite precision representation. Since round-off errors accumulate during numerical computations, they may significantly affect the evaluation of both arithmetic and Boolean expressions. In particular, *unstable guards*[1] occur when the guard of a conditional statement contains a floating-point expression whose round-off error makes the actual Boolean value of the guard differ from the value that would be obtained assuming real arithmetic. The presence of unstable guards amplifies the divergence between the output of a floating-point program and its ideal evaluation in real arithmetic. This divergence may lead to catastrophic consequences in safety-critical applications. Understanding how round-off errors and unstable guards affect the result and execution flow of floating-point programs requires a deep comprehension of floating-point arithmetic.

This paper presents a *fully automatic* integrated toolchain that generates and verifies guard-stable floating-point C code from its formal functional specification in real arithmetic. This toolchain consists of:

Research by the first three authors was supported by the National Aeronautics and Space Administration under NASA/NIA Cooperative Agreement NNL09AA00A.

[1] In the literature [15,31], unstable guards are often referred to as unstable tests.

© Springer Nature Switzerland AG 2020
B. Dongol and E. Troubitsyna (Eds.): IFM 2020, LNCS 12546, pp. 141–159, 2020.
https://doi.org/10.1007/978-3-030-63461-2_8

- PRECiSA [19,29], a static analyzer for floating-point programs[2],
- Frama-C [17], a collaborative tool suite for the analysis of C code, and
- the Prototype Verification System (PVS) [23], an interactive theorem prover.

The input of the toolchain is a PVS specification of a numerical algorithm in real arithmetic, the desired floating-point format (single or double precision), and initial ranges for the input variables. A formally verified program transformation is introduced to implement the real-valued specification using floating-point arithmetic in the chosen floating-point format. This transformation is an extended and improved version of the one presented in [31]. Numerically unstable guards are replaced with more restrictive ones that preserve the control flow of the real-valued original specification. These new guards take into consideration the round-off error that may occur when the expressions of the original program are evaluated in floating-point arithmetic. In addition, the transformation instruments the program to emit a warning when the floating-point flow may diverge with respect to the real number specification. This program transformation is designed to limit the overhead introduced by the new guards. Symbolic error expressions are used to avoid concrete numerical assumptions on the input variables. This symbolic approach is highly modular since the transformation is still correct even if the input ranges are modified.

The static analyzer PRECiSA is extended with a module implementing the proposed program transformation and with another module that generates the corresponding C code. This C code includes ANSI/ISO C Specification Language (ACSL) [1] annotations stating the relationship between the floating-point C implementation and its functional specification in real arithmetic. To this end, the round-off errors that occur in conditional guards and the overall round-off error of each function in the program are estimated by PRECiSA. PVS proof certificates are generated stating the correctness of these estimations. The correctness property of the C program states that if the program terminates without a warning, it follows the same computational path as the real-valued specification, i.e., all unstable guards are detected.

The Frama-C/WeakestPrecondition (WP) plug-in is used to generate verification conditions in the language of PVS and it is customized to automatically integrate the PVS certificates generated by PRECiSA into the proof of such verification conditions. While PVS is an interactive theorem prover, these verification conditions are automatically proved by ad-hoc strategies developed as part of this work. Therefore, neither expertise in theorem proving nor in floating-point arithmetic is required from the user to verify the correctness of the generated C program. The proposed approach is applied to a fragment of the Detect and AvoID Alerting Logic for Unmanned Systems (DAIDALUS) software library developed by NASA [21]. DAIDALUS is the reference implementation of detect-and-avoid for unmanned aircraft systems in the standard document RTCA DO-365 [25].

The remainder of the paper is organized as follows. Section 2 provides a brief overview of floating-point numbers, unstable guards, and the tool PRECiSA.

---

[2] The PRECiSA distribution is available at https://github.com/nasa/PRECiSA.

The proposed program transformation to detect guard instability is introduced in Sect. 3. Section 4 describes the integrated toolchain to automatically generate and verify a probably correct floating-point C program from a PVS real-valued specification. Section 5 discusses related work and Sect. 6 concludes the paper.

2   Preliminaries

Floating-point numbers [16] (or *floats*) are finite precision representations of real numbers widely used in computer programs. In this work, $\mathbb{F}$ denotes the set of floating-point numbers. The expression $R(\tilde{v})$ denotes the conversion of the float $\tilde{v}$ to reals, while the expression $F(r)$ denotes the floating-point number representing r, i.e., the rounding of r.

Definition 1 (Round-off error). *Let $\tilde{v} \in \mathbb{F}$ be a floating-point number that represents a real number $r \in \mathbb{R}$, the difference $| R(\tilde{v}) - r |$ is called the* round-off error *(or* rounding error*) of $\tilde{v}$ with respect to r.*

When a real number r is rounded to the closest float, the round-off error is bounded by half *unit in the last place* of r, $ulp(r)$, which represents the difference between the two closest consecutive floating-point numbers $\tilde{v}_1$ and $\tilde{v}_2$ such that $\tilde{v}_1 \le r \le \tilde{v}_2$ and $\tilde{v}_1 \neq \tilde{v}_2$. Round-off errors accumulate through the computation of mathematical operators. The IEEE-754 standard [16] states that every basic operation should be performed as if it would be calculated with infinite precision and then rounded to the nearest floating-point value. Therefore, an initial error that seems negligible may become significantly larger when combined and propagated inside nested mathematical expressions.

Let $\tilde{\mathbb{V}}$ be a finite set of variables representing floating-point values and $\mathbb{V}$ a finite set of variables representing real values such that $\tilde{\mathbb{V}} \cap \mathbb{V} = \emptyset$. It is assumed that there is a function $\chi_r : \tilde{\mathbb{V}} \to \mathbb{V}$ that associates to each floating-point variable $\tilde{x}$ a variable $x \in \mathbb{V}$ representing the real value of $\tilde{x}$. The set of arithmetic expressions over floating-point (respectively real) numbers is denoted as $\tilde{\mathbb{A}}$ (respectively $\mathbb{A}$). The function $R_{\tilde{\mathbb{A}}} : \tilde{\mathbb{A}} \to \mathbb{A}$ converts an arithmetic expression on floating-point numbers to the corresponding one on real numbers. This function is defined by replacing each floating-point operation with the corresponding one on real numbers and by applying R and χ_r to floating-point values and variables, respectively. Conversely, the function $F_{\tilde{\mathbb{A}}} : \mathbb{A} \to \tilde{\mathbb{A}}$ applies the rounding F to constants and variables and replaces each real-valued operator with the corresponding floating-point one.

The function $R_{\tilde{\mathbb{B}}} : \tilde{\mathbb{B}} \to \mathbb{B}$ is defined as the natural extension of $R_{\tilde{\mathbb{A}}}$ to Boolean expressions. Given a variable assignment $\sigma : \mathbb{V} \to \mathbb{R}$, $eval_{\mathbb{B}}(\sigma, B) \in \{true, false\}$ denotes the evaluation of the real Boolean expression B. Similarly, given $\tilde{\sigma} : \tilde{\mathbb{V}} \to \mathbb{F}$, $\widetilde{eval_{\tilde{\mathbb{B}}}}(\tilde{\sigma}, \tilde{B}) \in \{true, false\}$ denotes the evaluation of the floating-point Boolean expression $\tilde{B}$. Boolean expressions are also affected by rounding errors. When $\tilde{\phi} \in \tilde{\mathbb{B}}$ evaluates differently in real and floating-point arithmetic, $\tilde{\phi}$ is said to be *unstable*.

Definition 2 (Unstable Guard). *A guard $\tilde{\phi} \in \widetilde{\mathbb{B}}$ is said to be unstable if there exist two assignments $\tilde{\sigma} : \{\tilde{x}_1, \ldots, \tilde{x}_n\} \to \mathbb{F}$ and $\sigma : \{\chi_r(\tilde{x}_1), \ldots, \chi_r(\tilde{x}_n)\} \to \mathbb{R}$ such that for all $i \in \{1, \ldots, n\}$, $\sigma(\chi_r(\tilde{x}_i)) = R(\tilde{\sigma}(\tilde{x}_i))$ and $eval_{\mathbb{B}}(\sigma, R_{\widetilde{\mathbb{B}}}(\tilde{\phi})) \neq eval_{\widetilde{\mathbb{B}}}(\tilde{\sigma}, \tilde{\phi})$. Otherwise, the guard is said to be* stable.

The evaluation of a conditional statement *if $\tilde{\phi}$ then $\widetilde{ae}_1$ else $\widetilde{ae}_2$* is said to follow an *unstable path* when $\tilde{\phi}$ is unstable. When the flows coincide, the evaluation is said to follow a *stable path*. The presence of unstable guards amplifies the effect of round-off errors in numerical programs since the computational flow of a floating-point program may significantly diverge from the ideal execution of its representation in real arithmetic. Therefore, for establishing the correctness of a numerical program, it is essential to correctly estimate the round-off error associated with both stable and unstable paths.

PRECiSA [29] is a static analyzer for floating-point programs. PRECiSA accepts as input a floating-point program and automatically generates a sound over-approximation of the floating-point round-off error and a proof certificate in PVS ensuring its correctness. Given a program to analyze, for every possible combination of real and floating-point execution paths, PRECiSA computes a *conditional error bound* of the form $\langle \eta, \tilde{\eta} \rangle_t \twoheadrightarrow (r, \tilde{v}, e)$, where $\eta \in \widetilde{\mathbb{B}}$ is a symbolic path condition over the reals, $\tilde{\eta} \in \widetilde{\mathbb{B}}$ is a symbolic path condition over the floats, $r, e \in \mathbb{A}$ are symbolic arithmetic expressions over the reals, and $\tilde{v} \in \widetilde{\mathbb{A}}$ is a symbolic expression over the floats. Intuitively, $\langle \eta, \tilde{\eta} \rangle_t \twoheadrightarrow (r, \tilde{v}, e)$ indicates that if both conditions η and $\tilde{\eta}$ are satisfied, the output of the ideal real-valued program is r, the output of the floating-point implementation is $\tilde{v}$, and the round-off error is at most e, i.e., $|r - \tilde{v}| \leq e$. The flag t is used to indicate, by construction, whether a conditional error bound corresponds to an unstable path, when $t = \mathbf{u}$, or to a stable path, when $t = \mathbf{s}$. PRECiSA initially computes round-off error estimations in a symbolic form so that the analysis is modular. Given the initial ranges for the input variables, PRECiSA uses the Kodiak global optimizer [22,27] to maximize the symbolic error expression and obtain a concrete numerical enclosure for the error.

3   A Program Transformation to Detect Unstable Guards

This section presents a program transformation that converts a real-valued specification into a floating-point program instrumented to detect unstable guards. This program transformation significantly extends the expressivity of the input language of the transformation originally presented in [31]. In particular, it provides support for function calls, for-loops, predicates, and arithmetic expressions with inline conditionals. In addition, it improves the accuracy of the method to detect guard instability.

Let $\widetilde{\Omega}$ be a set of pre-defined floating-point operations, Σ a set of function symbols, Π a set of predicate symbols such that $\Sigma \cap \Pi = \varnothing$, and $\widetilde{V}$ a finite set of variables representing floating-point values, respectively. The syntax of *floating-point program expressions* in $\mathbb{S}$ is given by the following grammar.

$$\widetilde{A} \in \widetilde{\mathbb{A}} ::= \widetilde{d} \mid \widetilde{x} \mid \widetilde{\odot}(\widetilde{A}, \ldots, \widetilde{A}) \mid \widetilde{f}(\widetilde{A}, \ldots, \widetilde{A}) \mid \widetilde{B}? \, \widetilde{A} : \widetilde{A}$$

$$\widetilde{B} \in \widetilde{\mathbb{B}} ::= true \mid \widetilde{B} \wedge \widetilde{B} \mid \neg \widetilde{B} \mid \widetilde{A} < \widetilde{A} \mid \widetilde{A} \leq \widetilde{A} \mid \widetilde{p}(\widetilde{A}, \ldots, \widetilde{A})$$

$$\widetilde{S} \in \widetilde{\mathbb{S}} ::= \widetilde{A} \mid let \; \widetilde{x} = \widetilde{A} \; in \; \widetilde{S} \mid for(i_0, i_n, acc_0, \lambda(i, acc).\widetilde{S}) \mid if \; \widetilde{B} \; then \; \widetilde{S} \; else \; \widetilde{S}$$

$$\mid if \; \widetilde{B} \; then \; \widetilde{S} [elsif \; \widetilde{B} \; then \; \widetilde{S}]_{j=1}^{m} \; else \; \widetilde{S} \mid \omega$$

where $\widetilde{d} \in \mathbb{F}$, $\widetilde{x} \in \widetilde{\mathbb{V}}$, $\widetilde{f} \in \widetilde{\Sigma}$, $\widetilde{p} \in \widetilde{\Pi}$, $\widetilde{\odot} \in \widetilde{\Omega}$, $i_0, i_n, acc_0 \in \widetilde{\mathbb{A}}$, and $i, acc \in \widetilde{\mathbb{V}}$.

The expression $\phi? \, A_{then} : A_{else}$ denotes an inline conditional statement that can be used as a parameter in an arithmetic operator or in a function call. The conjunction $\wedge$, negation $\neg$, and $true$ have the usual classical logic meaning. The disjunction $\vee$ operator, the relations $>$, $\geq$, and the constant $false$ can be derived. The notation $[elsif \; \widetilde{B} \; then \; \widetilde{S}]_{j=1}^{m}$ denotes a list of m conditional $elsif$ branches. Bounded recursion is added to the language as syntactic sugar using the for construct. The expression $for(i_0, i_n, acc_0, \lambda(i, acc).body)$ emulates a for-loop where $i \in \widetilde{\mathbb{V}}$ is the control variable that ranges from i_0 to i_n, acc is the variable where the result is accumulated with initial value acc_0, and $body$ is the body of the loop. For instance, $for(1, 10, 0, \lambda(i, acc).i + acc)$ represents the value $f(1, 0)$, where f is the recursive function $f(i, acc) \equiv if \; i > 10 \; then \; acc \; else \; f(i+1, acc+i)$. The body of the for-loop is restricted to be of type integer. Therefore, it does not accumulate round-off errors. The transformation of more generic for-loops requires the computation of the round-off error of a recursive function, which is an open problem beyond the scope of this paper. The symbol ω denotes a warning exceptional statement.

A *floating-point program* $\widetilde{P}$ is defined as a set of *function declarations* of the form $\widetilde{f}(\widetilde{x}_1, \ldots, \widetilde{x}_n) = \widetilde{S}$, where $\widetilde{x}_1, \ldots, \widetilde{x}_n$ are pairwise distinct variables in $\widetilde{\mathbb{V}}$ and all free variables appearing in $\widetilde{S}$ are in $\{\widetilde{x}_1, \ldots, \widetilde{x}_n\}$. The natural number n is called the *arity* of $\widetilde{f}$. Henceforth, it is assumed that programs are well-formed in the sense that, in a program $\widetilde{P}$, for every function call $\widetilde{f}(\widetilde{A}_1, \ldots, \widetilde{A}_n)$ that occurs in the body of the declaration of a function $\widetilde{g}$, a unique function $\widetilde{f}$ of arity n is defined in $\widetilde{P}$ before $\widetilde{g}$. Hence, the only recursion allowed is the one provided by the for-loop construct. The set of floating-point programs is denoted by $\widetilde{\mathbb{P}}$.

A *real-valued program* has the same structure of a floating-point program where floating-point expressions are replaced with real-valued ones. A real-valued program does not contain any ω statements. The set of real-valued programs is denoted by $\mathbb{P}$. The function $F_{\widetilde{\mathbb{P}}} : \mathbb{P} \to \widetilde{\mathbb{P}}$ converts a real program P into a floating-point one by applying $F_{\widetilde{\mathbb{A}}}$ to the arithmetic expressions occurring in P.

The input of the transformation is a real-valued program P. The straightforward floating-point implementation of P is initially computed as $\widetilde{P} := F_{\widetilde{\mathbb{P}}}(P)$. Subsequently, the Boolean expressions in the guards of $\widetilde{P}$ are replaced with more restrictive ones that take into consideration the symbolic round-off error. This is done by means of two Boolean abstractions $\beta^+, \beta^- : \widetilde{\mathbb{B}} \to \widetilde{\mathbb{B}}$ defined as follows.

Definition 3. *Let $\epsilon_{var} : \widetilde{\mathbb{A}} \to \widetilde{\mathbb{V}}$ be a function that associates to an expression $\widetilde{ae} \in \widetilde{\mathbb{A}}$ a variable that represents its round-off error, i.e., $|\widetilde{ae} - R_{\widetilde{\mathbb{A}}}(\widetilde{ae})| \leq \epsilon_{var}(\widetilde{ae})$. The functions $\beta^+, \beta^- : \widetilde{\mathbb{B}} \to \widetilde{\mathbb{B}}$ are defined as follows, where $\diamond \in \{\leq, <\}$.*

$$\beta^+(\widetilde{ae} \diamond 0) := \begin{cases} \widetilde{ae} \diamond 0 & \textit{if } |\widetilde{ae} - R_{\widetilde{\mathbb{A}}}(\widetilde{ae})| \leq 0 \\ \widetilde{ae} \diamond -\epsilon_{var}(\widetilde{ae}) & \textit{otherwise} \end{cases}$$

$$\beta^-(\widetilde{ae} \diamond 0) := \begin{cases} \neg(\widetilde{ae} \diamond 0) & \textit{if } |\widetilde{ae} - R_{\widetilde{\mathbb{A}}}(\widetilde{ae})| \leq 0 \\ \neg(\widetilde{ae} \diamond \epsilon_{var}(\widetilde{ae})) & \textit{otherwise} \end{cases}$$

$$\beta^+(\tilde{\phi}_1 \wedge \tilde{\phi}_2) := \beta^+(\tilde{\phi}_1) \wedge \beta^+(\tilde{\phi}_2) \qquad \beta^-(\tilde{\phi}_1 \wedge \tilde{\phi}_2) := \beta^-(\tilde{\phi}_1) \vee \beta^-(\tilde{\phi}_2)$$

$$\beta^+(\neg\tilde{\phi}) := \beta^-(\tilde{\phi}) \qquad\qquad\qquad \beta^-(\neg\tilde{\phi}) := \beta^+(\tilde{\phi})$$

Let $\epsilon_{var}^\beta : \widetilde{\mathbb{B}} \to \wp(\widetilde{\mathbb{V}})$ denote a function computing the error variables introduced by applying β^+ and β^- to a Boolean expression. Given $\tilde{\phi}, \tilde{\phi}_1, \tilde{\phi}_2 \in \widetilde{\mathbb{B}}$, $\epsilon_{var}^\beta(\widetilde{ae} \diamond 0) :$ $= \{\epsilon_{var}(\widetilde{ae})\}$, where $\diamond \in \{\leq, <\}$, $\epsilon_{var}^\beta(\tilde{\phi}_1 \wedge \tilde{\phi}_2) := \epsilon_{var}^\beta(\tilde{\phi}_1) \cup \epsilon_{var}^\beta(\tilde{\phi}_2)$, and $\epsilon_{var}^\beta(\neg\tilde{\phi}) :$ $= \epsilon_{var}^\beta(\tilde{\phi})$. For each predicate $\tilde{p}(\tilde{x}_1,...,\tilde{x}_n) = \tilde{\phi}$ such that $\epsilon_{var}^\beta(\tilde{\phi}) = \{e_1, \dots, e_m\}$, $\tilde{\phi} \neq \beta^+(\tilde{\phi})$, and $\neg\tilde{\phi} \neq \beta^-(\tilde{\phi})$, two new predicates are introduced:

$$\tilde{p}^+(\tilde{x}_1, \dots, \tilde{x}_n, e_1, \dots, e_m) = \beta^+(\tilde{\phi}) \qquad \tilde{p}^-(\tilde{x}_1, \dots, \tilde{x}_n, e_1, \dots, e_m) = \beta^-(\tilde{\phi})$$

Thus, the Boolean abstractions for a predicate call are defined as follows:

$$\beta^+(\tilde{p}(\widetilde{ae}_1, \dots, \widetilde{ae}_n)) := \tilde{p}^+(\widetilde{ae}_1, \dots, \widetilde{ae}_n, e_1, \dots, e_m)$$

$$\beta^-(\tilde{p}(\widetilde{ae}_1, \dots, \widetilde{ae}_n)) := \tilde{p}^-(\widetilde{ae}_1, \dots, \widetilde{ae}_n, e_1, \dots, e_m).$$

Generic inequalities of the form $a < b$ are handled by replacing them with their equivalent sign-test form $a - b < 0$. The following lemma states that β^+ and β^- correctly approximate a floating-point Boolean expression and its negation, respectively.

Lemma 1. *Given $\tilde{\phi} \in \widetilde{\mathbb{B}}$, let $fv(\tilde{\phi})$ be the set of free variables in $\tilde{\phi}$. For all $\sigma :$ $fv(\phi) \to \mathbb{R}$, $\tilde{\sigma} : fv(\tilde{\phi}) \to \mathbb{F}$, and $\tilde{x} \in fv(\tilde{\phi})$ such that $F(\sigma(\chi_r(\tilde{x}))) = \tilde{\sigma}(\tilde{x})$, β^+ and β^- satisfy the following properties.*

1. $\widetilde{eval}_{\widetilde{\mathbb{B}}}(\tilde{\sigma}, \beta^+(\tilde{\phi})) \Rightarrow \widetilde{eval}_{\widetilde{\mathbb{B}}}(\tilde{\sigma}, \tilde{\phi}) \wedge eval_{\mathbb{B}}(\sigma, R_{\widetilde{\mathbb{B}}}(\tilde{\phi}))$.

2. $\widetilde{eval}_{\widetilde{\mathbb{B}}}(\tilde{\sigma}, \beta^-(\tilde{\phi})) \Rightarrow \widetilde{eval}_{\widetilde{\mathbb{B}}}(\tilde{\sigma}, \neg\tilde{\phi}) \wedge eval_{\mathbb{B}}(\sigma, \neg R_{\widetilde{\mathbb{B}}}(\tilde{\phi}))$.

Given a program expression $\tilde{S}$, the function $\tau : \widetilde{\mathbb{S}} \to \widetilde{\mathbb{S}} \times \wp(\widetilde{\mathbb{V}})$, defined in Fig. 1, returns a pair formed by the instrumented version of $\tilde{S}$ and the set of new error variables introduced by β^+ and β^-. The functions $\tau_{\mathbb{S}} : \widetilde{\mathbb{S}} \to \widetilde{\mathbb{S}}$ and $\tau_{\widetilde{\mathbb{V}}} : \widetilde{\mathbb{S}} \to \wp(\widetilde{\mathbb{V}})$ return the first and the second projection of the result of τ respectively.

In the case of the conditional (Eq. (3.2)), when the round-off error is null and it does not affect the evaluation of the Boolean expression, i.e., $\tilde{\phi} = \beta^+(\tilde{\phi})$ and $\neg\tilde{\phi} = \beta^-(\tilde{\phi})$, the transformation function τ is recursively applied to the subprograms $\tilde{S}_1$ and $\tilde{S}_2$. Otherwise, the test on $\tilde{\phi}$ is replaced by two more restrictive tests on $\beta^+(\tilde{\phi})$ and $\beta^-(\tilde{\phi})$. The *then* branch is taken when $\beta^+(\tilde{\phi})$ is satisfied. By

$$\tau(\tilde{d}) = \langle \tilde{d}, \varnothing \rangle \qquad \tau(\tilde{x}) = \langle \tilde{x}, \varnothing \rangle \qquad \tau(\tilde{\odot}(\tilde{A}_i)_{i=1}^n) = \langle \tilde{\odot}(\tau_{\mathbb{S}}(\tilde{A}_i))_{i=1}^n, \bigcup_{i=1}^n \tau_{\mathbb{V}}(\tilde{A}_i) \rangle \quad (3.1)$$

$$\tau(if\ \tilde{\phi}\ then\ \tilde{S}_1\ else\ \tilde{S}_2) = \begin{cases} \begin{aligned} &\langle if\ \tilde{\phi}\ then\ \tau_{\mathbb{S}}(\tilde{S}_1)\ else\ \tau_{\mathbb{S}}(\tilde{S}_2), \\ &\quad \tau_{\mathbb{V}}(\tilde{S}_1) \cup \tau_{\mathbb{V}}(\tilde{S}_2) \rangle \end{aligned} & \begin{aligned} &\text{if } \tilde{\phi} = \beta^+(\tilde{\phi}) \text{ and} \\ &\neg \tilde{\phi} = \beta^-(\tilde{\phi}) \end{aligned} \\[2em] \begin{aligned} &\langle if\ \beta^+(\tilde{\phi})\ then\ \tau_{\mathbb{S}}(\tilde{S}_1) \\ &\quad elsif\ \beta^-(\tilde{\phi})\ then\ \tau_{\mathbb{S}}(\tilde{S}_2) \\ &\quad else\ \omega, \\ &\quad \tau_{\mathbb{V}}(\tilde{S}_1) \cup \tau_{\mathbb{V}}(\tilde{S}_2) \cup \epsilon_{var}^{\beta}(\tilde{\phi}) \rangle \end{aligned} & \begin{aligned} &\text{if } \tilde{\phi} \ne \beta^+(\tilde{\phi}) \text{ or} \\ &\neg \tilde{\phi} \ne \beta^-(\tilde{\phi}) \end{aligned} \end{cases} \quad (3.2)$$

$$\tau(if\ \tilde{\phi}_1\ then\ \tilde{S}_1\ [elsif\ \tilde{\phi}_i\ then\ \tilde{S}_i]_{i=2}^{n-1}\ else\ \tilde{S}_n) = \quad (3.3)$$

$$\begin{cases} \begin{aligned} &\langle if\ \tilde{\phi}_1\ then\ \tau_{\mathbb{S}}(\tilde{S}_1) \\ &\quad [elsif\ \tilde{\phi}_i\ then\ \tau_{\mathbb{S}}(\tilde{S}_i)]_{i=2}^{n-1}\ else\ \tau_{\mathbb{S}}(\tilde{S}_n), \\ &\quad \bigcup_{i=1}^n \tau_{\mathbb{V}}(S_i) \rangle \end{aligned} & \begin{aligned} &\text{if } \forall 1 \le i \le n,\ \tilde{\phi}_i = \beta^+(\tilde{\phi}_i) \\ &\text{and } \neg \tilde{\phi}_i = \beta^-(\tilde{\phi}_i) \end{aligned} \\[3em] \begin{aligned} &\langle if\ \beta^+(\tilde{\phi}_1)\ then\ \tau_{\mathbb{S}}(\tilde{S}_1) \\ &\quad [elsif\ \beta^+(\tilde{\phi}_i) \wedge \bigwedge_{j=1}^{i-1} \beta^-(\tilde{\phi}_j)\ then\ \tau_{\mathbb{S}}(\tilde{S}_i)]_{i=2}^{n-1} \\ &\quad elsif\ \bigwedge_{j=1}^{n-1} \beta^-(\tilde{\phi}_j)\ then\ \tau_{\mathbb{S}}(\tilde{S}_n) \\ &\quad else\ \omega, \\ &\quad \bigcup_{i=1}^n (\tau_{\mathbb{V}}(\tilde{S}_i) \cup \epsilon_{var}^{\beta}(\tilde{\phi}_i)) \rangle \end{aligned} & \text{otherwise} \end{cases}$$

$$\quad (3.4)$$

$$\tau(let\ \tilde{x} = \tilde{A}\ in\ \tilde{S}) = \langle let\ \tilde{x} = \tau_{\mathbb{S}}(\tilde{A})\ in\ \tau_{\mathbb{S}}(\tilde{S}), \tau_{\mathbb{V}}(\tilde{S}) \rangle \quad (3.5)$$

$$\tau(for(i_0, i_n, acc_0, \lambda(i, acc).\tilde{S})) = \langle for(i_0, i_n, acc_0, \lambda(i, acc).\tau_{\mathbb{S}}(\tilde{S})), \tau_{\mathbb{V}}(\tilde{S}) \rangle \quad (3.6)$$

$$\tau(\tilde{g}(\tilde{A}_1, \ldots, \tilde{A}_n)) = \langle \tilde{g}^{\tau}(\tau_{\mathbb{S}}(\tilde{A}_1), \ldots, \tau_{\mathbb{S}}(\tilde{A}_n), e_1', \ldots, e_m'), \bigcup_{i=1}^n \{e_i'\} \rangle, \quad (3.7)$$

where $\tilde{g}^{\tau}(\tilde{x}_1, \ldots, \tilde{x}_n, e_1, \ldots, e_m) \in \bar{\tau}(P)$

and $\forall i = 1 \ldots m$, if $e_i = \epsilon_{var}(\tilde{a}\tilde{e}_i)$, then $e_i' = \epsilon_{var}(\tilde{a}\tilde{e}_i[\tilde{x}_j \leftarrow \tau_{\mathbb{S}}(\tilde{A}_j)]_{j=1}^n)$.

Fig. 1. Program transformation rules.

Property 1 in Lemma 1, this means that in the original program both $\tilde{\phi}$ and $R(\tilde{\phi})$ hold and, thus, the *then* branch is taken in both real and floating-point control flows. The *else* branch of the transformed program is taken when $\beta^-(\tilde{\phi})$ holds. This means, by Property 2 in Lemma 1, that in the original program the else branch is taken in both real and floating-point control flows. When neither $\beta^+(\tilde{\phi})$ nor $\beta^-(\tilde{\phi})$ is satisfied a warning ω is issued indicating that floating-point and real flows may diverge. The function ϵ_{var}^{β} is applied to $\tilde{\phi}$ to collect the new error variables introduced by the application of β^+ and β^-. The inline version of the conditional is transformed in the same way.

For the n-ary conditional (Eq. (3.4)), in the case the round-off error does not affect the evaluation of any of the Boolean expression, the transformation function τ is applied recursively to the subprograms $\widetilde{S}_1, \ldots, \widetilde{S}_2$. Otherwise, the guard $\tilde{\phi}_i$ of the i-th branch is replaced by the conjunction of $\beta^+(\tilde{\phi}_i)$ and $\beta^-(\tilde{\phi}_j)$ for all the previous branches $j < i$. By Lemma 1, it follows that the transformed program takes the i-th branch only when the same branch is taken in both real and floating-point control flows of the original program. A warning is issued by the transformed program when real and floating-point control flows of the original program differ. The new variables introduced by the application of β^+ and β^- in each branch are computed by the ϵ^{β}_{var} function.

In the case of the function call (Eq. (3.7)), new error variables $e'_1, \ldots, e'_m$ are introduced to model the instantiated error parameters where the formal parameters $\tilde{x}_1, \ldots, \tilde{x}_n$ are replaced by the actual parameters $\widetilde{A}_1, \ldots, \widetilde{A}_n$. These new variables are added to the set $\tau_{\widetilde{\mathbb{V}}}(\widetilde{S})$. Thus, when $\tilde{g}^\tau(\tilde{x}_1, \ldots, \tilde{x}_n, e_1, \ldots, e_m) \in \bar{\tau}(P)$ and for all $i = 1 \ldots m$, if $e_i = \epsilon_{var}(\widetilde{ae}_i)$, then $e'_i = \epsilon_{var}(\widetilde{ae}_i[\tilde{x}_j \leftarrow \tau_{\mathbb{S}}(\widetilde{A}_j)]^n_{j=1})$.

The function $\bar{\tau}$ transforms a real-valued program P into a floating-point program that is instrumented to detect unstable guards. It is defined as follows.

Definition 4 (Program Transformation). *Let $P \in \mathbb{P}$ be a real-valued program, the transformation $\bar{\tau} : \mathbb{P} \to \widetilde{\mathbb{P}}$ is defined as*

$$\bar{\tau}(P) = \bigcup \{\tilde{f}^\tau(\tilde{x}_1, \ldots, \tilde{x}_n, e_1, \ldots, e_k) = \textit{if } \bigvee\nolimits_{\tilde{g}^\tau(\tilde{y}) \in fc(\widetilde{S}')} (\tilde{g}^\tau(\tilde{y}) = \omega) \textit{ then } \omega \textit{ else } \widetilde{S}' \mid$$
$$\tilde{f}(\tilde{x}_1, \ldots, \tilde{x}_n) = \widetilde{S} \in F_{\widetilde{\mathbb{P}}}(P), \langle \widetilde{S}', \{e_1, \ldots, e_k\}\rangle = \tau(\widetilde{S})\},$$

where $fc(\widetilde{S})$ returns all the function calls occurring in $\widetilde{S}$. The new parameters $e_1, \ldots, e_k$ are called symbolic error parameters.

A check on each function call $\tilde{g}^\tau(\tilde{y})$ occurring in the body of $\tilde{f}$ is performed. If the returned value is warning, this is propagated as the result of $\tilde{f}$. The expression $\widetilde{S}'$ is the instrumented body of $\tilde{f}$ obtained by applying the transformation τ. Each function declaration is equipped with an additional set of arguments $e_1, \ldots, e_k$ which correspond to the symbolic error parameters introduced by the application of β^+ and β^- in the body of the function. Therefore, there is one new argument for each floating-point arithmetic expression occurring in the guard of a conditional. It can be argued that it would be sufficient to add, for each argument in the original function declaration, a variable representing its rounding error. In this case, the Boolean approximations β^+ and β^- could be implemented by using the symbolic error expression computed by PRECiSA. This approach has two main problems. First, such symbolic error expressions, being real-valued, cannot be evaluated precisely in a floating-point program. A trivial floating-point implementation would be affected by rounding error, thus compromising the soundness of the transformation. Second, correctly estimating the round-off error by using uniquely floating-point-operators is likely to produce a huge symbolic expression. This will lead to unintelligible code and, possibly, in a loss of performances since a complex arithmetic expression needs to be evaluated at runtime. In addition, the round-off error of computing the error expression itself needs to be considered. This may lead to an excessively coarse over-estimation resulting in a large number of false warnings. The choice of using symbolic error parameters to model the round-off error of arithmetic expressions avoids the aforementioned problems. This solution provides a good level of modularity since the symbolic expression is independent of the variables' initial ranges. Furthermore, this approach preserves the program structure of the original program.

The following theorem states the correctness of the program transformation $\bar{\tau}$. The straightforward floating-point implementation of the original program $F_{\widetilde{\mathbb{P}}}(P)$ and the transformed program $\bar{\tau}(P)$ return the same output if and only if the transformed program does not emit a warning.

Theorem 1. *Given $P \in \mathbb{P}$, for all $\tilde{f}(\tilde{x}_1, \ldots, \tilde{x}_n) = \widetilde{S} \in F_{\widetilde{\mathbb{P}}}(P)$, let $\tilde{f}^\tau(\tilde{x}_1, \ldots, \tilde{x}_n, e_1, \ldots, e_m) \in \bar{\tau}(P)$ be its transformed version. It holds that*

$$\tilde{f}^\tau(\tilde{x}_1, \ldots, \tilde{x}_n, e_1, \ldots, e_m) \neq \omega \iff \tilde{f}(\tilde{x}_1, \ldots, \tilde{x}_n) = \tilde{f}^\tau(\tilde{x}_1, \ldots, \tilde{x}_n, e_1, \ldots, e_m).$$

The proposed program transformation (including Lemma 1 and Theorem 1) has been formally specified and verified in PVS[3].

The intended semantics of the floating-point transformed program $\bar{\tau}(P)$ is the real-valued semantics of the original program P, i.e., the real-valued semantics of the transformed program $R_{\widetilde{\mathbb{P}}}(\bar{\tau}(P))$ is not relevant for the notion of correctness considered in this work. Therefore, even if the transformed program presents unstable guards with respect to $R_{\widetilde{\mathbb{P}}}(\bar{\tau}(P))$, Theorem 2 ensures that its floating-point control flow preserves the control flow of the original specification P on real arithmetic. The difference between the output of the real number specification P and the one of the transformed floating-point implementation $\bar{\tau}(P)$ is bounded by the error occurring in $F_{\widetilde{\mathbb{P}}}(P)$ taking into consideration only the stable cases $(t = \mathbf{s})$, as stated in the following theorem. In the following, $\mathcal{P}[\![\widetilde{P}]\!](\tilde{f})$ denotes the set of conditional error bounds computed by PRECiSA for the function $\tilde{f}$ defined in the program $\tilde{P}$.

Theorem 2 (Program Transformation Correctness). *Given $P \in \mathbb{P}$, for all $f(x_1, \ldots, x_n) = S \in P$, let $\tilde{f}^\tau(\tilde{x}_1, \ldots, \tilde{x}_n, e_1, \ldots, e_m) \in \bar{\tau}(P)$ be its transformed floating-point version. Let $\sigma : \{x_1 \ldots x_n\} \to \mathbb{R}$, and $\tilde{\sigma} : \{\tilde{x}_1 \ldots \tilde{x}_n\} \to \mathbb{F}$, such that for all $i \in \{1, \ldots, n\}$, $R(\tilde{\sigma}(\tilde{x}_i)) = \sigma(x_i)$, it holds that*

$$\tilde{f}^\tau(\tilde{x}_1, \ldots, \tilde{x}_n, e_1, \ldots, e_m) \neq \omega \iff |f(x_1, \ldots, x_n) - \tilde{f}^\tau(\tilde{x}_1, \ldots, \tilde{x}_n, e_1, \ldots, e_m)| \leq e_{\tilde{f}}$$

where $\tilde{f}^\tau(\tilde{x}_1, \ldots, \tilde{x}_n, e_1, \ldots, e_m) \in \bar{\tau}(P)$ *and* $e_{\tilde{f}} = max\{e \mid \langle \eta, \bar{\eta} \rangle_t \twoheadrightarrow (r, \tilde{v}, e) \in \mathcal{P}[\![F_{\mathbb{P}}(P)]\!](\tilde{f}), t = \mathbf{s}\}.$

---

[3] This formalization is available at https://shemesh.larc.nasa.gov/fm/PRECiSA.

Therefore, all the unstable cases of the original program are detected in the transformed program and they no longer influence the overall round-off error.

Example 1. Consider the following fragment of DAIDALUS[4], a software library that implements a detect-and-avoid logic for unmanned aircraft systems (UAS). A detect-and-avoid logic ensures that UAS remain well clear, e.g., safely separated, from traffic aircraft. The real-valued program $WCV \in \mathbb{P}$ consists of six functions. The function *wcv* determines if two aircraft (ownship and intruder), whose relative vertical position and velocity are given by (s_x, s_y, s_z) and (v_x, v_y, v_z), respectively, are in loss of horizontal (*hwcv*) and vertical (*vwcv*) well clear. The function *tcoa* computes the time to co-altitude of two vertically converging aircraft. When the aircraft are vertically diverging, the function returns 0. The function *tcpa* computes the time to (horizontal) closest point of approach. The function *taumod* is an estimation of *tcpa* that is less demanding on sensor and surveillance technology. The constants DTHR, TTHR, ZTHR and TCOA are distance and time thresholds used in the definition of the DAIDALUS well-clear logic.

$$tcoa(s_z, v_z) = \ if \ s_z v_z < 0 \ then \ -(s_z/v_z) \ else \ 0$$

$$tcpa(s_x, s_y, v_x, v_y) = \ if \ v_x \neq 0 \wedge v_y \neq 0 \ then \ -(s_x v_x + s_y v_y)/(v_x^2 + v_y^2) \ else \ 0$$

$$taumod(s_x, s_y, v_x, v_y) = \ if \ s_x v_x + s_y v_y < 0$$
$$then \ (\text{DTHR}^2 - s_x^2)/(s_x v_x + s_y v_y)$$
$$else \ -1$$

$$vwcv(s_z, v_z) = |s_z| \leq \text{ZTHR} \vee (tcoa(s_z, v_z) \geq 0 \wedge tcoa(s_z, v_z) \leq \text{TCOA})$$

$$hwcv(s_x, s_y, v_x, v_y) = \ let \ t = tcpa(s_x, s_y, v_x, v_y), \ tm = taumod(s_x, v_x, s_y, v_y) \ in$$
$$s_x v_x + s_y v_y < = \text{DTHR}^2$$
$$\vee \ ((s_x + tv_x)^2 + (sy + tv_y)^2 < = \text{DTHR}^2 \wedge 0 < = tm \wedge tm < = \text{TTHR})$$

$$wcv(s_x, s_y, s_z, v_x, v_y, v_z) = hwcv(s_x, s_y, v_x, v_y) \wedge vwcv(s_z, v_z)$$

The program $\bar{\tau}(WCV)$ is obtained by using the transformation in Fig. 1. The floating-point parameters are the rounding of the real ones, e.g., $s_x = \chi_r(\tilde{s}_x)$. The floating-point rounding of each constant is denoted with a tilde. All inequalities occurring in WCV have been rearranged to be in the form of a sign-test in the transformed program. Error variables are introduced by β^+ and β^- as parameters for each floating-point expression occurring in the guards. In addition, the error parameters of the function calls are propagated to the caller. The meaning of each error variable is shown as a comment in gray.

---

[4] DAIDALUS is available from https://shemesh.larc.nasa.gov/fm/DAIDALUS/.

$$\widetilde{tcoa}^{\top}(\tilde{s}_z, \tilde{v}_z, e_{tcoa}) = \quad if\ \tilde{s}_z\tilde{v}_z < -e_{tcoa}\ then\ -(\tilde{s}\tilde{/}\tilde{v}) \qquad \%|(\tilde{s}_z\tilde{v}_z) - (s_zv_z)| \le e_{tcoa}$$
$$elsif\ \tilde{s}_z\tilde{v}_z \ge e_{tcoa}\ then\ 0\ else\ \omega$$

$$\widetilde{tcpa}^{\top}(\tilde{s}_x, \tilde{s}_y, \tilde{v}_x, \tilde{v}_y, e_x, e_y) = \qquad\qquad \%|\tilde{v}_x - v_x| \le e_x,\ |\tilde{v}_y - v_y| \le e_y$$
$$if\ (\tilde{v}_x < -e_x \vee \tilde{v}_x > e_x) \wedge (\tilde{v}_y < -e_y \vee \tilde{v}_y > e_y)\ then\ -(\tilde{s}_x\tilde{v}_x\tilde{+}\tilde{s}_y\tilde{v}_y)\tilde{/}(\tilde{v}_x^2\tilde{+}\tilde{v}_y^2)$$
$$elsif\ (\tilde{v}_x \ge e_x \wedge \tilde{v}_x \le -e_x) \vee (\tilde{v}_y \ge e_y \wedge \tilde{v}_y \le -e_y)\ then\ 0\ else\ \omega$$

$$\widetilde{taumod}^{\top}(\tilde{s}_x, \tilde{s}_y, \tilde{v}_x, \tilde{v}_y, e_{tau}) = \qquad \%|(\tilde{s}_x\tilde{v}_x + \tilde{s}_y\tilde{v}_y) - (s_xv_x + s_yv_y)| \le e_{tau}$$
$$if\ \tilde{s}_x\tilde{v}_x + \tilde{s}_y\tilde{v}_y < -e_{tau}\ then\ (\widetilde{DTHR}^2\tilde{-}s_x^2)\tilde{/}(s_xv_x\tilde{+}s_yv_y)$$
$$elsif\ \tilde{s}_x\tilde{v}_x + \tilde{s}_y\tilde{v}_y \ge e_{tau}\ then\ -1\ else\ \omega$$

$$\widetilde{vwcv}^{+}(\tilde{s}_z, \tilde{v}_z, e_{tcoa}, e_1^v, e_2^v, e_3^v) = \quad if\ \widetilde{tcoa}^{\top}(\tilde{s}_z, \tilde{v}_z, e_{tcoa}) = \omega\ then\ \omega\ else$$
$$|\tilde{s}_z|\tilde{-}\widetilde{ZTHR} \le -e_1^v \qquad \%||\tilde{s}_z|\tilde{-}\widetilde{ZTHR}) - (|s_z| - ZTHR)| \le e_1^v$$
$$\vee\ (\widetilde{tcoa}^{\top}(\tilde{s}_z, \tilde{v}_z, e_{tcoa}) \ge e_2^v \qquad \%|\widetilde{tcoa}^{\top}(\tilde{s}_z, \tilde{v}_z, e_{tcoa}) - tcoa(s_z, v_z)| \le e_2^v$$
$$\wedge\ \widetilde{tcoa}^{\top}(\tilde{s}_z, \tilde{v}_z, e_{tcoa})\tilde{-}\widetilde{TCOA} \le -e_3^v)$$
$$\%|\widetilde{tcoa}^{\top}((\tilde{s}_z, \tilde{v}_z, e_{tcoa})\tilde{-}\widetilde{TCOA}) - (tcoa(s_z, v_z) - TCOA)| \le e_3^v$$

$$\widetilde{vwcv}^{-}(\tilde{s}_z, \tilde{v}_z, e_{tcoa}, e_1^v, e_2^v, e_3^v) = \quad if\ \widetilde{tcoa}^{\top}(\tilde{s}_z, \tilde{v}_z, e_{tcoa}) = \omega\ then\ \omega\ else$$
$$|\tilde{s}_z| - \widetilde{ZTHR} > e_1^v \wedge (\widetilde{tcoa}^{\top}(\tilde{s}_z, \tilde{v}_z, e_{tcoa}) < -e_2^v \vee \widetilde{tcoa}^{\top}(\tilde{s}_z, \tilde{v}_z, e_{tcoa})\tilde{-}\widetilde{TCOA} > e_3^v)$$

$$\widetilde{hwcv}^{+}(\tilde{s}_x, \tilde{v}_x, \tilde{s}_y, \tilde{v}_y, e_x, e_y, e_{tau}, e_1^h, e_2^h, e_3^h, e_4^h) =$$
$$let\ t = \widetilde{tcpa}^{\top}(\tilde{s}_x, \tilde{s}_y, \tilde{v}_x, \tilde{v}_y, e_x, e_y),\ tm = \widetilde{taumod}^{\top}(\tilde{s}_x, \tilde{s}_y, \tilde{v}_x, \tilde{v}_y, e_{tau})\ in$$
$$if\ t = \omega \vee tm = \omega\ then\ \omega\ else$$
$$\tilde{s}_x\tilde{v}_x\tilde{+}\tilde{s}_y\tilde{v}_y\tilde{-}\widetilde{DTHR}^2 \le -e_1^h\ \%|(\tilde{s}_x\tilde{v}_x\tilde{+}\tilde{s}_y\tilde{v}_y - \widetilde{DTHR}^2) - (s_xv_x + s_yv_y - DTHR^2)| \le e_1^h$$
$$\vee\ ((\tilde{s}_x\tilde{+}t\tilde{v}_x)^2\tilde{+}(\tilde{s}_y\tilde{+}t\tilde{v}_y)^2\tilde{-}\widetilde{DTHR}^2 \le -e_2^h$$
$$\%|((\tilde{s}_x\tilde{+}t\tilde{v}_x)^2\tilde{+}(\tilde{s}_y\tilde{+}t\tilde{v}_y)^2\tilde{-}\widetilde{DTHR}^2) - ((s_x + tv_x)^2 + (s_y + tv_y)^2 - DTHR^2)| \le e_2^h$$
$$\wedge\ tm \ge e_3^h \qquad \%|tm - taumod(s_x, s_y, v_x, v_y)| \le e_3^h$$
$$\wedge\ tm\tilde{-}\widetilde{TTHR} \le -e_4^h) \qquad \%|(tm\tilde{-}\widetilde{TTHR}) - (taumod(s_x, s_y, v_x, v_y) - TTHR)| \le e_4^h$$

$$\widetilde{hwcv}^{-}(\tilde{s}_x, \tilde{v}_x, \tilde{s}_y, \tilde{v}_y, e_x, e_y, e_{tau}, e_1^h, e_2^h, e_3^h, e_4^h) =$$
$$let\ t = \widetilde{tcpa}^{\top}(\tilde{s}_x, \tilde{s}_y, \tilde{v}_x, \tilde{v}_y, e_x, e_y),\ tm = \widetilde{taumod}^{\top}(\tilde{s}_x, \tilde{s}_y, \tilde{v}_x, \tilde{v}_y, e_{tau})\ in$$
$$if\ t = \omega \vee tm = \omega\ then\ \omega\ else\ (\tilde{s}_x\tilde{v}_x\tilde{+}\tilde{s}_y\tilde{v}_y\tilde{-}\widetilde{DTHR}^2 > e_1^h$$
$$\wedge\ ((\tilde{s}_x\tilde{+}t\tilde{v}_x)^2\tilde{+}(\tilde{s}_y\tilde{+}t\tilde{v}_y)^2\tilde{-}\widetilde{DTHR}^2 > e_2^h \vee tm \ge e_3^h \vee tm\tilde{-}\widetilde{TTHR} > e_4^h))$$

$$\widetilde{wcv}^{+}(\tilde{s}_x, \tilde{v}_x, \tilde{s}_y, \tilde{v}_y, \tilde{s}_z, \tilde{v}_z, e_{tcoa}, e_x, e_y, e_{tau}, e_1^h, e_2^h, e_3^h, e_4^h, e_1^v, e_2^v, e_3^v) =$$
$$let\ hv = \widetilde{hwcv}^{+}(\tilde{s}_x, \tilde{v}_x, \tilde{s}_y, \tilde{v}_y, e_x, e_y, e_{tau}, e_1^h, e_2^h, e_3^h, e_4^h),$$
$$vv = \widetilde{vwcv}^{+}(\tilde{s}_z, \tilde{v}_z, e_{tcoa}, e_1^v, e_2^v, e_3^v)\ in$$
$$if\ hv = \omega \vee vv = \omega\ then\ \omega\ else\ hv \wedge vv$$

$$\widetilde{wcv}^{-}(\tilde{s}_x, \tilde{v}_x, \tilde{s}_y, \tilde{v}_y, \tilde{s}_z, \tilde{v}_z, e_{tcoa}, e_x, e_y, e_{tau}, e_1^h, e_2^h, e_3^h, e_4^h, e_1^v, e_2^v, e_3^v) =$$
$$let\ hv = \widetilde{hwcv}^{-}(\tilde{s}_x, \tilde{v}_x, \tilde{s}_y, \tilde{v}_y, e_x, e_y, e_{tau}, e_1^h, e_2^h, e_3^h, e_4^h),$$
$$vv = \widetilde{vwcv}^{-}(\tilde{s}_z, \tilde{v}_z, e_{tcoa}, e_1^v, e_2^v, e_3^v)\ in$$
$$if\ hv = \omega \vee vv = \omega\ then\ \omega\ else\ hv \vee vv$$

4 Automatic Generation and Verification of Guard-Stable C Code

The toolchain presented in this section relies on several tools: the static analyzer PRECiSA, the global optimizer Kodiak [27][5], the static analyzer Frama-C, and the interactive prover PVS. The input to the toolchain is a real-valued program expressed in the PVS specification language, the desired floating-point precision (single and double precision are supported), and initial ranges for the input variables. The output is an annotated C program that is guaranteed to emit a warning when real and floating-point paths diverge in the original program and PVS certificates that ensure its correctness. An overview of the approach is depicted in Fig. 2.

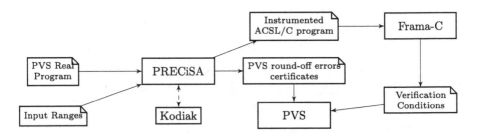

Fig. 2. Toolchain for automatically generate and verify guard-stable C code.

In this work, PRECiSA is extended to implement the transformation defined in Sect. 3 and to generate the corresponding C code. Given a real-valued program P and a desired floating-point format (single or double precision), PRECiSA applies the transformation presented in Sect. 3. The transformed program is then converted into C syntax and ANSI/ISO C Specification Language (ACSL) annotations are generated. ACSL [1] is a behavioral specification language for C programs centered on the notion of function contract. It is used to state pre- and post-conditions, assertions, and invariants.

For each function $\tilde{f}^\tau$ in the transformed program, a C procedure is auto-matically generated. In addition, each function f in the original specification is expressed as a logic axiomatic definition in ACSL syntax. This definition can be seen as a predicate modeling the real-valued expected behavior of the function. The floating-point version $\tilde{f}$ of f is also expressed as an ACSL definition.

An ACSL predicate called f_stable_paths is introduced to model under which conditions real and floating-point flows coincide. ACSL preconditions are added to relate each C floating-point expression with its logic real-valued counter-part through the error variable representing its round-off error. As mentioned in Sect. 3, a new error variable $e := \epsilon_{var}(\widetilde{ae})$ is introduced for each floating-point arithmetic expression $\widetilde{ae}$ occurring in the conditional guards. For each new error

---

[5] Kodiak is available from https://shemesh.larc.nasa.gov/fm/Kodiak/.

variable, a precondition stating that $|\widetilde{ae} - R_{\widetilde{\mathbb{A}}}(\widetilde{ae})| \leq e$ is added. A post-condition is introduced for each function stating that, when the transformed function $\tilde{f}^\tau$ does not emit a warning, the predicate f_stable_paths holds and the difference between $\tilde{f}^\tau$ and its real-number specification f is at most the round-off error computed for the stable paths of $\tilde{f}$. For the functions containing for-loops, a recursive real-valued version is generated as a logic axiomatic function in ACSL. An invariant is also computed in order to relate the result of each iteration of the for-loop with the corresponding call of the recursive real-valued function.

Example 2. Consider the real-valued specification *tcoa* and the instrumented function $\widetilde{tcoa}^\tau$ defined in Example 1. The pseudo-code of the annotated C code generated by PRECiSA is shown below, the pseudo-code of the ACSL annotation is printed in grey.

$/\!*@$ *logic auxiliary functions:*

$\quad$ *real tcoa*$(real\ s_z, real\ v_z) = s_z * v_z < 0\ ?\ -(s_z/v_z) : 0$

$\quad$ *double fp_tcoa*$(double\ \tilde{s}_z, double\ \tilde{v}_z) = \tilde{s}_z\tilde{*}\tilde{v}_z < 0\ ?\ \tilde{-}(\tilde{s}_z\tilde{/}\tilde{v}_z) : 0$

$\quad$ *predicate tcoa_stable_paths*$(real\ s_z, real v_z, double\ \tilde{s}_z, double\ \tilde{v}_z)=$

$\qquad (v_z \neq 0 \wedge s_z * v_z < 0 \wedge \tilde{v}_z \neq 0 \wedge \tilde{s}_z\tilde{*}\tilde{v}_z < 0) \vee (s_z * v_z \geq 0 \wedge \tilde{s}_z\tilde{*}\tilde{v}_z \geq 0)$

$\quad$ **requires** : $0 \leq e$

$\quad$ **ensures** :*result* $\neq \omega \implies$ $(result = fp\_tcoa(\tilde{s}_z, \tilde{v}_z)$

$\qquad \wedge \forall s_z, v_z(|(\tilde{s}_z\tilde{*}\tilde{v}_z) - (s_z * v_z)| \leq e \implies tcoa\_stable\_paths(s_z, v_z, \tilde{s}_z, \tilde{v}_z))*/$

double tau_tcoa $(double\ \tilde{s}_z, double\ \tilde{v}_z, double\ e)\{$

$\quad$ *if* $(\tilde{s}_z\tilde{*}\tilde{v}_z < -e)\{return\ \tilde{-}(\tilde{s}_z\tilde{/}\tilde{v}_z);\}$

$\quad$ *else* $\{\ if\ (\tilde{s}_z\tilde{*}\tilde{v}_z \geq e)\{return\ 0;\}$

$\qquad$ *else* $\{return\ \omega;\}\}\}$

As already mentioned, PRECiSA handles programs with symbolic parameters and generates a symbolic expression modeling an over-estimation of the round-off error that may occur. Given input ranges for the variables, a numerical evaluation of the symbolic expressions is performed in PRECiSA with the help of Kodiak, a rigorous global optimizer for real-valued expressions. Kodiak performs a branch-and-bound search that computes a sound enclosure for a symbolic error expression using either interval arithmetic or Bernstein polynomial basis. Therefore, it is possible to instantiate the error variables in the transformed program with numerical values representing a provably correct round-off error over-estimation.

Example 3. The following function instantiates the symbolic function shown in Example 2 assuming that $1 \leq s_z \leq 1000$ and $1 \leq v_z \leq 1000$.

$$/*@\textbf{ensures} : \forall s_z, v_z (1 \leq s_z \leq 1000 \wedge 1 \leq v_z \leq 1000 \wedge result \neq \omega \wedge$$
$$|\tilde{s}_z - s_z| \leq ulp(s_z)/2 \wedge |\tilde{v}_z - v_z| \leq ulp(v_z)/2)$$
$$\implies |result - tcoa(s_z, v_z)| \leq 2.78e - 12 * /$$
$$double\ tau\_tcoa\_num(double\ \tilde{s}_z, double\ \tilde{v}_z)\{$$
$$return\ tau\_tcoa\ (\tilde{s}_z, \tilde{v}_z, 1.72e - 10)\}$$

Besides the transformed C program, PRECiSA generates PVS theorems that act as formal certificates of the soundness of the computed estimations with respect to the floating-point IEEE-754 standard [16]. These theorems are automatically discharged in PVS by proof strategies that recursively inspect the round-off error expression and apply the corresponding lemmas included in the PVS floating-point round-off error formalization [7]. The instrumented C code for the program *WCV* defined in Example 1 and the corresponding PVS certificates are generated by PRECiSA[6] in 7.12 seconds. The C code consists of approximately 500 lines of code including all the ACSL annotations.

The tool suite Frama-C [17] is used to compute a set of verification conditions (VCs) stating the relationship between the transformed floating-point program and the original real-valued specification. Frama-C includes several static analyzers for the C language that support ACSL annotations. The Frama-C WP plug-in implements the weakest precondition calculus for ACSL annotations through C programs. For each annotation, Frama-C computes a set of verification conditions in the form of mathematical first-order logic formulas. These verification conditions can be proved by a combination of external automated theorem provers, proof assistants, and SMT solvers.

The WP plug-in has been customized to support the PVS certificates generated by PRECiSA in the proof of correctness of the C program. PRECiSA also provides a collection of PVS proof strategies that automatically discharge the VCs generated by Frama-C. To prove the VCs for a particular function f, it is necessary to use not only properties about floating-point numbers but also the contracts of the functions that are called in the body of f. These proofs are quite tedious and error-prone since several renaming and reformulation steps are applied by Frama-C to the annotated C code. The PVS strategies follow the syntactic structure of the input functions to determine which properties and contracts are needed to prove each of the VCs generated by Frama-C. Therefore, no expertise in floating-point arithmetic or in PVS is required to verify the correctness of the generated C code.

Example 4. Consider again the pseudo-code for *tcoa* depicted in Example 2. The verification conditions computed by Frama-C for the functions *tau_tcoa* and *tau_tcoa_num* are the following.

---

[6] This example is available at https://shemesh.larc.nasa.gov/fm/PRECiSA.

$\varphi_{tau\_tcoa} = \forall e, s_z, v_z, e_s, e_v \in \mathbb{R}, \tilde{s}, \tilde{v} \in \mathbb{F}$

$(result \neq \omega \wedge e \geq 0 \wedge |\tilde{v}_z - v_z| \leq e_v \wedge |\tilde{s}_z - s_z| \leq e_s \wedge |(\tilde{s}_z \tilde{*} \tilde{v}_z) - (v_z * s_z)| \leq e$
$\Rightarrow |result - tcoa(s_z, v_z)| \leq \epsilon_7(s_z, e_s, v_z, e_v)).$

$\varphi_{tau\_tcoa\_num} = \forall s_z, v_z \in \mathbb{R}, \tilde{s}_z, \tilde{v}_z \in \mathbb{F}, (result \neq \omega \wedge 1 \leq \tilde{s}_z \leq 1000 \wedge 1 \leq \tilde{v}_z \leq 1000$

$\wedge |s_z - \tilde{s}_z| \leq \frac{1}{2} ulp(s_z) \wedge |v_z - \tilde{v}_z| \leq \frac{1}{2} ulp(v_z) \wedge |(\tilde{s}_z \tilde{*} \tilde{v}_z) - (v_z * s_z)| \leq 1.72e\text{-}10)$
$\Rightarrow |result - tcoa(s_z, v_z)| \leq 2.78e\text{-}12$

The expression $\epsilon_7(s_z, e_s, v_z, e_v)$ denotes the symbolic error bound computed by PRECiSA, the variable e denotes the round-off error of the expression $\tilde{s}_z \tilde{*} \tilde{v}_z$, which is introduced when the Boolean approximations β^+ and β^- are applied. The proof of these verification conditions follows from the fact that when $result$ is not a warning ω, it is equal to $\widetilde{tcoa}(\tilde{s}_z, \tilde{v}_z)$ and from the numerical certificates output by PRECiSA stating that $|\widetilde{tcoa}(\tilde{s}_z, \tilde{v}_z) - tcoa(s_z, v_z)| \leq \epsilon_7(s_z, e_s, v_z, e_v)) = 2.78e\text{-}12$.

5 Related Work

Several tools are available for analyzing numerical aspects of C programs. In this work, the Frama-C [17] analyzer is used. Support for floating-point round-off error analysis in Frama-C is provided by the integration with the tool Gappa [12]. However, the applicability of Gappa is limited to straight-line programs without conditionals. Gappa's ability to verify more complex programs requires adding additional ACSL intermediate assertions and providing hints through annotation that may be unfeasible to automatically generate. The interactive theorem prover Coq can also be used to prove verification conditions on floating-point numbers thanks to the formalization defined in [6]. Nevertheless, Coq [2] tactics need to be implemented to automatize the verification process. Several approaches have been proposed for the verification of numerical C code by using Frama-C in combination with Gappa and/or Coq [3–5,13,18,30]. In [20], a preliminary version of the technique presented in this paper is used to verify a specific case study of a point-in-polygon containment algorithm. In contrast to the present work, the aforementioned techniques are not fully automatic and they require the user intervention in both the specification and verification processes.

Besides Frama-C, other tools are available to formally verify and analyze numerical properties of C code. Fluctuat [14] is a commercial static analyzer that, given a C program with annotations about input bounds and uncertainties on its arguments, produces an estimation of the round-off error of the program. Fluctuat detects the presence of possible unstable guards in the analyzed program, as explained in [15], but does not instrument the program to emit a warning in these cases. The static analyzer Astrée [9] detects the presence of run-time exceptions such as division by zero and under and over-flows by means of sound floating-point abstract domains. In contrast to the approach presented here, neither Fluctuat nor Astrée emit proof certificates that can be externally checked by an external prover.

Precision allocation (or tuning) tools, such as FPTuner [8], Precimonius [26], and Rosa [11], aim at selecting the lowest floating-point precision for the program variables that is enough to achieve the desired accuracy. Rosa soundly deals with unstable guards and with bounded loops when the variables appearing in the loop are restricted to a finite domain. In contrast with the approach presented in this paper, Rosa does not instrument the program to emit a warning when an unstable guard may occur. This means that the target precision may be difficult to reach without additional optimization rewritings and a program transformation as the one presented in this work. Program optimization tools aim at improving the accuracy of floating-point programs by rewriting arithmetic expressions in equivalent ones with a lower accumulated round-off error. Examples of these tools are Herbie [24], AutoRNP [32], Salsa [10], and CoHD [28].

6   Conclusion

Unstable guards, which occur when rounding errors affect the evaluation of conditional statements, are hard to detect and fix without the expert use of specialized tools. This paper presents a toolchain that automatically generates and verifies floating-point C code that soundly detects the presence of unstable guards with respect to an ideal real number specification.

The proposed toolchain relies on different formal tools and formal techniques that have been integrated to make the generation and verification processes fully automatic. As part of the proposed approach, the program transformation originally proposed in [31] has been enhanced and improved. The floating-point static analyzer PRECiSA [19,29] has been extended with two modules. One module implements the transformation defined in Sect. 3. The other module generates the corresponding C/ACSL code. Thus, given a PVS program specification written in real arithmetic and the desired precision, PRECiSA automatically generates a guard-stable floating-point version in C syntax enriched with ACSL annotations. Additionally, PVS proof certificates are automatically generated by PRECiSA to ensure the correctness of the round-off error overestimations used in the program transformation.

The absence of unstable guards in the resulting floating-point implementation and the soundness of the computed round-off errors are automatically verified using a combination of Frama-C, PRECiSA, and PVS. The Frama-C/WP [17] plug-in customization developed in this work enabled a seamless integration between the proof obligations generated by Frama-C and the PVS certificates generated by PRECiSA. Having externally checkable certificates increases the level of confidence in the proposed approach. In addition, no theorem proving expertise is required from the user since proof strategies, which have been implemented as part of this work, automatically discharge the verification conditions generated by Frama-C. To the best of authors' knowledge, this is the first automatic technique that is able to generate a formally-verified floating-point program instrumented to detect unstable guards from a real-valued specification. The proposed program transformation is designed to correctly detect any divergence of flow with respect to the original program. However, due to the error over-estimation used in the Boolean approximation functions, false warnings may arise. The number of false warnings depends on the accuracy of the round-off error approximation computed by PRECiSA, which has been shown in [29] to be the most precise round-off error estimator handling programs with let-in, conditionals, and function calls.

An interesting future direction is the integration of the proposed approach with numerical optimization tools such as Salsa [10] and Herbie [24]. This integration will improve the accuracy of the mathematical expressions used inside a program and, at the same time, prevent unstable guards that may cause unexpected behaviors. The proposed approach could also be combined with tuning precision techniques [8,11]. Since the program transformation lowers the overall round-off error, this would likely increase the chance of finding a precision allocation meeting the target accuracy. Finally, the authors plan to enhance the approach to support floating-point special values and exceptions such as under- and over-flows and division by zero.

References

1. Baudin, P.,et al.: ACSL: ANSI/ISO C Specification Language, version 1.12 (2016)
2. Bertot, Y., Castéran, P.: Interactive Theorem Proving and Program Development - Coq'Art: The Calculus of Inductive Constructions. Texts in Theoretical Computer Science. An EATCS Series, Springer, Berlin (2004)
3. Boldo, S., Clément, F., Filliâtre, J.C., Mayero, M., Melquiond, G., Weis, P.: Wave equation numerical resolution: a comprehensive mechanized proof of a C program. J. Autom. Reasoning **50**(4), 423–456 (2013)
4. Boldo, S., Filliâtre, J.C.: Formal verification of floating-point programs. In: Proceedings of ARITH18 2007, pp. 187–194. IEEE Computer Society (2007)
5. Boldo, S., Marché, C.: Formal verification of numerical programs: from C annotated programs to mechanical proofs. Math. Comput. Sci. **5**(4), 377–393 (2011)
6. Boldo, S., Melquiond, G.: Flocq: a unified library for proving floating-point algorithms in Coq. In: 20th IEEE Symposium on Computer Arithmetic, ARITH 2011, pp. 243–252. IEEE Computer Society (2011)
7. Boldo, S., Muñoz, C.: A high-level formalization of floating-point numbers in PVS. Technical report CR-2006-214298, NASA (2006)
8. Chiang, W., Baranowski, M., Briggs, I., Solovyev, A., Gopalakrishnan, G., Rakamarić, Z.: Rigorous floating-point mixed-precision tuning. In: Proceedings of the 44th ACM SIGPLAN Symposium on Principles of Programming Languages, POPL 2017, pp. 300–315. ACM (2017)
9. Cousot, P., et al.: The ASTREÉ analyzer. In: Sagiv, M. (ed.) Proceedings of the 14th European Symposium on Programming (ESOP 2005). Lecture Notes in Computer Science, vol. 3444, pp. 21–30. Springer, Berlin, Heidelberg (2005). https://doi.org/10.1007/978-3-540-31987-0_3

10. Damouche, N., Martel, M.: Salsa: an automatic tool to improve the numerical accuracy of programs. In: 6th Workshop on Automated Formal Methods, AFM 2017 (2017)
11. Darulova, E., Kuncak, V.: Sound compilation of reals. In: Proceedings of the 41st Annual ACM SIGPLAN-SIGACT Symposium on Principles of Programming Languages (POPL), pp. 235–248. ACM (2014)
12. de Dinechin, F., Lauter, C., Melquiond, G.: Certifying the floating-point implementation of an elementary function using Gappa. IEEE Trans. Comput. **60**(2), 242–253 (2011)
13. Goodloe, A., Muñoz, C., Kirchner, F., Correnson, L.: Verification of numerical programs: from real numbers to floating point numbers. In: Brat, G., Rungta, N., Venet, A. (eds.) NASA Formal Methods. NFM 2013. Lecture Notes in Computer Science, vol. 7871, pp. 441–446. Springer, Berlin, Heidelberg (2013). https://doi.org/10.1007/978-3-642-38088-4_31
14. Goubault, E., Putot, S.: Static analysis of numerical algorithms. In: Yi, K. (ed.) Proceedings of SAS 2006. Lecture Notes in Computer Science, vol. 4134, pp. 18–34. Springer, Berlin, Heidelberg. (2006)
15. Goubault, E., Putot, S.: Robustness analysis of finite precision implementations. In: Shan, C. (ed.) Programming Languages and Systems. APLAS 2013. Lecture Notes in Computer Science, vol. 8301, pp. 50–57. Springer, Cham (2013). https://doi.org/10.1007/978-3-319-03542-0_4
16. IEEE: IEEE standard for binary floating-point arithmetic. Technical report, Institute of Electrical and Electronics Engineers (2008)
17. Kirchner, F., Kosmatov, N., Prevosto, V., Signoles, J., Yakobowski, B.: Frama-C: a software analysis perspective. Formal Aspects Comput. **27**(3), 573–609 (2015)
18. Marché, C.: Verification of the functional behavior of a floating-point program: an industrial case study. Sci. Comput. Program. **96**, 279–296 (2014)
19. Moscato, M., Titolo, L., Dutle, A., Muñoz, C.: Automatic estimation of verified floating-point round-off errors via static analysis. In: Tonetta, S., Schoitsch, E., Bitsch, F. (eds.) Computer Safety, Reliability, and Security. SAFECOMP 2017. Lecture Notes in Computer Science, vol. 10488, pp. 213–229. Springer, Cham (2017). https://doi.org/10.1007/978-3-319-66266-4_14
20. Moscato, M.M., Titolo, L., Feliú, M., Muñoz, C.: Provably correct floating-point implementation of a point-in-polygon algorithm. In: ter Beek, M., McIver, A., Oliveira, J. (eds.) Formal Methods – The Next 30 Years. FM 2019. Lecture Notes in Computer Science, vol. 11800, pp. 21–37. Springer, Cham (2019). https://doi.org/10.1007/978-3-030-30942-8_3
21. Muñoz, C., Narkawicz, A., Hagen, G., Upchurch, J., Dutle, A., Consiglio, M.: DAIDALUS: detect and avoid alerting logic for unmanned systems. In: Proceedings of the 34th Digital Avionics Systems Conference (DASC 2015). Prague, Czech Republic (2015)
22. Narkawicz, A., Muñoz, C.: A formally verified generic branching algorithm for global optimization. In: Cohen, E., Rybalchenko, A. (eds.) Verified Software: Theories, Tools, Experiments. VSTTE 2013. Lecture Notes in Computer Science, vol. 8164, pp. 326–343. Springer, Berlin, Heidelberg (2013). https://doi.org/10.1007/978-3-642-54108-7_17
23. Owre, S., Rushby, J., Shankar, N.: PVS: a prototype verification system. In: Kapur, D. (ed.) Automated Deduction – CADE-11. CADE 1992. Lecture Notes in Computer Science, vol. 607, pp. 748–752. Springer, Berlin, Heidelberg (1992). https://doi.org/10.1007/3-540-55602-8_217

24. Panchekha, P., Sanchez-Stern, A., Wilcox, J.R., Tatlock, Z.: Automatically improving accuracy for floating point expressions. In: Proceedings of the 36th ACM SIGPLAN Conference on Programming Language Design and Implementation, PLDI 2015, pp. 1–11. ACM (2015)

25. RTCA SC-228: DO-365, Minimum Operational Performance Standards for Detect and Avoid (DAA) Systems (2017)

26. Rubio-González, C., et al.: Precimonious: tuning assistant for floating-point precision. In: International Conference for High Performance Computing, Networking, Storage and Analysis, SC'13, p. 27. ACM (2013)

27. Smith, A.P., Muñoz, C., Narkawicz, A.J., Markevicius, M.: A rigorous generic branch and bound solver for nonlinear problems. In: Proceedings of the 17th International Symposium on Symbolic and Numeric Algorithms for Scientific Computing, SYNASC 2015, pp. 71–78 (2015)

28. Thévenoux, L., Langlois, P., Martel, M.: Automatic source-to-source error compensation of floating-point programs. In: 18th IEEE International Conference on Computational Science and Engineering, CSE 2015, pp. 9–16. IEEE Computer Society (2015)

29. Titolo, L., Feliú, M., Moscato, M.: An abstract interpretation framework for the round-off error analysis of floating-point programs. In: Dillig, I., Palsberg, J. (eds.) Verification, Model Checking, and Abstract Interpretation. VMCAI 2018. Cham, pp. 516–537. Springer, Cham (2018). https://doi.org/10.1007/978-3-319-73721-8_24

30. Titolo, L., Moscato, M., Muñoz, C., Dutle, A., Bobot, F.: A formally verified floating-point implementation of the compact position reporting algorithm. In: Havelund, K., Peleska, J., Roscoe, B., de Vink, E. (eds.) Formal Methods. FM 2018. Lecture Notes in Computer Science, vol. 10951. Springer, Cham (2018). https://doi.org/10.1007/978-3-319-95582-7_22

31. Titolo, L., Muñoz, C., Feliú, M., Moscato, M.: Eliminating unstable tests in floating-point programs. In: Mesnard, F., Stuckey, P. (eds.) Logic-Based Program Synthesis and Transformation. LOPSTR 2018. Lecture Notes in Computer Science, vol. 11408, pp. 169–183. Springer, Cham (2018). https://doi.org/10.1007/978-3-030-13838-7_10

32. Yi, X., Chen, L., Mao, X., Ji, T.: Efficient automated repair of high floating-point errors in numerical libraries. PACMPL 3(POPL) **3**, 56:1–56:29 (2019)

Formal Methods for GPGPU
Programming: Is the Demand Met?

Lars B. van den Haak[1]([✉])[ID], Anton Wijs[1][ID], Mark van den Brand[1][ID],
and Marieke Huisman[2][ID]

[1] Eindhoven University of Technology, Eindhoven, The Netherlands
{l.b.v.d.haak,a.j.wijs,m.g.j.v.d.brand}@tue.nl
[2] University of Twente, Enschede, The Netherlands
m.huisman@utwente.nl

Abstract. Over the years, researchers have developed many formal
method tools to support software development. However, hardly any
studies are conducted to determine whether the actual problems developers encounter are sufficiently addressed. For the relatively young field of
GPU programming, we would like to know whether the tools developed so
far are sufficient, or whether some problems still need attention. To this
end, we first look at what kind of problems programmers encounter in
OpenCL and CUDA. We gather problems from Stack Overflow and categorise them with card sorting. We find that problems related to memory,
synchronisation of threads, threads in general and performance are essential topics. Next, we look at (verification) tools in industry and research,
to see how these tools addressed the problems we discovered. We think
many problems are already properly addressed, but there is still a need
for easy to use sound tools. Alternatively, languages or programming
styles can be created, that allows for easier checking for soundness.

Keywords: GPU · GPGPU · Formal methods · Verification · Bugs ·
CUDA · OpenCL

1 Introduction

General-purpose GPU (GPGPU) programming has been around for over 10 years
now, but is notoriously hard to do. In this work, we want to explore what kind
of problems people experience during GPGPU programming and understand
what the difficulties are in overcoming these problems. We accomplish this in
two steps. First we find the problems and next we analyse current solutions
in the domain of formal methods. We view this work as a way of identifying
further research challenges and directions in this domain, with the aim to ease
the difficulty of programming for a GPU.

To find the problems programmers encounter, we looked at Stack Overflow,
which is a widely known website where programmers can ask questions related
to programming. We took a sample of questions that are related to OpenCL

© Springer Nature Switzerland AG 2020
B. Dongol and E. Troubitsyna (Eds.): IFM 2020, LNCS 12546, pp. 160–177, 2020.
https://doi.org/10.1007/978-3-030-63461-2_9

and CUDA, the two dominant GPGPU programming languages, and categorise them using card sorting. These categories give us an up-to-date overview of (most) problems people encounter.

The next step is finding verification tools. Many tools have been developed that help people in their GPU programming work, like GPUVerify [11], Oclgrind [31], GKLEE [24], VerCors [12] and CUDA-MEMCHECK [1]. Although, only some of these have been picked up by developers of GPGPU programs. We look at scientific conferences and industry companies for tools. We narrow the scope to correctness issues and link the tools that solve these issues and indicate what improvements research can make.

In conclusion, in this work, we aim to help other researchers to focus their research on GPGPU programming problems that are not or incompletely addressed with and tools.

We make the following contributions.

1. An overview of common problems people struggle with whilst programming a GPGPU (Sect. 3).
2. Addressing problems of Sect. 3 where we think formal methods can make a direct contribution. We discuss solutions of existing tools and new research opportunities (Sect. 4).

2 Background

We base this section mostly on the CUDA Programming Guide [2]. GPUs are massive parallel compute devices, that work via the Single Instruction Multiple Threads (SIMT) execution model, which means that multiple threads are executing the same instruction in parallel, but with other data. In this paper, we consider mainly the CUDA and OpenCL programming languages. We work with the CUDA terms, but give the corresponding OpenCL terms in parentheses in this section. CUDA compiles to PTX [3], a pseudo-assembly language, which we call the *instruction level*, similarly OpenCL compiles to SPIR [4].

Functions that are executed on the GPU are called *kernels*. One can start kernels from the CPU, which we call the *host*. The GPU itself is called the *device*. Data stored on the RAM is not automatically accessible on the GPU and must be sent from the host to the device before invoking the kernel that uses the data. The programmer can schedule memory transfers and kernel executions in a queue.

Threads (Work-Items). When scheduling a kernel, you specify how many *threads* (*work-items*) are going to be executing this kernel. Threads are grouped together in *thread blocks* (*workgroups*) and all the thread blocks together form the *grid* (*NDRange*). From the hardware perspective, thread blocks are subdivided into *warps* (*sub-groups* or AMD calls them *wavefronts*), that typically have a size of 32 (64 on AMD devices) threads. Threads of a warp are executed in *lockstep*, meaning that they execute all the instruction at the same time.[1] If threads of a warp take different execution paths, e.g. due to if statements, the warp executes each path, but disables threads that are not on that path. This is called *thread divergence*, which can lead to performance loss.

A GPU consists of multiple *streaming multiprocessors*, which execute the warps in lockstep. Each thread block is assigned to one streaming multiprocessors.

Memory Model. A programmer has to manage the memory of a GPU manually. It has *global memory*, where transferred data from the host is stored, and any thread can access it. *Shared memory (local memory)* is shared in a thread block, which is faster than global memory. One can use it to share results within a thread block or to have faster access when data is reused. Per thread data is automatically stored in fast-access *registers*, or slow *local* memory in case not enough registers are available. For optimal global memory accesses, the accesses should be fully *coalesced*: this happens if threads of a warp call consecutive memory addresses and the first address is a multiple of the warp size.

Synchronization. When two threads do a read and write, or two writes to the same memory address, and this could happen simultaneously, this is called a *data race*. Data races lead to non-determinism and are considered, in most cases, a bug. A GPU can synchronize with a *barrier* on the thread block level, which ensures that all threads wait for each other before continuing execution. It also makes sure that after the synchronization, all writes to global and shared memory are performed, or depending on the barrier, only to shared memory. Thus, barriers can prevent *intra-block* data races in a thread block. All threads in a thread block must reach the same barrier, otherwise it results in undefined behaviour and is called *barrier divergence*.

In between threads of different thread blocks, synchronization is not possible with a (standard) global barrier, although Sorensen et al. [37] show how this can be constructed. Data races in between thread blocks are called *inter-block* data races. When lockstep execution of warps is not ensured also *intra-warp* data races can occur.

Synchronization can also be achieved via *fine-grained synchronization* using locks or atomics. Locks can make sure that only one thread has access to a specific memory address. Atomics allow for communication via memory, without risks of data races and GPUs typically implement them more efficiently than locks. A GPU has a weak memory model [6], which means that memory actions within a thread can be reordered by the hardware if there exist no dependencies within the thread. Therefore, when using fine-grained synchronization, specific memory actions may not yet be visible to other threads. Memory *fences* can be inserted to enforce a memory order, which might be needed to make sure that no *weak-memory* data races occur.

---

[1] Although this is not exactly true any more for Nvidia's Volta architecture and onward. See https://developer.nvidia.com/blog/inside-volta/.

Other Features. Some other features are less used, although we do want to mention them since they come up in this work. *Dynamic parallelism* allows parent kernels, to launch child kernels. A parent and child kernel have a consistent view of global memory at the start of the launch, but this is not guaranteed while executing. The parent kernel can synchronize with the child kernels it launched. A child kernel can recursively call a new child kernel. *Warp-level primitives* (*subgroup primitives*) are primitives that allow communication between threads in a warp, via the faster registers. For instance, one can use them to make a faster scan and reduction operation.

3   GPGPU Programming Problems

To know how formal methods can help solve GPGPU problems, we first need to know with what actual developers are struggling with. Therefore, we look at Stack Overflow, which is the go-to place for programming-related questions and is used by many programmers as a reference. Of the languages programmers use for GPGPU programming, CUDA (729 questions), OpenMP (471) and OpenCL (311) are the most popular, based on the number of question asked on Stack Overflow in 2019.[2] We focus on CUDA and OpenCL since OpenMP does not solely focusses on the GPU.

We first explain our approach for gathering and categorizing the results (Sect. 3.1). Next, we present the categories of programming problems we found, which we again ordered into themes and sub-themes for a clear overview (Sect. 3.2).

3.1   Approach

Gathering Problems. As argued above, we look at OpenCL and CUDA on Stack Overflow. Looking at the general tag `gpgpu`, `cuda` and `opencl`, we found that the 7 most related tags are `gpu`, `c++`, `nvidia`, `c`, `parallel-processing`, `thrust` and `nvcc`. The first five tags we consider too general, which would pollute our results. The tags `thrust` and `nvcc` are a specific CUDA library and compiler, which we do not want to focus on. Therefore, we stick with the tags `gpgpu`, `cuda` and `opencl`. On March 2, 2020 there are 17,539 questions on stack overflow that have the tag `cuda`, `opencl` or `gpgpu`.[3] We look at 376 Stack Overflow questions, which is a representative sample with a confidence level of 95% and a confidence interval of 5%s. Thus, with a 95% chance, we identify the problems which are present in at least 5% of the questions in the tags mentioned above.

Categorizing Problems. On the gathered questions, we performed open card sorting [27, Card-sorting: From Text To Themes], which creates categories in an unknown data set. We decided to look at the title, body and answers of the

---

[2] https://data.stackexchange.com/stackoverflow/query/1258739/gpgpu-tags.
[3] https://data.stackexchange.com/stackoverflow/query/1258838/gpgpu.

questions, to determine the categories. The first author, together with another PhD student, sorted the first 84 questions, where they achieved a mutual understanding of categories and held discussions for any corner cases. The next 43 cards were sorted separately, but in the same room, which allowed discussion on difficult cards. Eventually, this led to 26 different categories. The last 260 cards were sorted alone by the first author, and we ended up with 34 categories. For cards we could sort in multiple categories, we made new overlapping category or sorted them to the most appropriate category. After the sorting, we went over the relevant questions once more, to see if a newly made category would be more suitable.

Relevant Problems for Formal Methods. In the 34 categories, we make two distinctions. First, we mark problems that are interesting for GPGPU programming; these are 28 of the 34 categories. The non-relevant categories are related to (GPU) hardware, errors in the host code (unrelated to CUDA or OpenCL API calls), installing the correct CUDA and OpenCL drivers or libraries, setting up a development environment, linking libraries and questions related to OpenGL. In total, we found that 220 of the 376 questions were relevant to GPGPU programming.

We present the 28 GPGPU categories in the remainder of this section. We mark the ones (10) where we think formal methods are directly applicable to solve correctness problems underlying these questions.

3.2   Results

The results of the card sort are visible in Fig. 1. To organize the results, we have put some structure into them. We identified two themes: *memory* and *threads and synchronization*. We place the remaining categories in the *general* theme. Within each theme, we distinguish between bugs and performance-related questions as sub-themes. The results of this can be viewed in Fig. 2. We will explain each theme with its associated categories in the following subsections.

Memory. We first consider the *bugs* sub-theme categories: 'memory transfer bug', 'out of bounds' and 'memory bug'. An *out of bounds* error occurs when an array is indexed outside its bounds, which can be reported at runtime. A *memory transfer bug* happens when not all necessary data was transferred to the device and causes uninitialized memory accesses. We assign the category *memory bug* to questions where a memory error happened, but the cause was unclear from the post. We think that formal methods could help detect these bugs or possibly ensure programmers that such bugs are not present in their program. For instance, CUDA-MEMCHECK [1] and ESBMC-GPU [28] are tools that can detect these kinds of bugs.

Next we consider the memory *performance* sub-theme: 'manage memory spaces' and 'memory performance'. A GPU has to *manage* its own (faster) shared *memory space*. This management can be difficult and error-prone to do but is

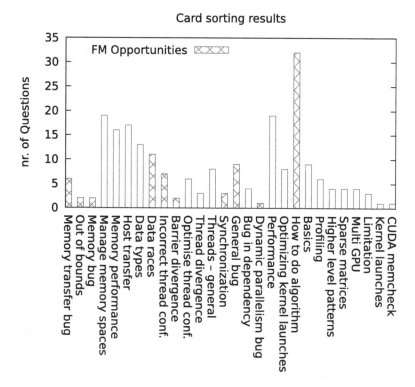

Fig. 1. Results of open card sorting 376 GPGPU related questions. We only show the 220 questions and categories relevant to GPGPU programming. The categories labelled *FM Opportunities* are the ones where we think formal methods could play a role in solving the underlying correctness issues.

an essential optimization strategy. We also added questions related to a better understanding of the memory model here. We label other questions as *memory performance* when they are related to access patterns (coalesced) or other ways to optimize memory usage.

The last two categories are 'host transfer' and 'data types'. Both are related to getting memory from the host to the device. The *host transfer* category is more general. It is related to doing transfers efficiently, asynchronously, transferring the data back, transferring arrays, parameters or constants, and handling arrays too big for global memory. We also assign questions related to aligning and pinning memory here. Actual bugs related to this we report in the 'memory transfer bug' category. We assign questions about overlapping transfers to the 'optimizing kernel launches' category. The *data types* category is more specific. It contains questions related to correctly transferring a composite data type ('struct' in C) and making sure it has a correct corresponding data type on the device. We also consider questions related to Structure of Arrays (SoA) or Arrays of Structures (AoS) here. Although we think that tools can help to

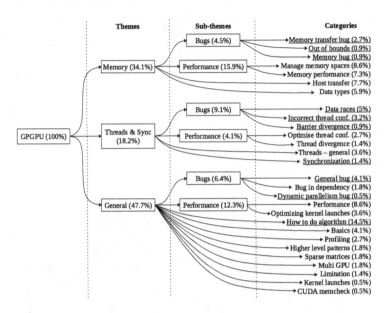

Fig. 2. Overview of the card sort, where we place the categories under themes and sub-themes. Similar to Fig. 1 we only show categories relevant to GPGPU programming. The underlined questions are the ones where we think formal methods could play a role in solving the underlying correctness issues. The percentages indicate how many questions are under a specific category, where 100% corresponds to all 220 relevant GPGPU questions.

solve problems in checking correct correspondence of *data types*, a programming language could do this automatically.

Threads and Synchronization. Under the *bug* sub-theme, we consider 'data races', 'incorrect thread configuration' and 'barrier divergence'. We assign the category *data race* to questions where this occurs. A data race is a problem that is hard to detect: it is non-deterministic by nature, and it is hard to reason about. *Incorrect thread configuration* happens when a programmer configures the wrong number of threads or goes over the maximum amount of threads possible. Some incorrect configurations will be reported at runtime, while others will run without errors but do not process all the input. We assign *barrier divergence* to questions, where not all threads in a thread block reach the same barrier. This is not allowed in the general GPU programming model and leads to undefined results. Data races and barrier divergence bugs are already the study of many formal method tools, like GPUVerify [11] and GKLEE [24]. We think formal methods can also reason about thread configurations, where a tool figures out if the indexing of the input by the threads corresponds with the size of the input or detects memory-related bugs which are caused by incorrect configurations. Another idea is to check whether kernels work the same for each thread configuration.

The 'optimise thread configuration' and 'threads divergence' categories are related to the *performance* sub-theme. When *optimising the amount of threads*, one can choose the number of threads per thread block and how much work each thread does, which both influence performance. *Thread divergence*, on the other hand, could lead to bad performance, which a programmer can sometimes avoid.

The *threads - general* category consists of questions related to understanding the execution model of threads, and what correct configurations are. *Synchronization* is used to prevent data races from happening by using barriers or atomics. General questions on how to use this, about using warp primitives or what can and cannot be synchronized we give this tag. We think formal methods can help people understand when barriers are necessary, or maybe even place barriers automatically. For instance, the Simulee [39] tool can detect unnecessary barriers.

General. First we consider the *bug* sub-theme. We have a *general bug* category, which means something is wrong in the program, but not one of the previously mentioned bugs. This can be incorrect usage of the available resources (e.g. registers), people computing something incorrectly, incorrect use of the Thrust library or it is not yet clear what is wrong. Formal methods, for instance VerCors [12], can check for functional correctness of programs when something is incorrectly calculated. *Bug in dependency* consists of all bugs in Thrust that were fixed in later versions of the library, and are therefore not considered for formal methods later on. *Dynamic parallelism bug* consists of a single question (SO/19527391), where a bug was encountered using dynamic parallelism, although it is unclear what exactly went wrong. Formal methods tools could also reason about correctness in this case, although dynamic parallelism would have to be supported.

General *performance* are questions, where people want to understand, given a program, algorithm or function, the performance and how to improve it. Questions about overlapping computations and memory transfers, and ideal scheduling of computation kernels we place in the *optimizing kernel launches* category.

We came across many questions where people wondered how a specific problem or algorithm should be programmed on the GPU, or if a library contained a specific functionality. We placed these in the *how to do algorithm* category. Formal methods could help to prove the equivalence between a sequential and parallel implementation.

The *basics* category has questions related to how certain concepts are called (e.g. what is a thread block), how they work, how specific API calls work, or some basic easy to fix mistakes that prevent correct compilation. Some questions arose about using *higher level patterns* in CUDA and OpenCL, for instance using templated functions. We think these problems are best solved by a beginners GPU programming book or by using a higher-level programming language.

Profiling are questions related to how to use the profiling tools available or how to measure runtimes correctly. *Sparse matrices* are questions on how to process matrices, or on how to use the cuSparse library. *Multi GPU* are questions related to how to use multiple GPUs for computations. The *limitation* category consists of questions related to the limitation of the CUDA/ OpenCL programming model. For example, the CUDA runtime library can only be called from the main scope of a C++ program (SO/55819758.) *Kernel launches* are questions related how to start a computation on the GPU correctly. *CUDA memcheck* is about using that specific tool for debugging.

3.3   Insights

Summarizing, we observe that 32.3% of the relevant questions are related to performance, 34.1% to memory, 20% to bugs and 18.2% to threads and synchronization. These are the areas developers on Stack Overflow are most interested in. Performance makes sense since programmers will use a GPU to get better performance, otherwise they would have used the CPU. Memory related questions are important since memory management works quite differently from CPU programs. The transferring of data is error-prone, and the management of memory without race conditions is hard to do. We also think that many developers are just interested in the result: have a faster parallel version of their original (sequential) code, which is related to our 'how to do algorithm' category. Concluding, there is potential for formal methods to help solve correctness related issues that GPGPU programmers experience. We will further discuss this in Sect. 4.

3.4   Threats to Validity

External Validity. There is a bias in the results since we look only at questions located at Stack Overflow. This may not address the general population of GPGPU developers. We suspect that there will be more questions by beginning GPGPU programmers, than by more experienced ones. Therefore, we might not discover the problems of more experienced users.

Internal Validity. As the categories have been manually created, there is an internal bias, meaning that if other people were to perform this study with the same questions, there could be a different outcome. We think that although the categories might be different, the general topics would be similar. Also, part of the categorizing is done together with another PhD student for exactly this reason.

4   Formal Verification Solutions

In Sect. 3, we looked at problems that programmers struggle with when coding in CUDA and OpenCL. In this section we focus on the problems where we think formal methods can make a direct contribution, and provide an overview of tools that (partially) solve these problems. Again, we focus mainly on correctness. First we explain how we selected these verification tools (Sect. 4.1). Next, we discuss for each of the selected problems the available solutions and possible research directions (Sect. 4.2).

4.1   Approach

In order to find as many tools as possible that target the verification of GPU applications, we took the following steps in finding them. First, we looked at the industry. We considered the websites of Nvidia, AMD (gpuopen.com), the Khronos group, and a list[4] found on the IWOCL conference site. Next we looked at important conferences, based on the Microsoft Academic's field ratings.[5] We looked in the areas of programming languages, software verification and parallel computing and selected the following conferences: PLDI, POPL, TACAS, CAV and IPDPS. For each these conferences, we looked through the years 2015–2020.

This was the initial set of tools we considered, and we snowballed, by looking at any tools that the original papers referenced. Lastly, we searched Google Scholar with the following query: "(cuda OR opencl OR gpu) AND (bugs OR problems OR verification OR formal)".

4.2   Available Solutions

In this section we consider the problems that we discussed in Sect. 3, where we identified categories. In Table 1, we provide an overview of the tools we found. We distinguish between three types of tools (inspired by Donaldson et al. [15, Chap. 1]): *Dynamic* tools check for one specific input. *Symbolic* tools execute the input symbolically, allowing for more different paths to be tested at once. *Static* tools make (sound) approximations of the source code and will try to prove existence or absence of bugs. We indicate if a tool checks for data races (*Race*), barrier divergence (*Bar*), memory problems (*Mem*), functional correctness (*Func*) or equivalence (*Eq*), or if it helps with synchronization (*Sync*) or thread configuration (*Thr*) in the 'Solves' column. With 'Auto', we refer to the degree of automation: is it completely automatic, or does the user need to be involved in the checking, for instance by writing annotations. The *Corr.* column indicates if the tool can prove the absence of bugs in certain settings. We also list any limitations or other remarks in the table.

Data Races. Ideally, a tool in this category reports existing data races with precise details or guarantees that data races are not present.

Many dynamic tools are practical and require no manual input, but do not guarantee the absence of data races. Solely for checking for a specific input, we think CURD is most suitable, it checks on instruction level, thus can also be used for higher-level languages. Only the approach of Leung et al. [22] gives some guarantees for a dynamic tool and can be used to 'prove' absence of data races for specific invariant kernels. One can combine this approach with other dynamic tools.

Symbolic tools, such as GKLEE and ESBMC-GPU, can test for more input, and one can (mostly) use them automatically although they can also suffer from

---

[4] https://www.iwocl.org/resources/opencl-libraries-and-toolkits/.
[5] https://academic.microsoft.com/home.

Table 1. Overview of different tools we discuss in this section. We indicate the type of tool, the problems (which we consider in this section) they solve, the degree of automation (Auto.), any correctness guarantees (Corr.) it can give, on which languages it works, and any limitations and other remarks.

Tool	Type	Solves	Auto.	Corr.	Languages	Limitations	Remarks
Oclgrind [31]	Dynamic	Race Bar Mem	High	×	SPIR		Simulates execution
CUDA Memcheck [1]	Dynamic	Race Bar Mem	High	×	CUDA	No global memory for Race	
GRACE [41]	Dynamic	Race	High	×	CUDA	No global memory and atomics for Race	
LDetector [26]	Dynamic	Race	High	×	CUDA	No atomics and intra-warp checks for Race	Does value checking, to determine a race, which might miss races
HAccRG [17]	Hardware	Race	-	×	CUDA		Needs a hardware implementation, but is now simply simulated. Can check fine-grained synchronization
BARRACUDA [16]	Dynamic	Race Bar	High	×	PTX	No intra-warp checks for Race	Can check fine-grained synchronization
CURD [29]	Dynamic	Race Bar	High	×	PTX		Faster version of BARRACUDA
Leung et al. [22]	Dynamic /Static	Race	-	±	CUDA	No atomics	Checks on races for one input and determines if memory accesses are the same for each input. If they are the same, this proves race freedom for all inputs
ARCHER [8]	Dynamic	Race	Medium	×	OpenMP		Runs dynamically on the CPU, not GPU specific
PUG [23]	Static	Race Bar Func	Low	✓	CUDA	Can't check floating point values for Func. Only asserts for Func. Only checks kernels	Scales badly for correctness checking. Can be unsound and incomplete. Needs annotations
GPUVerify [11]	Static	Race Bar Func	Low	✓	CUDA OpenCL	No indirect accesses Only asserts for Func. Only checks kernels	Needs annotations to deal with false positives for races. Is only sound for some CUDA features
VerCors [12]	Static	Race Bar Func	Low	✓	OpenCL	No support for floats (yet)	Needs annotations to prove correctness
GKLEE [24]	Symbolic	Race Bar Func	Medium	×	CUDA (LLVM-IR)	Can't check floating point values for Func. Only asserts for Func.	Difficult to scale for more threads. Generate's concrete tests for races
KLEE-CL [14]	Symbolic	Race Eq	Medium	×	OpenCL		Checks for equivalence on symbolic output, although false positives are possible for this
SESA [25]	Symbolic	Race	High	±	CUDA (LLVM-IR		Similar to GKLEE, but concretize values when possible to reduce runtimes. Can be sound and complete under specific circumstances
ESBMC-GPU [28]	Symbolic	Race Mem Func	High Medium	×	CUDA	Only asserts for Func.	Can be run automatically, but needs assertions for functional correctness checks
Xing et al. [40]	Static	Race	High	±	PTX		Can check fine-grained synchronization. It has to unrolls loops, which can cause unsoundness
Banerjee et al. [10]	Static	Race Eq	High	✓	OpenMP	Equivalent version should be similar	Equivalence checking is sound, but might not be possible for complex programs
WEFT [35]	Static	Race Bar	High	✓	PTX (CUDA)	No global memory and atomics for Race	It is based on a warp specialized programming model. It can only verify programs which are completely predictable, e.g. it cannot have dependencies on the input for memory locations and control flow. It will check named barriers, which are only accesible via PTX
CIVL [36]	Symbolic	Race Eq Mem	Medium	?	OpenMP CUDA Chapel	No atomics	Can use the languages interchangeably, but has no support for specific GPU capabilities. Need some annotations for checking
Alur et al. [7]	Symbolic	Thr	High	±	LLVM-IR (CUDA)		Can only prove block size independence for synchronization free programs
Simulee [39]	Dynamic	DR Bar Sync	High	×	LLVM-IR (CUDA)		Simulates a GPU memory model, and generates memory via evoluationary computing for it
Vericuda [21]	Static	Func	Low	✓	CUDA	Race-free	Needs annotations to prove correctness and can only prove this for race-free programs

longer verification times. GPUVerify is the most practical static verifier, although it needs annotations to overcome false positives. The tool from Xing et al. [40] is interesting and checks on instruction level, but uses loop unrolling, which makes it unsound. It could use ideas from GPUVerify, which generates loop invariants. VerCors can give the most guarantees but needs a serious effort in annotating. For example, see the work of Safari et al. [33], which verifies a prefix-sum algorithm.

WEFT, CIVL, Archer, and the tool of Banerjee et al. [10] serve a more specific purpose, like checking OpenMP or warp-specialised programs.

Overall, many steps have been made to verify data races in GPGPU programs. Checking on instruction level is a good idea since other programming languages benefit from this as well. We also think there are proper steps made to check for fine-grained synchronisation and memory fences which one need for this kind of synchronisation (e.g., BARRACUDA checks on this). From the benchmarks that the authors of the tools consider, it seems to be clear though that there is no tool that always detects or proves the absence of data races. Also, each author uses a different set of benchmarks. It would be interesting to test all the mentioned tools with the benchmark suite created by the work of Schmitz et al. [34], for a fair comparison between tools.

Memory Bugs. Here we look for solutions for the categories: 'memory bug', 'out of bounds' and 'memory transfer bug'. Thus, tools should check that memory addresses which are accessed are valid and initialised.

CUDA-MEMCHECK detects the above errors dynamically for CUDA. The OCLgrind tool does the same for OpenCL. ESBMC-GPU verifies on index out of bounds. CIVL checks on array index-out-of bounds. These tools can also check for memory leaks.

For these memory issues, we see an opportunity to check on the instruction level. The dynamic tools seem to cover the properties of interests, but this is not yet the case for the (symbolic) verification tools. For instance, it is unclear if ESBMC-GPU checks on accessing uninitialised memory. Lastly, only VerCors could guarantee correctness for the 'out of bounds' issues, but it will only check kernels, not host code and needs annotations.

Barriers and Synchronization. Barrier divergence is also a source of bugs, which can be verified by GPUVerify and GKLEE. CUDA-MEMCHECK detects this dynamically. Another interesting topic, which can help developers with 'synchronisation', is placing barriers automatically or notifying the user about unnecessary barriers. The Simulee tool checks for the latter, but no tool addressed the former to the best of our knowledge. Automatic barrier placement could be implemented together with race check tools to afterwards verify for race freedom.

Thread Configuration. The tool by Alur et al. [7] can verify if a synchronisation-free program is blocksize independent: does the program behave the same if the number of blocks is changed, but the total amount of threads stays the same. We think such an approach can be helpful for newer programmers. (And would be a good programming style to begin with.) By making one's program work for any block size, it is easier to optimise. Or even better, verify that one's program behaves the same for any number of threads[6]. A thread-invariant program lets one freely try different thread configurations without introducing new bugs. Thus, we see an opportunity for verification tools addressing this.

Dynamic Parallelism. As far as we know, there are no tools that support dynamic parallelism, although we are not sure if tools working at the instruction level, e.g. BARRACUDA, support this. Support for dynamic parallelism is the first step to ensure that a tool can check kernels using this concept. One can also come across new bugs like data races between parent and child kernels. Specific to dynamic parallelism is the fact that there is a maximum recursion depth of new kernels and a maximum number of child kernels. A formal methods tool can check both of these restrictions.

Functional Correctness. VerCors [13] allows deductive checking of functional correctness of programs, although it needs non-trivial annotations.

On a similar vein, the work of Kojima et al. [20] proposes a Hoare logic for GPU programs, which the Vericuda tool [21] verifies when one provides Hoare tuples. However, the latter tool requires that the checked program is data race free, which should be verified by another program.

ESBMC-GPU, CIVL, GPUVerify and GKLEE allow the programmer to place assertions. These assertions do not give complete correctness but allow more flexibility in checking certain aspects of the program.

We think VerCors has potential, although the need for annotations makes it difficult to use out of the box. An interesting research direction is making the reuse of annotations easier after a program has been slightly changed, e.g. due to an optimisation.

Equivalence Checking. Instead of fully verifying a specification, one can do equivalence checking: take a (simple), possibly sequential, version of a program, which you know is correct and prove that a parallel implementation is equivalent. The CIVL tool can do this. Kamil et al. [19] use a similar approach. They transform Fortran stencil codes to Halide (an image processing DSL), and proof functional equality, while being able to optimise the program in Halide further. The tool by Banerjee et al. [10] is similar. It verifies equivalence for parallelising loop transformations from OpenMP and also verifies data race freedom.

---

[6] https://developer.nvidia.com/blog/cuda-pro-tip-write-flexible-kernels-grid-stride-loops/.

4.3   Research Directions

We think much progress has already been made by formal methods that address many issues that developers encounter. We make the following observations.

In general, we think that checking on instruction level is valuable. Typically, all GPU programs will eventually compile to the instruction level, and thus allows the tool to be used for more programming languages.

No verification tool is completely sound yet, which might be impossible for the full flexibility of the CUDA and OpenCL languages, but should be the goal. Tools should support as many program features as possible while staying sound. Certainly, since programmers use a lot of low-level features when optimising code, this is an ambitious goal.

Most verification tools only check the GPU kernels, but the host code must also be correct. Bugs related to memory initialization, memory transfers and thread configuration are often made on the host side, can be hard to spot and should be relatively easy to tackle with verification tools.

Another take on this is to identify which patterns and programming features are sound to verify. This can give rise to a particular programming style, which can be enforced by a different (domain-specific) language.

In the papers presenting the various tools, those tools are compared with each other to show that for specific kernels, the new tool is, at that point in time, the best. It would be better to use a standard benchmark suite, like the suite by Schmitz et al. [34], which is uniformly used and addresses the errors we mention in this paper. Additionally, it should support all the CUDA and OpenCL features. This suite then makes it clear what errors tools can check and what programming features they do or do not support. For instance, we think that tools that deal with fine-grained synchronisation are essential.

5   Related Work

GPGPU Problems. The study by Wu et al. [39] is similar to our work. Instead of Stack Overflow, they look at open source repositories on Github to collect CUDA bugs. They identify 5 root causes for bugs, which is coarser than our results. We can match most of our categories with one of their root causes. Only their 'poor portability' we can not match, and is more related to specific platforms issues, which were questions we marked as irrelevant. Also, the nature of Stack Overflow means we have more questions related to solely understanding GPU programming (e.g. 'Basics' or 'How to do algorithm') and are not things you could find in commit messages. Because of that reason, the exact numbers on how often certain issues arise are hard to compare, but we don't think that is too important. Both of these methods give a good overview of what kind of bugs to expect whilst GPGPU programming.

The work of Donaldson et al. [9, Chap. 1] gives an overview of what kind of correctness issues occur with GPGPU programming and gives a comparison between the tools GPUVerify, GKLEE, Oclgrind and CUDA-MEMCHECK.

They name four different correctness issues: *data races, weak memory behaviours, lack of forward progress guarantees* and *floating point accuracy*. Of these issues, we have only come across *data races* in our study. We think the other issues are more particular for experienced users, and less so for novice users. As mentioned before, we think Stack Overflow attracts mostly novice users. The taxonomy made by Donaldson et al. of the considered tools inspired the current work, although we consider a wider range of tools overall.

Stack Overflow Studies. There were many other studies performed on Stack Overflow concerning other subjects, for example concurrency [5,30] mobile development [32] and machine learning [18]. In [5,30,32] topic modelling is used to categorize all the questions. We chose to not use topic modeling, since we think that we can make a finer subdivision of the categories with open card sorting. In [18] something more related to our work was done, but experts pre-determined the categories. In our case the goal was to discover problems, therefore it makes no sense to pre-determine the categories.

6   Discussion

In this work, we showed the problems GPGPU programmers struggle with, while programming for the GPU using OpenCL or CUDA. We see that memory, synchronization, threads and performance are essential topics for GPGPU programming. Next, we looked at (formal method) tools and how they address the correctness issues we found. In general, the research community addresses most problems, but we identified several interesting research directions.

Acknowledgements and Data Availibility Statement. We want to thank Jan Martens for his help with the card sorting.

The data used for the categorization with card sorting is available in the Figshare repository: https://doi.org/10.4121/12988781 [38].

References

1. CUDA-MEMCHECK, June 2020. https://docs.nvidia.com/cuda/cuda-memcheck
2. CUDA Programming Guide, July 2020. http://docs.nvidia.com/cuda/cuda-c-programming-guide/
3. Parallel Thread Execution ISA Version 7.0, July 2020. http://docs.nvidia.com/cuda/parallel-thread-execution/index.html
4. SPIR - The Industry Open Standard Intermediate Language for Parallel Compute and Graphics, July 2020. https://www.khronos.org/spir/
5. Ahmed, S., Bagherzadeh, M.: What do concurrency developers ask about? a large-scale study using stack overflow. In: Proceedings of the 12th ACM/IEEE International Symposium on Empirical Software Engineering and Measurement, ESEM 2018, pp. 1–10. Association for Computing Machinery, Oulu, October 2018. https://doi.org/10.1145/3239235.3239524

6. Alglave, J., et al.: GPU concurrency: weak behaviours and programming assumptions. In: Proceedings of the Twentieth International Conference on Architectural Support for Programming Languages and Operating Systems - ASPLOS 2015, pp. 577–591. ACM Press, Istanbul (2015). https://doi.org/10.1145/2694344.2694391

7. Alur, R., Devietti, J., Singhania, N.: Block-size independence for GPU programs. In: Podelski, A. (ed.) SAS 2018. LNCS, vol. 11002, pp. 107–126. Springer, Cham (2018). https://doi.org/10.1007/978-3-319-99725-4_9

8. Atzeni, S., et al.: ARCHER: effectively spotting data races in large OpenMP applications. In: 2016 IEEE International Parallel and Distributed Processing Symposium (IPDPS), pp. 53–62. IEEE, Chicago, May 2016. https://doi.org/10.1109/IPDPS.2016.68

9. Azad, H.S.: Advances in GPU Research and Practice, 1st edn. Morgan Kaufmann Publishers Inc., San Francisco (2016)

10. Banerjee, K., Banerjee, S., Sarkar, S.: Data-race detection: the missing piece for an end-to-end semantic equivalence checker for parallelizing transformations of array-intensive programs. In: Proceedings of the 3rd ACM SIGPLAN International Workshop on Libraries, Languages, and Compilers for Array Programming, ARRAY 2016, pp. 1–8. Association for Computing Machinery, Santa Barbara, June 2016. https://doi.org/10.1145/2935323.2935324

11. Betts, A., Chong, N., Donaldson, A., Qadeer, S., Thomson, P.: GPUVerify: a verifier for GPU kernels. In: Proceedings of the ACM International Conference on Object Oriented Programming Systems Languages and Applications, OOPSLA 2012, pp. 113–132. ACM, New York (2012). https://doi.org/10.1145/2384616.2384625

12. Blom, S., Huisman, M.: The VerCors tool for verification of concurrent programs. In: Jones, C., Pihlajasaari, P., Sun, J. (eds.) FM 2014. LNCS, vol. 8442, pp. 127–131. Springer, Cham (2014). https://doi.org/10.1007/978-3-319-06410-9_9

13. Blom, S., Huisman, M., Mihelčić, M.: Specification and verification of GPGPU programs. Sci. Comput. Program. **95**, 376–388 (2014). https://doi.org/10.1016/j.scico.2014.03.013

14. Collingbourne, P., Cadar, C., Kelly, P.H.J.: Symbolic testing of OpenCL code. In: Eder, K., Lourenço, J., Shehory, O. (eds.) HVC 2011. LNCS, vol. 7261, pp. 203–218. Springer, Heidelberg (2012). https://doi.org/10.1007/978-3-642-34188-5_18

15. Donaldson, A.F., Ketema, J., Sorensen, T., Wickerson, J.: Forward progress on GPU concurrency (invited talk). In: Meyer, R., Nestmann, U. (eds.) 28th International Conference on Concurrency Theory (CONCUR 2017). Leibniz International Proceedings in Informatics (LIPIcs), vol. 85, pp. 1:1–1:13. Schloss Dagstuhl–Leibniz-Zentrum fuer Informatik, Dagstuhl (2017). https://doi.org/10.4230/LIPIcs.CONCUR.2017.1

16. Eizenberg, A., Peng, Y., Pigli, T., Mansky, W., Devietti, J.: BARRACUDA: binary-level analysis of runtime RAces in CUDA programs. In: Proceedings of the 38th ACM SIGPLAN Conference on Programming Language Design and Implementation, PLDI 2017, pp. 126–140. Association for Computing Machinery, Barcelona, June 2017. https://doi.org/10.1145/3062341.3062342

17. Holey, A., Mekkat, V., Zhai, A.: HAccRG: hardware-accelerated data race detection in GPUs. In: 2013 42nd International Conference on Parallel Processing, pp. 60–69. IEEE, Lyon, October 2013. https://doi.org/10.1109/ICPP.2013.15

18. Islam, M.J., Nguyen, H.A., Pan, R., Rajan, H.: What do developers ask about ML libraries? A large-scale study using stack overflow. ArXiv: 1906.11940 (Cs), June 2019

19. Kamil, S., Cheung, A., Itzhaky, S., Solar-Lezama, A.: Verified lifting of stencil computations. In: Proceedings of the 37th ACM SIGPLAN Conference on Programming Language Design and Implementation, PLDI 2016, pp. 711–726. Association for Computing Machinery, Santa Barbara, June 2016. https://doi.org/10.1145/2908080.2908117
20. Kojima, K., Igarashi, A.: A hoare logic for GPU kernels. ACM Trans. Comput. Log. **18**(1), 3:1–3:43 (2017). https://doi.org/10.1145/3001834
21. Kojima, K., Imanishi, A., Igarashi, A.: Automated verification of functional correctness of race-free GPU programs. J. Autom. Reason. **60**(3), 279–298 (2018). https://doi.org/10.1007/s10817-017-9428-2
22. Leung, A., Gupta, M., Agarwal, Y., Gupta, R., Jhala, R., Lerner, S.: Verifying GPU kernels by test amplification. SIGPLAN Not. **47**(6), 383–394 (2012). https://doi.org/10.1145/2345156.2254110
23. Li, G., Gopalakrishnan, G.: Scalable SMT-based verification of GPU kernel functions. In: Proceedings of the Eighteenth ACM SIGSOFT International Symposium on Foundations of Software Engineering - FSE 2010, p. 187. ACM Press, Santa Fe (2010). https://doi.org/10.1145/1882291.1882320
24. Li, G., Li, P., Sawaya, G., Gopalakrishnan, G., Ghosh, I., Rajan, S.P.: GKLEE: concolic verification and test generation for GPUs. In: Proceedings of the 17th ACM SIGPLAN Symposium on Principles and Practice of Parallel Programming, PPoPP 2012, pp. 215–224. ACM, New York (2012). https://doi.org/10.1145/2145816.2145844
25. Li, P., Li, G., Gopalakrishnan, G.: Practical symbolic race checking of GPU programs. In: SC 2014: Proceedings of the International Conference for High Performance Computing, Networking, Storage and Analysis, pp. 179–190, November 2014. https://doi.org/10.1109/SC.2014.20
26. Li, P., et al.: LD: low-overhead GPU race detection without access monitoring. ACM Trans. Archit. Code Optim. **14**(1), 1–25 (2017). https://doi.org/10.1145/3046678
27. Menzies, T., Williams, L., Zimmermann, T.: Perspectives on Data Science for Software Engineering, 1st edn. Morgan Kaufmann Publishers Inc., San Francisco (2016)
28. Monteiro, F.R., et al.: ESBMC-GPU a context-bounded model checking tool to verify CUDA programs. Sci. Comput. Program. **152**, 63–69 (2018). https://doi.org/10.1016/j.scico.2017.09.005
29. Peng, Y., Grover, V., Devietti, J.: CURD: a dynamic CUDA race detector. In: PLDI 2018, pp. 390–403. Association for Computing Machinery, Philadelphia, June 2018. https://doi.org/10.1145/3192366.3192368
30. Pinto, G., Torres, W., Castor, F.: A study on the most popular questions about concurrent programming. In: Proceedings of the 6th Workshop on Evaluation and Usability of Programming Languages and Tools - PLATEAU 2015, pp. 39–46. ACM Press, Pittsburgh (2015). https://doi.org/10.1145/2846680.2846687
31. Price, J., McIntosh-Smith, S.: Oclgrind: an extensible OpenCL device simulator. In: Proceedings of the 3rd International Workshop on OpenCL - IWOCL 2015, pp. 1–7. ACM Press, Palo Alto (2015). https://doi.org/10.1145/2791321.2791333
32. Rosen, C., Shihab, E.: What are mobile developers asking about? A large scale study using stack overflow. Empir. Softw. Eng. **21**(3), 1192–1223 (2016). https://doi.org/10.1007/s10664-015-9379-3
33. Safari, M., Oortwijn, W., Joosten, S., Huisman, M.: Formal verification of parallel prefix sum. In: Lee, R., Jha, S., Mavridou, A. (eds.) NFM 2020. LNCS, vol. 12229, pp. 170–186. Springer, Cham (2020). https://doi.org/10.1007/978-3-030-55754-6_10

34. Schmitz, A., Protze, J., Yu, L., Schwitanski, S., Müller, M.S.: DataRaceOnAccelerator – a micro-benchmark suite for evaluating correctness tools targeting accelerators. In: Schwardmann, U., et al. (eds.) Euro-Par 2019. LNCS, vol. 11997, pp. 245–257. Springer, Cham (2020). https://doi.org/10.1007/978-3-030-48340-1_19

35. Sharma, R., Bauer, M., Aiken, A.: Verification of producer-consumer synchronization in GPU programs. In: PLDI 2015, pp. 88–98. Association for Computing Machinery, Portland, June 2015. https://doi.org/10.1145/2737924.2737962

36. Siegel, S.F., et al.: CIVL: the concurrency intermediate verification language. In: Proceedings of the International Conference for High Performance Computing, Networking, Storage and Analysis on - SC 2015, pp. 1–12. ACM Press, Austin (2015). https://doi.org/10.1145/2807591.2807635

37. Sorensen, T., Donaldson, A.F., Batty, M., Gopalakrishnan, G., Rakamaric, Z.: Portable inter-workgroup barrier synchronisation for GPUs. In: OOPSLA 2016, p. 20 (2016). https://doi.org/10.1145/3022671.2984032

38. van den Haak, L.B., Wijs, A., van den Brand, M., Huisman, M.: Card sorting data for Formal methods for GPGPU programming: is the demand met?, September 2020. https://doi.org/10.4121/12988781

39. Wu, M., Zhou, H., Zhang, L., Liu, C., Zhang, Y.: Characterizing and detecting CUDA program bugs. ArXiv: 1905.01833 (Cs), May 2019

40. Xing, Y., Huang, B.Y., Gupta, A., Malik, S.: A formal instruction-level GPU model for scalable verification. In: 2018 IEEE/ACM International Conference on Computer-Aided Design (ICCAD), pp. 1–8, November 2018. https://doi.org/10.1145/3240765.3240771

41. Zheng, M., Ravi, V.T., Qin, F., Agrawal, G.: GRace: a low-overhead mechanism for detecting data races in GPU programs. SIGPLAN Not. **46**(8), 135–146 (2011). https://doi.org/10.1145/2038037.1941574

Verification of Interactive Behaviour

Active Objects with Deterministic Behaviour

Ludovic Henrio[1], Einar Broch Johnsen[2], and Violet Ka I. Pun[2,3](✉)

[1] Univ. Lyon, EnsL, UCBL, CNRS, Inria, LIP, Lyon, France
`ludovic.henrio@ens-lyon.fr`
[2] University of Oslo, Oslo, Norway
`{einarj,violet}@ifi.uio.no`
[3] Western Norway University of Applied Sciences, Bergen, Norway
`Violet.Ka.I.Pun@hvl.no`

Abstract. Active objects extend the Actor paradigm with structured communication using method calls and futures. Active objects are, like actors, known to be data race free. Both are inherently concurrent, as they share a fundamental decoupling of communication and synchronisation. Both encapsulate their state, restricting access to one process at a time. Clearly, this rules out low-level races between two processes accessing a shared variable. However, is that sufficient to guarantee deterministic results from the execution of an active object program?

In this paper we are interested in so-called high-level races caused by the fact that the arrival order of messages between active objects can be non-deterministic, resulting in non-deterministic overall behaviour. We study this problem in the setting of a core calculus and identify restrictions on active object programs which are sufficient to guarantee deterministic behaviour for active object programs. We formalise these restrictions as a simple extension to the type system of the calculus and prove that well-typed programs exhibit deterministic behaviour.

1 Introduction

Concurrent programs are characterised by multiple threads executing over a program's state space, possibly in parallel on multicore or distributed hardware. Concurrency introduces non-determinism in the programs, which makes it hard to reason about program behaviour and easy to inadvertently introduce errors. Two major causes for errors in concurrent programs are *deadlocks* and *races*. One has to choose between making programs *more synchronous*, which makes them exhibit less behaviour but also makes them more deadlock-prone, and making program *more asynchronous*, which enables more behaviour and makes them less deadlock-prone. However, allowing more behaviour also allows more races to occur between the program threads.

Active object languages [1], which extend the Actor [2,3] model of concurrency with asynchronous method calls and synchronisation using futures, naturally lend themselves to an asynchronous program style because they decouple

© Springer Nature Switzerland AG 2020
B. Dongol and E. Troubitsyna (Eds.): IFM 2020, LNCS 12546, pp. 181–198, 2020.
https://doi.org/10.1007/978-3-030-63461-2_10

communication from synchronisation. Asynchronous method calls can be dispatched without any transfer of control between the active objects. Although asynchrony generally leads to non-determinism, languages based on the Actor model are known to be free from data races (e.g., [4]). This is because actors (and active objects) encapsulate internal state and restrict local state access to one method at a time, which eliminate such low-level races. However, these systems are prone to *high-level communication races* which result in a non-deterministic order of execution for methods on an actor in the system. These races may be triggered by asynchronous method calls (e.g., they are the only races in ASP [5]), by the synchronisation on the associated futures (e.g., [6,7]) to retrieve the return values from these method calls, and by cooperative scheduling inside the active objects (e.g., [8]). The occurrence of high-level races gives rise to the following question: *under which conditions are active object programs guaranteed to be deterministic?* That is, the programs always produce the same output given a particular input.

This paper studies the problem of active objects with guaranteed deterministic behaviour. Deterministic behaviour for a concurrent program boils down to confluence properties between execution steps. We formalise the execution of active objects systems in a core calculus to study their confluence properties. We combine certain characteristics of the underlying communication network and the local scheduling policy of each active object with restrictions on the program's topology, and show that these together suffice to prove confluence. We identify characteristics that can ensure determinacy, and show how to restrict existing languages to make them partially deterministic. We further show that a simple typing discipline suffices to statically enforce this topology and relate our findings to existing calculi and languages to shed light on how to approach the problem of designing a deterministic active object system in different languages.

The main contributions of the paper can be summarised as follows: We extend previous work on deterministic active object systems, which enforce a tree-shaped object graph, to handle explicit futures and cooperative scheduling, and show that a simple type system is sufficient to guarantee deterministic behaviour even when futures can be shared among objects in the tree-shaped topology.

Paper Overview. Section 2 motivates the problem addressed in this paper through an example. Section 3 introduces the active object calculus in which we study the problem, including its operational semantics and basic type system. Section 4 defines and proves confluence properties for our calculus. Section 5 addresses the problem of statically guaranteeing a tree structure in the program topology. Section 6 discusses related work, and in particular to what extent existing active object calculi and languages can guarantee deterministic behaviour. Section 7 concludes the paper.

2   Motivation and Example

An actor is a single-threaded unit of distribution that communicates with other actors by asynchronous message sending. The absence of multi-threading inside an actor and the fact that data is handled by a single actor prevents data races. However, race conditions can appear when two actors send messages to the same receiver, or when an actor chooses the next message to be processed. Thus, actors are a programming abstraction that limits non-determinism, but does not prevent it. Different adaptations of the actor principles entail different sources of non-deterministic behaviour for programs. To motivate our work on deterministic behaviour for active objects, which are actors synchronising on futures, we review below two classical parallel programming patterns implemented using active objects and discuss the races they exhibit.

```
1   Worker {
2       Array work(int i) { .... } // omitted
3   }
4   { // main
5       Worker w1 = new Worker();   // creation of active objects
6       Worker w2 = new Worker();
7       Fut<Array> f1 = w1!work(1); // asynchronous invocation
8       Fut<Array> f2 = w2!work(2);
9       Array r1 = get f1;          // synchronisation
10      Array r2 = get f2;          // synchronisation
11      average = (sum(r1) + sum(r2)) / (length(r1) + length(r2))
12  }
```

Fig. 1. Implementation with a master-worker pattern.

We consider two implementations of a program which computes the average over a sequence of values. Figure 1 shows an implementation using a master-worker pattern based on active objects. Two workers w1 and w2 are called asynchronously (Lines 7 and 8) to perform some work task, the main object then synchronises on the returns from the two invocations (Lines 9 and 10 use a get-statement to retrieve the return values) before it computes the average in Line 11. The implementation is presented in the core calculus of Sect. 3 using an additional basic type **Array** with sum and length operators.

Figure 2 shows an implementation of the same problem using a map-reduce pattern. In this implementation, partial results are reduced as they arrive. The workers send their results to a **Reducer** active object who computes the partial average of the results as they arrive and forwards the average to a receiving active object **out** (we omit its implementation). We see that the asynchronous method calls to the workers (Lines 27 and 28) are not associated with futures in this implementation, but include a reference to the **Reducer** instance so the partial results can be passed on directly. The computed result would be deterministic with a commutative and associative reduction operator—but this is not the case in our example. Observe that if the first partial average is computed over an empty array, a division-by-zero error will be triggered. This bug might only

```
1   Map {
2       int work(int i, Reducer red) {
3           .... // computation omitted
4           Fut<int> c = red!reduce(computedArray);
5           return 0
6       }
7   }
8   Reducer {
9       int expectedResults;   // number of expected results
10      OutputObject out;      // result is sent to out
11      int partialNb,partialAvg;
12      int NbWorks;           // number of received results
13
14      int reduce (Array oneResult) { // reduce computing partial average
15          int newPartialNb = partialNb+length(oneResult);
16          partialAvg = (partialAvg*partialNb+sum(oneResult))/newPartialNb;
17          partialNb = newPartialNb;
18          NbWorks = NbWorks + 1;
19          if (NbWorks == expectedResults) { out!send(partialAvg) } ;
20          return partialAvg
21      }
22  }
23  { // main. We suppose out is an active object expecting the result
24    Reducer red = new Reducer(2,out,0,0,0); //reducer creation with
                  initial values for fields
25    Worker m1 = new Map();
26    Worker m2 = new Map();
27    Fut<int> f1 = m1!work(1,red); // asynchronous invocation
28    Fut<int> f2 = m2!work(2,red)
29  }
```

Fig. 2. Implementation with a map-reduce pattern.

appear in some executions because messages are received in a non-deterministic order, which makes the reducer difficult to debug. In contrast, the master-worker implementation behaves deterministically; if a division-by-zero bug would occur in that implementation, it would occur in every execution.

Map-reduce is a popular pattern that is supported by powerful runtime frameworks like Hadoop. In the sequel, we identify why patterns such as map-reduce are potentially non-deterministic and design a type-system that ensures deterministic behaviour for active objects. This type system can type the master-worker implementation, but not the map-reduce one.

3   An Active Object Language

In this section we propose a core language for active objects. We adopt a Java-like syntax that is similar to ABS [8].

Notations. $\overline{T}$ denotes a list of elements T, unless stated otherwise this list is ordered. In the syntax x, y, u range over variable names, m method names, α, β active object identifiers, f future identifiers, and Act class names. The set of binary operators on values is represented by an abstract operator $\oplus$, it replaces all the classical operations on integer and booleans. Mappings are denoted $[\overline{x} \mapsto \overline{a}]$ which builds a map from the two lists $\overline{x}$ and $\overline{a}$ of identical length, $m[x \mapsto a]$ updates a map, associating the value a to the entry x, and $+$ merges two maps (taking values in the rightmost one in case of conflict). $\bar{q}\#q$ (resp. $q\#\bar{q}$) is the FIFO enqueue (resp. dequeue) operation.

$$
\begin{array}{llr}
P ::= \overline{\text{Act}\{\overline{T\ x}\ \ \overline{M}\}}\ \{\overline{T\ x}\ s\} & & \text{program} \\
M ::= T\ \text{m}(\overline{T\ x})\ \{\overline{T\ x}\ s\} & & \text{method} \\
s ::= \text{skip}\ \mid\ x = z\ \mid\ \text{if}\ v\ \{s\}\ \text{else}\ \{s\}\ \mid\ s\ ;\ s & & \text{statements} \\
\quad\mid\ \text{return}\ v\ \mid\ \text{await}\ e & & \\
z ::= e\ \mid\ v!\text{m}(\overline{v})\ \mid\ \text{new Act}(\overline{v})\ \mid\ \text{get}\ v & & \text{rhs of assignments} \\
\\
e ::= v\ \mid\ v \oplus v & & \text{expressions} \\
v ::= x\ \mid\ \text{null}\ \mid\ \textit{integer-and-boolean-values} & & \text{atoms} \\
B ::= \text{Int}\ \mid\ \text{Bool}\ \mid\ \text{Act} & & \text{basic type} \\
T ::= B\ \mid\ \text{Fut}\langle B \rangle & & \text{type}
\end{array}
$$

Fig. 3. Static syntax of the core language.

3.1 Syntax and Semantics

We design a simple active object model with one thread per object and where all objects are active (uniform active object model). Interested readers are referred to [1] for a complete description of the different request scheduling strategies in active object languages.

Figure 3 shows the syntax of our language. A program P is made of a set of classes, each having a set of fields and a set of methods, plus a main method. A method M has a name m, a set of parameters, and a body, made of a set of local variables and a statement. Types and terms are standard of active object languages, for instance **new** creates an active object, **get** accesses a future, and $v!\text{m}(\overline{v})$ performs a method invocation on an active object and thus systematically creates a future. The type constructor for future is $\text{Fut}\langle T \rangle$ like ABS or any explicit future construct. Sequence is denoted as ; and is associative with a neutral element **skip**. Consequently, each statement that is not **skip** can be rewritten as $s; s'$ with s neither **skip** nor a sequence. $\oplus$ denotes the (standard) operations on integers and booleans. Finally, including an *await* enables cooperative scheduling: it interrupts a thread until a condition is validated. Several design choices had to be made in our language we discuss them briefly below:

- For simplicity, we suppose that local variables and fields have disjoint names.
- We specify a service of requests in FIFO order with a causal ordering of request transmission, like in ASP [5], Rebeca [9] or Encore [10]. Also, FIFO communication is supported by many actor and active object implementations, and it reduces the possible interleaving of messages.
- Adding subtyping is outside the scope of our study.
- With more complex active object models, it is sometimes necessary to have a syntactic distinction between synchronous and asynchronous invocations.

For instance, ABS uses ! to identify asynchronous method invocations that create futures. Our core language adopts ABS syntax here but does not have synchronous invocation.

$$
\begin{array}{llr}
cn ::= & \overline{\alpha(a, p, \overline{q})} \ \overline{f(w)} & \text{configuration} \\
p ::= & \varnothing \mid q & \text{current request service} \\
q ::= & \{\ell \mid s\}_f & \text{request} \\
w ::= & x \mid \alpha \mid f \mid \texttt{null} \mid integer\text{-}values & \text{runtime values} \\
\ell, a ::= & [\overline{x} \mapsto \overline{w}] & \text{local store and object fields} \\
e ::= & w \mid v \oplus v & \text{expressions can now have runtime values} \\
s ::= & \texttt{skip} \mid x = z \mid \texttt{if } e \ \{s\} \ \texttt{else} \ \{s\} & \text{statements} \\
& \mid \ s \ ; \ s \mid \texttt{return } e \mid \texttt{await } e & \\
z ::= & e \mid v!\texttt{m}(\overline{v}) \mid \texttt{new Act}(\overline{v}) \mid \texttt{get } v & \text{expressions with side effects}
\end{array}
$$

Fig. 4. Runtime Syntax of the core language .

The operational semantics of our language is shown in Fig. 5; it expresses a small-step reduction semantics as a transition between runtime configurations. The syntax of configurations and runtime terms is defined in Fig. 4, statements are the same as in the static syntax except that they can contain runtime values like reference to an object or a future (inside assignment or $\texttt{get}$ statement). A configuration is an *unordered* set of active objects and futures. Each active object is of the form $\alpha(a, p, \overline{q})$ where α is the active object identifier, a stores the value of object fields, p is the task currently be executed, and $\overline{q}$ a list of pending tasks. The configuration also contains futures that are resolved by a value w (when a future is not yet resolved, it is not in the configuration). A task q is made of a set of local variables ℓ and a statement s to be executed, additionally each task is supposed to fulfil a future f. The currently performed task p is either empty $\varnothing$ or a single task q.

The semantics uses an auxiliary operator – bind – that creates a context for evaluating a method invocation. If the object α is of type $\texttt{Act}$, and $\texttt{m}$ is defined in $\texttt{Act}$, i.e., $\texttt{Act}\{.. T \ \texttt{m}(\overline{T \ x}) \ \{\overline{T \ y} \ s\}..\}$ is one class of the program P, then[1]: $\text{bind}(\alpha, (f, \texttt{m}, \overline{w})) \triangleq \{ [\texttt{this} \mapsto \alpha, \overline{x} \mapsto \overline{w}] \mid s \}$.

To deal with assignment, we use a dedicated operator for updating the current fields or local variables:

$$
\begin{array}{ll}
(a + \ell)[x \mapsto w] = a' + \ell' \iff & a' = a[x \mapsto w] \text{ and } \ell' = \ell, \text{ if } x \in \text{dom}(a), \\
& a' = a \text{ and } \ell' = \ell[x \mapsto w], \text{ otherwise}
\end{array}
$$

We also define a predicate checking whether a thread is enabled, i.e., can progress. A thread is disabled if it starts with an $\texttt{await}$ statement on a condition that is $\texttt{false}$.

$$
\text{disabled}(q) \iff \exists \ell \ e \ s \ f. \ (q = \{\ell | \texttt{await } e \ ; \ s\}_f \wedge [\![e]\!]_{a+\ell} = \texttt{false})
$$
$$
\text{enabled}(q) \iff \neg\text{disabled}(q)
$$

---

[1] It is not necessary to initialise the local variables in the local environment because of the way store update is defined.

$$\frac{w \text{ is not a variable}}{[\![w]\!]_\ell \ = \ w} \qquad \frac{x \in \text{dom}(\ell)}{[\![x]\!]_\ell \ = \ \ell(x)} \qquad \frac{[\![v]\!]_\ell \ = \ k \qquad [\![v']\!]_\ell \ = \ k'}{[\![v \oplus v']\!]_\ell \ = \ k \oplus k'}$$

CONTEXT
$$\frac{cn \rightarrow cn'}{cn \ cn'' \rightarrow cn' \ cn''}$$

ASSIGN
$$\frac{[\![e]\!]_{a+\ell} = w \qquad (a+\ell)[x \mapsto w] = a' + \ell'}{\alpha(a, \{\ell \mid x = e \ ; \ s\}_f, \overline{q'}) \rightarrow \alpha(a', \{\ell' \mid s\}_f, \overline{q'})}$$

NEW
$$\frac{[\![\overline{v}]\!]_{a+\ell} = \overline{w} \qquad \beta \ \text{fresh} \qquad \overline{y} = \textit{fields}(\text{Act})}{\begin{array}{c}\alpha(a, \{\ell \mid x = \text{new Act}(\overline{v}) \ ; \ s\}_f, \overline{q'}) \rightarrow \\ \alpha(a, \{\ell \mid x = \beta \ ; \ s\}_f, \overline{q'}) \ \beta([\overline{y} \mapsto \overline{w}], \varnothing, \varnothing)\end{array}}$$

INVK
$$\frac{[\![v]\!]_{a+\ell} = \beta \qquad [\![\overline{v}]\!]_{a+\ell} = \overline{w} \qquad \beta \neq \alpha \qquad f' \ \text{fresh} \qquad \text{bind}(\beta, m, \overline{w}) = \{\ell' \mid s\}}{\alpha(a, \{\ell \mid x = v!m(\overline{v}); s\}_f, \overline{q'}) \ \beta(a', p, \overline{q_\beta}) \rightarrow \alpha(a, \{\ell \mid x = f'; s\}_f, \overline{q'}) \ \beta(a', p, \overline{q_\beta}\#\{\ell' \mid s\}_{f'})}$$

INVK-SELF
$$\frac{[\![v]\!]_{a+\ell} = \alpha \qquad [\![\overline{v}]\!]_{a+\ell} = \overline{w} \qquad f' \ \text{fresh} \qquad \text{bind}(\alpha, m, \overline{w}) = \{\ell' \mid s\}}{\alpha(a, \{\ell \mid x = v!m(\overline{v}) \ ; \ s\}_f, \overline{q'}) \rightarrow \alpha(a, \{\ell \mid x = f' \ ; \ s\}_f, \overline{q'}\#\{\ell' \mid s\}_{f'})}$$

RETURN
$$\frac{[\![v]\!]_{a+\ell} = w}{\begin{array}{c}\alpha(a, \{\ell \mid \text{return } v \ ; \ s\}_f, \overline{q}) \rightarrow \\ \alpha(a, \varnothing, \overline{q}) \ f(w)\end{array}}$$

GET
$$\frac{[\![v]\!]_{a+\ell} = f'}{\begin{array}{c}\alpha(a, \{\ell \mid y = \text{get } v \ ; \ s\}_f, \overline{q'}) \ f'(w) \\ \rightarrow \alpha(a, \{\ell \mid y = w \ ; \ s\}_f, \overline{q'}) \ f'(w)\end{array}}$$

SERVE
$$\frac{\forall q' \in \overline{q_1}. \ \text{disabled}(q') \qquad \text{enabled}(q)}{\alpha(a, \varnothing, \overline{q_1}\#q\#\overline{q_2}) \rightarrow \alpha(a, q, \overline{q_1}\#\overline{q_2})}$$

AWAIT
$$\frac{\text{disabled}(q)}{\alpha(a, q, \overline{q'}) \rightarrow \alpha(a, \varnothing, q\#\overline{q'})}$$

Fig. 5. Semantics of the core language (rules IF-TRUE and IF-FALSE for reducing if omitted).

The semantics of a program features the classical elements of active object programming [8,11], the stateful aspects of the language are expressed as accesses to either local variables (ℓ) or object fields (a). The first three rules of the semantics define an evaluation operator $[\![e]\!]_{a+\ell}$ that evaluates an expression. Note that $[\![e]\!]_{a+\ell} = w$ implies that w can only be an object or future name, null, or an integer or boolean value. The semantics in Fig. 5 contains the following rules that are standard of active object languages.

ASSIGN deals with assignment to either local variables or object fields.
NEW creates a new active object at a fresh location β.
INVK (method invocation) creates a task and enqueues it in the target active object, and a future identifier f', a reference to the future can then be used by the invoker α.
INVK-SELF deals with the particular case where the target is the invoking object.
RETURN evaluates a return statement and resolves the corresponding futures, finishing a task so that a new task can be performed.

SERVE occurs when there is no current task, it picks the first one that can be activated from the list of pending tasks and starts its execution. This ensures a strict single-threaded execution of each request one after the other.

GET fetc.hes the value associated to a future.

AWAIT suspends a task, waiting for the object to be in a given state before continuing the task. Note that the awaited condition only depends on the internal state of the active object. This scheduling feature is called *cooperative scheduling* because several threads can be executing at the same time but only one progresses and the context switch between a thread and another is triggered by the program itself.

The *initial configuration* for running a program $\mathsf{Act}\{\overline{T\ x}\ \ \overline{M}\}\ \{\overline{T\ x}\ s\}$ consists of a single object performing a single task defined by the main method, the corresponding future f is useless as no other object will fetc.h the result (it can be any future identifier): $\alpha(\varnothing, \{\varnothing|s\}_f, \varnothing)$. We use $\to^*$ for the reflexive transitive closure of $\to$.

3.2   Type System

We define a simple type system for our language (the syntax of types is defined in Fig. 3). The type system is standard for a language with active objects and futures. The type checking rules are presented in Fig. 6. Classically, Act ranges over class names and types. Γ is used for typing environments. The typing rules have the form $\Gamma \vdash_T s$ for statements where T is the return type of the current method, $\Gamma \vdash e$ for expressions, $\Gamma \vdash M$ for methods, and $\Gamma \vdash P$ for programs. The static type checking is defined in the first twelve rules of the figure. We describe below the most interesting rules.

T-GET removes one future construct.

T-INVK creates a future type. This rule adds a future construct for the result of asynchronous method invocation.

T-PROGRAM Note that the main body return type can be chosen arbitrarily: there is no constraint on the typing of a **return** statement in the main block.

The *initial typing environment* Γ, which types the program, associates to each class name a mapping from method names to method signatures. If m is a method of class Act defined as follow T'' m $(\overline{T\ x})\{\overline{T'\ x'}\ s\}$, we will have $\Gamma(\mathsf{Act})(\mathsf{m}) = \overline{T} \to T''$.

The type system is extended for typing configurations, this is expressed in the last four rules of Fig. 6. A typing environment gives the type of each active object and future. Each element of the configuration is checked individually in a very standard manner. The only complex case happens when checking processes, i.e., statements of requests in the queue or being processed, the complexity only comes from the necessity to build the typing environment for the body of the methods.

$$\text{(T-Var)} \quad \frac{}{\Gamma \vdash x : \Gamma(x)}$$

$$\text{(T-Null)} \quad \frac{}{\Gamma \vdash \texttt{null} : Act}$$

$$\text{(T-Assign)} \quad \frac{\Gamma(x) = T' \quad \Gamma \vdash z : T'}{\Gamma \vdash_T x = z}$$

$$\text{(T-New)} \quad \frac{\Gamma \vdash \overline{v} : \overline{T} \quad \mathit{fields}(\texttt{Act}) = \overline{T}\ \overline{x}}{\Gamma \vdash \texttt{new Act}(\overline{v}) : Act}$$

$$\text{(T-Expression)} \quad \frac{\oplus : T \times T' \to T'' \quad \Gamma \vdash v : T \quad \Gamma \vdash v' : T'}{\Gamma \vdash v \oplus v' : T''}$$

$$\text{(T-Get)} \quad \frac{\Gamma \vdash v : \mathsf{Fut}\langle B \rangle}{\Gamma \vdash \texttt{get}\ v : B}$$

$$\text{(T-Return)} \quad \frac{\Gamma \vdash e : T}{\Gamma \vdash_T \texttt{return}\ e}$$

$$\text{(T-Invk)} \quad \frac{\Gamma(\texttt{Act})(\texttt{m}) = \overline{T} \to T' \quad \Gamma \vdash v : Act \quad \Gamma \vdash \overline{v} : \overline{T}}{\Gamma \vdash v!\texttt{m}(\overline{v}) : \mathsf{Fut}\langle T' \rangle}$$

$$\text{(T-Seq)} \quad \frac{\Gamma \vdash_T s \quad \Gamma \vdash_T s'}{\Gamma \vdash_T s\ ;\ s'}$$

$$\text{(T-Skip)} \quad \frac{}{\Gamma \vdash_T \texttt{skip}}$$

$$\text{(T-Program)} \quad \frac{\Gamma[\overline{x'} \mapsto \overline{T'}] \vdash_{T_0} s \quad \forall \texttt{Act}\{\overline{T\ x}, \overline{M}\} \in \texttt{Act}\{\overline{T\ x}, \overline{M}\}.\forall M \in \overline{M}.\Gamma[\overline{x} \mapsto \overline{T}][\texttt{this} \mapsto \texttt{Act}] \vdash M}{\Gamma \vdash \texttt{Act}\{\overline{T\ x}, \overline{M}\}\ \{T'\ x'\ s\}}$$

$$\text{(T-Method)} \quad \frac{\Gamma[\overline{x} \mapsto \overline{T}][\overline{x'} \mapsto \overline{T'}] \vdash_T s}{\Gamma \vdash T''\ \texttt{m}\ (\overline{T\ x})\{T'\ x'\ s\}}$$

$$\text{(T-Config)} \quad \frac{\forall \alpha(a, p, \overline{q}) \in \overline{\alpha(a, p, \overline{q})}.\ \Gamma \vdash \alpha(a, p, \overline{q}) \quad \forall f(w) \in \overline{f(w)}.\ \Gamma \vdash w : \Gamma(f)}{\Gamma \vdash \overline{\alpha(a, p, \overline{q})}\ \overline{f(w)}}$$

$$\text{(T-Obj)} \quad \frac{\begin{array}{c}\Gamma(\alpha) = \texttt{Act} \quad \mathit{fields}(\texttt{Act}) = \overline{T}\ \overline{x} \\ \Gamma' = \Gamma[\texttt{this} \mapsto \texttt{Act}][\overline{x} \mapsto \overline{T}] \quad \forall x \in \mathrm{dom}(a).\ \Gamma' \vdash a(x) : \Gamma'(x) \\ \forall \{[\overline{y} \mapsto \overline{w}] | s\}_f \in p \cup \overline{q}.\ \exists \overline{T'}.\ \left(\Gamma' \vdash \overline{w} : \overline{T'}\ \wedge\ \Gamma'[\overline{y} \mapsto \overline{T'}] \vdash_{\Gamma(f)} s\right)\end{array}}{\Gamma \vdash \alpha(a, p, \overline{q})}$$

$$\text{(T-ObjRef)} \quad \frac{}{\Gamma \vdash \alpha : \Gamma(\alpha)}$$

$$\text{(T-FutRef)} \quad \frac{}{\Gamma \vdash f : \Gamma(f)}$$

Fig. 6. Type system (operator $\oplus$ has a predefined signature, rule for if omitted).

Properties of the Type System. Our type system verifies *subject reduction*.

Property 1 (Subject Reduction). *If* $\Gamma \vdash cn$ *and* $cn \to cn'$ *then* $\Gamma' \vdash cn'$ *with* $\Gamma \subseteq \Gamma'$.

Proof (Sketch). The proof is by straightforward induction over the application of transition rules. For example the correct typing of the future value is ensured by the fact that the **return** statement is well-typed in the initial configuration (i.e., it has the return type of the method). This also ensures that the **get** statement is well-typed (accordingly to the future type and the return type of the method), and thus the GET reduction rule obtains the return type without the future construct. Then, it is easy and classical to prove that every bind succeeds (because the target method exists). The proof is standard and thus omitted from the paper. □

4   Confluence Properties

In the following, we will state under which conditions a program written in our language can behave deterministically. We first identify the configurations modulo renaming of futures and active object identifiers. For this we let σ range over renaming of futures and active object identifiers (mapping names to names), and use $cn\sigma$ to apply the renaming σ to the configuration cn.

Definition 1 (Equivalence). *The configurations cn_1 and cn_2 are equivalent, denoted as $cn_1 \equiv cn_2$, if and only if $\exists \sigma. cn_1 = cn_2\sigma$.*

Note that it is trivial to prove that two equivalent configuration can do the same reduction step (according to the SOS rules) and reach equivalent configurations. Our properties will rely on the topology of active objects. For this we first define the set of active objects referenced by a term of the language as follows.

Definition 2 (References). *We state that active object β is referenced by active object α in configuration cn, written $\beta \in \mathbf{refs}_{cn}(\alpha)$, if inside configuration cn, the content of the active object α holds a reference to active object β. More precisely*

$$refs(\ell) = \{\beta | \beta \in range(\ell)\}$$

$$refs(\{\ell | s\}) = \{\beta | \beta \in range(\ell)\}$$

$$refs(\alpha(a, q, \overline{q'})) = refs(a) \cup refs(q) \cup \bigcup_{q' \in \overline{q'}} refs(q')$$

$$\mathbf{refs}_{cn}(\alpha) = refs(\alpha(a, q, \overline{q'})) \text{ if } \alpha(a, q, \overline{q'}) \in cn$$

For example, consider the configuration

$$cn_1 = \alpha([x \mapsto \beta], \{[y \mapsto \beta] \mid y := \mathbf{new}\ \mathrm{Act}(\overline{v}); y!m()\}, \varnothing) \quad \gamma(\varnothing, \varnothing, \varnothing)$$
$$\beta([z \mapsto f], \{[w \mapsto 1] \mid y := w + 1\}, \{[g \mapsto \gamma] \mid h = g!m()\}) \quad f(3)$$

We have $\mathbf{refs}_{cn_1}(\alpha) = \{\beta\}$, $\mathbf{refs}_{cn_1}(\beta) = \{\gamma\}$ and $\mathbf{refs}_{cn_1}(\gamma) = \varnothing$

We can now define when a configuration has a tree structure. To be precise, we should call such a configuration a *forest* as there is no requirement on the unicity of the tree root.

Definition 3 (Tree Structure). *We say that a configuration has a tree structure when no two objects reference the same third one.*

$$\mathbf{Tree}(cn) = \forall \alpha\beta \in cn. \mathbf{refs}_{cn}(\alpha) \cap \mathbf{refs}_{cn}(\beta) = \varnothing$$

The configuration cn_1 given as example above verifies $\mathbf{Tree}(cn_1)$ because active object α only references active object β, active object β only references γ, and active object γ references nothing. If the object field x of α was mapped to γ instead of β, we would have two active objects referencing γ and the property $\mathbf{Tree}(cn_1)$ would be `false`.

(T-NEW)

$$\dfrac{\textit{fields}(\texttt{Act}) = \overline{T}\ \overline{x} \qquad \Gamma \Vdash \overline{v} : \overline{T} \qquad \forall v \in \overline{v}.\,\Gamma \Vdash v : \texttt{ActB} \implies v = \texttt{null}}{\Gamma \Vdash \mathbf{new}\ \texttt{Act}(\overline{v}) : \texttt{Act}}$$

(T-INVK)

$$\dfrac{\Gamma \Vdash \overline{v} : \overline{T} \qquad \begin{array}{c}\Gamma \Vdash v : \texttt{Act} \qquad \Gamma(\texttt{Act})(\mathtt{m}) = \overline{T} \to T' \\ \forall v' \in \overline{v}.\,\Gamma(\exists \texttt{ActB}.\,\Vdash v' : \texttt{ActB}) \implies v' = \texttt{null} \qquad \nexists \texttt{ActB}.\,T' = \texttt{ActB}\end{array}}{\Gamma \Vdash v!\mathtt{m}(\overline{v}) : \texttt{Fut}\langle T'\rangle}$$

Fig. 7. Type system modified for no reference passing (each operator $\oplus$ has a predefined signature, rule for if-statement is omitted). $T \neq \texttt{Act}$ means T is not an object type.

Now, we can state one crucial property of our language; it is a partial confluence property constrained by the structure of the references between active objects. We first prove a local confluence property. It relies on the fact that the only conflicting reductions of the calculus is the concurrent sending of request to a same target active object, from two different active objects. As a consequence, if each object is referenced by a single object, then there is no conflicting reduction and we have local confluence.

Property 2 (Local Confluence). For any configuration cn such that $\texttt{Tree}(cn)$, if there exists cn_1 and cn_2 such that $cn \to cn_1$ and $cn \to cn_2$, then there exists cn_1' and cn_2' such that $cn_1 \to cn_1' \wedge cn_2 \to cn_2' \wedge cn_1' \equiv cn_2'$.

Proof (Sketch). The proof of local confluence is classically done by case analysis on each pair of reduction rules that can be applied. We start by eliminating the CONTEXT rule that is used to extract a sub-configuration and apply it automatically in the proof, which is detailed in an accompanying technical report [12].

□

Finally, as a consequence of the previous property, we can state the following partial confluence theorem. When at each point of the execution, the graph of dependencies between active objects forms a tree, the program behaves deterministically.

Theorem 1 (Global Confluence). *Let cn be any configuration such that $\forall cn'.\, cn \to^* cn' \Rightarrow \texttt{Tree}(cn')$.*

If there exists cn_1 and cn_2 such that $cn \to^* cn_1$ and $cn \to^* cn_2$, then there exists cn_1' and cn_2' such that $cn_1 \to^* cn_1' \wedge cn_2 \to^* cn_2' \wedge cn_1' \equiv cn_2'$.

5   Static Tree Structure Guarantee

In this section we define a type system that is sufficient to ensure the tree structure of active objects and show that every well typed program according to the type system defined in this section is confluent.

The type system in Fig. 6 is modified by revising rules T-NEW and T-INVK, which handles object creations and method invocations, as shown in Fig. 7. The modified type system is denoted as $\Vdash$. The two revised rules ensure that references to an object cannot be passed upon object creation or method invocation, thus only the creator of an object keeps a reference to it.

Note that this is useless in a tree-structure setting because an object cannot call itself and it cannot pass its reference to an external object either. Note that, however, we could add a synchronous call on this to the calculus (stacking a method invocation), which would not raise any problem (just extending syntax). Alternatively an asynchronous self call that adds the invocation at the head of the queue like *await* would also be safe and maintain confluence property (but with a strange semantics). To keep the typing rules simple, we use ActA, ActB, ..., to represents the types of different objects. Alternatively, we could use subtyping relatively to a generic object type.

To show that a well-typed program in our language is confluent, we first show that the type system $\Vdash$ verifies subject reduction and reduction maintains the tree property.

Property 3 (Subject Reduction of $\Vdash$). If $\Gamma \Vdash cn$ and $cn \rightarrow cn'$ then $\Gamma' \Vdash cn'$, where $\Gamma \subseteq \Gamma'$.

Proof (Sketch) The proof is by classical induction over the application of transition rules, and is detailed in an accompanying technical report [12]. The proof also ensures that any return-type and thus any future is not an object, i.e., its type is not an Act. More concretely, we never have $\Gamma(f) = $ Act.   □

Property 4 (Reduction Maintains Tree Property) Consider the type-system of our language modified according to Fig. 7 and extended to configurations.

$$(\Gamma \Vdash cn \wedge cn \rightarrow cn' \wedge \mathtt{Tree}(cn)) \quad \Longrightarrow \quad \mathtt{Tree}(cn')$$

Proof. This is due to the fact that the type system prevents the communication of an object reference to a newly created object or as method parameter, or as method result. In fact we prove by induction a stronger property:

$$(\Gamma \Vdash cn \wedge cn \rightarrow cn' \wedge \mathtt{Tree}(cn) \wedge \forall f(w) \in cn. \, w \neq \alpha)$$
$$\Longrightarrow \mathtt{Tree}(cn') \wedge \forall f(w) \in cn'. \, w \neq \alpha$$

INVK. Let $cn = \alpha_1(a_1, \{\ell_1 \mid x = v!m(\overline{v}) \; ; \; s_1\}_f, \overline{q_1}) \quad \alpha_2(a_2, p, \overline{q_2})$. We are given that $\mathtt{Tree}(cn)$, i.e., $\mathbf{refs}_{cn}(\alpha_1) \cap \mathbf{refs}_{cn}(\alpha_2) = \varnothing$, and $\Gamma \Vdash cn$, which implies $\Gamma_1 \Vdash_{T_1} v!m(\overline{v})$ for some Γ_1 and T_1. This further gives us by rule T-INVK that (i) $\Gamma_1 \Vdash_{T_1} v : \mathtt{Act}$, (ii) $\Gamma_1 \Vdash_{T_1} \overline{v} : \overline{T}$, (iii) $\Gamma(\mathtt{Act})(\mathtt{m}) = \overline{T} \rightarrow T'$, (iv) $\nexists \mathtt{ActB}. \, T' = \mathtt{ActB}$, and (v) $\forall v' \in \overline{v}. \, \Gamma'(\exists \mathtt{ActB}. \Vdash v' : \mathtt{ActB}) \Longrightarrow v' = \mathtt{null}$.

We are further given by rule INVK that $cn \rightarrow cn'$ and $cn' = \alpha_1(a_1, \{\ell_1 \mid x = f_m \; ; \; s_1\}_f, \overline{q_1})$ $\alpha_2(a_2, p, \overline{q_2}\#\{\ell_m \mid s_m\}_{f_m})$ where $[\![v]\!]_{a_1+\ell_1} = \alpha_2$ and $\alpha_2 \neq \alpha_1$, $[\![\overline{v}]\!]_{a_1+\ell_1} = \overline{w}$, $\mathsf{bind}(\alpha_2, m, \overline{w}) = \{\ell_m \mid s_m\}$, and f_m is fresh. Given (v) above, we have $\mathit{refs}(\ell_m) = \varnothing$; thus $\forall \gamma. \mathit{refs}(\gamma) \cap \mathit{refs}(\ell_m) = \varnothing$. This, together with $\mathsf{Tree}(cn)$, implies $\mathsf{Tree}(cn')$ because ℓ_m is the only new term in cn' that can contain references to active objects. Also $\forall f(w) \in cn'. w \neq \alpha$ because the set of resolved future is the same in cn and cn'.

RETURN. Let $cn = \alpha(a, \{\ell \mid \mathtt{return}\ e \; ; \; s\}_f, \overline{q})$. We are given that $\mathsf{Tree}(cn)$, and $\Gamma \Vdash cn$. We are further given by rule RETURN that $cn \rightarrow cn'$, where $cn' = \alpha(a, \varnothing, \overline{q})\ f(w)$ and $[\![e]\!]_{a+\ell} = w$. Since $\mathsf{Tree}(cn)$, it is easy to see that $\mathsf{Tree}(cn')$. By Property 3, we have $\Gamma' \Vdash cn'$ where $\Gamma \subseteq \Gamma'$ implying that $\Gamma' \Vdash w : \Gamma'(f)$, where $\Gamma'(f) = T$. From the remark on return-types in the proof of Property 3, it is clear a well-typed future can never be of any type Act, i.e., $\nexists \mathsf{Act}.T = \mathsf{Act}$. Since $f(w)$ is the only future that is changed, $\forall f(w) \in cn'. w \neq \alpha$ holds.

The remaining cases are straightforward.

□

Now, we can prove that the type system $\Vdash$ is sufficient to ensure the tree structure required for confluence.

Property 5 (Tree Structure). Consider the type-system of our language modified according to Fig. 7. If for a program P, $\Gamma \Vdash P$ then the execution of P verifies the conditions of the global confluence theorem, and P has a deterministic behaviour.

Proof. Consider cn_0 is the initial configuration for the program P, we can prove that $\forall cn. cn_0 \rightarrow^* cn \implies \mathsf{Tree}(cn)$. This is a direct consequence of Property 4 and of the fact that cn_0 forms a tree. By application of Property 2 we obtain global confluence.

□

It is easy to see that in the examples of Sect. 2, the master-worker example in Fig. 1 can be typed with our type system. On the other hand, the transmission of object references (Lines 27 and 28) in the map-reduce example in Fig. 2 makes it impossible to type with our type system. This reflects the fact that only the first one is deterministic.

Ensuring the confluence property in a more flexible way would require a more dynamic view of the object dependencies, for example by a more powerful static analysis or a linear type system that would allow the creator to forget a reference and send it to another object. These more dynamic systems are not studied in this article and left for future work.

6   Related Work

We review the closest related work and discuss how different actor calculi could be made partially confluent by following the approach advocated in this paper. Table 1 summarises the features of some of the languages we discuss, with respect to the key points that make our approach feasible in practice. FIFO channels are mandatory to ensure determinacy of communication between two given objects. Futures can be safely added to the language to handle responses to messages in a deterministic manner *provided they can only be accessed in a blocking manner.* In the following, when a language appears to us as a meaningful target for our approach, we explain briefly how our result is applicable. We consider that for the other languages, the decisions made in the design of the language are somehow contradictory with the principles of our approach.

Table 1. Deterministic characteristics for a few actor and active object languages.

Language	FIFO channels	Blocking future synchronisation	Cooperative scheduling
ProActive and ASP	YES	YES	NO
Rebeca	YES	NO	NO
AmbientTalk	NO	NO	NO
ABS	NO	YES	Non-deterministic
Encore	YES	YES	Non-deterministic
Akka	YES	Discouraged	Non-deterministic
Lustre with futures	YES	YES	NO

ProActive [13] uses active objects to implement remotely accessible, asynchronous objects. The ASP calculus [5] formalises the ProActive Java library. This paper also identifies partial confluence properties for active objects, which can be seen as a follow-up to [5], except that our futures are explicit, where ASP features implicit futures. Compared to the original work, the presented core language is more streamlined, making this contribution easier to adapt to many programming languages.

Applying our Approach to ProActive. This paper can be seen both as an extension of [5] and as an adaptation to explicit futures. Additionally we partially address cooperative scheduling via a restricted *await* primitive. We also identify a simple type system that allows us to ensure deterministic behaviour of programs.

Rebeca [9] and its variants mostly consist of actors communicating by asynchronous messages over FIFO queues, which makes model-checking for Rebeca programs less prone to state-explosion than most distributed systems [14]. Ensuring a tree structure of Rebeca actors would then be sufficient to guarantee deterministic behaviour; unfortunately the absence of futures in Rebeca forces callbacks to be used to transmit results of computations, and it is very challenging to maintain a tree-structure in the presence of callbacks.

AmbientTalk [15], based on the E Programming Language [16], implements an actor model with a communicating event-loop. It targets embedded systems and uses asynchronous reaction to future resolution, which prevents deadlocks at the price of more non-determinism, creating a race between the reaction to the future resolution and the rest of the computation in the same actor.

Creol [17] and languages inheriting from it, JCoBox [18], ABS [8] and Encore [10], rely on *cooperative scheduling* allowing the single execution thread of the active object to interrupt the service of one request and start (or recover) another at explicitly defined program points. A main difference between ABS and Encore is that the former is built upon Erlang [19] that does not ensure FIFO ordering of messages, while the latter is built upon Pony [20] that ensures causal ordering of messages. In addition, Encore supports an advanced capability-based type system [21] which enables race-free data sharing between active objects. Confluence properties for cooperative scheduling in ABS have previously been studied, based on controlling the local scheduler [22,23].

Applying our Approach to Languages à la *ABS*. ABS is a good candidate for our approach because of the numerous formal developments it supports. However, ABS features much less determinism than our core language because communications are unordered, and cooperative scheduling entails unpredictable interleaving between the treatment of different messages. For example, Encore is similar to ABS but already ensures FIFO ordering of messages, it would thus be easier to adapt our work to Encore.

Concerning cooperative scheduling in JCoBox, ABS and Encore, we can state that *await* on a future creates a non-blocking future access and should be proscribed if determinism is expected. Other *await* statements (on the internal state of an active object) can be kept in the language, but the cooperative scheduling policy has to be adapted to make it deterministic.

Futures are becoming increasingly mainstream and are now available through libraries in many languages, including Java, Scala, C++, and Rust. Akka [24,25] is a scalable library for actors on top of Java and Scala. Communication in Akka is FIFO which allows scheduling to be performed deterministically. Concerning return-values, Akka used to favour asynchronous reaction to future resolution which is not deterministic by nature. In the newest release, Akka 2.6.0, callbacks are the preferred strategy for returning values. By nature, callbacks entail a non-tree structure of object dependencies and create race-conditions between the handling of callbacks and of standard requests.

Lohstroh et al. [26] recently proposed a deterministic actor language. The key ingredient for determinism is the *logical timing* of messages based on a protocol which combines physical and logical timing to ensure determinacy. Unfortunately the resulting language is only deterministic when each message reaching the same actor is tagged with a different time, which may not be easy to ensure. Additionally, to the best of our knowledge, there is no proof of correctness of the used scheduling protocol and its adaptation to the context of the paper. We believe our approach could provide the right abstractions to prove correctness of such scheduling approaches for determinacy, adapting the proof of confluence provided in this paper and relating it to the scheduling protocol could prove the confluence property of [26].

Ownership type systems [27] can enforce a given object topology. Their application to active objects [28], especially inside the Encore language [10,21], ensures the separation between different memory spaces. Ownership types guarantee that each passive (or data) object is referenced by a single active object. Ownership types are in general adapted to enforce a tree topology, and these works could be extended to active objects so that their dependencies form a tree (and passive objects are still owned by a single active object). This significant extension of type systems is outside the scope of this paper but would allow more programs in our calculus to be accepted by the type checker and proven deterministic. Other modern type system features, especially linearity and borrowing [29], should also be considered for the same reasons. In particular we envisage the use of linear types and borrowing techniques to extend our results to computations where the tree structure of active objects may change over time.

Outside the actor community, the addition of futures in Lustre has been proposed in 2012 [30]. In this work, the authors provide an asynchronous computation primitive based on futures inside a synchronous language. As futures have good properties with respect to parallelism and determinism, they obtain a language that is equivalent to the synchronous language but with more parallelism. Our approach is very close to futures in Lustre for two reasons: firstly, both set up a programming model that ensure deterministic behaviour by using futures and asynchronous invocations, secondly, the way futures are encoded in Lustre corresponds in fact to an actor-like program where the dependency between actors form a tree and communication is over FIFO channels.

Applying our Approach to Lustre with Futures. We prove here that, in an asynchronous setting, futures in Lustre still have a deterministic behaviour (the same behaviour as synchronous programs). Additionally, our *await* primitive could be used in Lustre with future to enable cooperative scheduling.

7   Conclusion

This paper has given guidelines on how to implement deterministic active objects and ensure that in any given framework a program behaves deterministically if this is desired. We formalised a basic active object calculus where communication between objects is performed by asynchronous method invocations on FIFO channels, replies by means of futures, and synchronisation by a blocking wait on future access. We added a deterministic cooperative scheduling policy, allowing a thread to be suspended and recovered *depending on the internal state of the object*. These conditions are the necessary prerequisites for our approach to be applicable; in such system we identify precisely the possible races. Our first result can be summarised as: *in our calculus the only source of non-determinacy is the concurrent sending of messages from two active objects to the same third one.* Then we showed that with the given semantics we can design a type system that ensure determinacy of results by enforcing a tree structure for objects. For example, if the active objects were using a communication library ensuring FIFO ordering and deterministic scheduling, our type system would ensure that the correctly typed active objects using this library behave deterministically.

The current results are still restrictive in the programs that can be expressed and the rigidity of its properties; however, we believe that we have a minimal and reliable basis for further studies. In the future, we plan to introduce more dynamic trees for example using linearity and borrowing types, but also primitive to attach and detach tree to the object dependence graph, in order to constantly ensure a tree structure, but allow the structure of the tree to evolve at runtime.

References

1. de Boer, F., et al.: A survey of active object languages. ACM Comput. Surv. **50**(5), 76:1–76:39 (2017)
2. Baker Jr., H.G., Hewitt, C.: The incremental garbage collection of processes. In: Proceedings of the Symposium on Artificial Intelligence and Programming Languages, pp. 55–59. ACM (1977)
3. Agha, G.: Actors: A Model of Concurrent Computation in Distributed Systems. MIT Press (1986)
4. Torres Lopez, C., Marr, S., Gonzalez Boix, E., Mössenböck, H.: A study of concurrency bugs and advanced development support for actor-based programs. In: Ricci, A., Haller, P. (eds.) Programming with Actors. LNCS, vol. 10789, pp. 155–185. Springer, Cham (2018). https://doi.org/10.1007/978-3-030-00302-9_6
5. Caromel, D., Henrio, L., Serpette, B.: Asynchronous and deterministic objects. In: Proceedings of the 31st ACM SIGPLAN-SIGACT Symposium on Principles of Programming Languages, pp. 123–134. ACM Press (2004)
6. Fernandez-Reyes, K., Clarke, D., Henrio, L., Johnsen, E.B., Wrigstad, T.: Godot: all the benefits of implicit and explicit futures. In: Proceedings of the 33rd European Conference on Object-Oriented Programming (ECOOP 2019). LIPIcs, vol. 134, pp. 2:1–2:28. Schloss Dagstuhl - Leibniz-Zentrum für Informatik (2019)
7. de Boer, F.S., Clarke, D., Johnsen, E.B.: A complete guide to the future. In: De Nicola, R. (ed.) ESOP 2007. LNCS, vol. 4421, pp. 316–330. Springer, Heidelberg (2007). https://doi.org/10.1007/978-3-540-71316-6_22
8. Johnsen, E.B., Hähnle, R., Schäfer, J., Schlatte, R., Steffen, M.: ABS: a core language for abstract behavioral specification. In: Aichernig, B.K., de Boer, F.S., Bonsangue, M.M. (eds.) FMCO 2010. LNCS, vol. 6957, pp. 142–164. Springer, Heidelberg (2011). https://doi.org/10.1007/978-3-642-25271-6_8
9. Sirjani, M., de Boer, F.S., Movaghar-Rahimabadi, A.: Modular verification of a component-based actor language. J. Univ. Comput. Sci. **11**(10), 1695–1717 (2005)
10. Brandauer, S., et al.: Parallel objects for multicores: a glimpse at the parallel language ENCORE. In: Bernardo, M., Johnsen, E.B. (eds.) SFM 2015. LNCS, vol. 9104, pp. 1–56. Springer, Cham (2015). https://doi.org/10.1007/978-3-319-18941-3_1
11. Caromel, D., Henrio, L.: A Theory of Distributed Objects. Springer, Heidelberg (2004)
12. Henrio, L., Johnsen, E.B., Pun, K.I.: Active Objects with Deterministic Behaviour (long version). Research Report 8, Western Norway University of Applied Sciences (2020)
13. Baduel, L., et al.: Programming, composing, deploying for the grid. In: Cunha, J.C., Rana, O.F. (eds.) Grid Computing: Software Environments and Tools, pp. 205–229. Springer, London (2006). https://doi.org/10.1007/1-84628-339-6_9
14. Jaghoori, M.M., Sirjani, M., Mousavi, M.R., Khamespanah, E., Movaghar, A.: Symmetry and partial order reduction techniques in model checking Rebeca. Acta Informatica **47**(1), 33–66 (2010)

15. Dedecker, J., Van Cutsem, T., Mostinckx, S., D'Hondt, T., De Meuter, W.: Ambient-oriented programming in ambienttalk. In: Thomas, D. (ed.) ECOOP 2006. LNCS, vol. 4067, pp. 230–254. Springer, Heidelberg (2006). https://doi.org/10.1007/11785477_16

16. Miller, M.S., Tribble, E.D., Shapiro, J.: Concurrency among strangers. In: De Nicola, R., Sangiorgi, D. (eds.) TGC 2005. LNCS, vol. 3705, pp. 195–229. Springer, Heidelberg (2005). https://doi.org/10.1007/11580850_12

17. Johnsen, E.B., Owe, O.: An asynchronous communication model for distributed concurrent objects. Softw. Syst. Model. 6(1), 35–58 (2007)

18. Schäfer, J., Poetzsch-Heffter, A.: JCoBox: generalizing active objects to concurrent components. In: D'Hondt, T. (ed.) ECOOP 2010. LNCS, vol. 6183, pp. 275–299. Springer, Heidelberg (2010). https://doi.org/10.1007/978-3-642-14107-2_13

19. Armstrong, J.: Programming Erlang: Software for a Concurrent World. Pragmatic Bookshelf Series. Pragmatic Bookshelf (2007)

20. Clebsch, S., Drossopoulou, S., Blessing, S., McNeil, A.: Deny capabilities for safe, fast actors. In: Proceedings of the 5th International Workshop on Programming Based on Actors, Agents, and Decentralized Control, AGERE 2015, pp. 1–12. Association for Computing Machinery, New York (2015)

21. Castegren, E., Wrigstad, T.: Reference capabilities for concurrency control. In: Proceedings of the 30th European Conference on Object-Oriented Programming (ECOOP 2016). LIPIcs, vol. 56, pp. 5:1–5:26. Schloss Dagstuhl - Leibniz-Zentrum für Informatik (2016)

22. Bezirgiannis, N., de Boer, F., Johnsen, E.B., Pun, K.I., Tapia Tarifa, S.L.: Implementing SOS with active objects: a case study of a multicore memory system. In: Hähnle, R., van der Aalst, W. (eds.) FASE 2019. LNCS, vol. 11424, pp. 332–350. Springer, Cham (2019). https://doi.org/10.1007/978-3-030-16722-6_20

23. Tveito, L., Johnsen, E.B., Schlatte, R.: Global reproducibility through local control for distributed active objects. In: Wehrheim H., Cabot J. (eds.) FASE 2020. LNCS, vol. 12076, pp. 140–160. Springer, Cham (2020). https://doi.org/10.1007/978-3-030-45234-6_7

24. Haller, P., Odersky, M.: Scala actors: unifying thread-based and event-based programming. Theoret. Comput. Sci. 410(2–3), 202–220 (2009)

25. Wyatt, D.: Akka Concurrency. Artima (2013)

26. Lohstroh, M., Lee, E.A.: Deterministic actors. In: 2019 Forum for Specification and Design Languages, FDL 2019, Southampton, United Kingdom, September 2–4, 2019, pp. 1–8. IEEE (2019)

27. Clarke, D., Noble, J., Wrigstad, T. (eds.): Aliasing in Object-Oriented Programming. Types, Analysis and Verification. LNCS, vol. 7850. Springer, Heidelberg (2013). https://doi.org/10.1007/978-3-642-36946-9

28. Clarke, D., Wrigstad, T., Östlund, J., Johnsen, E.B.: Minimal ownership for active objects. In: Ramalingam, G. (ed.) APLAS 2008. LNCS, vol. 5356, pp. 139–154. Springer, Heidelberg (2008). https://doi.org/10.1007/978-3-540-89330-1_11

29. Haller, P., Odersky, M.: Capabilities for uniqueness and borrowing. In: D'Hondt, T. (ed.) ECOOP 2010. LNCS, vol. 6183, pp. 354–378. Springer, Heidelberg (2010). https://doi.org/10.1007/978-3-642-14107-2_17

30. Cohen, A., Gérard, L., Pouzet, M.: Programming parallelism with futures in Lustre. In: ACM International Conference on Embedded Software (EMSOFT 2012), Tampere, Finland. ACM, October 7–12, 2012. Best paper award

History-Based Specification and Verification of Java Collections in KeY

Hans-Dieter A. Hiep[(✉)][iD], Jinting Bian[(✉)], Frank S. de Boer[(✉)], and Stijn de Gouw[(✉)]

CWI, Science Park 123, 1098 XG Amsterdam, The Netherlands
{hdh,j.bian,frb,stijn.de.gouw}@cwi.nl

Abstract. In this feasibility study we discuss reasoning about the correctness of Java interfaces using histories, with a particular application to Java's `Collection` interface. We introduce a new specification method (in the KeY theorem prover) using histories, that record method invocations including their parameters and return value, on an interface. We outline the challenges of proving client code correct with respect to arbitrary implementations, and describe a practical specification and verification effort of part of the `Collection` interface using KeY (including source and video material).

Keywords: Formal verification · Interface specification · KeY

1 Introduction

Throughout the history of computer science, a major challenge has been how to assert that software is free of bugs and works as intended. In particular, correctness of software libraries is of the utmost importance because these are the building blocks of millions of programs, and they run on the devices of billions of users. Formal verification gives precise, mathematical proof of correctness of software, with respect to specifications of intended behavior expressed in formal logic. Formal verification can guarantee correctness of software (as opposed, for instance, to testing) but can be challenging in practice, as it frequently requires significant effort in specification writing and constructing proof.

Such effort can very well pay off, as is clearly demonstrated by the use of formal methods which led to the discovery of a major flaw in the design of TimSort—a crash caused by indexing an array out of bounds. TimSort is the default sorting library in many widely-used programming languages such as Java and Python, and platforms like Android. A fixed version, which is now used in all these platforms, was derived and has been proven correct [10] using KeY, a state-of-the-art theorem proving technology [1]. Use of formal methods further led to the discovery of some major flaws in the `LinkedList` implementation provided by Java's Collection Framework—erratic behavior caused by an integer overflow. A fixed version of the core methods of the linked list implementation in Java has also been formally proven correct using KeY [11].

© Springer Nature Switzerland AG 2020
B. Dongol and E. Troubitsyna (Eds.): IFM 2020, LNCS 12546, pp. 199–217, 2020.
https://doi.org/10.1007/978-3-030-63461-2_11

However, some of the methods of the linked list implementation contain an interface type as parameter and were out of scope of the work in [11]. As example we could take the `retainAll` method. Verification of `LinkedList`'s implementation of `retainAll` requires the verification of the inherited `retainAll` method from `AbstractCollection`. The implementation in `AbstractCollection` (see Listing 1) shows a difficult method to verify: the methody body implements an interface method, acts as a client of the supplied `Collection` instance by calling `contains`, but it also acts as a client of the `this` instance by calling `iterator`. Moreover, as `AbstractCollection` is an abstract class and does not provide a concrete implementation of the interface, implementing `iterator` is left to a subclass such as `LinkedList`. Thus arises the need for an approach to specify interfaces which allows us to verify its (abstract) implementations and its clients.

```
public boolean retainAll(Collection c) {
    boolean modified = false;
    Iterator it = iterator();
    while (it.hasNext())
        if (!c.contains(it.next())) {
            it.remove();
            modified = true;
        }
    return modified;
}
```

Listing 1. A difficult method to verify: `retainAll` in `AbstractCollection`.

More generally, libraries form the basis of the "programming to interfaces" discipline, which is one of the most important principles in software engineering. Interfaces abstract from state and other internal implementation details, and aids modular program development. However, tool-supported programming logics and specification languages are predominantly state-based which as such cannot be directly used for interfaces. The main contribution of this paper is to show the feasibility of an approach which overcomes this limitation, by integrating history-based reasoning with existing specification and verification methods. This work is the next step towards our ultimate goal of completely specifying and verifying complex software libraries such as the Java Collection Framework, including its `LinkedList` class and `addAll`, `removeAll` and `retainAll` methods.

The formal semantic justification of our approach is provided by the fully abstract semantics for Java introduced in [15] which characterizes exactly the minimal information about a method implementation in a class in a Java library that captures its external use. This minimal information consists of *histories* (also called *traces*) of method calls and returns, and provides a formal semantic justification of the basic observation that such histories completely determine the concrete state of any implementation and thus can be viewed as constituting the generic abstract state space of an interface. This observation naturally leads to the development of a history-based specification language for interfaces.

The background of our approach is given in Sect. 2. An important use case, which leads us to formal requirements on interface specifications, is to reason about the correctness of clients, viz. programs that use instances of an interface by calling methods on it. In Sect. 3 we analyze concrete examples that motivates the design choices that leads us to the core of our approach: we associate to each instance of an interface a history that represents the sequence of method calls performed on the object since its creation. For each method call, the parameters and return value are recorded symbolically in the history. This crucially allows us to define abstractions over histories, called *attributes*, used to describe all possible behaviors of objects regardless of its implementation.

Our methodology is to embed histories and attributes in the KeY theorem prover [1] by encoding them as Java objects, thereby avoiding the need to change the KeY system itself. Interface specifications can then be written in the state-based specification language JML [13] by referring to histories and its attributes to describe the intended behavior of implementations. This methodology is described in Sect. 4. Further, a distinguishing feature of histories is that they support a *history-based reference implementation* for each interface which is defined in a systematic manner. This allows an important application of our methodology: the verification of the satisfiability of interface specifications themselves. This is done for part of the `Collection` interface in Sect. 5. We provide source and video material of the verification effort to make the construction of the proofs fully reproducible.

We now discuss related work. It can be empirically established that Java libraries, and Java's Collection Framework in particular, are heavily used and have many implementations [8]. Recently, several issues with parts of the Collection Framework were revealed [10,11]. Such issues are hard to discover at run-time due to their heap size requirements, necessitating a static approach to analysis. Static verification of the Collection Framework was already initiated almost two decades ago, see e.g. the work by Huisman *et al.* [12,14]. What complicates static verification is that it requires formal specifications. Two known approaches are by Huisman [12] and Knüppel *et al.* [16], but their specifications are not complete nor demonstrate the verification of various clients and implementations. Generally speaking, there seems to be no obvious strategy in specifying Java interfaces so that its clients and its implementations can be verified statically by means of a theorem prover. However, for the purpose of run-time verification, numerous approaches exist to specify and check Java programs, such as [3–6]. Most of these approaches are based on histories. LARVA [7], a tool also mainly developed for run-time verification, was extended in e.g. [2] to optimize away checks at run-time that can be established statically. But, there, static guarantees are limited by expressivity (no fully-fledged theorem prover is used) and interfaces are not handled by the static analysis. Closest to the nature of this work is [17] by Welsch and Poetzsch-Heffter, who reason about backwards compatibility of Java libraries in a formal manner using histories to capture and compare the externally observable behavior of two libraries. In [17], however, two programs are compared, and not a program against a formal specification.

2   Background

In this section, we first provide the context of our work on history-based specification and verification, by giving an overview of the relevant basic concepts, followed by a brief overview of the specification language JML and theorem prover KeY, which are used to realize our approach.

At the lowest level of abstraction, a history is a sequence of events. So the question arises: what events does it contain, and how are the events related to a given program? To concretize this, we first note that in our setting we focus on histories for single-threaded object-oriented programs, and classes and interfaces of Java libraries in particular. For such programs, there are two main kinds of histories: (a) a single global history for the entire program, and (b) a local history *per object*. The first kind, a global history, does not result in a modular specification and verification approach: such a history is specific to a particular program and thus cannot be reused in other programs, since as soon as other objects or classes are added this affects the global history. A global history is therefore not suitable for specifying and verifying Java libraries, since libraries are reused in many different client programs. Hence, in our setting, we tend towards using a local history for each object separately.[1]

Following the concept of information hiding, we assume that an object encapsulates its own state, i.e. other objects cannot directly access its fields, but only indirectly by calling methods. This is not a severe limitation: one can introduce getter and setter methods rather than reading and writing a field directly. But this assumption is crucial to enable any kind of (sound) reasoning about objects: if objects do not encapsulate their own state, any other object that has a reference to it can simply modify the values of the fields directly in a malicious fashion where the new internal state breaks the class invariant of the object[2] without the object being able to prevent (or even being aware of) this.

Assuming encapsulation, each object has full control over its own internal state, it can enforce invariants over its own fields and its state can be completely determined by the sequence of method calls invoked on the object. How an object realizes the intended behavior of each method may differ per implementation: to a client of the object, the internal method body is of no concern, including any calls to other objects that may be done in the method body. We name the calls that an object invokes on other objects inside a method outgoing calls (their direction is out of the object, into another object), and we name the calls made to the object on methods it exposes incoming calls. The above discussion makes clear that the semantics of an object-oriented program can be described purely in terms of its behavior on incoming method calls. Indeed, formally, this is confirmed by Jeffrey and Rathke's work [15] which presents a fully abstract semantics for Java based on traces.

---

[1] A more sophisticated approach will be introduced for inner classes (see Sect. 3).

[2] Roughly speaking, a class invariant is a property that all objects of the class must satisfy before and after every method call. Class invariants typically express consistency properties of the object.

KeY and JML. KeY [1] is a semi-interactive theorem prover for Java programs (typically $> 95\%$ of the proof steps are automated). The input for KeY is a Java program together with a formal specification in a KeY-dialect of JML. The user proves the specifications method-by-method. KeY generates appropriate proof obligations and expresses them in a sequent calculus, where the formulas inside the sequent are multi-modal dynamic logic formulas in which Java program fragments are used as the modalities. To reduce such dynamic logic formulas to first-order formulas, KeY symbolically executes the Java program in the modality (it has rules for nearly all sequential Java constructs). Once the program is fully symbolically executed, only formulas without Java program fragments remain.

JML, the Java Modeling Language [13], is a specification language for Java that supports the design by contract paradigm. Specifications are embedded as Java comments alongside the program. A method precondition in JML is given by a **requires** clause, and a postcondition is given by **ensures**. JML also supports class invariants. A class invariant is a property that all instances of a class should satisfy. In the design by contract setting, each method is proven in isolation (assuming the contracts of methods that it calls), and the class invariant can be assumed in the precondition and must be established in the postcondition, as well as at all call-sites to other methods. To avoid manually adding the class invariant at all these points, JML provides an **invariant** keyword which implicitly conjoins the class invariant to all pre- and postconditions. Method contracts may also contain an **assignable** clause stating the locations that may be changed by the method (if the precondition is satisfied), and an **accessible** clause that expresses the locations that may be read by the method (if the precondition is satisfied). Our approach uses all of the above concepts.

Our methodology is based on a symbolic representation of histories. We encode histories as Java objects to avoid modifying the KeY system and thus avoid the risk of introducing an inconsistency. Such representation allows the expression of relations between different method calls and their parameters and return values, by implementing abstractions over histories, called *attributes*, as Java methods. These abstractions are specified using JML.

3   Specification and Verification Challenges for Collection

In this section, we highlight several specification and verification challenges with histories that occur in real-world programs. We guide our discussion with examples based on Collection, the central interface of the Java Collection Framework. However, note that our approach, and methodology in general, can be applied to all interfaces, as our discussion can be generalized from Collection.

A collection contains elements of type Object and can be manipulated independently of its implementation details. Typical manipulations are adding and removing elements, and checking whether it contains an element. Sub-interfaces of Collection may have refined behavior. In case of interface List, each element is also associated to a unique position. In case of interface Set, every element is contained at most once. Further, collections are extensible: interfaces can also be implemented by programs outside of the Java Collection Framework.

How do we specify and verify interface methods using histories?
We focus our discussion on the core methods add, remove, contains, and
iterator of the Collection interface. These four methods comprise the events
of our history. More precisely, we have at least the following events:

- add(o) = b,
- remove(o) = b,
- contains(o) = b,
- iterator() = i,

where o is an element, b is a Boolean return value indicating the success of the
method, and i is an object implementing Iterator. Abstracting from the implementations of these methods we can still *compute* the contents of a collection
from the history of its add and remove events; the other events do not change the
contents. This computation results in a representation of the contents of a collection by a multiset of objects. For each object its multiplicity then equals the
number of successful add events minus the number of successful remove events.
Thus, the contents of a collection (represented by a multiset) is an attribute.

For example, for two separate elements o and o',
$$\text{add}(o) = \textbf{true}, \text{ add}(o') = \textbf{true}, \text{ add}(o') = \textbf{false}, \text{ remove}(o') = \textbf{true}$$
is a history of some collection (where the left-most event happens first). The
multiplicity of o in the multiset attribute of this history is 1 (there is one successful add event), and the multiplicity of o' is 0 (there is one successful add
event, and one successful remove event).

The main idea is to associate each instance to its own history. Consequently,
we can use the multiset attribute in method contracts. For example, we can
state that the add method ensures that after returning **true** the multiplicity of
its argument is increased by one, that the contains method returns **true** when
the argument is contained (i.e. its multiplicity is positive), and that the remove
method ensures that the multiplicity of a contained object is decreased by one.

How can we specify and verify client-side properties of interfaces?
Consider the client program in Listing 2, where x is a Collection and y is an
Object. To specify the behavior of this program fragment, we could now use the
multiset attribute to express that the contents of the Collection instance x is
not affected.

```
if (x.add(y)) x.remove(y);
```

Listing 2. Adding and removing an element does not affect contents.

Another example of this challenge is shown in Listing 3: can we prove the termination of a client? For an arbitrary collection, it is possible to obtain an object
that can traverse the collection: this is an instance of the Iterator interface containing the core methods hasNext and next. To check whether the traversal is
still on-going, we use hasNext. Subsequently, a call to next returns an object
that is an element of the backing collection, and continues the traversal. Finally,
if all objects of the collection are traversed, hasNext returns false.

```
Iterator it = x.iterator();
while (it.hasNext()) it.next();
```

Listing 3. Iterating over the collection.

How do we deal with intertwined object behaviors?

Since an iterator by its very nature directly accesses the internal representation of the collection it was obtained from[3], the behavior of the collection and its iterator(s) are intertwined: to specify and reason about collections with iterators a notion of *ownership* is needed. The behavior of the iterator itself depends on the collection from which it was created.

How do we deal with non-local behavior in a modular fashion?

Consider the example in Listing 4, where the collection x is assumed non-empty. We obtain an iterator and its call to next succeeds (because x is non-empty). Consequently, we perform the calls as in Listing 2: this leaves the collection with the same elements as before the calls to add and remove. However, the iterator may become invalidated by a call that modifies the collection; then the iterator it is no longer valid, and we should not call any methods on it—doing so throws an exception.

```
Iterator it = x.iterator(); it.next();
if (x.add(y)) x.remove(y); // may invalidate iterator it
```

Listing 4. Invalidating an iterator by modifying the owning collection.

Invalidation of an iterator is the result of non-local behavior: the expected behavior of the iterator depends on the methods called on its owning collection and also all other iterators associated to the same collection. The latter is true since the Iterator interface also has a remove method (to allow the in-place removal of an element) which should invalidate all other iterators. Moreover, a successful method call to add or remove (or any mutating method) on the collection invalidates all its iterators.

We can resolve both phenomena by generalizing the above notion of a history, strictly local to a single object, without introducing interference. We take the iterator to be a 'subobject' of a collection: the methods invoked on the iterator are recorded in the history of its owning collection. More precisely, we also have the following events recorded in the history of Collection:

- hasNext$(i) = b$,
- next$(i) = o$,
- remove(i),

where b is a Boolean return value indicating the success of the method, and i is an iterator object. Now, not only can we express what the contents of a collection

---

[3] To iterate over the content of a collection, iterators are typically implemented as so-called inner classes that have direct access to the fields of the enclosing object.

is at the moment the iterator is created and its methods are called, but we can also define the validity of an iterator as an attribute of the history of the owning collection.

4   History-Based Specification in KeY

We start with an overview of our methodology: through what framework can we see the different concepts involved? The goal is to specify interface method contracts using histories. This is done in a number of steps:

1. We introduce histories by Java classes that represent the inductive data type of sequences of events, and we introduce attributes of histories encoded by static Java methods. These attributes are defined inductively over the structure of a history. The attributes are used within the interface method contracts (of `Collection`) to specify the intended behavior of every implementation (of `Collection`) in terms of history attributes.
2. Attributes are deterministic and thus represent a function. Certain logical properties of and between attributes hold, comparable to an equational specification of attributes. These are represented by the method contracts associated to the static Java methods that encode the attributes.
3. Finally, we append an event to a history by creating a new history object in a static factory method. The new object consists of the new event as head, and the old history object as tail. The contract for these static methods also expresses certain logical properties of and between attributes, of the new history related to the old history.

The main motivation of our methodology is derived from the fact that the KeY theorem prover uses the Java Modeling Language as the specification language and that both JML and the KeY system do not have built-in support for specification of interfaces using histories. Instead of extending JML and KeY, we introduce Java encodings of histories that can be used for the specification of the `Collection` interface, which as such can also be used by other tools [4].

Remark 1. JML supports model fields which are used to define an abstract state and its representation in terms of the concrete state given (by the fields) in a concrete class. For clients, only the interface type `Collection` is known rather than a concrete class, and thus a represents clause cannot be defined. Ghost variables cannot be used either, since ghost variables are updated by adding set statements in method bodies and interfaces do not have method bodies. What remains are model methods, which we use as our specification technique.

4.1   The `History` Class for `Collection`

In principle our histories are a simple inductive data type of a sequence of events. Inductive data types are convenient for defining attributes by induction. However, no direct support for inductive definitions is given in either Java or KeY.

Thus, we encode histories by defining a concrete `History` class in Java itself, specifically for `Collection`. The externally observable behavior of any implementation of the `Collection` interface is then represented by an instance of the `History` class, and specific attributes (e.g., patterns) of this behavior are specified by pure methods (which do not affect the global state of the given program under analysis). Every instance represents a particular history value.

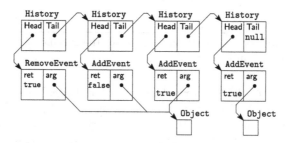

Fig. 1. A number of history objects. The left-most represents the history of a collection in which **add** is called three times followed by a remove. Intuitively, this history captures the behavior of a set (the addition of an object already contained returns **false**).

The `History` class implements a singly-linked list data structure: a history consists of a head `Event` and a tail `History`. The class `Event` has sub-classes, one for each method of the `Collection` interface. Moreover, there are sub-classes for each method of the `Iterator` interface that additionally track the iterator instance sub-objects. These events are also part of the history of a `Collection`. See Fig. 1 and Listing 5.

Each sub-class of the `Event` class comprises the corresponding method's arguments and return value as data. For the `Collection` interface we have the events: `AddEvent`, `RemoveEvent`, `ContainsEvent`, `IteratorEvent`. `AddEvent` has an `Object` field `arg` for the method argument, and a Boolean field `ret` for the return value, that corresponds to the method declaration of `boolean add(Object)`. `RemoveEvent` and `ContainsEvent` are similar. `IteratorEvent` has an `Object` field `ret` for the return value, for `Iterator iterator()`, which is seen as a creation event for the iterator sub-object.

For the `Iterator` interface we have the events: `IteratorHasNextEvent`, `IteratorNextEvent`, `IteratorRemoveEvent`. `IteratorHasNextEvent` has a field `inst` for the sub-object instance of `Iterator`, and a Boolean field `ret` for the return value, that corresponds to the method declaration of `boolean hasNext()`. `IteratorNextEvent` has an instance field and an `Object` field `ret`, corresponding to the method declaration `Object next()`. `IteratorRemoveEvent` only has an instance field, since `void remove()` returns nothing.

```
public class History {
    Event Head; /*@ nullable @*/ History Tail; /*@ ghost int length; @*/
    // (attributes and their method contracts...)
    // (factory methods... e.g.)
    /*@ pure */ static History addEvent(/*@ nullable */ History h,
            /*@ nullable */ Object o, boolean ret) {
        return new History(new AddEvent(o, ret), h);
    }
}
```

Listing 5. The `History` class structure. Later on, the specification of the `addEvent` factory method is given in Listing 10.

Remark 2. As part of the `History` class, we define *footprint()* as a JML model method. The footprint of a history is a particular set of heap locations; if those locations are not modified then the value of attributes of the history remains unchanged. In our case, the footprint is the set of fields of events and the singly-linked history list, but we do not include in our footprint the fields of the objects that are elements of the collection, since those never influence any attribute value of a history (we never cast elements of a collection to a specific sub-class to access its fields).

We treat the history as an immutable data type[4]: once an object is created, its fields are never modified. History updates are encoded by the creation of a new history, with an additional new event as head, pointing to the old history as tail. Immutability allows us to lift any computed attribute of a history in some heap over heap modifications that do not affect the footprint of the given history. This turns out to be crucial in verifying that an implementation is correct with respect to interface method contracts, where we update a history to reflect that an incoming method call was performed. Such a contract expresses a particular relation between the history's attributes in the heap before and after object creation and history update: the value of an attribute of the old history in the heap before remains the same in the heap after these heap modifications.

4.2 Attributes of `History`

To avoid tying ourselves to a particular history representation, the linked list of events in the history itself is not exposed and cannot be used in specifications. Rather, the history is accessed exclusively through "observer symbols", also called "query methods", that map the history to a value. Such observer symbols we call *attributes*. Attributes are defined as **strictly pure** methods, since their computation cannot affect the heap. Strictly pure methods are also easier to work with than non-strict or non-pure methods, especially when these methods are used in specifications of the `Collection` interface: these methods evaluate in one heap without modifying it.

---

[4] By immutable, we mean an object for which its fields after construction are never modified, and its reference type fields point only to immutable objects.

The advantage of the use of KeY is that pure methods that appear in specifications as observer symbols can be translated into a modal JavaDL expression, and this allows, more generally, reasoning about pure methods [9]. The rule in the proof system, that replaces observer symbols associated to pure method by a modal expression that expresses the result of a separate symbolic execution of calling the method, is called *query evaluation* [1, Sect. 11.4].

Attributes are defined inductively over the history. In order to prove their termination we also introduce a ghost field *length* that represents the length of the history. A ghost field logically assigns to each object a value used for the purpose of verification, but is not present at run-time. In each call on the tail of the history its length decreases, and the length is always positive, thus realizing a so-called decreasing term.

Attributes are functions of the history. Functionality of an attribute amounts to showing dependence (only on the footprint of a history), determinism (uniqueness of result) and termination. To verify that an attribute is deterministic involves two steps: we first symbolically execute the method body, until we obtain a proof obligation in which we have to show that the post-condition holds. The post-condition consequently contains, as observer symbol, the same method applied to the same formal parameters: we use query evaluation to perform *another* symbolic execution of the same method. We need to prove that their outcomes are identical, to verify that the method is deterministic. Not every method can be proven to be deterministic: e.g. if a method body contains a call to a method that cannot be unfolded and that has an unspecified result, then the two symbolic executions (first directly, and secondly through an evaluated query of the observer symbol) need not pick the same result in each method call.

Contents of a `Collection`: The multiset attribute of a `Collection` represents its content and is defined inductively over the structure of the history: the events corresponding to a successful `add` and `remove` call of the `Collection` interface increase and decrease the multiplicity of their argument. Note that removing an element never brings it down to a negative multiplicity. Moreover, `remove` of the `Iterator` interface also decreases the multiplicity; but no longer an argument is supplied because the removed element is the return value the previous `next` call of the corresponding iterator sub-object. Thus, we define an attribute for each iterator that denotes the object returned by the last `next` call. Calling `remove` on an iterator without a preceding `next` call is not allowed, so neither is calling `remove` consecutively multiple times.

```
/*@ normal_behavior
  @ requires h != null && \invariant_for(h);
  @ ensures \result == History.Multiset(h,o) && \result >= 0;
  @ measured_by h.length;
  @ accessible h.footprint(); // dependency contract
  @*/
/*@ strictly_pure */ static int Multiset(
      /*@ nullable */ History h, /*@ nullable */ Object o) {
   if (h == null) return 0;
```

```
    else {
        int c = History.Multiset(h.Tail, o);
        if (h.Head instanceof AddEvent &&
            ((AddEvent) h.Head).arg == o &&
            ((AddEvent) h.Head).ret == true) { // important
            return c + 1;
        } else ...
        return c;
} }
```

Listing 6. Part of `Multiset` method of the `History` class, with one JML contract.

Listing 6 shows part of the implementation of the *Multiset* attribute that is computed by the `Multiset` static method. It is worthwile to observe that `AddEvent` is counted only when its result is **true**. This makes it possible to compute the *Multiset* attribute based on the history: if the return value is omitted, one cannot be certain whether an add has affected the contents. With this design, further refinements can be made into lists and sets.

Iterating over a `Collection`: Once an iterator is obtained from a collection, the elements of the collection can be retrieved one by one. If the `Collection` is subsequently modified, the iterator becomes invalidated. An exception to this rule is if the iterator instance itself directly modifies the collection, i.e. with its own `Iterator.remove()` method (instead of `Collection.remove(Object)`): calling that method invalidates all *other* iterators. We have added an attribute *Valid* that is true exactly for iterators that are valid (definition omitted).

For each iterator, there is another multiset attribute, *Visit* (definition omitted), that tracks the multiplicities of the objects already visited. Intuitively, this visited attribute is used to specify the **next** method of an iterator. Namely, **next** returns an element that had not yet been visited. Calling `Iterator.next` increases the *Visit* multiplicity of the returned object by one and leaves all other element multiplicities the same. Intuitively, the iterator increases the size of its *Visit* multiset attribute during traversal, until it completely covers the whole collection, represented by the *Multiset* attribute: then the iterator terminates.

Although these two attributes are useful in defining an implementation of an iterator, they are less useful in showing client-side correctness of code that uses an iterator. To show termination of a client that iterates over a collection, we introduce two *derived* attributes: *CollectionSize* and *IteratorSize*. One can think of the collection's size as a sum of the multiplicties of all elements, and similar for an iterator size of its visited multiset.

4.3   The Collection interface

```
public interface Collection {
    /*@ model_behavior
    @ requires true;
    @ model nullable History history();
    @*/
    // (interface methods and their method contracts ...)
}
```

Listing 7. The *history*() model method of the Collection interface.

The Collection interface has an associated history that is retrieved by an abstract model method called *history*(). This model method is used in the contracts for the interface methods, to specify what relation must hold of the attribute values of the history in the heap before and after executing the interface method.

As a typical example we show the specification of the **add** method in terms of the *Multiset* attribute of the new history (after the call) and the old history (prior to the call). The specification of **add** closely corresponds to the informal Javadoc specification written above it. Similar contracts are given for the **remove**, **contains**, and **iterator** methods. In each contract, we implicitly assume a single event is added to the history corresponding to a method call on the interface. The assignable clause is important, as it rules out implementations from modifying its past history: this ensures that the attributes of the old history object in the heap before executing the method have the same value in the heap after the method finished execution.

```
/** Ensures that this collection contains the specified element (optional
 * operation). Returns true if this collection changed as a result of the call.
 * Returns false if this collection does not permit duplicates and already
 * contains the specified element. ... **/
/*@ public normal_behavior
@ ensures history() != null;
@ ensures History.Multiset(history(),o) ==
      History.Multiset(\old(history()), o) + (\result ? 1 : 0);
@ ensures History.Multiset(history(),o) > 0;
@ ensures (\forall Object o1; o1 != o; History.Multiset(history(),o1) ==
      History.Multiset(\old(history()), o1));
@ assignable \set_minus(\everything, (history() == null) ? \empty :
      history().footprint());
@*/
boolean add( /*@ nullable */ Object o);
```

Listing 8. The use of *Multiset* in the specification of **add** in the Collection interface.

It is important to note that the value of \result is unspecified. The intended meaning of the result is that it is **true** if the collection is modified. There are at least two implementations: that of a set, and that of a list. For a set, the result is **false** if the multiplicity prior to the call is positive, for a list the result is always **true**. Thus it is not possible to specify the result any further in the `Collection` interface that is compatible with both `Set` and `List` sub-interfaces. In particular, consider the following refinements [1, Sect. 7.4.5] of `add`:

- The `Set` interface *also* specifies that $\backslash result$ is **true** if and only if the multiset attribute before execution of the method is zero, i.e.
  ensures $History.Multiset(\backslash old(history()), o) == 0 \iff \backslash result == $ **true**;
- The `List` interface *also* specifies that $\backslash result$ is **true** unconditionally, i.e.
  ensures $\backslash result == $ **true**;

As in another approach [16], one could use a static field that encodes a closed enumeration of the possible implementations, e.g. set or list, and specify $\backslash result$ directly. Such closed world perspective does not leave room for other implementations. In our approach we can obtain refinements of interfaces that inherit from `Collection`, while keeping the interface open to other possible implementations, such as Google Guava's `Multiset` or Apache Commons' `MultiSet`.

4.4   History-Based Refinement

Given an interface specification we can extract a history-based implementation, that is used to verify there exists a correct implementation of the interface specification. The latter establishes that the interface specification itself is satisfiable. Since one could write inconsistent interface specifications for which there does not exist a correct implementation, this step is crucial.

The state of the history-based implementation `BasicCollection` consists of a single *concrete* history field **this.h**. Compare this to the model method of the interface, which only exists *conceptually*. By encoding the history as a Java object, we can also directly work with the history at run-time instead of only symbolically. The concrete history field points to the most recent history, and we can use it to compute attributes. The implementation of a method simply adds for each call a new corresponding event to the history, where the return value is computed depending on the (attributes of the) old history and method arguments. The contract of each method is inherited from the interface.

```
public boolean add(/*@ nullable */ Object o) {
    boolean ret = true;
    this.h = History.addEvent(this.h, o, ret);
    return ret;
}
```

Listing 9. One of the possible implementations of *add* in `BasicCollection`.

See Listing 9 for an implementation of `add`, that inherits the contract in Listing 8. Note that due to underspecification of $\backslash result$ there are several possible implementations, not a unique one. For our purposes of showing that the interface specification is satisfiable, it suffices to prove that *at least one correct implementation exists*.

For each method of the interface we have specified, we also have a static factory method in the history class which creates a new history object that consists of the previous history as tail, and the event corresponding to the method call of the interface as head. We verify that for each such factory method, the relation between the attributes of the old and the resulting history holds.

```
/*@ normal_behavior
 @ requires h != null ==> \invariant_for(h);
 @ ensures \result != null && \invariant_for(\result);
 @ ensures History.Multiset(\result,o) ==
    History.Multiset(h,o) + (ret ? 1 : 0);
 @ ensures (\forall Object o1; o1 != o;
    History.Multiset(\result,o1) == History.Multiset(h,o1));
 @ ensures \result.Tail == \old(h); */
/*@ pure */ static History addEvent(
    /*@ nullable */ History h, /*@ nullable */ Object o, boolean ret);
```

Listing 10. The contract for the factory method for `AddEvent` in class `History`.

For example, the event corresponding to `Collection`'s `add` method is added to a history in Listing 10 (see also Listing 5). We have proven that the *Multiset* attribute remains unchanged for all elements, except for the argument o if the return value is **true** (see Listing 6). This property is reflected in the factory method contract. Similarly, we have a factory method for other events, e.g. corresponding to `Collection`'s `remove`.

5   History-Based Verification in KeY

This section describes our verification work which we performed to show the feasibility of our approach. We use KeY version 2.7-1681 with the default settings. For the purpose of this article, we have recorded est. 2.5 h of video[5] showing how to produce some of our proofs using KeY. A repository of all our produced proof files is available on Zenodo[6] and includes the KeY version we used.

The proof statistics are shown in Table 1. These statistics must be interpreted with care: shorter proofs (in the number of nodes and interactive steps) may exists, and the reported time depends largely on the user's experience with the tool. The reported time does not include the time to develop the specifications.

We now describe a number of proofs, that also have been formally verified using KeY. Note that the formal proof produced in KeY consists of many low-level proof steps, of which the details are too cumbersome to consider here.

To verify clients of the interface, we use the interface method contracts. In particular, the verification challenge in Listing 2 makes use of the contracts of

---

[5] https://doi.org/10.6084/m9.figshare.c.5015645.
[6] https://doi.org/10.5281/zenodo.3903203.

Table 1. Summary of proof statistics. Nodes and branches are measures of proof trees, I.step is the number of interactive proof steps, Q.inst is the number of quantifier instansiation rules, O.Contract is the number of method contracts applied, Dep. is the number of dependency contracts applied, Loop inv. is the number of loop invariants, and Time is an estimated wall-clock duration for interactively producing the proof tree.

Nodes	Branches	I.step	Q.inst	O.Contract	Dep.	Loop inv.	Time
171,543	3,771	1,499	965	79	263	1	388 min

add and remove, to establish that the contents of the Collection parameter passed to the program in Listing 2 remains unchanged. More technically, during symbolic execution of a Java program fragment in KeY, one can replace the execution of a method by its associated method contract. The contract we have formulated for add and remove is sufficient in proving the client code in Listing 2: the multiset remains unchanged. In the proof, the user has to interactively replace occurrences of history attributes by their method contracts. Method contracts for attributes can in turn be verified by unfolding the method body, thereby inductively establishing their equational specifications. The specification of the latter is not shown here, but can be found in the source files.

For the verification challenge in Listing 3, we make use of the contracts for iterator and the methods of the Iterator interface. The iterator method returns a fresh Iterator sub-object that is valid upon creation, and its owner is set to be the collection. The history of the owning collection is updated after each method call to an iterator sub-object. Each iterator has as derived attribute *IteratorSize*, the size of the visited multiset. It is a property of the *IteratorSize* attribute that it is not bigger than *CollectionSize*, the size of the overall collection. To verify termination of a client using the iterator in Listing 3, we can specify a loop invariant that maintains the validity and ownership of the iterator, and take as decreasing term the value of *CollectionSize* minus *IteratorSize*. Since each call to next causes the visited multiset to become larger, this term decreases. Since an iterator cannot iterate over more objects than the collection contains, this term is non-negative. We never needed to verify that the equational specification for the involved attributes hold and this can be done separately from verifying the client, thus allowing modular verification.

One of the complications of our history-based approach is reasoning about invariant properties of (immutable) histories, caused by potential aliasing. This currently cannot be automated by the KeY tool. We manually introduce a general but crucial lemma, that addresses the issue, as illustrated by the following verification condition that arises when verifying the reference implementation.

One verification condition is a conjunct of the method contract for the add method of Collection, namely that in the post-condition, $Multiset(history(), o) == Multiset(\backslash old(history()), o) + (\backslash result \, ? \, 1 : 0)$ should hold. We verify that BasicCollection's add method is correct with respect to this contract. Within BasicCollection, the model method *history()* is defined by the field this.h, which is updated during the method call with a newly created history using the factory method `History.addEvent`. We can use the contract of the `addEvent` factory method to establish the relation between the multiset value of the new and old history (see Listing 10); this contract is in turn simply verified by unfolding the method body of the multiset attribute and performing symbolic execution, which computes the multiplicity recursively over the history and adds one to it precisely if the returned value is true. Back in `BasicCollection`, after the update of the history field **this**.h, we need to prove that the post-condition of the interface method holds (see Listing 8); but we already have obtained that this property holds after the static factory method `add` before **this**.h was updated.

$$\forall \ \textbf{int} \ n; \ (n \geq 0 \rightarrow \forall \ \textit{History} \ g;$$
$$(g.\langle inv \rangle \wedge g.\langle created \rangle = \textbf{true} \wedge g.\textit{history\_length} = n \rightarrow$$
$$\textbf{this}.h \notin g.\textit{footprint}())) $$

The update of the history field, as a pointer to the `History` linked list, does not affect this structure itself, i.e. the values of attributes are not affected by changing the history field. This is an issue of aliasing, but we know that the updated pointer does not affect the attribute values of *any* `History` linked list. This can not be proven automatically: we need to interactively introduce a cut formula (shown above) that the history field does not occur in the footprint of the history object itself. The formula can be proven by induction on the length of the history.

6 Conclusion

Programming to interfaces is one of the core principles in object-oriented programming and central to the widely-used Java Collection Framework, which provides a hierarchy of interfaces and classes that represent object containers. But current practical static analysis tools, including model checkers and theorem provers such as KeY, are primarily state-based. Since interfaces do not expose a state or concrete representation, a major question is how to support interfaces.

The main contribution of this paper is a new systematic method for history-based reasoning and reusable specifications for Java programs that integrates seamlessly in the KeY theorem prover, without affecting the underlying proof system (this ensures our method introduces no inconsistencies). Our approach includes support for reasoning about interfaces from the client perspective, as well as about classes that implement interfaces. To show the feasibility of our novel method, we specified part of the Collection Framework with promising results. We showed how we can reason about clients with these specifications, and showed the satisfiability of the specifications by a witness implementation of the interface. We also showed how to handle inner classes with a notion of ownership. This is essential for showing termination of clients of the `Iterator`.

This work is the next step in the formal verification of Java's Collection Framework. With our novel method we can continue our specification and verification work on `LinkedList`, including methods with arguments of interface type such as `addAll`, and its inherited methods `removeAll` and `retainAll`.

A direction for future work is to further improve practicality of history-based specification and verification: for example, (a) considering client-side correctness with multiple (potentially aliasing) objects implementing the same interface, (b) considering client-side correctness that involves objects that implement multiple (potentially interfering) interfaces, (c) developing techniques to show that certain combinations of interfaces are inconsistent, such as an object implementing both `List` and `Set`, (d) considering implementations that initialize the value of attributes by an arbitrary value at creation time (e.g. a non-empty collection when it is constructed) which necessitates an object creation event, and (e) encoding histories as built-in abstract data types with special proof rules, to avoid modeling histories as Java objects.

Acknowledgements. The authors thank the anonymous reviewers for their helpful comments and suggestions.

References

1. Ahrendt, W., Beckert, B., Bubel, R., Hähnle, R., Schmitt, P.H., Ulbrich, M. (eds.): Deductive Software Verification - The KeY Book. Programming and Software Engineering, vol. 10001. Springer, Cham (2016). https://doi.org/10.1007/978-3-319-49812-6

2. Azzopardi, S., Colombo, C., Pace, G.J.: CLARVA: model-based residual verification of Java programs. In: Model-Driven Engineering and Software Development (MODELSWARD), pp. 352–359. SciTePress (2020)

3. de Boer, F.S., de Gouw, S., Vinju, J.J.: Prototyping a tool environment for run-time assertion checking in JML with communication histories. In: Formal Techniques for Java-Like Programs (FTfJP), pp. 6:1–6:7. ACM (2010)

4. Burdy, L., et al.: An overview of JML tools and applications. Int. J. Softw. Tools Technol. Transf. **7**(3), 212–232 (2004). https://doi.org/10.1007/s10009-004-0167-4

5. Chen, F., Rosu, G.: Mop: an efficient and generic runtime verification framework. In: Object-Oriented Programming, Systems, Languages, and Applications (OOPSLA), pp. 569–588. ACM (2007)

6. Cheon, Y., Perumandla, A.: Specifying and checking method call sequences of Java programs. Softw. Qual. J. **15**(1), 7–25 (2007)

7. Colombo, C., Pace, G.J., Schneider, G.: LARVA – safer monitoring of real-time Java programs (tool paper). In: Software Engineering and Formal Methods (SEFM), pp. 33–37. IEEE Computer Society (2009)

8. Costa, D., Andrzejak, A., Seboek, J., Lo, D.: Empirical study of usage and performance of Java collections. In: Proceedings of the 8th ACM/SPEC International Conference on Performance Engineering, pp. 389–400 (2017)

9. Darvas, Á., Leino, K.R.M.: Practical reasoning about invocations and implementations of pure methods. In: Dwyer, M.B., Lopes, A. (eds.) FASE 2007. LNCS, vol. 4422, pp. 336–351. Springer, Heidelberg (2007). https://doi.org/10.1007/978-3-540-71289-3_26

10. de Gouw, S., de Boer, F.S., Bubel, R., Hähnle, R., Rot, J., Steinhöfel, D.: Verifying OpenJDK's sort method for generic collections. J. Autom. Reason. **62**(1), 93–126 (2019)

11. Hiep, H.-D.A., Maathuis, O., Bian, J., de Boer, F.S., van Eekelen, M., de Gouw, S.: Verifying OpenJDK's **LinkedList** using KeY. TACAS 2020. LNCS, vol. 12079, pp. 217–234. Springer, Cham (2020). https://doi.org/10.1007/978-3-030-45237-7_13

12. Huisman, M.: Verification of Java's AbstractCollection class: a case study. In: Boiten, E.A., Möller, B. (eds.) MPC 2002. LNCS, vol. 2386, pp. 175–194. Springer, Heidelberg (2002). https://doi.org/10.1007/3-540-45442-X_11

13. Huisman, M., Ahrendt, W., Grahl, D., Hentschel, M.: Formal specification with the Java Modeling Language. In: [1], pp. 193–241. Springer, Cham (2016)

14. Huisman, M., Jacobs, B., van den Berg, J.: A case study in class library verification: Java's vector class. Int. J. Softw. Tools Technol. Transf. **3**(3), 332–352 (2001)

15. Jeffrey, A., Rathke, J.: Java JR: fully abstract trace semantics for a core Java language. In: Sagiv, M. (ed.) ESOP 2005. LNCS, vol. 3444, pp. 423–438. Springer, Heidelberg (2005). https://doi.org/10.1007/978-3-540-31987-0_29

16. Knüppel, A., Thüm, T., Pardylla, C., Schaefer, I.: Experience report on formally verifying parts of OpenJDK's API with KeY. In: Workshop on Formal Integrated Development Environment (F-IDE). EPTCS, vol. 284, pp. 53–70. OPA (2018)

17. Welsch, Y., Poetzsch-Heffter, A.: A fully abstract trace-based semantics for reasoning about backward compatibility of class libraries. Sci. Comput. Program. **92**, 129–161 (2014)

Modular Integration of Crashsafe Caching into a Verified Virtual File System Switch

Stefan Bodenmüller[✉], Gerhard Schellhorn, and Wolfgang Reif

Institute for Software and Systems Engineering, University of Augsburg,
Augsburg, Germany
{stefan.bodenmueller,schellhorn,reif}@informatik.uni-augsburg.de

Abstract. When developing file systems, caching is a common technique to achieve a performant implementation. Integrating write-back caches into a file system does not only affect functional correctness but also impacts crash safety properties of the file system. As parts of written data are only stored in volatile memory, special care has to be taken when integrating write-back caches to guarantee that a power cut during running operations leads to a consistent state. This paper shows how non-order-preserving caches can be added to a virtual file system switch (VFS) and gives a novel crash-safety criterion matching the characteristics of such caches. Broken down to individual files, a power cut can be explained by constructing an alternative run, where all writes since the last synchronization of that file have written a prefix. VFS caches have been integrated modularly into Flashix, a verified file system for flash memory, and both functional correctness and crash-safety of this extension have been verified with the interactive theorem prover KIV.

Keywords: POSIX-compliant File Systems · Write-Back Caching ·
Crash-Safety · Refinement · Interactive Verification

1 Introduction

This paper addresses the modular specification of a caching mechanism to a virtual filesystem switch (VFS) and the formal verification of crash-safety.

The original VFS is the standard top-level layer of any file system adhering to the POSIX standard [15] for all file systems used by Linux. Standard file systems like ext2,3,4 or ReiserFS use it, as well as file systems specific for raw flash memory, such as JFFS, YAFFS, or UBIFS.

In our Flashix project, we have developed a POSIX-compliant, modular file system for flash memory, using UBIFS as a blueprint, that was verified to be functionally correct and crash-safe. This includes a verified implementation of VFS without caching described in [8,9]. The implementation is one of ten components of the verified development, which altogether generates approximately

Supported by the Deutsche Forschungsgemeinschaft (DFG), "Verifikation von Flash-Dateisystemen" (grants RE828/13-1 and RE828/13-2).

© Springer Nature Switzerland AG 2020
B. Dongol and E. Troubitsyna (Eds.): IFM 2020, LNCS 12546, pp. 218–236, 2020.
https://doi.org/10.1007/978-3-030-63461-2_12

18k of C-Code that can be run in the Linux kernel or via the FUSE interface. Initially, the implementation was sequential, in recent work we have developed a concept for adding concurrency to components [16], which has led to a concurrent implementation of wear leveling and garbage collection (both necessary for Flash memory). Allowing concurrent calls for the top-level POSIX operations is work in progress.

VFS is responsible for the generic aspects of file systems: mapping directory paths to individual nodes, checking access rights, and breaking up writing data into files into updates for individual data pages. VFS is specific to Linux, although Windows uses a similar concept called IFS.

Our implementation VFS does not use a cache so far. However, since writing data to a cache in RAM is about two orders of magnitude more efficient than writing data to flash memory, caching is essential for efficiency: updating a file (e.g. editing a file with a text editor) several times will write the last version only when using a cache instead of persisting each update. It also reduces the need to read data from flash memory significantly.

We have addressed integrating caches into a verified file system before. Write-through caches are simple as they just store a redundant part of the persistent data in RAM. On a crash, nothing is lost, and an invariant stating that cached data are always identical to a part of the persistent data will suffice for verification. In [13] we have looked at order-preserving write-back caches that are used near the hardware level to queue data before persisting them in larger chunks. We have shown that these can be integrated into the hierarchy of components still allowing modular verification of each component separately.

Caching in VFS is rather different, since it is not order-preserving, so for the top-level POSIX operations, a new weaker crash safety criterion compared to [13] is necessary. We define *write-prefix crash consistency*, which states, that individual files still satisfy a prefix property: On a crash, all writes since the last fsync (that cleared the cache of this individual file) are retracted. Instead, *all* of them have written a prefix of their data after recovery from the crash.

This paper also demonstrates, that adding caching to VFS can be done without reimplementing VFS or breaking the implementation hierarchy represented as a formal refinement tower. In Software Engineering terms, we use the decorator pattern [10] to add VFS caches as a single new component. Functional correctness then just requires to verify the new component separately. Crash-Safety however, which is the main topic of this paper, was quite hard to verify, since VFS uses a data representation that is optimized for efficiency, and has a specific interface to the individual file systems that exploits it. This interface is called AFS (abstract file system) in this paper.

Our result has two limitations. First, we assume that concurrent writes to a single file are prohibited. Without this restriction, very little can be said about the file content after a crash. Linux does not enforce this, but assumes that applications will use file locking (using the flock operation) to ensure this. Second, we assume that emptying caches when executing the fsync-command is done with a specific strategy that empties caches bottom-up. This strategy is the default strategy implemented in VFS, but individual file systems can override this behavior e.g. with persisting the least recently used page first. Within these limitations, however, our result enables to write applications that use the file system in a crash-safe way: check-sums written before the actual data can be used to detect writes, that have not been persisted completely. Such a transaction concept would be similar to using group nodes for order-preserving caches as used by the file system itself [6].

This paper is organized as follows. Section 2 gives background on the general concept of a refinement tower: components ("machines") specified as interfaces that are refined to implementations, that call subcomponents, which are again specified and implemented the same way. Section 3 shows the data structures and operations of the VFS and AFS machines that are relevant for manipulating file content. Section 4 then shows the extension, that adds caching to VFS.

Section 5 defines the correctness criterion of write-prefix crash consistency and Sect. 6 gives some insight into its verification, that was done using our interactive verification system KIV [5]. We cannot fully go into the details of the proofs, which are very complex, the interested reader can find the full KIV proofs online [12]. Finally, Sect. 7 gives related work and concludes.

2   Formal Approach

The specification of the Flashix file system shown in Fig. 1a is organized into specifications of machines. An abstract state machine is an abstract data type, that consists of a state and some operations with inputs and outputs, that modify the state. Each operation is specified with a contract. Machines are used to either specify an interface abstractly (white boxes) or to describe an implementation (gray), from which code is generated. Both are connected by using the contract approach to data refinement (dotted lines in Fig. 1). The theory has been extended with proof obligations for crash safety, as detailed in [7].

To specify contracts uniformly, we prefer the style of abstract state machines (ASMs [2]) over using relational specifications as in Z [4]: we use a precondition together with an imperative program over algebraically specified data types that establishes the postcondition. The program is close to real code for implementations, but it may be as abstract as "**choose** *nextstate, output* **with** *postcondition*" in interfaces, using the **choose** construct of ASMs. Implementations may call operations of submachines (—⊙— in Fig. 1), which again are abstractly specified and then implemented as a separate component.

Altogether we get the refinement tower shown in Fig. 1a. At the top-level is a specification of a POSIX-compliant interface to a file system. This uses an algebraic tree to represent the directory structure and a sequence of bytes (or words, the exact size is a parameter of the specification) to represent file content. The POSIX interface is implemented by VFS, which uses a different data representation: Directory structure is now represented by numbered nodes, which are linked by referencing these numbers. Refinement guarantees that the nodes always form a tree, resulting in a consistent file system.

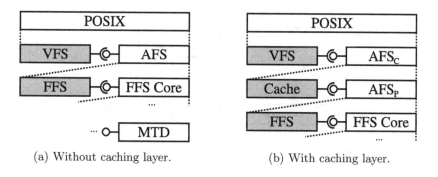

(a) Without caching layer.   (b) With caching layer.

Fig. 1. Flashix refinement tower.

Files are now represented as a *header* and several *pages*, which are arrays of bytes of the same fixed size. Since file content is cached write-back by VFS while the directory structure only uses write-through caches, which are easy to verify, we will ignore directory structure in the following: more information can be found in [8,9]; the KIV specifications online [12] also have a full list.

VFS calls operations specific to each file system implementation via an interface we call AFS (abstract file system). Again this is specified abstractly, and the operations relevant for accessing file data will be defined in the next section.

Our implementation of AFS then is specific to flash memory (called FFS in the figure). Again it is implemented using subcomponents. Altogether we get a refinement tower with 11 layers. In earlier work, we have verified the various components [6,14] to be crash-safe refinements according to the theory in [7,16]. The bottom layer of this development is the MTD interface, that Linux uses to access raw flash memory.

To add caching in VFS, we extend the refinement tower as shown in Fig. 1b. Instead of implementing AFS directly with FFS, we use an intermediate implementation Cache of AFS (AFS_C in the figure) that caches the data and calls operations of an identical copy of AFS (called AFS_P) to persist cached data. Details on this implementation will be given in Sect. 4.

3   Data Representation in VFS

The task of VFS is to implement POSIX operations like creating or deleting files and directories, or opening files and writing buffers to them by elementary operations on individual nodes, that represent a single directory or file. Each of these nodes is identified by a natural number $ino \in \mathsf{Ino}$, where $\mathsf{Ino} \simeq \mathbb{N}$. The operations on single nodes are implemented by each file system separately, and we specify them via the AFS interface.

The state of AFS is specified as abstract as possible by two finite maps ($Key \nrightarrow Value$ denotes a map from finitely many keys to values) with disjoint domains to store directories and files.

$$\textbf{state} \quad dirs : \mathsf{Ino} \nrightarrow \mathsf{Dir} \quad \textit{files} : \mathsf{Ino} \nrightarrow \mathsf{File} \quad \text{where } \mathsf{Ino} \simeq \mathbb{N}$$

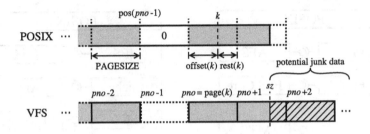

Fig. 2. Representation of file contents in POSIX and in VFS.

Since we are interested in adding write-back caches for file content, while directory structure only uses write-through caches, we just specify files

$$\text{data File} = \text{file}(\text{meta} : \text{Meta}, \ \text{size} : \mathbb{N}, \ \text{content} : \mathbb{N} \nrightarrow \text{Page})$$

Details on the representation of a file are shown in Fig. 2. The uniform representation as a sequence of bytes is broken up into file size, metadata (access rights), and several pages. Each Page is an array of size PAGESIZE. Byte k of a file is accessed via $\text{offset}(k)$ in $\text{page}(k)$, which are the remainder and quotient when dividing k by PAGESIZE. We also use $\text{rest}(k)$ to denote the length of the rest of the page above $\text{offset}(k)$. We have $\text{rest}(k) = \text{PAGESIZE} - \text{offset}(k)$, when the offset is non-zero. Otherwise $\text{rest}(k) = 0$, k is (page-)*aligned*, and predicate $\text{aligned}(k)$ is true. The start of page pno is at $\text{pos}(pno) = pno * \text{PAGESIZE}$. The pages are stored as a map, a missing page (e.g. page $pno - 1$ in the figure) indicates that the page contains zeros only. This sparse representation allows to create a file with a large size, without allocating all the pages immediately (which is important, e.g. for streaming data). Another important detail is that there may be irrelevant data beyond the file size. It is possible that the page $\text{page}(sz)$ at the file size sz contains random junk data (hatched part of the page) above $\text{offset}(sz)$ instead of just zeros. Extra (hatched) pages with a page number larger than $\text{page}(sz)$ are possible as well. Allowing such junk data is necessary for efficient recovery from a crash: writing data at the end of a file is always done by writing pages first, and finally incrementing the size. If a crash happens in between, then removing the extra data when rebooting would require to scan all files, which would be prohibitively expensive.

With this data representation AFS offers a number of operations that are called by VFS, using parameters of type Inode as input and output (passed by reference). An inode has the form

$$\text{data Inode} = \text{inode}(\text{ino} : \text{Ino}, \ \text{meta} : \text{Meta}, \ \text{isdir} : \text{Bool},$$
$$\text{nlink} : \mathbb{N}, \ \text{size} : \mathbb{N})$$

The boolean isdir distinguishes between directories and files, the nlink-field gives the number of hard links for a file (nlink = 1 for a directory). size stores the file size for files, and the number of entries for a directory.

```
afs_rpage(inode, pno; pbuf, exists; err) {
    exists := pno ∈ files[inode.ino].content;
    if exists then
        pbuf := files[inode.ino].content[pno];
    else
        pbuf := ⊥;
    err := false;
or err := true;
}

afs_wpage(inode, pno, pbuf; ; err) {
    files[inode.ino].content[pno] := pbuf;
    err := false;
or err := true;
}

afs_wsize(inode, sz; ; err) {
    files[inode.ino].size := sz;
    err := false;
or err := true;
}

afs_fsync(inode; ; err) {
    err := false;
or err := true;
}
```

```
afs_wbegin(inode; ; err) {
    let sz = inode.size in
    let cont = files[inode.ino].content,
        pno = page(inode.size),
        aligned = aligned(inode.size) in
    if pno ∈ cont ∧ ¬ aligned then
        cont[pno] := truncate(cont[pno], sz);
    files[inode.ino].content := cont upto sz;
    err := false;
or err := true;
}

afs_truncate(n; inode; err) {
    let sz = inode.size in
    let cont = files[inode.ino].content,
        sz_T = min(n, sz),
        pno = page(inode.size),
        aligned = aligned(inode.size) in
    if sz ≤ n ∧ pno ∈ cont ∧ ¬ aligned then
        cont[pno] := truncate(cont[pno], sz_T);
    files[inode.ino].content := cont upto sz_T;
    files[inode.ino].size := n;
    inode.size := n;
    err := false;
or err := true;
}
```

Fig. 3. File operations of AFS.

The relevant AFS operations for modifying file content are specified in Fig. 3. The operations use semicolons to separate input, in/out, and output parameters. We give a short description, which also gives some preconditions.

- **afs_rpage** reads the content of the page with number pno into a buffer $pbuf$: Page. The file is determined as the inode number of an inode $inode$, that points to a file. If the page does not exist, the buffer is set to all zeros (abbreviated as $\perp$), and the $exists$ flag is set to false. The flag is ignored by VFS but will be relevant for implementing a cache in the next section.
- **afs_wpage** writes the content of $pbuf$ to the respective page. Note that the page is allowed to be beyond file size (which is not modified).
- The file size is changed with the operation **afs_wsize**. This operation does not check, whether there are junk pages above the new file size.
- **afs_fsync** synchronizes a file. If a crash happens directly after this operation, the file accessed by $inode$ must retain its content. On this abstract level, the operation does nothing. Its implementation, which uses an order-preserving write-back cache (see [13]) must empty this cache.
- **afs_truncate** is used to change the file size to n, checking that there are no junk data that would end up being part of the file below the new file size. This operation first discards all pages above the minimum sz_T of n and the old sz: The expression $cont$ upto sz_T keeps pages below sz_T only. For efficiency, the operation then distinguishes two cases, shown in Fig. 4. The first case a) is when the new size n is at least the old sz. In this case, the page $page(sz)$ may contain junk data, which must be overwritten by zeros

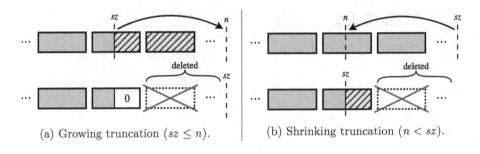

(a) Growing truncation ($sz \leq n$).   (b) Shrinking truncation ($n < sz$).

Fig. 4. Effects of a truncation to n on a file with size sz.

since this range becomes part of the file. Overwriting the part above $sz_T = sz$ with zeros is the result of the function call $\mathtt{truncate}(cont[pno], sz_T)$. This call can be avoided, if the part is empty or if the old size was aligned. The second case b) is when the new file size is less than the old. In this case, the page above the new filesize simply become junk, it does not need to be modified. The implementation of the **afs_truncate** operation, therefore, avoids writing pages to persistent store whenever this is possible[1].

- **afs_wbegin** is an optimized version of **afs_truncate** for the case $n = sz$. It is called at the start of writing content to a file in VFS. It makes sure that writing beyond the old file size will not accidentally create a page, which contains junk.

All operations are allowed to non-deterministically (**or**) return $err = \mathtt{true}$. This allows the implementation to return errors, e.g. when there is not enough memory available, which can not be specified on this level of abstraction. The implementation will resolve the nondeterminism to success whenever possible.

On the basis of the AFS operations, VFS implements two POSIX operations that modify file content, **vfs_truncate** and **vfs_write**. The first operation changes file size by just calling **afs_truncate**. Writing a buffer buf (an array of arbitrary size) of length n at position pos has the following steps:

- **afs_wbegin** is called first, to make sure that writing does not accidentally read junk data.
- Then the buffer is split at page boundaries, and individual pages are written by calling **afs_wpage**. Writing starts with the lowest page at $\mathtt{page}(pos)$ and proceeds upwards. If pos is not page-aligned, the first write requires to read the original page first by calling **afs_rpage** and to merge the original content below $\mathtt{offset}(pos)$ with the initial piece of buf of length $\mathtt{rest}(pos)$. Merging is necessary too for the last page when $pos + n$ is not aligned.
- Writing pages stops as soon as the first call to **afs_wpage** returns an error. If this is the case, the number n is decremented to the number of bytes actually written.

---

[1] deleting a page does not write it, but adds a "page deleted" entry to the journal.

- Finally, if *pos* + *n* is larger than the old file size, **afs_wsize** is called, to modify the file size, and **vfs_write** returns the number *n* of bytes written.

We will see in the next section that when adding caches it is crucially important that VFS implements writing by traversing the pages from low to high page numbers. We will also find, that the data representation of VFS, where all calls are optimized for efficiency, which in particular results in an asymmetric **afs_truncate** (Fig. 4) is one of the main difficulties for adding caches correctly.

4   Integration of Caches into Flashix

Initially, Flashix was developed without having caches for high-level data structures in mind. To add such caches to Flashix we introduce a new layer between the Virtual File System Switch and the Flash File System, visualized in Fig. 5. This layer is implemented as a *Decorator* [10], i.e. it implements the same interface as the FFS and delegates calls from the VFS to the FFS. The VFS communicates with a Cache Controller which in turn communicates with the FFS and manages caches for inodes, pages, and an auxiliary cache for truncations.

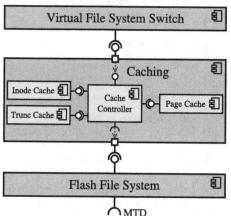

Fig. 5. Flashix component hierarchy.

The Inode- and Page-Cache components internally store maps from unique identifiers to the corresponding data structures. They all offer interfaces to the Cache Controller for adding resp. updating, reading, and deleting cache entries. The Cache Controller is responsible for processing requests from the VFS by either delegating these requests to the FFS or fulfilling them with the help of the required caches. It also has to keep the caches consistent with data stored on flash, i.e. update cached data when changes to corresponding data on flash have been made.

Similar to the Linux VFS, the caching layer includes further caches for data structures forming the basic structure of the file system. These caches however only operate in write-through mode to speed up read accesses. Otherwise, the integrity of the file system tree after a crash could be compromised since *structural operations* are usually highly dependent on one another and affect multiple data objects.

Compared to structural operations, updates to file data can be considered mostly in isolation. This means that in particular reads and writes to different files do not interfere with each other. Therefore we allow write-back caching of POSIX operations that modify the content of a file, namely *write* and *truncate*. Hence, the Cache Controller does not forward page writes to the FFS and instead only stores the pages in the Page Cache. Updates to the size of a file are also performed in the Inode Cache only as garbage data could be exposed in the event of a power cut otherwise. To distinguish between up-to-date data and cached updates, entries of the Page Cache or the Inode Cache include an additional *dirty* flag. For the Page Cache, this results in a mapping from inode numbers and page numbers to entries consisting of a page-sized buffer and a boolean flag.

Figure 6 lists the central operations of the PCache component using the state $pcache\colon \mathsf{Ino} \times \mathsf{Nat} \nrightarrow \mathsf{Bool} \times \mathsf{Page}$. Analogously the component ICache is defined. It stores a mapping $icache\colon \mathsf{Ino} \nrightarrow \mathsf{Bool} \times \mathsf{Inode}$ from inode numbers to entries containing the inode itself and a dirty flag.

Writing pages or file sizes results in putting the new data *dirty* in the particular caches. These operations of the controller component Cache are shown in Fig. 7 on the right. Reading pages on the other hand returns the page in question stored in PCache or, if it has not been cached yet, it tries to read it from flash (Fig. 7 on the left). But reading from flash yields the correct result only if there was no prior truncation that would have deleted the relevant page, i.e. an entry for this file exists in TCache and applying this truncation would delete the requested page (if $\min(sz_T, sz_F) \leq \mathsf{pos}(pno)$, i.e. *pno* is beyond the cached truncate size sz_T and the current persisted size of the file sz_F). If reading the page

```
state   pcache:  Ino × Nat ↛ Bool × Page

pcache_set(ino, pno, pbuf, dirty){
let key = ino × pno in
  pcache[key] := dirty × pbuf;
}

pcache_get(ino, pno; pbuf, dirty; hit) {
let key = ino × pno in
  hit := key ∈ pcache;
  if hit then
    dirty := pcache[key].dirty;
    pbuf := pcache[key].page;
}

pcache_delete(ino, pno) {
let key = ino × pno in
  pcache := pcache -- key;
}

pcache_mark_clean(ino, pno) {
let key = ino × pno in
  pcache[key].dirty := false;
}
```

Fig. 6. Core of the PCache component.

from flash is correct and the page actually stores any relevant data (*exists* is true), the resulting page is stored *clean* in PCache to handle repeated read requests.

For truncations of files, there are several steps Cache needs to perform. These steps are implemented with the operations **cache_truncate** and **cache_wbegin** as shown in Fig. 8 on the left. First, when an actual user truncation is executed, ICache needs to be updated by setting the size to the size the file is truncated to. Second, cached pages beyond sz resp. n have to be removed from PCache and the truncate sizes in TCache have to be updated. For this purpose, the two subcomponents provide dedicated truncation operations **pcache_truncate** resp. **tcache_update**. **tcache_update** aggregates multiple truncations by caching the minimal truncate size n for each file only. Additionally, the persisted size sz of a file is stored in TCache to determine whether it is allowed to read a page from flash in **cache_rpage**. Finally, if the truncate is growing, i.e. $sz \leq n$, the page at size sz may need to be filled with zeros. The auxiliary operation

```
cache_rpage(ino, pno; pbuf, exists; err) {
let hit = false, dirty = false in
  pcache_get(ino, pno; pbuf, dirty; hit);
  if hit then
    exists := true, err := false;
  else let sz_T = 0, sz_F = 0 in
    tcache_get(ino; sz_T, sz_F; hit);
    if hit ∧ min(sz_T, sz_F) ≤ pos(pno) then
      pbuf := ⊥, exists := false, err := false;
    else
      afs_rpage(ino, pno; pbuf; exists, err);
      if ¬ err ∧ exists then
        dirty := false;
      pcache_set(ino, pno, pbuf, dirty);
}
```

```
cache_wpage(ino, pno, pbuf; ; err) {
err := false;
let dirty = true in
  pcache_set(ino, pno, pbuf, dirty);
}
```

```
cache_wsize(inode, sz; ; err) {
err := false;
let dirty = true in
  inode.size := sz;
  icache_set(inode, dirty);
}
```

Fig. 7. Cache operations for reading and writing pages and updating file sizes.

cache_get_tpage is used to determine if this page is existent. This is the case if the page is either cached in PCache or can be read from flash but would not have been truncated according to TCache. If necessary, the page is then filled with zeros beyond offset(sz) using the truncate function and the result is stored in PCache.

The synchronization of files, i.e. transferring cached updates to the persistent storage, is also coordinated by Cache. Clients can use the POSIX *fsync* operation to trigger synchronization of a specific file. It is common practice that cached data is also synchronized concurrently, however, this is left for future work.

The implementation of *fsync* in Cache is shown in Fig. 8 on the right. The general idea of this implementation is to first remove all pages from flash that would have been deleted by truncations on this file since the last synchronization and then mimic a VFS *write* that persists all *dirty* pages in PCache and updates the file size to the size stored in ICache if necessary.

The operation **cache_fbegin** is responsible for synchronizing truncations and prepares the subsequent writing of pages and updating the file size in **cache_fpages** resp. **cache_finode**. When using this synchronization strategy, it is sufficient to aggregate multiple truncations by truncating to the minimal size the file was truncated to, and only if this minimal truncation size is lower than the current file size on flash. As truncation is the only possibility to delete pages (except for deleting the file as a whole), this **afs_truncate** call deletes all obsolete pages. The following **afs_wbegin** call ensures that the whole file content beyond sz_T resp. sz_F is zeroed so that writing pages and increasing the file size on flash is possible safely. Since AFS enforces an initial **afs_wbegin** before writing pages or updating the file size and Cache is a refinement of AFS, it is guaranteed that there are dirty pages only in PCache or dirty inodes in ICache if there is an entry in TCache for the file that is being synchronized. Hence there is nothing to do if *hit* after **tcache_get** is false.

cache_fpages iterates over all possibly cached pages of the file and writes *dirty* pages with **afs_wpage**, marking them *clean* in PCache after writing them successfully. Similar to the implementation of **vfs_write** explained in Sect. 3, this iteration is executed bottom-up, starting at page 0 up to the

```
cache_truncate(n; inode; err) {
let ino = inode.ino, sz = inode.size in
let sz_T = min(n, sz) in
let pno = page(sz_T), pbuf = ⊥,
    hit = false, dirty = true in
  cache_get_tpage(ino, pno; pbuf; hit, err);
  if ¬ err then
    pcache_truncate(ino, sz_T);
    if hit ∧ sz ≤ n ∧ ¬ aligned(sz) then
      pbuf := truncate(pbuf, sz);
      pcache_set(ino, pno, pbuf, dirty);
    tcache_update(ino, n, sz);
    inode.size := n;
    icache_set(inode, dirty);
}


cache_wbegin(inode; ; err) {
let ino = inode.ino, sz = inode.size in
let pno = page(sz), pbuf = ⊥, hit = false in
  cache_get_tpage(ino, pno; pbuf; hit, err);
  if ¬ err then
    pcache_truncate(ino, sz);
    if hit ∧ ¬ aligned(sz) then
      pbuf := truncate(pbuf, sz);
      let dirty = true in
        pcache_set(ino, pno, pbuf, dirty);
    tcache_update(ino, sz, sz);
}


cache_get_tpage(ino, pno; pbuf; hit, err) {
err := false;
let dirty = false in
  pcache_get(ino, pno; pbuf, dirty; hit);
  if ¬ hit then let sz_T = 0, sz_F = 0 in
    tcache_get(ino; sz_T, sz_F; hit);
    if ¬ hit ∨ pos(pno) < min(sz_T, sz_F) then
      afs_rpage(ino, pno; pbuf; hit, err);
}
```

```
cache_fsync(inode; ; err) {
let sz_F = 0, sync_data = false in
  cache_fbegin(inode; sz_F; sync_data, err);
  if ¬ err ∧ sync_data then
    cache_fpages(inode; ; err);
  if ¬ err ∧ sync_data then
    cache_finode(inode, sz_F; ; err);
}


cache_fbegin(inode; sz_F; sync_data, err) {
err := false;
let hit = false, sz_T = 0 in
  tcache_get(inode.ino; sz_T, sz_F; hit);
  sync_data := hit;
  if sync_data then
    if sz_T < sz_F then
      afs_truncate(sz_T; inode; err);
      sz_F := sz_T;
    if ¬ err then
      afs_wbegin(inode; ; err);
    if ¬ err then
      tcache_delete(inode.ino);
}


cache_fpages(inode; ; err) {
err := false;
let ino = inode.ino, pno = 0, pno_max = 0 in
  pcache_max_pageno(ino; ; pno_max);
  while ¬ err ∧ pno ≤ pno_max do
    let pbuf = ⊥, hit = false, dirty = false in
      pcache_get(ino, pno; pbuf, dirty; hit);
      if hit ∧ dirty then
        afs_wpage(ino, pno, pbuf; ; err);
        if ¬ err then
          pcache_mark_clean(ino, pno);
      pno := pno + 1;
}


cache_finode(inode, sz_F; ; err) {
if sz_F < inode.size then
  afs_wsize(inode, inode.size; ; err)
else
  err := false
}
```

Fig. 8. File truncation (left) and synchronization (right) operations of Cache.

maximal page cached in PCache (returned by **pcache_max_pageno**). Finally, **cache_finode** updates the file size with **afs_wsize** if the cached size is greater than the persisted size sz_F.

5 Functional Correctness and Crash-Safety Criterion

Due to our modular approach, verifying the correctness of integrating caches into Flashix as shown in Fig. 1b requires to prove a single additional data refinement $\text{Cache}(\text{AFS}_P) \sqsubseteq \text{AFS}_C$ only. The proofs are done with a forward simulation $R \subseteq AS \times CS$ using commuting diagrams with states $AS \equiv dirs_C \times files_C$ of AFS_C and $CS \equiv dirs_P \times files_P \times icache \times pcache \times tcache$ of $\text{Cache}(\text{AFS}_P)$.

$$R \quad \equiv \quad dirs_C = dirs_P \wedge files_C = ((files_P \downarrow tcache) \oplus pcache) \oplus icache$$

Basically, R states that for each $(as, cs) \in R$ the cached AFS state as can be constructed from cs by applying all cached updates to the persistent AFS state, i.e. pruning all files at their cached truncate size ($\_ \downarrow tcache$), overwriting all pages with their cached contents ($\_ \oplus pcache$), and updating the cached file sizes ($\_ \oplus icache$). As no structural operations are cached, $dirs_C$ and $dirs_P$ are identical.

While AFS$_C$ functionally matches the original specification of AFS, it is easy to see that AFS$_C$ differs quite heavily from AFS$_P$ in terms of its crash behavior. A crash in AFS$_P$, for example, has the effect of removing orphaned files [7], i.e. those files that are not accessible from the file system tree anymore but still opened in VFS for reading/writing at the event of the crash. However, if there are pending writes that have not been synchronized yet, a crash in AFS$_C$ additionally may revert parts of these writes as all data only stored in the volatile state of Cache is lost.

Usually, we express the effect of a crash in *specification* components in terms of a state transition given by a *crash predicate* $\lightning \subseteq S \times S$ and prove that the *implementations* of these components match their specification. But as soon as write-back caches - especially non-order-preserving ones - are integrated into a refinement hierarchy, it is typically not feasible to express the loss of cached data explicitly. This is the case for AFS$_C$ and thus for POSIX, too. So instead of verifying crash-safety in a state-based manner, we want to explain the effects of a crash by constructing an alternative run where losing cached data does not have any effect on the state of AFS$_C$. If such an alternative run can always be found, crash-safety holds since all regular (non-crashing) runs of AFS$_C$ yield consistent states, and thus a crash results in a consistent state as well.

Definition 1 (Write-Prefix Crash Consistency). *A file system is write-prefix crash consistent (WPCC) iff a crash keeps the directory tree intact and for each file f a crash has the effect of retracting all write and truncate operations to f since the last state it was synchronized and re-executing them, potentially resulting in writing prefixes of the original runs.*

This property results from the fact that files are synchronized individually by the *fsync* operation. Thus, all runs of operations that modify the content of a file, either cached or persistent, can be decoupled from runs of structural operations or operations accessing the content of other files.

To prove that Flashix satisfies *WPCC* we need to show that for each possible occurrence of a crash in Cache(AFS$_P$) we can construct a matching alternative run for each file in AFS$_C$ and lift this to runs in VFS(AFS$_C$). As it turns out, for an arbitrary file f the only critical case is when a crash occurs during the execution of **cache_fsync** for this file. In all other cases, updates to the content of f have been stored in cache only, thus the persistent content of f in AFS$_P$ is unchanged since the last successful execution of **cache_fsync** for f. So we can choose a VFS(AFS$_C$) run in which all *writes* and *truncates* to f have failed and hence have not written or deleted any data. Constructing such a run is always possible as AFS$_C$ is *crash-neutral*, i.e. all operations of AFS$_C$ are specified to have a run that fails without any changes to the state (see Fig. 3 and [7]).

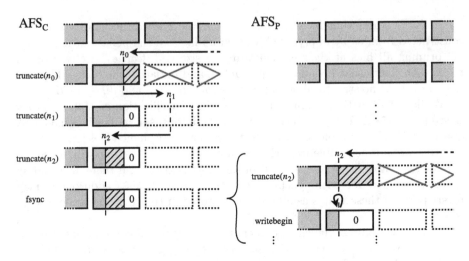

Fig. 9. Effect of a sequence of *truncate* operations and a following *fsync* on the states of one file in AFS$_C$ (left) and AFS$_P$ (right), including intermediate states of AFS$_P$ during *fsync*. The state of `Cache` is ommitted.

However, showing that $WPCC$ holds for crashes during **cache_fsync** is hard. Initially, our goal was to prove this property locally on the level of AFS$_C$ resp. of `Cache` and AFS$_P$ only. For example, one approach was to construct matching prefix runs of AFS$_C$ by commuting and merging of operation calls. While we will not go into details of the many pitfalls we ran into, the main problem with these approaches was that the synchronization of aggregated *truncates*, as states resulting from prefix runs of **cache_fsync** could not be reconstructed by any combination of `VFS` prefixes from the corresponding AFS$_C$ run.

For example, given the sequence of three **afs_truncate** calls followed by an **afs_fsync** call as visualized in Fig. 9, starting with a synchronized file, i.e. the contents (and sizes) of the affected file are equal in AFS$_C$ and AFS$_P$. Considering this run in AFS$_C$ on the left, the first truncation shrinks the file to a new size n_0 deleting all pages above `page`(n_0). Since `aligned`(n_0) is false, `rest`(n_0) bytes of junk data remain in `page`(n_0) for the moment. This junk data is removed not before the second truncation as it increases the file size then to n_1 and the remainder of `page`(n_0) is filled with zeros. When finally the third truncation shrinks the file again to n_2 with $n_2 < n_0$ but `page`(n_0) = `page`(n_2), which yields a mixed page containing valid data, junk, and zeros.

These truncations do not have any effect on the persistent state of AFS$_P$ as `Cache` handles all requests. Conversely, a call to **afs_fsync** in AFS$_C$ leaves its state unchanged but its implementation `Cache` triggers a number of calls to AFS$_P$. First, the file is truncated to n_2, the minimal truncation size since its last synchronized state. Second, junk data above n_2 is removed with **afs_wbegin** to prepare a potential synchronization of pages beyond n_2.

Comparing the state after **afs_wbegin** in AFS$_P$ with the state after all truncations in AFS$_C$, one can see that the sizes and the valid part of the content match but there is some junk data left in AFS$_C$ that is not in AFS$_P$. In fact, if a crash occurs in a state after this **afs_wbegin** call and before the synchronization of page(n_2) with **afs_wpage**, we cannot construct a VFS prefix run of AFS$_C$ that yields the state of AFS$_P$. Fortunately, the abstraction from VFS(AFS$_C$) to POSIX ignores bytes written beyond the file size anyway and the implementation Cache(AFS$_P$) may at most remove more junk data than AFS$_C$, so the implementation actually matches our crash-safety criterion under the POSIX abstraction as intended. But in order to prove this, we need to explicitly consider runs of AFS$_C$ in the context of VFS.

In the following section, we give a brief overview of the concrete proof strategy we pursued to construct such a *write-prefix* run.

6 Proving Crash-Safety

The main effort for proving that Flashix is actually *write-prefix crash consistent* was to show that a crash during **cache_fsync** actually has the effect of write-prefix runs of VFS. Given the implementation of **cache_fsync** and the fact that the operations of AFS$_P$ are atomic with respect to crashes, effectively two cases need to be considered, namely a crash occurs

1. between **afs_truncate** and **afs_wbegin** or
2. between persisting pages $k - 1$ and k with **afs_wpage**.

Two additional cases are crashes before **afs_truncate** or after **afs_wsize**. These can be viewed as crashing before resp. after the complete **cache_fsync** operation since no persistent changes happen in these ranges. Note that we do not explicitly consider crashes immediately after **afs_wbegin** or before **afs_wsize** as separate cases, but instead we handle these as variants of case 2.

For case 1 finding a write-prefix run is quite obvious. As **cache_fsync** only executed a single persisting truncation to sz_T, only **vfs_truncate** calls to sz_T were successful in the alternative VFS run as well. For **vfs_truncate** calls to sizes n greater than sz_T the run is chosen in which **afs_truncate** fails, so we get a failing run of **vfs_truncate** too. For **vfs_write** calls the run is chosen in which the initial **afs_wbegin** fails which results in not calling any further AFS$_C$ operations (cf. Sect. 3).

Verifying case 2 requires more effort. As an example consider the crashed run shown in the upper half of Fig. 10. We omit irrelevant arguments of operations and abbreviate **wbegin**, **wpage**, **wsize**, and **truncate** with **wb**, **w**, **ws**, and **t**, respectively. The run contains **vfs_truncate** and **vfs_write** calls, followed by an interrupted synchronization **fsync**^{i}. The former operations are performed in Cache only, so calls to AFS$_P$ are performed not until synchronization. **fsync** crashes after an ascending sequence $\mathbf{w}^*|_k$ of **wpage** operations, which contains only writes to pages $< k$. As for case 1, the write-prefix run we construct in the lower half of Fig. 10 contains successful executions of **vfs_truncate** calls to the

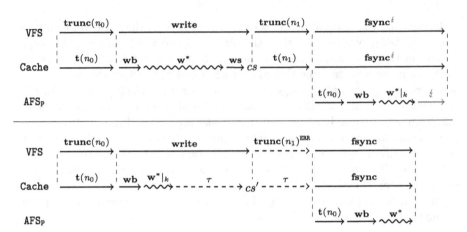

Fig. 10. Construction of a write-prefix run (lower half) matching a run with a crash in **cache_fsync** that occurs just before writing page k (upper half).

minimal truncate size. In the example, this is the size n_0, so the first truncation is performed as before. For the second truncation to n_1 on the other hand we choose a failing run of **vfs_truncate** (failing operation runs are marked with ^{ERR}), which results in a stutter step τ in Cache, i.e. no operation is executed in Cache.

The main aspect of $WPCC$ is that alternative **vfs_write** runs write just as far as the interrupted **fsync** was able to persist pages. Hence, the alternative run successfully performs **wbegin** and a prefix of the original **wpage** sequence $\mathbf{w}^*$, namely the prefix of writes $\mathbf{w}^*|_k$ to pages $< k$. All other writes to pages $\geq k$ are again replaced by stutter steps τ in Cache. Depending on the range the original **vfs_write** has written to, the restricted sequence $\mathbf{w}^*|_k$ may be empty or the full sequence $\mathbf{w}^*$. However, the alternative run will not execute (stutter) for updates of the file size via **wsize**. With a complete system run constructed this way, a full **fsync** run has the same effect as the crashed execution if the original run (except for differences in junk data resulting from the problematic nature of synchronizing truncations discussed in Sect. 5), and thus the alternative run finishes in a synchronized state.

Proving that the runs constructed this way match the original crashed runs is done with a forward simulation $\cong^k \subseteq CS \times CS$ using commuting diagrams. Relation $\cong^k$ links all vertically aligned states in Fig. 10.

$$\cong^k \;\equiv\; \begin{aligned}&((\mathit{files}_{\mathrm{P}} \downarrow \mathit{tcache}) \oplus \mathit{pcache}|_k).\mathtt{seq}(ino) \\ &= (((\mathit{files_P}' \downarrow \mathit{tcache}') \oplus \mathit{pcache}') \oplus \mathit{icache}').\mathtt{seq}(ino)\end{aligned}$$

where $\mathit{pcache}|_k$ restricts pcache to entries for pages $i < k$ and $\mathit{files}.\mathtt{seq}(\mathrm{Ino})$ extracts the content of the file ino as a sequence of bytes up to the current size of ino in files. Intuitively, two Cache states cs and cs' are $cs \cong^k cs'$ if a synchronization interrupted at page k of cs yields the same content (up to

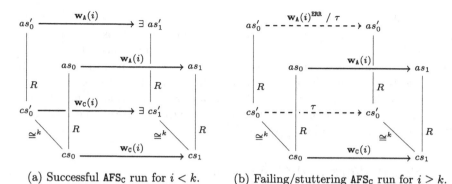

(a) Successful $\mathsf{AFS_C}$ run for $i < k$.   (b) Failing/stuttering $\mathsf{AFS_C}$ run for $i \geq k$.

Fig. 11. Commuting diagrams of a **wpage** run writing page i.

the file size) as a complete synchronization of cs'. Note that $cs \cong^k cs'$ enforces implicitly that the file size of ino is identical in cs and cs' and hence the cached truncate sizes in $tcache$ and $tcache'$, as well as the cached size in $icache'$, must be equal.

For the **wpage** calls the commuting diagrams as shown in Fig. 11 in the bottom plane are required. **wpage** operations of AFS and Cache are denoted $\mathbf{w_A}$ and $\mathbf{w_C}$, respectively. When writing a page $< k$, re-executing this operation maintains $\cong^k$ (Fig. 11a). In contrast, writing pages $\geq k$ maintains $\cong^k$ if the alternative run stutters (Fig. 11b). Since VFS is defined on $\mathsf{AFS_C}$, these commuting properties must be lifted from Cache to $\mathsf{AFS_C}$ in order to construct commuting diagrams for VFS runs. This is why the commuting diagrams are extended by R-corresponding $\mathsf{AFS_C}$ runs, yielding the front and back sides of Fig. 11. So in addition we show that, given a run $as_0 \xrightarrow{\mathbf{w_A}(i)} as_1$ as it is part of **vfs_write** or **vfs_truncate**, there is an R-corresponding run of Cache. Conversely, we have to show that the resulting alternative run of Cache can be lifted to an R-corresponding run of $\mathsf{AFS_C}$ as well. Depending on the operation, up to two versions of this lifting are necessary if the run is stuttering: an $\mathsf{AFS_C}$ run that stutters and a failing run of the $\mathsf{AFS_C}$ operation. For **wpage**, the former is used to skip writes of pages $> k$ while the latter is required to stop the loop of **vfs_write** when trying to write page k.

To construct a valid alternative VFS run, analogous commuting diagrams for **wbegin**, **wsize**, and **truncate** have been proven, not all commuting diagrams were necessary for each operation though. The proofs of commuting diagrams for **vfs_write** and **vfs_truncate** then base upon the step by step application of these commutative properties. Considering the final states of the runs shown in Fig. 10, $tcache$, $pcache|_k$, $tcache'$, $pcache'$, and $icache'$ do not contain any *dirty* data for ino and so applying them to $files_P$ resp. $files_P'$ does not have any effect. Consequently, in theses states $cs \cong^k cs'$ reduces to $files_P.\mathtt{seq}(ino) = files_P'.\mathtt{seq}(ino)$, which is exactly the property we wanted to achieve.

All in all, the verification of the crash-safety properties alone (not including earlier attempts) took about two months and comprises approx. 300 theorems. Most of the time was spent proving the commuting diagrams for $\cong^k$ on the level of Cache, since many different cases have to be considered. Lifting these to AFS_C could be done mainly by reusing the commuting diagrams for R together with some auxiliary lemmata over the Cache and AFS operations, which in turn enabled proving the commuting diagrams for VFS without major issues. For more details, the full proofs can be found online [12].

7   Related Work and Conclusion

In this paper we have shown how to integrate caching of file content as done by VFS into the modular development of a verified file system. We have defined the correctness criterion of *write-prefix crash consistency* for crash safety, and have verified it with KIV, thus giving applications a formal criterion that can be used to verify that applications are crash-safe.

For reasons of space we could not formally address how caching of VFS interacts with the order-preserving cache (called "write buffer" in [13]) as used by lower levels of the implementation. However, informally the answer is as follows. AFS_P operations are implemented atomically, i.e. a page is either persisted as a whole or not at all. This is necessary to imply linearizability of AFS_P operations in a concurrent context. Removing the data of the write buffer on a crash has the effect of undoing some AFS_P operations according to [7]. Therefore, discarding the write buffer has the same effect as crashing slightly earlier, and thus *WPCC* still holds.

We have also not discussed concurrent top-level calls of POSIX operations. We have augmented the specification to allow this, and are working on a verification using the approach given in [16], which has already been used to allow concurrent garbage collection. For the theory presented here to work, the implementation ensures that modifications to each file (write, truncate, fsync) are done sequentially only.

We have discussed lots of related work on verified file systems in general in earlier work [13,16], here we discuss two related approaches, that generate running code and have addressed the correctness of write-back caching in file systems. These are BilbyFS [1] and DFSCQ [3]. BilbyFS is a file system for flash memory too. It implements caching mechanisms and gives a specification of the *sync* operation on the level of AFS and proves the functional correctness of this operation. However, the verification of crash-safety or caching on the level of VFS is not considered.

DFSCQ is a sequentially implemented file system not targeted to work specifically with flash memory. Similar to our approach, structural updates to the file system tree are persisted in order. DFSCQ also uses a page cache, however, it does not specify an order in which cached pages are written to persistent store. Therefore it is not provable that a crash leads to a POSIX-conforming alternate run. Instead a weaker crash-safety criterion is satisfied, called *metadata-prefix* specification: it is proved that a consistent file system results from a crash, where some subset of the page writes has been executed.

In our context, the weaker criterion should be provable for any (functional correct) implementation of VFS caches, since we ensure that all AFS_P operations are atomic (calls can never overlap) and the refinement proof of VFS $\sqsubseteq$ POSIX has lemmas for all AFS operations, that ensure that even these (and not just the VFS operations) preserve the abstraction relation to a consistent file system.

Our earlier crash-safety criterion for order-preserving caches can be viewed as the sequential case of buffered durable linearizability [11], which allows to undo a postfix of the history of invokes and responses for operations, thus allowing pending operations of the resulting prefix to have a new result. The criterion is also sufficient to specify the AFS_C interface in a concurrent context (since the operations are linearizable). However, it is stronger than the criterion given here, as it does not allow to re-execute several sequentially executed operations (only one can be pending in the prefix).

Future work on the file system will be to add a background process that calls fsync to empty caches when no user operations are executed. To imitate the behavior of Linux VFS, the crucial extension necessary there will be to allow fsync-calls of this process to be interrupted when the user calls an operation.

References

1. Amani, S., et al.: Cogent: verifying high-assurance file system implementations. In: Proceedings of ASPLOS, pp. 175–188. ACM (2016)
2. Börger, E., Stärk, R.F.: Abstract State Machines–A Method for High-Level System Design and Analysis. Springer, Heidelberg (2003). https://doi.org/10.1007/978-3-642-18216-7
3. Chen, H., et al.: Verifying a high-performance crash-safe file system using a tree specification. In: Proceedings of the 26th Symposium on Operating Systems Principles (SOSP), pp. 270–286 (2017)
4. Derrick, J., Boiten, E.: Refinement in Z and in Object-Z : Foundations and Advanced Applications. FACIT, 2nd edn. Springer, London (2014)
5. Ernst, G., Pfähler, J., Schellhorn, G., Haneberg, D., Reif, W.: KIV – overview and VerifyThis competition. Softw. Tools Technol. Transf. (STTT) **17**(6), 677–694 (2015)
6. Ernst, G., Pfähler, J., Schellhorn, G., Reif, W.: Inside a verified flash file system: transactions and garbage collection. In: Gurfinkel, A., Seshia, S.A. (eds.) VSTTE 2015. LNCS, vol. 9593, pp. 73–93. Springer, Cham (2016). https://doi.org/10.1007/978-3-319-29613-5_5
7. Ernst, G., Pfähler, J., Schellhorn, G., Reif, W.: Modular, crash-safe refinement for ASMs with submachines. Sci. Comput. Program. **131**, 3–21 (2016). Abstract State Machines, Alloy, B, TLA, VDM and Z (ABZ 2014)
8. Ernst, G., Schellhorn, G., Haneberg, D., Pfähler, J., Reif, W.: A formal model of a virtual filesystem switch. In: Proceedings of Software and Systems Modeling (SSV). EPTCS, pp. 33–45 (2012)

9. Ernst, G., Schellhorn, G., Haneberg, D., Pfähler, J., Reif, W.: Verification of a virtual filesystem switch. In: Cohen, E., Rybalchenko, A. (eds.) VSTTE 2013. LNCS, vol. 8164, pp. 242–261. Springer, Heidelberg (2014). https://doi.org/10.1007/978-3-642-54108-7_13
10. Gamma, E., Helm, R., Johnson, R., Vlissides, J.: Design Patterns: Elements of Reusable Object-Oriented Software. Addison-Wesley, Boston (1995)
11. Izraelevitz, J., Mendes, H., Scott, M.L.: Linearizability of persistent memory objects under a full-system-crash failure model. In: Gavoille, C., Ilcinkas, D. (eds.) DISC 2016. LNCS, vol. 9888, pp. 313–327. Springer, Heidelberg (2016). https://doi.org/10.1007/978-3-662-53426-7_23
12. KIV models and proofs for VFS Caching (2020). https://kiv.isse.de/projects/VFSCaching.html
13. Pfähler, J., Ernst, G., Bodenmüller, S., Schellhorn, G., Reif, W.: Modular verification of order-preserving write-back caches. In: Polikarpova, N., Schneider, S. (eds.) IFM 2017. LNCS, vol. 10510, pp. 375–390. Springer, Cham (2017). https://doi.org/10.1007/978-3-319-66845-1_25
14. Pfähler, J., Ernst, G., Schellhorn, G., Haneberg, D., Reif, W.: Formal specification of an erase block management layer for flash memory. In: Bertacco, V., Legay, A. (eds.) HVC 2013. LNCS, vol. 8244, pp. 214–229. Springer, Cham (2013). https://doi.org/10.1007/978-3-319-03077-7_15
15. The Open Group Base Specifications Issue 7, IEEE Std 1003.1, 2018 Edition. The IEEE and The Open Group (2017)
16. Schellhorn, G., Bodenmüller, S., Pfähler, J., Reif, W.: Adding concurrency to a sequential refinement tower. In: Raschke, A., Méry, D., Houdek, F. (eds.) ABZ 2020. LNCS, vol. 12071, pp. 6–23. Springer, Cham (2020). https://doi.org/10.1007/978-3-030-48077-6_2

Formal Verification

Formal Verification of Executable Complementation and Equivalence Checking for Büchi Automata

Julian Brunner[(✉)] [ID]

Technische Universität München, Munich, Germany
brunnerj@in.tum.de

Abstract. We develop a complementation procedure and an equivalence checker for nondeterministic Büchi automata. Both are formally verified using the proof assistant Isabelle/HOL. The verification covers everything from the abstract correctness proof down to the generated SML code.

The complementation follows the rank-based approach. We formalize the abstract algorithm and use refinement to derive an executable implementation. In conjunction with a product operation and an emptiness check, this enables deciding language-wise equivalence between nondeterministic Büchi automata. We also improve and extend our library for transition systems and automata presented in previous research.

Finally, we develop a command-line executable providing complementation and equivalence checking as a verified reference tool. It can be used to test the output of other, unverified tools. We also include some tests that demonstrate that its performance is sufficient to do this in practice.

Keywords: Formal verification · Omega automata · Complementation

1 Introduction

Büchi complementation is the process of taking a Büchi automaton, and constructing another Büchi automaton which accepts the complementary language. It is a much-researched topic [10,15,20,37,38]. In fact, it has been so popular that there are now several meta-papers [41,43] chronologuing the research itself. Much of this research has focused on the state complexity of the resulting automata (see Sect. 2.3). However, Büchi complementation also has compelling applications. Model checking usually requires having the property to be checked against as either a formula or a deterministic Büchi automaton, as those are easily negated and complemented, respectively [15]. However, having access to a general complementation procedure, it becomes possible to decide

Research supported by DFG grant CAVA (Computer Aided Verification of Automata, ES 139/5-1, NI 491/12-1, SM 73/2-1) and CAVA2 (Verified Model Checkers, KR 4890/1-1, LA 3292/1-1).

B. Dongol and E. Troubitsyna (Eds.): IFM 2020, LNCS 12546, pp. 239–256, 2020.
https://doi.org/10.1007/978-3-030-63461-2_13

language containment between arbitrary nondeterministic Büchi automata. This not only allows for more general model checking, but also enables checking if two automata are equivalent in terms of their language.

Unfortunately, complementation algorithms are complicated and their correctness proofs are involved. This is common in the model checking setting and there are examples of algorithms widely believed to be correct turning out not to be [8,18,40]. The situation is especially troubling as these tools act as trust multipliers. That is, the trust in the correctness of one tool is used to justify confidence in the correctness of the many entities that it checks. Motivated by this situation, our goal is to formally verify one such complementation algorithm.

We use the proof assistant Isabelle/HOL [34] for this. Thanks to its LCF-like architecture, Isabelle/HOL and the formalizations it facilitates grant very strong correctness guarantees. Our contributions are as follows.

1. Formalization of rank-based complementation [20] theory
2. Formally verified complementation implementation
3. Formally verified equivalence checker
4. Extension and continued development of automata library [7,9]

In previous work, Stephan Merz formalized complementation of weak alternating automata [33]. He also started working on a formalization of Büchi complementation. However, this only covers the first part of the complementation procedure and was never finished or published. Thus, our work constitutes what we believe to be the first formally verified implementation of Büchi complementation. The verification gaplessly covers everything from the abstract correctness proof to the executable SML code.

The equivalence checker can be used as a command-line tool to check automata in the Hanoi Omega-Automata format [1]. It takes the role of a trusted reference implementation that can be used to test the correctness of other tools, like those translating from LTL formulae to automata. With an equivalence checker, it is possible to test whether several algorithms produce automata with identical languages, given the same formula. It is also possible to test if an algorithm that simplifies automata preserves their language.

2   Theory

We follow the rank-based complementation construction described in [20]. The central concept here is the *odd ranking*, a function f that certifies the rejection of a word w by the automaton A. The complement automaton $\overline{A}$ is then designed to nondeterministically search for such an odd ranking, accepting if and only if one exists. Thus, the complement automaton accepts exactly those words that the original automaton rejects.

$$w \notin \mathcal{L}\, A \iff \exists f.\, \mathrm{odd\_ranking}\, A\, w\, f \iff w \in \mathcal{L}\, \overline{A} \qquad (1)$$

Having access to complement and product operations as well as an emptiness check, we can then decide language containment.

$$\mathcal{L}\, A \subseteq \mathcal{L}\, B \iff \mathcal{L}\, A \cap \overline{\mathcal{L}\, B} = \emptyset \iff \mathcal{L}\left(A \times \overline{B}\right) = \emptyset \qquad (2)$$

Checking for containment in both directions then leads to a decision procedure for language-wise equivalence of Büchi automata.

2.1   Notation

We introduce some basic notation. Let $w \in \Sigma^\omega$ be an infinite sequence and $w_k \in \Sigma$ be the symbol at index k in w. Let $A = (\Sigma, Q, I, \delta, F)$ be a nondeterministic Büchi automaton with alphabet Σ, states Q, initial states $I :: Q$ set, successor function $\delta :: \Sigma \to Q \to Q$ set, and acceptance condition $F :: Q \to$ bool. Let $\mathcal{L}\ A \subseteq \Sigma^\omega$ denote the language of automaton A.

2.2   Complementation

We want to realize complementation according to Eq. 1. For this, we need to define odd rankings and the complement automaton. We also need to define run DAGs as a prerequisite for odd rankings.

A run DAG is a graph whose nodes are pairs of states and natural numbers. Given an automaton A and a word w, we define it inductively as follows.

Definition 1 (Run DAG). $G = (V, E)$ *with* $V \subseteq Q \times \mathbb{N}$ *and* $E \subseteq V \times V$

$$
\begin{aligned}
p \in I &\implies (p, 0) \in V \\
(p, k) \in V \implies q \in \delta\ w_k\ p &\implies (q, k+1) \in V \\
(p, k) \in V \implies q \in \delta\ w_k\ p &\implies ((p, k), (q, k+1)) \in E
\end{aligned}
$$

Intuitively, each node $(p, k) \in V$ represents A being in state p after having read k characters from w. With that, the run DAG contains all possible paths that A can take while reading w.

We can now define odd rankings. An odd ranking is a function assigning a rank to each node in the run DAG. Given an automaton A and a word w, we require the following properties to hold for odd rankings.

Definition 2 (Odd Ranking).   odd_ranking $A\ w\ f$ *with* $f :: V \to \mathbb{N}$

$$
\begin{aligned}
&\forall v \in V. & &f\ v \leq 2|Q| \\
&\forall (u, v) \in E. & &f\ u \geq f\ v \\
&\forall (p, k) \in V. & &F\ p \implies \text{even}\ (f\ (p, k)) \\
&\forall r \in \text{paths}\ G.\ \textit{the path } r \textit{ eventually gets stuck in an odd rank} & &
\end{aligned}
$$

Intuitively, the rank of a node indicates the distance to a node from which no more accepting states are visited [15].

The final definition concerns the actual complement automaton. Given an automaton $A = (\Sigma, Q, I, \delta, F)$, we define its complement as follows.

Definition 3 (Complement Automaton). $\overline{A} = (\Sigma, Q_C, I_C, \delta_C, F_C)$

$$\delta_1 \quad :: \quad \Sigma \to (Q \rightharpoonup \mathbb{N}) \to (Q \rightharpoonup \mathbb{N}) \text{ set}$$

$$g \in \delta_1 \; a \; f \iff \text{dom } g = \bigcup p \in \text{dom } f. \; \delta \; a \; p \; \wedge$$
$$\forall p \in \text{dom } f. \; \forall q \in \delta \; a \; p. \; f \; p \geq g \; q \; \wedge$$
$$\forall q \in \text{dom } g. \; F \; q \implies \text{even } (g \; q)$$

$$\delta_2 \quad :: \quad \Sigma \to (Q \rightharpoonup \mathbb{N}) \to Q \text{ set} \to Q \text{ set}$$

$$\delta_2 \; a \; g \; P \quad = \quad \begin{cases} \{q \in \text{dom } g \mid \text{even } (g \; q)\} & \textit{if } P = \{\} \\ \{q \in \bigcup p \in P. \; \delta \; a \; p \mid \text{even } (g \; q)\} & \textit{otherwise} \end{cases}$$

$$Q_C \quad :: \quad ((Q \rightharpoonup \mathbb{N}) \times Q \text{ set}) \text{ set}$$
$$Q_C \quad = \quad \delta_C^* \; \Sigma \; I_C$$

$$I_C \quad :: \quad Q_C \text{ set}$$
$$I_C \quad = \quad (\lambda p \in I. \; 2 \, |Q|, \emptyset)$$

$$\delta_C \quad :: \quad \Sigma \to Q_C \to Q_C \text{ set}$$
$$\delta_C \; a \; (f, P) \quad = \quad \{(g, \delta_2 \; a \; g \; P) \mid g \in \delta_1 \; a \; f\}$$

$$F_C \quad :: \quad Q_C \to \text{bool}$$
$$F_C \; (f, P) \quad = \quad (P = \emptyset)$$

Since the complement automaton is designed to nondeterministically search for an odd ranking, many of the properties from Definition 2 reappear here. Instead of a ranking on the whole run DAG ($V \to \mathbb{N}$), the complement automaton deals with *level rankings*. These assign ranks to only the reachable nodes in the current level ($Q \to \mathbb{N}$). Furthermore, each state keeps track of which paths have yet to visit an odd rank (Q set). This encodes the property of every path getting stuck in an odd rank, with the acceptance condition requiring this set to become empty infinitely often. Together, these lead to the state type ($Q \to \mathbb{N}$) × Q set.

2.3   Complexity and Optimizations

Much of the interest in Büchi complementation focuses on its state complexity [15,38,43]. That is, one considers the number of states in the complement automaton as a function of the number of states in the original automaton. For an automaton with n states, the original construction by Büchi [10] resulted in $2^{2^{O(n)}}$ states [15]. The complementation procedure derived from Safra's determinization construction [37] reduces this to $2^{O(n \log n)}$ or n^{2n} states [15]. The algorithm from [20] generates a complement automaton with at most $(6n)^n$ states [15]. In the quest for closing the gap between the known lower and upper bounds, various optimizations to this algorithm have been proposed. The optimization in [15] lowers the bound to $\mathcal{O}((0.96n)^n)$ states. The algorithm is then adjusted further in [38] to lower the bound to $\mathcal{O}((0.76n)^n)$ states.

This being the first attempt at formalizing Büchi complementation, we chose not to implement these more involved optimizations. Instead, we favor the original version of the algorithm as presented in [20]. We do however implement one optimization mentioned in [20]. In Definition 3, for each successor q of p, the function δ_1 considers for q all ranks lower than or equal to the rank of p. We restrict δ_1 so that it only considers for q a rank that is equal to or one less than the rank of p. This does not change the language of the complement automaton and significantly restricts the number of successors generated for each state.

It is worth noting that in practice, factors other than asymptotical state complexity can also play a role. For instance, it turns out that determinization-based complementation often generates fewer states than rank-based complementation [41]. This is despite the fact that rank-based complementation is optimal in terms of asymptotical state complexity.

2.4 Equivalence

We want to realize equivalence according to Eq. 2. For this, we need to define a product operation and an emptiness check on Büchi automata.

The product construction follows the textbook approach, where the product of two nondeterministic Büchi automata results in one nondeterministic generalized Büchi automaton. For the emptiness check, we use Gabow's algorithm for strongly-connected components [16]. This enables checking emptiness of generalized Büchi automata directly, skipping the degeneralization to regular Büchi automata that is usually necessary for nested-DFS-based algorithms.

3   Formalization

With the theoretical background established, we now describe the various aspects of our formalization. This section will mostly give a high-level overview, highlighting challenges and points of interest while avoiding technical details. However, specific parts of the formalization will be presented in greater detail.

3.1   Isabelle/HOL

Isabelle/HOL [34] is a proof assistant based on Higher-Order Logic (HOL), which can be thought of as a combination of functional programming and logic. Formalizations done in Isabelle are trustworthy due to its LCF architecture. It guarantees that all proofs are checked using a small logical core which is rarely modified but tested extensively over time, reducing the trusted code base to a minimum.

Code generation in Isabelle/HOL is based on a shallow embedding of HOL constants in the target language. Equational theorems marked as code equations are translated into rewrite rules in the target language [17]. This correspondence embodies the specification of the target language semantics. As this process does not involve the LCF kernel, the code generator is part of the trusted code base.

3.2   Basics

The most basic concept needed for our formalization is that of sequences. The HOL standard library already includes extensive support for both finite and infinite sequences. They take the form of the types list and stream.

Definition 4 (Sequences)

$$\textbf{datatype } \alpha \text{ list} = [] \mid \alpha \mathbin{\#} \alpha \text{ list}$$
$$\textbf{codatatype } \alpha \text{ stream} = \alpha \mathbin{\#\#} \alpha \text{ stream}$$

The new datatype package [3, 4] allows for codatatypes like stream. The libraries of both list and stream include many common operations and their properties.

We also make use of a shallow embedding of linear temporal logic (LTL) on streams that is defined using inductive and coinductive predicates. This is used to define a predicate holding infinitely often in an infinite sequence.

Definition 5 (Infinite Occurrence). infs P w $\iff$ alw (ev (holds P)) w

3.3   Transition Systems and Automata

In our formalization, we both use and extend the *Transition Systems and Automata* library [7,9]. The development of this library was in fact motivated by the idea of formalizing Büchi complementation and determinization. Since then, it has been used in several other formalizations [6,8,9,35,36,39].

The goal of this library is to support many different types of automata while avoiding both duplication and compromising usability. This is achieved via several layers of abstraction as well as the use of Isabelle's locale mechanism. For an in-depth description, see [9]. Since then, an additional abstraction layer has been introduced to consolidate various operations on automata like intersection, union, and degeneralization. However, describing this in detail is outside the scope of this paper. Thus, we will only introduce the concepts and constants that are used in later sections. We start with the definition of a transition system.

Definition 6 (Transition System)

$$\textbf{locale } \text{transition\_system} =$$
$$\textbf{fixes } \text{execute} :: transition \Rightarrow state \Rightarrow state$$
$$\textbf{fixes } \text{enabled} :: transition \Rightarrow state \Rightarrow \text{bool}$$

It fixes type variables for transitions and states as well as constants to determine which transitions are enabled in each state and which target states they lead to. This locale forms the backbone of the library. Note that it may look like it can only be used to model (sub-)deterministic transition systems. However, by instantiating the type variable *transition*, we can actually model many different types of transition systems, including nondeterministic ones [9].

We can then define concepts concerning sequences of transitions.

Definition 7 (Targets and Traces)

$$target = \text{fold execute} :: transition \text{ list} \Rightarrow state \Rightarrow state$$
$$trace = \text{scan execute} :: transition \text{ list} \Rightarrow state \Rightarrow state \text{ list}$$
$$strace = \text{sscan execute} :: transition \text{ stream} \Rightarrow state \Rightarrow state \text{ stream}$$

Given a sequence of transitions and a source state, these functions give the target state and the finite and infinite sequence of traversed states, respectively. Note how each of these is simply a lifted version of execute.

We can also define constants for finite and infinite paths, respectively.

Definition 8 (Paths)

inductive path :: $transition$ list $\Rightarrow state \Rightarrow$ bool **where**
    path $[]$ p
    enabled a p $\implies$ path r (execute a p) $\implies$ path $(a \# r)$ p
coinductive spath :: $transition$ stream $\Rightarrow state \Rightarrow$ bool **where**
    enabled a p $\implies$ spath r (execute a p) $\implies$ spath $(a \# \# r)$ p

These constants are (co)inductively defined predicates that capture the notion of all the transitions in a sequence being enabled at their respective states. Like before, these are lifted versions of enabled, which is also reflected in their types.

3.4 Run DAGs

Having established all the basics and foundations, we can now turn to the actual formalization of Büchi complementation. We start with formalizing Definition 1 concerning run DAGs. We do this by instantiating the transition system locale from Definition 6. This yields definitions for all the required graph-related concepts, like finite and infinite paths as well as reachability.

We then establish a tight correspondence between these definitions and the ones concerning automata. This requires mostly elemental induction and coinduction proofs. Only minor technical work was required to translate between paths in the automaton being labeled and paths in its run DAG being indexed.

3.5 Odd Rankings

Having formalized run DAGs, we can now formalize Definition 2 concerning odd rankings. The resulting formal definition does not differ significantly from its informal counterpart and will thus not be repeated here.

We prove the left equivalence from Eq. 1, which states that an odd ranking f exists if and only if the automaton A rejects the word w.

$$w \notin \mathcal{L}\, A \iff \exists f.\, \text{odd\_ranking}\ A\ w\ f$$

We follow the proof given in [20].

The direction $\Longleftarrow$ is fairly straightforward. Given an odd ranking, we immediately have that all infinite paths in the run DAG get trapped in an odd rank. Together with the fact that odd ranks are not accepting, we obtain that all infinite paths in the automaton are not accepting. Formally proving this is mainly technical work consisting of establishing the correspondence between the run DAG and the automaton. However, there is one exception. In [20], the fact that all infinite paths get trapped in some rank is merely stated as part of the definition of rankings. While this is intuitively obvious from the fact that ranks are natural numbers and always decreasing along a path, it still requires rigorous proof in a formal setting. Thus, we need to define the notion of decreasing infinite sequences and prove this property via well-founded induction on the ranks.

The direction $\Longrightarrow$ is a lot more involved. It requires defining an infinite sequence of subgraphs of the run DAG in order to construct an odd ranking. Again, we follow the proof given in [20]. As before, we were able to follow the high-level ideas of this proof in the formalized version, with some parts requiring more fine-grained reasoning or additional technical work. However, we want to highlight one particular technique that is used several times in the proof and that required special attention in the formalized version. While most of our descriptions focus on high-level ideas, we also want to take this opportunity to present one part of the formalization in greater detail.

The idea in question concerns itself with the construction of infinite paths in graphs and transition systems. We already encountered this type of reasoning in [8]. Assume that there is a state with property P, and that for every state with property P we can find a path to another state with property P. Then, there exists an infinite path that contains infinitely many states with property P. Intuitively, this seems obvious, which is why in informal proofs, statements like these require no further elaboration. However, in a formal setting, this requires rigorous reasoning, resulting in the following proof.

Lemma 1 (Recurring Condition)

> **lemma** recurring_condition:
>   **assumes** "$P\ p$" "$\forall p.\ P\ p \implies \exists r.\ r \neq [] \wedge$ path $r\ p \wedge P$ (target $r\ p$)"
>   **obtains** r **where** "spath $r\ p$" "infs P ($p\,\#\#$ strace $r\ p$)"
> **proof** −
>   **obtain** f **where** "$f\ p \neq []$" "path ($f\ p$) p" "P (target ($f\ p$) p)"
>   **if** "$P\ p$" **for** p **by** ...
>   **let** $?g =$ "$\lambda p.$ target ($f\ p$) p"
>   **let** $?r =$ "$\lambda p.$ flat (smap f (siterate $?g\ p$))"
>   **have** "$?r\ p = f\ p$ @- $?r$ ($?g\ p$)" **if** "$P\ p$" **for** p **by** ...
>   **show** *?thesis*
>   **proof**
>   **show** "spath ($?r\ p$) p" **by** ...
>   **show** "infs P ($p\,\#\#$ strace ($?r\ p$) p)" **by** ...
>   **qed**
> **qed**

This theorem is stated for general transition systems and corresponds closely to the informal one presented earlier. That is, we assume that P holds at some state p. We also assume that for every state p where P holds, we can find a nonempty path r leading to a state target r p where P holds again. We prove that from these assumptions, one can obtain an infinite path r such that for the states it traverses, P holds infinitely often. The proof consists of three major steps.

1. Skolemization of the assumption. We obtain a function f that for each state in which P holds, gives a nonempty path that leads to another state in which P holds. This can be done by either explicitly invoking the choice theorems derived from Hilbert's epsilon operator, or by using `metis`.
2. Definition of the state iteration function $?g$ and the infinite path $?r$. We define a function $?g$ that for each state p gives the target state of the path given by f. Iterating $?g$ yields all those states along the infinite path where P holds. We can then define $?r$, which is the infinite path obtained by concatenating all the finite paths given by f from each state in the iteration of $?g$.
3. Proving the required properties of $?r$. We now prove both that $?r$ is an infinite path and that for the states it traverses, P holds infinitely often. Both of these proofs require specific coinduction rules for the constants spath and infs. This is because the coinduction cannot consume the infinite sequence one item at a time, instead having to operate on finite nonempty prefixes. However, these coinduction rules are generally useful and once proven, can be reused and improve compositionality.

In the end, a surprising amount of work is necessary to prove a seemingly obvious statement. While it is easy to dismiss this as a shortcoming of either formal logic in general or of a particular proof assistant, we do not think that this is the case. Instead, we believe that situations like these point out areas where informal proofs rely on intuition, thereby hiding the actual complexity of the proof. Since this can lead to subtle mistakes, the ability of formal proofs to make it visible is valuable and one of the reasons for our confidence in them. It is also worth noting that these situations do not persistently hinder the construction of formal proofs. By proving the statement in its most general form, this needs to be done only once for this type of reasoning to become available everywhere.

3.6   Complement Automaton

Next, we formalize Definition 3 concerning the complement automaton. As in the previous section, the resulting formal definition differs only slightly from the informal one and will thus not be repeated here.

We prove the right equivalence from Eq. 1, which states that the complement automaton $\overline{A}$ accepts a word w if and only if an odd ranking f exists.

$$\exists f. \text{ odd\_ranking } A \, w \, f \iff w \in \mathcal{L} \, \overline{A} \qquad (3)$$

We follow the proof given in [20].

There are two main challenges to formalizing this proof. The first one is converting between different representations of rankings. On the side of the odd ranking, a ranking is a function assigning ranks to the nodes in the run DAG. On the side of the complement automaton, a ranking is an infinite sequence of level rankings in the states of the accepting path. While this seems simple enough conceptually, it requires attention to detail and much technical work in the formalization. The second challenge consists of proving that two ways of stating the same property are equivalent. The last condition in the definition of the odd ranking states that all paths eventually get stuck in an odd rank. On the side of the complement automaton, this property takes the form of a set that keeps track of which paths have yet to visit an odd rank. The acceptance condition of the complement automaton then requires this set to infinitely often become empty, ensuring that no path visits even ranks indefinitely. This again requires coinduction and the construction of infinite paths.

Together with the theorem from the previous section, we obtain the correctness theorem of complementation.

Theorem 1 (Complement Language)

$$\textbf{theorem } \text{complement\_language}:$$
$$\textbf{assumes } \text{"finite (nodes } A\text{)"}$$
$$\textbf{shows } \text{"} \mathcal{L} \, \overline{A} = \Sigma^\omega \setminus \mathcal{L} \, A \text{"}$$

3.7 Refinement Framework

We want our complementation algorithm and equivalence checker to be executable. When developing formally verified algorithms, there is a trade-off between efficiency of the algorithm and simplicity of the proof. For complex algorithms, a direct proof of an efficient implementation tends to get unmanageable, as implementation details obfuscate the main ideas of the proof.

A standard approach to this problem is stepwise refinement [2], which modularizes the correctness proof. One starts with an abstract version of the algorithm and then refines it in correctness-preserving steps to the concrete, efficient version. A refinement step may reduce the nondeterminism of a program, replace abstract mathematical specifications by concrete algorithms, and replace abstract datatypes by their implementations. For example, selection of an arbitrary element from a set may be refined to getting the head of a list. This approach separates the correctness proof of the algorithm from the correctness proof of the implementation. The former can focus on algorithmic ideas without implementation details getting in the way. The latter consists of a series of refinement steps, each focusing on a specific implementation detail, without having to worry about overall correctness.

In Isabelle/HOL, stepwise refinement is supported by the Refinement Framework [24–26, 32] and the Isabelle Collections Framework [23, 29]. The former implements a refinement calculus [2] based on a nondeterminism monad [44], while the latter provides a library of verified efficient data structures. Both frameworks come with tool support to simplify their usage for algorithm development and to automate canonical tasks such as verification condition generation.

3.8   Implementation

Now that the abstract correctness of our complementation procedure is proven, we want to derive an executable algorithm from our definitions. We use the aforementioned refinement framework to refine our definitions that involve partial functions and sets to executable code working on association lists. For instance, the abstract correctness proof is most naturally stated on the complement state type $(Q \rightharpoonup \mathbb{N}) \times Q$ set. However, the isomorphic type $Q \rightharpoonup (\mathbb{N} \times \text{bool})$ is more suitable for the implementation. Thus, this and several other preliminary steps are taken to bring the definition into the correct shape. We also introduce the language-preserving optimization mentioned in Sect. 2.3 at this stage. The correctness proof of this optimization involves establishing a simulation relation between the original automaton and its optimized version.

Once these manual refinement steps are completed, we then use the automatic refinement tool [21, 22]. It allows us to automatically refine an abstract definition to an executable implementation. It does this by instantiating abstract data structures like sets and partial functions with concrete ones like lists, hash sets, and association lists. Since refinement is compositional and the structure of the algorithm is not affected by these substitutions, refinement proofs only have to be done once for each concrete data structure. As many of these data structures have already been formalized in the library, very little has to be proven manually by the user. For instance, choosing to implement a set with a hash set instead of a list can be as simple as adding a type annotation. In particular, none of the refinement proofs have to be adjusted or redone.

At this stage, we have an executable definition that takes a successor function and gives the successor function of the complement automaton. However, we also want to be able to generate the complement automaton as a whole in an explicit representation. To do this, we make use of the DFS Framework [30, 31]. It comes with a sample instantiation that collects all unique nodes in a graph. We define the graph induced by a given automaton and generate an executable definition of its successor function. We can then run the previously verified DFS algorithm on this graph to explore the complement automaton. The correctness proof of this algorithm then states that these are indeed all of the reachable states.

The complement automaton now has the state type $(Q \times (\mathbb{N} \times \text{bool}))$ list. This is the association list implementation of the type $Q \rightharpoonup \mathbb{N} \times \text{bool}$ mentioned earlier. Since this type is rather unwieldy, we use the result of the exploration phase to rename all the complement states using natural numbers. We then use the states explored by the DFS algorithm to collect all of the transitions in the automaton. The end result is an explicit representation of the complement automaton with label type α and state type $\mathbb{N}$. We have $\overline{A} = (\Sigma, I, \delta, F)$ with $\Sigma :: \alpha$ list, $I :: \mathbb{N}$ list, $\delta :: (\mathbb{N} \times \alpha \times \mathbb{N})$ list, and $F :: \mathbb{N}$ list.

3.9 Equivalence

We now want to use our complementation algorithm to build an equivalence checker as outlined in Sect. 2.4. In order to decide language containment and thus equivalence, we still need a product operation and an emptiness check. To this end, we add more operations to the automata library [7]. We already added several operations for deterministic Büchi automata, deterministic co-Büchi automata, and deterministic Rabin automata as part of [9,39]. We now also add intersection, union, and degeneralization constructions for nondeterministic Büchi automata. Thanks to the new intermediate abstraction layer mentioned in Sect. 3.3, these operations generalize to all other nondeterministic automata in the library. The main challenge here was finding an abstraction for degeneralization that enables sharing this part of the formalization between both deterministic and nondeterministic automata. In the end, this was achieved by stating the main idea of degeneralization on streams rather than automata.

As mentioned in Sect. 2.4, we use an emptiness check based on Gabow's algorithm for strongly-connected components. For this, we reuse a formalization originally developed as part of the CAVA model checker [13,14]. This formalization [27,28] includes both the abstract correctness proof of the algorithm, as well as executable code. Furthermore, it supports checking emptiness of generalized Büchi automata directly, enabling us to skip the degeneralization step that would usually be necessary after the product. This turns out to be significantly faster.

We now assemble these parts into an equivalence checker and then refine it to be executable. In contrast to complementation, this algorithm is much more compositional, simplifying both the abstract correctness proof and the refinement steps. We ran into one issue with the correctness theorem in the formalization of Gabow's algorithm [27,28] not being strong enough due to some technicalities. We would like to thank the author Peter Lammich for quickly generalizing the theorem after this issue was discovered.

3.10 Integration

With all the pieces in place, it is now time to integrate everything into a command-line tool. Having refined all of our definitions to be executable, we can already export SML code from Isabelle. In order for these algorithms to function as part of a stand-alone tool, we need the ability to input and output automata. For this, we have decided to use the Hanoi Omega-Automata format [1], also called HOA. It is used by other automata tools such as Spot [11], Owl [19], and GOAL [42]. The handling of command-line parameters as well as HOA parsing and printing are implemented manually in SML. This piece of code wraps the verified algorithm in a command-line tool and is the only unverified part of the final executable.

The result is a command-line tool with two modes of operation: complementation and equivalence checking. Complementation takes an input automaton in the HOA format and outputs the complement automaton either as a transition list or in the HoA format. Equivalence checking takes two input automata in the HoA format and outputs a truth value indicating their equivalence.

Our formalization is available as part of the Archive of Formal Proofs [5].

4   Evaluation

We evaluate the performance of both our complementation implementation and our equivalence checker. As a benchmark for raw complementation performance, we run our implementation on randomly-generated automata. The results are shown in Fig. 1.

States	Samples	Completion Rate	Average Time
5	393 438	100.00 %	0.006 s
10	41 496	99.98 %	0.110 s
15	15 616	98.30 %	3.112 s
20	16 950	36.58 %	22.695 s

Fig. 1. Complementation Performance. We use Spot's `randaut` tool to generate random automata with a given number of states. We then run our complementation implementation on them. The time limit was set to 60 s.

Furthermore, we compare the performance of our complementation implementation to Spot [11] and GOAL [42]. The results are shown in Fig. 2.

Tool	Completion Rate	Average Time	States
Spot (`--complement --ba`)	100.00 %	0.006 s	12.76
GOAL (`rank -tr`)	84.13 %	0.837 s	91.3
GOAL (`rank -rd`)	69.01 %	5.661 s	6 010
Our Tool	79.36 %	0.683 s	6 010

Fig. 2. Complementation Performance Comparison. We use Spot's `randltl` and `ltl2tgba` tools to generate automata from random LTL formulae. Automata with a state count other than 10 are discarded and the rest is complemented with various tools. Out of 5741 samples, 3962 could be complemented by all tools within the time limit of 60 s. To ensure comparability, we use the latter set of automata for the average time and complement states statistics.

Our tool implements the same algorithm as GOAL with the rank decrement option (`rank -rd`), which is also reflected in the identical number of states of the complement automata. However, our implementation has significantly shorter execution times thanks to extensive profiling efforts and use of efficient data structures from the Isabelle Collections Framework [23,29]. In fact, this effect is so large that it somewhat makes up for the worse asymptotical state complexity when compared to GOAL with the tight rank option (`rank -tr`). The latter has significant startup overhead, but performs better on automata that are difficult to complement. While the performance of Spot is superior to either of the other tools, we want to emphasize that absolute competitiveness with unverified tools is not the goal of our work. As long as our tool is fast enough to process practical examples, it can serve its purpose as a verified reference implementation.

We also evaluate the performance of the equivalence checker. To do so, we generate random LTL formulae and translate them to Büchi automata via both Spot [11] and Owl [19]. We then use our equivalence checker on these automata. The results are shown in Fig. 3.

States	Samples	Completion Rate	Average Time
$(0, 5]$	73 001	100.00 %	0.004 s
$(5, 10]$	16 024	98.49 %	0.632 s
$(10, 15]$	4 128	88.32 %	3.607 s
$(15, 20]$	1 347	64.88 %	5.203 s
$(20, \infty)$	1 370	39.12 %	8.543 s
total	95 870	97.88 %	0.347 s

Fig. 3. Equivalence Checker Performance. We use Spot's `randltl` tool to generate random LTL formulae. We then use Spot's `ltl2tgba` tool as well as Owl's `ltl2dra` translation in conjunction with Spot's `autfilt` tool to obtain two translations of the same formula. Finally, we use our equivalence checker to check if both automata do indeed have the same language. The time limit was set to 60 s. The state count shown is that of the larger of the two automata.

When running the equivalence checker on automata that are not equivalent, the performance is often better. This is due to the fact that the algorithm searches for an accepting cycle in either $A \times \overline{B}$ or $\overline{A} \times B$. As soon as such a cycle is found, it can abort and return a negative answer. Since both complement and product are represented implicitly, this avoids constructing the full state space.

Finally, we use the same testing procedure on translations of the well-known "Dwyer"-patterns [12]. We were able to successfully check 52 out of the 55 formulae with the following exceptions. One formula resulted in automata of sizes 13 and 8, respectively, whose equivalence could not be verified within the time limit of 600 s. Two more formulae were successfully translated by Owl's `ltl2dra` translation procedure, but Spot's `autfilt` tool could not translate them to a nondeterministic Büchi automaton within the time limit of 600 s. Note that Spot's `autfilt` tool was also set up to simplify the resulting automata, as otherwise, they would quickly grow to be too large. Out of the 52 checked formulae, 49 could be processed in a matter of milliseconds, with two taking about a second and one taking 129 s.

From these tests we conclude that the performance of our tool is good enough to serve as a verified reference tool for examples of practical relevance. Note that tools like Spot include many more optimizations and heuristics that enable them to complement into much smaller automata as well as check the equivalence of much larger automata. However, it is not our goal to compete with Spot, but rather to provide a verified reference tool that is fast enough to be useful for testing other tools.

It turns out that we do not have to look far to find an illustration for this point. While gathering data for this section, our equivalence checker discovered a language mismatch between Spot's and Owl's translation of the same LTL formula. The developers of Owl confirmed that this was indeed a bug in the implementation of its `ltl2dra` translation procedure and promptly fixed it. Manifestation of this issue was very rare, first occurring after about 50 000 randomly-generated formulae. This demonstrates the need for verified reference implementations, as even extensively tested software can still contain undetected issues.

5 Conclusion

We developed a formally verified and executable complementation procedure and equivalence checker. The formal theory acts as a very detailed and machine-checkable description of rank-based complementation. Additionally, our formalization includes executable reference tools. These come with a strong correctness guarantee as everything from the abstract correctness down to the executable SML code is covered by the verification. This high confidence in their correctness justifies their use to test other, unverified tools.

We also contributed additional functionality as well as an improved architecture to the automata library. This emphasizes the software engineering aspect of formal theory development where theories can be reused and become more and more useful as they mature.

For future work, it would be desirable to formalize an algorithm that generates a complement automaton with fewer states. As mentioned in Sect. 2.3, this concerns both asymptotical state complexity as well as performance in practice. It would also be of interest to verify the bounds on asymptotical state complexity.

References

1. Babiak, T., et al.: The Hanoi omega-automata format. In: Kroening, D., Păsăreanu, C.S. (eds.) CAV 2015. LNCS, vol. 9206, pp. 479–486. Springer, Cham (2015). https://doi.org/10.1007/978-3-319-21690-4_31
2. Back, R.-J., von Wright, J.: Refinement Calculus - A Systematic Introduction. Texts in Computer Science. Springer, New York (1998). https://doi.org/10.1007/978-1-4612-1674-2
3. Biendarra, J., et al.: Foundational (Co)datatypes and (Co)recursion for higher-order logic. In: Dixon, C., Finger, M. (eds.) FroCoS 2017. LNCS (LNAI), vol. 10483, pp. 3–21. Springer, Cham (2017). https://doi.org/10.1007/978-3-319-66167-4_1
4. Blanchette, J.C., Hölzl, J., Lochbihler, A., Panny, L., Popescu, A., Traytel, D.: Truly modular (Co)datatypes for isabelle/HOL. In: Klein, G., Gamboa, R. (eds.) ITP 2014. LNCS, vol. 8558, pp. 93–110. Springer, Cham (2014). https://doi.org/10.1007/978-3-319-08970-6_7

5. Brunner, J.: Büchi complementation. In: Archive of Formal Proofs (2017). https://www.isa-afp.org/entries/Buchi_Complementation.html
6. Brunner, J.: Partial order reduction. In: Archive of Formal Proofs (2018). https://www.isa-afp.org/entries/Partial_Order_Reduction.html
7. Brunner, J.: Transition systems and automata. In: Archive of Formal Proofs (2017). https://www.isa-afp.org/entries/Transition_Systems_and_Automata.html
8. Brunner, J., Lammich, P.: Formal verification of an executable LTL model checker with partial order reduction. J. Autom. Reason. **60**, 3–21 (2018). https://doi.org/10.1007/s10817-017-9418-4
9. Brunner, J., Seidl, B., Sickert, S.: A verified and compositional translation of LTL to deterministic rabin automata. In: ITP 2019 (2019). https://doi.org/10.4230/LIPIcs.ITP.2019.11
10. Richard Büchi, J.: On a decision method in restricted second order arithmetic. In: Proceedings of the International Congress on Logic, Methodology, and Philosophy of Science, p. 1962, Berkeley, California, USA (1960)
11. Duret-Lutz, A., Lewkowicz, A., Fauchille, A., Michaud, T., Renault, É., Xu, L.: Spot 2.0 — a framework for LTL and ω-automata manipulation. In: Artho, C., Legay, A., Peled, D. (eds.) ATVA 2016. LNCS, vol. 9938, pp. 122–129. Springer, Cham (2016). https://doi.org/10.1007/978-3-319-46520-3_8
12. Dwyer, M.B., Avrunin, G.S., Corbett, J.C.: Property specification patterns for finite-state verification. In: Proceedings of the Second Workshop on Formal Methods in Software Practice (1998). https://doi.org/10.1145/298595.298598
13. Esparza, J., Lammich, P., Neumann, R., Nipkow, T., Schimpf, A., Smaus, J.-G.: A fully verified executable LTL model checker. In: Sharygina, N., Veith, H. (eds.) CAV 2013. LNCS, vol. 8044, pp. 463–478. Springer, Heidelberg (2013). https://doi.org/10.1007/978-3-642-39799-8_31
14. Esparza, J., Lammich, P., Neumann, R., Nipkow, T., Schimpf, A., Smaus, J.: A fully verified executable LTL model checker. In: Archive of Formal Proofs 2014 (2014). https://www.isa-afp.org/entries/CAVA_LTL_Modelchecker.shtml
15. Friedgut, E., Kupferman, O., Vardi, M.Y.: Büchi complementation made tighter. Int. J. Found. Comput. Sci. **17**(4), 851–868 (2006). https://doi.org/10.1142/S0129054106004145
16. Gabow, H.N.: Path-based depth-first search for strong and biconnected components. Inf. Process. Lett. **74**(3–4), 107–114 (2000). https://doi.org/10.1016/S0020-0190(00)00051-X
17. Haftmann, F., Nipkow, T.: Code generation via higher-order rewrite systems. In: Blume, M., Kobayashi, N., Vidal, G. (eds.) FLOPS 2010. LNCS, vol 6009, pp. 103–117. Springer, Berlin, Heidelberg (2010).https://doi.org/10.1007/978-3-642-12251-4_9
18. Holzmann, G.J., Peled, D.A., Yannakakis, M.: On nested depth first search. In: The Spin Verification System, Proceedings of a DIMACS Workshop (1996). https://doi.org/10.1090/dimacs/032/03
19. Křetínský, J., Meggendorfer, T., Sickert, S.: Owl: a library for ω-Words, automata, and LTL. In: Lahiri, S.K., Wang, C. (eds.) ATVA 2018. LNCS, vol. 11138, pp. 543–550. Springer, Cham (2018). https://doi.org/10.1007/978-3-030-01090-4_34
20. Kupferman, O., Vardi, M.Y.: Weak alternating automata are not that weak. ACM Trans. Comput. Log. **2**(3), 408–429 (2001). https://doi.org/10.1145/377978.377993
21. Lammich, P.: Automatic data refinement. In: Archive of Formal Proofs (2013).https://www.isa-afp.org/entries/Automatic_Refinement.shtml

22. Lammich, P.: Automatic data refinement. In: Blazy, S., Paulin-Mohring, C., Pichardie, D. (eds.) ITP 2013. LNCS, vol. 7998, pp. 84–99. Springer, Heidelberg (2013). https://doi.org/10.1007/978-3-642-39634-2_9

23. Lammich, P.: Collections framework. In: Archive of Formal Proofs (2009). https://www.isa-afp.org/entries/Collections.shtml

24. Lammich, P.: Refinement for monadic programs. In: Archive of Formal Proofs (2012). https://www.isa-afp.org/entries/Refine_Monadic.shtml

25. Lammich, P.: Refinement to imperative/HOL. In: Urban, C., Zhang, X. (eds.) ITP 2015. LNCS, vol. 9236, pp. 253–269. Springer, Cham (2015). https://doi.org/10.1007/978-3-319-22102-1_17

26. Lammich, P.: The imperative refinement framework. In: Archive of Formal Proofs (2016). https://www.isa-afp.org/entries/Refine_Imperative_HOL.shtml

27. Lammich, P.: Verified efficient implementation of Gabow's strongly connected component algorithm. In: Klein, G., Gamboa, R. (eds.) ITP 2014. LNCS, vol. 8558, pp. 325–340. Springer, Cham (2014). https://doi.org/10.1007/978-3-319-08970-6_21

28. Lammich, P.: Verified efficient implementation of Gabow's strongly connected components algorithm. In: Archive of Formal Proofs (2014). https://www.isa-afp.org/entries/Gabow_SCC.shtml

29. Lammich, P., Lochbihler, A.: The Isabelle collections framework. In: Kaufmann, M., Paulson, L.C. (eds.) ITP 2010. LNCS, vol. 6172, pp. 339–354. Springer, Heidelberg (2010). https://doi.org/10.1007/978-3-642-14052-5_24

30. Lammich, P., Neumann, R.: A framework for verifying depth- first search algorithms. In: CPP 2015 (2015). https://doi.org/10.1145/2676724.2693165

31. Lammich, P., Neumann, R.: A framework for verifying depth- first search algorithms. In: Archive of Formal Proofs (2016). https://www.isa-afp.org/entries/DFS_Framework.shtml

32. Lammich, P., Tuerk, T.: Applying data refinement for monadic programs to Hopcroft's algorithm. In: Beringer, L., Felty, A. (eds.) ITP 2012. LNCS, vol. 7406, pp. 166–182. Springer, Heidelberg (2012). https://doi.org/10.1007/978-3-642-32347-8_12

33. Merz, S.: Weak alternating automata in Isabelle/HOL. In: Aagaard, M., Harrison, J. (eds.) TPHOLs 2000. LNCS, vol. 1869, pp. 424–441. Springer, Heidelberg (2000). https://doi.org/10.1007/3-540-44659-1_26

34. Nipkow, T., Wenzel, M., Paulson, L.C. (eds.): Isabelle/HOL. A Proof Assistant for Higher-Order Logic. LNCS, vol. 2283. Springer, Heidelberg (2002). https://doi.org/10.1007/3-540-45949-9

35. Sachtleben, R.: Formalisation of an adaptive state counting algorithm. In: Archive of Formal Proofs (2019). https://www.isaafp.org/entries/Adaptive_State_Counting.html

36. Sachtleben, R., et al.: A mechanised proof of an adaptive state counting algorithm. In: ICTSS 2019. https://doi.org/10.1007/978-3-030-31280-0_11

37. Safra, S.: On the complexity of omega-automata. In: 29th Annual Symposium on Foundations of Computer Science (1988). https://doi.org/10.1109/SFCS.1988.21948

38. Schewe, S.: Büchi complementation made tight. In: STACS 2009 (2009). https://doi.org/10.4230/LIPIcs.STACS.2009.1854

39. Seidl, B., Sickert, S.: A compositional and unified translation of LTL into !-Automata. In: Archive of Formal Proofs (2019). https://www.isa-afp.org/entries/LTL_Master_Theorem.html

40. Siegel, S.F.: What's wrong with on-the-fly partial order reduction. In: Dillig, I., Tasiran, S. (eds.) CAV 2019. LNCS, vol. 11562, pp. 478–495. Springer, Cham (2019). https://doi.org/10.1007/978-3-030-25543-5_27

41. Tsai, M.-H., et al.: State of büchi complementation. Log. Method Comput. Sci. 104 (2014). https://doi.org/10.2168/LMCS-10(4:13)2014

42. Tsay, Y.-K., Chen, Y.-F., Tsai, M.-H., Wu, K.-N., Chan, W.-C.: GOAL: a graphical tool for manipulating Büchi automata and temporal formulae. In: Grumberg, O., Huth, M. (eds.) TACAS 2007. LNCS, vol. 4424, pp. 466–471. Springer, Heidelberg (2007). https://doi.org/10.1007/978-3-540-71209-1_35

43. Vardi, M.Y.: The Büchi complementation saga. In: STACS 2007 (2007). https://doi.org/10.1007/978-3-540-70918-3_2

44. Wadler, P.: Comprehending monads. Math. Struct. Comput. Sci. 4, 461–493 (1992). https://doi.org/10.1017/S0960129500001560

A Generic Approach to the Verification of the Permutation Property of Sequential and Parallel Swap-Based Sorting Algorithms

Mohsen Safari[✉] and Marieke Huisman

Formal Methods and Tools, University of Twente, Enschede, The Netherlands
{m.safari,m.huisman}@utwente.nl

Abstract. Sorting is one of the fundamental operations in computer science, and many sequential and parallel algorithms have been proposed in the literature. Swap-based sorting algorithms are one category of sorting algorithms where elements are swapped repeatedly to achieve the desired order. Since these algorithms are widely used in practice, their (functional) correctness, i.e., proving sortedness and permutation properties, is of utmost importance. However, proving the permutation property using automated program verifiers is much more challenging as the formal definition of this property involves existential quantifiers. In this paper, we propose a generic pattern to verify the permutation property for any sequential and parallel swap-based sorting algorithm automatically. To demonstrate our approach, we use VerCors, a verification tool based on separation logic for concurrent and parallel programs, to verify the permutation property of bubble sort, selection sort, insertion sort, parallel odd-even transposition sort, quick sort, two in-place merge sorts and TimSort for any arbitrary size of input.

Keywords: Sorting algorithms · Deductive verification · Separation logic

1 Introduction

Sorting is one of the fundamental and frequently used operations in computer science. Sorting algorithms take a list of elements as input and rearrange them into a particular order as output. Sorting has many applications in searching, data structures and data bases. Because of its importance, the literature contains many sorting algorithms with different complexity. One category of sorting algorithms is swap-based sorting, where the elements are swapped repeatedly until the desired order is achieved (e.g., bubble sort).

Because of the increase in the amount of data and emerging multi-core architectures, also parallel versions of sorting algorithms have been proposed. For

This work is supported by NWO grant 639.023.710 for the Mercedes project.

B. Dongol and E. Troubitsyna (Eds.): IFM 2020, LNCS 12546, pp. 257–275, 2020.
https://doi.org/10.1007/978-3-030-63461-2_14

instance, odd-even transposition sort [16] has been proposed as a parallel version of the bubble sort algorithm. Parallelizing algorithms on many-core processors (e.g., GPGPUs) is an active area of research, and it has been shown that parallel (GPU-based) implementations of sorting algorithms [14,15,18,19,21,23] outperform their sequential (CPU-based) counterparts.

Due to the frequent use of both sequential and parallel sorting algorithms, their correctness is of utmost importance, which means that they must have the following properties: (1) sortedness: the output is ordered, and (2) permutation: the output is a permutation of the input (i.e., the elements do not change).

To establish these two properties of sorting algorithms, one can use dynamic approaches (e.g., testing) and run the programs with concrete inputs to find bugs. However, this does not guarantee the absence of bugs. In contrast, with static verification, the complete state space of a program is analyzed without running it. In deductive verification, a program is annotated with intermediate (invariant) properties. Then, using a program logic, the annotated code is translated into proof obligations which are discharged by an automated theorem prover.

Using deductive program verification, proving the permutation property is harder than the sortedness property. This might be surprising at first glance, since in the swap-based sorting algorithms, the main operation is only swapping two elements repeatedly. But the permutation property typically requires reasoning about existential quantifiers, which is challenging for the underlying automated theorem provers.

As discussed by Filliatre [9], there are three common solutions: (1) in a higher order logic, one can state the existence of a bijection; (2) one can use multisets, a collection of unordered lists of elements where multiple instances can occur; and (3) one can define a permutation as the smallest equivalence relation containing the transpositions (i.e., the exchanges of elements). In [9,11], it is shown that the third approach is the best solution for automated proofs of the permutation property, but it is still not easy to define it formally. The literature contains various examples of permutation proofs, following the third approach [3,10,11,22,24,25]. In these papers, a permutation is formally defined and some of its properties (e.g., transitivity) are proved using deductive program verifiers, such as KeY [1] or Why3 [12] or interactive theorem provers like Coq [7]. However, they are ad hoc and there is a new proof for each algorithm.

In this paper, we recognize that there is a *uniform pattern* and we exploit this to prove the permutation property of any sequential and parallel swap-based sorting algorithm. We do this using VerCors [4], which is a deductive verification tool for reasoning about the correctness of concurrent programs. There are several advantages of our approach w.r.t. the previous work. First, none of the existing papers verified the permutation property of embarrassingly parallel sorting algorithms (e.g., in GPGPU). We demonstrate that our uniform approach also works for such algorithms by proving the permutation property of the parallel odd-even transposition sort algorithm. Second, the technique works for all languages supported in the tool such as C, Java and OpenCL, which means it is possible to prove the permutation property of sorting algorithms in a variety of real-world languages. Third, in our permutation proof pattern, we use ghost variables[1] to keep track of value changes, which can be reused when establishing sortedness. Forth, we illustrate the generality of our approach by proving the permutation property of a vast collection of well-known sorting algorithms all together in one place.

Contributions. The main contributions of this paper are:

1. We outline a generic approach to verify the permutation property of any sequential and parallel swap-based sorting algorithm automatically.
2. We illustrate our technique by proving the permutation property of bubble sort, selection sort, insertion sort, parallel odd-even transposition sort, quick sort, two in-place merge sorts and TimSort, using the VerCors verifier.

Organization. Section 2 explains VerCors and its logic, by a verification example. Section 3 discusses the proposed generic approach to prove the permutation property and Sect. 4 applies it to an extensive collection of well-known sorting algorithms. Section 5 discusses related work and Sect. 6 concludes the paper.

2   VerCors

This section describes VerCors and the logic behind it along with a simple program verification example. VerCors[2] is a verifier to specify and verify (concurrent and parallel) programs written in a high-level language such as (subsets of) Java, C, OpenCL, OpenMP and PVL, where PVL is VerCors' internal language for prototyping new features. VerCors can be used to verify memory and thread safety and functional correctness of programs. The program logic behind Ver-Cors is based on permission-based separation logic [2,5]. Programs are annotated with pre- and postconditions in permission-based separation logic. Permissions are used to capture which heap memory locations may be accessed by which threads, and verify memory and thread safety. Permissions are written as fractional values in the interval $(0, 1]$ (cf. Boyland [6]): any fraction in the interval $(0, 1)$ indicates a read permission, while 1 indicates a write permission.

Verification Example. Listing 1 shows a specification of a simple program that increments all the elements in an array by one. To specify permissions, we use predicates $Perm(L, \pi)$ where L is a heap location and π a fractional value in the interval $(0, 1]$[3]. Pre- and postconditions, (denoted by keywords `requires` and `ensures`, respectively in lines 2–4), should hold at the beginning and the end of the function, respectively. The keyword `context_everywhere` is used to specify a property that must hold throughout the function (line 1). As precondition, we have write permissions in all locations in the array (line 2). The postconditions

---

[1] A ghost variable is used for verification purposes and is not part of the program.

[2] See https://utwente.nl/vercors.

[3] The keywords `read` and `write` can also be used instead of fractions in VerCors.

List. 1. A simple sequential program

```
1   /*@  context_everywhere array != NULL && array.length == size;
2        requires (\forall* int k; k>=0 && k<size; Perm(array[k], write));
3        ensures (\forall* int k; k>=0 && k<size; Perm(array[k], write));
4        ensures (\forall int k; k>=0 && k<size; array[k] == \old(array[k])+1);
        @*/
5   void Inc(int[] array, int size) {
6
7     loop_invariant i>=0 && i<=size;
8     loop_invariant (\forall* int k; k>=0 && k<size; Perm(array[k], write));
9     loop_invariant (\forall int k; k>=0 && k<i; array[k] == \old(array[k])+1);
10    for(int i = 0; i < size; i++){
11        array[i] = array[i] + 1;
12  }
```

indicate first, we have write permissions in all locations in the array (line 3), and second, all values in the array are increased by one (line 4). Note that we use \forall* as universal separating conjunction over permission predicates and \forall as standard universal conjunction over logical predicates. Moreover, the keyword \old is used for an expression to refer to the value of that expression before entering a function (lines 4 and 9). The loop invariants specify that in each iteration we have write permissions to the array (line 8) and all values from index 0 up to index $i - 1$ are increased by one (line 9). Then, the postcondition follows from these loop invariants.

3   Permutation Verification of Swap-Based Sorting

In this section, we describe our generic approach to verify the permutation property of sequential and parallel swap-based sorting algorithms.

3.1   Swap-Based Sorting Algorithms

An algorithm is a swap-based sorting algorithm if *by only swapping* the elements it satisfies the following:

- INPUT: An array *Input* of integers[4] of size N.
- OUTPUT: An array *Output* of integers of size N such that
  - sortedness: $\forall i. \, 0 \leq i < N-1: Output[i] \leq Output[i + 1]$
  - permutation:
    $\forall i \in Input: occurrence(Input, i) == occurrence(Output, i).$

where $occurrence(A, i)$ counts the number of occurrences of i in A.

---

[4] We specify the type of *Input* as integers, but it can be other types as well.

Algorithm 2. Parallel

1: *invar: Output == inp_seq_cur*
2: *invar: Input == inp_seq_chain[0]*
3: *invar: properties to prove sortedness*
4: **par**(*tid = 0.. K*)

⋮

5:   *swap(Output, f_1(tid), f_2(tid))*
6:   **atomic**
7:     *inp_seq_cur = swap-seq(*
8:     *inp_seq_cur, f_1(tid), f_2(tid))*
9:   **end atomic**

⋮

10: **end par**
11: *inp_seq_chain = inp_seq_chain +*
12:   *seq<seq<int>> {inp_seq_cur}*

Algorithm 1. Sequential

1: *invar: Output == inp_seq_cur*
2: *invar: Input == inp_seq_chain[0]*
3: *invar: properties to prove sortedness*
4: **loop(0 .. M)**

   . . .

5:   *swap(Output, i, j)*
6:   *inp_seq_cur = swap-seq(inp_seq_cur,*
7:                 *i, j)*

   . . .

8:   *inp_seq_chain = inp_seq_chain +*
9:     *seq<seq<int>> {inp_seq_cur}*
10: **end loop**

Fig. 1. Annotated pseudocode of sequential and parallel swap-based sorting algorithms.

3.2 Functional Correctness of Swap-Based Sorting Algorithms

To prove the correctness of swap-based sorting algorithms, we use ghost variables, in particular as sequences in VerCors. The most important advantage of using ghost variables is that it allows us to reason about *both* sortedness and permutation properties in the same specification. Moreover, establishing the proof based on ghost sequences helps us to also apply our technique on other data types rather than arrays such as linked lists. To demonstrate that, first we discuss which ghost variables we define and how they are beneficial in verifying sortedness. Then, we explain in detail how these ghost variables can be used to describe a generic verification pattern to verify the permutation property.

Figure 1 provides general sketches of the core (annotated) part of sequential and parallel swap-based sorting algorithms. Initially, we assume that *Input* and *Output* contain the same elements. The key operation in both sequential and parallel algorithms is the *swap* function where two elements are swapped. In the sequential algorithms, there is at most one swap at a time, but there might be multiple swaps in one iteration (e.g., sequential odd-even sort). In the parallel version there might be multiple simultaneous swaps, where f_1 and f_2 are two functions that assign a thread to two elements for swapping according to a thread id (i.e., *tid*). Note that in the parallel version, there can be a loop inside or outside the *par* block. By swapping the elements, a new rearrangement of the input array is generated. To keep track of these rearrangements of the elements, we define a ghost variable, *inp_seq_chain* (type sequence of sequences), as a chain of sequences that the first sequence in this chain is *Input*. We also define another ghost variable, *inp_seq_cur*, as the sequence that always stores the current rearrangement (i.e., last sequence in the chain).

List. 2. The *occurrence* function

```
1  /*@ ensures \result≥0 && \result≤|xs|;
2      ensures (\forall int i; 0≤i && i<|xs|; element != xs[i]) <==> \result
           == 0;
3      ensures (\forall int i; 0≤i && i<|xs|; element == xs[i]) <==>
4              \result == |xs|;
5      ensures element in xs <==> \result>0; @*/
6  static pure int occurrence(seq<int> xs, int element) = |xs| ≤ 0 ? 0 :
7      ( head(xs) == element ? (1+occurrence(tail(xs), element)) :
8          occurrence(tail(xs), element) );
```

Next, in the sequential version, we define a function, *swap-seq* and apply it to *inp_seq_cur* to update the current sequence exactly in the same way as the *swap* function does over *Output* (lines 6–7). Finally, we specify a loop invariant that shows that the array and the sequence are the same in each iteration (line 1). Moreover, in each iteration, after the swapping(s), we add the new current sequence to the chain of sequences (lines 8–9)[5]. This proposed pattern is also applicable for proving the correctness of recursive swap-based sorting algorithms (e.g., quick sort). In the parallel version, the principle is the same, but as there might be simultaneous swaps, we update the current sequence atomically (lines 6–9). Note that the exact location where we add the updated sequence to the chain depends on the algorithms and might be different from the sketches. For instance, if there is a loop inside the parallel block then we add the sequence to the chain at the end of the loop inside the parallel block. Notice that in the parallel algorithm (Fig. 1) the *swap* function over *Output* (line 5) is outside the atomic block. This matches for instance the parallel odd-even transposition sort. However, in other parallel sorting algorithms, we might need to include the *swap* function inside the atomic block to avoid data races[6]. Note that in the tool we use permission-based separation logic to prove data race-freedom of the algorithms.

These constructs allow us to prove the sortedness and permutation properties of any sequential and parallel swap-based sorting algorithm. By defining a chain of sequences, a user can provide key properties as invariants to reason about how the values change in the chain from *Input* to the last sequence (which is *Output*) to prove sortedness (line 3). To prove the permutation property, first we define a function *occurrence* (as shown in Listing 2) that counts the number of occurrences of an element in a sequence[7]. The postcondition of the function specifies (the boundary of) the result of the function in general (line 1) and in

---

[5] Note that depending on the algorithm, the new arrangement might be added to the chain after one swap *or* multiple swaps.

[6] A data race is a situation when two or more threads may access the same memory location simultaneously where at least one of them is a write.

[7] The **head** operation returns the first element of a sequence and **tail** returns a new sequence by eliminating the first element.

List. 3. The *permutation* function

```
1   static pure boolean permutation(seq<int> xs, seq<int> ys) = (|xs| == |ys|)
        &&
2       (\forall int i; 0≤i && i<|xs|; occurrence(xs, xs[i]) == occurrence(ys, xs[i
            ]));
```

three different conditions where the element exists in the sequence (line 5) or does not exist (lines 2) or the sequence only contains that element (lines 3–4).

Next, we define a predicate that states that a sequence is a permutation of another sequence if and only if the size of both are the same and the number of occurrences of each element in both are the same (Listing 3).

Next, we use VerCors to prove a property that for any sequence if we swap two arbitrary elements, the result is a permutation of the original sequence:

Property 3.1 For any sequence xs:
$(\forall i, j. 0 \le i \le j < |xs|$:
$(\forall l. 0 \le l < |xs| : occurrence(xs, xs[l]) = occurrence(swap\text{-}seq(xs, i, j), xs[l])))$.

Proof. We define a lemma in VerCors to prove the property. We explain the steps that we have in the lemma (in VerCors) exactly as implemented[8].

If i equals to j both xs and $swap\text{-}seq(xs, i, j)$ are the same. Thus, the property holds and VerCors can infer it. If i is less than j, we split xs and $swap\text{-}seq(xs, i, j)$ into disjoint sequences in VerCors according to i and j as follows:

$$xs = xs[0..i-1] + xs[i] + xs[i+1..j-1] + xs[j] + xs[j+1..|xs|-1] \quad (1)$$

$$swap\text{-}seq(xs, i, j) = xs[0..i-1] + xs[j] + xs[i+1..j-1] + xs[i] \\ + xs[j+1..|xs|-1] \quad (2)$$

We rewrite (1) and (2) in terms of the *occurrence* function and prove (by another lemma in VerCors) that this function distributes over concatenation of sequences as follows:

$$occurrence(xs + ys + ... + ts, element) = occurrence(xs, element) \\ + occurrence(ys, element) + ... + occurrence(ts, element) \quad (3)$$

Then we note that we have the following equalities:

$$occurrence(xs, element) = occurrence(xs[0..i-1] + xs[i] \\ + xs[i+1..j-1] + xs[j] + xs[j+1..|xs|-1], element) \quad (4)$$

---

[8] The full proof of all properties in VerCors is available at https://github.com/Safari1991/Permutation.

$$occurrence(swap\text{-}seq(xs, i, j), element) = occurrence(xs[0..i-1]$$
$$+ xs[j] + xs[i+1..j-1] + xs[i] + xs[j+1..|xs|-1], element) \tag{5}$$

By applying property (3) to Eqs. (4) and (5) and using commutativity of "+" on integers, VerCors can conclude that both right-hand sides of (4) and (5) are equal, hence also their left-hand sides are equal.   □

This allows us to specify that after each swap, the new sequence is a permutation of the previous one. As a corollary we prove that the *occurrence* function is symmetric:

Corollary 3.1. For any sequence xs:
$(\forall i, j.0 \le i \le j < |swap\text{-}seq(xs, i, j)| : (\forall l.0 \le l < |swap\text{-}seq(xs, i, j)| :$
$occurrence(swap\text{-}seq(xs, i, j), swap\text{-}seq(xs, i, j)[l])$
$= occurrence(xs, swap\text{-}seq(xs, i, j)[l])))$.

Property 3.1 does not specify that the current sequence is a permutation of the input array (i.e., the first sequence in the chain). To establish that, we use VerCors to also prove that the *occurrence* function is transitive:

Property 3.2. For any equal-sized sequences xs, ys and ts:
$(\ (\forall l.0 \le l < |xs| \rightarrow occurrence(xs, xs[l]) = occurrence(ys, xs[l])) \ \wedge$
$(\forall l.0 \le l < |ys| \rightarrow occurrence(ys, ys[l]) = occurrence(ts, ys[l])) \ ) \Rightarrow$
$(\forall l.0 \le l < |xs| \rightarrow occurrence(xs, xs[l]) = occurrence(ts, xs[l]))$

Proof. The proof is trivial using Corollary 3.1 and VerCors can infer this without intermediate proof steps.   □

Using Properties 3.1 and 3.2 we can show that the permutation property is preserved for each new rearrangement of the input array during the algorithms:

Permutation Invariant. After each swap in the sequential and parallel swap-based sorting algorithms $permutation(inp\_seq\_chain[0], inp\_seq\_cur)$ holds.

To understand why this is an invariant: (1) At the beginning, $inp\_seq\_chain[0]$ and inp_seq_cur are equal to *Input*, hence the invariant holds. (2) assume that the invariant holds between sequences $inp\_seq\_chain[0]$ (which is *Input*) and $inp\_seq\_chain[M-1]$ (which is inp_seq_cur). Then, after each swap, we can apply Properties 3.1 and 3.2 to show that the invariant is preserved. Therefore, after the last swap when we add the updated inp_seq_cur ($inp\_seq\_chain[M]$) to the chain, the invariant still holds. In the pseudocode of sequential and parallel swap-based sorting algorithms, we only need to apply the two properties before a swap. This is sufficient to prove the permutation property of the algorithms. Figure 2 illustrates this and completes the generic pattern. As we can see, the pattern can be generated automatically and the only parts that a user needs to fill out are the arguments i and j which are specific to the algorithms.

4   Case Studies: Proving Permutation of Swap-Based Sorting Algorithms

In this section, we show how we apply the technique described above, to verify multiple parallel and sequential swap-based sorting algorithms. In particular, we discuss how we prove the permutation property of parallel odd even transposition sort as well as sequential bubble sort, selection sort and insertion sort. Moreover, we illustrate how we use our approach to prove the permutation property of recursive in-place sorting algorithms quick sort and merge sort. In addition, we benefit from the verification of insertion sort and merge sort to verify the permutation property of TimSort[9].

Algorithm 1. Sequential

1: *invar: Output == inp_seq_cur*
2: *invar: Input == inp_seq_chain[0]*
3: *invar: properties to prove sortedness*
4: *invar: permutation(inp_seq_chain[0],*
5: *inp_seq_cur)*
6: **loop(0 .. M)**
...
7:    *swap(Output, i, j)*
8:    *applying Prop. 3.1 to inp_seq_cur*
9:    *applying Prop. 3.2 to*
10:   *inp_seq_chain[0], inp_seq_cur and*
11:   *swap-seq(inp_seq_cur, i, j)*
12:   *inp_seq_cur = swap-seq(inp_seq_cur,*
13:   *i, j)*
...
14:   *inp_seq_chain = inp_seq_chain +*
15:   *seq<seq<int>> {inp_seq_cur}*
16: **end loop**

Algorithm 2. Parallel

1: *invar: Output == inp_seq_cur*
2: *invar: Input == inp_seq_chain[0]*
3: *invar: properties to prove sortedness*
4: *invar: permutation(inp_seq_chain[0],*
5: *inp_seq_cur)*
6: **par(tid = 0.. K)**
...
7:    *swap(Output, f₁(tid), f₂(tid))*
8:    **atomic**
9:       *applying Prop. 3.1 to inp_seq_cur*
10:      *applying Prop. 3.2 to*
11:      *inp_seq_chain[0], inp_seq_cur and*
12:      *swap-seq(inp_seq_cur, f₁(tid),*
13:      *f₂(tid))*
14:      *inp_seq_cur = swap-seq(*
15:      *inp_seq_cur, f₁(tid), f₂(tid))*
16:   **end atomic**
...
17:   **end par**
18: *inp_seq_chain = inp_seq_chain +*
19:   *seq<seq<int>> {inp_seq_cur}*

Fig. 2. Annotated pseudocode of sequential and parallel swap-based sorting algorithms.

4.1   Permutation Verification of Bubble, Selection and Insertion Sort

In this section, we use our generic pattern to verify the permutation property of bubble sort, selection sort, and insertion sort, as illustrated in Fig. 3. In bubble

---

[9] The full specifications of all case studies are available at https://github.com/Safari1991/Permutation.

Algorithm 3. Bubble sort

1: *invar: Output == inp_seq_cur*
2: *invar: Input == inp_seq_chain[0]*
3: *invar: permutation(inp_seq_chain[0],*
4:              *inp_seq_cur)*
5: **loop**(k: 0 .. N-2)
6:   *invar: Output == inp_seq_cur*
7:   *invar: Input == inp_seq_chain[0]*
8:   *invar: permutation(inp_seq_chain[0],*
9:              *inp_seq_cur)*
10: **loop**(t: 0 .. N-k-2)
11:   **if** *Output[t] > Output[t+1]*
12:    *swap(Output, t, t+1)*
13:    *applying Prop. 3.1 to inp_seq_cur*
14:    *applying Prop. 3.2 to*
15:    *inp_seq_chain[0], inp_seq_cur and*
16:    *swap-seq(inp_seq_cur, t, t+1)*
17:    *inp_seq_cur = swap-seq(*
18:            *inp_seq_cur, t, t+1)*
19:   **end if**
20: **end loop**
21: *inp_seq_chain = inp_seq_chain +*
22:    *seq<seq<int>> {inp_seq_cur}*
23: **end loop**

Algorithm 4. Selection sort

1: *invar: Output == inp_seq_cur*
2: *invar: Input == inp_seq_chain[0]*
3: *invar: permutation(inp_seq_chain[0],*
4:              *inp_seq_cur)*
5: **loop**(k: 0 .. N-2)
6:   *minIdx = k;*
7:   *invar: Output == inp_seq_cur*
8:   *invar: Input == inp_seq_chain[0]*
9:   *invar: properties to prove sortedness*
10:   *invar: permutation(inp_seq_chain[0],*
11:              *inp_seq_cur)*
12: **loop**(t: k+1 .. N-1)
13:   **if** *Output[t] < Output[minIdx]*
14:    *minIdx = t*
15:   **end if**
16: **end loop**
17: *swap(Output, k, minIdx)*
18: *applying Prop. 3.1 to inp_seq_cur*
19: *applying Prop. 3.2 to*
20: *inp_seq_chain[0], inp_seq_cur and*
21: *swap-seq(inp_seq_cur, k, minIdx)*
22: *inp_seq_cur = swap-seq(*
23:            *inp_seq_cur, k, minIdx)*
24: *inp_seq_chain = inp_seq_chain +*
25:    *seq<seq<int>> {inp_seq_cur}*
26: **end loop**

Algorithm 5. Insertion sort

1: *invar: Output == inp_seq_cur*
2: *invar: Input == inp_seq_chain[0]*
3: *invar: properties to prove sortedness*
4: *invar: permutation(inp_seq_chain[0], inp_seq_cur)*
5: **loop**(k: 1 .. N-1)
6:   *invar: Output == inp_seq_cur*
7:   *invar: Input == inp_seq_chain[0]*
8:   *invar: properties to prove sortedness*
9:   *invar: permutation(inp_seq_chain[0], inp_seq_cur)*
10: **loop**(t: k ..1)
11:   **if** *Output[t-1] > Output[t]*
12:    *swap(Output, t-1, t)*
13:    *applying Prop. 3.1 to inp_seq_cur*
14:    *applying Prop. 3.2 to inp_seq_chain[0], inp_seq_cur and*
15:    *swap-seq(inp_seq_cur, t-1, t)*
16:    *inp_seq_cur = swap-seq(inp_seq_cur, t-1, t)*
17:   **end if**
18: **end loop**
19: *inp_seq_chain = inp_seq_chain + seq<seq<int>> {inp_seq_cur}*
20: **end loop**

Fig. 3. Proving permutation property of bubble sort, selection sort and insertion sort using the proposed pattern.

Algorithm 6. Quick sort

```
 1: if low < high
 2:     pivot = Output[high], idx = low-1
 3:     invar: Output == inp_seq_cur
 4:     invar: Input == inp_seq_chain[0]
 5:     invar: permutation(inp_seq_chain[0], inp_seq_cur)
 6:     loop(k: low .. high-1)
 7:        if Output[k] ≤ pivot
 8:           idx++
 9:           swap(Output, idx, k)
10:           applying Prop. 3.1 to inp_seq_cur and applying Prop. 3.2 to
11:           inp_seq_chain[0], inp_seq_cur and swap-seq(inp_seq_cur, idx, k)
12:           inp_seq_cur = swap-seq(inp_seq_cur, idx, k)
13:        end if
14:     end loop
15:     swap(Output, idx+1, high)
16:     applying Prop. 3.1 to inp_seq_cur and applying Prop. 3.2 to
17:     inp_seq_chain[0], inp_seq_cur and swap-seq(inp_seq_cur, idx+1, high)
18:     inp_seq_cur = swap-seq(inp_seq_cur, idx+1, high)
19:     inp_seq_chain = inp_seq_chain + seq<seq<int>> {inp_seq_cur}
20:     pivotIdx = idx+1
21:     recursive call for Output[low ... pivotIdx-1]
22:     recursive call for Output[pivotIdx+1 ... high]
23: end if
```

and insertion sort, there are two nested loops and a swap happens inside the inner loop. In selection sort, there are also two nested loops, but a swap happens in the outer loop. In all three algorithms, we follow exactly the approach as discussed in Sect. 3. We have the same invariants (for both loops) and we apply the same properties before a swap. The only differences are the two locations of elements to be swapped, which we set according to the algorithms themselves.

4.2 Permutation Verification of Quick Sort

The proposed pattern can also be used for recursive in-place sorting algorithms. To show this, we use the pattern to verify the permutation property of the quick sort algorithm as illustrated in Algorithm 6. This recursive algorithm is initialized with $low = 0$ and $high = |Output| - 1$. Each recursive call puts the last element (the pivot), in the correct position in the sorted array in such a way that all smaller elements will be to the left of the pivot and all larger elements will be to the right of the pivot. The function recursively applies the same function to both subarrays to the left and right of the pivot (lines 23–24), resulting in a sorted array. As we can see there are two swaps, one inside the loop and the other one outside the loop (lines 9 and 16). Again, we apply the properties before each swap and we add the new sequence (i.e., inp_seq_cur) to the chain (i.e., inp_seq_chain) after the second swap (line 21). In this way, we prove permutation of the quick sort algorithm.

Algorithm 7. In-place merge1

```
1:  start2 = mid+1
2:  if Output[mid] ≤ Output[start2]
3:    return
4:  end if
5:  invar: Output == inp_seq_cur
6:  invar: Input == inp_seq_chain[0]
7:  invar: permutation(inp_seq_chain[0],
8:                      inp_seq_cur)
9:  while(start ≤ mid && start2 ≤ right)
10:   if Output[start] ≤ Output[start2]
11:     start+=1
12:   else
13:     idx = start2
14:     while(idx != start)
15:       swap(Output, idx-1, idx)
16:       applying Prop. 3.1 to inp_seq_cur
17:       applying Prop. 3.2 to
18:       inp_seq_chain[0], inp_seq_cur and
19:       swap-seq(inp_seq_cur, idx-1, idx)
20:       inp_seq_cur = swap-seq(inp_seq_cur,
21:                               idx-1, idx)
22:       idx-=1
23:     end while
24:     start+=1, mid+=1, start2+=1
25:   end if else
26:  end while
27:  inp_seq_chain = inp_seq_chain +
28:     seq<seq<int>> {inp_seq_cur}
```

Fig. 4. Annotated pseudocode of an in-place merging (left) and an example (right). Green values in the example indicates that the comparison implies some swaps. (Color figure online)

4.3 Permutation Verification of Merge Sort

Merge sort is another example of a recursive sort that splits the elements into smaller parts (recursively) and merges them into a sorted array. Thus, the main part of the algorithm is merging two sorted subarrays. Figure 4 presents the (annotated) pseudocode and an example of an in-place merging. The example shows how the merge operates on two sorted subarrays (from indices 0–3 and 4–7). Initially, *start* points to the first element in the array (i.e., index 0), and *right* indicates the last element (i.e., index $N - 1$). Moreover, the variable *start2* points to the first location in the right subarray (i.e., index $mid + 1$) where *mid* equals $(start+right)/2$. Then, the elements in these two locations are compared and if $Output[start] > Output[start2]$, we should insert the element in location *start2* into location *start* by shifting all elements in between by one location to the right (lines 12–25 of the pseudocode). Otherwise, we increase *start* by 1 (line 11). This process repeats until the array is sorted. As we can see in the pseudocode, the shifting is implemented as swapping two adjacent elements from location *start2* to *start* consecutively. In this way, we can reuse the proposed pattern again to verify the permutation property of this algorithm.

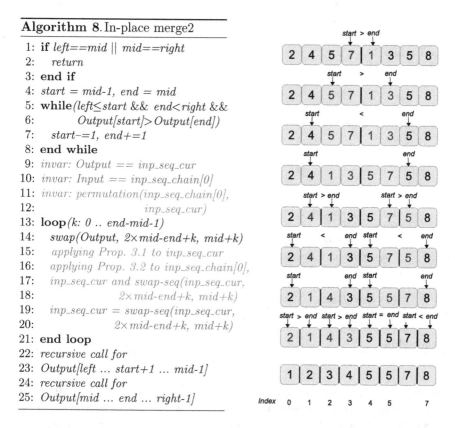

Algorithm 8. In-place merge2

1: **if** *left==mid* || *mid==right*
2:    *return*
3: **end if**
4: *start = mid-1, end = mid*
5: **while** *(left≤start && end<right &&*
6:       *Output[start]> Output[end])*
7:    *start-=1, end+=1*
8: **end while**
9: *invar: Output == inp_seq_cur*
10: *invar: Input == inp_seq_chain[0]*
11: *invar: permutation(inp_seq_chain[0],*
12:           *inp_seq_cur)*
13: **loop** *(k: 0 .. end-mid-1)*
14:    *swap(Output, 2×mid-end+k, mid+k)*
15:    *applying Prop. 3.1 to inp_seq_cur*
16:    *applying Prop. 3.2 to inp_seq_chain[0],*
17:    *inp_seq_cur and swap-seq(inp_seq_cur,*
18:           *2×mid-end+k, mid+k)*
19:    *inp_seq_cur = swap-seq(inp_seq_cur,*
20:           *2×mid-end+k, mid+k)*
21: **end loop**
22: *recursive call for*
23: *Output[left ... start+1 ... mid-1]*
24: *recursive call for*
25: *Output[mid ... end ... right-1]*

Fig. 5. Another in-place merging: annotated pseudocode (left) and an example (right). Red values should be swapped with green values in each recursion. (Color figure online)

Figure 5 presents another (annotated) pseudocode and an example of an in-place merge [8,17] which is more efficient than the previous one in complexity. In this algorithm, initially *left* points to index zero, *right* equals N and the two variables, *start* and *end* point to the last and first elements of the subarrays, respectively[10]. Variable *start* decreases and *end* increases by one until *Output[start] <= Output[end]* (lines 5–8). When *Output[start] <= Output[end]*, we should swap the two subarrays in ranges (*start, mid*) (as red

---
[10] In the example, the middle element initially is in index 4, because *right* equals N.

Algorithm 9. In-place TimSort

1: *RUN = 64, k=0*
2: *invar: Output == inp_seq_cur*
3: *invar: Input == inp_seq_chain[0]*
4: *invar: permutation(inp_seq_chain[0], inp_seq_cur)*
5: **while***(k < N)*
6:      *end = min(k+RUN-1, N-1)*
7:      *insertion sort(Output[k ... end]*
8:      *k+=RUN*
9: **end while**
10: *chunk = RUN*
11: *invar: Output == inp_seq_cur*
12: *invar: Input == inp_seq_chain[0]*
13: *invar: permutation(inp_seq_chain[0], inp_seq_cur)*
14: **while***(chunk < N)*
15:      *left = 0*
16:      *invar: Output == inp_seq_cur*
17:      *invar: Input == inp_seq_chain[0]*
18:      *invar: permutation(inp_seq_chain[0], inp_seq_cur)*
19:      **while***(left < N)*
20:          *mid = left+chunk-1, right = min(left+2×chunk-1, N-1)*
21:          **if***(mid < N-1)*
22:              *merge1(Output, left, mid, right)*
23:              *// or merge2(Output, left, mid+1, right+1)*
24:          **end if**
25:          *inp_seq_chain = inp_seq_chain + seq<seq<int>> {inp_seq_cur}*
26:          *left+=2×chunk*
27:      **end while**
28:      *chunk×=2*
29: **end while**

---

values in the example on the right) and [*mid, end*) (as green values in the example), as in line 13–21 of the pseudocode. As we can see, we do swaps one by one between the first elements in the two ranges, then between the second elements, and so on. As a result, all elements in the left subarray become smaller than all the elements in the right subarray. This means that the subarrays are now independent and the same process can be applied for both of them. Therefore, we recursively call this process for the two subarrays to sort the full array (lines 22–25). Thus, the merge function is also recursive in addition to the main function of merge sort. Since there are swaps in this algorithm, we reuse the generic pattern and verify the permutation property of this algorithm as well. The only point is that, since the merging function is recursive, we add the new rearrangement of the elements (i.e., *inp_seq_cur*) to the chain (i.e., *inp_seq_chain*) in the main function of merge sort instead of in the merge function itself.

4.4   Permutation Verification of TimSort

Amongst the sorting algorithms, insertion sort performs better in practice when the number of elements are small (e.g., 64). Merge sort performs well when the size of two subarrays is power of 2. TimSort [20] benefits from this as a combination of insertion and merge sort. Algorithm 9 presents a simplified (annotated) version of this algorithm. It first sorts small groups of elements (e.g., 64) as runs (lines 5–9). Then, the algorithm repeatedly merges these equal-size sorted runs using the merging function (lines 14–29). That means, in the first iteration, the algorithm merges each two consecutive runs into a larger size of runs, and it repeats merging for each two consecutive (larger) runs until the full array is sorted. Note that we can use both merge functions discussed above for TimSort.

Since we already proved permutation of insertion and merge sort, we can easily prove the permutation property of TimSort. In fact, we prove permutation of two (in-place) TimSort algorithms using the two verified merge functions.

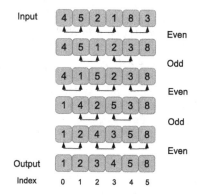

Fig. 6. An example of odd-even transposition sort. Values in green should be swapped. (Color figure online)

4.5   Permutation Verification of Parallel Odd-Even Transposition Sort

Odd-even transposition sort is a parallel version of bubble sort. It consists of two phases: odd and even. Algorithm 10 presents the annotated pseudocode while Fig. 6 shows an example of the execution of the algorithm. In the algorithm, *Output* is initialized to *Input*. In the even phase (lines 7–18), even locations $(2 \times tid)$ are compared to their right neighbor $(2 \times tid + 1)$ in line 8 and swapped if they are greater (line 9). In the odd phase (lines 20–31), odd locations $(2 \times tid + 1)$ are compared and swapped in the same way with their right neighbor $(2 \times tid + 2)$ in lines 21–22. This process repeats inside a loop (line 5) until all elements are sorted, i.e., there is no swap (indicated by a boolean, *isSorted*).

Algorithm 10. Parallel odd-even transposition sort

```
 1: boolean isSorted = false;
 2: invar: Output == inp_seq_cur
 3: invar: Input == inp_seq_chain[0]
 4: invar: permutation(inp_seq_chain[0], inp_seq_cur)
 5: while !isSorted do
 6:    isSorted = true;
 7:    Par(tid = 0.. N/2) // thread id from 0 to N/2-1
 8:       if 2 × tid + 1 < N && Output[2 × tid] > Output[2 × tid + 1] then
 9:          Swap(Output, 2 × tid, 2 × tid + 1);
10:          atomic
11:             applying Property 3.1 to inp_seq_cur and applying Property 3.2 to
12:             inp_seq_chain[0], inp_seq_cur and swap-seq(inp_seq_cur, 2 × tid, 2 × tid + 1)
13:             inp_seq_cur = swap-seq(inp_seq_cur, 2 × tid, 2 × tid + 1)
14:          end atomic
15:          isSorted = false
16:       end if
17:    end par
18:    inp_seq_chain = inp_seq_chain + seq<seq<int>> {inp_seq_cur}
19:    Par(tid = 0.. N/2) // thread id from 0 to N/2-1
20:       if 2 × tid + 2 < N && Output[2 × tid + 1] > Output[2 × tid + 2] then
21:          Swap(Output, 2 × tid + 1, 2 × tid + 2);
22:          atomic
23:             applying Property 3.1 to inp_seq_cur and applying Property 3.2 to
24:             inp_seq_chain[0], inp_seq_cur and swap-seq(inp_seq_cur, 2 × tid + 1, 2 × tid + 2)
25:             inp_seq_cur = swap-seq(inp_seq_cur, 2 × tid + 1, 2 × tid + 2)
26:          end atomic
27:          isSorted = false
28:       end if
29:    end par
30:    inp_seq_chain = inp_seq_chain + seq<seq<int>> {inp_seq_cur}
31: end while
```

To prove permutation, we use the pattern proposed in Algorithm 2 (Fig. 2) for both phases. We only fill out the two locations that need to be swapped (i.e., $2 \times tid$ and $2 \times tid + 1$ in line 14, $2 \times tid + 1$ and $2 \times tid + 2$ in line 27). By applying the properties before a swap (lines 12–14 and 25–27), we establish the permutation property indicated as an invariant in line 4.

5   Related Work

There are several papers on proving sortedness and permutation properties of concrete sorting algorithms. In [10, 22, 24], the authors prove correctness of various sorting algorithms using the Why3 [12] platform[11]. Why3 is a program verifier which has its own language for programming and specification (i.e., WhyML)

---

[11] The verified sorting algorithms using Why3 are available at http://pauillac.inria.fr/~levy/why3/sorting.

based on first-order logic. It is mainly used as backend for other verifiers. To prove sortedness and permutation properties, suitable lemmas and invariants are defined and used in the extensive Why3 library[12]. However, they do not propose a generic approach to verify sortedness and permutation properties. Moreover, they do not verify any parallel sorting algorithms and they only prove the correctness of several sequential sorting algorithms.

Beckert et al. [3] prove JDK's dual pivot quick sort algorithm using KeY [1]. KeY is a program verifier for Java programs. The annotated Java programs are transformed into the internal dynamic logic representation of KeY, and then proof obligations are discharged to its first-order theorem prover which is based on sequent calculus. They benefit from sequences to prove sortedness and permutation properties of the algorithm. To prove the permutation property, they provide suitable invariants and prove some lemmas in the tool. They mention that proving the permutation property is by far the hardest part of their verification, which requires more interaction with the tool than the sortedness property. They neither outline a generic pattern nor verify any parallel sorting algorithms. In addition, they only verify quick sort in Java.

De Gouw et al. [13] found a bug in the TimSort implementation in one of OpenJDK's libraries while verifying the code using KeY. They show the effectiveness of (semi) automatic verification in finding bugs in a complex algorithm.

Filliâtre et al. [11] verify three sorting algorithms, insertion sort, quick sort and heap sort, in the Coq proof assistant. To prove the permutation property, they propose to express that the set of permutations is the smallest equivalence relation containing the transpositions (i.e., the exchanges of elements). We follow their approach to formally define permutation and prove its properties to prove any sequential and parallel swap-based sorting algorithms automatically.

Tushkanova et al. [25] discuss two specification languages, Java Modeling Language (JML) and Krakatoa Modeling Language (KML), to verify selection sort in Java automatically. To prove the permutation property, they use bags to show that the input and output array have the same content. Their approach is different from ours as we opt to not use bags to have a uniform pattern for verifying both sortedness and permutation.

6   Conclusion

Sorting algorithms are widely use in practice and their correctness is an important issue. To prove correctness of sorting algorithms, we should prove sortedness and permutation properties. Proving the permutation property is harder than sortedness, because it requires reasoning about existential quantifiers. In this paper, we propose a uniform approach to verify the permutation property of any sequential and parallel swap-based sorting algorithms. To demonstrate that our technique is generic, we prove the permutation property of bubble sort, selection sort, insertion sort, parallel odd-even transposition sort, in-place (recursive) quick sort, two merge sorts and TimSort using the VerCorse verifier.

---

[12] See http://why3.lri.fr/stdlib/array.html.

As future work, we plan to augment the proofs by providing the sortedness property for complex sorting algorithms such as odd-even transposition sort and TimSort using the proposed pattern.

References

1. Ahrendt, W., Beckert, B., Bubel, R., Hähnle, R., Schmitt, P.H., Ulbrich, M.: Deductive Software Verification - The KeY Book, Lecture Notes in Computer Science, vol. 10001. Springer, Heidelberg (2016). https://doi.org/10.1007/978-3-319-49812-6
2. Amighi, A., Haack, C., Huisman, M., Hurlin, C.: Permission-based separation logic for multithreaded Java programs. LMCS **11**(1), 1–66 (2015)
3. Beckert, B., Schiffl, J., Schmitt, P.H., Ulbrich, M.: Proving JDK's dual pivot quicksort correct. In: Paskevich, A., Wies, T. (eds.) VSTTE 2017. LNCS, vol. 10712, pp. 35–48. Springer, Cham (2017). https://doi.org/10.1007/978-3-319-72308-2_3
4. Blom, S., Darabi, S., Huisman, M., Oortwijn, W.: The VerCors tool set: verification of parallel and concurrent software. In: Polikarpova, N., Schneider, S. (eds.) IFM 2017. LNCS, vol. 10510, pp. 102–110. Springer, Cham (2017). https://doi.org/10.1007/978-3-319-66845-1_7
5. Bornat, R., Calcagno, C., O'Hearn, P., Parkinson, M.: Permission accounting in separation logic. In: POPL, pp. 259–270 (2005)
6. Boyland, J.: Checking interference with fractional permissions. In: Cousot, R. (ed.) SAS 2003. LNCS, vol. 2694, pp. 55–72. Springer, Heidelberg (2003). https://doi.org/10.1007/3-540-44898-5_4
7. The Coq proof assistant. https://coq.inria.fr/
8. Dvořák, S., Durian, B.: Merging by decomposition revisited. Comput. J. **31**(6), 553–556 (1988)
9. Filliâtre, J.C.: Deductive program verification. Ph.D. thesis, Université de Paris-Sud, vol. 11 (2011)
10. Filliâtre, J.C.: Deductive program verification with Why3 a tutorial (2013). https://www.lri.fr/~marche/DigiCosmeSchool/filliatre.html
11. Filliâtre, J.C., Magaud, N.: Certification of sorting algorithms in the Coq system. In: TPHOLs (1999). http://www-sop.inria.fr/croap/TPHOLs99/proceeding.html
12. Filliâtre, J.-C., Paskevich, A.: Why3—where programs meet provers. In: Felleisen, M., Gardner, P. (eds.) ESOP 2013. LNCS, vol. 7792, pp. 125–128. Springer, Heidelberg (2013). https://doi.org/10.1007/978-3-642-37036-6_8
13. de Gouw, S., Rot, J., de Boer, F.S., Bubel, R., Hähnle, R.: OpenJDK's Java.utils.Collection.sort() is broken: the good, the bad and the worst case. In: Kroening, D., Păsăreanu, C.S. (eds.) CAV 2015. LNCS, vol. 9206, pp. 273–289. Springer, Cham (2015). https://doi.org/10.1007/978-3-319-21690-4_16
14. Govindaraju, N., Gray, J., Kumar, R., Manocha, D.: GPUTeraSort: high performance graphics co-processor sorting for large database management. In: Proceedings of the 2006 ACM SIGMOD International Conference on Management of Data, pp. 325–336 (2006)
15. Greb, A., Zachmann, G.: GPU-ABiSort: optimal parallel sorting on stream architectures. In: PDP, pp. 10-pp. IEEE (2006)
16. Habermann, A.: Parallel Neighbor Sort. Computer Science Report. Carnegie-Mellon University, Pittsburgh (1972)

17. Kim, P.-S., Kutzner, A.: Stable minimum storage merging by symmetric comparisons. In: Albers, S., Radzik, T. (eds.) ESA 2004. LNCS, vol. 3221, pp. 714–723. Springer, Heidelberg (2004). https://doi.org/10.1007/978-3-540-30140-0_63
18. Kipfer, P., Westermann, R.: Improved GPU sorting. GPU Gems **2**, 733–746 (2005)
19. Merrill, D.G., Grimshaw, A.S.: Revisiting sorting for GPGPU stream architectures. In: PACT, pp. 545–546 (2010)
20. Peters, T.: Timsort (2002). https://bugs.python.org/file4451/timsort.txt
21. Satish, N., Harris, M., Garland, M.: Designing efficient sorting algorithms for many-core GPUs. In: PDP, pp. 1–10. IEEE (2009)
22. Schoolderman, M.: Verification of Goroutines using Why3. Master's thesis, Institute for Computing and Information Sciences, RU Nijmegen (2016)
23. Sintorn, E., Assarsson, U.: Fast parallel GPU-sorting using a hybrid algorithm. J. Parallel Distrib. Comput. **68**(10), 1381–1388 (2008)
24. Tafat, A., Marché, C.: Binary heaps formally verified in Why3. Research Report RR-7780, INRIA (October 2011). https://hal.inria.fr/inria-00636083
25. Tushkanova, E., Giorgetti, A., Kouchnarenko, O.: Specifying and proving a sorting algorithm. Technical Report, University of Franche-Comte (October 2009). https://hal.archives-ouvertes.fr/hal-00429040

Synthesizing Clock-Efficient Timed Automata

Neda Saeedloei[1]([⊠]) and Feliks Kluźniak[2]([⊠])

[1] Towson University, Towson, USA
nsaeedloei@towson.edu
[2] LogicBlox, Atlanta, USA
feliks.kluzniak@logicblox.com

Abstract. We describe a new approach to synthesizing a timed automaton from a set of timed scenarios. The set of scenarios specifies a set of behaviours, i.e., sequences of events that satisfy the time constraints imposed by the scenarios. The language of the constructed automaton is equivalent to that set of behaviours. Every location of the automaton appears in at least one accepting run, and its graph is constructed so as to minimise the number of clocks. The construction allows a new clock allocation algorithm whose cost is linear in the number of edges.

1 Introduction

Construction of complex systems, in particular real-time systems, is a very difficult undertaking. It is more or less generally agreed that it cannot be successful unless the specification of the system either constitutes, or can be used to derive a *formal model* of the system (or at least of its essential aspects)—a model that can be used to formally verify that the specified system will actually have the required/expected properties.

A well-researched approach to building formal models of real-time systems is that of constructing timed automata [3], whose properties can then be formally verified, e.g., by model checking [8]. This approach can be considered successful, though it has its problems: verification of a timed automaton can be computationally expensive, and the cost crucially depends on the properties of the automaton, such as the number of clocks [2].

Another kind of difficulty is that the task of constructing a complex timed automaton is itself not easy and quite error-prone. Hence the interest in automatic synthesis of automata from some more "user friendly" notation, for example from specifications expressed in various forms of scenarios [9,10,18,19] and more recently by means of learning [5,11,12].

In this paper we study the problem of synthesizing timed automata from *timed scenarios*: a simple and intuitive notation that is properly formalised and well-understood [15]. We take into account the need to make the resulting automaton suitable for verification (by keeping the numbers of clocks small), as well as some of the practical problems of writing scenarios for a complex system.

© Springer Nature Switzerland AG 2020
B. Dongol and E. Troubitsyna (Eds.): IFM 2020, LNCS 12546, pp. 276–294, 2020.
https://doi.org/10.1007/978-3-030-63461-2_15

Development of the specification for a complex system is usually a collaborative effort. The task is often divided into several smaller tasks, each of which is performed independently by a team of engineers or specialists. A complete specification of the system is obtained by integrating these individual specifications.

Several important questions arise in this context. For instance: how do the partial specifications relate to each other? What is the minimum set of high level assumptions that all teams can agree on so that each of them can work independently? How can we ensure the mutual consistency of these partial specifications, so that they can be integrated into a reasonable whole?

We assume that each team specifies various aspects of a system by using timed scenarios. A timed scenario is essentially a sequence of event names along with a set of constraints between the times at which the named events occur. It specifies a set of behaviours that are composed of this sequence of events and satisfy the constraints: we say that each of these behaviours is *supported* by the scenario. (The notion of "behaviour" is equivalent to that of Alur's "timed word", i.e., a constituent of the language accepted by a timed automaton [3].)

Each timed scenario begins in some state of the specified system, and ends in some state. Such states are interpreted as "important", "visible" or even "expected", and can be viewed as the high level "interfaces" between timed scenarios. If a timed scenario ends in some state, and another begins in the same state, then the two can be *composed* (see Definition 5) to create a longer timed scenario.

In the remainder of the paper we will use the term *modes* to refer to these "important states".

So, the process of specifying a particular aspect of a system takes the form of building a set of partial timed scenarios that would describe the various behaviours relevant to that aspect. The teams that are responsible for different aspects of the system must all agree on the modes (i.e., the "important" states). This is the minimum amount of information that a team must have about the work of the other teams, in order to function independently with at least some degree of confidence that all the scenarios can be integrated at the end.

Once all such partial timed scenarios are obtained, we compose them to obtain a maximal set of "complete" timed scenarios. Such scenarios specify all those behaviours that begin in some initial mode and end in some final mode of the system, and that are composed of the partial behaviours supported by the partial timed scenarios. We exclude from this set all those scenarios that are inconsistent [15], thus obtaining a set Ξ of consistent complete timed scenarios.

We then build an automaton such that every behaviour supported by a timed scenario in Ξ will be accepted by the automaton and, conversely, every behaviour accepted by the automaton will be supported by some timed scenario in Ξ. In other words, the language of the automaton is—in a well-defined sense— equivalent to the set of behaviours supported by Ξ. We call such an automaton *correct* with respect to Ξ, and denote the class of all such automata by $\mathcal{TA}(\Xi)$.

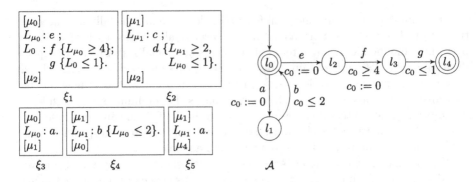

Fig. 1. A few timed scenarios and their synthesized timed automaton

For example, if we assume that μ_0 is the initial mode and μ_0 and μ_2 are the final modes, then the five timed scenarios of Fig. 1 are synthesized into the timed automaton $\mathcal{A}$ (the notation for timed scenarios is explained in detail in Sect. 3.1). It turns out (see Sects. 3.3 and 3.4) that inclusion of ξ_2 and ξ_5 in the construction of $\mathcal{A}$ would make $\mathcal{A}$ contain locations that would not appear in any accepting run.

Under the assumption that the original constraints in a timed scenario cannot be changed, i.e., replaced by an equivalent set, we propose a method of synthesis that generates an automaton $\mathcal{A}$ in $\mathcal{TA}(\varXi)$ with the *optimal number of clocks* (in the sense of Sect. 3.5). The construction makes it possible to use a novel clock allocation algorithm that is very efficient. In addition, all the locations of $\mathcal{A}$ are reachable, that is, every location appears in at least one accepting run of $\mathcal{A}$.

In our earlier work [14] we proposed a form of timed scenarios (called Timed Event Sequences or TES) and developed a synthesis method for constructing a timed automaton from a set of TES. A set of restrictions on the given set of TES ensured that the resulting synthesized automaton was acyclic. Since we did not address the question of the consistency of timed scenarios, some of the locations in the synthesized automaton would not appear in any accepting run. The number of clocks was optimal [13] *for the underlying graph of the automaton.*

We have recently developed [16] a new scheme for "untangling" the underlying graph of an automaton: this can further decrease the number of clocks. The scheme can be applied to the automata synthesised by the method described here (Sect. 3.7). This, together with allowing cycles and with the reachability of all locations, is a significant improvement over our earlier results [14].

2   Timed Automata

A *timed automaton* [3] is a tuple $\mathcal{A} = \langle E, Q, q_0, Q_f, C, T \rangle$, where E is a finite alphabet, Q is the (*finite*) set of locations, $q_0 \in Q$ is the initial location, $Q_f \subseteq Q$ is the set of final locations, C is a finite set of *clocks* (i.e., clock variables), and $T \subseteq Q \times Q \times E \times 2^C \times 2^{\varPhi(C)}$ is the set of transitions. In each transition $(q, q', e, \lambda, \phi)$, λ is the set of clocks to be reset with the transition and $\phi \subset \varPhi(C)$

is a set of clock constraints over C of the form $c \sim a$, where $\sim \in \{\leq, <, \geq, >, =\}$, $c \in C$, and a is a constant in the set of rational numbers, $\mathbb{Q}$.

A *clock valuation* for a set C of clocks is a mapping from C to $\mathbb{R}^{\geq 0}$. A clock valuation ν for C *satisfies* a set of clock constraints ϕ over C iff every clock constraint in ϕ evaluates to true after each clock variable c is replaced with $\nu(c)$.

For $\tau \in \mathbb{R}, \nu + \tau$ denotes the clock valuation which maps every clock c to the value $\nu(c) + \tau$. For $Y \subseteq C$, $[Y \mapsto \tau]\nu$ denotes the clock valuation for C which assigns τ to each $c \in Y$ and agrees with ν over the rest of the clocks.

A *timed word* over an alphabet E is a pair (σ, τ) where $\sigma = \sigma_1 \sigma_2 \ldots$ is a finite [1,6] or infinite word over E and $\tau = \tau_1 \tau_2 \ldots$ is a finite or infinite sequence of (time) values such that (i) $\tau_i \in \mathbb{R}^{\geq 0}$, (ii) $\tau_i \leq \tau_{i+1}$ for all $i \geq 1$, and (iii) if the word is infinite, then for every $t \in \mathbb{R}^{\geq 0}$ there is some $i \geq 1$ such that $\tau_i > t$.

A run of $\mathcal{A}$ over a timed word (σ, τ) is a sequence of the form $\langle q_0, \nu_0 \rangle \xrightarrow[\tau_1]{\sigma_1}$ $\langle q_1, \nu_1 \rangle \xrightarrow[\tau_2]{\sigma_2} \langle q_2, \nu_2 \rangle \xrightarrow[\tau_3]{\sigma_3} \ldots$, where for all $i \geq 0$, $q_i \in Q$ and ν_i is a clock valuation such that (i) $\nu_0(c) = 0$ for all clocks $c \in C$ and (ii) for every $i > 1$ there is a transition in T of the form $(q_{i-1}, q_i, \sigma_i, \lambda_i, \phi_i)$, such that $(\nu_{i-1} + \tau_i - \tau_{i-1})$ satisfies ϕ_i, and ν_i equals $[\lambda_i \mapsto 0](\nu_{i-1} + \tau_i - \tau_{i-1})$.

A run over a finite timed word is accepting if it ends in a final location [1,6]. (We do not consider infinite accepting runs in this paper.)

The language of $\mathcal{A}$, $L(\mathcal{A})$, is the set $\{(\sigma, \tau) \mid \mathcal{A} \text{ has an accepting run over } (\sigma, \tau)\}$.

3   Synthesizing Timed Automata from Scenarios

3.1   Timed Scenarios

(Parts of this subsection briefly recount our earlier work [15].)

Definition 1. *Let Σ be a finite set of symbols called* events. *A behaviour $\mathcal{B}$ over Σ is a sequence $(e_0, t_0)(e_1, t_1)(e_2, t_2) \ldots$, such that $e_i \in \Sigma$, $t_i \in \mathbb{R}^{\geq 0}$ and $t_{i-1} \leq t_i$ for $i \in \{1, 2 \ldots\}$.*

We often say "event i of $\mathcal{B}$" (or "the i-th event") to denote event i of the sequence $e_0 e_1 e_2 \ldots$. A behaviour can, but need not, be an infinite sequence.

The intended interpretation of (e_i, t_i) is that the i-th occurrence of an event is an occurrence of event e_i, and takes place t_i time units after the initial occurrence of an event (namely, e_0).

Let $\mathcal{M}$ be a finite set of modes, interpreted as the *visible states* or *important states* of a system that is being specified. We assume each mode $\mu \in \mathcal{M}$ is associated with a label L_μ. Let $\mathcal{L}_\mathcal{M}$ be the set of all such labels and $\mathcal{L}$ be a set of labels such that $\mathcal{L} \supset \mathcal{L}_\mathcal{M}$. We assume there is a special symbol *none* $\in \mathcal{L} \setminus \mathcal{L}_\mathcal{M}$ and that $\mathcal{L}_n = \mathcal{L} \setminus \{none\}$. The elements of $\mathcal{L}$ can be associated with events and are interpreted as symbolic representations of the times at which these events occur (they are analogous to clocks in timed automata).

We use $\Phi(\mathcal{L})$ to denote the set of *constraints* of the form $\alpha \sim a$, where $\alpha \neq none$ is a label in $\mathcal{L}$, $\sim \in \{\leq, \geq, =\}^1$, and a is a constant in the set of rational numbers, $\mathbb{Q}$.

Let $S \subseteq \mathcal{L} \times \Sigma \times 2^{\Phi(\mathcal{L}_n)}$ be the set of *annotated events* of the form (α, e, ϕ), where $\alpha \in \mathcal{L}$, e is an event in Σ and ϕ is a set of constraints in $\Phi(\mathcal{L}_n)$. If $\alpha \neq none$, then the label α is said to be *defined* by the annotated event (α, e, ϕ). We also say that the event is *labeled* by α.

We use S^* to denote the set of all sequences (finite or infinite) formed from elements of S. The subset of S^* that contains only all the sequences of length n will be denoted by S^n.

In all the definitions below we will assume the sets Σ, $\mathcal{M}$ and $\mathcal{L}$ are given, that $\mu_0 \in \mathcal{M}$ is the initial mode, and that $\mathcal{M}_F \subseteq \mathcal{M}$ is the set of final modes.

Definition 2. *A timed scenario is a tuple* $\xi = (\mu^i, \psi, \mu^f)$*, where* μ^i *and* μ^f *are some modes in* $\mathcal{M}$ *and* $\psi = (\alpha_0, e_0, \phi_0)(\alpha_1, e_1, \phi_1) \ldots$ *is a non-empty sequence of annotated events in* S^* *such that* $\alpha_0 = L_{\mu^i}$ *and* $\alpha_k \in \mathcal{L}$*, for* $k \geq 1$*. Moreover, for every* $\beta \sim a \in \phi_k$*, if* $\beta \in \mathcal{L} \setminus \mathcal{L}_\mathcal{M}$*, then there exists a* $j < k$ *such that* $\alpha_j = \beta$*.*

The intended interpretation is that the system is in mode μ^i when the first event of ξ occurs, and the mode of the system changes to μ^f when the last event of ξ occurs. Moreover, each α_k, for $k \geq 0$, is interpreted as the time of event e_k: in particular, α_0 is the time of event e_0, which is also the time of leaving mode μ^i. A constraint in ϕ_k of the form $\beta \sim a$ means that the time difference between the kth event and the latest preceding event whose label is β must satisfy the constraint. If $\beta \in \mathcal{L} \setminus \mathcal{L}_\mathcal{M}$, then there must exist some earlier annotated event *in this scenario* whose label is β. (If $\beta \in \mathcal{L}_\mathcal{M}$, then it might be defined in other scenarios, as will become clear below.)

Informally, a timed scenario ξ describes a set of behaviours in which the times of events satisfy the constraints in ξ. We say that such behaviours are supported by ξ (see Definition 6).

For a scenario $\xi = (\mu^i, \psi, \mu^f)$, with $\psi = (\alpha_0, e_0, \phi_0)(\alpha_1, e_1, \phi_1) \ldots$, we will use $eseq(\xi)$ to denote the sequence of events $e_0 e_1 \ldots$, $imode(\xi)$ to denote μ^i, and $fmode(\xi)$ to denote μ^f. The term "event i of ξ" will denote event i in $eseq(\xi)$.

In the remainder of the paper, we will use "scenarios" instead of "timed scenarios". A scenario will be written as a sequence of events, preceded and followed by a mode in square brackets. Events are separated by semicolons, and the last event is followed by a period. If a label is *none*, we simply drop it.

For example, ξ_1 of Fig. 1 is a representation of $(\mu_0, (L_{\mu_0}, e, \emptyset)(L_0, f, \{L_{\mu_0} \geq 4\})(none, g, \{L_0 \leq 1\}), \mu_2)$. Label L_{μ_0} is treated as the time of leaving mode μ_0, that is, the time of event 0 (i.e., e) in ξ_1. The constraint $L_{\mu_0} \geq 4$ on event 1 (i.e., f) means that, for every behaviour supported by ξ_1, the time difference between events 0 and 1 must be at least 4 units of time.

In ξ_4 of Fig. 1, label L_{μ_0} used in $L_{\mu_0} \leq 2$ can be the time of event 0 in ξ_1 or event 0 in ξ_3. This will become clear after Definition 4.

---

[1] To keep the presentation compact, we do not allow sharp inequalities [15].

$$\boxed{\begin{array}{l}[\mu_0]\\ L_{\mu_0}:a\ ;\\ L_{\mu_1}:b\ \{L_{\mu_0}\leq 2\}.\\ [\mu_0]\end{array}}$$

$$\xi_3 \circ \xi_4$$

$$\boxed{\begin{array}{l}[\mu_1]\\ L_{\mu_1}:b\ \{L_{\mu_0}\leq 2\};\\ L_{\mu_0}:a.\\ [\mu_1]\end{array}}$$

$$\xi_4 \circ \xi_3$$

$$\boxed{\begin{array}{l}[\mu_1]\\ L_{\mu_1}:b\ ;\\ \qquad a\ \{L_{\mu_1}\geq 3\};\\ \qquad b\ \{L_{\mu_1}\leq 2\}.\\ [\mu_2]\end{array}}$$

Fig. 2. Composition of ξ_3 and ξ_4 of Fig. 1   **Fig. 3.** An inconsistent scenario

Definition 3. *Let* $\xi = (\mu^i, \psi, \mu^f)$ *be a scenario.* ξ *is* closed *iff, for any k-th annotated event* (α_k, e_k, ϕ_k) *in* ψ, *and for every* $\beta \sim a \in \phi_k$, *there exists a $j < k$ such that the j-th annotated event of ψ is* (β, e_j, ϕ_j) *for some e_j and ϕ_j. A scenario is* open *if it is not closed.*

Scenario ξ_1 of Fig. 1 is closed, but ξ_2 is open, because the constraint $L_{\mu_0} \leq 1$ on event 1 (i.e., d) refers to the time of an event from some other scenario.

Definition 4. ξ *is* complete *iff* ξ *is closed,* $imode(\xi) = \mu_0$ *and* $fmode(\xi) \in \mathcal{M}_F$.

Definition 5. *Let* $\xi = (\mu^i_\xi, \psi_\xi, \mu^f_\xi)$ *and* $\eta = (\mu^i_\eta, \psi_\eta, \mu^f_\eta)$ *be two scenarios of lengths n and m, respectively. If* $\mu^f_\xi = \mu^i_\eta$, *then* η *can be* composed *with* ξ. *The result is the scenario* $\xi \circ \eta = (\mu^i_\xi, \psi_\xi\psi_\eta, \mu^f_\eta)$ *of length $n+m$, where $\psi_\xi\psi_\eta \in S^{n+m}$ is the concatenation of ψ_ξ and ψ_η.*

For instance, ξ_3 and ξ_4 of Fig. 1 can be composed in two ways (see Fig. 2). In $\xi_3 \circ \xi_4$, L_{μ_0} refers to the time of leaving μ_0, which is the time of event 0 (i.e., a). In $\xi_4 \circ \xi_3$, L_{μ_0} in the constraint of event 0 does not refer to the time of event 1, because it can only refer to the time of a preceding event. $\xi_4 \circ \xi_3$ is open, but $\xi_3 \circ \xi_4$ is closed. If μ_0 is both the initial and a final mode, then $\xi_3 \circ \xi_4$ is complete.

Definition 6. *Let* ξ *be a closed scenario. A behaviour* $\mathcal{B} = (e_0, t_0)(e_1, t_1) \ldots$ *over* Σ *is* supported *by* ξ *iff* $eseq(\xi) = e_0e_1 \ldots$ *and every constraint $\alpha \sim a$ on event j in ξ evaluates to true after α is replaced by $t_j - t_i$, where event i is the last event before j in ξ whose label is α.*

Definition 7. *Let* ξ *be a closed scenario. The* semantics *of* ξ, *denoted by* $[\![\xi]\!]$, *is the set of behaviours that are supported by* ξ.

Open scenarios have no semantics. If ξ is complete, then all the behaviours in $[\![\xi]\!]$ are finite.

Definition 8. *Two closed scenarios,* ξ *and* ξ' *are* equivalent *iff* $[\![\xi]\!] = [\![\xi']\!]$.

Definition 9. *Let* ξ *be a closed scenario.* ξ *is* consistent *iff* $[\![\xi]\!] \neq \emptyset$. ξ *is* inconsistent *iff it is not consistent.*

Two inconsistent scenarios are obviously equivalent.

Scenario ξ_1 of Fig. 1 is consistent. Scenario ξ of Fig. 3 is inconsistent: $[\![\xi]\!] = \{(b, t_0)(a, t_1)(b, t_2) | t_0 = 0 \wedge t_2 \geq t_1 \geq t_0 \wedge t_1 - t_0 \geq 3 \wedge t_2 - t_0 \leq 2\}$ is empty.

Definition 10. *Let Ξ be a finite set of finite scenarios. We define*
$Composed(\Xi) = \{\xi = \xi_1 \circ \xi_2 \circ \cdots \circ \xi_n \mid \xi_j \in \Xi \text{ for } 1 \leq j \leq n\},$
$Comp(\Xi) \quad = \{\xi \mid \xi \in Composed(\Xi) \wedge \xi \text{ is complete}\},$
$Cons(\Xi) \quad = \{\xi \mid \xi \in Comp(\Xi) \wedge \xi \text{ is consistent}\}.$

Definition 11. *Let Ξ be a finite set of finite scenarios. We define the set of behaviors supported by Ξ as $Supp(\Xi) = \bigcup_{\eta \in Cons(\Xi)} [\![\eta]\!]$.*

3.2 A Bird's Eye View

Let $\mathcal{TA}$ be the class of all timed automata. Let $\mathcal{M}$ be a set of modes, with the initial mode $\mu_0 \in \mathcal{M}$ and a set of final modes $\mathcal{M}_F \subseteq \mathcal{M}$. Let $\mathcal{L}$ be a set of labels, and Ξ be a finite set of finite scenarios (over the alphabet Σ) whose initial and final modes belong to $\mathcal{M}$ and whose labels belong to $\mathcal{L}$.

We define $\mathcal{TA}(\Xi) = \{\mathcal{A} \mid \mathcal{A} \in \mathcal{TA} \text{ and } L(\mathcal{A}) = Supp(\Xi)\}$. Given Ξ, the objective is to synthesize an automaton $\mathcal{A} \in \mathcal{TA}(\Xi)$. Obviously, such an automaton is not unique, so one can be more specific about the precise goal: the method of synthesis may depend on the desired properties of the resulting automaton. Our goals, listed in the order of importance, are as follows:

1. Every location of $\mathcal{A}$ should appear in at least one accepting run of $\mathcal{A}$.
2. The number of clocks should be as low as it is possible to make it without analysing the semantics of the constraints.
3. The number of locations should not be unduly large.

Our general strategy is to construct a finite representation of $Cons(\Xi)$ in the form of a tree $\mathcal{T}^\Xi$ that can be almost directly converted to an automaton. The tree is then modified to decrease the number of clocks.

To obtain $Cons(\Xi)$, we construct a representation of $Comp(\Xi)$ and then remove from it all those scenarios that are not consistent.

$Comp(\Xi)$ can be computed by taking the members of Ξ and repeatedly composing them in all possible ways to generate longer scenarios (as long as these are sure to be complete: see Sect. 3.3). This is done by building a tree rooted at a node that represents μ_0, i.e., is labeled with μ_0. Although the tree will represent the potentially large set $Comp(\Xi)$, we keep it compact by making sure that a member of Ξ never appears more than once on any branch.

For example, given the set Ξ of scenarios of Fig. 1, $Comp(\Xi)$ can be represented by the tree of Fig. 4, where each node that corresponds to the beginning or end of (each instance of) an original scenario is labeled with the appropriate mode. Observe that after generating the leaf labeled with μ_0, it would be possible to further extend the branch with scenario ξ_3, followed by ξ_4 and so on. We avoid this by marking the leaf as a "looping" leaf. In the final automaton this leaf will be unified with its "looping ancestor", that is, the ancestor whose

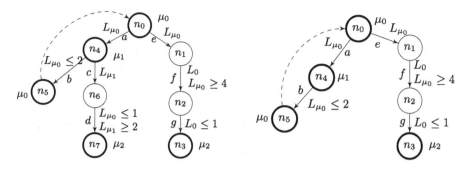

Fig. 4. The tree of Fig. 1

Fig. 5. The tree of Fig.4 after removing inconsistent paths

mode is μ_0 (the root, in this case), and therefore there will be a cycle. (The correspondence between the two nodes is shown by the dashed line.) Notice that ξ_5 is not added at node n_4.

Assuming V is the set of nodes of the tree, we use the partial function $VM : V \to \mathcal{M}$ to denote the labeling function described above.

3.3 Constructing $\mathcal{T}^{\Xi}$

The construction of $\mathcal{T}^{\Xi}$ is performed in two steps. Step 2 is repeated until it is no longer possible to expand the tree.

1. We initialize $\mathcal{T}^{\Xi}$ with a node n_0 and assign label μ_0 to it, i.e., $VM(n_0) = \mu_0$. The node is marked as a non-looping leaf.
2. Let n_l be a non-looping leaf in $\mathcal{T}^{\Xi}$, let p be the path from n_0 to n_l, and let *Candidates* $\subset \Xi$ be the set of scenarios whose initial mode is $VM(n_l)$.
   (a) For every $\xi \in$ *Candidates*, if ξ contains an annotated event (β, e, ϕ) such that there is a constraint $\alpha \sim a$ in ϕ for which:
       – there is no previous definition of label α in ξ, and
       – α is not defined on p,
       then remove ξ from *Candidates*.
   (b) Every remaining $\xi \in$ *Candidates* is "grafted" onto the tree at n_l. Grafting is carried out as follows:
       – In $\mathcal{T}^{\Xi}$, beginning at n_l, we create a path p' whose length is the length of ξ. Every transition r in p' is annotated with the label, event and constraints of the corresponding annotated event (β, e, ϕ) in ξ.
       – Let $n_{l'}$ be the final node of p'. We set $VM(n_{l'}) = fmode(\xi)$.
       – If there is a node n_j on p such that $VM(n_j) = VM(n_{l'})$, then we mark $n_{l'}$ as a *looping leaf* and n_j as its *looping ancestor*. Otherwise we mark $n_{l'}$ as a non-looping leaf.

Step 2a ensures that every branch represents a closed scenario.

Given Ξ, we use $\mathcal{T}^{\Xi} = \langle \Sigma, V, n_0, R \rangle$ to denote its tree. V is a finite set of nodes; $n_0 \in V$ is the initial node, and $R \subseteq V \times V \times \Sigma \times \mathcal{L} \times 2^{\Phi(\mathcal{L}_n)}$ is the set of transitions of the form $(n_i, n_j, e, \beta, \phi)$, where n_i and n_j are nodes in V, e is an event in Σ, β is a label in $\mathcal{L}$, and ϕ is a set of constraints in $2^{\Phi(\mathcal{L}_n)}$.

In our examples different transitions will often be associated with different events. This will allow us to refer to a transition by the name of its event and to refer to a path by the sequence of the events that appear in its transitions.

We use the following auxiliary notation:

- if $r = (n_i, n_j, e, \beta, \phi) \in R$, then $source(r) = n_i$, $target(r) = n_j$, $event(r) = e$, $label(r) = \beta$, and $constraints(r) = \phi$;
- if $n \in V$, then $out(n) = \{r \mid source(r) = n\}$ and $in(n) = \{r \mid target(r) = n\}$;
- $act\_target(r) = target(r)$ if $target(r)$ is not a looping leaf, otherwise $act\_target(r)$ is the looping ancestor of $target(r)$.

Definition 12. *A sequence of transitions $r_0 r_1 \ldots r_n$ in $\mathcal{T}^\Xi$ is a g-path iff, for $0 \le i < n$, $source(r_{i+1}) = act\_target(r_i)$.*

Intuitively, a g-path corresponds to a path in the final automaton. Notice that a path in the tree is also a g-path.

Let $p = r_1 \ldots r_k$ be a g-path in the tree. We define $origin(p) = source(r_1)$, $end(p) = act\_target(r_k)$, and $transitions(p) = \{r_1, \ldots, r_k\}$.

Let p_1 and p_2 be two g-paths such that $end(p_1) = origin(p_2)$. $p_1 \oplus p_2$ denotes their concatenation: $origin(p_1 \oplus p_2) = origin(p_1)$ and $end(p_1 \oplus p_2) = end(p_2)$.

Definition 13. *Given $\mathcal{T}^\Xi$, we introduce the following notions:*

- *A node n is* final *iff $VM(n) \in \mathcal{M}_F$.*
- *A g-path p is* complete *iff $origin(p) = n_0$ and $end(p)$ is final.*
- *Let n be a looping leaf with label μ, and let n_a be its looping ancestor. The path that begins at n_a and ends at n is an* open cycle. *We sometimes call n_a the* origin *of the open cycle.*
- *Let p be a path that begins at the root and ends at a leaf, r be a transition on p and $\alpha \sim a$ be a constraint in $constraints(r)$. We say α is* well-defined *iff there is a transition r' that appears before r on p and $label(r') = \alpha$.*

Observe that a final node can (but need not) be a leaf, even a looping leaf.

Some of the nodes in $\mathcal{T}^\Xi$ might not be on a complete g-path: the corresponding locations will not appear in accepting runs, so we must remove them.

Definition 14. *A node n is* alive *iff n is final or there is a g-path from n to a final node. A node that is not alive is* dead.

Removal of dead nodes in $\mathcal{T}^\Xi$ is quite similar to standard garbage collection. We remove all nodes that are not marked as "alive" by the following algorithm:

1. Mark all the nodes in $\mathcal{T}^\Xi$ as "dead".
2. Initialize LN to the set of identifiers of final nodes.
3. While $LN \neq \emptyset$:
   (a) Remove some n from LN. Mark node n in $\mathcal{T}^\Xi$ as "alive".
   (b) If n is a looping ancestor, add to LN the identifiers of those looping leaves associated with n that are not marked as "alive".
   (c) If n has a parent node that is not marked as "alive", add the identifier of the parent to LN.

In the tree of Fig. 4 the nodes labeled by VM are drawn with thick lines. Assuming that μ_0 is the initial mode and μ_0, μ_2 are the final modes, the paths that begin at n_0 and end at n_3, n_5 or n_7 are complete. n_0 is the looping ancestor of n_5, and the path between n_0 and n_5 is an open cycle. Notice that the node corresponding to ξ_5 would be dead and was removed after the initial construction.

Observation 1 $\mathcal{T}^\Xi$ *has the following properties:*

1. *If p is a path from n_0 to a leaf, and r is a transition on p, such that $label(r) = L_\mu \in \mathcal{L}_\mathcal{M}$, then no other transition on p is labeled with L_μ.*
2. *If r is a transition, and $constraints(r)$ includes a label $L_\mu \in \mathcal{L}_\mathcal{M}$, then there is a unique transition $r' \neq r$ on the path from n_0 to r, such that $label(r') = L_\mu$.*
3. *If r is a transition, such that $constraints(r)$ includes a label $L \in \mathcal{L} \setminus \mathcal{L}_\mathcal{M}$, and n is the latest labeled ancestor node of r, then there is a transition $r' \neq r$ on the path from n to r, such that $label(r') = L$.*
4. *Every label α that appears in a constraint on a transition r is well-defined.*

We can think of labels in $\mathcal{L} \setminus \mathcal{L}_\mathcal{M}$ as "local labels": local to a scenario, or— equivalently—to a path between two labeled nodes in $\mathcal{T}^\Xi$; $\mathcal{L}_\mathcal{M}$ would then be the set of "global labels".

Let a label L appear in a constraint on some transition r. If $L \in \mathcal{L}_\mathcal{M}$, then, by pt. 2 of Observation 1, L is defined only once on the path from the root to r. If $L \in \mathcal{L} \setminus \mathcal{L}_\mathcal{M}$, then there might be many definitions of L on this path: in this case L in the constraint associates with the latest definition of L on the path.

The distinction between local and global labels ensures that in the target automaton an occurrence of a clock in a constraint always refers to the same clock reset (see Observation 5). This is important both for checking the consistency of scenarios (Sect. 3.4) and for our specialized clock allocation algorithm (Sect. 3.5).

Let p be a g-path in $\mathcal{T}^\Xi$ that begins at n_0 and ends at some labeled node. The g-path represents a closed scenario ξ_p. If p is complete, ξ_p is complete. We have removed dead nodes, so p is complete. $\mathcal{T}^\Xi$ can be viewed as an encoding of all the complete scenarios that can be composed from members of Ξ.

We use $\mathcal{S}(\mathcal{T}^\Xi)$ to denote the set of all complete scenarios represented by $\mathcal{T}^\Xi$.

Observation 2 *Let Ξ be a finite set of finite scenarios, then $\mathcal{S}(\mathcal{T}^\Xi) = Comp(\Xi)$.*

In the remainder of the paper, whenever we refer to a tree, we assume it is obtained from a set of scenarios by means of the method described in Sect. 3.3.

3.4   Checking the Consistency of $\mathcal{T}^{\Xi}$

Now that we have built $\mathcal{T}^{\Xi}$ to represent all the complete scenarios, we must remove paths that correspond to inconsistent scenarios, to ensure that the final automaton does not have locations that never appear in an accepting run.

To check the consistency of the complete scenarios encoded by $\mathcal{T}^{\Xi}$ we use the method described in our earlier work [15]. The check is carried out in two steps: first we consider the complete paths, then the open cycles.

First step. Let p be a complete path in $\mathcal{T}^{\Xi}$. If ξ_p is inconsistent, our method allows us to identify the offending constraint (the first constraint in ξ_p that makes it inconsistent): if it is on transition r, we remove the subtree whose trunk is r.

As a result of such pruning we may obtain a smaller tree. Some of its nodes might no longer be alive (see Definition 14): we must remove them.

As an example consider the tree of Fig. 4 once more. The tree has three complete paths. Let p_1 be the path that begins at n_0 and ends at n_3, p_2 be the path that begins at n_0 and ends at n_7, and p_3 be the open cycle with origin n_0 which is also a complete path. $\xi_{p_1} = \xi_1$ (see Fig. 1) is consistent. p_2 and p_3 correspond to scenarios $\xi_{p_2} = \xi_3 \circ \xi_2$ and $\xi_{p_3} = \xi_3 \circ \xi_4$, shown in Fig. 6.

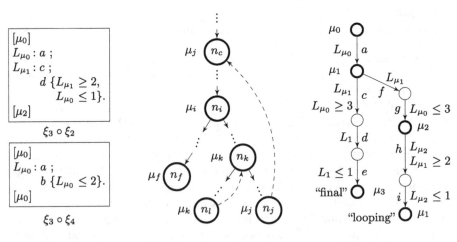

Fig. 6. Complete scenarios

Fig. 7. Nested open cycles

Fig. 8. A tree

ξ_{p_2} is inconsistent. Our method identifies the second constraint on transition d as the offending constraint, so transition d and node n_7 are removed. This renders n_6 dead, so c and n_6 are removed. ξ_{p_3} is consistent, and all the remaining nodes are alive. Figure 5 shows the resulting tree.

Second step. In the second step we consider the scenarios that correspond to paths that include open cycles: if there is no complete consistent path that includes an open cycle, then at least a part of the cycle must be removed. We use the tree of Fig. 7 to illustrate one such situation. Let n_f and n_k be the final nodes, p be the path between the root and n_c, c_1 be the open cycle with origin n_c (with looping leaf n_j), p' be the path between n_c and n_f, and p'' be the path between n_c and n_k. Assume that the consistency of the scenarios corresponding to the two complete paths (between the root and n_f, and between the root and n_k) is established in the first step. In the second step we first check the consistency of scenario $\xi_{p \oplus c_1 \oplus p'}$.

The consistency of $p \oplus p'$ and $p \oplus p''$ has already been established, so if $\xi_{p \oplus c_1 \oplus p'}$ is inconsistent, the inconsistency must have been introduced by the inclusion of c_1. In that case we remove transitions that belong to c_1, but not those that belong to p' or p'' (i.e., we remove the path between n_k and n_j). Observe that the first offending constraint in this case might well be on some transition between n_c and n_f.

If $\xi_{p \oplus c_1 \oplus p'}$ is consistent, then c_1 is not removed, but we must consider any nested cycles. Assume c_2 is the open cycle with origin n_k and looping leaf n_l, and c_{11} is the path between n_c and n_k. We check the consistency of $\xi_{p \oplus c_{11} \oplus c_2}$. If the scenario is inconsistent, c_2 is removed (recall that n_k is final).

While checking the consistency of a path that includes an open cycle it is enough to consider only one unrolling of each cycle: if it does not introduce an inconsistency, then in the final automaton there will be an accepting run that goes through the cycle at least once.

After removing an open cycle we prune away any resulting dead branches.

We use $\mathcal{T}_c^\Xi$ to denote the tree obtained from $\mathcal{T}^\Xi$ after removing the inconsistent paths. $\mathcal{S}(\mathcal{T}_c^\Xi)$ denotes the set of complete scenarios represented by $\mathcal{T}_c^\Xi$.

Observation 3 $\mathcal{S}(\mathcal{T}_c^\Xi)$ *is the set of all the complete, consistent scenarios that can be built from elements of* Ξ.

With a slight abuse of notation, the set of behaviors represented by $\mathcal{T}_c^\Xi$ will be denoted by $Supp(\mathcal{T}_c^\Xi) = \bigcup_{\xi \in \mathcal{S}(\mathcal{T}_c^\Xi)} \llbracket \xi \rrbracket$.

From now on we assume that all our trees are consistent.

3.5 A Specialized Clock Allocation Algorithm for $\mathcal{T}_c^\Xi$

Most of the definitions in the remainder of this subsection are adapted from our previous work [13] and are specialized for the case of trees.

Recall that $\mathcal{L}_n = \mathcal{L} \setminus \{none\}$. For a given $\mathcal{T}_c^\Xi$ we define the following functions:

- $used : R \to 2^{\mathcal{L}_n}$ maps transition r to the set $\{\alpha \mid \alpha \sim a \in constraints(r)\}$.
- $needed : R \to 2^{\mathcal{L}_n}$ maps transition r to a set of labels. $\alpha \in needed(r)$ iff there is a g-path $r_0 r_1 \ldots r_k$, $k \geq 0$, such that $r = r_0$, $\alpha \in used(r_k)$ and, for any $0 < i < k$, $\alpha \neq label(r_i)$.
  If $\alpha \in needed(r)$, we say α *is needed* on r. Intuitively, $needed(r)$ identifies labels whose values are used on r or on some subsequent transitions.

- $born : R \rightarrow 2^{\mathcal{L}_n}$ maps transition r to a set of labels. $\alpha \in born(r)$ iff $\alpha = label(r)$ and $\alpha \in needed(r')$ for some $r' \in out(target(r))$.

  We say that a label α *is born* on transition r if $born(r) = \{\alpha\}$.

  Notice that $born(r)$ is either a singleton or the empty set. Moreover, $\alpha \in born(r)$ implies $\alpha \in needed(r)$.

- $last\_ref : R \rightarrow 2^{\mathcal{L}_n}$ maps transition r to the set $\{\alpha \mid \alpha \in needed(r) \wedge (\alpha \in born(r) \vee \forall_{r' \in out(act\_target(r))} \, \alpha \notin needed(r'))\}$.

Note: If a label α is defined on some transition of an open cycle, then, by Observation 1, its value cannot possibly be needed on any transition outgoing from the origin of the open cycle. So there is no need to use act_target in the definition of $born$.

As noted above, a label that is born on a transition is needed on that transition. For instance, in the tree of Fig. 8, $born(a) = \{L_{\mu_0}\}$, $born(f) = \{L_{\mu_1}\}$ and $born(d) = \{L_1\}$. L_{μ_0} is in $needed(a)$, L_{μ_1} is in $needed(f)$, and L_1 is in $needed(d)$.

However, a label is born on a transition only if it is used on some subsequent transition. In the tree of Fig. 8, even though label L_{μ_1} is defined on transition c, it is not born on c, because it is not subsequently used.

Finally, a label is included in $last\_ref$ on transition r only if it is used there, but is not needed on any subsequent transition. For instance, in the tree of Fig. 8 L_{μ_0} is in $last\_ref(c)$, but not in $last\_ref(g)$: after unifying the looping leaf with its looping ancestor (labeled with μ_1), L_{μ_0} will be needed on c. (It is worth noticing that if L_{μ_0} were not referenced on transition c, then it would be needed on f, g, h and i, but would not belong to $last\_ref(r)$ for any transition r.)

Definition 15. *Let T_c^{Ξ} be a tree and α be a label in $\mathcal{L}_n$. A g-path $r_0 r_1 \ldots r_n$ in T_c^{Ξ} ($n > 0$) is a path of α iff the following four conditions are satisfied:*

- $\alpha \in born(r_0)$,
- $\alpha \in needed(r_n)$,
- *for every $0 < i < n$, $\alpha \notin born(r_i)$,*
- $\alpha \notin born(r_n) \vee \alpha \in used(r_n)$.

In the tree of Fig. 8, $afghic$ and ac are two of several paths of label L_{μ_0}. Similarly, fgh is a path of label L_{μ_1}. de and d are the only paths of label L_1, while h and hi are the only paths of L_{μ_2}.

Observation 4 *Let T_c^{Ξ} be a tree, $\alpha \in \mathcal{L}_{\mathcal{M}}$, and p and p' be two paths of α. If p and p' overlap, then there must exist a transition r such that $\alpha \in born(r)$ and r is the initial transition of both p and p'.*

Intuitively, if a label $\alpha \in \mathcal{L}_{\mathcal{M}}$ has two overlapping paths that are partly disjoint, then the paths must share at least their first transition and then continue, at some point diverging as branches of a fork.

Notice that a label $\alpha \in \mathcal{L}_n \setminus \mathcal{L}_\mathcal{M}$ cannot have two partly disjoint paths that begin on the same transition (see pt. 3 of Observation 1).[2]

Definition 16. *Let $P(\alpha, r)$ be the set of all paths of label α that begin on transition r. The function range $: \mathcal{L}_n \times R \to 2^R$ maps (α, r) to $\bigcup_{p \in P(\alpha, r)}$ transitions(p).*

Intuitively, $range(\alpha, r)$ is the set of all transitions on which the value of α defined on r is needed. If $range(\alpha, r) \neq \emptyset$, we often say that this range of α begins at r.

In the tree of Fig. 8 there is one range of L_{μ_0}, namely $\{a, c, f, g, h, i\}$: it begins at a. Similarly, $\{f, g, h\}$ is the only range of L_{μ_1}, and it begins at f.

It is worth pointing out that if a label α is defined on a transition r of an open cycle c, then $range(\alpha, r)$ can contain only transitions of those g-paths that begin at r and do not pass through the origin of c (pts. 1, 3 and 4 of Observation 1).

Definition 17. *Let $\mathcal{R}$ be a range of $\alpha \in \mathcal{L}_n$ and $\mathcal{R}'$ be a range of $\alpha' \in \mathcal{L}_n$, such that $\mathcal{R} \neq \mathcal{R}'$.[3] We define conflict$(\mathcal{R}, \mathcal{R}') = \{r \in \mathcal{R} \cap \mathcal{R}' \mid (\alpha \in born(r) \implies \alpha' \notin last\_ref(r)) \lor (\alpha' \in born(r) \implies \alpha \notin last\_ref(r))\}$.*

Definition 18. *Let $\mathcal{R}$ and $\mathcal{R}'$ be two different ranges. $\mathcal{R}$ and $\mathcal{R}'$ conflict iff conflict$(\mathcal{R}, \mathcal{R}') \neq \emptyset$.*

If R and R' conflict, we say that they *are conflicting*, or that R *conflicts with* R' (and vice versa). If $r \in conflict(\mathcal{R}, \mathcal{R}')$, we say that $\mathcal{R}$ and $\mathcal{R}'$ *conflict on* r.

In the tree of Fig. 8 the range of L_1 does not conflict with the ranges of L_{μ_0}, L_{μ_1} or L_{μ_2} (and would not conflict even if L_{μ_0} were used on transition d). The range of L_{μ_0} conflicts with the ranges of L_{μ_1} and L_{μ_2}.

Observation 5 *Let α be a label that appears in used(r) for some transition r in $\mathcal{T}_c^\Xi$. Then there is a unique transition r' on the path from the root to r, such that $r \in range(\alpha, r')$.*

3.5.1 Clock Allocation We assume the existence of a set $\mathcal{C}$ of clocks (i.e., "clock" variables).

Definition 19. *Let $\mathcal{T}_c^\Xi$ be a tree with the set R of transitions and the set $\mathcal{L}$ of labels. A clock allocation for $\mathcal{T}_c^\Xi$ is a relation alloc $\subset R \times \mathcal{L}_n \times \mathcal{C}$ such that $(r, \alpha, c) \in alloc \Rightarrow \alpha \in needed(r)$.*

---

[2] By Observation 1, if $\alpha \in \mathcal{L}_\mathcal{M}$, there is no transition r such that $\alpha \in born(r) \cap used(r)$. However, this is quite possible for $\alpha \in \mathcal{L}_n \setminus \mathcal{L}_\mathcal{M}$: in that case, the last transition of a path of α can be the same as the first transition of another path of α.

[3] α may, but need not, be different from α'.

Recall that $\mathcal{L}_n = \mathcal{L} \setminus \{none\}$. Inclusion of (r, α, c) in *alloc* represents the fact that on transition r clock c is associated with label α.

Definition 20. *A clock allocation alloc is* incorrect *iff there are two conflicting ranges $\mathcal{R}$ and $\mathcal{R}'$, of some labels α and α' (where $\alpha \neq \alpha'$)[4], some $c \in \mathcal{C}$ and some $r \in conflict(\mathcal{R}, \mathcal{R}')$ such that $(r, \alpha, c) \in alloc \wedge (r, \alpha', c) \in alloc$.*
alloc is correct *iff it is not incorrect.*

Intuitively, if two labels are needed on a single transition r then a correct allocation associates them with two different clocks, unless r is the transition on which the range of one label ends and the range of the other label begins (in which case it is correct to associate both labels with the same clock).

Definition 21. *The clock allocation alloc is* complete *iff, for every transition r and every $\alpha \in needed(r)$, there is a clock $c \in \mathcal{C}$ such that $(r, \alpha, c) \in alloc$.*

Definition 22. *We define the number of clocks used in an allocation by:*
$cost(alloc) = |\{c \in \mathcal{C} \mid \exists_{r \in R} \exists_{\alpha \in \mathcal{L}_n} (r, \alpha, c) \in alloc\}|$.

Definition 23. *Let alloc be a complete and correct clock allocation for T_c^{Ξ}. The allocation alloc is* optimal *if there is no complete correct allocation alloc' for T_c^{Ξ} such that $cost(alloc') < cost(alloc)$.*

This definition is the right one if we cannot modify the graph and do not take into account the semantics of the constraints. It is, in general, possible to construct "pathological" examples in which the number of clocks can be smaller than defined here (e.g., if all the constraints always evaluate to true). See our earlier work [13] for details and a more formal treatment of this notion of optimality.

We are now ready to present our new clock allocation algorithm. We assume the values of functions *needed*, *born* and *last_ref* are computed by a standard data-flow algorithm [13] whose cost is $O(e^3)$ (where e is the number of edges).

Algorithm 1 finds a clock allocation that is optimal *for the given tree T_c^{Ξ}*. Its simplicity is due to Observations 5 and 1. If we assume that set operations are carried out in constant time, then its cost is $O(e)$. Our general clock allocation algorithm [13] is based on graph colouring, which is NP-complete in general, but is cheaper on specialised kinds of graphs.

Algorithm 1: Allocating clocks in T_c^{Ξ}

Input : A tree $T_c^{\Xi} = \langle E, V, n_0, R \rangle$ and a set $\mathcal{C}$ of clocks.
Output: The allocation relation *alloc*.

1 $alloc := \emptyset$;
2 $doNode(n_0, \emptyset, \mathcal{C})$

---

[4] In our setting two ranges of the same label can overlap, but cannot be conflicting.

Procedure doNode(node n, set of pairs $assoc$, set of clocks $pool$)

1 **foreach** $r \in out(n)$ **do**
2 $\quad \lfloor \; doTrans(r, assoc, pool)$

Procedure doTrans(transition r, set of pairs $assoc$, set of clocks $pool$)

1 $newAssoc := \{(\alpha, c) \in assoc \mid \alpha \in ((needed(r) \setminus born(r)) \cup last\_ref(r))\};$
2 $newPool := pool \cup \{c \mid \exists_{\alpha \in \mathcal{L}}(\alpha, c) \in (assoc \setminus newAssoc)\};$
3 **foreach** $(\alpha, c) \in newAssoc$ **do**
4 $\quad \lfloor \; alloc := alloc \cup \{(r, \alpha, c)\};$

5 **foreach** $\alpha \in last\_ref(r)$ **do**
6 $\quad$ Let d be the clock such that $(\alpha, d) \in newAssoc;$
7 $\quad newAssoc := newAssoc \setminus \{(\alpha, d)\};$
8 $\quad \lfloor \; newPool := newPool \cup \{d\};$

9 **if** $born(r) \neq \emptyset$ **then**
10 $\quad$ Let $\beta \in born(r);$ /* $born(r)$ is a singleton   */
11 $\quad$ Let d be the clock in $newPool$ with the smallest number;
12 $\quad newPool := newPool \setminus \{d\};$
13 $\quad newAssoc := newAssoc \cup \{(\beta, d)\};$
14 $\quad \lfloor \; alloc := alloc \cup \{(r, \beta, d)\};$

15 $doNode(target(r), newAssoc, newPool)$

3.6 Obtaining the Final Automaton

After allocating clocks we should rewrite the constraints in $\mathcal{T}_c^{\Xi}$ in terms of clocks.

Let r be a transition. If $\alpha \in born(r)$ and $(r, \alpha, c_i) \in alloc$, we annotate r with the clock reset $c_i := 0$. If $\beta \sim a \in constraints(r)$ and $(r, \beta, c_j) \in alloc$, we replace the constraint by $c_j \sim a$.

$\mathcal{T}_a^{\Xi}$ denotes the automaton that is obtained after this step. If $\mathcal{T}_c^{\Xi}$ includes open cycles, then $\mathcal{T}_a^{\Xi}$ is not yet the target automaton: we must first form cycles. This step can be performed by unifying the looping leaves with their corresponding looping ancestors. $\mathcal{A}^{\Xi}$ denotes the resulting automaton.

The automaton on the right hand side of Fig. 1 is obtained after optimally allocating clocks in the tree of Fig. 5 and forming the cycles. Observe that clock c_0 is associated with both labels L_0 and L_{μ_0} and that n_5 is unified with n_0. (Final locations are drawn as double circles.)

The timed automaton of Fig. 9 corresponds to the tree of Fig. 8. Algorithm 1 replaces the four labels of the tree with two clocks. The allocation is optimal.

Observation 6 *Let Ξ be a set of finite scenarios over Σ and let $\mathcal{A}^{\Xi}$ be the final timed automaton synthesized from scenarios in Ξ. Then $Supp(\Xi) = L(\mathcal{A}^{\Xi})$.*

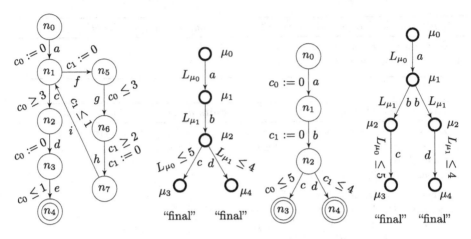

Fig. 9. An automaton for the tree of Fig. 8   **Fig. 10.** A tree, its automaton, and its equivalent tree

3.7   Untangling $\mathcal{T}_c^{\Xi}$

The clock allocation obtained by Algorithm 1 is optimal *under the assumption that the underlying graph cannot be changed.*

We recently explored the possibility of reducing the number of clocks even further, by modifying the underlying graph [16]. We found out that the graph of an automaton can often be "untangled" in order to decrease the number of conflicting ranges, and hence the number of clocks.

We present a very brief overview of the method. Under the assumption that the original constraints in a timed automaton $\mathcal{A}$ cannot be changed, we determine $\mathcal{A}$'s *real cost* $C(\mathcal{A})$, i.e., the maximum of the smallest number of clocks that must be maintained on any path through the automaton. If this is smaller than the number of clocks in an optimal clock allocation [13] for $\mathcal{A}$, then we know that there is at least one language-equivalent automaton, $\mathcal{A}'$, for which it is possible to allocate only $C(\mathcal{A})$ clocks.

The method can be applied directly to $\mathcal{T}_c^{\Xi}$ before we perform clock allocation. This is illustrated by a simple example. Consider the tree on the left-hand side of Fig. 10 and its corresponding automaton, shown in the middle of the figure, obtained after clocks are optimally allocated by Algorithm 1. Observe that the automaton has two clocks. Using our new method [16] we "untangle" the paths of the tree and obtain the tree shown on the right-hand side of the figure. Algorithm 1 will allocate only one clock for this tree: both L_{μ_0} and L_{μ_1} can be replaced by a single clock, as $range(L_{\mu_0}, a)$ is disjoint from $range(L_{\mu_1}, b)$ (a range for L_{μ_1} begins only on the rightmost transition with event b).

4 Related Work and Conclusions

For over three decades scenarios (including various forms of scenarios with time) have been proposed and used for specifying (and also synthesizing formal models of) complex systems [4,7,9,19]. The problem of synthesizing a *timed automaton* from scenarios has also been considered [17,18].

Our scenarios are different from those proposed by Somé et al. [18]: ours do not include "conditions". These "conditions" are not related to time and assert some facts about the status/mode of the described system.

Our synthesis method is completely different from theirs: in particular, we do not allow a part of a scenario to be composed with a part of another scenario. This enables us to precisely define the semantics of a set of scenarios Ξ and synthesize a timed automaton whose semantics are isomorphic to those of Ξ.

The method of Somé et al. assigns a clock to every location of the synthesized automaton and resets it in all the incoming transitions of that location. We perform optimal clock allocation (in the sense of Sect. 3.5). By modifying the graph (Sect. 3.7) we can often decrease the number of clocks still further.

Finally, our method performs a consistency check of scenarios and excludes the inconsistent scenarios (or combination thereof) from the construction. As a result, every location of the automaton appears in at least one accepting run.

Salah et al. [17] synthesize an executable specification for a real-time system by integrating scenarios into a timed automaton. Both the syntax and the semantics of their scenarios are different from ours (the latter are defined in terms of labeled transition systems). The construction of the automaton is also completely different from ours, and the automaton includes ϵ-transitions.

To summarize, we developed a novel approach for synthesizing a timed automaton from a set of scenarios. The language of the automaton is the set of all behaviours supported by the set of scenarios. Every location of the automaton appears in some accepting run of the automaton. The number of clocks is as low as it is possible to obtain without considering the semantics of clock constraints, and our new clock allocation algorithm is simple and efficient.

References

1. Abdulla, P.A., Deneux, J., Ouaknine, J., Worrell, J.: Decidability and complexity results for timed automata via channel machines. In: Caires, L., Italiano, G.F., Monteiro, L., Palamidessi, C., Yung, M. (eds.) ICALP 2005. LNCS, vol. 3580, pp. 1089–1101. Springer, Heidelberg (2005). https://doi.org/10.1007/11523468_88
2. Alur, R.: Timed automata. In: Halbwachs, N., Peled, D. (eds.) CAV 1999. LNCS, vol. 1633, pp. 8–22. Springer, Heidelberg (1999). https://doi.org/10.1007/3-540-48683-6_3
3. Alur, R., Dill, D.L.: A theory of timed automata. Theor. Comput. Sci. **126**(2), 183–235 (1994)
4. Alur, R., Martin, M., Raghothaman, M., Stergiou, C., Tripakis, S., Udupa, A.: Synthesizing finite-state protocols from scenarios and requirements. In: Yahav, E. (ed.) HVC 2014. LNCS, vol. 8855, pp. 75–91. Springer, Cham (2014). https://doi.org/10.1007/978-3-319-13338-6_7

5. An, J., Chen, M., Zhan, B., Zhan, N., Zhang, M.: Learning one-clock timed automata. TACAS 2020. LNCS, vol. 12078, pp. 444–462. Springer, Cham (2020). https://doi.org/10.1007/978-3-030-45190-5_25

6. Baier, C., Bertrand, N., Bouyer, P., Brihaye, T.: When are timed automata determinizable? In: Albers, S., Marchetti-Spaccamela, A., Matias, Y., Nikoletseas, S., Thomas, W. (eds.) ICALP 2009. LNCS, vol. 5556, pp. 43–54. Springer, Heidelberg (2009). https://doi.org/10.1007/978-3-642-02930-1_4

7. Bollig, B., Katoen, J.-P., Kern, C., Leucker, M.: Replaying play in and play out: synthesis of design models from scenarios by learning. In: Grumberg, O., Huth, M. (eds.) TACAS 2007. LNCS, vol. 4424, pp. 435–450. Springer, Heidelberg (2007). https://doi.org/10.1007/978-3-540-71209-1_33

8. Clarke Jr., E.M., Grumberg, O., Peled, D.A.: Model Checking. MIT Press, Cambridge (1999)

9. Damas, C., Lambeau, B., Roucoux, F., van Lamsweerde, A.: Analyzing critical process models through behavior model synthesis. In: Proceedings of the 31st International Conference on Software Engineering, pp. 441–451. IEEE Computer Society (2009)

10. Giese, H.: Towards scenario-based synthesis for parametric timed automata. In: Proceedings of the 2nd International Workshop on Scenarios and State Machines: Models, Algorithms, and Tools (SCESM), Portland, USA (2003)

11. Grinchtein, O., Jonsson, B., Leucker, M.: Learning of event-recording automata. Theor. Comput. Sci. **411**(47), 4029–4054 (2010)

12. Lin, S., André, É., Liu, Y., Sun, J., Dong, J.S.: Learning assumptions for compositional verification of timed systems. IEEE Trans. Software Eng. **40**(2), 137–153 (2014)

13. Saeedloei, N., Kluźniak, F.: Clock allocation in timed automata and graph colouring. In: Proceedings of the 21st International Conference on Hybrid Systems: Computation and Control (part of CPS Week), HSCC 2018, pp. 71–80 (2018)

14. Saeedloei, N., Kluźniak, F.: From scenarios to timed automata. In: Cavalheiro, S., Fiadeiro, J. (eds.) SBMF 2017. LNCS, vol. 10623, pp. 33–51. Springer, Cham (2017). https://doi.org/10.1007/978-3-319-70848-5_4

15. Saeedloei, N., Kluźniak, F.: Timed scenarios: consistency, equivalence and optimization. In: Massoni, T., Mousavi, M.R. (eds.) SBMF 2018. LNCS, vol. 11254, pp. 215–233. Springer, Cham (2018). https://doi.org/10.1007/978-3-030-03044-5_14

16. Saeedloei, N., Kluźniak, F.: Untangling the Graphs of Timed Automata to Streamline the Number of Clocks. https://tigerweb.towson.edu/nsaeedloei/untangling.pdf

17. Salah, A., Dssouli, R., Lapalme, G.: Compiling real-time scenarios into a timed automaton. In: Kim, M., Chin, B., Kang, S., Lee, D. (eds.) FORTE 2001. IIFIP, vol. 69, pp. 135–150. Springer, Boston, MA (2002). https://doi.org/10.1007/0-306-47003-9_9

18. Somé, S., Dssouli, R., Vaucher, J.: From scenarios to timed automata: building specifications from users requirements. In: Proceedings of the Second Asia Pacific Software Engineering Conference, pp. 48–57. IEEE Computer Society (1995)

19. Uchitel, S., Brunet, G., Chechik, M.: Synthesis of partial behavior models from properties and scenarios. IEEE Trans. Softw. Eng. **35**(3), 384–406 (2009)

Static Analysis

Lock and Fence When Needed: State Space Exploration + Static Analysis = Improved Fence and Lock Insertion

Sander de Putter and Anton Wijs(✉)

Eindhoven University of Technology, Eindhoven, The Netherlands
{s.m.j.d.putter,a.j.wijs}@tue.nl

Abstract. When targeting modern parallel hardware architectures, constructing correct and high-performing software is complex and time-consuming. In particular, reorderings of memory accesses that violate intended sequentially consistent behaviour are a major source of bugs. Applying synchronisation mechanisms to repair these should be done sparingly, as they negatively impact performance.

In the past, both static analysis approaches and techniques based on explicit-state model checking have been proposed to identify where synchronisation fences have to be placed in a program. The former are fast, but the latter more precise, as they tend to insert fewer fences. Unfortunately, the model checking techniques suffer a form of state space explosion that is even worse than the traditional one.

In this work, we propose a technique using a combination of state space exploration and static analysis. This combination is in terms of precision comparable to purely model checking-based techniques, but it reduces the state space explosion problem to the one typically seen in model checking. Furthermore, experiments show that the combination frequently outperforms both purely model checking and static analysis techniques. In addition, we have added the capability to check for atomicity violations, which is another major source of bugs.

1 Introduction

When developing parallel software it is very challenging to guarantee the absence of bugs. Achieving the intended execution order of instructions while obtaining high performance is extremely hard. This is particularly the case on parallel hardware architectures where memory accesses may be reordered. Reorderings that break the intended sequential and atomic behaviour are a major source of bugs [31]. These can be avoided by appropriately using synchronisation mechanisms such as fences, semaphores, hardware-level atomic operations, and software/hardware transactional memory [37]. However, overusing these can cause contention, as experimentally demonstrated in [4], which negatively impacts performance and therefore defeats the purpose of using parallelism in the first place.

Sequential consistency is arguably the best understood concurrency model. An (execution) trace of a concurrent program is *Sequentially Consistent* (SC) iff

© Springer Nature Switzerland AG 2020
B. Dongol and E. Troubitsyna (Eds.): IFM 2020, LNCS 12546, pp. 297–317, 2020.
https://doi.org/10.1007/978-3-030-63461-2_16

all memory accesses are performed in program order, atomicity constraints are respected, and accesses of all threads are serviced as if from a single First In First Out queue [27]. As this model does not deviate from the software developers' specification it is very intuitive.

SC is very restrictive and does not benefit from modern compiler and processor optimisations. It is sufficient, however, that traces produce results that are *observably* equivalent to SC traces. Traces that do not do this, which we refer to as *non-SC* traces, produce results different from SC traces, i.e., they read and write combinations of values from/ to memory locations that an SC trace cannot produce. Such traces violate the behaviour intended by the software developer.

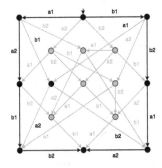

Fig. 1. Interleaving under weak memory models

In earlier work, either explicit-state model checking or static analysis was used to detect non-SC behaviour. Static analysis techniques [4–6,16,19,28,39], based on the seminal work of Shasha and Snir [36], estimate the possible SC behaviour, and derive which violations can occur when accesses are reordered according to what the memory model allows. These techniques are fundamentally limited regarding their accuracy. In particular, when pointers and guards (if-statements) are used, over-approximations cannot in general be avoided (are two pointers pointing to the same object? And when does the condition of an if-statement evaluate to **true**?).

An alternative is to use explicit-state model checking for fence insertion [1, 2, 8, 14, 23, 25, 29]. In those approaches, program specifications are extended to allow the model checker to systematically traverse *all* behaviour allowed by the memory model. For instance, to specify the memory store behaviour via thread-local caches, allowed by *Total Store Order* (TSO) [33, 38] and weaker models, additional store buffers must be modelled. The benefit of these approaches is their accuracy. However, their main issue is scalability; exploring non-SC executions makes the state space explosion problem even worse. Not surprisingly, very weak memory models such as ARMv7 [7] and POWER [22] have not yet been considered. In Fig. 1, all possible interleavings are given for four memory accesses performed by two threads: the first should execute $a1$ followed by $a2$, the second should execute $b1$ followed by $b2$. Starting at the initial state (the one with the incoming arrow), the typical diamond of interleavings is indicated by the black states and transitions between them. This diamond represents all possible SC traces. If the memory model under consideration can also reorder $a2$ before $a1$ and reorder $b2$ before $b1$, then the grey states and transitions also need to be explored. Clearly, as the number of accesses and threads increases, the number of states grows even more rapidly than when only considering SC traces.

Contributions. We propose to combine the state space exploration approach used by techniques based on explicit-state model checking, with the core concept of static analysis approaches, the latter working as a *postprocessing* procedure, to keep the precision of model checking while restricting state space exploration to

SC traces. First, we apply a model checker to explore the state space of a program specification. This specification describes all possible interleavings of program instructions, and its state space contains all possible SC executions, as is common for model checking.[1] This state space is used to extract an abstract event graph (AEG), which more accurately represents conflicts between the memory accesses of instructions than statically derived ones. Next, this graph is analysed using our postprocessing tool. Experiments show that constructing the AEG via state space exploration benefits the overall runtime performance, even compared to a state-of-the-art static analysis approach.

Besides this different workflow, compared to earlier work, we also support the specification of *atomic instructions*, thereby incorporating the atomicity checking originally addressed in [36]. When code does not enforce atomicity, non-SC behaviour can still occur, and only inserting fences does not suffice. In our approach, sets of accesses that are supposed to be executed atomically, i.e., without interruption by other threads, are marked for synchronisation if they are involved in non-SC behaviour. In the final code, these atomic instructions can be enforced by means of locks.

Our technique is the first *model checking-based* technique to support memory models as weak as ARMv7. We have implemented it by translating state machine specifications to MCRL2, such that the MCRL2 model checking toolset [15] can be used, and developed a new tool for the postprocessing. We demonstrate our technique for the memory models TSO, *Partial Store Order* (PSO) [38] and ARMv7/POWER, but it can be straightforwardly adapted to other memory models. During postprocessing, the technique reasons about the (un)safety of thread program paths by means of path rewrite rules.

Finally, it should be stressed that we reason about programs in which initially *no synchronisation primitives* are used. Therefore, the current work is *not* about reasoning about the semantics and SC guarantees of fences, atomic instructions, transactions, etc. When we talk about (atomic) instructions, we are referring to computation steps that are *specified* as atomic; whether they need to be implemented using some synchronisation primitive still needs to be determined. We acknowledge that in order to make an implementation correct, it is crucial to know the semantics and guarantees of those primitives; there are excellent studies on those for Java, C/C++11, and OpenCL [11,12,26], and various architectures [7,33,35], and applying their insights can be seen as the next step. Here, we focus on detecting the need for synchronisation. Earlier work on SC violation checking, such as [4,6,29], reasons about synchronisation primitives as well, but this is not really needed if one entirely relies on automatic insertion of synchronisation points.

---

[1] In order for this analysis to terminate, it is important that the system is *finite-state*, or at least has a finite-state quotient that can be derived prior to state space generation [32]. It may perform infinite executions, though, i.e., have cyclic behaviour between its states.

This work is also not about optimally implementing synchronisation. An architecture may provide several types of fences, with various guarantees and performance penalties. We aim to optimise the number of places in which a program needs synchronisation, not how that should be implemented. Related work [4] provides methods for that.

Structure of the Paper. In Sect. 2, we consider parallel program specifications, and recall the notions of SC, access conflicts and cycle detection in AEGs. We define the notion of (un)safety of thread program paths in Sect. 3, and present how we extract an AEG from a state space constructed by an explicit-state model checker in Sect. 4. The non-SC detection procedure is discussed in Sect. 5. Experimental results are discussed in Sect. 6. Finally, conclusions and pointers to future work are given in Sect. 7.

2   Preliminaries

Parallel Program Specifications. We assume that a parallel program involving shared variables is specified. Figure 2 gives an overview of the concepts related to such a program used in this work. A program consists of a set of threads $\mathbb{T}$, each performing a (possibly infinite) sequence of *instructions* called a *thread program*. Such a specification can, for instance, be given as a PROMELA [21] or MCRL2 model [15], in which the processes represent the threads, and each instruction represents an atomic execution step. Each instruction is either of the form e, $e; x_1 = e_1; \ldots; x_n = e_n$ or $x_1 = e_1; \ldots; x_n = e_n$ $(n \geqslant 1)$, with e and the e_i *expressions*, and the x_i memory locations. First, an optional *condition* e is checked (an expression evaluating to **true** or **false**). If the condition evaluates to **true**, or there is no condition, zero or more *assignments* can be performed that assign the outcome of interpreting e_i to x_i. For brevity, we do not define the form of expressions here (the usual logical and arithmetic operators can be used to combine variable references), and we assume that expressions are type correct. The data types we consider are Integer, Boolean, and arrays of Integers or Booleans. Extending this basic setup is not fundamentally relevant for the purpose of the current paper.

Program Behaviour. To reason about SC behaviour of a concurrent program we consider its execution on, and its effects on the memory of, a multi-core machine. To this end we assume that the state of the machine is defined by the values stored in its storage locations. The set of storage *locations* of a machine is denoted by $\mathbb{L}$. A location may be a register or a memory location (associated to some variable). Figure 2 presents that an instruction executes zero or more *accesses* to locations.

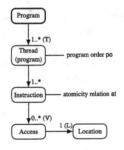

Fig. 2. Overview of a program

An *access* reads from, or writes to, a location $x \in \mathbb{L}$ and reads or writes a value. We write Rx and Wx to refer to a read and write access from/to x, respectively. When both the type (read or write) and the location are irrelevant, we use $a, b, \ldots$. An access is performed *atomically*, i.e., two accesses on the same location behave as if they occur in some serial order. The set of accesses of a thread $t \in \mathbb{T}$ is denoted by $\mathbb{V}_t$. The set of all accesses of a program is defined as $\mathbb{V} = \bigcup_{t \in \mathbb{T}} \mathbb{V}_t$.

For SC checking, only shared memory locations are relevant, i.e., those that can be accessed by multiple threads. Therefore, when we refer to memory locations, it is always implied that they are shared, and accesses always address shared locations.

The execution order of accesses in the program, or the *program order*, is defined by a per-thread total order $\mathsf{po} \subseteq \mathbb{V} \times \mathbb{V}$. Accesses of different threads are unrelated, hence po is the union of the (thread-local) total execution orders of accesses of all the threads.

The instructions of a specification are defined using an equivalence relation $\mathsf{at} \subseteq \mathbb{V} \times \mathbb{V}$ identifying classes of accesses that are to be performed (observably) atomically. Like po, at only relates accesses of the same thread. With $[\alpha]$, we refer to the (atomic) set of accesses associated with an instruction α. With $[e]$ consisting of read accesses for all locations referenced in expression e, we define $[\alpha]$ as $[e; x_1 = e_1; \ldots; x_n = e_n] = [e] \cup \bigcup_{1 \leq i \leq n} \{Wx_i\} \cup [e_i]$ and $[x_1 = e_1; \ldots; x_n = e_n] = \bigcup_{1 \leq i \leq n} \{Wx_i\} \cup [e_i]$. With $\langle\!\langle \alpha \rangle\!\rangle$, we refer to the set of read accesses performed to evaluate the condition of α: $\langle\!\langle e; x_1 = e_1; \ldots; x_n = e_n \rangle\!\rangle = [e]$ and $\langle\!\langle x_1 = e_1; \ldots; x_n = e_n \rangle\!\rangle = \varnothing$.

A *thread execution trace* π is a sequence of accesses $a \prec_t b \prec_t \ldots$, with $\prec_t$ a irreflexive, antisymmetric, non-transitive binary relation, describing the order in which accesses of thread t are (visibly) performed. The set of accesses in π is called $[\pi]$. A *program execution trace* is an interleaving of thread execution traces, ordered by $\prec$ (which is also, for convenience in Sect. 4, non-transitive).

Programmers *rely* on a programming paradigm where executions appear to be interleavings of instructions, and the instructions appear to be executed in programmed order without interruption. That is, they expect their program to be *sequentially consistent* [27]. The following definition is based on the one given by Shasha and Snir [36].

Definition 1 (Sequential Consistency). *A program execution trace* $\pi = a \prec b \prec \ldots$ *is sequentially consistent (SC) iff* $\prec$ *can be extended to a total order* $\prec\!\!\prec$ *that satisfies:*

1. $\mathsf{po} \subseteq \prec\!\!\prec$, *so that if* $a \mathsf{\,po\,} b$ *then* $a \prec\!\!\prec b$;
2. at-*equivalent accesses occur in consecutive places in the sequence defined by* $\prec\!\!\prec$: *if* $a \mathsf{\,at\,} b$ *but* $\neg(a \mathsf{\,at\,} c)$, *then either* $c \prec\!\!\prec a$ *and* $c \prec\!\!\prec b$, *or* $a \prec\!\!\prec c$ *and* $b \prec\!\!\prec c$.

By condition 2 of Definition 1, an SC trace retains atomicity of instructions.

In practice, it is sufficient that a trace is observably equivalent to an SC trace, which is the case if it computes the same values as an SC trace. The potential values of a location $x \in \mathbb{L}$ may depend on the order in which two accesses on x are executed. In this case, those accesses are said to be in conflict. In the literature, various types of conflicts have been formalised [6,7], but for fence insertion analysis, the symmetric *competing pairs* relation (cmp) [4], stemming from data race detection algorithms [24], typically suffices. We have a cmp b iff a and b access the same location and at least one of them is a write. A trace π is observably equivalent to an SC trace π' if we can obtain π' by commuting consecutive accesses in π that are not conflicting.

We recall the SC violation detection theory of Shasha and Snir [36], rephrased to be in line with recent work [4,6,7]. To detect non-SC behaviour, an *abstract event graph* (AEG) for a program can be constructed, in which the nodes are accesses and edges represent po and cmp. Shasha and Snir prove that cycles in the AEG with at least one cmp-edge and one po-edge represent all possibilities for non-SC executions if we run the program on an architecture without the guarantee that po is always respected (i.e., that has a weak memory model).

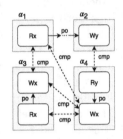

Fig. 3. Example cycles

Consider the cycle $\sigma_1 = \alpha_1 : \mathrm{R}x \xrightarrow{\mathsf{po}} \cdots \xrightarrow{\mathsf{po}}$ $\alpha_2 : \mathrm{W}y \xrightarrow{\mathsf{cmp}} \alpha_4 : \mathrm{R}y \xrightarrow{\mathsf{po}} \alpha_4 : \mathrm{W}x \xrightarrow{\mathsf{cmp}} \alpha_1 : \mathrm{R}x$ in Fig. 3, with $\alpha : a$ indicating access a of instruction α. The grey boxes indicate the atomic instructions, i.e., they define at. Given the direction of σ_1, the involved accesses would lead to non-SC behaviour if either the trace $\pi_1 = \alpha_4 : \mathrm{W}x \prec \alpha_1 :$ $\mathrm{R}x \prec \alpha_2 : \mathrm{W}y \prec \alpha_4 : \mathrm{R}y$ or the trace $\pi_2 = \alpha_2 : \mathrm{W}y \prec \alpha_4 : \mathrm{R}y \prec \alpha_4 : \mathrm{W}x \prec \alpha_1 :$ $\mathrm{R}x$ is executed, since they contradict the po-order between $\alpha_4 : \mathrm{R}y$ and $\alpha_4 :$ $\mathrm{W}x$, and between $\alpha_1 : \mathrm{R}x$ and $\alpha_2 : \mathrm{W}y$, respectively. That both traces are non-SC can be seen when trying to obtain an SC trace by commuting consecutive, non-conflicting accesses. For instance, in π_1, the accesses of α_4 would need to be commuted next to each other, but $\alpha_1 : \mathrm{R}x$ and $\alpha_2 : \mathrm{W}y$ prevent $\alpha_4 : \mathrm{W}x$ from moving to the right and $\alpha_4 : \mathrm{R}y$ from moving to the left, respectively, due to conflicts, unless we reorder $\alpha_1 : \mathrm{R}x$ and $\alpha_2 : \mathrm{W}y$, but then those instructions would be removed from each other and the trace would still not be SC. Traces π_1 and π_2 are not possible on architectures respecting po. However, as we discuss in Sect. 3, for some architectures, a compiler may ignore the po-order of some accesses, thereby breaking the cycle, and making non-SC traces possible. In [4,6,28], a po-path from access a to access b is called *unsafe* for an architecture if the latter's memory model allows b to be executed before a. The remedy to prevent non-SC behaviour is to *enforce* unsafe po-paths that are part of a cycle, by placing a delay, i.e., indicating that synchronisation is required, somewhere along the unsafe po-path.[2] The delays ensure the cycle remains.

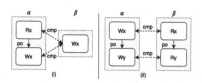

Fig. 4. Atomicity breaking examples

Shasha and Snir demonstrate that in the analysis, redundant work can be avoided by only considering cycles that are *simple* (they involve each vertex and edge at most once) and that have no chords. A chord is an edge between vertices in the cycle that are not each other's neighbour in the cycle. For instance, in Fig. 3, we also have cycles $\sigma_2 = \alpha_1 : Rx \xrightarrow{po} \cdots \xrightarrow{po} \alpha_2 : Wy \xrightarrow{cmp} \alpha_4 : Ry \xrightarrow{po} \alpha_4 : Wx \xrightarrow{cmp} \alpha_3 : Wx \xrightarrow{cmp} \alpha_1 : Rx$ and $\sigma_3 = \alpha_1 : Rx \xrightarrow{po} \cdots \xrightarrow{po} \alpha_2 : Wy \xrightarrow{cmp} \alpha_4 : Ry \xrightarrow{po} \alpha_4 : Wx \xrightarrow{cmp} \alpha_3 : Rx \xrightarrow{po} \alpha_3 : Wx \xrightarrow{cmp} \alpha_1 : Rx$, but both have the chord $\alpha_4 : Wx \xrightarrow{cmp} \alpha_1 : Rx$. The po-path $\alpha_3 : Rx \xrightarrow{po} \alpha_3 : Wx$ will be considered when the cycle $\sigma_4 = \alpha_4 : Wx \xrightarrow{cmp} \alpha_3 : Rx \xrightarrow{po} \alpha_3 : Wx \xrightarrow{cmp} \alpha_4 : Wx$ is analysed, hence analysis of σ_2 and σ_3 is redundant. We call a cycle *critical* if it is simple, has no chords, and contains at least one unsafe po-path.

Concerning atomicity, in Fig. 4, graph (i) represents the common situation of an instruction α reading and writing from/to the same location, for instance to increment a counter. A write to the same location can lead to an atomicity violation: If this write is performed between the read and write of the instruction, the effect of the former write will be lost. Shasha and Snir explain that for atomicity checking, it is even needed to go against the direction of po-edges inside instructions. By doing so, we get one cycle in graph (i), $\alpha : Rx \xrightarrow{cmp} \beta : Wx \xrightarrow{cmp} \alpha : Wx \xleftarrow{po} \alpha : Rx$, and two cycles in graph (ii), namely $\alpha : Wx \xrightarrow{cmp} \beta : Rx \xrightarrow{po} \beta : Ry \xrightarrow{cmp} \alpha : Wy \xleftarrow{po} \alpha : Wx$ and $\beta : Rx \xrightarrow{cmp} \alpha : Wx \xrightarrow{po} \alpha : Wy \xrightarrow{cmp} \beta : Ry \xleftarrow{po} \beta : Rx$. The cycles in graph (ii) represent the reading instruction retrieving an inconsistent state in which only one location has been updated. The remedy is to enforce po-edges against their direction, resulting in cyclic dependencies. These cannot be resolved in practice using fences, but require locks [36]. Recent work [1, 2, 4, 6–8, 14, 16, 19, 23, 25, 28, 29, 39] does not address this, allowing non-SC behaviour due to atomicity violations.

Next, we consider unsafety of po-paths w.r.t. a given weak memory model. The information is obtained from [4, 6, 7, 18]. The novelty is that we apply path rewriting.

---

[2] We use the term 'delay' here to refer to the *remedy* for non-SC behaviour [36], and not, as for instance later done in [4,6,7], to refer to the *problem*, i.e., the unsafe behaviour itself.

3   Guarantees of Weak Memory Models

Over the years, various weak memory multiprocessor architectures have been developed, for instance with x86 [33], SPARC [38], ARMv7 [7], ARMv8 [20] and POWER [22] processors. For each, suitable memory models have been derived, to reason about the access reorderings they may apply [3,6,18]. For the x86 and some SPARC processors, the TSO memory model is applicable, while other SPARC architectures support the PSO model. The POWER and ARMv7 processors can apply many types of reordering, requiring a very weak memory model.

To reason about the order of accesses, we use a relation $<$, which is initially equal to po^-, the transitive reduction of po, i.e., $a\,\mathsf{po}^-b$ cannot be decomposed into multiple po-connections between accesses from a to b. With $<$, we define *paths* of accesses $a < b < \ldots$. Paths should not be confused with traces: a trace is a concrete execution of accesses, while a path indicates the order in which accesses may be executed. For accesses a and b, we say that $a < b$ is *safe* for a memory model iff any trace executing a and b executes a before b. This is formally expressed as $a\,\mathsf{ppo}\,b$, with ppo a safe subrelation of po [4,6].

Table 1. Intra-thread safety guarantees under various memory models $(x \neq y)$

Case	Subtrace	SC	TSO	PSO	ARMv7
1	$W.xj < R.xk$	✓	✗	✗	✗
2	$W.xj < R.yk$	✓	✗	✗	✗
3	$R.xj < R.xk$	✓	✓	✓	✗
4	$R.xj < R.yk$	✓	✓	✓	✓ $\Longleftrightarrow$ R.yk addr R.xj
5	$W.xj < W.xk$	✓	✓	✓	✓
6	$W.xj < W.yk$	✓	✓	✗	✗
7	$R.xj < W.xk$	✓	✓	✓	✓ $\Longleftrightarrow$ W.xk addr R.xj ∨ W.xk dp R.xj
8	$R.xj < W.yk$	✓	✓	✓	✓ $\Longleftrightarrow$ W.yk addr R.xj ∨ W.yk dp R.xj

Table 1 gives an overview of the guarantees provided by the aforementioned memory models for accesses performed by the same thread.[3] Case 5 expresses that the order of two writes to the same location is guaranteed under all memory models. For cases 4, 7 and 8 of ARMv7/POWER, a reordering is allowed if the latter access is not dependent on the former. We define the following (intra-thread) dependency relations [6,7]:

1. The *address* relation addr relates address dependent accesses. We have $b\,\mathsf{addr}$ a iff a is a read access and is done to (possibly via local variables) compute an address for access b (for instance an address of an array element). For example, in order to access in an array v element v[i], first, the value of i must be retrieved.

---

[3] We ignore rdw and detour dependencies between threads under ARMv7/POWER [7], since those cannot be checked thread-locally. The penalty is that we under-approximate the guarantees of those memory models, but the effect seems marginal, as experimentally observed in [7].

2. The relation dp combines two dependency relations. We have b dp a iff either
   - b needs to write a value dependent on a (for example, to perform x = y, the value of y must be retrieved before assigning it to x), or
   - a is a read needed to evaluate a condition which must hold for the program branch containing b to be executed (for example, in if (x==0) {y = z}, the write to y and the read from z are both dp-dependent on the read from x).

Note that case 4 for ARMv7 requires only addr-dependency. A read access b may be performed even before a condition that guards b has been evaluated, unless b is address dependent on the read access(es) of the condition. For example, in if (x==0) {y=z}, the read access from z can be performed before the read from x. This is called *speculative execution*. Cases 7 and 8 for ARMv7 imply that speculative writing is never allowed, i.e., in the example, the writing to y cannot be done before the read from x.

Next, we define safety of po-*paths*, i.e., paths of accesses with $< = $ po$^-$, in terms of string rewriting. Table 1 can be used to define rewrite rules for TSO, PSO and ARMv7/POWER: if a model does not guarantee the order of accesses a and b (i.e., $a < b$), then the rewrite rule $(a < b) \Rightarrow (b < a)$ is applicable. We refer to the set of rewrite rules for a model as Σ, and say that a po-path is safe w.r.t. Σ iff it is safe under a model with rewrite rules Σ. The transitive closure of $<$ is $<^+$.

Definition 2 (po-path safety). *Given a* po-*path q between accesses a and b ($a <^+ b$ with $< = $ po$^-$), and a set of rewrite rules Σ, we say that q is safe w.r.t. Σ iff it cannot be rewritten, using the rewrite rules in Σ, to a path q' with $b <^+ a$.*

In other words, safety of a po-path between accesses a and b w.r.t. Σ can be determined by applying a path rewriting algorithm that tries to reorder a and b.

We already covered the case of two writes related via cmp. For accesses a and b with at most one being a write, if we have both a po b and a cmp b, then order guarantee of $a < b$ does not depend on cmp under any of the memory models. For instance, if a and b are not related via either addr or dp, a is a write and b is a read, then b can use the result of a before a is globally visible. Concerning cmp-related accesses of *different* threads, ARMv7/POWER has a property called *store atomicity relaxation* (ARMv8 [20,35] no longer allows this). Because of this, a cmp-edge in the AEG between a write a and a read b must be considered as unsafe in the direction from a to b [6]. To remedy this, a so-called *A-cumulative* fence must be placed along the po-path following the cmp-edge in the cycle [6]. The other memory models do not have this problem.

4   Deriving **po** and **cmp** via State Space Exploration

Given a formal parallel program specification M, containing a specification
of the individual threads, i.e., which
atomic instructions each thread performs
in which SC order, and the variables
(thread-local and program-global) each
instruction accesses, we can construct
its state space using an explicit-state
model checker. As mentioned in Sect. 2,
M can be expressed using a formal modelling language such as PROMELA [21] or
MCRL2 [15]. In the next example, we use
a state machine to specify a thread.

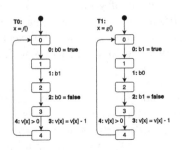

Fig. 5. State machines T0 and T1

Example 1. Figure 5 provides the specification of two threads T0 and T1, each
with a local variable **x**. The initial value of this variable is provided by function
f and g, respectively. We assume that f and g are too complex to derive by
means of static analysis whether or not they return the same value. From the
initial states of T0 and T1, i.e., 0, five steps can be repeatedly executed. First, T0
sets the global boolean variable **b0** to **true** (initially it has the value **false**), after
which it waits for global boolean variable **b1** to be **true** as well. Execution can
continue as soon as this is the case; before that, execution is blocked (this has
the same semantics as the condition statement in PROMELA [21], for instance).
Next, **b0** is set to **false** again, and the value of element **x** in the global integer
array **v** is decremented (all elements in **v** are initially set to some positive value).
Finally, if **v[x]** is still bigger than **0**, the process is repeated. Thread T1 works
similarly to T0, except that **b0** and **b1** are swapped. Note that the use of **b0** and
b1 effectively works as a synchronisation mechanism; for each thread, execution
can only proceed from state 1 to state 2 if the other thread has also proceeded
to state 1. It is not guaranteed that when this has happened, both threads will
proceed to state 2, as one thread may set one of the boolean variables back to
false before the other thread has moved to state 2. However, this issue is not
important for the example.

We define a state space as a tuple $\mathcal{G}_M = (\mathcal{S}, \mathcal{A}, \mathcal{T}, \hat{s})$, with $\hat{s}$ the initial state,
in which all thread specifications are in their initial state and all variables are
set to their initial value, $\mathcal{S}$ the set of states reachable from $\hat{s}$ ($\hat{s} \in \mathcal{S}$), $\mathcal{A}$ a set of
labels, and $\mathcal{T} : \mathcal{S} \times \mathcal{A} \times \mathcal{S}$ the transition relation. With $s \xrightarrow{a} s'$, we express that
from state s, a transition labelled a exists to a state s'. The set $out(s)$ is defined
as $out(s) = \{a \mid \exists s' \in \mathcal{S}.s \xrightarrow{a} s'\}$.[4]

---

[4] Note that we define state spaces by means of *Labelled Transition Systems*, in which
transitions are labelled with events. However, the technique we propose in this paper
can be adapted to Kripke structures, by encoding via state predicates the events that
are performed.

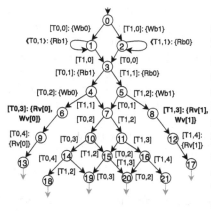

Fig. 6. A state space fragment

We construct the state space of a specification at the level of instructions, i.e., with each transition, exactly one instruction is associated. If M consists of n threads $t_1, \ldots, t_n$ in parallel composition, then every state s in $\mathcal{G}_M$ encodes, besides values for all variables in M, the local states $s_1, \ldots, s_n$ of the threads. For each enabled instruction α from s_i $(1 \leqslant i \leqslant n)$ that locally leads to state s'_i in t_i, there is a transition $s \xrightarrow{t_i, \alpha, [\alpha]} s'$, with s' being the state in which t_i is in s'_i, all other threads t_k $(k \neq i)$ are in s_k, and the variables have been updated as defined by α. Since we use $\mathcal{G}_M$ to analyse memory access behaviour, we need to know when read accesses are performed to evaluate a condition, also when it evaluates to **false**. For that reason, for each state s in $\mathcal{G}_M$ and each instruction α of t_i blocked in s, we have a self-loop $s \xrightarrow{t_i, \alpha, \langle\!\langle \alpha \rangle\!\rangle} s$.

Note that $\mathcal{G}_M$ allows us to precisely reason about accesses, even if pointers are used or dynamic accessing of array elements. For instance, in Fig. 5, the accessed location in $\mathbf{v[x]>0}$ is determined by the value of $\mathbf{x}$. Because, of this, $[\alpha]$ depends on the current state s. In the example, in any system state in which $\mathbf{T0}$ is in state 2 and $\mathbf{x}$ has the value $\mathbf{0}$, we have $[\mathbf{v[x]>0}] = \{\mathrm{Rv[0]}\}$. A model checker will make this explicit.

The state space will contain all possible interleavings of instructions in the specified order. All traces in $\mathcal{G}_M$ are therefore SC (Definition 1). Next, we wish to derive an AEG, as is done, for instance, in [4,11,12,26], but we derive it from the state space, as opposed to the specification (or the source code) of a program. Before we explain how to derive pr and cmp, consider the example state space fragment in Fig. 6, which is part of the state space of $\mathbf{T0}$ and $\mathbf{T1}$ (from Example 1) in parallel composition, when $f() = \mathbf{0}$ and $g() = \mathbf{1}$. The transition labels provide the sets of accesses, with instructions named by pairs 'thread, instruction identifier'. To make the figure more clear, only the sets of accesses are indicated, for instance [**T0**,0], and their definition is given only once, for instance $\{Wb0\}$ for [**T0**,0]. For this example, this suffices, as $\mathbf{x}$ is never updated, and hence there is no instruction α for which $[\alpha]$ changes over time. The two outgoing transitions from initial state 0 are associated with instruction $\mathbf{0}$ of **T0** and **T1**. If we traverse the transition for **T0**,0, we enter state 1. State 1 has a self-loop for $\langle\!\langle \mathbf{T0}, 1 \rangle\!\rangle$, representing the read access of $\mathbf{b1}$ to discover that $\mathbf{b1}$ evaluates to **false**. Beyond state 2, selfloops are not displayed, to simplify the figure.

For each thread t, instruction α of t and access $a \in [\alpha]$, we construct exactly one vertex $\langle t, \alpha, a \rangle$ in the AEG. The edges are derived from $\mathcal{G}_M$. As each access (of some instruction and thread) has one AEG vertex, the program order relation may appear cyclic if the thread specification contains cycles (as in Fig. 5).

We model this with a *program relation* pr. It offers the benefit of being able to represent infinite behaviour, as long as the number of instructions is finite. Unsafety of pr-paths is similar to unsafety of po-paths. To define pr, we first consider pairs of accesses from the same instruction α of thread t. We have to define how these are ordered. We want to be as non-restrictive as possible, so we restrict pr only by addr and dp (see Sect. 3): for every instruction α and accesses $a, b \in [\alpha]$, we have a pr b iff b addr a or b dp a, i.e., a only must precede b if b depends on a. In the AEG, if a pr b, we add a pr-edge from $\langle t, \alpha, a \rangle$ to $\langle t, \alpha, b \rangle$.

Next, using this definition of pr, we define $\bot(A)$, with $A \subseteq [\alpha]$ of an instruction α, as $\{a \in A \mid \neg \exists b \in A.b \text{ pr } a\}$, i.e., the accesses in A that are first in the pr-order. With $\top(A)$, we refer to the accesses last in the pr-order: $\top(A) = \{a \in A \mid \neg \exists b \in A.a \text{ pr } b\}$.

Finally, we extend pr by relating accesses from different instructions executed by the same thread. If we can establish that the execution of an instruction α enables the execution of at least some accesses of instruction β, then we pr-relate the accesses of α executed last with the accesses of β executed first. In the example of Fig. 6, since the execution of access $[T0, 0] = \{Wb0\}$ from state 0 leads to a state in which $\langle\!\langle T0, 1 \rangle\!\rangle$ is executable, i.e., Rb1, both accesses are performed by T0, and $\langle\!\langle T0, 1 \rangle\!\rangle$ was not enabled in state 0, the execution of $[T0, 0]$ enables $\langle\!\langle T0, 1 \rangle\!\rangle$. Since Wb0 $\in \top([T0, 0])$ and Rb1 $\in \bot(\langle\!\langle T0, 1 \rangle\!\rangle)$, we conclude that Wb0 pr Rb1 and $\langle T0, 0, Wb0 \rangle \xrightarrow{\text{pr}} \langle T0, 1, Rb1 \rangle$. Similarly, when traversing the transition for T0,1 from state 3, we can conclude $\langle T0, 1, Rb1 \rangle \xrightarrow{\text{pr}} \langle T0, 2, Wb0 \rangle$. In general, for any two instructions α, β of a thread t, we have:

$$\langle t, \alpha, a \rangle \xrightarrow{\text{pr}} \langle t, \beta, b \rangle \iff \exists s, s' \in \mathcal{S}.\exists A \in \{[\alpha], \langle\!\langle \alpha \rangle\!\rangle\}, B \in \{[\beta], \langle\!\langle \beta \rangle\!\rangle\}.s \xrightarrow{t, \alpha, A} s'$$
$$\wedge (t, \beta, B) \in out(s') \setminus out(s) \wedge a \in \top(A) \wedge b \in \bot(B)$$

Note that the pr relation is non-transitive, corresponding closely with po$^-$.

Next, we need to derive cmp. A straightforward way is to relate every pair of accesses (a, b) performed by different threads that access the same location, if at least one access is a write, and that is essentially the approach taken by static analysis techniques. With state space exploration, we can define cmp more precisely. Note that the above condition is the same as the one for data races, except that there is a data race only if accesses execute *at the same time*. In terms of traces, this means that it must be possible to execute b immediately after a, and vice versa, i.e., we can have both $a \prec b$ and $b \prec a$. We observe that for AEG construction, this aspect is also relevant. Consider the situation that accesses a, b *cannot* be executed at the same time, i.e., no traces are possible in which either $a \prec b$ or $b \prec a$. In that case, if there would be a cmp-edge between a and b, it might be possible to construct cycles in which $a \xrightarrow{\text{cmp}} b$ or $b \xrightarrow{\text{cmp}} a$ is an edge, but that would represent an execution in which a is directly followed by b or b followed by a, respectively (recall the example in Fig. 3 of Sect. 2), behaviour that is not possible.

The following theorem addresses how to determine, by analysing the state space, whether two accesses of different threads can directly follow each other in an SC trace.

Theorem 1. *Given a state space $\mathcal{G}_M = (\mathcal{S}, \mathcal{A}, \mathcal{T}, \hat{s})$, two accesses a, b and instructions α, β with $a \in [\alpha]$, $b \in [\beta]$, to be executed by threads t_1, t_2 of M, respectively ($t_1 \neq t_2$). There exists a trace π with $a \prec b$ or $b \prec a$ iff there exists a state $s \in \mathcal{S}$ with $(t_1, \alpha, A) \in out(s)$ and $(t_2, \beta, B) \in out(s)$, where $A \in \{[\alpha], \langle\!\langle\alpha\rangle\!\rangle\}$, $B \in \{[\beta], \langle\!\langle\beta\rangle\!\rangle\}$ and $a \in A$, $b \in B$.[5]*

It follows that cmp-edges can be added to the AEG by checking for each pair of outgoing transitions of every reachable state whether they are executed by different threads and have conflicting accesses. In Fig. 6, state 1 shows that $\langle\!\langle\mathsf{T0}, 1\rangle\!\rangle$ and $[\mathsf{T1}, \mathsf{0}]$ conflict. Therefore, we add $\langle\mathsf{T0}, 1, \mathsf{Rb1}\rangle \xrightarrow{\text{cmp}} \langle\mathsf{T1}, \mathsf{0}, \mathsf{Wb1}\rangle$ to the AEG. In contrast, state 15 demonstrates that $[\mathsf{T0}, 3] = \{\mathsf{Rv[0]}, \mathsf{Wv[0]}\}$ and $[\mathsf{T1}, 3] = \{\mathsf{Rv[1]}, \mathsf{Wv[1]}\}$ can happen simultaneously, but they have no conflicting accesses.

The above procedure works for SC, but not yet for weaker memory models. For instance, if we have three instructions α, β, γ, two threads t, t', and states $s_0, \ldots, s_3 \in \mathcal{S}$, with $s_0 \xrightarrow{t, \alpha, [\alpha]} s_1 \xrightarrow{t, \beta, [\beta]} s_2$, $s_0 \xrightarrow{t', \gamma, [\gamma]} s_3$ and $s_1 \xrightarrow{t', \gamma, \langle\!\langle\gamma\rangle\!\rangle} s_1$, then there is no SC trace in which for any accesses $b \in [\beta]$, $c \in [\gamma] \setminus \langle\!\langle\gamma\rangle\!\rangle$ we have either $b \prec c$ or $c \prec b$, but if b can be reordered before some accesses of α, b and accesses of γ may suddenly conflict.

To both detect all cmp-edges for weak memory models *and* identify which pr-paths are unsafe, we first repeatedly apply access reordering on all accesses in the program, as explained in Sect. 3, with $<$ intially set to pr, and keep track for each instruction α which accesses of other instructions can be reordered to be executed at the same time α is executed. This leads to a set of accesses $[\alpha]^+ \supseteq [\alpha]$. The procedure is continued until a fix-point has been reached, i.e., the $[\alpha]^+$ have been identified. While the reordering is performed, we construct a relation ppr with a ppr$^+$ b iff there exists no unsafe pr-path from a to b: if at any point we have $a < b$ and b cannot be reordered before a, we know that a ppr b. When a fix-point has been reached, we know there exists an unsafe pr-path from access a to access b if $\neg(a$ ppr$^+$ $b)$. The cmp-relation can be constructed by comparing the accesses in $[\alpha]^+$ and $[\beta]^+$ of each two instructions α, β that are associated with different threads and are related to transitions with a common source state.

Example 2. Consider again Example 1 with threads $\mathsf{T0}$, $\mathsf{T1}$. Figure 7 presents AEGs, for convenience at the instruction level, that can be constructed when using model checking (on the left) and when only using static analysis (on the right). For the moment, ignore the fences and the grey colouring. The vertices contain the instructions, solid edges represent pr-edges between accesses performed by those instructions, and dashed edges represent cmp-edges between some of those accesses. In the AEG on the left, the accesses to $\mathsf{v[0]}$ and $\mathsf{v[1]}$ have been distinguished, and it has been observed that $\mathsf{T0}$ and $\mathsf{T1}$ never conflict on accessing v. Hence, those accesses are not related by cmp. In the AEG on the right, the accesses to v of each thread have been symbolically represented by $\mathsf{v[x]}$, and it is concluded that conflicts can happen, hence the extra cmp-edges.

---

[5] A proof can be found at http://www.win.tue.nl/~awijs/seqcon-analyser.

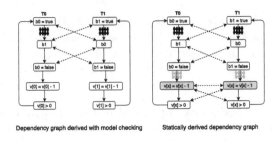

Fig. 7. AEGs (at instruction level) for T0 and T1 (Fig. 1), with $f()=0$, $g()=1$, obtained with (left) and without (right) model checking, including locks and fences for TSO.

5   Detecting and Ruling Out Non-SC Behaviour

Shasha and Snir provided a definition of critical cycle that allows efficient detection in an AEG [36]. We generalise this definition to use the non-transitive, cyclic pr, distinguish safe and unsafe pr-paths, and support unsafe cmp-edges.

Definition 3 (Critical cycle). *A cycle σ in a* pr $\cup$ cmp *AEG is critical iff*:

c1. *σ contains for each thread t at most one* pr-*path*;
c2. *σ contains at consecutive start and end points of* pr-*paths and/or* cmp-*edges up to three accesses to the same location*;
c3. *For at least one thread t, its* pr-*path in σ is unsafe, or there is an unsafe* cmp-*edge*;
c4. *At least two threads are involved in σ*;
c5. *For each* pr-*path $\alpha_0 : a_0 \xrightarrow{pr} \cdots \xrightarrow{pr} \alpha_n : a_n$ in σ, we have for all $0 \leqslant i < j \leqslant n$ that either $i = 0$ and $j = n$, or $\alpha_i : a_i \neq \alpha_j : a_j$.*

By c1, c3 and c4, a pr $\cup$ cmp cycle consists of at least one pr-path, connected at its start and end accesses via cmp-edges with at least one access of at least one other thread. Furthermore, for each pr-path, no proper subpath is a cycle (c5), but it may itself be a cycle. If some proper subpath is a cycle, it means that a shorter path can be constructed by removing that subpath. By c1, no chords exist in pr: if a thread t is involved in a cycle both with a pr-path $a \xrightarrow{pr} \cdots \xrightarrow{pr} b$ and a pr-path $c \xrightarrow{pr} \cdots \xrightarrow{pr} d$, then there are multiple chords, for instance $a \xrightarrow{pr} \cdots \xrightarrow{pr} d$. Finally, c2 ensures that no chords in cmp exist. If a location is involved more than three times in a cycle, such a chord must exist [36]. In Fig. 3, σ_2 and σ_3 violate c2, since x is involved four times, which points to the existence of the chord $\alpha_4 : Wx \xdashrightarrow{cmp} \alpha_1 : Rx$.

When no atomicity checking is performed, there is actually an additional condition, namely that the cycle involves at least two locations [4]. The weak memory models we consider ensure SC *per location*, i.e., cycles in which all accesses access the same location do not represent non-SC behaviour. However, for atomicity checking, such cycles cannot be ignored, as explained in Sect. 2 (see Fig. 4).

Theorem 2. *A trace π of a program specification M is non-SC iff it traverses a* pr $\cup$ cmp *path through the AEG of M that contains a critical cycle.*[6]

Note that enforcing an unsafe pr-path p' results in enforcing any unsafe pr-path p containing p'. Any cycle σ satisfying c1 to c4 of Definition 3 contains a cycle σ' satisfying c1 to c5. If p is part of σ and p' is part of σ', then p is enforced due to p' being enforced. Therefore, it suffices to enforce unsafe pr-paths in critical cycles as defined by Definition 3.

For the detection of critical cycles, algorithms for finding elementary circuits can be used. We use Tarjan's algorithm [40], extended to detect cycles meeting c1-c5 of Definition 3. To support atomicity checking, all that is needed is to allow cycle detection to move against the pr-order between at-related accesses, as is explained in Sect. 2 and [36]. The ppr-relation allows us to identify the existence of unsafe pr-paths in constant time.

With each instruction in the program, we associate a counter. Each time a critical cycle is detected, we record the involved unsafe pr-paths and cmp-edges as sequences of the involved instructions, and increment their counters. If we do atomicity checking, we furthermore mark an instruction for locking if its execution in the unsafe path violates pr. Once all cycles have been detected, the sequences of instructions that include an instruction marked for locking are removed, since a lock will make an unsafe path safe. The counters of all involved instructions are decremented each time a sequence is removed. For the remaining sequences, we sort the instructions by the counter values, select the instruction α with the highest value, and place a delay after $\perp([\alpha])$, to ensure that any path involved α is enforced. We remove each sequence involving α, decrement the counters of the other instructions, and repeat until all counters have the value 0.

Although the constructed AEGs are more precise than statically derived ones, we do not claim that our fencing procedure is optimal. In fact, experiments demonstrate that it is not (see Sect. 6). Future work involves optimising this procedure as far as possible.

Example 3. Consider the fences and the grey colouring in Fig. 7, which result from analysing the system under TSO. In both AEGs, the critical cycle $\sigma_1 =$ T0 : Wb0 $\xrightarrow{\text{pr}}$ T0 : Rb1 $\xrightarrow{\text{cmp}}$ T1 : Wb1 $\xrightarrow{\text{pr}}$ T1 : Rb0 $\xrightarrow{\text{cmp}}$ T0 : Wb0 requires that the two black fences are placed. On the right, additional critical cycles are detected, due to the inaccuracy of the AEG. The grey nodes represent the instructions for which it is detected that locks are needed, when atomicity checking is performed. In other words, v[x]=v[x]-1 can only be executed if a lock on v[x] has been acquired. The involved cycles are actually not directly visible, due to the AEG being given at the instruction level, but the two instructions v[x]=v[x]-1 conflict with each other, forming two cycles $\sigma_2 =$ T0 : Wv[x] $\xleftarrow{\text{pr}}$ T0 : Rv[x] $\xrightarrow{\text{cmp}}$ T1 : Wv[x] $\xrightarrow{\text{cmp}}$ T0 : Wv[x] and $\sigma_3 =$ T1 : Wv[x] $\xleftarrow{\text{pr}}$ T1 : Rv[x] $\xrightarrow{\text{cmp}}$ T0 : Wv[x] $\xrightarrow{\text{cmp}}$ T1 : Wv[x], both going against the pr-direction. As locks strictly provide more guarantees than fences [5], placing

---

[6] A proof sketch can be found at http://www.win.tue.nl/~awijs/seqcon-analyser.

locks means that no more unresolved violations exist. Alternatively, if no atomicity checking is performed, the cycles $\sigma_4 = \texttt{T0 : Wb0} \xrightarrow{\text{pr}} \texttt{T0 : Rv[x]} \xrightarrow{\text{cmp}} \texttt{T1 :}$ $\texttt{Wv[x]} \xrightarrow{\text{pr}} \cdots \xrightarrow{\text{pr}} \texttt{T1 : Rb0} \xrightarrow{\text{cmp}} \texttt{T0 : Wb0}$ and $\sigma_5 = \texttt{T1 : Wb1} \xrightarrow{\text{pr}} \texttt{T1 :}$ $\texttt{Rv[x]} \xrightarrow{\text{cmp}} \texttt{T0 : Wv[x]} \xrightarrow{\text{pr}} \cdots \xrightarrow{\text{pr}} \texttt{T0 : Rb1} \xrightarrow{\text{cmp}} \texttt{T1 : Wb1}$ require that the grey fences are placed. If the instructions $\texttt{v[x]=v[x]-1}$ are locked, this is not required, as $\texttt{Wb0}$ in [b0=false] and $\texttt{Wb1}$ in [b1=false] are separated from the $\texttt{Rv[x]}$'s by those locks.

6   Experimental Results

We have implemented our technique using the MCRL2 toolset [15] for state space exploration. State machine models are first translated to MCRL2 specifications, from which a state space can be generated and written to disk. In addition, we have developed a new tool SEQCON-ANALYSER in C++, that reads the state space, constructs an AEG, and suggests where to place fences and locks, based on critical cycle detection.

We conducted experiments to compare SEQCON-ANALYSER with existing fence insertion tools, and to analyse their scalability. We decided to compare SEQCON-ANALYSER with the static analysis tool MUSKETEER [4] and the model checking tool REMMEX [29]. These tools offer a good representation of the current state-of-the-art in static-analysis- and model checking-based approaches to automatic fence insertion, respectively. For instance, in [4], MUSKETEER clearly outperforms the static analysis tools DFENCE [30], MEMORAX [1], OFFENCE [6], TRENCHER [14] and PENSIEVE [39], using several instances of four of the models, Dekker, Peterson, Lamport, and Szymanski, that we also used in our experiments. Hence, we have not involved the other static analysis tools in our experiments.

Besides the four models already mentioned, we selected six additional models from the BEEM benchmark set [34], Anderson, Bakery, Elevator2, Leader_filters, Mcs, and Msmie, and manually translated several instances of each of those models, written in the DVE language [10], to suitable input for SEQCON-ANALYSER, MUSKETEER and REMMEX.[7]

Table 2 presents the experimental results, comparing our technique without atomicity checking (S–A) with MUSKETEER (M) and REMMEX (R), tools that do not support atomicity checking. In addition, we report the results obtained when performing atomicity checking with our tool (S+A). We report the number of delay insertions under TSO, PSO and ARMv7 whenever possible (REMMEX does not support ARMv7) in the form ('number of locks' / 'number of non-cumulative fences' / 'number of A-cumulative fences'). We acknowledge that ARMv8 is more recent, but the weaker ARMv7 is very suitable to demonstrate the efficiency of our technique when applied on very weak memory models.

We conducted our experiments on the DAS-5 cluster [9]. Each node runs CENTOS 7.4, and has a 2.4 GHz Intel Haswell E5-2630-v3 CPU and 64 GB of memory. In the table, we list for each model the number of threads ($|\mathbb{T}|$), the

---

[7] See http://www.win.tue.nl/~awijs/seqcon-analyser for the models and our tool.

Table 2. Scalability results for (M)USKETEER, (R)EMMEX, and SEQCON-ANALYSER without (s−A) and with (s+A) atomicity checking. Runtimes in seconds, averages of ten executions. o.o.m.: out of memory (> 64 GB), o.o.t.: out of time (> 20 h.), *: executed with option −no-loop-duplication, -: no result possible due to lack of suitable error states.

case	|T|	|I|	|L|	state space gen. #states	time	TSO M	TSO R	TSO s−A	TSO s+A	PSO M	PSO R	PSO s−A	PSO s+A	ARMv7 M	ARMv7 s−A	ARMv7 s+A
Anderson.1	2	12	3	350,119	41.89	0.03 (/6)*	o.o.m.	0.04 (/4)	0.05 (4/2/)	0.04 (/6)*	o.o.m.	0.05 (/4)	0.05 (/4)	0.06 (/2/6)*	0.07 (/7)	0.07 (4/5)
Anderson.4	4	24	5	9,956	2.56	o.o.m.	o.o.m.	17.23 (/8)	17.36 (8/4/)	o.o.m.	o.o.m.	39.61 (/12)	40.07 (8/8/)	o.o.m.	54.68 (/12)	55.68 (8/8)
Anderson.6	6	36	7	2,633,730	1,086.73	o.o.m.	o.o.m.	855.68 (/12)	855.54 (12//)	o.o.m.	o.o.m.	1,936.00 (/12)	1,910.83 (12//)	o.o.m.	4,337.74 (/18)	4,358.88 (12/0/12)
Anderson.8	7	42	8	50,799,077	25,322.92	o.o.m.	o.o.m.	4,425.45 (/14)	4,340.08 (14//)	o.o.m.	o.o.m.	9,524.06 (/14)	9,625.17 (14/7/)	o.o.m.	24,017.29 (/21)	23,694.51 (14/14)
Bakery.1	2	18	4	1,622	0.45	0.17 (/10)	o.o.m.	0.07 (/4)	0.07 (2/1/)	0.23 (/12)	o.o.m.	0.12 (/5)	0.09 (2/3/)	0.34 (/29)	0.32 (/12)	0.32 (2/10)
Bakery.3	3	27	6	41,185	14.52	o.o.m.	o.o.m.	1.21 (/5)	1.37 (/5)	o.o.m.	o.o.m.	1.55 (/7)	1.55 (3/4/)	3.98 (/18)	3.98 (/12)	4.01 (3/15)
Bakery.5	4	36	8	9,604,719	3,933.80	o.o.m.	o.o.m.	10.65 (/7)	10.67 (/7)	o.o.m.	o.o.m.	12.66 (/9)	12.70 (4/9/)	o.o.m.	386.54 (/72)	391.62 (4/0/20)
Dekker.1	2	16	3	20	0.02	0.01 (/4)	1.20 (/2)	0.01 (/2)	0.04 (/2)	0.01 (8/)	0.77 (/2)	0.02 (/3)	0.02 (/3)	0.02 (/8/8)	0.02 (/3/2)	0.02 (3/2)
Dekker.2	3	24	4	62	0.03	0.04 (/6)	o.o.m.	0.04 (/3)	0.04 (/3)	0.20 (/12)	o.o.m.	0.22 (/7)	0.22 (/7)	0.64 (/11/10)	0.32 (/57)	0.28 (/57)
Dekker.3	4	32	5	212	0.06	2.55 (/8)	o.o.m.	0.23 (/4)	0.23 (/4)	9.94 (/16)	o.o.m.	1.56 (/11)	1.52 (/11)	59.26 (18/13)	2.44 (/79)	2.46 (/79)
Dekker.5	6	48	7	3,104	0.83	0.04 (/11)	o.o.m.	2.62 (/6)	2.62 (/6)	0.07 (/24)	o.o.m.	31.81 (/17)	31.79 (/17)	0.08 (24/46)	54.57 (11/13)	54.59 (11/13)
Elevator2.1	3	13	7	1,664	0.38	0.59 (/3)	-	0.04 (/4)	0.03 (/)	0.62 (/3)	-	0.06 (/2)	0.06 (5/1/)	0.81 (/8/5)	0.17 (/6)	0.18 (6/4)
Elevator2.2	3	26	13	174,080	38.85	o.o.m.	-	0.15 (/)	0.17 (/)	0.01 (/13)	-	3.35 (/14)	3.58 (21/2/)	o.o.m.	6.81 (/214)	7.11 (21/5)
Elevator2.3	3	22	16	7,561,216	2,369.50	o.o.m.	1.92 (/4)	0.24 (/)	0.27 (/)	0.01 (/13)	4.68 (/4)	0.56 (/2)	0.61 (14/1/)	o.o.m.	4.31 (/6)	4.53 (15/4)
Lamport.1	2	22	4	106	0.04	0.03 (/4)	o.o.m.	0.01 (/2)	0.02 (/2)	0.01 (/9)	o.o.m.	0.06 (/4)	0.06 (/4)	0.01 (/6/7)	0.08 (/6)	0.10 (/6)
Lamport.2	3	33	5	1,283	0.24	0.01 (/6)	o.o.m.	0.23 (/6)	0.18 (/6)	0.01 (/13)	o.o.m.	0.80 (/6)	0.80 (/6)	0.01 (/11/11)	1.08 (/9)	1.08 (/9)
Lamport.3	4	44	6	12,924	2.57	0.01 (/8)	o.o.m.	1.11 (/4)	1.11 (/4)	0.02 (/17)	o.o.m.	5.64 (/8)	5.51 (/8)	0.02 (/16/15)	8.00 (/12)	8.05 (/12)
Lamport.5	6	66	8	6,352,764	260.78	0.15 (/12)	o.o.m.	12.20 (/6)	12.48 (/6)	0.92 (/25)	o.o.m.	64.57 (/12)	64.61 (/12)	1.30 (23/28)	144.84 (/18)	147.70 (1/23)
Leader_filters.2	3	27	15	432	0.09	5.89 (/3)	o.o.m.	0.07 (/3)	0.07 (/3)	8.26 (/3)	o.o.m.	0.10 (/6)	0.10 (/6)	10.11 (/16)	0.12 (/6)	0.11 (/6)
Leader_filters.4	4	40	15	7,289	1.19	o.o.m.	o.o.m.	0.88 (/4)	0.88 (/4)	o.o.m.	o.o.m.	1.03 (/4)	1.03 (/4)	o.o.m.	1.41 (/12)	1.43 (/12)
Leader_filters.5	5	50	18	64,646	11.00	o.o.m.	o.o.m.	3.70 (/10)	3.70 (/10)	o.o.m.	o.o.m.	4.29 (/10)	4.30 (/10)	o.o.m.	5.88 (/15)	5.90 (/15)
Leader_filters.7	6	60	18	3,383,790	111.07	o.o.m.	o.o.m.	11.49 (/6)	11.94 (/6)	o.o.m.	o.o.m.	13.17 (/6)	13.15 (/6)	o.o.m.	23.31 (/18)	23.28 (/18)
Mcs.1	3	33	7	767	0.20	o.o.m.	o.o.m.	3.27 (/3)	3.26 (/6)	o.o.m.	o.o.m.	21.28 (/17)	21.49 (12/6/)	o.o.m.	30.03 (/20)	30.74 (12/19)
Mcs.3	4	44	9	11,599	2.84	o.o.m.	o.o.m.	19.14 (/7)	19.73 (9/3/)	o.o.m.	o.o.m.	78.54 (/19)	78.84 (13/8/)	o.o.m.	117.30 (/28)	118.71 (13/16)
Mcs.5	5	55	11	236,227	71.19	o.o.m.	o.o.m.	108.22 (/8)	110.34 (11/4/)	o.o.m.	o.o.m.	649.97 (/25)	697.02 (17/13/)	o.o.m.	1,076.28 (/39)	1,090.33 (17/27)
Msmie.1	5	79	6	2,334	1.18	o.o.m.	o.o.m.	49.74 (/7)	54.19 (8/3/)	o.o.m.	o.o.m.	4,559.18 (/27)	4,911.42 (38/5/)	o.o.m.	7,180.24 (/61)	7,518.20 (38/23)
Msmie.2	13	168	5	10,558	8.93	o.o.m.	o.o.m.	2,318.31 (/7)	2,568.96 (19/16/)	o.o.m.	o.o.m.	o.o.t.	o.o.t.	o.o.m.	o.o.t.	o.o.t.
Peterson.1	2	8	3	14	0.02	0.01 (/3)	0.81 (/2)	0.02 (/2)	0.02 (/2)	0.01 (/6)	1.07 (/4)	0.03 (/2)	0.03 (/2)	0.01 (/5)	0.04 (/2)	0.04 (/2)
Peterson.2	3	12	4	62	0.02	0.01 (/6)	10.50 (/3)	0.03 (/3)	0.02 (/3)	0.01 (/12)	68.12 (/6)	0.03 (/4)	0.03 (/4)	0.01 (/10)	0.04 (/3)	0.04 (/3)
Peterson.3	4	16	5	1,264	0.06	0.01 (/13)	3,754.04 (/4)	0.15 (/4)	0.13 (/4)	0.08 (/20)	o.o.m.	0.17 (/4)	0.17 (/4)	0.05 (/18)	0.21 (/4)	0.17 (/4)
Peterson.5	6	24	7	6,232	1.19	0.34 (/27)	o.o.m.	1.56 (/6)	1.56 (/6)	11.53 (/42)	o.o.m.	1.87 (/6)	1.86 (/6)	8.18 (/34)	2.67 (/6)	2.68 (/6)
Szymanski.1	2	20	2	52	0.02	0.01 (/2)	2.33 (/2)	0.03 (/2)	0.03 (/2)	0.01 (/9)	o.o.m.	0.44 (/4)	0.44 (/4)	0.02 (/2)	0.80 (/28)	0.80 (2/8)
Szymanski.2	3	30	3	354	0.10	0.01 (/3)	o.o.m.	4.02 (/9)	3.87 (/9)	0.03 (/13)	o.o.m.	5.56 (9/)	5.56 (9/)	10.17 (/3/14)	10.27 (/3/14)	10.27 (3/14)
Szymanski.3	4	40	4	2,376	0.77	0.15 (/4)	o.o.m.	74.71 (/6)	74.41 (/6)	1.24 (/17)	o.o.m.	104.82 (/6)	104.88 (/6)	9.70 (/14/5)	186.79 (/23)	189.70 (/23)
Szymanski.5	6	60	6	49,328	21.11	663.51 (/19)	o.o.m.	1,070.38 (/13)	1,072.20 (/)	o.o.m.	o.o.m.	1,373.15 (13/)	1,377.78 (13/)	o.o.m.	2,723.08 (/29)	2,730.82 (1/29)

error states.

number of instructions ($|I|$), and the number of memory locations ($|\mathbb{L}|$). For state space generation, we used version 201908.0 of the MCRL2 toolset, and report the number of states and the runtime. For our technique, on the one hand, the runtime of state space generation should be added to the runtime needed for critical cycle detection to obtain the overall time, but on the other hand, state space generation is only needed once per case, to perform cycle detection for all memory models, with and without atomicity checking. For the cycle detection phase, we have excluded the time needed to read the state space, as it obfuscates the time for the actual computation. In the future, we plan to avoid storing and reading state spaces entirely. Translating a state machine model to MCRL2 can be done instantly.

In Table 2, the best results in each category, in terms of number of fences, and runtime in case of a tie, are written in bold. It should be mentioned that for the Anderson instances, MUSKETEER had to be run with the –no-loop-duplication option enabled, as the standard option reported (erroneously) that no fences were required.

Even though the models are relatively small, the positive effect of state space exploration is apparent. Constructing the state space helps to keep the AEG smaller, and hence to reduce the number of critical cycles. State spaces grow exponentially, but so does the number of critical cycles in the AEG. Frequently, state space exploration plus critical cycle detection with SEQCON-ANALYSER has an overall runtime that is not drastically worse than MUSKETEER, and in case of Dekker.3, the combined time is even shorter. It is important to note here that various techniques exist to speed up state space exploration considerably (for instance, by using symbolic [13,17] or GPU exploration [42,43]), whereas much fewer techniques exist to speed up the enumeration of elementary circuits in a graph. In other words, it is in practice beneficial to involve state space exploration, as the techniques above can be applied to further reduce the runtime.

The performance of REMMEX is as expected; since it has to explore all behaviour, SC and non-SC, it quickly runs out of memory. For the Elevator2 cases, no results could be obtained. REMMEX needs to be given an error state representing a violation of a safety property, after which it checks for the reachability of that state under the given memory model. However, for those cases, no suitable safety properties could be identified. With MUSKETEER, we also experienced out-of-memory frequently, which was not expected. The tool first constructs the entire set of critical cycles before deriving fences. This is not strictly needed, as alternatively, the output of Tarjan's algorithm [40], used by MUSKETEER, could be directly processed to store where fences are needed. If the implementation of MUSKETEER would be changed in this regard, the runtimes for the 'o.o.m.' cases of MUSKETEER would still be much higher than those of SEQCON-ANALYSER, as it always took several hours to fill the memory, and the number of fences would often be higher.

Finally, regarding the number of locks and fences, SEQCON-ANALYSER does not always identify the smallest number of fences, even though it works with AEGs that are in general more precise than those of MUSKETEER. This is due to the sub-optimal placement of fences to resolve all detected non-SC issues. In future work, we will continue on improving this aspect. The optimisation problem of resolving all non-SC behaviour with fences also frequently results in each tool suggesting different fence locations. For instance, the four fences suggested by SEQCON-ANALYSER for Anderson.1 are not suggested by MUSKETEER. Furthermore, it is interesting to note that in multiple cases, the number of locks is influenced by the memory model. Unfortunately, MUSKETEER does not support atomicity checking, so we cannot directly assess this, but with a pure static analysis technique, this effect would not be observed; if each pair of conflicting accesses is related by cmp, then for each memory model, the same atomicity issues would be detected.

7   Conclusions

We have proposed a technique for automatic delay insertion, combining state space generation and static analysis. It has the precision of model checking-based techniques, yet better scalability, and frequently even outperforms MUSKETEER, a state-of-the-art static analysis technique. Furthermore, it supports atomicity checking. We addressed TSO, PSO, and ARMv7, but an arbitrary set of intra-thread order guarantees can be specified. These may depend on relations such as addr and dp, but also on others. In the future, it will be interesting to support the CAT language [7], to make SEQCON-ANALYSER more configurable in this respect. Furthermore, we will investigate to what extent delay suggestions can be updated when a model is transformed, along the lines of [41].

References

1. Abdulla, P.A., Atig, M.F., Chen, Y.-F., Leonardsson, C., Rezine, A.: MEMORAX, a precise and sound tool for automatic fence insertion under TSO. In: Piterman, N., Smolka, S.A. (eds.) TACAS 2013. LNCS, vol. 7795, pp. 530–536. Springer, Heidelberg (2013). https://doi.org/10.1007/978-3-642-36742-7_37
2. Abdulla, P.A., Atig, M.F., Ngo, T.-P.: The best of both worlds: trading efficiency and optimality in fence insertion for TSO. In: Vitek, J. (ed.) ESOP 2015. LNCS, vol. 9032, pp. 308–332. Springer, Heidelberg (2015). https://doi.org/10.1007/978-3-662-46669-8_13
3. Adve, S., Gharachorloo, K.: Shared memory consistency models: a tutorial. Computer 29(12), 66–76 (1996)
4. Alglave, J., Kroening, D., Nimal, V., Poetzl, D.: Don't sit on the fence: a static analysis approach to automatic fence insertion. ACM Trans. Program. Lang. Syst. 39(2), 6 (2017)
5. Alglave, J., Maranget, L.: Stability in weak memory models. In: Gopalakrishnan, G., Qadeer, S. (eds.) CAV 2011. LNCS, vol. 6806, pp. 50–66. Springer, Heidelberg (2011). https://doi.org/10.1007/978-3-642-22110-1_6
6. Alglave, J., Maranget, L., Sarkar, S., Sewell, P.: Fences in weak memory models. In: Touili, T., Cook, B., Jackson, P. (eds.) CAV 2010. LNCS, vol. 6174, pp. 258–272. Springer, Heidelberg (2010). https://doi.org/10.1007/978-3-642-14295-6_25

7. Alglave, J., Maranget, L., Tautschnig, M.: Herding cats: modelling, simulation, testing, and data mining for weak memory. ACM Trans. Program. Lang. Syst. **36**(2), 7:1–7:74 (2014)

8. Atig, M.F., Bouajjani, A., Parlato, G.: Getting rid of store-buffers in TSO analysis. In: Gopalakrishnan, G., Qadeer, S. (eds.) CAV 2011. LNCS, vol. 6806, pp. 99–115. Springer, Heidelberg (2011). https://doi.org/10.1007/978-3-642-22110-1_9

9. Bal, H., et al.: A medium-scale distributed system for computer science research: infrastructure for the long term. IEEE Comput. **49**(5), 54–63 (2016)

10. Barnat, J., et al.: DiVinE 3.0 – an explicit-state model checker for multithreaded C & C++ programs. In: Sharygina, N., Veith, H. (eds.) CAV 2013. LNCS, vol. 8044, pp. 863–868. Springer, Heidelberg (2013). https://doi.org/10.1007/978-3-642-39799-8_60

11. Batty, M., Donaldson, A., Wickerson, J.: Overhauling SC atomics in C11 and OpenCL. In: POPL, pp. 634–648. ACM (2016)

12. Bender, J., Palsberg, J.: A formalization of Java's concurrent access modes. In: OOPSLA, pp. 142:1–142:28. ACM (2019)

13. Biere, A., Kröning, D.: SAT-based model checking. Handbook of Model Checking, pp. 277–303. Springer, Cham (2018). https://doi.org/10.1007/978-3-319-10575-8_10

14. Bouajjani, A., Derevenetc, E., Meyer, R.: Checking and enforcing robustness against TSO. In: Felleisen, M., Gardner, P. (eds.) ESOP 2013. LNCS, vol. 7792, pp. 533–553. Springer, Heidelberg (2013). https://doi.org/10.1007/978-3-642-37036-6_29

15. Bunte, O., et al.: The mCRL2 toolset for analysing concurrent systems. In: Vojnar, T., Zhang, L. (eds.) TACAS 2019. LNCS, vol. 11428, pp. 21–39. Springer, Cham (2019). https://doi.org/10.1007/978-3-030-17465-1_2

16. Burckhardt, S., Musuvathi, M.: Effective program verification for relaxed memory models. In: Gupta, A., Malik, S. (eds.) CAV 2008. LNCS, vol. 5123, pp. 107–120. Springer, Heidelberg (2008). https://doi.org/10.1007/978-3-540-70545-1_12

17. Chaki, S., Gurfinkel, A.: BDD-based symbolic model checking. Handbook of Model Checking, pp. 219–245. Springer, Cham (2018). https://doi.org/10.1007/978-3-319-10575-8_8

18. Colvin, R.J., Smith, G.: A wide-spectrum language for verification of programs on weak memory models. In: Havelund, K., Peleska, J., Roscoe, B., de Vink, E. (eds.) FM 2018. LNCS, vol. 10951, pp. 240–257. Springer, Cham (2018). https://doi.org/10.1007/978-3-319-95582-7_14

19. Fang, X., Lee, J., Midkiff, S.: Automatic fence insertion for shared memory multiprocessing. In: ICS, pp. 285–294. ACM Press (2003)

20. Flur, S., et al.: Modelling the ARMv8 architecture, operationally: concurrency and ISA. In: POPL, pp. 608–621. ACM (2016)

21. Holzmann, G.: The SPIN Model Checker: Primer and Reference Manual. Addison-Wesley Professional, Boston (2003)

22. IBM: Power ISA Version 2.06 Revision B (2010)

23. Jonsson, B.: State-space exploration for concurrent algorithms under weak memory orderings. ACM SIGARCH Comput. Archit. News **36**, 65–71 (2009)

24. Kahlon, V., Sinha, N., Kruus, E., Zhang, Y.: Static data race detection for concurrent programs with asynchronous calls. In: FSE, pp. 13–22. ACM (2009)

25. Kuperstein, M., Vechev, M., Yahav, E.: Partial-coherence abstractions for relaxed memory models. In: PLDI, pp. 187–198. ACM Press (2011)

26. Lahav, O., Vafeiadis, V., Kang, J., Hur, C.K., Dreyer, D.: Repairing sequential consistency in C/C++11. In: PLDI, pp. 618–632. ACM (2017)

27. Lamport, L.: How to make a multiprocessor computer that correctly executes multiprocess programs. IEEE Trans. Comput. **28**(9), 690–691 (1979)

28. Lee, J., Padua, D.: Hiding relaxed memory consistency with a compiler. IEEE Trans. Comput. **50**, 824–833 (2001)

29. Linden, A., Wolper, P.: A verification-based approach to memory fence insertion in PSO memory systems. In: Piterman, N., Smolka, S.A. (eds.) TACAS 2013. LNCS, vol. 7795, pp. 339–353. Springer, Heidelberg (2013). https://doi.org/10.1007/978-3-642-36742-7_24

30. Liu, F., Nedev, N., Prisadnikov, N., Vechev, M., Yahav, E.: Dynamic synthesis for relaxed memory models. In: PLDI, pp. 429–440. ACM (2012)

31. Lu, S., Park, S., Seo, E., Zhou, Y.: Learning from mistakes: a comprehensive study on real world concurrency bug characteristics. In: ASPLOS, pp. 329–339. ACM Press (2008)

32. Neele, T., Willemse, T.A.C., Groote, J.F.: Solving parameterised boolean equation systems with infinite data through quotienting. In: Bae, K., Ölveczky, P.C. (eds.) FACS 2018. LNCS, vol. 11222, pp. 216–236. Springer, Cham (2018). https://doi.org/10.1007/978-3-030-02146-7_11

33. Owens, S., Sarkar, S., Sewell, P.: A better x86 memory model: x86-TSO. In: Berghofer, S., Nipkow, T., Urban, C., Wenzel, M. (eds.) TPHOLs 2009. LNCS, vol. 5674, pp. 391–407. Springer, Heidelberg (2009). https://doi.org/10.1007/978-3-642-03359-9_27

34. Pelánek, R.: BEEM: benchmarks for explicit model checkers. In: Bošnački, D., Edelkamp, S. (eds.) SPIN 2007. LNCS, vol. 4595, pp. 263–267. Springer, Heidelberg (2007). https://doi.org/10.1007/978-3-540-73370-6_17

35. Pulte, C., Flur, S., Deacon, W., French, J., Sarkar, S., Sewell, P.: Simplifying ARM concurrency: multicopy-atomic axiomatic and operational models for ARMv8. In: POPL, pp. 19:1–19:29. ACM (2018)

36. Shasha, D., Snir, M.: Efficient and correct execution of parallel programs that share memory. ACM Trans. Prog. Lang. Syst. **10**(2), 282–312 (1988)

37. Shavit, N., Touitou, D.: Software transactional memory. Distrib. Comput. **10**(2), 99–116 (1997). https://doi.org/10.1007/s004460050028

38. SPARC International Inc: The SPARC architecture manual (version 9) (1994)

39. Sura, Z., Fang, X., Wong, C.L., Midkiff, S., Lee, J., Padua, D.: Compiler techniques for high performance sequentially consistent Java programs. In: PPOPP, pp. 2–13. ACM Press (2005)

40. Tarjan, R.: Enumeration of the elementary circuits of a directed graph. SIAM J. Comput. **2**(3), 211–216 (1973)

41. Wijs, A., Engelen, L.: REFINER: towards formal verification of model transformations. In: Badger, J.M., Rozier, K.Y. (eds.) NFM 2014. LNCS, vol. 8430, pp. 258–263. Springer, Cham (2014). https://doi.org/10.1007/978-3-319-06200-6_21

42. Wijs, A., Bošnački, D.: GPUexplore: many-core on-the-fly state space exploration using GPUs. In: Ábrahám, E., Havelund, K. (eds.) TACAS 2014. LNCS, vol. 8413, pp. 233–247. Springer, Heidelberg (2014). https://doi.org/10.1007/978-3-642-54862-8_16

43. Wijs, A., Neele, T., Bošnački, D.: GPUexplore 2.0: unleashing GPU explicit-state model checking. In: Fitzgerald, J., Heitmeyer, C., Gnesi, S., Philippou, A. (eds.) FM 2016. LNCS, vol. 9995, pp. 694–701. Springer, Cham (2016). https://doi.org/10.1007/978-3-319-48989-6_42

Tight Error Analysis in Fixed-Point Arithmetic

Stella Simić[1]([✉])[iD], Alberto Bemporad[1][iD], Omar Inverso[2][iD],
and Mirco Tribastone[1][iD]

[1] IMT School for Advanced Studies, Lucca, Italy
stella.simic@imtlucca.it
[2] Gran Sasso Science Institute, L'Aquila, Italy

Abstract. We consider the problem of estimating the numerical accuracy of programs with operations in fixed-point arithmetic and variables of arbitrary, mixed precision and possibly non-deterministic value. By applying a set of parameterised rewrite rules, we transform the relevant fragments of the program under consideration into sequences of operations in integer arithmetic over vectors of bits, thereby reducing the problem as to whether the error enclosures in the initial program can ever exceed a given order of magnitude to simple reachability queries on the transformed program. We present a preliminary experimental evaluation of our technique on a particularly complex industrial case study.

Keywords: Fixed-point arithmetic · Static analysis · Numerical error analysis · Program transformation

1 Introduction

Numerical computation can be exceptionally troublesome in the presence of non-integer arithmetics, which cannot be expected to be exact on a computer. In fact, the finite representation of the operands can lead to undesirable conditions such as rounding errors, underflow, numerical cancellation and the like. This numerical inaccuracy will in turn propagate, possibly non-linearly, through the variables of the program. When the dependency between variables becomes particularly intricate (e.g., in control software loops, simulators, neural networks, digital signal processing applications, common arithmetic routines used in embedded systems, and generally in any numerically-intensive piece of code), programmers must thus exercise caution not to end up too far away from their intended result.

The analysis of the numerical accuracy of programs is of particular relevance when its variables are subject to non-determinism or uncertainty (as often is the case for the mentioned classes of programs), calling for formal methods to analyse

Partially supported by MIUR projects PRIN 2017TWRCNB SEDUCE (Designing Spatially Distributed Cyber-Physical Systems under Uncertainty) and PRIN 2017FTXR7S IT-MATTERS (Methods and Tools for Trustworthy Smart Systems).

B. Dongol and E. Troubitsyna (Eds.): IFM 2020, LNCS 12546, pp. 318–336, 2020.
https://doi.org/10.1007/978-3-030-63461-2_17

the property at hand as precisely as possible, while avoiding explicit low-level representations which would quickly render the analysis hopelessly infeasible.

Fixed-point [31] arithmetic can be desirable in several applications because it is cheaper than floating-point, provides a constant resolution over the entire representation range, and allows to adjust the precision for more or less computational accuracy. For instance, it has been shown that carefully tailored fixed-point implementations of artificial neural networks and deep convolutional networks can have greater efficiency or accuracy than their floating-point counterparts [21,25]. Programming in fixed-point arithmetic, however, does require considerable expertise for choosing the appropriate precision for the variables, for correctly aligning operands of different precision when needed, and for the separate bookkeeping of the radix point, which is not explicitly represented. Fixed-point arithmetics is natively supported in Ada, and the ISO/IEC has been proposing language extensions [1] for the C programming language to support the fixed-point data type, which have already been implemented in the GNU compiler collection; similar efforts are being made for more modern languages, sometimes in the form of external libraries. Yet, crucially, fixed-point arithmetic is often not supported by the existing verification pipelines.

Here we aim at a tight error analysis in fixed-point arithmetic. Intuitively, our approach is straightforward. For each fixed-point operation we re-compute the same value in a greater precision, so that the error bound on a specific computation can be estimated by computing the difference between the two values; such errors are in turn propagated through the re-computations. If the precision of the re-computed values is sufficient enough, this yields an accurate error bound for each variable in the initial program, at any point of the program.

Rather than implementing the above error semantics as a static analysis, we devise a set of rewrite rules to transform the relevant fragments of the initial program into sequences of operations in integer arithmetics over vectors of bits, with appropriate assertions to check a given bound on the error. This reduces the problem as to whether the error enclosures in the initial program can ever exceed a given order of magnitude to (possibly multiple) simple reachability queries on the transformed program. The translated program can be analysed by any program analyser that supports integer arithmetic over variables of mixed precision, from bit-precise symbolic model checkers to abstraction-based machinery. The non-fixed-point part of the program is unchanged, thus allowing standard safety or liveness checks at the same time.

We evaluate our approach on an industrial case study related to the certification of a real-time iterative quadratic programming (QP) solver for embedded model predictive control applications. The solver is based on the Alternating Direction Method of Multipliers (ADMM) [7], that we assume is implemented in fixed-point arithmetics for running the controller at either a high sampling frequency or on very simple electronic control modules. Certification of QP solvers is of paramount importance in industrial control applications, if one needs to guarantee that a control action of accurate enough quality is computed within the imposed real-time constraint. Analytical bounds on convergence quality of a gradient-projection method for QP in fixed-point arithmetic was established in [28]. Certification algorithms for a dual active-set method and a block-pivoting algorithm for QP have been proposed in [8] and [9], respectively, based on polyhedral computations, that analyze the behavior of the solver in a parametric way, determining *exactly* the maximum number of iterations (and, therefore, of flops) the solver can make in the worst case, without taking care however of roundoff errors and only considering changes of problem parameters in the linear term of the cost function and in the right hand side of the constraints. To the best of our knowledge, exact certification methods do not exist for ADMM, which is a method gaining increasing popularity within the control, machine learning, and financial engineering communities [29]. Our experiments show that it is possible to successfully compute tight error bounds for different configurations of the case study using a standard machine and bit-precise bounded model checking.

The rest of the paper is organized as follows. In Sect. 2 we briefly introduce the semantics of operations over fixed-point variables. In Sect. 3 we derive the expressions for error propagation arising from the considered operations. Section 4 gives an overview of our workflow and illustrates the details of the proposed program transformation. In Sect. 5 we show how our approach performs on a case study and in Sect. 7 we report our findings and ideas for future development. Section 6 gives an overview of the related work.

2   Fixed-Point Arithmetic

The precision or format of a fixed-point variable x is $p.q$ when its integer and fractional parts are represented using p and q binary digits, respectively. We denote such a variable by $x_{(p.q)} = \langle a_{p-1}, \ldots, a_0.a_{-1}, \ldots, a_{-q} \rangle$. Since the position of the radix point is not part of the representation, the storage size for a fixed-point variable is $p+q$, plus a sign bit in case of signed arithmetics. It is customary to use a two's complement representation with sign extension for signed values.

Operations on fixed-point numbers are carried out much like on regular integers [31]. The sum or difference of two fixed-point numbers takes one extra bit in the integer part to hold the result, e.g., $z_{(p+1.q)} = x_{(p.q)} \pm y_{(p.q)}$, if the operands are in the same format. If the formats differ, then format conversion of one or both operands need to be carried out upfront to obtain the same format.

The product of two fixed-point numbers is also performed as in integer arithmetics. In this case the two operands are not required to be in the same format. The format to store the result uses the sum of the integer parts of the operands plus one extra bit for its integer part and the sum of the fractional precisions of the operands for the fractional part, i.e. $z_{(p+p'+1.q+q')} = x_{(p.q)} \times y_{(p'.q')}$. Similarly, a division operation does not require the operands to be in the same precision, but it does require extending the dividend by the overall length of the divisor before the actual integer division takes place. The result, if representable, requires a precision equal to the sum of the integer part of the dividend and the fractional part of the divisor plus one extra bit for its integer part, and a precision equal to the sum of the integer part of the divisor and the fractional part of

```
1   fixedpoint x(3.2), y(3.2), z(3.2);
2   x(3.2) = 7.5₁₀;                          // +111.10, 011110
3   y(3.2) = 0.5₁₀;                          // +000.10, 000010
4   z(3.2) = x(3.2) + y(3.2);           // +0.0, +000.00, 000000
```

Listing 1: Overflow in fixed-point arithmetics.

the dividend for its fractional part, i.e. $z_{(p+q'+1.q+p')} = x_{(p.q+p'+q')}/y_{(p'.q')}$. The result of a division operation is not representable in fixed-point if the fractional part is periodic. Non-representable quotients need to be quantized to allow a finite fixed-point representation.

An arithmetic right shift of a variable $x_{(p.q)}$ by a non-negative integer k, for $k \leq p + q$ has the effect of trimming down the least significant k bits and extending the variable by k sign bits while shifting the radix point by k positions to the right. This results in a variable in the same precision of the operand, $x'_{(p.q)} = x_{(p.q)} \gg k$. An arithmetic left shift of variable $x_{(p.q)}$ by a non-negative integer k trims down the most significant k bits and extends the fractional part of the operand by k zeros, while shifting the dot by k positions to the right. This produces a variable in the same precision as the operand, $x'_{(p.q)} = x_{(p.q)} \ll k$.

It may be necessary to convert a variable $x_{(p.q)}$ to one with a different format $x'_{(p'.q')}$. While converting to a greater integer or fractional format does not usually cause problems, converting to a smaller one may cause errors because this operation amounts to trimming down the representation starting from the most significant digit, which may cause overflow, an example of which can be seen in Listing 1. Here, variable $z_{(3.2)}$ in line 4 is not large enough to store the correct result of adding the values of variables $x_{(3.2)}$ and $y_{(3.2)}$. Indeed, the correct result (8.0_{10}) would require a variable with 4 integer bits to store this value.

```
1   fixedpoint x(3.2), y(3.2), z(3.2);
2   x(3.2) = 0.5₁₀;                                    // +000.10, 000010
3   y(3.2) = * ;                      // assume +0.25, +000.01, 000001
4   z(3.2) = x(3.2) * y(3.2);                //+0.0, +000.00, 000000
```

Listing 2: A fixed-point program with a numerical error.

Assigning a variable to one with a lower fractional precision amounts to trimming down the representation starting from the least significant digit and may cause a numerical error. An example is shown in Listing 2, in which the value of variable $y_{(3.2)}$ is non-deterministic, i.e. it symbolises any possible value taken by y, provided it can be stored in the given precision. If we consider a run of this program in which $y_{(3.2)}$ is assigned to the value 0.25_{10}, the correct result of multiplying $x_{(3.2)}$ and $y_{(3.2)}$, namely 0.125_{10}, would require 3 fractional bits of precision, such as (3.3). Hence, having to store the result in $z_{(3.2)}$ forces the least significant bit to be dropped and the obtained result is 0.0_{10}.

3   Error Propagation in Fixed-Point Arithmetic

To track errors due to quantization and operations between operands which themselves carry errors from previous computations, we need to express the errors arising from the single operations in the program (Sect. 2). We denote the error of a variable $x_{(p.q)}$ with $\bar{x}_{(\bar{p}.\bar{q})}$ and denote with $M(x)_{(m_i^x.m_f^x)}$ the exact value that would have been calculated, had all the operations leading to the computation of x been carried out precisely. Using the identity $M(x)_{(m_i^x.m_f^x)} = x_{(p.q)} + \bar{x}_{(\bar{p}.\bar{q})}$ we will derive the expressions for the errors in arithmetic operations as functions of the values of the operands and of their errors, as proposed in [23], but adapted to our fixed-point semantics.

We assume that all error variables $\bar{x}$ have the same format $(e_i.e_f)$ and that it is sufficiently large not to cause overflow or underflow (Sect. 4). We further assume that the resulting variables of all computations have an adequate precision to store the correct result (Sect. 2).

Addition/subtraction. Let $x_{(p+1.q)} = y_{(p.q)} \diamond z_{(p.q)}$ for $\diamond \in \{+, -\}$. Keeping in mind that $\diamond$ introduces no error itself, since we guarantee a sufficient number of bits for the result, the value of the error of x can be expressed as:

$$
\begin{aligned}
\bar{x}_{(e_i.e_f)} = M(x)_{(m_i^x.m_f^x)} - x_{(p+1.q)} &= \left(M(y)_{(m_i^y.m_f^y)} \diamond M(z)_{(m_i^z.m_f^z)}\right) - \left(y_{(p.q)} \diamond z_{(p.q)}\right) \\
&= \left(M(y)_{(m_i^y.m_f^y)} - y_{(p.q)}\right) \diamond \left(M(z)_{(m_i^z.m_f^z)} - z_{(p.q)}\right) = \bar{y}_{(e_i.e_f)} \diamond \bar{z}_{(e_i.e_f)}.
\end{aligned}
\tag{1}
$$

Multiplication. Let $x_{(p.q)} = y_{(p'.q')} \times z_{(p''.q'')}$ with $p = p' + p'' + 1$ and $q = q' + q''$. We derive the expression for the error of multiplication:

$$
\begin{aligned}
\bar{x}_{(e_i.e_f)} = M(x)_{(m_i^x.m_f^x)} - x_{(p.q)} &= \left(M(y)_{(m_i^y.m_f^y)} \times M(z)_{(m_i^z.m_f^z)}\right) - x_{(p.q)} \\
&= \left[\left(\bar{y}_{(e_i.e_f)} + y_{(p'.q')}\right) \times \left(\bar{z}_{(e_i.e_f)} + z_{(p''.q'')}\right)\right] - x_{(p.q)} \\
&= \bar{y}_{(e_i.e_f)} \times \bar{z}_{(e_i.e_f)} + \bar{y}_{(e_i.e_f)} \times z_{(p''.q'')} + \\
&\quad + y_{(p'.q')} \times \bar{z}_{(e_i.e_f)} + \left(y_{(p'.q')} \times z_{(p''.q'')} - x_{(p.q)}\right) \\
&= \bar{y}_{(e_i.e_f)} \times \bar{z}_{(e_i.e_f)} + \bar{y}_{(e_i.e_f)} \times z_{(p''.q'')} + y_{(p'.q')} \times \bar{z}_{(e_i.e_f)}.
\end{aligned}
\tag{2}
$$

Division. Let $x_{(p.q)} = y_{(p'.q')}/z_{(p''.q'')}$ with $p = p' + q'' + 1$ and $q = p'' + q'$. Division requires the fractional part of y to be zero-padded up to the length of z (Sect. 2). We do not consider this format, as it has no impact on the error equation. Moreover, the $/$ operator may introduce quantization errors for periodic quotients: if the quotient has precision $(p.q)$, this yields an error e (bounded by 2^{-q}) with respect to the quotient of the exact $\div$ operator:

$$\bar{\mathbf{x}}_{(e_i.e_f)} = \mathbf{M}(\mathbf{x})_{(m_i^x.m_f^x)} - \mathbf{x}_{(p.q)} = (\mathbf{M}(\mathbf{y})_{(m_i^y.m_f^y)} \div \mathbf{M}(\mathbf{z})_{(m_i^z.m_f^z)}) - \mathbf{x}_{(p.q)}$$

$$= (\bar{\mathbf{y}}_{(e_i.e_f)} + \mathbf{y}_{(p'.q')}) \div (\bar{\mathbf{z}}_{(e_i.e_f)} + \mathbf{z}_{(p''.q'')}) - \mathbf{y}_{(p'.q')}/\mathbf{z}_{(p''.q'')}$$

$$= (\bar{\mathbf{y}}_{(e_i.e_f)} + \mathbf{y}_{(p'.q')}) \div (\bar{\mathbf{z}}_{(e_i.e_f)} + \mathbf{z}_{(p''.q'')}) - (\mathbf{y}_{(p'.q')} \div \mathbf{z}_{(p''.q'')} - e) \quad (3)$$

$$= (\mathbf{z}_{(p''.q'')} \times \bar{\mathbf{y}}_{(e_i.e_f)} - \bar{\mathbf{z}}_{(e_i.e_f)} \times \mathbf{y}_{(p'.q')})$$

$$\div [\mathbf{z}_{(p''.q'')} \times (\bar{\mathbf{z}}_{(e_i.e_f)} + \mathbf{z}_{(p''.q'')})] + e.$$

Right Shift. To compute the error due to a right shift $\mathbf{x}_{(p.q)} = \mathbf{y}_{(p.q)} \gg k$, let us first notice that the mathematical computation of this operation would only result in shifting the radix point to the left (which is equivalent to dividing by 2^k), and would maintain the value of the underlying integer, since this operation would be carried out in infinite precision without truncating any bits. Let $\ggg$ denote the operation that simply truncates the least significant bits and shortens the variable. We will express $\gg$ as a composition of $\ggg$ and a rescaling of the variable. Let $\mathbf{y}'_{(p'.q')} = \mathbf{y}_{(p.q)} \ggg k$, where $(p'.q') = (p.q-k)$ if $k \le q$ and $(p'.q') = (p+q-k.0)$ otherwise. The expression for the error is derived as follows:

$$\bar{\mathbf{x}}_{(e_i.e_f)} = \mathbf{M}(\mathbf{x})_{(m_i^x.m_f^x)} - \mathbf{x}_{(p.q)} = (\mathbf{M}(\mathbf{y})_{(m_i^y.m_f^y)} \gg k) - \mathbf{x}_{(p.q)}$$

$$= \mathbf{M}(\mathbf{y})_{(m_i^y.m_f^y)} \times 2^{-k} - (\mathbf{y}_{(p.q)} \ggg k) \times 2^{-k}$$

$$= (\mathbf{M}(\mathbf{y})_{(m_i^y.m_f^y)} - \mathbf{y}'_{(p'.q')}) \times 2^{-k} = (\bar{\mathbf{y}}_{(e_i.e_f)} + \mathbf{y}_{(p.q)} - \mathbf{y}'_{(p'.q')}) \times 2^{-k}.$$

$$(4)$$

Left shift. To derive the error of $\mathbf{x}_{(p.q)} = \mathbf{y}_{(p.q)} \ll k$ we introduce $\lll$ to denote the extention of a variable by zero bits in its fractional part and express $\ll$ as a composition of $\lll$ and a rescaling of the variable. Let $\mathbf{y}'_{(p.q+k)} = \mathbf{y}_{(p.q)} \lll k$. Notice that the values of $\mathbf{y}'_{(p.q+k)}$ and $\mathbf{y}_{(p.q)}$ coincide. Then we have:

$$\bar{\mathbf{x}}_{(e_i.e_f)} = \mathbf{M}(\mathbf{x})_{(m_i^x.m_f^x)} - \mathbf{x}_{(p.q)} = (\mathbf{M}(\mathbf{y})_{(m_i^y.m_f^y)} \ll k) - \mathbf{x}_{(p.q)}$$

$$= \mathbf{M}(\mathbf{y})_{(m_i^y.m_f^y)} \times 2^k - (\mathbf{y}_{(p.q)} \lll k) \times 2^k = (\mathbf{M}(\mathbf{y})_{(m_i^y.m_f^y)} - \mathbf{y}'_{(p.q+k)}) \times 2^k$$

$$= (\mathbf{M}(\mathbf{y})_{(m_i^y.m_f^y)} - \mathbf{y}_{(p.q)}) \times 2^k = \bar{\mathbf{y}}_{(e_i.e_f)} \times 2^k.$$

$$(5)$$

So far we have been under the assumption that the result of every operation is stored in a sufficient precision. This allowed us to express the errors in terms of the values of the operands and their errors, without additional error introduced by the finite representation of the result (except for division). In general, we can account for errors due to insufficient precision by storing the result in a long enough temporary variable, and then performing a precision conversion. The total error will then be the composition of the two computed errors.

Fractional Precision Conversion. Here we give the expression for the error due to a fractional precision conversion $\mathbf{x}_{(p.q')} = \mathbf{y}_{(p.q)}$, for $q' \le q$:

$$\bar{\mathbf{x}}_{(e_i.e_f)} = \mathbf{M}(\mathbf{x})_{(m_i^x.m_f^x)} - \mathbf{x}_{(p.q)} = \mathbf{M}(\mathbf{y})_{(m_i^y.m_f^y)} - \mathbf{x}_{(p.q)}$$

$$= \bar{\mathbf{y}}_{(e_i.e_f)} + \mathbf{y}_{(p.q)} - \mathbf{x}_{(p.q')} = (\mathbf{y}_{(p.q)} - \mathbf{x}_{(p.q')}) + \bar{\mathbf{y}}_{(e_i.e_f)} \qquad (6)$$

Integer Precision Conversion. In the case of an integer precision conversion $\mathbf{x}_{(p'.q)} = \mathbf{y}_{(p.q)}$, for $p' \leq p$, we do not give an expression for the error since here an error would mean overflow, which we treat as undesired behavior.

4   Program Analysis

The overall workflow of our approach is shown in Fig. 1. Given a fixed-point program P_{FP} and an error bound 2^{-f} on its variables, we wish to know whether any computation of P_{FP} can ever exceed the given error bound.

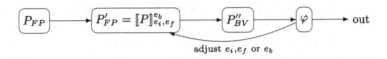

Fig. 1. Analysis flow for programs over fixed-point arithmetics.

To that end, we first transform P_{FP} into an expanded fixed-point program P'_{FP} with additional statements for computing and propagating the error, and assertions that the numerical errors do not exceed the given error bound. We denote this transformation function with $[\![\cdot]\!]^{e_b}_{e_i,e_f}$, where e_i, e_f, and e_b are parameters of the encoding that represent the integer and fractional precision of the error variables and the maximum number of least significant non-zero digits for the error variables, respectively. Notice that checking that numerical errors do not exceed 2^{-f} is equivalent to checking whether all but the last e_b bits of error variables are zero, for $e_b = e_f - f$. By construction, P'_{FP} will contain a reachable assertion failure if and only if either P_{FP} can exceed the given error bound, or (e_i, e_f) is not a sufficient precision for an accurate error analysis, or if overflow occurs.

However, the program is not ready for the analysis yet. We need to encode P'_{FP} into a bit-vector program P''_{BV}. This amounts to transforming all fixed-point variables into bit-vectors whose length is the sum of their integer and fractional parts, and on which operations are carried out as in integer arithmetics. P''_{BV} can then be analysed by any software verifier that supports integer arithmetic over variables of mixed precision. For instance, a bounded model checker would translate P''_{BV} into a propositional formula and feed it to a SAT solver.

If an assertion failure is reached, stating that the chosen precision $(e_i.e_f)$ does not suffice to hold the error of a variable, we adjust these parameters (and, consequently, e_b) and re-encode. As a first choice for e_i and e_f we can perform light-weight static analysis on the program and choose values s.t. $e_i \geq p$, $e_f \geq q$, where p and q are the integer and fractional precisions of any variable in P_{FP}, and $e_f \geq k$ where k is the magnitude appearing in any right shift.

4.1   Input Program

Let $x_{(p.q)}$ be a fixed-point variable, k a non-negative integer constant, $*$ a symbolic value, and $\diamond \in \{+, -, \times, /\}$ and $\circ \in \{\gg, \ll\}$ the arithmetic operations over fixed-point variables. For the input program P_{FP} we adopt a C-like syntax extended with an extra datatype `fixedpoint` for fixed-point variables:

$$v ::= x_{(p.q)} \mid k \mid *$$
$$s = \texttt{fixedpoint } x_{(p.q)} \mid (v = v) \mid (v = v \diamond v) \mid (v = v \circ k)$$

Assignment ($=$) of one variable to another can be across the same or different formats. In the latter case it acts as an implicit format conversion operation. For assignment to a constant or non-deterministic value, we assume that value to be in the same precision as the target variable. For binary operations, if one of the two operands is a constant we assume the same precision of the other operand. Without loss of generality, we assume that the operations do not occur in nested expressions (e.g. $x = z \times y + w$), and that $\pm$ is always performed on operands of the same precision. Nested or mixed-precision operations can be accommodated via intermediate assignments to temporary variables to hold the result of the sub-expressions or adjust the precisions of the operands, respectively.

Besides fixed-point specific features, the input program P_{FP} can contain any standard C-like elements such as scalars, arrays, loops, etc. For simplicity, however, in the rest of the section we assume that all function calls have been inlined, and `main` is the only function defined. Finally, we include verification-oriented primitives for symbolic initialisation ($x = *$) and assertion checking (`assert(condition)`) to express safety properties of interest, in form of predicates over the variables of the program.

4.2   Program Transformation

Here we describe the process of encoding the input program into a modified fixed-point program. We will denote with x' a temporary variable that does not belong to the initial program, but is introduced during the encoding. The purpose of such variables is to store the actual result of an operation without overflow or numerical error, thus they will always be given sufficient precision. Variables denoted with $\bar{x}$ will be introduced to represent the error that arises from the computation of x. All other variables introduced by the translation will be denoted by letters of the alphabet not appearing in P_{FP}. We point out here that our chosen quantization mode is truncation, but other rounding modes may be considered with slight adjustments.

Error variables are themselves fixed-point variables, but their manipulation is more involved. If we were to treat error variables as we do program variables, by keeping track of the errors arising from their computation, we would incur a recursive definition and have to compute errors of higher degree. Hence, we denote with $\oplus$, $\ominus$, $\otimes$ and $\oslash$ the four arithmetic operations on error variables and with c_1, c_2 and d three functions needed for the manipulation of error components and we define their macros in Fig. 5, discussed later.

Figures 2, 3, 4 and 5 display the translation rules for function $[\![\cdot]\!]_{e_i,e_f}^{e_b}$, for which we omit the parameters for simplicity. First, we consider all statements of the input program containing operations in which the format of the result variable is different from the one needed to hold the correct result. These are the statements that appear in the left-hand side of the first 8 rules of Fig. 2. For each of them, we declare an auxiliary variable, designed to hold the exact result of the considered operation, we introduce an additional statement assigning the

$$
\begin{array}{c}
\text{RANGE}
\end{array}
$$

$$
\begin{array}{l}
[\![\mathbf{x}_{(p.q)} = \mathbf{y}_{(p'.q')} \gg k;]\!] \\
{[k \leq p', k \leq q']} \\
{[p \neq p' - k \vee q \neq q']}
\end{array}
\rightarrow
\begin{array}{l}
[\![\texttt{fixedpoint } x'_{(p'-k.q')};]\!] \\
[\![x'_{(p'-k.q')} = \mathbf{y}_{(p'.q')} \gg k;]\!] \\
[\![\mathbf{x}_{(p.q)} = \mathbf{x}'_{(p'-k.q')};]\!]
\end{array}
$$

$$
\begin{array}{l}
[\![\mathbf{x}_{(p.q)} = \mathbf{y}_{(p'.q')} \gg k;]\!] \\
{[k > p', k \leq q']} \\
{[p \neq 0 \vee q \neq q']}
\end{array}
\rightarrow
\begin{array}{l}
[\![\texttt{fixedpoint } x'_{(0.q')};]\!] \\
[\![x'_{(0.q')} = \mathbf{y}_{(p'.q')} \gg k;]\!] \\
[\![\mathbf{x}_{(p.q)} = \mathbf{x}'_{(0.q')};]\!]
\end{array}
$$

$$
\begin{array}{l}
[\![\mathbf{x}_{(p.q)} = \mathbf{y}_{(p'.q')} \gg k;]\!] \\
{[k > q']} \\
{[p \neq p' - k \vee q \neq q']}
\end{array}
\rightarrow
\begin{array}{l}
[\![\texttt{fixedpoint } x'_{(p'-k.q')};]\!] \\
[\![x'_{(p'-k.q')} = \mathbf{y}_{(p'.q')} \gg k;]\!] \\
[\![\mathbf{x}_{(p.q)} = \mathbf{x}'_{(p'-k.q')};]\!]
\end{array}
$$

$$
\begin{array}{l}
[\![\mathbf{x}_{(p.q)} = \mathbf{y}_{(p'.q')} \ll k;]\!] \\
{[p \neq p' + k \vee q \neq q']}
\end{array}
\rightarrow
\begin{array}{l}
[\![\texttt{fixedpoint } x'_{(p'+k.q')};]\!] \\
[\![x'_{(p'+k.q')} = \mathbf{y}_{(p'.q')} \ll k;]\!] \\
[\![\mathbf{x}_{(p.q)} = \mathbf{x}'_{(p'+k.q')};]\!]
\end{array}
$$

$$
\begin{array}{l}
[\![\mathbf{x}_{(p.q)} = \mathbf{y}_{(p'.q')} + \mathbf{z}_{(p'.q')};]\!] \\
{[p \neq p' + 1 \vee q \neq q']}
\end{array}
\rightarrow
\begin{array}{l}
[\![\texttt{fixedpoint } x'_{(p'+1.q')};]\!] \\
[\![x'_{(p+1.q)} = \mathbf{y}_{(p'.q')} + \mathbf{z}_{(p'.q')};]\!] \\
[\![\mathbf{x}_{(p.q)} = \mathbf{x}'_{(p'+1.q')};]\!]
\end{array}
$$

$$
\begin{array}{l}
[\![\mathbf{x}_{(p.q)} = \mathbf{y}_{(p'.q')} - \mathbf{z}_{(p'.q')};]\!] \\
{[p \neq p' + 1 \vee q \neq q']}
\end{array}
\rightarrow
\begin{array}{l}
[\![\texttt{fixedpoint } x'_{(p'+1.q')};]\!] \\
[\![x'_{(p+1.q)} = \mathbf{y}_{(p'.q')} - \mathbf{z}_{(p'.q')};]\!] \\
[\![\mathbf{x}_{(p.q)} = \mathbf{x}'_{(p'+1.q')};]\!]
\end{array}
$$

$$
\begin{array}{l}
[\![\mathbf{x}_{(p.q)} = \mathbf{y}_{(p'.q')} \times \mathbf{z}_{(p''.q'')};]\!] \\
{[p \neq p' + p'' + 1 \vee q \neq q' + q'']}
\end{array}
\rightarrow
\begin{array}{l}
[\![\texttt{fixedpoint } x'_{(p'+p''+1.q'+q'')};]\!] \\
[\![x'_{(p'+p''+1.q'+q'')} = \mathbf{y}_{(p'.q')} \times \mathbf{z}_{(p''.q'')};]\!] \\
[\![\mathbf{x}_{(p.q)} = \mathbf{x}'_{(p'+p''+1.q'+q'')};]\!]
\end{array}
$$

$$
\begin{array}{l}
[\![\mathbf{x}_{(p.q)} = \mathbf{y}_{(p'.q')} / \mathbf{z}_{(p''.q'')};]\!] \\
{[p \neq p' + q'' + 1 \vee q \neq p'' + q']}
\end{array}
\rightarrow
\begin{array}{l}
[\![\texttt{fixedpoint } x'_{(p'+q''+1.p''+q')};]\!] \\
[\![x'_{(p'+q''+1.p''+q')} = \mathbf{y}_{(p'.q')} / \mathbf{z}_{(p''.q'')};]\!] \\
[\![\mathbf{x}_{(p.q)} = \mathbf{x}'_{(p'+q''+1.p''+q')};]\!]
\end{array}
$$

$$
\begin{array}{l}
[\![\mathbf{x}_{(p.q)} = \mathbf{y}_{(p'.q')};]\!] \\
{[p \neq p' \wedge q \neq q']}
\end{array}
\rightarrow
\begin{array}{l}
[\![\texttt{fixedpoint } x'_{(p.q')};]\!] \\
[\![x'_{(p.q')} = \mathbf{y}_{(p'.q')};]\!] \\
[\![\mathbf{x}_{(p.q)} = \mathbf{x}'_{(p.q')};]\!]
\end{array}
$$

Fig. 2. Rewrite function $[\![\cdot]\!]$: first set of rules to be applied.

result of said operation to the new variable and finally we introduce a statement to convert the new result variable to the original one. The last rule of Fig. 2 concerns precision conversion, involving both the integer and fractional part. We translate it by declaring an auxiliary variable and dividing the integer and fractional conversions into two separate steps. We point out here that all newly declared variables introduced by the encoding are implicitly initialized to 0.

When declaring a fixed-point variable z in the original program, by rule DECLARATION in Fig. 3, in the translated program this will be accompanied by a declaration of an extra variable $\bar{z}$ representing the error in the computation of z. The group of rules ASSIGNMENT describes assignment to a constant, a non-deterministic value, or another variable in the same precision. In particular, * indicates any possible value representable in the precision of the target variable. In both cases, the error variable $\bar{x}$ will have value zero, as no error is generated by such an assignment. When a variable y is assigned to another variable x with the same precision, the error of the former is propagated unchanged to the latter.

The INTEGER PRECISION CAST rules handle assignments between variables with different integer precisions. When assigning a variable to one with greater integer precision, the old variable is lengthened (by sign extension or zeros, depending on the representation), so there is no loss of precision and no error is introduced by this operation. Hence, the error of the new variable is equal to that of the previous one. The case of an assignment to lower integer precision may result in overflow. For this kind of assignment we introduce an assertion to check that the values of the old and the new variable are equal. The error of the new variable coincides with the error of the old variable, as this assignment entails no additional error, once the assertion is checked. The assertion statement may be left out of the encoding if we do not wish to check for overflow.

The FRACTIONAL PRECISION CAST rules encode statements for fractional conversion. The first rule handles the case of assignment of a variable y to one with a greater fractional precision x. This translates to extending y by a number of bits equal to the difference in precision. We indicate this operation with an internal operator $\lll$, already introduced in Sect. 3. As this operation introduces no error, the error variable of the result will be equal to that of the operand.

The conversion of a variable y to one with a lower fractional precision x translates to a declaration of 4 new variables, the assignment of x to the trimmed-down value of y (here we use operator $\ggg$ introduced earlier) and a number of statements to compute the error. First, x and y are aligned in order to perform subtraction. This operation can be carried out error-free and stored in t, since the value of y' does not exceed that of y by construction. The value of t is then stored in a new variable $\bar{y}$ by extending it to obtain the usual precision for error variables. The total error $\bar{x}$ is the sum of $\bar{y}$ and $\bar{\bar{y}}$, as derived in Eq. 6, where $\bar{\bar{y}}$ corresponds to y − x. Finally, we check whether the absolute value of $\bar{x}$ exceeds the given error bound by cutting off the last e_b bits and checking if the remaining bits are all zero. We use here our internal operator abs that computes the absolute value of the underlying integer and returns its properly scaled value.

DECLARATION

$$[\![\texttt{fixedpoint } z_{(p.q)};]\!] \to \texttt{fixedpoint } z_{(p.q)}, \ \bar{z}_{(e_i.e_f)};$$

ASSIGNMENT

$$[\![x_{(p.q)} = k;]\!] \to \begin{array}{l} x_{(p.q)} = k; \\ \bar{x}_{(e_i.e_f)} = 0; \end{array}$$

$$[\![x_{(p.q)} = *;]\!] \to \begin{array}{l} x_{(p.q)} = *; \\ \bar{x}_{(e_i.e_f)} = 0; \end{array}$$

$$[\![x_{(p.q)} = y_{(p.q)};]\!] \to \begin{array}{l} x_{(p.q)} = y_{(p.q)}; \\ \bar{x}_{(e_i.e_f)} = \bar{y}_{(e_i.e_f)}; \end{array}$$

INTEGER PRECISION CAST

$$\begin{array}{l} [\![x_{(p.q)} = y_{(p'.q)};]\!] \\ [p > p'] \end{array} \to \begin{array}{l} x_{(p.q)} = y_{(p'.q)}; \\ \bar{x}_{(e_i.e_f)} = \bar{y}_{(e_i.e_f)}; \end{array}$$

$$\begin{array}{l} [\![x_{(p.q)} = y_{(p'.q)};]\!] \\ [p < p'] \end{array} \to \begin{array}{l} x_{(p.q)} = y_{(p'.q)}; \\ \texttt{assert}(y_{(p'.q)} = x_{(p.q)}); \\ \bar{x}_{(e_i.e_f)} = \bar{y}_{(e_i.e_f)}; \end{array}$$

FRACTIONAL PRECISION CAST

$$\begin{array}{l} [\![x_{(p.q)} = y_{(p.q')}]\!] \\ [q > q'] \end{array} \to \begin{array}{l} x_{(p.q)} = y_{(p.q')} \lll q - q'; \\ \bar{x}_{(e_i.e_f)} = \bar{y}_{(e_i.e_f)}; \end{array}$$

$$\begin{array}{l} [\![x_{(p.q)} = y_{(p.q')};]\!] \\ [q < q', q' \le e_f] \end{array} \to \begin{array}{l} \texttt{fixedpoint } y'_{(p.q')}, \bar{\bar{y}}_{(e_i.e_t)}, s_{(e_i.e_t)}, t_{(p.q')}; \\ x_{(p.q)} = y_{(p.q')} \ggg q' - q; \\ y'_{(p.q')} = x_{(p.q)} \lll q' - q; \\ t_{(p.q')} = y_{(p.q')} - y'_{(p.q')}; \\ \bar{\bar{y}}_{(e_i.e_f)} = t_{(p.q')} \lll e_t - q'; \\ \bar{x}_{(e_i.e_f)} = \bar{y}_{(e_i.e_f)} \oplus \bar{\bar{y}}_{(e_i.e_f)}; \\ s_{(e_i.e_f)} = \texttt{abs}(\bar{x}_{(e_i.e_f)}); \\ \texttt{assert}((s_{(e_i.e_f)} \ggg eb) = 0); \end{array}$$

ADDITION/SUBTRACTION

$$\begin{array}{l} [\![x_{(p.q)} = y_{(p'.q')} \pm z_{(p'.q')};]\!] \\ [p = p' + 1 \land q = q'] \end{array} \to \begin{array}{l} \texttt{fixedpoint } s_{(e_i.e_f)}; \\ x_{(p.q)} = y_{(p'.q')} \pm z_{(p'.q')}; \\ \bar{x}_{(e_i.e_f)} = \bar{y}_{(e_i.e_f)} \oplus \bar{z}_{(e_i.e_f)}; \\ s_{(e_i.e_f)} = \texttt{abs}(\bar{x}_{(e_i.e_f)}); \\ \texttt{assert}((s_{(e_i.e_f)} \ggg eb) = 0); \end{array}$$

MULTIPLICATION

$$\begin{array}{l} [\![x_{(p.q)} = y_{(p'.q')} \times z_{(p''.q'')};]\!] \\ [p = p' + p'' + 1 \land q = q' + q''] \end{array} \to \begin{array}{l} \texttt{fixedpoint } s_{(e_i.e_f)}; \\ x_{(p.q)} = y_{(p'.q')} \times z_{(p''.q'')}; \\ \bar{x}_{(e_i.e_f)} = (\bar{y}_{(e_i.e_f)} \otimes \bar{z}_{(e_i.e_f)}) \oplus \\ \quad (y_{(p'.q')} \otimes \bar{z}_{(e_i.e_f)}) \oplus \\ \quad (z_{(p''.q'')} \otimes \bar{y}_{(e_i.e_f)}); \\ s_{(e_i.e_f)} = \texttt{abs}(\bar{x}_{(e_i.e_f)}); \\ \texttt{assert}((s_{(e_i.e_f)} \ggg eb) = 0); \end{array}$$

DIVISION

$$\begin{array}{l} [\![x_{(p.q)} = y_{(p'.q')} / z_{(p''.q'')};]\!] \\ [p = p' + q'' + 1 \land q = p'' + q'] \end{array} \to \begin{array}{l} \texttt{assert}(z_{(p''.q'')} \ne 0); \\ \texttt{fixedpoint } t_{(p'.q'+p''+q'')}, t'_{(p''+p+1.q''+q)}; \\ \texttt{fixedpoint } v_{(q.0)}, \bar{x}_{(0.q)}, u_{(e_i.e_f)}, s_{(e_i.e_f)}; \\ t_{(p'.q'+p''+q'')} = y_{(p'.q')} \lll p'' + q''; \\ x_{(p.q)} = t_{(p'.q'+p''+q'')} / z_{(p''.q'')}; \\ t'_{(p''+p+1.q''+q)} = z_{(p''.q'')} \times x_{(p.q)}; \\ v_{(q.0)} = 1 - (t_{(p'.q'+p''+q'')} - t'_{(p''+p+1.q''+q)}); \\ \bar{x}_{(0.q)} \equiv v_{(q.0)}; \\ u_{(e_i.e_f)} = c_1(\bar{x}_{(0.q)}); \\ \bar{x}_{(e_i.e_f)} = [(\bar{y}_{(e_i.e_f)} \otimes z_{(p''.q'')}) \ominus \\ \quad (t_{(p'.q'+p''+q'')} \otimes \bar{z}_{(e_i.e_f)})] \oslash \\ \quad [z_{(p''.q'')} \otimes (z_{(p''.q'')} \oplus \bar{z}_{(e_i.e_f)})] \oplus u_{(e_i.e_f)}; \\ s_{(e_i.e_f)} = \texttt{abs}(\bar{x}_{(e_i.e_f)}); \\ \texttt{assert}((s_{(e_i.e_f)} \ggg eb) = 0); \end{array}$$

Fig. 3. Rewrite function $[\![\cdot]\!]$ for declarations, assignments, precision conversions and $+$, $-$, $\times$ and $/$ operations.

LEFT SHIFT

$$\begin{array}{r} [\![\mathtt{x}_{(p.q)} = \mathtt{y}_{(p'.q')} \ll k;]\!] \\ {[p = p' + k, q = q']} \end{array} \rightarrow \begin{array}{l} \mathtt{fixedpoint}\ \mathtt{y'}_{(p'.q'+k)}, \hat{\mathtt{x}}_{(e_i+k.e_f-k)}; \\ \mathtt{y'}_{(p'.q'+k)} = \mathtt{y}_{(p'.q')} \lll k; \\ \mathtt{x}_{(p'+k.q')} \equiv \mathtt{y'}_{(p'.q'+k)}; \\ \hat{\mathtt{x}}_{(e_i+k.e_f-k)} \equiv \bar{\mathtt{y}}_{(e_i.e_f)}; \\ \bar{\mathtt{x}}_{(e_i.e_f)} = c_1(\hat{\mathtt{x}}_{(e_i+k.e_f-k)}); \end{array}$$

RIGHT SHIFT

$$\begin{array}{r} [\![\mathtt{x}_{(p.q)} = \mathtt{y}_{(p'.q')} \gg k;]\!] \\ {[k \le p', k \le q']} \\ {[p = p' - k, q = q']} \end{array} \rightarrow \begin{array}{l} \mathtt{fixedpoint}\ \mathtt{y'}_{(p'.q'-k)}, \mathtt{s}_{(e_i.e_f)}; \\ \mathtt{y'}_{(p'.q'-k)} = \mathtt{y}_{(p'.q')} \ggg \mathtt{k}; \\ \mathtt{x}_{(p'-k.q')} \equiv \mathtt{y'}_{(p'.q'-k)}; \\ \bar{\mathtt{x}}_{(e_i.e_f)} = \mathtt{d}(\mathtt{y}_{(p'.q')}, \mathtt{y'}_{(p'.q'-k)}, \mathtt{k}); \\ \mathtt{s}_{(e_i.e_f)} = \mathtt{abs}(\bar{\mathtt{x}}_{(e_i.e_f)}); \\ \mathtt{assert}((\mathtt{s}_{(e_i.e_f)} \ggg \mathtt{eb}) = 0); \end{array}$$

$$\begin{array}{r} [\![\mathtt{x}_{(p.q)} = \mathtt{y}_{(p'.q')} \gg k;]\!] \\ {[k > p', k \le q']} \\ {[p = 0, q = q']} \end{array} \rightarrow \begin{array}{l} \mathtt{fixedpoint}\ \mathtt{y'}_{(p'.q'-k)}, \mathtt{x'}_{(p'.q')}, \mathtt{y''}_{(p'+k.q'-k)}, \mathtt{s}_{(e_i.e_f)}; \\ \mathtt{y'}_{(p'.q'-k)} = \mathtt{y}_{(p'.q')} \ggg \mathtt{k}; \\ \mathtt{y''}_{(p'+k.q'-k)} = \mathtt{y'}_{(p'.q'-k)}; \\ \mathtt{x'}_{(p'.q')} \equiv \mathtt{y''}_{(p'+k.q'-k)}; \\ \mathtt{x}_{(0.q')} = \mathtt{x'}_{(p'.q')}; \\ \bar{\mathtt{x}}_{(e_i.e_f)} = \mathtt{d}(\mathtt{y}_{(p'.q')}, \mathtt{y'}_{(p'.q'-k)}, \mathtt{k}); \\ \mathtt{s}_{(e_i.e_f)} = \mathtt{abs}(\bar{\mathtt{x}}_{(e_i.e_f)}); \\ \mathtt{assert}((\mathtt{s}_{(e_i.e_f)} \ggg \mathtt{eb}) = 0); \end{array}$$

$$\begin{array}{r} [\![\mathtt{x}_{(p.q)} = \mathtt{y}_{(p'.q')} \gg k;]\!] \\ {[k > q', 2k < p' + q']} \\ {[p = p' + q' - 2k, q = k]} \end{array} \rightarrow \begin{array}{l} \mathtt{fixedpoint}\ \mathtt{y'}_{(p'+q'-k.0)}, \mathtt{s}_{(e_i.e_f)}; \\ \mathtt{y'}_{(p'+q'-k.0)} = \mathtt{y}_{(p'.q')} \ggg k; \\ \mathtt{x}_{(p'+q'-2k.k)} \equiv \mathtt{y'}_{(p'+q'-k.0)}; \\ \bar{\mathtt{x}}_{(e_i.e_f)} = \mathtt{d}(\mathtt{y}_{(p'.q')}, \mathtt{y'}_{(p'+q'-k.0)}, \mathtt{k}); \\ \mathtt{s}_{(e_i.e_f)} = \mathtt{abs}(\bar{\mathtt{x}}_{(e_i.e_f)}); \\ \mathtt{assert}((\mathtt{s}_{(e_i.e_f)} \ggg \mathtt{eb}) = 0); \end{array}$$

$$\begin{array}{r} [\![\mathtt{x}_{(p.q)} = \mathtt{y}_{(p'.q')} \gg k;]\!] \\ {[k > q', 2k \ge p' + q']} \\ {[p = 0, q = k]} \end{array} \rightarrow \begin{array}{l} \mathtt{fixedpoint}\ \mathtt{y'}_{(k.0)}, \mathtt{s}_{(e_i.e_f)}; \\ \mathtt{y'}_{(k.0)} = \mathtt{y}_{(p'.q')} \ggg k; \\ \mathtt{x}_{(0.k)} \equiv \mathtt{y'}_{(k.0)}; \\ \bar{\mathtt{x}}_{(e_i.e_f)} = \mathtt{d}(\mathtt{y}_{(p'.q')}, \mathtt{y'}_{(k.0)}, \mathtt{k}); \\ \mathtt{s}_{(e_i.e_f)} = \mathtt{abs}(\bar{\mathtt{x}}_{(e_i.e_f)}); \\ \mathtt{assert}((\mathtt{s}_{(e_i.e_f)} \ggg \mathtt{eb}) = 0); \end{array}$$

Fig. 4. Rewrite function $[\![\cdot]\!]$ for left and right shift operations.

Rule ADDITION/SUBTRACTION translates $\mathtt{x}_{(p'+1.q')} = \mathtt{y}_{(p'.q')} \pm \mathtt{z}_{(p'.q')}$ into the same statement plus a statement for the computation of the error of $\mathtt{x}$. Notice that the expression for the error, namely the sum/difference of the errors of the operands, is the one derived in Eq. 1. We use the special operator $\oplus$ instead of $\pm$ since computations between error variables are carried out differently than those between program variables. Finally, as for fractional precision conversion, we check if the obtained error exceeds the error bound. Similarly, in rule MULTIPLICATION, the translation of $\mathtt{x}_{(p'+p''+1.q'+q'')} = \mathtt{y}_{(p'.q')} \times \mathtt{z}_{(p''.q'')}$ introduces a new statement for the computation of the error of $\mathtt{x}$, whose expression is derived in Eq. 2. As before, we use operators $\oplus$ and $\otimes$ instead of the usual ones. Finally, we check the error bound as before.

A statement $\mathtt{x}_{(p'+q''+1.q'+q'')} = \mathtt{y}_{(p'.q')}/\mathtt{z}_{(p''.q'')}$ is translated by rule DIVISION as follows. The dividend is extended to a new variable $\mathtt{t}$, division is performed between the obtained variable and the original divisor and the result is stored in $\mathtt{x}$. The encoding then introduces an extra variable $\mathtt{t'}$, assigned to the product of x and z. If t' coincides with t then the quotient is representable and no quantization error is introduced, otherwise an error bounded by 2^{-q} (the resolution of x) is introduced. Variable v is introduced to contain the value 0 if the result is representable and 1 otherwise. This value is rescaled in a new variable $\bar{x}$, which will remain 0 if $v = 0$ and will be 2^{-q} if $v = 1$. This variable is then converted to format $(e_i.e_f)$ by function c_1 and added to the overall error $\bar{x}$, as derived in Eq. 3. Again, we check the error bound condition.

In rule LEFT SHIFT in Fig. 4 we translate $x_{(p'+k.q')} = y_{(p'.q')} \ll k$ by first padding y with k zeros in its fractional part and storing the result in a new variable y' (we use our internal operator $\lll$ to indicate this). We then change the format of y' by moving the radix point by k positions to the right. To indicate this we use an internal operator $\equiv$ and store the result in x. Since no bits are lost, the error due to the shift is a rescaling of the error of y, as derived in Eq. 5, and a conversion of its format to $(e_i.e_f)$ by function c_1, defined later.

When right-shifting a variable $y_{(p'.q')}$ by k bits, the required format of the result $x_{(p.q)}$ may vary, based on k and the format of y. Indeed, this operation translates into a cut of the least significant k bits, possibly removing bits even from the integer part if $k > q'$ (third rule), plus the rescaling of the obtained variable, moving the radix point by k positions to the left, possibly exceeding the integer part of the variable if $k > p'$ (second rule). We only allow right shifting by a number of bits less or equal to the overall length of the variable (this condition is checked by performing light-weight static analysis on the input program). The computation of the error, as derived in Eq. 4, is expanded in the definition of d, defined in Fig. 5 and the obtained error is checked against the error bound.

Figure 5 defines the operators used for manipulating error components in our encoding. Function d is used to compute the error in the right-shift rules in Fig. 4. Esentially, it computes the difference between the exact value of the shifted variable and the one obtained by trimming it, scales this value appropriately and stores it in the chosen precision for error variables, as shown in Eq. 4. The sum and difference of error components computed in d are again the specialised ones for error variables.

Functions c_1 and c_2 convert a variable in any precision to one in the chosen precision for error components. c_1, used when the fractional part of the argument is shorter than e_f, reaches an assertion failure if the integer part of the argument is too large to be stored in e_i bits (error overflow). c_2 may reach either an assertion failure for error underflow, if the fractional part of the argument can not be stored in e_f bits, or an assertion failure for error overflow.

The operator $\oplus$ computes the exact result of a sum/difference of two variables by assigning it an extra bit and then relies on c_2 to convert this result to the desired precision. Similarly, the operator $\otimes$ first computes the exact product and then converts it to the desired format. To perform $\oslash$, the dividend needs to be extended by the length of the divisor and the quotient is computed. In case of non-representable quotients an extra error term is computed and added to the already computed quotient, and the resulting variable is converted to the

$$[\![\mathbf{x}_{(e_i.e_f)} = \\ \mathbf{d}(\mathbf{y}_{(p'.q')}, \mathbf{y'}_{(m_i.m_f)}, \mathbf{k})]\!];$$
$\rightarrow$
$$
\begin{aligned}
&\texttt{fixedpoint } \mathbf{t}_{(e_i.e_f)}, \mathbf{t'}_{(e_i.e_f)}, \mathbf{u}_{(e_i.e_f)}; \\
&\texttt{fixedpoint } \mathbf{u'}_{(e_i.e_f)}, \mathbf{t''}_{(e_i-k.e_f+k)}; \\
&\mathbf{u}_{(e_i.e_f)} = \mathbf{c}_1(\mathbf{y}_{(p'.q')}); \\
&\mathbf{t}_{(e_i.e_f)} = \mathbf{u}_{(e_i.e_f)} \oplus \bar{\mathbf{y}}_{(e_i.e_f)}; \\
&\mathbf{u'}_{(e_i.e_f)} = \mathbf{c}_1(\mathbf{y'}_{(m_i.m_f)}); \\
&\mathbf{t'}_{(e_i.e_f)} = \mathbf{t}_{(e_i.e_f)} \ominus \mathbf{u'}_{(e_i.e_f)}; \\
&\mathbf{t''}_{(e_i-k.e_f+k)} \equiv \mathbf{t'}_{(e_i.e_f)}; \\
&\mathbf{x}_{(e_i.e_f)} = \mathbf{c}_2(\mathbf{t''}_{(e_i-k.e_f+k)});
\end{aligned}
$$

$$[\![\mathbf{x}_{(e_i.e_f)} = \\ \mathbf{c}_1(\mathbf{y}_{(m_i.m_f)});]\!] \\ [m_f < e_f]$$
$\rightarrow$
$$
\begin{aligned}
&\texttt{fixedpoint } \mathbf{t'}_{(m_i.e_f)}; \\
&\mathbf{t'}_{(m_i.e_f)} = \mathbf{y}_{(m_i.m_f)} \lll \mathbf{e}_f - \mathbf{m}_f; \\
&\mathbf{x}_{(e_i.e_f)} = \mathbf{t'}_{(m_i.e_f)}; \\
&\texttt{assert}(\mathbf{x}_{(e_i.e_f)} = \mathbf{t'}_{(m_i.e_f)});
\end{aligned}
$$

$$[\![\mathbf{x}_{(e_i.e_f)} = \\ \mathbf{c}_2(\mathbf{y}_{(m_i.m_f)});]\!] \\ [m_f \geq e_f]$$
$\rightarrow$
$$
\begin{aligned}
&\texttt{fixedpoint } \mathbf{t'}_{(m_i.e_f)}, \mathbf{t''}_{(m_i.m_f)}; \\
&\mathbf{t'}_{(m_i.e_f)} = \mathbf{y}_{(m_i.m_f)} \ggg \mathbf{m}_f - \mathbf{e}_f; \\
&\mathbf{t''}_{(m_i.m_f)} = \mathbf{t'}_{(m_i.e_f)} \lll \mathbf{m}_f - \mathbf{e}_f; \\
&\texttt{assert}(\mathbf{t''}_{(m_i.m_f)} = \mathbf{y}_{(m_i.m_f)}); \\
&\mathbf{x}_{(e_i.e_f)} = \mathbf{t'}_{(m_i.e_f)}; \\
&\texttt{assert}(\mathbf{x}_{(e_i.e_f)} = \mathbf{t'}_{(m_i.e_f)});
\end{aligned}
$$

$$[\![\mathbf{x}_{(e_i.e_f)} = \\ \mathbf{l}_{(e_i.e_f)} \oplus \mathbf{r}_{(e_i.e_f)};]\!]$$
$\rightarrow$
$$
\begin{aligned}
&\texttt{fixedpoint } \mathbf{s}_{(e_i+1.e_f)}; \\
&\mathbf{s}_{(e_i+1.e_f)} = \mathbf{l}_{(e_i.e_f)} \pm \mathbf{r}_{(e_i.e_f)}; \\
&\mathbf{x}_{(e_i.e_f)} = \mathbf{c}_2(\mathbf{s}_{(e_i+1.e_f)});
\end{aligned}
$$

$$[\![\mathbf{x}_{(e_i.e_f)} = \\ \mathbf{l}_{(m_i.m_f)} \otimes \mathbf{r}_{(n_i.n_f)};]\!]$$
$\rightarrow$
$$
\begin{aligned}
&\texttt{fixedpoint } \mathbf{p}_{(m_i+n_i+1.m_f+n_f)}; \\
&\mathbf{p}_{(m_i+n_i+1.m_f+n_f)} = \mathbf{l}_{(m_i.m_f)} \times \mathbf{r}_{(n_i.n_f)}; \\
&\mathbf{x}_{(e_i.e_f)} = \mathbf{c}_2(\mathbf{p}_{(m_i+n_i+1.m_f+n_f)});
\end{aligned}
$$

$$[\![\mathbf{x}_{(e_i.e_f)} = \\ \mathbf{l}_{(m_i.m_f)} \oslash \mathbf{r}_{(n_i.n_f)}]\!];$$
$\rightarrow$
$$
\begin{aligned}
&\texttt{fixedpoint } \mathbf{q}_{(m_i+n_f+1.n_i+m_f)}, \mathbf{v}_{(n_i+m_f.0)}; \\
&\texttt{fixedpoint } \mathbf{l'}_{(m_i.m_f+n)}, \mathbf{u}_{(0.n_i+m_f)}; \\
&\texttt{fixedpoint } \mathbf{l''}_{(m_i+n+2.m_f+n)}, \mathbf{q'}_{(m_i+n_f+2.n_i+m_f)}; \\
&\mathbf{l'}_{(m_i.m_f+n)} = \mathbf{l}_{(m_i.m_f)} \lll n; \\
&\mathbf{q}_{(m_i+n_f+1.n_i+m_f)} = \mathbf{l'}_{(m_i.m_f+n)} \div \mathbf{r}_{(n_i.n_f)}; \\
&\mathbf{l''}_{(m_i+n+2.m_f+n)} = \mathbf{q}_{(m_i+n_f+1.n_i+m_f)} \times \mathbf{r}_{(n_i.n_f)}; \\
&\mathbf{v}_{(n_i+m_f.0)} = 1 - (\mathbf{l''}_{(m_i+n+2.m_f+n)} = \mathbf{l'}_{(m_i.m_f+n)}); \\
&\mathbf{u}_{(0.n_i+m_f)} \equiv \mathbf{v}_{(n_i+m_f.0)}; \\
&\mathbf{q'}_{(m_i+n_f+2.n_i+m_f)} = \mathbf{q}_{(m_i+n_f+1.n_i+m_f)} + \mathbf{u}_{(0.n_i+m_f)}; \\
&\mathbf{x}_{(e_i.e_f)} = \mathbf{c}_2(\mathbf{q'}_{(m_i+n_f+2.n_i+m_f)}); \\
&n = n_i + n_f
\end{aligned}
$$

Fig. 5. Rewrite function $[\![\cdot]\!]$: expansions for $\mathbf{d}$, $\mathbf{c}_1$, $\mathbf{c}_2$, $\oplus$, $\ominus$, $\otimes$ and $\oslash$.

desired precision. Notice that these operations differ from the ones on program variables in that they do not compute errors due to lack of precision. Indeed, they are tailored to reach an assertion failure when the computed exact (when representable) results can not be stored in the designated error variables. Should this happen during the verification phase, new values for error precisions can be chosen and the process repeated.

In the case that the control flow of the input program depends on conditions regarding variables with inexact values, our encoding may be extended to model the error arising from incorrect branching and loops. Following the ideas described above, the error of an incorrect branching choice is translated into a doubling of the conditional block of statements under examination and the values of the output variables are compared. In the first block, the original conditional statement is maintained, while the second considers the conditional statement on the exact values of the variables appearing in it.

Notice that our encoding always assures an exact computation of all representable values and gives an over-approximation only for the errors arising from the computation of quotients. To assure this accuracy, we either make sure an assertion failure is reached if a variable is too short to contain the value it is supposed to, or we assign e large enough precision to hold the result.

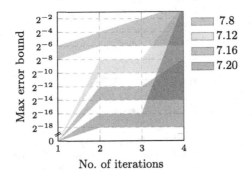

Fig. 6. Maximum absolute error enclosures

5   Experimental Evaluation

We evaluate our approach on an industrial case study of a real-time iterative quadratic programming (QP) solver based on the Alternating Direction Method of Multipliers (ADMM) [7] for embedded control. We consider the case where some of the coefficients of the problem are nondeterministic, to reflect the fact that they may vary at run time, to model changes of estimates produced from measurements and of the set-point signals to track. We studied 16 different configurations of this program by setting the precision to (7.8), (7.12), (7.16), and (7.20) for all the variables except for the 8 non-deterministic variables representing the uncertain parameters, which we restricted to a precision of (3.4) (using a signed bit-vector of 8 bits). Thus, each program configuration has $2^{8\cdot8} = 2^{64} \approx 1.85 \cdot 10^{19}$ different possible assignments. For each such configuration we considered up to 1,2,3, and 4 iterations of the ADMM algorithm. For i iterations the number of arithmetic operations amounted to $38 + i * 111$, of which $10 + i * 61$ sums/subtractions and $15 + i * 42$ multiplications.

In order to work out tight upper and lower bounds on the error on the output variables of the program, we analysed each configuration repeatedly, considering different error bounds starting from 2^0 and going down in steps of 2^{-2}, stopping as soon as a pass is followed by a fail, or when even the last check ($e_f - f = 0$, see Sect. 4) succeeds. In the first case, we have successfully found upper and lower bounds; in the second case, we have that the error is exactly zero.

The experimental results are summarised in Fig. 6, where we report the maximum error upper and lower bounds obtained with our approach. In one iteration, the analysis of the program with precision (7.8) fails with error bound 2^{-8} and succeeds with 2^{-6}; for all the other precisions, the analysis always succeeds, so the error is exactly zero. Larger intervals than 2^{-2} are reported when the check of a specific error bound was taking too long for a specific configuration (time-out was set to 6 days but generally did not exceed 24 h).

For the analysis we used a SAT-based bounded model checker, namely CBMC 5.4 [10], which relies on MiniSat 2.2.1 [13] for propositional satisfiability checking; for the program rewriting part we used CSeq [15]. For all the experiments we used a dedicated machine equipped with 128 GB of physical memory and a dual Xeon E5-2687W 8-core CPU clocked at 3.10 GHz with hyper-threading disabled, running 64-bit GNU/Linux with kernel 4.9.95.

6 Related Work

A large body of work on numerical error analysis leverages traditional static analyses and representations, e.g., based on interval arithmetic or affine arithmetic [30]; abstraction-based techniques, originally proposed for program synthesis, are [11,12] and [23]. Different tools based on abstract interpretation are currently available for estimating errors arising from finite-precision computations [6,16], while an open source library allows users to experiment with different abstract domains [26]. Probabilistic error analysis based on abstraction for floating-point computations has been studied in [14,22].

In general, abstraction-based techniques manipulate abstract objects that over-approximate the state of the program (i.e., either its variables or the error enclosures thereof) rather than representing it precisely. For this reason they are relatively lightweight, and can scale up to large programs. However, the approximation can become too coarse over long computations, and yield loose error enclosures. Bounded model checking has been used for under-approximate analysis of properties in finite-precision implementations of numerical programs [2,5,18,20]. Under-approximation and over-approximation are somehow orthogonal: bounded model checking approaches can be bit-precise, but are usually more resource intensive.

Interactive theorem provers are also a valid tool for reasoning about numerical accuracy of finite precision computations. Specifically, fixed-point arithmetic is addressed in [3] while [17] and [4] reason about floating-point arithmetic.

Our approach allows a separation of concerns from the underlying verification technique. The bit-vector program on its own provides a tight representation of the propagated numerical error, but the program can be analysed by any verification tool that supports bit-vectors of arbitrary sizes. Therefore, a more or less accurate error analysis can be carried out. For instance, if the priority is on certifying large error bounds, one could try to analyse our encodings using an abstraction-based technique for over-approximation; if the priority is on analysing the sources of numerical errors, then using a bit-precise approach such as bounded model checking would be advisable.

Numerical properties, such as numerical accuracy and stability are of great interest to the embedded systems community. Examples of works dealing with the accuracy of finite-precision computations are [27] and [24], which tackle the problem of controller accuracy, [14] gives probabilistic error bounds in the field of DSP, while [18] uses bounded model checking to certify unattackability of sensors in a cyber-physical system.

7   Conclusion

We have presented a technique for error analysis under fixed-point arithmetic via reachability in integer programs over bit-vectors. It allows the use of standard verification machinery for integer programs, and the seamless integration of error analysis with standard safety and liveness checks. Preliminary experiments show that it is possible to successfully calculate accurate error bounds for different configurations of an industrial case study using a bit-precise bounded model checker and a standard workstation.

In the near future, we plan to optimise our encoding, for example by avoiding redundant intermediate computations, and to experiment with parallel or distributed SAT-based analysis [19]. We also plan to evaluate whether verification techniques based on more structured encodings of the bit-vector program can improve performance. In that respect, it would be interesting to compare word-level encodings such as SMT against our current SAT-based workflow.

Our current approach considers fixed-point arithmetic as a syntactic extension of a standard C-like language. However, it would be interesting to focus on programs that only use fixed-point arithmetics, for which it would be possible to have a direct SMT encoding in the bit-vector theory, for instance. Under this assumption, we are currently working on a direct encoding for abstract interpretation (via Crab [26]) to evaluate the efficacy of the different abstract domains on the analysis of our bit-vector programs, and in particular on the accuracy of the error bound that such techniques can certificate.

A very difficult problem can arise in programs in which numerical error alters the control flow. For example, reachability (and thus safety) may be altered by numerically inaccurate results. We will be considering future extensions of our approach to take into account this problem.

References

1. Programming languages – C - Extensions to support embedded processors. EEE, New York (1987). iSO/IEC Technical Report 18037:2008(E)

2. Abreu, R.B., Cordeiro, L.C., Filho, E.B.L.: Verifying fixed-point digital filters using SMT-based bounded model checking. CoRR abs/1305.2892 (2013)
3. Akbarpour, B., Tahar, S., Dekdouk, A.: Formalization of fixed-point arithmetic in HOL. Formal Methods Syst. Des. **27**(1–2), 173–200 (2005)
4. Ayad, A., Marché, C.: Multi-prover verification of floating-point programs. In: Giesl, J., Hähnle, R. (eds.) IJCAR 2010. LNCS (LNAI), vol. 6173, pp. 127–141. Springer, Heidelberg (2010). https://doi.org/10.1007/978-3-642-14203-1_11
5. de Bessa, I.V., Ismail, H.I., Cordeiro, L.C., Filho, J.E.C.: Verification of delta form realization in fixed-point digital controllers using bounded model checking. In: SBESC, pp. 49–54. IEEE (2014)
6. Blanchet, B., Cousot, P., Cousot, R., Feret, J., Mauborgne, L., Miné, A., Monniaux, D., Rival, X.: A static analyzer for large safety-critical software. CoRR (2007)
7. Boyd, S., Parikh, N., Chu, E., Peleato, B., Eckstein, J.: Distributed optimization and statistical learning via the alternating direction method of multipliers. Found. Trends Mach. Learn. **3**(1), 1–122 (2011)
8. Cimini, G., Bemporad, A.: Exact complexity certification of active-set methods for quadratic programming **62**(12), 6094–6109 (2017)
9. Cimini, G., Bemporad, A.: Complexity and convergence certification of a block principal pivoting method for box-constrained quadratic programs. Automatica **100**, 29–37 (2019)
10. Clarke, E.M., Kroening, D., Lerda, F.: A tool for checking ANSI-C programs. In: TACAS, pp. 168–176 (2004)
11. Darulova, E., Kuncak, V.: Sound compilation of reals. In: POPL, ACM (2014)
12. Darulova, E., Kuncak, V., Majumdar, R., Saha, I.: Synthesis of fixed-point programs. In: EMSOFT, pp. 22:1–22:10. IEEE (2013)
13. Eén, N., Sörensson, N.: An extensible SAT-solver. In: Giunchiglia, E., Tacchella, A. (eds.) SAT 2003. LNCS, vol. 2919, pp. 502–518. Springer, Heidelberg (2004). https://doi.org/10.1007/978-3-540-24605-3_37
14. Fang, C.F., Rutenbar, R.A., Chen, T.: Fast, accurate static analysis for fixed-point finite-precision effects in DSP designs. In: ICCAD, pp. 275–282. IEEE/ACM (2003)
15. Fischer, B., Inverso, O., Parlato, G.: CSEQ: a concurrency pre-processor for sequential C verification tools. In: ASE, pp. 710–713. IEEE (2013)
16. Goubault, E., Putot, S.: Static analysis of finite precision computations. In: Jhala, R., Schmidt, D. (eds.) VMCAI 2011. LNCS, vol. 6538, pp. 232–247. Springer, Heidelberg (2011). https://doi.org/10.1007/978-3-642-18275-4_17
17. Harrison, J.: Floating-point verification using theorem proving. In: Bernardo, M., Cimatti, A. (eds.) SFM 2006. LNCS, vol. 3965, pp. 211–242. Springer, Heidelberg (2006). https://doi.org/10.1007/11757283_8
18. Inverso, O., Bemporad, A., Tribastone, M.: Sat-based synthesis of spoofing attacks in cyber-physical control systems. In: ICCPS, pp. 1–9. IEEE/ACM (2018)
19. Inverso, O., Trubiani, C.: Parallel and distributed bounded model checking of multi-threaded programs. In: PPoPP, pp. 202–216. ACM (2020)
20. Ivancic, F., Ganai, M.K., Sankaranarayanan, S., Gupta, A.: Numerical stability analysis of floating-point computations using software model checking. In: MEMOCODE, pp. 49–58. IEEE (2010)
21. Lin, D.D., Talathi, S.S., Annapureddy, V.S.: Fixed point quantization of deep convolutional networks. In: ICML. JMLR Workshop and Conference Proceedings, vol. 48, pp. 2849–2858. JMLR.org (2016)
22. Lohar, D., Prokop, M., Darulova, E.: Sound probabilistic numerical error analysis. In: Ahrendt, W., Tapia Tarifa, S.L. (eds.) IFM 2019. LNCS, vol. 11918, pp. 322–340. Springer, Cham (2019). https://doi.org/10.1007/978-3-030-34968-4_18

23. Martel, M., Najahi, A., Revy, G.: Toward the synthesis of fixed-point code for matrix inversion based on cholesky decomposition. In: DASIP, pp. 1–8. IEEE (2014)
24. Martinez, A.A., Majumdar, R., Saha, I., Tabuada, P.: Automatic verification of control system implementations. In: EMSOFT, pp. 9–18. ACM (2010)
25. Moussa, M., Areibi, S., Nichols, K.: On the arithmetic precision for implementing back-propagation networks on FPGA: a case study. In: Omondi, A.R., Rajapakse, J.C. (eds.) FPGA Implementations of Neural Networks. Springer, Boston (2006). https://doi.org/10.1007/0-387-28487-7_2
26. Navas, J.A., Schachte, P., Søndergaard, H., Stuckey, P.J.: Signedness-agnostic program analysis: precise integer bounds for low-level code. In: Jhala, R., Igarashi, A. (eds.) APLAS 2012. LNCS, vol. 7705, pp. 115–130. Springer, Heidelberg (2012). https://doi.org/10.1007/978-3-642-35182-2_9
27. Pajic, M., Park, J., Lee, I., Pappas, G.J., Sokolsky, O.: Automatic verification of linear controller software. In: EMSOFT. pp. 217–226. IEEE (2015)
28. Patrinos, P., Guiggiani, A., Bemporad, A.: A dual gradient-projection algorithm for model predictive control in fixed-point arithmetic. Automatica (2015)
29. Stellato, B., Banjac, G., Goulart, P., Bemporad, A., Boyd, S.: OSQP: an operator splitting solver for quadratic programs. Mathematical Programming Computation (2020). http://arxiv.org/abs/1711.08013
30. Stol, J., De Figueiredo, L.H.: Self-validated numerical methods and applications. In: Monograph for 21st Brazilian Mathematics Colloquium, IMPA. Citeseer (1997)
31. Yates, R.: Fixed-point arithmetic: an introduction. Digital Signal Labs (2009)

Detection of Polluting Test Objectives
for Dataflow Criteria

Thibault Martin[1]([⊠]) [iD], Nikolai Kosmatov[1,2] [iD], Virgile Prevosto[1] [iD],
and Matthieu Lemerre[1] [iD]

[1] Université Paris-Saclay, CEA, List, Palaiseau, France
{thibault.martin,nikolai.kosmatov,virgile.prevosto,
matthieu.lemerre}@cea.fr, nikolaikosmatov@gmail.com
[2] Thales Research and Technology, Palaiseau, France

Abstract. Dataflow test coverage criteria, such as all-defs and all-uses,
belong to the most advanced coverage criteria. These criteria are defined
by complex artifacts combining variable definitions, uses and program
paths. Detection of polluting (i.e. inapplicable, infeasible and equivalent) test objectives for such criteria is a particularly challenging task.
This short paper evaluates three detection approaches involving dataflow
analysis, value analysis and weakest precondition calculus. We implement and compare these approaches, analyze their detection capacities
and propose a methodology for their efficient combination. Initial experiments illustrate the benefits of the proposed approach.

1 Introduction

Among a large range of test coverage criteria proposed in the literature, dataflow
(coverage) criteria [1,2], such as all-defs and all-uses, belong to the most
advanced. These criteria are defined by complex artifacts combining a (program)
location where a variable is defined, a location where it is used, and a path from
the definition to the use such that the variable is not redefined in between (called
a *def-clear path*). Like for many other criteria (e.g. conditions, mutations), some
test objectives are not relevant (or *polluting*): they should be removed to properly ensure or evaluate test coverage [3,4]. Polluting test objectives for dataflow
criteria include *inapplicable* test objectives [5], where a def-use pair cannot be
linked by a def-clear path. They also include *infeasible* test objectives, where a
def-use pair can be linked by at least one def-clear path, but none of these paths
is feasible (i.e. can be activated by a test case). Finally, they include *duplicate* (or
equivalent) test objectives, which are always covered simultaneously: it suffices
to keep only one objective for each equivalence class.

While creating a list of (candidate) test objectives for dataflow criteria can
look easy, detection of polluting objectives for such criteria is challenging, due
to a complex definition, mixing reachability and def-clear paths. Yet it is crucial
to avoid a waste of time during test generation (trying to cover polluting test
objectives) and to allow a correct computation of coverage ratios (by ignoring

© Springer Nature Switzerland AG 2020
B. Dongol and E. Troubitsyna (Eds.): IFM 2020, LNCS 12546, pp. 337–345, 2020.
https://doi.org/10.1007/978-3-030-63461-2_18

polluting objectives in the total number of objectives). While applying dataflow criteria for testing [2,6–10] and detection of polluting test objectives for simpler criteria (see [3,11] for some recent results and related work) were previously studied, evaluating and combining various program analysis techniques for their detection for dataflow criteria—the purpose of this work—was not investigated.

Contributions. This short paper evaluates three approaches to detecting polluting test objectives for dataflow criteria, involving dataflow analysis, (abstract interpretation based) value analysis, and weakest precondition calculus. We implement these approaches inside the LTEST open-source testing toolset [12]. We evaluate and compare them by some initial experiments and analyze their detection capacities and limitations. We focus on the key ingredients of dataflow criteria: def-use pairs. The detection capacities we observed appear to be different from similar experiments made previously for other criteria. Finally, we propose a methodology for an efficient combination of several techniques.

2   Background and Motivating Example

Background. A large range of test coverage criteria have been defined [1]. Recent work proposed HTOL (Hyperlabel Test Objective Language) [4], a generic specification language for test objectives, that can express most of these criteria. We present here only the subset of HTOL that is useful to express dataflow criteria.

Given a program P, a *label* ℓ (in the sense of [13]) is a pair (loc, φ) where loc is a location in P and φ is a predicate. Label ℓ is *covered* by a test case t when the execution of t reaches loc and satisfies φ. While labels can express many simple criteria, test objectives for more complex criteria, including dataflow criteria, need a more general notion, hyperlabels. In our context, we use labels only for reachability, thus we always consider $\varphi = true$ and simplify the notation $\ell \triangleq (loc, true)$ as $\ell \triangleq loc$, that is, a usual label in the sense of C.

Hyperlabels [4] extend labels by relating them with several constructions, that include, among others, sequences, conjunctions and disjunctions. Given two labels ℓ and ℓ' and a predicate ψ, a *sequence* hyperlabel $h \triangleq \ell \xrightarrow{\psi} \ell'$ is covered by a test case t when the execution of t covers both labels ℓ and ℓ' (in that order), such that the path section between them satisfies predicate ψ. A *conjunction* $h_1 \cdot h_2$ requires both hyperlabels h_1, h_2 to be covered by (possibly distinct) test cases. A *disjunction* $h_1 + h_2$ requires covering at least one of hyperlabels h_1, h_2.

A key test objective of dataflow criteria is a def-use pair. For a given variable v and two labels ℓ, ℓ', we say that (ℓ, ℓ') is a *def-use pair for v* if ℓ is a definition of v and ℓ' is a use (i.e. a read) of v. It is linked by a *def-clear path for v* if there is a path from ℓ to ℓ' such that v is not redefined (strictly) between ℓ and ℓ'. A def-use pair (ℓ, ℓ') (for v) is *covered* by a test case t when the execution of t covers both labels (i.e.—in our context—passes through both locations) ℓ, ℓ' so that the path between them is a def-clear path (for v). When there is no ambiguity, we omit the variable name.

Thus, the test objective to cover a def-use pair (ℓ, ℓ') can be expressed by a sequence (hyperlabel) $h \triangleq \ell \xrightarrow{dc(v)} \ell'$, where predicate $dc(v)$ requires the path to be def-clear for variable v. Dataflow criteria rely on such sequences and require to cover all or some of them in various ways. Therefore we focus in this paper on detection of polluting sequences.

```
1   int f(){
2       int res=0, x=1, a;
3       ℓ1: a = ...;
4       if (Cond){
5           ℓ2: a = a + 1;
6           ℓ3: res = a;
7           x = 0;
8       }
9       if (x){
10          ℓ4: res += 2*a;
11          ℓ5: res *= a;
12      }
13      return res;
14  }
```

Def-use pairs for variable a:

$$h_1 \triangleq \ell_1 \xrightarrow{dc(a)} \ell_2 \qquad h_5 \triangleq \ell_2 \xrightarrow{dc(a)} \ell_3$$

$$h_2 \triangleq \ell_1 \xrightarrow{dc(a)} \ell_3 \qquad h_6 \triangleq \ell_2 \xrightarrow{dc(a)} \ell_4$$

$$h_3 \triangleq \ell_1 \xrightarrow{dc(a)} \ell_4 \qquad h_7 \triangleq \ell_2 \xrightarrow{dc(a)} \ell_5$$

$$h_4 \triangleq \ell_1 \xrightarrow{dc(a)} \ell_5$$

All-uses criterion objectives for a:

$$h_8 \triangleq h_1 \cdot h_2 \cdot h_3 \cdot h_4 \qquad h_9 \triangleq h_5 \cdot h_6 \cdot h_7$$

All-defs criterion objectives for a:

$$h_{10} \triangleq h_1 + h_2 + h_3 + h_4 \qquad h_{11} \triangleq h_5 + h_6 + h_7$$

Fig. 1. Example of def-use pairs and objectives for all-uses and all-defs for variable a.

Polluting Test Objectives. While the generation of candidate def-use pairs by combining definitions and uses for each variable can seem to be a simple task, many of them are irrelevant, or polluting, for various reasons. First, a def-use pair (ℓ, ℓ') for variable v is *inapplicable* if there is no structurally possible def-clear path from ℓ to ℓ' for v. Second, a def-use pair (ℓ, ℓ') is *infeasible* if such def-clear paths exist (structurally) but are all infeasible (i.e. cannot be executed by any test case). Inapplicable and infeasible def-use pairs are both *uncoverable*. Finally, a def-use pair (ℓ, ℓ') is *equivalent* to another def-use pair (ℓ, ℓ'') if for every test case t, the execution of t covers either both pairs or none of them.

Recent research showed that value analysis and weakest precondition calculus can be efficient to detect polluting test objectives for several (non dataflow) criteria [3,11] expressed in HTOL. For dataflow criteria, model-checking was applied to detect infeasible test objectives [14]. Continuing those efforts, this work adapts several existing program analysis techniques to detect polluting test objectives for dataflow criteria, implements and evaluates them.

Generating only relevant test objectives for dataflow criteria for an arbitrary program is undecidable. Indeed, it requires to identify which uses can be reached from a specific definition. If it were possible, one could apply it to solve the general reachability problem for a label ℓ in a given program P : {code1; ℓ : code2;} by considering program P' : {ℓ_0 :int new=0; code1; ℓ : return new; code2;} with a fresh variable **new** and checking whether the def-use pair (ℓ_0, ℓ) is generated for P'.

Motivating Example. Figure 1 gives a simple C code illustrating various cases of polluting objectives. The upper right of the figure shows all (candidate) def-use pairs for variable a ($h_1, \ldots, h_7$), that include polluting objectives. The all-uses criterion requires to cover all possible def-use pairs for each definition. For the definition ℓ_1 (resp., ℓ_2), this corresponds to the conjunctive hyperlabel h_8 (resp., h_9). The all-defs criterion requires to cover at least one def-use pair for each definition, which is illustrated by the disjunctive hyperlabel h_{10} (resp., h_{11}). We see that sequences are key ingredients to express test objectives of these dataflow criteria, and we focus on them below. Naturally, detecting polluting sequences will automatically simplify the combined hyperlabels.

In this example, h_2 is inapplicable: structurally, there is no def-clear path from ℓ_1 to ℓ_3 since all such paths pass through ℓ_2. This sequence should be strictly speaking discarded, i.e. erased from the combined objectives.

In addition, we can see that h_6 and h_7 are both infeasible since no test case can cover ℓ_2 and ℓ_4 (or ℓ_5) at the same time because of x. In this case, the combined objective h_9 becomes infeasible as well. It is also easily seen that having $Cond$ always false (or true) also makes some objectives infeasible.

Finally, since ℓ_4 and ℓ_5 lie in the same consecutive block, sequences h_3, h_4 are equivalent: a test case t either covers both of them, or none of them; and so are h_6, h_7. Keeping only one in each group would be sufficient both for test generation or infeasibility detection. We can keep h_3 for h_3, h_4. If h_3 is infeasible, h_4 is as well. If h_3 is covered by some test case t, h_4 is covered too[1].

For simplicity, we assume here that the C code has been normalized (like it is automatically done in FRAMA-C [15]), in particular, expressions contain no side effects and each function has a unique return point.

3 Detection Techniques

3.1 Dataflow Analysis for Inapplicable and Equivalent Sequences

Inapplicable Sequences. A simple approach to generate sequences expressing def-use pairs consists in performing a simple run through the Abstract Syntax Tree (AST) and creating a sequence for each definition and use of the same variable in the program. This approach leads to a significant number of inapplicable objectives. Their detection for an arbitrary program (e.g. with goto's) is non trivial. For Fig. 1, we would generate $h_1, ..., h_7$, including the inapplicable objective h_2.

To avoid generating this kind of objectives, we use a standard dataflow analysis [16]. This analysis propagates (over the program statements) a state associating to each variable v the set Defs_v of labels corresponding to definitions of v that may reach this point through a def-clear path. This dataflow analysis, denoted M_{NA}, is very efficient to identify Non-Applicable sequences.

Figure 2 illustrates this method for Fig. 1 and variable a. The Defs_a set near a node shows the set of definitions that may have assigned to a the value that a has at this node. So, after visiting ℓ_2, the definition of a at ℓ_1 is replaced with that at ℓ_2. Hence, at ℓ_3, we will create one sequence (h_5) for this use of a, and h_2

---

[1] unless the flow is interrupted by a runtime error between ℓ_4 and ℓ_5; hence we recommend keeping the first sequence h_3, so that a test case covering it either covers h_4 as well, or detects a runtime error, that is thus detected and can be fixed.

will not be generated. Notice that at node x, the state contains both definitions of a after the merge of both branches.

Equivalent Sequences. We distinguish two kinds of equivalent sequences. The first kind is trivial. If a variable v is used more than once in the same expression, assuming expressions do not contain side effects, the value of v will be the same for each occurrence. We consider each corresponding def-use pair only once.

The second kind is more complex and relies on the notions of *dominance* and *post-dominance* [17]. For two statements S_1 and S_2, we say that: S_1 *dominates* S_2 if all paths from the entry point of the function to S_2 pass through S_1; S_2 *post-dominates* S_1 if all paths from S_1 to the return point of the function pass through S_2.

We enrich the state propagated by M_{NA} by a set associating to each variable v the set Uses_v of (labels corresponding to the) uses of v that must (i.e. are guaranteed to) reach this point through a def-clear path. Before creating a sequence with a use at ℓ'', we check its associated Uses set. If it contains a label ℓ' for the same variable, it means that ℓ' dominates ℓ''. Then we check if ℓ'' post-dominates ℓ' using standard dataflow analysis. If so, for each definition ℓ in our state, def-use pairs $(\ell, \ell'), (\ell, \ell'')$ are equivalent. Figure 2 illustrates that the Uses_a state at ℓ_5 contains ℓ_4, and since ℓ_5 also post-dominates ℓ_4, h_4 (resp., h_7) is found equivalent to h_3 (resp., h_6). Notice that after the merge of branches at the last node, Uses_a is empty. We denote this method by M_{Eq}.

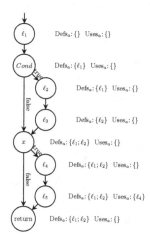

Fig. 2. Dataflow analysis for Fig. 1.

```
1    int f(void)
2    {
3        /*@ ghost int Cᵃ₆ = 0; */
4        int res = 0, x = 1, a;
5        /*@ ghost Cᵃ₆ = 0; */
6        ℓ₁: a = ...;
7        if (Cond) {
8            /*@ ghost Cᵃ₆ = 0; */
9            ℓ₂: a = a + 1;
10           /*@ ghost Cᵃ₆ = 1; */
11           ℓ₃: res = a;
12           x = 0;
13       }
14       if (x) {
15           /*@ check Cᵃ₆ != 1; */
16           ℓ₄: res += 2 * a;
17           ℓ₅: res *= a;
18       }
19       return res;
20   }
```

Fig. 3. Figure 1 instrumented for h_6.

3.2   Static Analysis for Uncoverable Sequences

Consider a sequence hyperlabel h_i expressing a def-use pair $\ell \xrightarrow{dc(v)} \ell'$ for v. Let $\mathcal{C}_i^v$ be a fresh variable associated to sequence h_i, that will represent its status: 0

for uncovered, and 1 for partially covered, i.e. after seeing only its definition, but not its use. More precisely, C_i^v is initialized to 0 at the beginning of the function. When we reach ℓ we set it to 1, meaning that we covered the first member of our sequence h_i. If $dc(v)$ is violated (i.e. if we encounter another definition on our path) we set C_i^v back to 0. If we can prove that $C_i^v \neq 1$ is always true at ℓ', then we show that covering h_i is impossible, that is, h_i is inapplicable or infeasible. A similar method was used in [14] with a model-checking approach.

Figure 3 illustrates this method for Fig. 1 for $h_6 = \ell_2 \xrightarrow{dc(a)} \ell_4$. We express the instrumented code in ACSL [15] as ghost code, used to provide additional code for analyzers, without interfering with the original code semantics. We create the ghost variable C_6^a that stands for the status of sequence h_6 over variable a (cf. lines 3, 5, 8, 10 in Fig. 3). We also generate an ACSL check clause $C_6^a \neq 1$ before ℓ_4 (line 15). If it is proved, then covering h_6 is impossible. Notice that h_7 would be proved infeasible as well, since they are equivalent.

To detect polluting sequences automatically, we apply static analysis techniques on the instrumented program, more precisely, Value Analysis based on abstract interpretation and Weakest Precondition calculus. The resulting detection techniques are denoted M_{VA} and M_{WP}.

Ex./ Size	Indi- cator	Cand. obj.gen.	Polluting objective detection							
			M_{NA}	M_{Eq}	M_{VA}	M_{WP}	$M_{NA,Eq}$	$M_{NA,Eq,VA}$	$M_{NA,Eq,WP}$	$M_{NA,Eq,VA,WP}$
cwe787 34 loc	time	0.3s	0.3	0.3s	4.9s	28.3s	0.3s	1.1s	5,6s	6,4s
	#seq.	207	144	144	144	108	171	171	171	171
	%seq.		69.6%	47.8%	69.6%	52.2%	82.6%	82.6%	82.6%	82.6%
2048 376 loc	time	0.6s	0.5s	0.5s	6.3s	1m45	0.5s	2.9s	50.2s	52.7s
	#seq.	560	159	187	161	14	293	295	294	295
	%seq.		28.4%	33.4%	28.8%	2.5%	52.3%	52.7%	52.5%	52.7%
papa- bench 1399 loc	time	1.2s	1.3s	1.3s	3.4s	1m7s	1.2s	4.1s	42.4s	45.3s
	#seq.	376	41	106	102	21	139	181	139	181
	%seq.		10.9%	28.2%	27.1%	5.6%	37.0%	48.1%	37.0%	48.1%
debie1 5165 loc	time	1.5s	1.5s	1.5s	1m20s	9m3s	1.5s	37.7s	4m2s	4m43s
	#seq.	2149	815	825	876	181	1272	1320	1280	1323
	%seq.		37.9%	38.4%	40.8%	8.4%	59.2%	61.4%	59.6%	61.6%
gzip 4790 loc	time	3.3s	2.7s	2.9s	22m20s	71m14s	2.6s	4m40s	29m28s	33m58s
	#seq.	7299	3710	2042	3806	1264	4738	4834	4741	4835
	%seq.		50.8%	28.0%	52.1%	17.3%	64.9%	66.2%	65.0%	66.2%
itc- benchm. 11825 loc	time	8.4s	8.4s	8.2s	32.3s	16m57s	8.2s	33.2s	11m45s	12m18s
	#seq.	3776	301	892	1145	152	1107	1703	1174	1708
	%seq.		8.0%	23.6%	30.3%	4.0%	29.3%	45.1%	31.1%	45.2%
Mono- cypher 1913 loc	time	28.2s	1.4s	7.0s	MO	TO	0.9s	16m32s	64m31s	80m10s
	#seq.	45707	38880	23839	–	–	43410	43414	43410	43414
	%seq.		85.1%	52.2%	–	–	95.0%	95.0%	95.0%	95.0%
Average	%seq.		41.5%	35.9%	41.5%	15%	60.0%	64.4%	60.4%	64.5%

Fig. 4. Polluting objectives detected by different techniques and their combinations.

4   Implementation and Evaluation

Implementation. We implemented the detection techniques described in Sect. 3 in LTEST[2] [12], a set of tools for coverage oriented testing, mostly written in OCaml as plugins of FRAMA-C [15], a program analysis platform for C code.

---

[2] available at https://github.com/ltest-dev/LTest.

One of the tools, LANNOTATE, creates test objectives for a given criterion. It supports various dataflow criteria (such as def-use, all-defs, all-uses) and generates (candidate) objectives inside each function. We implemented dataflow analysis techniques M_{NA} and M_{Eq} in LANNOTATE to filter out, resp., Non-Applicable and Equivalent objectives. It does not support pointers yet, and overapproximates arrays (meaning that an assignment at index i is seen as an assignment to the entire array). We implemented M_{VA} and M_{WP} in another tool, LUNCOV. detecting uncoverable objectives. It performs interprocedural analysis and relies on FRAMA-C plugins EVA for value analysis and WP for weakest precondition.

Experiments. In our evaluation, we address the following research questions:

RQ1: Is dataflow analysis with M_{NA} and M_{Eq} effective to detect inapplicable and equivalent test objectives? Can it scale to real-world applications?

RQ2: Can sound static analysis techniques M_{VA}, M_{WP} effectively find uncoverable objectives? Can they scale to real-world applications?

RQ3: Is it useful to combine these approaches? What is the best combination?

We use a set of real-life C benchmarks[3] of various size (up to 11 kloc) and nature, and focus on sequences encoding def-use pairs (cf. Sect. 2). Figure 4 illustrates the results. For each benchmark, we first generate all candidate def-use pairs using LANNOTATE without any additional analysis (see the third column in Fig. 4). Next, we apply the techniques, first separately (columns M_{NA}–M_{WP}) and then in combination (last four columns). We report execution time, the number of sequences (i.e. def-use pairs) detected as polluting, and the percentage it represents over the total number of candidate objectives. The last line gives an average percentage. TO and MO denote a timeout (set to 10 h) and memory-out. Experiments were run on an Intel(R) Xeon(R) E-2176M with 32 GB RAM.

Notice that M_{VA} requires an entry point function and an initial context to start the analysis, meaning that objectives are identified as uncoverable with respect to these starting point and initial context. Value analysis can require a certain expertise to find optimal settings for a better analysis. As we want our tool to be as automatic as possible, we used default parameters. As for M_{WP}, it does not require a global entry point but can be made more precise by providing contracts, i.e. pre- and postconditions and loops annotations. Again, in our experiments, annotations were not written for the same reason. Hence, an expert user can probably further improve the reported results. Similarly, using FRAMA-C plugins dedicated to generating ACSL annotations might improve these results as well. However, this demands some adaptations of our own implementation and is left for future work.

Results. Regarding **RQ1**, dataflow analysis techniques M_{NA} and M_{Eq} are very fast and very effective. M_{NA} detects an average rate of 41.5% (of all objectives) as inapplicable. M_{Eq} detects an average of 35.9% as equivalent. The rate of M_{NA} (between 8% and 85.1%) strongly depends on the example. Together, they identify a very significant number of polluting objectives (column $M_{NA,Eq}$).

---

[3] taken from https://git.frama-c.com/pub/open-source-case-studies.

Regarding **RQ2**, M_{VA} performs really well on smaller programs, and becomes more expensive for larger examples (e.g. it runs out of memory for Monocypher). It detects between 27.1% and 69.6% (with an average of 41.5%). M_{WP} is by far the slowest method of detection. It takes up to 7m14s, times out on Monocypher, and detects almost no new uncoverables compared to M_{VA} (see below).

Regarding **RQ3**, while it is natural to expect benefits of a combination of different analyses, the results were somewhat surprising. Unlike in the previous work for other (non dataflow) criteria [3,11], the weakest precondition based technique brings only very slight benefits (see columns $M_{NA,Eq,VA}$–$M_{NA,Eq,VA,WP}$). We believe it is due to the complex nature of dataflow criteria where infeasibility is less likely to be detected by local reasoning. It is left as future work to study whether these results can be significantly improved using additional annotations. Using $M_{NA,Eq}$ before M_{VA} or M_{WP} to filter out some objectives is clearly very efficient (and makes it possible for M_{VA}, M_{WP} to terminate on the Monocypher example). Overall, our results show that the best combination appears to be $M_{NA,Eq,VA}$, whereas executing M_{WP} in addition is very costly and detects at most 0.2% more sequences. When execution time is very limited, $M_{NA,Eq}$ can be already very effective.

5   Conclusion and Future Work

Polluting test objectives can be an important obstacle to efficiently applying test coverage criteria, both for test generation or computation of coverage ratios. We adapted, implemented and evaluated several sound techniques to detect (a subset of) such objectives for dataflow criteria. Combining dataflow analysis to detect inapplicable and equivalent objectives with value analysis to identify uncoverable ones appears to be the best trade-off for effective and fast detection. While this work provided a comparative analysis of the detection power of the analysis techniques, future work includes an evaluation of their results with respect to the *real set* of polluting objectives (or its overapproximation computed by replaying a rich test suite). Future work also includes a better support of the C language constructs (pointers and arrays) in the implemented tools, improving the analyses, notably M_{WP}, by automatically generating additional annotations, as well as extending this study to subsumed (i.e. implied) test objectives and to other coverage criteria.

Acknowledgements. This work was partially supported by ANR (grant ANR-18-CE25-0015-01). We thank Sébastien Bardin, and the anonymous reviewers for valuable comments.

References

1. Ammann, P., Offutt, J.: Introduction to Software Testing. Cambridge University Press, Cambridge (2017)
2. Rapps, S., Weyuker, E.J.: Data flow analysis techniques for test data selection. In: ICSE, pp. 272–278 (1982)

3. Bardin, S., et al.: Sound and quasi-complete detection of infeasible test requirements. In: ICST, pp. 1–10 (2015)
4. Marcozzi, M., Delahaye, M., Bardin, S., Kosmatov, N., Prevosto, V.: Generic and effective specification of structural test objectives. In: ICST, pp. 436–441 (2017)
5. Frankl, P.G., Weyuker, E.J.: An applicable family of data flow testing criteria. IEEE Trans. Softw. Eng. **14**(10), 1483–1498 (1988)
6. Rapps, S., Weyuker, E.J.: Selecting software test data using data flow information. IEEE Trans. Softw. Eng. **11**(4), 367–375 (1985)
7. Harrold, M.J., Soffa, M.L.: Interprocedural data flow testing. SIGSOFT Softw. Eng. Notes **14**(8), 158–167 (1989)
8. Weyuker, E.J.: The cost of data flow testing: an empirical study. IEEE Trans. Softw. Eng. **16**, 121–128 (1990)
9. Clarke, L.A., Podgurski, A., Richardson, D.J., Zeil, S.J.: A formal evaluation of data flow path selection criteria. IEEE Trans. Softw. Eng. **15**(11), 1318–1332 (1989)
10. Su, T., et al.: A survey on data-flow testing. ACM Comput. Surv. **50**(1), 1–35 (2017)
11. Marcozzi, M., Bardin, S., Kosmatov, N., Papadakis, M., Prevosto, V., Correnson, L.: Time to clean your test objectives. In: ICSE, pp. 456–467 (2018)
12. Marcozzi, M., Bardin, S., Delahaye, M., Kosmatov, N., Prevosto, V.: Taming coverage criteria heterogeneity with LTest. In: ICST, pp. 500–507 (2017)
13. Bardin, S., Kosmatov, N., Cheynier, F.: Efficient leveraging of symbolic execution to advanced coverage criteria. In: ICST, pp. 173–182 (2014)
14. Su, T., Fu, Z., Pu, G., He, J., Su, Z.: Combining symbolic execution and model checking for data flow testing. In: ICSE, pp. 654–665 (2015)
15. Kirchner, F., Kosmatov, N., Prevosto, V., Signoles, J., Yakobowski, B.: Frama-C: a software analysis perspective. Formal Aspects Comput. **27**(3), 573–609 (2015). https://doi.org/10.1007/s00165-014-0326-7
16. Kildall, G.A.: A unified approach to global program optimization. In: PoPL, pp. 194–206 (1973)
17. Prosser, R.T.: Applications of Boolean matrices to the analysis of flow diagrams. In: Eastern Joint IRE-AIEE-ACM Computer Conference (1959)

Domain-Specific Approaches

Meeduse: A Tool to Build
and Run Proved DSLs

Akram Idani[(⊠)]

University of Grenoble Alpes, CNRS, LIG, 38000 Grenoble, France
Akram.Idani@univ-grenoble-alpes.fr

Abstract. Executable Domain-Specific Languages (DSLs) are a promising paradigm in software systems development because they are aiming at performing early analysis of a system's behavior. They can be simulated and debugged by existing Model-Driven Engineering (MDE) tools leading to a better understanding of the system before its implementation. However, as the quality of the resulting system is closely related to the quality of the DSL, there is a need to ensure the correctness of the DSL and apply execution engines with a high level of trust. To this aim we developed Meeduse, a tool in which the MDE paradigm is mixed with a formal method assisted by automated reasoning tools such as provers and model-checkers. Meeduse assists the formal definition of the DSL static semantics by translating its meta-model into an equivalent formal B specification. The dynamic semantics can be defined using proved B operations that guarantee the correctness of the DSL's behavior with respect to its safety invariant properties. Regarding execution, Meeduse applies the ProB animator in order to animate underlying domain-specific scenarios.

Keywords: B Method · Domain-specific languages · MDE

1 Introduction

Model Driven Engineering (MDE) tools allow a rapid prototyping of domain-specific Languages (DSLs) with automated editor generation, integrated type-checking and contextual constraints verification, etc. This technique is powerful and provides a framework to implement the dynamic semantics of the language or to build compilers that translate the input formalism into another one (*e.g.* bytecode, programming language or another DSL). However, the major drawback of this approach is that the underlying verification and validation activities are limited to testing, which makes difficult the development of bug-free language analysers and compilers. When these tools are used for safety-critical or high-assurance software, [20] attests that *"validation by testing reaches its limits and needs to be complemented or even replaced by the use of formal methods such as model checking, static analysis, and program proof"*. Formal methods demonstrated their capability to guarantee the safety properties of languages

© Springer Nature Switzerland AG 2020
B. Dongol and E. Troubitsyna (Eds.): IFM 2020, LNCS 12546, pp. 349–367, 2020.
https://doi.org/10.1007/978-3-030-63461-2_19

and associated tools [7]; nonetheless, there is a lack of available tools to bridge the gap between MDE and formal methods for the development of DSLs.

In our works we apply the B method [1] to formally define the semantics that make a DSL executable and hence guarantee the correctness of its behaviour. The challenge of executing a DSL is not new and was widely addressed in the literature at several abstraction levels with various languages [5,12,23,29]. An executable DSL would not only represent the expected system's structure but it must itself behave as the system should run. The description of this behaviour also applies a language with its own abstract syntax and semantic domain. Unfortunately, most of the well-known existing DSL development approaches apply languages and tools that are not currently assisted by formal proofs.

In [16] we showed that there is an equivalence between the static semantics of DSLs and several constructs of the B method. In this paper we present Meeduse, a MDE platform built on our previous works [13,16] and whose intention is to circumvent the aforementioned shortcomings of MDE tools. It allows to formally check the semantics of DSLs by applying tools of the B method: AtelierB [6] for theorem proving and ProB [21] for animation and model-checking. The Meeduse approach translates the meta-model of a given DSL, designed in the Eclipse Modeling Framework (EMF [27]), into an equivalent formal B specification and then injects a DSL instance into this specification. The strength of Meeduse is that it synchronises the resulting B specification with the DSL instance and hence the animation of the B specification automatically leads to a visual execution of the DSL. This approach was successfully applied on a realistic railway case study [14,15] and also to formalize and execute a real-life DSL transformation [17] which is that of transforming truth tables into binary decision diagrams. This paper shows how the B method can be integrated within MDE and presents by practice Meeduse.

Section 2 presents a simple textual DSL built in a MDE tool and discusses its underlying semantics. Section 3 gives an overall view about the Meeduse approach and architecture and shows how the B method is integrated within a model-driven architecture. Section 4 applies two approaches to define the DSL semantics: the meta-model based approach and the CP-net approach. Section 5 summarizes two realistic applications of Meeduse and discusses their results. Finally, Section 6 draws the conclusions and the perspectives of this work.

2   A Simple DSL

For illustration we apply a well-known DSL builder (Xtext [2]) that allows to define textual languages using LL(*) grammars and generate a full infrastructure, including an ANTLR parser API with a type-checker and auto-completion facilities. We define a simple DSL that represents configuration files edited by operating system administrators to configure GPU servers. These servers are packed with graphics cards, called Graphics Processing Units (GPUs) that are used for high performance computing. Roughly speaking, in a GPU architecture, significant jobs are broken down into smaller computations (called here processes) that can be executed in parallel by the different GPUs.

Figure 1 gives the Xtext grammar of our DSL; it defines three non-terminal rules: Server (the axiom), Gpu and Process. Every rule starts by the definition of a naming identifier (name=ID) representing object declaration. The declaration of a server object is followed by two declaration lists: that of GPUs (gpus+=Gpu)* and that of processes (processes+=Process)*. A GPU has a fixed number of slots: free slots are defined by an Integer value (size=INT) and the occupied slots directly refer to their occupying processes (usedBy+=[Process]*).

```
Server:  name=ID (gpus+=Gpu)* (pocesses+=Process)*;
Gpu:     name=ID ':' size=INT '(slots)' '<-' (usedBy+=[Process])* ';';
Process: name=ID ;
```

Fig. 1. Example of an Xtext grammar.

Given a grammar, Xtext applies ANTLR to generate a Java API for a parser that can build and walk the abstract syntax tree (AST). One interesting feature of Xtext is that it defines the language AST by means of an EMF meta-model [27], which makes possible the integration of MDE tools that are built on top of EMF like OCL constraints checker, etc. Figure 2 provides the EMF meta-model of our DSL. It is composed of three classes, each of which is issued from a grammar rule. The grammar axiom is the root class of this meta-model and the associations represent the various object relationships.

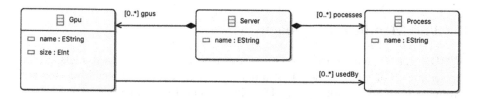

Fig. 2. The GPU server meta-model

Figure 3 presents the textual editor produced by Xtext for our DSL. In this file, the system administrator defined a server (GPUServer) with two GPUs (GPU1 and GPU2), and five processes (from p1 to p5). Process p2 is assigned to GPU1 and process p1 is assigned to both GPU1 and GPU2.

The DSL's grammar and the corresponding meta-model define the static semantics. Regarding the dynamic semantics, we informally define them with the following process scheduling actions:

- **enqueue/purge**: respectively assign and de-assign processes to a GPU server. Technically action **enqueue** declares a process in the DSL file, and action **purge** removes a process from this file. When assigned to the server the initial state of the process is Waiting.

```
1 GPUServer
2       GPU1 : 0 (slots) <-  p1 p2 ;
3       GPU2 : 3 (slots) <-  p1 |;
4
5 p1 p2 p3 p4 p5
```

```
p1 - GPUServer.p1
p2 - GPUServer.p2
p3 - GPUServer.p3
p4 - GPUServer.p4
p5 - GPUServer.p5
```

Fig. 3. Generated Xtext textual editor

- **ready**: assigns a GPU with at least one free slot to a waiting process. The process becomes then Active. If all GPUs are busy, the process enters in an intermediary state called Ready.
- **swap**: releases a slot by deactivating the corresponding process (the process becomes Waiting) and allocates the freed GPU slot to some ready process (the latter becomes then Active).

These actions must guarantee the following safety properties:

- The number of free slots cannot be negative;
- A process cannot be running on more than one GPU;
- If there is a Ready process then all GPUs are busy;
- A process cannot be Active and Ready or Active and Waiting or Ready and Waiting at the same time;
- An Active process is assigned to a GPU;
- Waiting and Ready processes are not assigned to GPUs.

3   The Meeduse Approach

In MDE, the implementation of DSLs is derived from their meta-models and as the semantics of meta-models is standardized [24] (by the Object Management Group − OMG), the underlying DSL implementation and associated tool-set code generation follow well established rules. This makes the integration of MDE tools easy and transparent. In fact, there are numerous MDE tools with various purposes: model-to-model transformation, model-to-code generation, constraint-checkers, graphical concrete syntax representation, bi-directional DSL mappings, etc. All these tools have the ability to work together using shared DSLs, as far as the semantics of these DSLs are defined by means of meta-models. The overall principle of a model-driven architecture is that once a meta-model is instantiated, MDE tools can be synchronised using the resulting model resource.

3.1   Main Approach

Figure 4 shows how Meeduse integrates the formal B method within MDE tools in order to build proved DSLs and execute their dynamic semantics. The left hand side of the figure represents a model-driven architecture where a meta-model (*e.g.* Fig. 2) is extracted by Xtext from a DSL grammar (*e.g.* Fig. 1).

When an input textual file is parsed, a model resource is created as an instance of the meta-model. Then every modification of the model resource implies a modification of the textual file, and vice-versa. Thanks to the standard semantics of meta-models, Meeduse can be synchronised with any model resource, which opens a bridge between MDE tools (Xtext or others) and formal tools like animators and model-checkers.

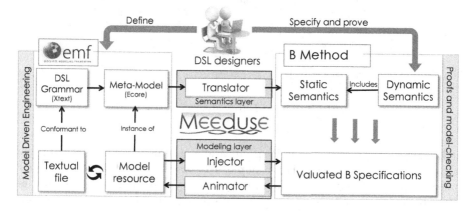

Fig. 4. The Meeduse approach.

3.2 Semantics Layer

The Meeduse approach starts by translating the meta-model of a DSL into the B language. This translation is done by component "Translator" of Fig. 4. The resulting formal model represents the static semantics of the DSL. It defines the structural features of the meta-model using B data structures: sets, variables and typing invariants. This translation applies a classical UML-to-B transformation technique, because all constructs of a meta-model have an equivalent in UML. For this purpose component "Translator" embeds B4MSecure [13], an open-source MDE platform whose advantage, in comparison with other UML-to-B tools, [8,26] is that it offers an extensibility facility allowing to easily add new UML-to-B rules or to specialize existing rules depending on the application context. In Meeduse the application context of UML-to-B rules is that of EMF meta-models.

A meta-class Class is translated into an abstract set named CLASS representing possible instances and a variable named Class representing the set of existing instances. Basic types (*e.g.* integer, boolean, etc.) become B types (Z, Bool, etc.), and attributes and references lead to functional relations depending on their multiplicities. Additional structural invariant properties can be written in B based on the generated B data. Figure 5 gives clauses SETS, VARIABLES and INVARIANT generated by Meeduse from the meta-model of Fig. 2.

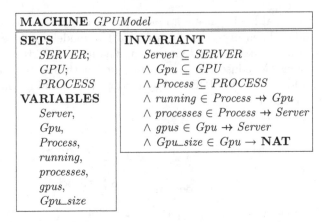

Fig. 5. Formal DSL static semantics.

During the extraction of the B specifications, the user can strengthen some properties of the meta-model. For example, attribute size is defined as an integer in the meta-model, but we translate its type into type NAT in order to limit its values to positive numbers as stated in the safety properties. The user can also complete the multiplicities over one-direction associations and apply to them specific names. For example, from our grammar Xtext generated a one-direction association from class Gpu to class Process with role usedBy. This means that the parser doesn't look at all to the opposite side of the association and hence it doesn't check the number of GPUs on which a process is running. During the translation of this association into B we assigned multiplicity 0..1 to its opposite side and we gave to it name *running*. This choice led to the partial relation named *running* from set Process to set Gpu.

Operations of this B specification, that may be generated automatically or even introduced manually, must preserve the structural invariant of Fig. 5. For this simple example, the generated invariant addresses four main static properties: (*i*) a process cannot be running on more than one GPU, (*ii*) the number of free slots is greater or equal to 0, (*iii*) processes are assigned to only one server at the same time, and (*iv*) GPUs cannot be shared by several servers. The proof of correctness guarantees that every provided operation never produces a wrong model − regarding this invariant − such as that of Fig. 3 where property (*iii*) is violated. Indeed, a proof-based formal approach is expected to provide error-free domain-specific operations.

3.3   Modeling Layer

The modeling layer is ensured by components "Injector" and "Animator". The "Injector" injects a model resource, issued from any EMF-based modeling tool (Xtext, Sirius, GMF, etc.) into the B specification produced from the meta-model. This component introduces enumerations into abstract data structures like abstract sets, and produces valuations of the B machine variables. Figure 6 presents clauses SETS and INITIALISATION generated by component "Injector" from an input model resource where five processes are scheduled and such that GPU1 is running p2 and GPU2 is running p4 and p5. In this model, GPU2 is busy and GPU1 has one remaining free slot.

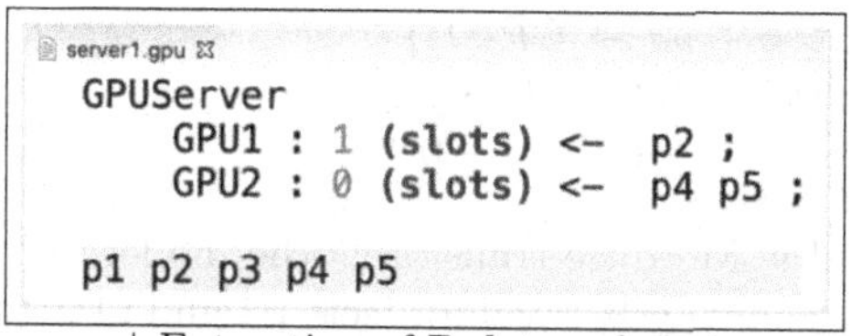

```
 server1.gpu ⊠
    GPUServer
        GPU1 : 1 (slots) <-  p2 ;
        GPU2 : 0 (slots) <-  p4 p5 ;

    p1 p2 p3 p4 p5
```

↓ Extraction of B data values ↓

SETS
  $SERVER=\{GPUServer\}$;
  $GPU=\{GPU1,\ GPU2\}$;
  $PROCESS=\{p1,\ p2,\ p3,\ p4,\ p5\}$

INITIALISATION
  $Server := \{GPUServer\}$
  $\|\ Gpu := \{GPU1,\ GPU2\}$
  $\|\ Process := \{p1,\ p2,\ p3,\ p4,\ p5\}$
  $\|\ running := \{(p2 \mapsto GPU1),(p4 \mapsto GPU2),\ (p5 \mapsto GPU2)\}$
  $\|\ processes := \{(p1 \mapsto GPUServer),\ (p2 \mapsto GPUServer),$
  $\qquad\qquad (p3 \mapsto GPUServer),\ (p4 \mapsto GPUServer),$
  $\qquad\qquad (p5 \mapsto GPUServer)\}$
  $\|\ gpus := \{(GPU1 \mapsto GPUServer),\ (GPU2 \mapsto GPUServer)\}$
  $\|\ Gpu\_size := \{(GPU1 \mapsto 1),\ (GPU2 \mapsto 0)\}$

Fig. 6. Valuation of the B machine.

In our approach the execution environment of the DSL is composed of Meeduse coupled with ProB, and the domain-specific actions (*e.g.* enqueue/purge, ready and swap) are defined as B operations that can be animated by the domain expert. At the beginning of the animation, the injector produces a B specification whose initial state is equivalent to the input model resource. If the input model is wrong (such as that of Fig. 3) ProB would detect it and the animation is stopped. In fact, our objective is to safely execute the DSL. Given a correct input model, component "Animator" keeps the equivalence between the state of the B specifications and the input model resource all along the animation process. When a new state is reached, Meeduse translates it back to the model resource and all MDE tools synchronised with this resource are automatically updated.

The "Animator" applies a constraint solving approach to compute for every variable the difference between its value before (v) and its value after (v') the animation of a B operation. Then, it applies the equivalent transformation to the corresponding element in the model resource. Formula $v - v'$ computes the values that are removed by the operation, and $v' - v$ computes the added ones. Suppose, for example, that from the initial state of Fig. 6 the animation of a given operation produces the following computation results for variables *running* and *Gpu_size*:

1. $running - running' = \emptyset$
2. $running' - running = \{(p3 \mapsto GPU1)\}$
3. $Gpu\_size - Gpu\_size' = \{(GPU1 \mapsto 1)\}$
4. $Gpu\_size' - Gpu\_size = \{(GPU1 \mapsto 0)\}$

Having these results, Meeduse transforms the model resource as follows: (1) and (2) create a link **running** between objects **p3** and **GPU1**; (3) and (4) modify the value of attribute **size** of object **GPU1** from 1 to 0. Figure 7 shows how the input textual file is updated after these modifications: process **p3** is now running on **GPU1** and all GPUs became busy.

```
server1.gpu ⊠
 GPUServer
     GPU1 : 0 (slots) <-  p2 p3 ;
     GPU2 : 0 (slots) <-  p4 p5 ;

 p1 p2 p3 p4 p5
```

Fig. 7. Example of an output model.

The reverse translation from a given state of the B machine into the EMF model resource is limited by the constructs of meta-models that Meeduse is able to translate into B. If the user adds programmatically some concepts to the DSL implementation that are not introduced within the EMF meta-model, then these concepts are missed during the animation. This may happen, for example, when the DSL encompasses stateful computations that are hand written by the developer using the Java implementation generated by Xtext. Despite that Meeduse does not provide a checking facility to ensure that a given model can be animated, it guarantees that all concepts of the meta-model that are translated into B are covered during the animation.

3.4 Meeduse Contributions

Figure 8 is a screenshot of Meeduse where the left hand side presents the textual DSL editor, and the right hand side shows: (1) the list of B operations that can be enabled, and (2) the current B variable valuations. The B specification used in this illustration applies B operations that define the domain-specific actions based on the B data structure extracted from the meta-model. Operation **ready** can be applied to **p1** or **p3** because both are waiting. These processes can also be purged using operation **purge**. Regarding the active processes (**p2**, **p4** and **p5**) they can be deactivated by operation **swap**. Playing with these operations in Meeduse automatically modifies the model resource and then the textual file is automatically updated. For example, Fig. 7 would result from the animation of **ready[p3]**. When ProB animates a B operation, Meeduse gets the new variable valuations and then it translates back these valuations to the model resource in order to keep the equivalence between these valuations and the model resource. The result is an automatic visual animation directly showed in the MDE tools that are synchronised with the model resource.

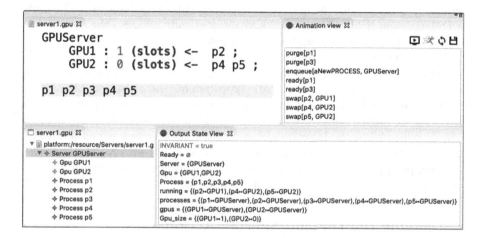

Fig. 8. DSL execution in Meeduse.

Several formal tools provide graphic animation and visualization techniques [11,19,22], which is intended to favour the communication between a formal methods engineer and the domain expert by using domain-specific visualizations. The contribution of Meeduse in comparison with these techniques is that the input model is provided by the domain expert using a dedicated language. Indeed, in tools like BMotion Studio [19], the domain-specific visualizations (textual or graphical) are created by the formal methods engineers who often would like to remedy the poor readability of their own specifications. We believe that visual animation may result in representations that lack of real-user perspective.

Furthermore, in visual animation tools, mapping a given graphical or textual representation to the formal specification is a rather time-consuming task (several days or several weeks as mentioned in [19]) and the creation of custom visualizations is often done when the formal model reaches an advanced stage during the modeling process. This may be counterproductive because the identification of misunderstandings often leads to enhancements of the formal specifications which in turn impacts the implementation of the visualization. In Meeduse, since the naming of the B data, generated from the DSL's static semantics, are not modified, the formal methods engineers do not need at all to manage the visualizations by themselves. The Meeduse approach does not require any manual mapping between the domain-specific representations and the formal specification.

Meeduse presents also an advancement in comparison with existing approaches where DSLs are mixed with formal methods [4,28]. In these works, once the formal model is defined (manually [4] or semi-automatically [28]), they don't offer any way to animate jointly the formal model and the domain model. These techniques start from a DSL definition, produce a formal specification and then they get lost in the formal process. In [28], the authors propose to use classical visual animation by applying BMotion Studio [19] to the formal specifications generated from the DSL. Our approach applies well-known MDE tools for DSL creation (EMF, Xtext, etc.) and automatically manages the equivalence between the formal model and the domain model.

Specifying typing and semantics rules within Xtext in a formal style was investigated by the Xsemantics tool [3]. The tool aims at filling the gap between the theory and the implementation of static type systems and operational semantics for Xtext-based DSLs. However, it does not provide formal tools for proving the correctness of these semantics. The detection of errors is done after they happen while Meeduse keeps the input model in a safe state-space regarding its invariant properties. We believe that the alignment of Meeduse with Xsemantics is an intersting perspective because typing rules as defined by Xsemantics can be seen in our case as invariants that must not be violated.

4   Defining the Domain-Specific Actions

The dynamic semantics of the DSL can be defined as additional B specifications with specific invariants and operations that use the data structures issued from the static semantics. Meeduse offers two strategies to define these specifications: (1) the meta-model based approach that generates presetted utility operations from the meta-model, and (2) the CP-net approach in which the domain-specific actions are first defined using coloured Petri-nets and then translated into B.

4.1   The Meta-model Based Approach

The meta-model based approach generates a list of presetted utility operations: getters, setters, constructors and destructors. Figure 9 gives operations extracted for class Process in order to manage link running with class Gpu.

Operation Process_SetGpu creates a link between a GPU (parameter $aGpu$) with a given process (parameter $aProcess$) if the process is not already linked to the GPU ($\{(aProcess \mapsto aGpu)\} \not\subseteq running$). Process_UnsetGpu is the reverse operation; it removes the link if it already exits.

The utility operations are correct by construction with respect to the invariants produced automatically from the meta-model structure. Indeed, if the structural invariants are not manually modified, the AtelierB prover should be able to

Process_SetGpu(*aProcess, aGpu*) =
   PRE
      aProcess ∈ *Process* ∧ *aGpu* ∈ *Gpu*
      ∧ {(*aProcess* ↦ *aGpu*)} ⊄ *running*
   THEN
      running := ({*aProcess*} ⊲ *running*)
            ∪ {(*aProcess* ↦ *aGpu*)}
   END;

Process_UnsetGpu(*aProcess*) =
   PRE
      aProcess ∈ *Process*
      ∧ *aProcess* ∈ dom(*running*)
   THEN
      running := {*aProcess*} ⊲ *running*
   END;

Fig. 9. Example of basic setters.

prove the correctness of the utility operations regarding these invariants. Otherwise, the operations for which the proof fails must be updated also manually. For our example, the structural invariants were automatically generated and then the resulting utility operations didn't require any manual modification. Meeduse generated a B specification whose length is about 245 lines of code, with 27 utility operations from which the AtelierB prover generated 43 proof obligations and proved them automatically.

The advantage of these utility operations is that they guarantee the preservation of the static semantics. In the following, we will use the inclusion mechanism of the B method in order to apply them for the formal specification of the domain-specific actions (`enqueue`, `purge`, `ready` and `swap`). Figure 10 gives the header part and the invariant clause of the proposed specification.

MACHINE *DynamicSemantics*
INCLUDES *GPUModel*
VARIABLES
   Ready
INVARIANT
   Ready ⊆ *Process* ∧
   dom(*running*) ∩ *Ready* = ∅ ∧
   (∃ *gpu* . (*gpu* ∈ *Gpu* ∧ *Gpu_size*(*gpu*) > 0) ⇒ *Ready* = ∅)

Fig. 10. Machine DynamicSemantics.

As mentioned in the informal description of our simple DSL, there are active, ready and waiting processes. In this specification, states active and waiting are somehow implicit. The domain of relation *running* (**dom**(*running*)) represents active processes. Thus, processes that are not active, are even ready, if they are member of set *Ready* or waiting, otherwise. For space reason, we give only the example of operation `ready` (Fig. 11). This operation selects a waiting process (*pp* ∈ *Process* − (**dom**(*running*) ∪ *Ready*)) and then it decides to activate it (if there exists a free slot) or to change its state to ready (if all GPUs are busy).

The activation of a process calls two utility operations from machine *GPUModel*: Process_SetGPU and GPU_SetSize.

The AtelierB prover generated from machine DynamicSemantics 39 proof obligations; 32 were proved automatically and 7 required the use of the interactive prover. These proofs attest that the domain specific actions, written in B, preserve the invariants of both dynamic and static semantics.

---

ready =
    ANY *pp* **WHERE** *pp* ∈ *Process* - (**dom**(*running*) ∪ *Ready*) **THEN**
      IF ∃ *gpu* . (*gpu* ∈ *Gpu* ∧ *Gpu_size*(*gpu*) > 0) **THEN**
        ANY *gg* **WHERE** *gg* ∈ *Gpu* ∧ *Gpu_size*(*gg*) > 0 **THEN**
          Process_SetGpu(*pp*,*gg*) ;
          Gpu_SetSize(*gg*, *Gpu_size*(*gg*) - 1)
        END
      ELSE
        Ready := *Ready* ∪ {*pp*}
      END
    END ;

Fig. 11. Operation ready.

4.2 The CP-net Approach

Meeduse offers a translation of coloured Petri-net models (CP-nets [18]) into B in order to help build the dynamic semantics using a readable graphical notation. CP-nets combine the strengths of classical Petri-nets (*i.e.* formal semantics) with the strengths of high-level visual languages (*i.e.* communication and readability) [10]. A CP-net model is an executable representation of a system consisting of the states of the system and the events or transitions that cause the system to change its state. Despite of a small basic vocabulary, CP-nets allow great flexibility in modeling a variety of application domains, including communication protocols, data networks, distributed algorithms, embedded systems, etc. All these domains apply their own DSLs and hence the CP-net approach of Meeduse coupled with DSLs, can have a wide range of applications.

The two main notions of CP-nets are: Places and Transitions. Places represent abstractions on data values (called tokens or colours in the CP-net vocabulary). A place is related to a data-type (called colour-set) that can be simple (*i.e.* Integer, Boolean, etc.) or complex (*i.e.* sequences, products, etc.). In Meeduse, colour-sets refer to the possible types provided by the B language. Regarding transitions, they are linked to input and output places. When fired, a transition consumes tokens from its input places and introduces tokens into its output places. In our approach, places represent B variables and transitions are B operations. We identify three kinds of places: existing, new and derived.

- Existing: refer to the B variables extracted from the meta-model (Fig. 5). These places must be assigned to the variables of the B machine.
- New: refer to additional variables that are useful to define the DSL's behaviour, such as the Ready state of processes. For these places the user must provide its type and initial value using the B language.
- Derived: refer to variables whose values are defined from other B data, such as the Active set of processes. Derivation rules are also written in B.

Figure 12 is a screen-shot of the CP-net component of Meeduse. It shows the invariant properties, the definition of free slots and the derivation rules for derived places. The figure also gives the CP-net of operation **ready** together with the corresponding B specification. This operation is designed by means of two CP-net transitions with different guards $[freeSlots \neq \emptyset]$ and $[freeSlots = \emptyset]$. Places Gpu_size and running refer to existing variables and place Ready introduces a new one that is a subset of variable $Process$. This place is initialized to the empty set. Places Waiting and Active are derived with the following rules: Waiting $= Process - (Active \cup Ready)$ and $Active = \mathbf{dom}(running)$. When the

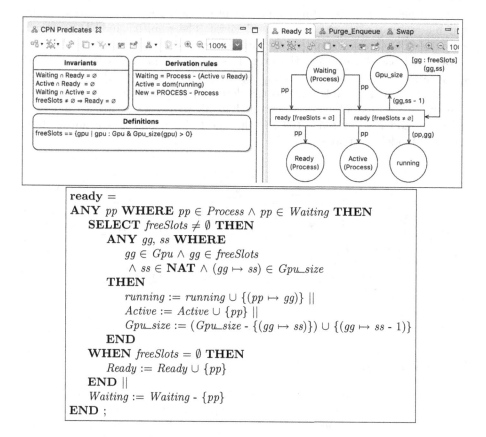

```
ready =
ANY pp WHERE pp ∈ Process ∧ pp ∈ Waiting THEN
    SELECT freeSlots ≠ ∅ THEN
        ANY gg, ss WHERE
            gg ∈ Gpu ∧ gg ∈ freeSlots
            ∧ ss ∈ NAT ∧ (gg ↦ ss) ∈ Gpu_size
        THEN
            running := running ∪ {(pp ↦ gg)} ||
            Active := Active ∪ {pp} ||
            Gpu_size := (Gpu_size - {(gg ↦ ss)}) ∪ {(gg ↦ ss - 1)}
        END
    WHEN freeSlots = ∅ THEN
        Ready := Ready ∪ {pp}
    END ||
    Waiting := Waiting - {pp}
END ;
```

Fig. 12. The CP-net component of Meeduse.

GPU server is busy, transition `ready[freeSlots = ∅]` can be triggered, which consumes a token `pp` from place Waiting and introduces it into place Ready. If there exists a free slot, transition `ready[freeSlots ≠ ∅]` consumes token `pp` but introduces it in place Active. In this case, the transition also looks at a couple of tokens `(gg,ss)` from place Gpu_size such that `gg ∈ freeSlots`. The couple is consumed and replaced by couple `(gg,ss-1)`, and tokens `pp` and `gg` are introduced together in place running. In the B specification, a token t is selected from a place P, whose colour-set is C, using substitution: **ANY** t **WHERE** $t \in C \wedge t \in P \wedge$ *condition* **THEN**. Guards are translated into guards of the **SELECT/WHEN** substitutions. Regarding actions, they represent the consumption and production mechanism of CP-nets using set union and set subtraction.

In the CP-net approach the additional data structures, invariants, definitions and operations are injected in the B specification of the meta-model. The B specification produced by this technique is about 135 lines, for which the AtelierB prover generated 69 proof obligations: 53 were proved automatically and 16 interactively. Figure 13 gives the CP-nets of the other operations: purge, enqueue and swap.

We believe that the CP-net approach provides a good visualization of the dynamic semantics thanks to graphical views. The resulting models are much more accessible for stakeholders who are not trained in the B method than the meta-model based approach. However, this approach produces less concise B specifications (*e.g.* 11 lines for Fig. 11 against 16 lines for Fig. 12) and generates several additional variables due to the derived places that are often required. The number of proof obligations for the dynamic semantics is then greater than the meta-modeling approach (69 POs for the CP-net approach against 39 for the meta-modeling approach).

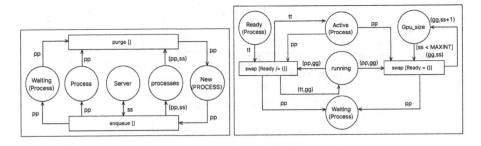

Fig. 13. Enqueue, purge and swap.

5   Evaluation

Two realistic case studies were developed and showed the viability of the tool: (1) a railway DSL for which the CP-net approach was fully exploited [14,15], and (2) a model-to-model transformation that applies the meta-model based approach to transform a given DSL into another one [17].

5.1   A Formal Railway DSL

In contrast with the textual language developed in this paper, this application of Meeduse defines a graphical DSL that can be used by railway experts to design railroad topologies and simulate train behaviours (Fig. 14). This work starts from two main observations: first, in railway control and safety systems the use of formal methods is a strong requirement; and second, graphical representations of domain concepts are omnipresent in railway documents thanks to their ability to share standardized information with common knowledge about several mechanisms (*e.g.* track circuits, signalling rules, etc.). Meeduse showed its strength to mix both aspects in the same tool.

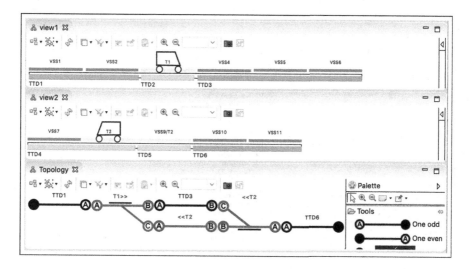

Fig. 14. Application of Meeduse to a railway case study.

We fully applied the CP-net approach to define the dynamic semantics of this DSL and represent train movements, assignment of routes to trains, modifications of switches positions, etc. This application deals with several safety-critical invariants for which theorem proving was applied in order to guarantee an accident-free behavior. The CP-net models were introduced incrementally using three proved refinement levels. The numbers of proofs generated from these refinements are presented in Table 1.

Table 1. Proof obligations generated from the railway DSL

	POs	Automatic	Manual
Level 1	17	11	6
Level 2	32	25	7
Level 3	62	41	21

5.2   A Formal DSL Transformation

We applied Meeduse to define a real-life DSL transformation [17]. Figure 15 shows the input and output models of the transformation: the input model is a truth table and the output model is a binary decision diagram (BDD). This application, carried out during the 12th edition of the transformation tool contest (TTC'19) won the award of best verification and the third audience award. The meta-model based approach was applied to take benefit of the utility operations and define B operations that consume truth table elements and progressively produce a binary decision diagram.

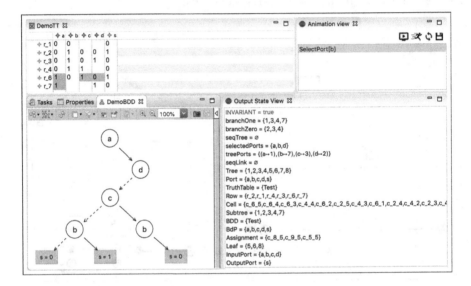

Fig. 15. Application of Meeduse to DSL transformation.

The B machine of the meta-model is about 1162 lines of code. 260 proof obligations were generated and automatically proved by the AtelierB prover, which guarantees that the static features of the output BDD are preserved during the DSL transformation. Regarding the dynamic semantics, they were specified by five B operations that are defined in an additional B machine whose length is about 150 lines of code. The correctness of the dynamic semantics was ensured by model-checking, rather than by theorem proving because on the one hand it is less time consuming, and on the other hand, it deals with bounded state spaces that can be exhaustively checked by the ProB [21] model-checker. The model-checking proof shows that both input and output models are equivalent.

6   Conclusion

When an executable DSL is not formally checked, it may lead to a succession of failures: failures of modeling operations (*e.g.* define a negative value for free slots) may result in failures of domain-specific operations (*e.g.* assign more processes to a GPU than its capacity), which in turn may result in failures of the coordination operations (*e.g.* wrong process scheduling algorithms). This paper gave an overview of Meeduse, a tool dedicated to build and run correct DSLs by formally defining their underlying static and dynamic semantics. It allows to develop DSL tools intended to be used by domain experts whose requirement is to apply domain-specific notations to model critical systems and to correctly simulate their behaviour. In addition to the benefits of the tool for DSL development, the proposed technique is a more pragmatic domain-centric animation than visual animation techniques provided by formal tools because the domain-centric representations are provided by the domain expert himself who has a greater knowledge of the application domain than the formal methods engineer.

Several state-based formal methods can get along with the tool as far as these methods are assisted by publicly available parsers and animators. Some research works have been devoted in the past to apply a formal method, such as MAUD [25] or ASM [9], for the verification of a DSL's semantics. Although these works are close to Meeduse, they don't cover the joint execution of the DSL and the formal model. The transformations they propose can be integrated within Meeduse in order to enhance them with our technique for DSL animation and be able to experiment several target formal languages in a single framework. The use of B is mainly motivated by our long experience with the UML and B mappings and the availability of B4MSecure [13].

Currently we are working on two main perspectives: (1) provide a palette of proved DSLs (such as the BPMN language, or a DSL for home-automation) that are powered by Meeduse in order to make the underlying formal semantics much more accessible to non-practitioners of formal methods, and (2) propose a technique for DSLs composition that favours the execution of several DSLs together and make them collaborate. This perspective would lead to the execution of several instances of ProB with the aim to animate jointly several heterogeneous models.

References

1. Abrial, J.R.: The B-book: Assigning Programs to Meanings. Cambridge University Press, New York (1996)
2. Bettini, L.: Implementing Domain-Specific Languages with Xtext and Xtend, 2nd edn. Packt Publishing, Birmingham (2016)
3. Bettini, L.: Implementing type systems for the IDE with Xsemantics. J. Log. Algebraic Meth. Program. **85**(5, Part 1), 655–680 (2016)
4. Bodeveix, J.-P., Filali, M., Lawall, J., Muller, G.: Formal methods meet domain specific languages. In: Romijn, J., Smith, G., van de Pol, J. (eds.) IFM 2005. LNCS, vol. 3771, pp. 187–206. Springer, Heidelberg (2005). https://doi.org/10.1007/11589976_12
5. Bousse, E., Leroy, D., Combemale, B., Wimmer, M., Baudry, B.: Omniscient debugging for executable DSLs. J. Syst. Softw. **137**, 261–288 (2018)
6. Clearsy: Atelier B. https://www.atelierb.eu/en/

7. Dave, M.A.: Compiler verification: a bibliography. SIGSOFT Softw. Eng. Notes **28**(6), 2 (2003)

8. Dghaym, D., Poppleton, M., Snook, C.: Diagram-led formal modelling using iUML-B for hybrid ERTMS level 3. In: Butler, M., Raschke, A., Hoang, T.S., Reichl, K. (eds.) ABZ 2018. LNCS, vol. 10817, pp. 338–352. Springer, Cham (2018). https://doi.org/10.1007/978-3-319-91271-4_23

9. Gargantini, A., Riccobene, E., Scandurra, P.: Combining formal methods and MDE techniques for model-driven system design and analysis. Adv. Softw. **3**(1&2) (2010)

10. Gehlot, V., Nigro, C.: An introduction to systems modeling and simulation with colored petri nets. In: Proceedings of the 2010 Winter Simulation Conference, WSC 2010, USA, 5–8 December 2010, pp. 104–118 (2010)

11. Hallerstede, S., Leuschel, M., Plagge, D.: Validation of formal models by refinement animation. Sci. Comput. Program. **78**(3), 272–292 (2013)

12. Hartmann, T., Sadilek, D.A.: Undoing operational steps of domain-specific modeling languages. In: Proceedings of the 8th OOPSLA Workshop on Domain-Specific Modeling, DSM 2008, University of Alabama at Birmingham (2008)

13. Idani, A., Ledru, Y.: B for modeling secure information systems. In: Butler, M., Conchon, S., Zaïdi, F. (eds.) ICFEM 2015. LNCS, vol. 9407, pp. 312–318. Springer, Cham (2015). https://doi.org/10.1007/978-3-319-25423-4_20

14. Idani, A., Ledru, Y., Ait Wakrime, A., Ben Ayed, R., Bon, P.: Towards a tool-based domain specific approach for railway systems modeling and validation. In: Collart-Dutilleul, S., Lecomte, T., Romanovsky, A. (eds.) RSSRail 2019. LNCS, vol. 11495, pp. 23–40. Springer, Cham (2019). https://doi.org/10.1007/978-3-030-18744-6_2

15. Idani, A., Ledru, Y., Ait Wakrime, A., Ben Ayed, R., Collart-Dutilleul, S.: Incremental development of a safety critical system combining formal methods and dsmls. In: Larsen, K.G., Willemse, T. (eds.) FMICS 2019. LNCS, vol. 11687, pp. 93–109. Springer, Cham (2019). https://doi.org/10.1007/978-3-030-27008-7_6

16. Idani, A., Ledru, Y., Vega, G.: Alliance of model-driven engineering with a proof-based formal approach. Innov. Syst. Softw. Eng., 1–19 (2020). https://doi.org/10.1007/s11334-020-00366-3

17. Idani, A., Vega, G., Leuschel, M.: Applying formal reasoning to model transformation: the meeduse solution. In: Proceedings of the 12th Transformation Tool Contest, co-located with STAF 2019, Software Technologies: Applications and Foundations. CEUR Workshop Proceedings, vol. 2550, pp. 33–44 (2019)

18. Jensen, K.: Coloured Petri Nets: Basic Concepts, Analysis Methods and Practical Use, vol. 1. Springer, Heidelberg (2010). https://doi.org/10.1007/978-3-662-03241-1

19. Ladenberger, L., Bendisposto, J., Leuschel, M.: Visualising event-b models with b-motion studio. In: Alpuente, M., Cook, B., Joubert, C. (eds.) FMICS 2009. LNCS, vol. 5825, pp. 202–204. Springer, Heidelberg (2009). https://doi.org/10.1007/978-3-642-04570-7_17

20. Leroy, X.: Formal verification of a realistic compiler. Commun. ACM **52**, 107–115 (2009)

21. Leuschel, M., Butler, M.: ProB: an automated analysis toolset for the B method. Softw. Tools Technol. Transf. (STTT) **10**(2), 185–203 (2008)

22. Li, M., Liu, S.: Integrating animation-based inspection into formal design specification construction for reliable software systems. IEEE Trans. Reliab. **65**, 1–19 (2015). https://doi.org/10.1109/TR.2015.2456853

23. Mayerhofer, T., Langer, P., Wimmer, M., Kappel, G.: xMOF: executable DSMLs based on fUML. In: Erwig, M., Paige, R.F., Van Wyk, E. (eds.) SLE 2013. LNCS, vol. 8225, pp. 56–75. Springer, Cham (2013). https://doi.org/10.1007/978-3-319-02654-1_4

24. OMG: OMG Meta Object Facility (MOF) Core Specification, Version 2.4.1 (June 2013). http://www.omg.org/spec/MOF/2.4.1

25. Rivera, J., Durán, F., Vallecillo, A.: Formal specification and analysis of domain specific models using Maude. Simulation **85**, 778–792 (2009)

26. Snook, C., Savicks, V., Butler, M.: Verification of UML models by translation to UML-B. In: Aichernig, B.K., de Boer, F.S., Bonsangue, M.M. (eds.) FMCO 2010. LNCS, vol. 6957, pp. 251–266. Springer, Heidelberg (2011). https://doi.org/10.1007/978-3-642-25271-6_13

27. Steinberg, D., Budinsky, F., Paternostro, M., Merks, E.: EMF: Eclipse Modeling Framework, vol. 2. Addison-Wesley, Boston (2008)

28. Tikhonova, U., Manders, M., van den Brand, M., Andova, S., Verhoeff, T.: Applying model transformation and event-b for specifying an industrial DSL. In: MoDeVVa@ MoDELS, pp. 41–50 (2013)

29. Wachsmuth, G.: Modelling the operational semantics of domain-specific modelling languages. In: Lämmel, R., Visser, J., Saraiva, J. (eds.) GTTSE 2007. LNCS, vol. 5235, pp. 506–520. Springer, Heidelberg (2008). https://doi.org/10.1007/978-3-540-88643-3_16

Chain of Events: Modular Process Models for the Law

Søren Debois[1]([✉]), Hugo A. López[2,4], Tijs Slaats[2], Amine Abbad Andaloussi[3],
and Thomas T. Hildebrandt[2]

[1] Department of Computer Science, IT University of Copenhagen,
København, Denmark
`debois@itu.dk`
[2] Department of Computer Science, Copenhagen University, København, Denmark
`{lopez,slaats,amab,hilde}@di.ku.dk`
[3] Technical University of Denmark, Kgs. Lyngby, Denmark
`amab@dtu.dk`
[4] DCR Solutions A/S, Copenhagen, Denmark

Abstract. In this paper, we take technical and practical steps towards
the modularisation of compliant-by-design executable declarative process models. First, we demonstrate by example how the specific language of timed DCR graphs is capable of modelling complex legisla-
tion, with examples from laws regulating the functioning of local governments in Denmark. We then identify examples of law paragraphs that
are beyond these modelling capabilities. This incompatibility arises from
subtle and—from a computer science perspective—non-standard interactions between distinct paragraphs of the law, which must then become
similar interactions between model fragments. To encompass these situations, we propose a notion of *networks of processes*, where the processes
are allowed to interact and regulate their interaction through the novel
mechanisms of *exclusion* and *linking*. Networks are parametric in the
underlying process formalism, allowing interactions between processes
specified in arbitrary and possibly distinct trace-language semantics formalisms as the individual models. Technically, we provide a sufficient
condition for a good class of network compositions to realise *refinement*
of the constituent processes. Finally, parts of the theoretical framework
(networks and exclusion) have been implemented by our industry partners, and we report on a preliminary evaluation suggesting that inter-
model synchronisation is indeed both necessary and helpful in practical
modelling scenarios.

Keywords: Law · Compliance by design · Process modelling ·
Refinement

T. T. Hildebrandt—work supported by the Innovation Fund Denmark project *EcoKnow*
(7050-00034A), the Danish Council for Independent Research project *Hybrid Business
Process Management Technologies* (DFF-6111-00337), and the European Union's Horizon 2020 research and innovation programme under the Marie Sklodowska-Curie grant
agreement BehAPI No. 778233.

B. Dongol and E. Troubitsyna (Eds.): IFM 2020, LNCS 12546, pp. 368–386, 2020.
https://doi.org/10.1007/978-3-030-63461-2_20

1   Introduction

Casework is often governed by law, e.g., in municipal governments or in the finance sector. In these settings, adherence to the law—legal compliance—is an essential part of "correctness". However, in systems supporting casework, the law is rarely a first-class object, and guarantees of compliance are hard to come by.

This problem is compounded by the practical difficulty that compliance is a property of a *collection* of IT system. A modern European municipal government of even a medium-sized city will have a system landscape rivalling enterprises in complexity and heterogeneity: Disparate systems acquired and updated at disparate schedules over decades. To reason formally about compliance in such a setting, it is not enough to know that any single system is in compliance, we must know that the composite overall system is in compliance.

The law itself is *also* a collection of interacting entities; typically paragraphs or sections. Research into formalisation of law has established as paramount the need for a trustworthy and understandable correspondence between the constructs in the formal notation on the one hand, and the natural language texts that express the rules in the original legal sources on the other [6,14]. Such a correspondence is necessary to ensure that guarantees provided by the formal language will, quite literally, "hold up in court"; but also to allow for updating models when the law inevitably changes. The quest for such correspondences have given rise to the *isomorphism principle* [5,6] (see also discussion in [7]) that formal models of the law must be in one-one correspondence with the structure of that law—e.g., that each paragraph in a law text corresponds uniquely to a model fragment in the formal specification.

This paper studies models for the law with the aim of directly constructing declarative, executable workflow specifications from it. E.g., when the law states that "the parents must consent to a government interview with their child", the executable workflow specification must have activities "consent" and "interview", and we must be able to prove that in the model, the latter is always preceded by the former. We specifically consider the Danish Consolidation Act on Social Services [1], which regulates in minute detail the operations of Danish Municipalities. We formalise fragments of this law in the Timed Dynamic Condition Response graphs (DCR graphs) declarative modelling language [11,18,20], as they are already actively being used to to create executable models of law to for public digital case management systems [25].

We find that while individual paragraphs of the law are straightforward to model, *interactions* between paragraphs are difficult or impossible to model if one is to take the isomorphism principle seriously. To address this shortcoming, we propose the meta-formalism of "Networks" for expressing such interactions via the novel constructs of *linking* and *exclusion*. These constructs allow (a) one-to-many interactions between constraints in the underlying processes and (b) selectively disregarding such constraints in interactions.

The meta-formalism of Networks is *independent* of the exact formalisms used to specify individual process/paragraphs, i.e., it is a hybrid process notation [31]. It is only required that each component notation has a labelled transition system semantics. Thus, it is technically possible for a network to combine processes/paragraphs formalised in disparate notations, e.g., some as DCR, some as DECLARE [3,30], some as finite automata, and some as BPMN [29].

Our key technical result is a sufficient condition for Networks to give rise to *refinement* in the sense of [11,34]. This theorem has been verified in Isabelle/HOL; the formalisation is available online [32]. Lemmas and Theorems etc. that have been so verified are marked out with a filled-in box, like this one: ∎

Parts of the theoretical framework (networks and exclusion) have been implemented by our industry partners, and we report on interviews with practitioners who find the notions of inter-model synchronisation indeed both necessary and helpful in practical modelling scenarios. In summary, we make the following contributions.

1. We demonstrate the use of timed DCR graphs to model excerpts of a real law, showing examples of both sections that can be modelled straightforwardly and those that require interaction.
2. We define a notion of Networks with novel concepts of "exclusion" and "linking" tailored to the complex and unusual requirements that modelling the law under the isomorphism principle poses on compositionality.
3. We show how this notion of compositionality formally gives a syntactic means of achieving refinement in the sense introduced in [11] of models expressed in possibly distinct formalisms.
4. We report on a preliminary qualitative evaluation of an implementation of DCR networks with exclusion as part of the a process engine used to digitalise administrative processes in municipal governments.

Altogether, the present paper takes significant steps, both technical and practical, towards achieving compliant-by-design executable declarative process models of government workflows.

Related Work.   We share motivation with the study of Compliant-by-Design business processes [15]. Here, formal languages expressing laws and regulations is an active line of research, and a variety of approaches exist, e.g., logics [15–17], Petri Nets [24], and declarative process languages [10]. We are unaware of Compliance-by-Design work that include references as language primitives.

The relationship between natural language specifications and (declarative) business processes has been recently studied in the BPM community with works for Declare [2], deontic logics [12] and DCR graphs [26]. While these works apply NLP techniques to identify rules between process activities, they do not consider the inter-dependencies between rules. The exception is [35], that identifies subsumption, redundancy and conflict between rules. The present work takes a different tack, by providing a mechanism to modularise rules.

An approach similar to linking has been proposed for Petri Net variants in [13,22,23]. Here process fragments, modelled as Petri nets, are loosely coupled through event and data dependencies. Our approach is different in that we employ a declarative process language (DCR graphs), we link event executions instead of data, and fragment composition is based on multicast synchronisation. Finally, several works in logic programming have studied modularity and composition (see [8] for an overview). Networks and links resemble union and overriding union operators in modular logic programs.

2 Timed Dynamic Condition Response Graphs

We briefly recall Timed DCR graphs as introduced in [20]. Informally, a DCR graph comprises a set of events E, a *marking* assigning state to each event, and a set of inter-event relations. Together, the two determine (a) whether a given event is *enabled* for execution, (b) how such execution would update the marking; and (c) what events are required to happen within what deadlines.

Time is advanced in discrete steps called "ticks", and time spans are measured in integral numbers of such ticks. Deadlines in a timed DCR graph is measured in how many ticks may elapse before some event must happen; when that number is 0, time cannot advance any further without either executing the event or violating the semantics of the DCR graph.

Intuitively, the marking indicates for each event e when (if ever) it was last executed; when (if ever) it must eventually be executed or excluded—its deadline—; and whether the event is currently included or excluded. Excluded events cannot be executed, and are disregarded as obstacles to other events executing.

Similarly, the relations govern enabledness and marking update: A *timed condition* $(e, k, e') \in \;\rightarrow\bullet$ means that event e' can only execute if event e is excluded or it was previously executed and that the last execution was at least k time units ago. A *timed response* $(e, k, e') \in \;\bullet\rightarrow$ means that whenever event e executes, it imposes the requirement on e' to either become and stay excluded, or to execute within at most k time units. A *milestone* $(e, e') \in \;\rightarrow\diamond$ means that event e' can only execute if event e is not currently required to be executed or excluded. An *exclusion* (resp. *inclusion*) relation $(e, f) \in \;\rightarrow\%$ resp. $(e, f) \in \;\rightarrow+$ toggles the inclusion state of f to false resp. true whenever e is executed.

All in all, the meaning of a DCR graph is the set of sequences of event executions and time increments it is willing to allow.

We give a brief formal account of timed DCR graphs below; however, the reader who either knows DCR graphs already, or is satisfied to learn by example is invited to skip ahead to the next Section.

Notation. Let ω be the set of finite natural numbers and zero. Let ∞ be the set $\omega \cup \{\omega\}$, where we refer to ω as infinity. We write $X \rightharpoonup Y$ for a partial function from X to Y. When $f : X \rightarrow Y$ is a (possibly partial) function, we write $f[x \mapsto y]$ for the function $f' : X \rightarrow Y$ identical to f except $f'(x) = y$. Finally, for a binary relation R, take $e\, R = \{f | (e, f) \in R\}$ and vice versa.

Definition 1. *A timed DCR Graph G is given by a tuple* $(E, M, \rightarrow\bullet, \bullet\rightarrow, \rightarrow\diamond$ $, \rightarrow+, \rightarrow\%, L, l)$ *where*

1. E is a finite set of events
2. $M \in (E \rightharpoonup \omega) \times (E \rightharpoonup \infty) \times \mathcal{P}(E)$ is the timed marking
3. $\rightarrow\bullet \subseteq E \times \omega \times E$, is the timed condition relation
4. $\bullet\rightarrow \subseteq E \times \infty \times E$, is the timed response relation
5. $\rightarrow\diamond, \rightarrow+, \rightarrow\% \subseteq E \times E$ are the milestone, include and exclude relations
6. L is the set of labels
7. $l : E \rightarrow L$ is a labelling function, which assigns to each event e a label $l(e)$.

We write the components of a marking M as $M = (t_{ex}, t_{re}, In)$. The minimal included response deadline $minr_G$ is defined by $minr_G = min\{t_{re}(e) \mid t_{re}(e) \in \omega \wedge e \in In\}$.

The marking defines for each event e an integer $k = t_{ex}(r)$ indicating how long ago it was executed or $\bot = t_{ex}(r)$ if not; a deadline $t_{re}(r)$ for the event to be executed or $\bot$; and a boolean In indicating whether the event is "included".

Definition 2. *Let G be a timed DCR graph. We say that the event e is enabled, writing* enabled(M, e) *iff*

1. $e \in In$
2. $\forall e' \in In . (e', k, e) \in \rightarrow\bullet \implies t_{ex}(e') \neq \bot \wedge k \leq t_{ex}(e')$
3. $\forall e' \in In . e' \rightarrow\diamond e \implies t_{re}(e') = \bot$

We say that the time-step n is enabled, writing enabled(M, n) *when $minr_G \geq n$.*

That is, for e to be enabled, (1) it must be included; (2) whenever it is conditional upon an included event e' with delay k, then this e' was executed at least k time steps ago; and (3) every included milestone e' for e is not pending. A time-step n is enabled iff no included event has a deadline closer than n time units.

Definition 3. *Let G be a timed DCR graph. The effect of executing an enabled event e in $M = (t_{ex}, t_{re}, In)$ is a new marking given by:*

$$\text{effect}_G(M, e) = (t_{ex}[e \mapsto 0], \ t'_{re}, \ In \setminus (e \rightarrow\%) \cup (e \rightarrow+))$$

where $t'_{re}(f) = min\{k \mid (e, k, f) \in \bullet\rightarrow\}$ when $(e, k, f) \in \bullet\rightarrow$ and $t'_{re}(f) = t_{re}[e \mapsto 0](f)$ otherwise. Similarly, the result of advancing time by n time-units is the new marking given by:

$$\text{effect}_G(M, n) = ((+n) \circ t_{ex}, (-n) \circ t_{re}, In)$$

where $(+n)$ respectively $(-n)$ denote the function $\omega_\bot \rightarrow \omega_\bot$ which preserve $\bot$ and otherwise takes k to $k + n$ respectively $max(k - n, 0)$.

That is, executing e updates the marking by (i) setting the last-executed time $t_{ex}(e)$ of e to 0 (now); (ii) clearing any existing deadline of e, then setting new deadlines for events with responses from e; and (iii) making not-included all events excluded by e, then making included all events included by e. Similarly, when the time-step n is enabled, we "advance time" by adding n to all executed time-stamps, and subtracting n from all deadlines. (An equivalent variation of this semantics make Timed DCR Graphs finite, see [20] for details.)

Definition 4 (Labelled transition system). *An event or time step $\alpha \in E \cup \mathbb{N}$ has a transition $M \xrightarrow{\alpha} M'$ iff enabled(M, α) and effect$_G(M, \alpha) = M'$. A run of a graph G is a finite or infinite sequence of transitions*

$$G_0 \xrightarrow{\alpha_1} G_1 \xrightarrow{\alpha_2} G_2 \xrightarrow{\alpha_3} \cdots$$

We write runs(G) *for the set of all possible runs for a graph G. An accepting run is a run such that for all $i \leq k$ and all $e \in E$, if $t_{re}^i(e) \in \omega$ and $e \in In^i$, then there exists $j > i$ s.t. either $e \notin In^j$ or $\alpha_i = e$ Finally, a trace is a finite or infinite sequence $\lambda_1 \lambda_2 \ldots$ of labels and natural numbers, such that there exists and accepting run $G_0 \xrightarrow{\alpha_1} G_1 \xrightarrow{\alpha_2} \cdots$ where $\lambda_i = l(\alpha_i)$ or $\lambda_i = \alpha_i = n \in \mathbb{N}$*

Note that in this definition, a trace is a run where events have been replaced with their labels, but time advances (natural numbers) have been left in. The indirection of labels is a source of expressive power; see [11] for details.

We write DCR graphs as $[M]\ R$, where M is the marking and R is a list of relations separated by vertical bars. E.g.:

$$[\mathsf{A} : (7, \mathsf{t}, \bot), \mathsf{B} : (\bot, \mathsf{t}, 3)]\ \mathsf{A} \rightarrow\!\!\bullet\ \mathsf{B}\ |\ \mathsf{A} \bullet\!\xrightarrow{10}\ \mathsf{B}$$

Here, the marking $\mathsf{A} : (7, \mathsf{t}, \bot)$ that A was executed 7 time-steps ago, it is currently included (t), and there is no deadline for it ($\bot$). Conversely, in $\mathsf{B} : (\bot, \mathsf{t}, 3)$, we see that B was not executed, but does have a deadline of 3. Formally, the marking $\mathsf{A} : (7, \mathsf{t}, \bot)$ should be read as $t_{ex}(\mathsf{A}) = 7$, $\mathsf{A} \in \mathsf{In}$ is true, and $t_{re}(\mathsf{A}) = \bot$.

While [20] did not allow multiple distinct deadlines between the same two events, the present notion of DCR graphs relaxes this limitation by preferring the minimum of multiple deadlines. This is to ensure that the above calculus-like notation is always well-defined, i.e., that one can freely write terms such as $\mathsf{A} \bullet\!\xrightarrow{5}\ \mathsf{B}\ |\ \mathsf{A} \bullet\!\xrightarrow{10}\ \mathsf{B}$.

3   Models of Law

We now provide examples of modelling law fragments as DCR graphs. We shall see how DCR graphs neatly model individual sections of a real-world law. In Sect. 4, we re-use these models when considering references between sections.

As a real-world example, we shall consider fragments of the Danish Consolidation Act for Social Services [33] (CASS). Municipalities in Denmark have processed an average of 9.337,33 CASS cases in the last 3 years. Revising the outcome of these cases is standard procedure: In the first semester of 2018, 887 cases (9,5% of the total cases) were revised, and the outcome of 483 cases (5,1% of the total cases) was changed [27, 28].

3.1   A Condition: CASS §63(1)

This paragraph describes the situations in which a municipal government must intervene to provide medical attention for a child:

> CASS §63(1): *"If the custodial parent fails to have a child or young person examined or treated for a life-threatening disease or a disease involving the risk of substantial and permanent impairment of function, the children and young persons committee may decide to undertake such examination or treatment."*

To model this paragraph as a DCR graph, or in any event-based formalism, we have to understand from this description what are the *events* of the graph. The custodial parent "fail[ing] to have a child or young person examined or treated" is not an event happening at a particular moment in time but rather a continuous state of affairs. The key to modelling this situation is to recognise that the event is not the failure itself, but rather the *formal recognition* by the municipal government that this failure is indeed happening. That decision *is* an event: It happens at a specific moment in time where a document declaring such recognition is signed.

With that in mind, we find in 63(1) the events (that the municipal government formally recognises) a *"failure to undertake examination or treatment"* and *"compulsory examination or treatment"*. How are these events related? The phrasing of the paragraph indicates that only if there is such failure may the government step in: in process terms, the failure is a condition for the compulsory examination or treatment. On the other hand, the phrasing does not *require* the government to act. Altogether, we arrive at the following DCR graph:

$$P_{63(1)} \stackrel{\text{def}}{=} [\text{failure}_{63(1)} : (\bot, \text{t}, \bot), \text{exam}_{63(1)} : (\bot, \text{t}, \bot)] \; \text{failure}_{63(1)} \rightarrow\!\bullet \; \text{exam}_{63(1)}$$

In this graph, both events are marked as not executed ($\bot$), included (t) and not pending ($\bot$). The graph has a single condition constraint $\text{failure}_{63(1)} \rightarrow\!\bullet$ $\text{exam}_{63(1)}$, indicating that the event $\text{exam}_{63(1)}$ can execute only if $\text{failure}_{63(1)}$ has previously executed. In this section, we shall not distinguish between an event and its label, formally taking $\ell(\text{failure}_{63(1)}) = \text{failure}_{63(1)}$ and $\ell(\text{exam}_{63(1)}) = \text{exam}_{63(1)}$.

Here, subscripts such as "63(1)" are simply part of the events name and do not have any special significance. They will become helpful in the next section, when we need to distinguish between near-identical events in distinct paragraphs/graphs.

Considering the possible runs of $P_{63(1)}$, we find among others the following:

$$\langle \text{failure}_{63(1)}, \text{exam}_{63(1)} \rangle \tag{1}$$

On the other hand the singleton $\text{exam}_{63(1)}$ is not a run: The condition prohibits execution $\text{exam}_{63(1)}$ without first executing $\text{failure}_{63(1)}$.

3.2   Static Obligations and Inclusion State: CASS §50(3)

This paragraph describes how, during a so-called Child Protection Examination (CPE), the child being considered for protection must in fact be heard.

> CASS §50(3): *"The examination shall include a consultation with the child or young person. The consultation may be dispensed with if factors such as the maturity of the child or young person or the nature of the case strongly suggests that the decision should be made without prior consultation. If the consultation cannot be conducted, steps shall be taken to establish the views of the child or young person. [...]"*

Again we identify events: a "consultation with the child or young person" ($\mathsf{consult}_{50(3)}$); the declaration that "the consultation may be dispensed with" ($\mathsf{omit}_{50(3)}$); and the (formal documentation of) "the views of the young person or child", established by some other means than consultation ($\mathsf{views}_{50(3)}$).

The text describes a usual course of action of consulting the child, and an alternative for special cases (marked as *"steps shall be taken"*). These situations are usually modelled with an event indicating the declaration of special circumstances, which then excludes the common case and includes the special case:

$$P_{50(3)} \stackrel{\text{def}}{=} [\mathsf{consult}_{50(3)} : (\bot, \mathsf{t}, \omega), \ \mathsf{omit}_{50(3)} : (\bot, \mathsf{t}, \bot), \ \mathsf{views}_{50(3)} : (\bot, \mathsf{f}, \omega)]$$
$$\mathsf{omit}_{50(3)} \rightarrow \% \ \mathsf{consult}_{50(3)} \mid \mathsf{omit}_{50(3)} \rightarrow + \ \mathsf{views}_{50(3)}$$

In $P_{50(3)}$, the marking (line 1) says that $\mathsf{consult}_{50(3)}$ and $\mathsf{views}_{50(3)}$ are initially required to happen eventually (ω). Event $\mathsf{views}_{50(3)}$ is initially not included. While not included it cannot be executed, so the requirement to eventually happen in the marking does not count. The relations (line 2) say that if event $\mathsf{omit}_{50(3)}$ happens, then (left) $\mathsf{consult}_{50(3)}$ is excluded and (right) $\mathsf{views}_{50(3)}$ is included, reversing that state of affairs: While both still technically pending, it is now $\mathsf{consult}_{50(3)}$ which is not included and considered irrelevant, whereas $\mathsf{views}_{50(3)}$ is included and relevant, and thus required to eventually happen.

3.3   Time and Obligations: CASS §50(7)

Part of the requirements for the CPE process described in CASS §50 describes how quickly the municipal government should react to reports (typically from medical staff or school staff) that a child may be in need of special support:

> CASS §50(7): *"The examination must be completed within four (4) months after the municipal council has become aware that a child or young person may be in need of special support. Where, exceptionally, an examination cannot be completed within 4 months, the municipal council shall prepare a provisional assessment and complete the examination as soon as possible thereafter. "*

We find three events in this text: "the municipal council has become aware that a child or young person may be in need of special support" ($\mathsf{report}_{50(7)}$), the completion of the examination (line 1, $\mathsf{compl}_{50(7)}$), and the preparation of a provisional assessment (line 4–5, $\mathsf{prov}_{50(7)}$).

We model this paragraph as a graph with relations enforcing the obligation to either complete the examination, or produce a provisional assessment within 4 months from report's reception.

$$P_{50(7)} \stackrel{\text{def}}{=} [\mathsf{report}_{50(7)} : (\bot, \mathsf{t}, \bot), \mathsf{compl}_{50(7)} : (\bot, \mathsf{t}, \bot), \mathsf{prov}_{50(7)} : (\bot, \mathsf{t}, \bot)]$$

$$\mathsf{report}_{50(7)} \bullet \xrightarrow{\omega} \mathsf{compl}_{50(7)} \mid \mathsf{report}_{50(7)} \rightarrow\bullet \mathsf{prov}_{50(7)}$$

$$\mid \mathsf{report}_{50(7)} \bullet \xrightarrow{4m} \mathsf{prov}_{50(7)} \mid \mathsf{compl}_{50(7)} \rightarrow\% \mathsf{prov}_{50(7)}$$

That is, if a report is received ($\mathsf{report}_{50(7)}$ is executed), the examination must eventually (ω) be concluded. To model the special case of provisional assessments, we combine deadlines and exclusion: we require that a provisional assessment ($\mathsf{prov}_{50(7)}$) is produced within 4 months after receiving the report, but remove that requirement using an exclusion once the actual examination completes ($\mathsf{compl}_{50(7)}$).

4 Modelling References

We now take legal texts whose specifications introduce referential information.

> CASS §48(1): *"Before the municipal council makes a decision under sections 51, 52, 52a, 56, 57a, 57b, 58, 62 and 63, section 65(2) and (3) and sections 68–71 and 75, the child or young person must be consulted on these matters. The consultation may be dispensed with if the child or young person was consulted immediately beforehand in connection with the performance of a child protection examination, cf. section 50 below. [...]"*

The article continues by describing the circumstances for a consultation to be omitted, under which a guardian must be present etc. We will ignore these details for brevity, and focus on the formal relations between paragraph instead.

There are several such references. First, §48(1) requires a consultation before "making a decision" under a range of other paragraphs, including §63 (see Sect. 3.1). Recall that §63(1) tasked the municipal government with undertaking medical examination or treatment for young persons if their custodian failed to do so. For §63, the "decision" referred to in §48(1) refers to the municipal government deciding to (unilaterally) undertake such exams or treatments, that is, executing the event $\mathsf{exam}_{63(1)}$.

Second, §48(1) explicitly states that if a child consultation was made under §50, the consultation otherwise required by §48(1) is not necessary. According to domain specialists, in the situation where both §48 and §50 takes effect, the various consultations required are all considered "the same".

These two kinds of references begets the question: How do we model such references in DCR graphs? We shall see in this section that the latter kind can be considered simply a renaming (since the activities are literally considered "the same"); however, the former kind requires special treatment.

For starters, let us ignore exactly how §48 will be connected to other paragraphs and make a straightforward model of the requirement that before making (certain) decisions about a child, that child must be consulted. In this case, it is straightforward to identify in §48(1) the events "make a decision" ($\mathsf{decide}_{48(1)}$) and "consult the child" ($\mathsf{consult}_{48(1)}$). Notice how $\mathsf{consult}_{48(1)}$ is not the same as the $\mathsf{consult}_{50(3)}$ in $P_{50(3)}$—this is where the subscripts become helpful. In this case, the model simply contains a condition, stipulating the requirement that the consultation must come before the decision:

$$P_{48(1)} \overset{\text{def}}{=}$$
$$[\mathsf{consult}_{48(1)} : (\bot, \mathsf{t}, \bot), \mathsf{decide}_{48(1)} : (\bot, \mathsf{t}, \bot)]\mathsf{consult}_{48(1)} \rightarrow\bullet \mathsf{decide}_{48(1)} \quad (2)$$

It is tempting to think that we can model this reference by simply *identifying* the event $\mathsf{decide}_{48(1)}$ in $P_{48(1)}$ with event $\mathsf{exam}_{63(1)}$ in $P_{63(1)}$. However, this will not be sufficient, as the decision in §48(1) must *also* be identified with other decisions in the other paragraphs listed (51, 52, 52a and so forth). By transitivity, we would identify them all, but that is non-sensical: the decision to remove a child from the home in §58 is obviously not identical the decision to conduct a medical examination in §63(1). *Those two things are not at all the same.*

However, if proceedings are underway for the same child for *both* of §58 and §63(1) simultaneously, then the consultation mentioned in §48(1) applies for both of them. That means that there should be only *one* such consultation, simultaneously catering to *all* the relevant proceedings.

Altogether, we find that we cannot identify all decisions mentioned in §48(1), however, we must identify the consultations for those decisions in order to maintain a strict correspondence with the law; in order to uphold the isomorphism principle [5,6]. In DCR terms, we have a set of events in distinct graphs (the decisions), each of which is conditional on the same precondition, specified in a distinct other graph. To capture this idea, we introduce *networks*.

4.1   Networks

Networks formalise a notion of "synchronising process models". While we intend to use them with DCR graphs as the underlying process model—and this is how our industry partner is using them—they are intrinsically formalism agnostic: Any formalism with trace-based semantics can be used as the basic processes, and there is no requirement that all underlying processes are specified in the same formalism.

We abstract the underlying formalism into the following notion of a *process notation*. Assume a fixed universe $\mathcal{U}$ of actions.

Definition 5. *A* process notation *$A = (\mathcal{P}, \mathsf{excluded}, \mathsf{step})$ comprises a set $\mathcal{P}$ of process models; a function $\mathsf{excluded} : \mathcal{P} \rightarrow 2^{\mathcal{U}}$, and a function $\mathsf{alph} : \mathcal{P} \rightarrow 2^{\mathcal{U}}$; and a transition predicate $\mathsf{step} : \mathcal{P} \times \mathcal{U} \times \mathcal{P}$. We require that $(P, l, Q) \in \mathsf{step}$ implies*

$R, S ::=$	P	process notation	$\mid$	$l \triangleright l_1, \cdots, l_n. R$ link
	$\mid R \parallel S$	network parallel	$\mid$	0 unit

$\beta ::= l \mid \triangleright \beta$ (regular/limited) action

Fig. 1. Syntax of Networks

both $l \in \mathsf{alph}(P)$ and $\mathsf{alph}(P) = \mathsf{alph}(Q)$, and if also (P, l, Q') then $Q = Q'$, that is, step is action-deterministic.

Intuitively, alph gives a finite bound on the actions a process may exhibit, and we require this bound to be preserved by step-transitions. Similarly, $\mathsf{excluded}$ tells us which actions are excluded in a given process; this set is allowed to change as the process evolves.

DCR graphs with injective labelling is a process notation; in this notation "actions" are DCR trace labels.

Lemma 6. Take $\mathcal{P}$ to be the set of timed DCR graphs with labels in $\mathcal{U}$ and injective labelling functions. Let $\mathsf{excluded}$ be the function which given a timed DCR graph G with events E, marking M, and labelling l returns the set of labels of events of E that are not in In, that is, $\mathsf{excluded}\, G = \{l(e) \mid e \in E \setminus In\}$. Finally take $(G, l, G') \in \mathsf{step}$ iff there exists some event $e \in E$ s.t. $\ell(e) = l$ and $G \xrightarrow{e} G'$. Then $(\mathcal{P}, \mathsf{excluded}, \mathsf{step})$ is a process notation.

Note that because of the assumption that the labelling functions are injective, (1) the step predicate is action deterministic, and (2) it is not possible have distinct events e, f where $\ell(e) = \ell(f)$ yet $e \in In$ but $f \notin In$. That is, if $l \in \mathsf{excluded}\, G$, then the graph G has exactly one event labelled l, and that event is excluded.

Network themselves are vaguely reminiscent of CSP [21], and are similar to the notion of networks for DCR graphs of [19]. However, they differ radically from both with the introduction of limited actions, exclusion, and links.

The key features of Networks is synchronisation on limited and unlimited actions. Intuitively, an unlimited action is a "real" action, exhibited by an underlying process. Conversely, a limited action indicates that while the network does not wish to independently execute that action, it is willing to follow along if someone else does. Limited actions allow a network to deny actions to other networks, by refusing to engage in them.

We use this mechanism to formalise a notion of linking, where a single label exhibited by one process is considered a required synchronisation partner for *multiple distinct* actions in other processes, but will not independently exhibit that action. This construct will be helpful in modelling paragraphs of the law like §48(1), which imposes constraints on multiple other paragraphs.

Notation. Network actions are formed by tagging an underlying action $l \in \mathcal{U}$ as either "limited" or "unlimited". We write limited actions $\triangleright l$ and unlimited

$$\text{alph}(N) = \begin{cases} \emptyset & \text{if } N = 0 \\ \text{alph}(P) & \text{if } N = P \\ \{l_1, \ldots, l_n\} \cup (\text{alph}(M) \backslash \{l\}) & \text{if } N = l \triangleright l_1, \ldots, l_n. \, M \\ \text{alph}(N_1) \cup \text{alph}(N_2) & \text{if } N = N_1 \parallel N_2 \end{cases}$$

$$\text{actions}(N) = \text{alph}(N) \cup \{\triangleright x \mid x \in \text{alph}(N)\}$$

Fig. 2. Alphabet and labels of a DCR network

$$\frac{(P, l, Q) \in \text{step}}{P \xrightarrow{l} Q} \ [\text{N-PROC}] \qquad \frac{l \in \text{excluded } P}{P \xrightarrow{\triangleright l} P} \ [\text{N-EXCL}]$$

$$\frac{R \xrightarrow{\beta} S \quad \gamma(\beta) = l \quad 1 \le i \le n}{l \triangleright l_1, \ldots, l_n. \, R \xrightarrow{\triangleright l_i} l \triangleright l_1, \ldots, l_n. \, S} \ [\text{N-LINK}]$$

$$\frac{R \xrightarrow{\beta} S \quad \gamma(\beta) \notin \{l, l_1, \ldots, l_n\}}{l \triangleright l_1, \cdots, l_n. \, R \xrightarrow{\beta} l \triangleright l_1, \ldots, l_n. \, S} \ [\text{N-PASSTHRU}]$$

$$\frac{R_1 \xrightarrow{\beta} R_2 \quad S_1 \xrightarrow{\beta'} S_2 \quad \gamma(\beta) = \gamma(\beta')}{R_1 \parallel S_1 \xrightarrow{\beta \sqcup \beta'} R_2 \parallel S_2} \ [\text{N-SYNC}] \qquad \frac{R_1 \xrightarrow{\beta} R_2 \quad \gamma(\beta) \notin \text{alph}(S)}{R_1 \parallel S \xrightarrow{\beta} R_2 \parallel S} \ [\text{N-PAR}]$$

Fig. 3. Transition semantics of networks (symmetric rule for [N-PAR] is elided.)

ones simply l. For either, we define the function γ to extract the underlying process action, $\gamma(l) = \gamma(\triangleright l) = l$. For two network actions β_1, β_2 with the same underlying action $\gamma(\beta_1) = \gamma(\beta_2) = l$ we define their combination $\triangleright l \sqcup \triangleright l = \triangleright l$, $\triangleright l \sqcup l = l$, $l \sqcup \triangleright l = l$, and $l \sqcup l = l$—that is, the unlimited action "wins".

The syntax of *Networks* is defined in Fig. 1. A network R is a collection of possibly linked processes. We present the semantics Networks in Fig. 3. The definition uses the auxiliary notion of the *alphabet* of a network, the set of labels it syntactically mentions, and its *actions*, which is just its alphabet lifted to both unlimited and limited actions. We give these auxiliary definitions in Fig. 2.

We briefly explain the rules of Fig. 3. In [N-PROC] we see that the network which is just a single process in some notation exhibits the actions of that process. In [N-EXCL] we see that this network *also* may exhibit a limited network action for an otherwise excluded underlying process action. Then, a network $l \triangleright l_1, \cdots, l_n. \, R$ has two ways to fire a transition: In [N-LINK], we assume that the underlying network R fires an action l. The linked network then fires, instead of l, any of the actions l_i. However, this linked action is limited, as indicated by the triangle. In [N-PASSTHRU], we assume instead that the action l' has nothing in common with neither l nor the linked actions $l_1, \ldots, l_n$; in this case, the linked network exhibits also the (unlimited) action l'. Finally, the synchronisation rule for parallel composition of networks $R_1 \parallel R_2$ is given in [N-SYNC] and [N-PAR]. In [N-SYNC], we require either both sides to exhibit an action, and the underlying process action of either to be the same. This allows a limited and unlimited action to synchronise, with the composite process exhibiting the "least limited" of the two actions. In [N-PAR], we allow the composite process to exhibit a network action when either does, provided the underlying process action does not occur syntactically in the other.

Definition 7 (Network LTS). *A Network R defines an LTS where states are networks, and there is a transition (R, l, R') whenever $R \xrightarrow{l} R'$. A run of R is a sequence*

$$R = R_1 \xrightarrow{\beta_1} R_2 \xrightarrow{\beta_2} \cdots R_{k-1} \xrightarrow{\beta_{k-1}} R_k$$

A trace trace(r) *of a run r is the sequence $\beta_1, \ldots, \beta_k$ of actions of the run. The language of the network R is defined as the set traces of those of its runs that are everywhere unlimited (where no $\beta_i = \triangleright l$ for any l), that is,*

$$\mathsf{lang}(R) = \{ \mathsf{trace}(r) \mid r \text{ is an unlimited run of } R \} .$$

Note that we do not accept limited actions in traces: limited actions cannot happen independently, but require a corroborating un-limited action.

4.2   Modelling with Networks

Using Networks underpinned by timed DCR graphs, we can return to the question how to model inter-paragraph references using the models in Sect. 3. Note the subtle difference that in that Sect. 3 we were considering runs, whereas now we are considering traces. The difference is imperceptible since the models of Sect. 3 all had every event labelled by itself, that is $\ell(e) = e$. For this reason, we allow ourselves in this section to treat "labels" and "events" interchangeably, and we will speak only of events.

For modelling §48(1), we simply *link* the decide$_{48(1)}$ event with the relevant events from other paragraphs:

$$R \stackrel{\text{def}}{=} P_{63(1)} \parallel \mathsf{decide}_{48(1)} \triangleright \mathsf{exam}_{63(1)}. P_{48(1)} \tag{3}$$

This R *does not* admit the trace $\langle \mathsf{failure}_{63(1)}, \mathsf{exam}_{63(1)} \rangle$ even though we saw in (1) that $P_{63(1)}$ does. In R, even if $P_{63(1)}$ allows the action exam$_{63(1)}$, for the entirety of R to also allow that action, the right-hand side decide$_{48(1)}$ $\triangleright$ exam$_{63(1)}$. $P_{48(1)}$ must synchronise via either the [N-SYNC] or [N-PAR] rule. Since both sides of the parallel has exam$_{63(1)}$ in their alphabet, only [N-SYNC] applies. This means that if the parallel were to have the action exam$_{63(1)}$, also the right-hand side link would have either of the actions exam$_{63(1)}$ or $\triangleright$exam$_{63(1)}$. Looking at the link rules [N-LINK] and [N-PASSTHRU], we see that the right-side can exhibit exam$_{63(1)}$ iff $P_{48(1)}$ can exhibit exam$_{63(1)}$, but this is *not* possible because of the condition from consult$_{50(3)}$ to decide$_{48(1)}$ in that graph, see (2).

On the other hand, the network R *does* have the trace

$$\langle \mathsf{failure}_{63(1)}, \mathsf{consult}_{48(1)}, \mathsf{exam}_{63(1)} \rangle .$$

We mentioned briefly above §58 which under extreme circumstances allows the government to remove a child from the home. Assuming a process P_{58}, with the event remove$_{58}$ signifying the decision to undertake such removal. We can then build the network where a child is both subject to proceedings §63 and §58.

$$R_2 \stackrel{\text{def}}{=} P_{63(1)} \parallel P_{58} \parallel \text{decide}_{48(1)} \triangleright \text{exam}_{63(1)}, \text{remove}_{58}. \, P_{48(1)} \qquad (4)$$

Again, this model would not admit any trace where exam$_{63(1)}$ or remove$_{58}$ happened without a prior consult$_{48(1)}$. It would admit various interleavings of the §63 and §58 proceedings and the §48(1) requirements.

The dependency on §50(3). Returning to §50(3), we recall that §48 allowed use of a §50(3) consultation to replace its own, and that practitioners consider both events "the same". This has an obvious model: the one where we simply rename events so that those two identical consultations are identical. This is represented via the syntactical substitution for a free name, here written $P\{e/f\}$:

$$R_3 \stackrel{\text{def}}{=} P_{63(1)} \parallel P_{58} \parallel P_{50(3)} \parallel$$
$$\text{decide}_{48(1)} \triangleright \text{exam}_{63(1)}, \text{remove}_{58}. \, \big(P_{48(1)}\{\text{consult}_{50(3)}/\text{consult}_{48(1)}\}\big) \quad (5)$$

It is irrelevant whether the renaming happens inside or outside the link construct.

5   A Theory of Links and Refinement

We now relate the networks to the notion of refinement originally introduced for DCR graphs [11] and later generalised to arbitrary process models with trace semantics [34]. Under the right circumstances, networks provide a syntactic mechanism for establishing refinements, thus providing a useful approximation for what in DCR graphs is a computationally hard problem.

Notation. Given a sequence s, we define the projection onto a set X as $s|_X$ as simply the (possibly non-contiguous) sub-sequence of s for which each element is in X. We lift this notion to sets of sequences pointwise.

Definition 8 (Network Refinement). *Let R, S be DCR networks. We say that R is a refinement of S iff* $\text{lang}(R)|_{\text{alph}(S)} \subseteq \text{lang}(S)$. ∎

To establish refinement, we confine the set of actions that may become limited.

Definition 9. *Let N be a network and $X \subseteq \mathcal{U}$ a finite set of labels. We call X unlimited for N iff for all β with $\gamma(\beta) \in X$ and $N \xrightarrow{\beta} N'$ for some N' then β is unlimited. X is globally unlimited for N if X is unlimited for every M reachable from N.* ∎

Lemma 10. *Let $P \in \mathcal{P}$ be a process, and let N be the network consisting exactly of P. Then X is unlimited for N iff in every P' reachable (under the process notation step-relation) from P, x is not excluded for all $x \in X$.* ∎

We shall see in Lemma 11 below how an unlimited set for a network ensures the existence of an unlimited sub-trace on one side of a parallel composition of networks. The proof relies on action-determinacy of networks, which in turn necessitates that requirement of Definition 5. We conjecture that this requirement of action-determinacy is can be dispensed with at the cost of a somewhat more complicated proof development.

Lemma 11. *Let R_0, S_0 be networks and let $X \subseteq \mathcal{U}$ be a set of labels. Suppose that X is globally unlimited for R_0 and that $\mathsf{alph}(R_0) \cap \mathsf{alph}(S_0) \subseteq X$. Let r be a run of $R_0 \parallel S_0$:*

$$R_0 \parallel S_0 \xrightarrow{\beta_1} R_1 \parallel S_1 \xrightarrow{\beta_2} \cdots \xrightarrow{\beta_{k-1}} R_{k-1} \parallel S_{k-1} \xrightarrow{\beta_k} R_k \parallel S_k \qquad (6)$$

Consider the sequence $(\beta_i, R_{i+1})_{1 \le i < k}$ and take $i_1, \dots, i_m$ to be the indices identifying a maximal subsequence of this sequence such that $\beta_{i_j} \in X$. Then this subsequence identifies a run r^1 of R_0:

$$R_0 = R_{i_1} \xrightarrow{\beta_{i_1}} R_{i_2} \xrightarrow{\beta_{i_2}} \cdots R_{i_{k'-1}} \xrightarrow{\beta_{i_{k'-1}}} R_{k'} \qquad (7)$$

Moreover, $\mathsf{trace}(r^1) = \mathsf{trace}(r)|_{\mathsf{actions}(R_1)}$. ∎

Theorem 12. *Let R be a network, assume that X is globally unlimited for R, and that $\mathsf{alph}(R) \cap \mathsf{alph}(S) \subseteq X$. Then $R \parallel S$ is a refinement of R.*

Proof. We must prove that for any trace $\mathsf{trace}(r) \in \mathsf{lang}(R \parallel S)$ we have also $\mathsf{trace}(r)|_{\mathsf{alph}(R)} \in \mathsf{lang}(R)$. By definition of language, every action in $\mathsf{trace}(r)$ is unlimited, so $\mathsf{trace}(r)|_{\mathsf{alph}(R)} = \mathsf{trace}(r)|_{\mathsf{actions}(R)}$. But $\mathsf{trace}(r)|_{\mathsf{actions}(R)}$ is a trace of R by Lemma 11; and projection preserves unlimited-ness, hence we must have $\mathsf{trace}(r)|_{\mathsf{actions}(R)} \in \mathsf{lang}(R)$. ∎

Corollary 13. *Let P be a DCR Graph in which all events with a label in $l, \boldsymbol{l}$ are included in all reachable markings. Let R be a Network with $\mathsf{alph}(R) \cap \mathsf{alph}(P) = \{l\} \cup \boldsymbol{l}$. Then the network $P \parallel l \triangleright \boldsymbol{l}. R$ refines P.*

What does Theorem 12 and Corollary 13 mean for modelling? Looking at R_2 and R_3 from Eqs. (4) and (5), it is straightforward to prove using Theorem 12 that both R_2 and R_3 are in fact refinements of $P_{63(1)}$.

Corollary 14. *R_2 and R_3 both refine $P_{63(1)}$.*

This confirms our intuition that (our model of) §48(1) does not in fact modify §63(1) *beyond* adding the requirement to have a consultation before deciding.

6   Implementation and Evaluation

A subset of networks with limited actions, exclusions and network composition but not the link construct, has been implemented by DCR Solutions A/S, a Danish vendor of adaptive case management systems, and used at Syddjurs Municipality (a Danish Municipal government) to implement a administrative processes compliant to CASS in DCR graphs. We report on a **qualitative evaluation** of this subset. The objective of the evaluation is to (a) determine whether DCR networks are *relevant* for practitioners; (b) estimate its *usability* as a modelling construct; and (c) discover its *limitations* as perceived by practitioners.

The evaluation comprises a structured 2 h interview with a Syddjurs Municipality staff member ("the subject") responsible for developing executable DCR models supporting municipal casework and subsequent analysis of responses. The subject has 3 years experience modelling with DCR models, and had used the DCR Network implementation for at least 2 months. The interview was conducted on February 7th, 2020; interview script, answers, and analysis results are available on-line at [4].

We posed two sets of questions consecutively in a single session. With the first set, we inquired into the background of the expert and the relevance of the investigated approach (a). With the second set, we sought to compare law digitalisation before and after the introduction of DCR networks (b), and to examine the consequences of using the implementation (b, c). In the interview, the subject reflected on his past and current experience with modelling the law.

We analysed a recording of the interview using a qualitative inductive approach supported by grounded theory [9]. With the support of qualitative data analysis tool "Atlas.ti", we applied *initial coding* to identify the pertinent aspects in the interview. We then used *focused coding* to gather the open-codes into more abstract concepts based on their similarity traits. Finally, we used *axial coding* to establish the relationships between the identified codes.

Outcome. The *relevance* (a) of DCR networks was justified by a set of domain requirements. The subject highlighted the presence of references in almost all law text and the need to model the interaction between distinct law paragraphs. When reflecting on *past* modelling experience, the subject mentioned the lack of mechanisms to model communication between process models representing distinct law paragraphs. In practice, these mechanisms are needed to automatically trigger related processes and model constraints between events in related models. In the absence of such mechanisms,case-workers must synchronise processes manually, incurring overhead and in some cases leading them to bypass the case management system altogether.

To investigate *usability* (b), the subject was guided to compare his past and current modelling experiences. We note that this interview cannot distinguish usability of the concept of DCR networks from usability of the tooling used by the subject. The subject described areas where the proposed implementation was helpful: the support to automate triggering of events, and for inter-model constraints between them. According to the subject, these mechanisms facilitate modelling the interplay between different processes, and also support process decomposition, making it possible to divide extant models into smaller fragments, each describing a specific law section.

With regards to *limitations* (c), the subject raised the lack of explicit mechanisms to visualise references between events of different processes, making it difficult to track and maintain dependencies between different models. Moreover, the subject felt limited by the absence of simulation tools for DCR networks. Last but not least, he underlined the necessity to extend the existing approach to support data flow between process models.

7   Conclusion

We have taken technical and practical steps towards achieving compliant-by-design executable process descriptions. We used timed DCR graphs to model excerpts of a real law, showing examples of both sections that can be modelled straightforwardly and those that required interaction between models. For the latter, recalling the isomorphism principle, we defined a notion of compositional Networks with novel concepts of "exclusion" and "linking". We then showed how Networks formally provides a syntactic means of achieving refinement in the sense introduced in [11], here for models expressed in possibly distinct formalisms. This development has been verified in Isabelle/HOL, with theories available on-line [32]. Finally, we reported on a preliminary interview-based evaluation with practitioners, which confirms the necessity of treating references in models. Altogether, we have taken both technical and a practical step towards executable declarative process models of government workflows.

Acknowledgments. The authors gratefully acknowledge helpful discussions with Nicklas Healy of Syddjurs Municipality.

References

1. Bekendtgørelse af lov om social service, Børne- og Socialministeriet (August 2017)
2. van der Aa, H., Di Ciccio, C., Leopold, H., Reijers, H.A.: Extracting declarative process models from natural language. In: Giorgini, P., Weber, B. (eds.) CAiSE 2019. LNCS, vol. 11483, pp. 365–382. Springer, Cham (2019). https://doi.org/10.1007/978-3-030-21290-2_23
3. van der Aalst, W.M.P., Pesic, M.: DecSerFlow: towards a truly declarative service flow language. In: Bravetti, M., Núñez, M., Zavattaro, G. (eds.) WS-FM 2006. LNCS, vol. 4184, pp. 1–23. Springer, Heidelberg (2006). https://doi.org/10.1007/11841197_1
4. Andaloussi, A.A.: Evaluation of DCR networks: Interview recordings and full analysis (February 2020). http://doi.org/10.5281/zenodo.3724874
5. Bench-Capon, T.J.M.: Deep models, normative reasoning and legal expert systems, pp. 37–45. Association for Computing Machinery, New York, USA (1989)
6. Bench-Capon, T.J.M., Coenen, F.P.: Isomorphism and legal knowledge based systems. Artif. Intell. Law 1(1), 65–86 (1992)
7. Bench-Capon, T., et al.: A history of AI and Law in 50 papers: 25 years of the international conference on AI and Law. Art. Intell. Law 20(3), 215–319 (2012)
8. Bugliesi, M., Lamma, E., Mello, P.: Modularity in logic programming. J. Log. Program. 19–20, 443–502 (1994)

9. Charmaz, K.: Constructing Grounded Theory. Introducing Qualitative Methods series. SAGE Publications, Thousand Oaks (2014)

10. Chesani, F., Mello, P., Montali, M., Riguzzi, F., Sebastianis, M., Storari, S.: Checking compliance of execution traces to business rules. In: Ardagna, D., Mecella, M., Yang, J. (eds.) BPM 2008. LNBIP, vol. 17. Springer, Heidelberg (2009). https://doi.org/10.1007/978-3-642-00328-8_13

11. Debois, S., Hildebrandt, T.T., Slaats, T.: Replication, refinement & reachability: complexity in dynamic condition-response graphs. Acta Informatica **55**(6), 489–520 (2017). https://doi.org/10.1007/s00236-017-0303-8

12. Dragoni, M., Villata, S., Rizzi, W., Governatori, G.: Combining natural language processing approaches for rule extraction from legal documents. In: Pagallo, U., Palmirani, M., Casanovas, P., Sartor, G., Villata, S. (eds.) AICOL 2015, AICOL 2016, AICOL 2016, AICOL 2017, AICOL 2017. LNCS, vol. 10791. Springer, Cham (2018). https://doi.org/10.1007/978-3-030-00178-0_19

13. Eberle, H., Unger, T., Leymann, F.: Process fragments. In: Meersman, R., Dillon, T., Herrero, P. (eds.) OTM 2009. LNCS, vol. 5870. Springer, Heidelberg (2009). https://doi.org/10.1007/978-3-642-05148-7_29

14. Gordon, T.F., Governatori, G., Rotolo, A.: Rules and norms: requirements for rule interchange languages in the legal domain. In: Governatori, G., Hall, J., Paschke, A. (eds.) RuleML 2009. LNCS, vol. 5858. Springer, Heidelberg (2009). https://doi.org/10.1007/978-3-642-04985-9_26

15. Governatori, G., Sadiq, S.: The journey to business process compliance. IGI Global (2009)

16. Governatori, G., Rotolo, A.: Norm compliance in business process modeling. In: Dean, M., Hall, J., Rotolo, A., Tabet, S. (eds.) RuleML 2010. LNCS, vol. 6403. Springer, Heidelberg (2010). https://doi.org/10.1007/978-3-642-16289-3_17

17. Hashmi, M., Governatori, G., Wynn, M.T.: Normative requirements for business process compliance. In: Davis, J., Demirkan, H., Motahari-Nezhad, H. (eds.) ASSRI 2013. LNBIP, vol. 177. Springer, Cham (2014). https://doi.org/10.1007/978-3-319-07950-9_8

18. Hildebrandt, T., Mukkamala, R.R.: Declarative Event-Based Workflow as Distributed Dynamic Condition Response Graphs. PLACES **69**, 59–73 (2010). EPTCS

19. Hildebrandt, T., Mukkamala, R.R., Slaats, T.: Safe distribution of declarative processes. In: Barthe, G., Pardo, A., Schneider, G. (eds.) SEFM 2011. LNCS, vol. 7041, pp. 237–252. Springer, Heidelberg (2011). https://doi.org/10.1007/978-3-642-24690-6_17

20. Hildebrandt, T.T., Mukkamala, R.R., Slaats, T., Zanitti, F.: Contracts for cross-organizational workflows as timed dynamic condition response graphs. J. Log. Algebr. Program. **82**(5–7), 164–185 (2013)

21. Hoare, C.A.R.: Communicating sequential processes. Commun. ACM **21**(8), 666–677 (1978)

22. Holfter, A., Haarmann, S., Pufahl, L., Weske, M.: Checking compliance in data-driven case management. In: Di Francescomarino, C., Dijkman, R., Zdun, U. (eds.) BPM 2019. LNBIP, vol. 362. Springer, Cham (2019). https://doi.org/10.1007/978-3-030-37453-2_33

23. Kindler, E., Petrucci, L.: Towards a standard for modular Petri Nets: a formalisation. In: Franceschinis, G., Wolf, K. (eds.) PETRI NETS 2009. LNCS, vol. 5606. Springer, Heidelberg (2009). https://doi.org/10.1007/978-3-642-02424-5_5

24. Lohmann, N.: Compliance by design for artifact-centric business processes. Inf. Syst. **38**(4), 606–618 (2013)

25. López, H.A., Debois, S., Slaats, T., Hildebrandt, T.T.: Business process compliance using reference models of law. In: Wehrheim, H., Cabot, J. (eds.) FASE 2020. LNCS, vol. 12076. Springer, Cham (2020). https://doi.org/10.1007/978-3-030-45234-6_19

26. López, H.A., Marquard, M., Muttenthaler, L., Strømsted, R.: Assisted declarative process creation from natural language descriptions. In: EDOC Workshops, pp. 96–99. IEEE (2019)

27. National Social Appeals Board (Ankestyrelsen): Annual report for the 2018 case process (May 2019). https://ast.dk/publikationer/arsopgorelse-2018

28. National Social Appeals Board (Ankestyrelsen): Appeals Board decisions on the Services Act in Q2 to Q4 2018 (...) (May 2019). https://bit.ly/3glQOBK

29. Object Management Group BPMN Technical Committee: Business Process Model and Notation, Version 2.0 (2013)

30. Pesic, M., Schonenberg, H., Van der Aalst, W.: DECLARE: full support for loosely-structured processes. In: EDOC, p. 287 (October 2007)

31. Slaats, T., Schunselaar, D.M.M., Maggi, F.M., Reijers, H.A.: The semantics of hybrid process models. In: Debruyne, C., et al. (eds.) OTM 2016. LNCS, vol. 10033. Springer, Cham (2016). https://doi.org/10.1007/978-3-319-48472-3_32

32. Debois, S.: Formalisation: Modular Process Models for the Law (June 2019). https://www.itu.dk/people/debois/thys/ifm20

33. The Danish Ministry of Social Affairs and the Interior: Consolidation Act on Social Services (September 2015). http://english.sm.dk/media/14900/consolidation-act-on-social-services.pdf. Executive Order no. 1053

34. Slaats, T., Debois, S., Hildebrandt, T.: Open to change: a theory for iterative test-driven modelling. In: Weske, M., Montali, M., Weber, I., vom Brocke, J. (eds.) BPM 2018. LNCS, vol. 11080, pp. 31–47. Springer, Cham (2018). https://doi.org/10.1007/978-3-319-98648-7_3

35. Winter, K., Rinderle-Ma, S.: Deriving and combining mixed graphs from regulatory documents based on constraint relations. In: Giorgini, P., Weber, B. (eds.) CAiSE 2019. LNCS, vol. 11483, pp. 430–445. Springer, Cham (2019). https://doi.org/10.1007/978-3-030-21290-2_27

Reformulation of SAT into a Polynomial Box-Constrained Optimization Problem

Stéphane Jacquet[✉] and Sylvain Hallé

Laboratoire d'informatique formelle, Université du Québec à Chicoutimi,
Saguenay, Canada
stephane.jacquet1@uqac.ca

Abstract. In order to leverage the capacities of non-linear constraint solvers, we propose a reformulation of SAT into a box-constrained optimization problem where the objective function is polynomial. We prove that any optimal solution of the numerical problem corresponds to a solution of the Boolean formula, and demonstrate a stopping criterion that can be used with a numerical solver.

1 Introduction

Boolean satisfiability (SAT) is probably the most well known NP-complete problem, which consists in its simplest form of finding appropriate values for variables of a propositional logic formula φ in Conjunctive Normal Form (CNF) such that it evaluates to true ($\top$). This problem is typically solved symbolically at the logical level through different techniques.

However, in recent years, different *reformulations* have been suggested to solve SAT by turning it into a numerical problem to be solved by numerical techniques. For example, a linear algebra approach has been attempted in [6]; the reformulation transforms a SAT instance into a system of linear equations. In [8], a relaxation of the Boolean variables is mixed with gradient-based algorithms. The work from [5] offers a reformulation through an optimization of degree 4 by adding as many variables as the number of clauses in the Boolean formula. In [7], the reformulation is done by defining an extension of the DeMorgan Laws.

The present work suggests a reformulation of SAT in order to use the capacities of *non-linear* solvers. The principle, illustrated in Fig. 1, works as follows. First, a Boolean formula φ over $\mathbb{B}^n$ is transformed into a real-valued polynomial $\hat{\varphi}$ over the interval $[0;1]^n$, using a transformation called τ, described in Sect. 2 (top arrow). For example, a CNF formula $\varphi = (a \vee b) \wedge (a \vee \neg b)$ will result in the function $\hat{\varphi} = (a + b - ab) + (a + 1 - b - a(1 - b))$. The SAT problem turns into the problem of maximizing $\hat{\varphi}$, a box-constrained optimization task that can be offloaded to a numerical solver (right arrow). Section 3 then formally proves that a real-valued solution provided by such a solver, such as $\hat{a} = (0.99, 0.99)$, can be converted into an optimal solution over the integers 0 and 1 using a backwards transformation ρ (bottom arrow); in our example, this would yield the point $(1, 1)$. Proposition 5 will show that the result applies even if a solver

© Springer Nature Switzerland AG 2020
B. Dongol and E. Troubitsyna (Eds.): IFM 2020, LNCS 12546, pp. 387–394, 2020.
https://doi.org/10.1007/978-3-030-63461-2_21

converges to a solution with coordinates that do not lie close to 0 or 1. Finally, Theorem 2 will show that such a solution exists if and only if the corresponding SAT instance admits it as a solution (left arrow).

In the context of this article, the objective function is non-linear (since $\hat{\phi}$ is polynomial of degree superior or equal to two as soon as there is a clause with two literals or more). The gradient of a function gives a direction where the function takes higher values [12]. When this gradient is not accessible, algorithms like the Nelder-Mead algorithm [11], genetic algorithms [13] or any algorithms from the derivative-free optimization field [1] are efficient. However, in the present work, the gradient is available, which makes it suitable for iterative algorithms. This paper lists a couple theoretical results that could be used when using a gradient-based algorithm. A few of those theoretical results have been listed in this paper; for example, some algorithms have been developed specifically for polynomial optimization [4,10], which is what one gets after reformulating SAT using the construction presented in this article.

The paper is structured as follows. Section 2 describes the transformation rules to define the reformulation. Section 3 studies the properties of the polynomial obtained after the transformation. Section 4 analyses the links between the SAT problem and its reformulation. It also contains theoretical results that can be used to anticipate numerical results over reformulation. Section 5 summarizes the theoretical results and talks about other difficulties that could occur in future numerical tests.

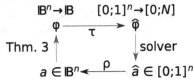

Fig. 1. A summary of the approach followed in this paper.

2   SAT as an Optimization Problem

In this section, we will describe how to transform a SAT instance into a polynomial function to maximize. Let $a_1, \ldots a_n$ be the n Boolean variables occurring in an arbitrary SAT instance. For convenience, we shall equate the values $\bot$ and $\top$ with integers 0 and 1, respectively. We will note $a = (a_1; \ldots; a_n)$. The set $\mathbb{B}$ will be interpreted as the subset of $\mathbb{R}$ containing only the values 0 and 1.

A Boolean variable a (which takes the values 0 or 1) will be assimilated with its bounded real variable *relaxation*, by allowing it to take a value in the interval $[0;1]$. For the sake of readability, we shall use the same symbol for a Boolean variable and its relaxation; it should be clear enough in the formulas whether a variable is Boolean or real.

Equipped with this notation, we can lift the notion of relaxation from Boolean variables to Boolean formulas. The transformation will be done using a function $\tau : (\mathbb{B}^n \to \mathbb{B}) \to ([0;1]^n \to [0;N])$, which takes as input a Boolean formula with N clauses, and produces as its output a real-valued polynomial expressed in terms of the relaxations of the Boolean variables.

Definition 1. *Let a be an arbitrary propositional variable, and φ_1 and φ_2 be arbitrary Boolean formulas. The transformation function $\tau : (\mathbb{B}^n \to \mathbb{B}) \to ([0;1]^n \to [0;N])$ defined recursively as follows:*

$$\tau(b) = b, \text{ for } b \in \mathbb{B} \tag{1}$$

$$\tau(a) = a \tag{2}$$

$$\tau(\neg a) = 1 - a \tag{3}$$

$$\tau(\varphi_1 \vee \varphi_2) = \tau(\varphi_1) + \tau(\varphi_2) - \tau(\varphi_1)\tau(\varphi_2) \tag{4}$$

$$\tau(\varphi_1 \wedge \varphi_2) = \tau(\varphi_1) + \tau(\varphi_2) \tag{5}$$

The introduction gave an example of a transformation using those five rules. It can be easily shown that applying them to a given CNF formula φ produces a unique polynomial, which will be written $\tau(\varphi)$. To simplify the notation, we shall also note this polynomial $\hat{\varphi}$. Three remarks should be made. First, one should be careful on the fact that two equivalent Boolean formulas (i.e. which have the same solutions) that have different CNF representations may have different transformation through τ. This is shown with the following example: $\tau(a \vee a) = 2a - a^2 \neq \tau(a) = a$ but $a \vee a$ is logically equivalent to a. Second, note how τ transforms logical conjunction into an *addition* instead of a multiplication; this goes against the "probabilistic" interpretation that $P(A \wedge B) = P(A)P(B)$ when A and B are independant. This decision has been done to reduce the degree of the polynomial. With a multiplication, the degree of the polynomial will be equal to the number of literals in the CNF representation of φ. With the addition, the degree will be much smaller and described in Proposition 1.

Finally, since $\hat{\varphi}$ takes as arguments elements of $[0;1]^n$, and not $\mathbb{B}^n$, the simplification $a^2 = a$ (commonly occurring in operations over $\{0,1\}$) is not used.

The objective of this work is to solve the following optimization problem:

$$(P): \max_{a \in [0;1]^n} \hat{\varphi}(a).$$

This is a case of an optimization problem that has what are called *box constraints*, meaning that all its variables are bounded by real values –the interval $[0;1]$ in that case. In addition, the objective function is polynomial, which means that its gradient can be calculated and used in the solving process.

3   Properties of $\hat{\varphi}$

It remains to determine how solutions to (P) can be used to produce solutions to the original SAT instance, and under what conditions. This is the purpose of the next two sections. First, we need to establish a few results on the properties of the polynomial function $\hat{\varphi}$ on $[0;1]^n$. This will then help to solve (P). A first observation can be made about the degree of the polynomial $\hat{\varphi}$ when φ is k-SAT (i.e. when each clause contains at most k literals).

Proposition 1. *Let $k \in \mathbb{N}^*$ (i.e. positive integer). If φ is k-SAT, then the degree of $\hat{\varphi}$ is k.*

The proof is trivial and can be done by induction. This result is important as it bounds the degree of the polynomial. Furthermore, since any SAT instance has a polynomial reduction into 3-SAT [9], this guarantees the existence of a reformulation of SAT into an optimization problem for a polynomial of degree at most 3.

We shall then observe that $\hat{\varphi}$ is "well-behaved" —among other things, that it maps the real hypercube $[0;1]^n$ on $[0;N]$, that the discrete hypercube $\mathbb{B}^n$ on $\{0,\ldots,N\}$, where N is the number of clauses in φ and to understand how $\hat{\varphi}$ behaves on the boundaries of the set $[0;1]^n$, noted:

$$\partial([0;1]^n) = \{(a_1,\ldots,a_n) \in [0;1]^n : \exists i \in \{1,\ldots,n\}, a_i \in \mathbb{B}\}.$$

Proposition 2. *Let $\hat{\varphi}$ be a polynomial resulting from the transformation of a SAT instance φ containing $N \in \mathbb{N}^*$ clauses. Then: i) if $a \in [0;1]^n$ then $\hat{\varphi}(a) \in [0;N]$; ii) if $a \in \mathbb{B}^n$ then $\hat{\varphi}(a) \in \{0;\ldots;N\}$; iii) if $a \in]0;1[^n$ then $\hat{\varphi}(a) \in]0;N[$.*

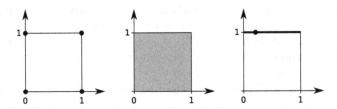

Fig. 2. On the left, studying $\hat{\varphi}$ on $\mathbb{B}^n$. In the middle, studying $\hat{\varphi}$ on $]0;1[^n$. On the right, studying $\hat{\varphi}$ on $\partial([0;1]^n)$.

Proof. It should be noted that, with two variables, the case *ii)* corresponds to the first graph on Fig. 2, while *iii)* corresponds to the second one. For i), let $a \in [0;1]^n$. If φ is a clause, then it can be shown by induction on the length of the clause that $\tau(\varphi) \in [0;1]$. Then, if φ contains N clauses, using equation (5), it can be shown by induction on the number of clauses that $\tau(\varphi) \in [0;N]$. For ii), the proof is very similar to i). Let $a \in \mathbb{B}^n$. If φ is a clause, it can be shown by induction on the length of the clause that $\tau(\varphi) \in \mathbb{B}$. Then, if φ contains N clauses, then the transformation through τ of each clauses evaluated in a will be in $\mathbb{B}$ and thus the sum of the N terms being in $\{0;\ldots;N\}$. The proof of *iii)* is almost identical to *ii)*.   □

Let us now study the eventuality where there exists a solution to (P) on the boundaries of $\partial([0;1]^n)$. Of particular interest is the case where $\hat{\varphi}(a) = N$, $a \in [0;1]^n$ but a contains at least one variable that is neither 0 nor 1. This can be illustrated by the SAT instance $\varphi = (a \lor b) \land (\neg a \lor b)$, which yields $\hat{\varphi} = (a + b - ab) + ((1-a) + b - (1-a)b)$. This polynomial admits an optimal solution at $(1/2, 1) \in \partial([0; 1]^2)$. However, one can observe that in this case, the value of a has no impact on the value of φ. A solver using the gradient may notice that $\partial \hat{\varphi} / \partial a = 0$, and thus never change this variable from any value it was initially set to. More importantly, it should be noted that in this case, both $(0; 1)$ and $(1; 1)$ are also optimal solutions of $\hat{\varphi}$. This result corresponds to the third plot of Fig. 2; as a matter of fact, if $\hat{\varphi}$ takes the value N on the dot, then it takes the value N on the whole edge in bold.

Can this observation be generalized to any Boolean formula? It turns out that the answer is yes. In order to prove it, let us define the function $\Psi : [0; 1]^n \mapsto \mathcal{P}(\mathbb{B}^n)$ defined for all $a \in [0; 1]^n$ by $\Psi(a) = \{x \in \mathbb{B}^n : \forall i \in A(a), x_i = a_i, \forall i \notin A(a), x_i \in \mathbb{B}\}$, where $A(a) = \{i \in \{1, \ldots, n\} : a_i \in \mathbb{B}\}$. Intuitively, given a non-Boolean solution a, $\Psi(a)$ returns the set of "corners" of the hypercube $\mathbb{B}^n$ adjacent to a. If we use again the third plot of Fig. 2, then the dot has coordinates $(0.25; 1)$ and $\Psi(0.25; 1) = \{(0; 1), (1; 1)\}$. First, we need to prove that the result is true for a formula containing only one clause.

Proposition 3. *Let φ be a clause; if there is a $\in \partial([0; 1]^n)$ such that $\hat{\varphi}(a) = 1$, then for all $x \in \Psi(a)$, $\hat{\varphi}(x) = 1$.*

Proof. Let $k \in \{1, \ldots, n\}$. We can consider that all the variables are positive literals in the formula. If not, the one with a negative literal can be redefined as the opposite of that variable. If needed, it is possible to rename the variables such that $\varphi = a_1 \vee \ldots \vee a_k$.

We show the result by finite induction on the length of the clause. For $k = 1$, then $\varphi = a_1$ and $\hat{\varphi}(a) = a_1$. If, for some $a \in \partial([0; 1]^n)$, $\hat{\varphi}(a) = 1$, then $a_1 = 1$; so, for all $x \in \Psi(a)$, $a_1 = 1$. This shows that for all $x \in \Psi(a)$, we have that $\hat{\varphi}(x) = 1$.

Let $k \in \{1, \ldots, n-1\}$ and let us assume that for any clause of length k, if $a \in \partial([0; 1]^n)$ is such that $\hat{\varphi}(a) = 1$, then for all $x \in \Psi(a)$, $\hat{\varphi}(x) = 1$. Consider a clause of length $k + 1$. It can be written $\varphi \vee a_{k+1}$ where φ is a clause of length k. So $\tau(\varphi \vee a_{k+1}) = \tau(\varphi) + \tau(a_{k+1}) - \tau(\varphi)\tau(a_{k+1})$. If for some $a \in \partial([0; 1]^n)$, $\tau(\varphi \vee a_{k+1})(a) = 1$, so necessarily, $\tau(\varphi)(a) = 1$ or $\tau(a_{k+1})(a) = 1$. In the first case, by the induction hypothesis, for all $x \in \Psi(a)$, $\tau(\varphi \vee a_{k+1})(x) = 1$. The second case is identical to the initial step ($k = 1$). □

Using Proposition 3, the result can now be generalized for logical formulas which are conjunctions of clauses.

Theorem 1. *If φ contains N clauses and $a \in \partial([0; 1]^n)$ is such that $\hat{\varphi}(a) = N$, then for all $x \in \Psi(a)$, $\hat{\varphi}(x) = N$.*

Proof. Let $a \in \partial([0; 1]^n)$ is such that $\hat{\varphi}(a) = N$. The theorem will be proven by induction on $N \in \mathbb{N}^*$, the number of clauses of φ written in CNF. The case $N = 1$ is solved with Proposition 3.

Let $N \geq 1$ and suppose that, for φ containing N clauses, if $a \in \partial([0; 1]^n)$ is such that $\hat{\varphi}(a) = 1$, then for all $x \in \Psi(a)$, $\hat{\varphi}(x) = 1$. Let us define a formula with $N + 1$ clauses. It can be written $\varphi \wedge C$, where φ contains N clauses and

C is a clause. Then $\tau(\varphi \wedge C) = \tau(\varphi) + \tau(C)$. Let $a \in \partial([0;1]^n)$ such that $\tau(\varphi \wedge C)(a) = N + 1$. Then $\tau(\varphi)(a) + \tau(C)(a) = N + 1$. Using Property 2, then necessarily, $\tau(\varphi)(a) = N$ and $\tau(C)(a) = 1$. Since C is a clause, by Proposition 3, for all $x \in \Psi(a)$, we have $\tau(C)(x) = 1$. In addition, by the induction hypothesis, we can assert that for all $x \in \Psi(a)$, $\tau(\varphi)(x) = N$. This proves that for all $x \in \Psi(a)$, $\tau(\varphi \wedge C)(x) = \tau(\varphi)(x) + \tau(C)(x) = N + 1$. □

4   From $\hat{\varphi}$ to φ

The previous result is important: it shows that, even when a non-Boolean optimum of $\hat{\varphi}$ is found, it can be turned into a solution that has only Boolean values and which is also optimal. It remains to prove that a solution to (P) can be used to construct a solution to the original SAT instance. The following theorem focuses about the case where a solver converges to a solution in $\mathbb{B}^n$.

Theorem 2. *For all $a \in \mathbb{B}^n$, $\varphi(a) = 1$ if, and only if, $\hat{\varphi}(a) = N$.*

The proof, very similar to the proof of Proposition 2, is omitted. Theorem 2 is what justifies the transformation of a Boolean formula φ to the function $\tau(\varphi)$. Finding a solution of the SAT problem described by φ is therefore equivalent to finding the optimal value (equal to N) of the function $\hat{\varphi}$.

However, in practice, a numerical solver will typically find a solution a that does not land perfectly on elements of $\mathbb{B}^n$, but more likely on values very close to 0 or 1. Likewise, the value taken by $\hat{\varphi}$ will be a real number close to, but not equal to N. In such a situation, Theorem 2 does not apply. A natural workaround would be to round each Boolean value to its nearest integer (0 or 1). To this end, let us define the "round" function ρ such that $\rho(x) = 0$ if $x < 1/2$, and $\rho(x) = 1$ otherwise. This function can be lifted to $\mathbb{R}^n$ by defining $\rho(x_1, \ldots, x_n) = (\rho(x_1), \ldots, \rho(x_n))$.

It is not clear at the onset that taking the round of each variable produces a solution that is optimal. Case in point, it is well known that in integer programming, rounding a solution after relaxation can lead to an non-optimal solution [3]. Fortunately, this is not the case with $\hat{\varphi}$, as we shall prove in Theorem 3. From this point, $||.||$ will be the euclidean norm.

Theorem 3. *Let $C > 0$ be a number that satisfies the Lipschitz condition of $\hat{\varphi}$ on $[0;1]^n$, and let $\hat{a} \in [0;1]^n$. If $\hat{\varphi}(\hat{a}) - C||\hat{a} - \rho(\hat{a})|| > N - 1$, then $\rho(\hat{a})$ is a solution of the logical formula φ.*

Proof. Since $\hat{\varphi}$ is a polynomial function on a compact set, it is Lipschitz. Let $C > 0$ be its Lipschitz constant. Suppose the solver found a solution $\hat{a} \in [0;1]^n$. Because $\hat{\varphi}$ is C-Lipschitz, $|\hat{\varphi}(\hat{a}) - \hat{\varphi}(\rho(\hat{a}))| \leq C||\hat{a} - \rho(\hat{a})||$, which means that:

$$\hat{\varphi}(\hat{a}) - C||\hat{a} - \rho(\hat{a})|| \leq \hat{\varphi}(\rho(a)) \leq \hat{\varphi}(\hat{a}) + C||\hat{a} - \rho(\hat{a})||.$$

But $\rho(\hat{a}) \in \mathbb{B}^n$, so using Proposition 2.*ii*) then $\hat{\varphi}(\rho(\hat{a})) \in \{0; \ldots; N\}$. This means that if $\hat{\varphi}(\hat{a}) - C||\hat{a} - \rho(\hat{a})|| > N - 1$, then necessarily $\hat{\varphi}(\rho(\hat{a})) = N$. Thus it guarantees that $\rho(\hat{a})$ is a solution of formula φ using Theorem 2. □

The proof of Theorem 3 claims the existence of a Lipschitz constant C without giving its value. However, using the definition of τ (in Definition 1), it is possible to find a Lipschitz constant of $\hat{\varphi}$, which depends only on n (the number of variables) and N (the number of clauses). Lemma 1, which is a consequence of the mean value theorem with several variables, provides a constant C, which we then use to prove that $\hat{\varphi}$ is C-Lipschitz.

Lemma 1. *If $\hat{\varphi}$ is differentiable and $C = \sup\limits_{a \in [0;1]^n} \|\nabla\hat{\varphi}(a)\|$, then $\hat{\varphi}$ is C-Lipschitz.*

Proposition 4. *If φ is a CNF Boolean formula containing N clauses depending of n variables, then $\hat{\varphi}$ is $N\sqrt{n}$-Lipschitz.*

Proof. This proof requires new notations. Consider a clause C where the variable a_i, $i \in \{1; \ldots; n\}$, appears. We will note C^{-a_i} the clause C where a_i has been removed. Also, considering the formula φ, we will define $V_{a_i} \subseteq \{1; \ldots; N\}$ the index of the clauses where a_i is a positive literal and $W_{a_i} \subseteq \{1; \ldots; N\}$ the index of the clauses where a_i is a negative literal. By definition of V_{a_i} and W_{a_i}, it can be observed that for all $i \in \{1; \ldots; N\}$, $|V_{a_i}| + |W_{a_i}| \leq N$.

It can be then shown that for all $i \in \{1, \ldots, n\}$ and all $a \in [0; 1]^n$,

$$\frac{\partial\hat{\varphi}}{\partial a_i}(a) = \sum_{k \in V_{a_i}} (1 - \hat{C}_k^{-a_i}(a)) - \sum_{k \in W_{a_i}} (1 - \hat{C}_k^{-a_i}(a)).$$

Then,

$$\left| \frac{\partial\hat{\varphi}}{\partial a_i}(a) \right| \leq \left| \sum_{k \in V_{a_i}} (1 - \hat{C}_k^{-a_i}(a)) \right| + \left| \sum_{k \in W_{a_i}} (1 - \hat{C}_k^{-a_i}(a)) \right| \leq |V_{a_i}| + |W_{a_i}|$$

Hence $\|\nabla\hat{\varphi}(a)\|^2 \leq \sum_{i=1}^{n} \left(\frac{\partial\hat{\varphi}}{\partial a_i}(a) \right)^2 \leq \sum_{i=1}^{n} (|V_{a_i}| + |W_{a_i}|)^2 \leq \sum_{i=1}^{n} N^2 \leq nN^2.$

By Lemma 1, this means that $\sup\limits_{a \in [0;1]^n} \|\nabla\hat{\varphi}(a)\| \leq N\sqrt{n}$. $\square$

We note that the Lipschitz constant $C = N\sqrt{n}$ is elegantly simple, especially considering the rather complex polynomials produced by τ in practice. Combining Theorem 3 with Proposition 4 leads to the following proposition:

Proposition 5. *If there is $\hat{a} \in \mathbb{B}^n$ such that $\hat{\varphi}(\hat{a}) - N\sqrt{n}\|\hat{a} - \rho(\hat{a})\| > N - 1$, then $\rho(\hat{a})$ is a solution of the Boolean formula φ.*

This result can be used by an iterative numerical solver as a *stopping criterion*. As soon as a solution $\hat{a}$ satisfying the condition of Proposition 5 is found, the solver can stop; there is no point in iterating further to find a better solution, since we already have the guarantee that $\rho(\hat{a})$ is a solution of the SAT instance. This criterion is specific to the transformation τ we use in this work.

5   Conclusion

In this work, a reformulation of a SAT instance has been suggested. This transformation leads to an optimization problem where the objective function is a polynomial function. The link between feasible solutions of the initial SAT problem and the optimal solution of that reformulation has been made.

As future work, numerical experiments should be performed to test the capacity of this reformulation to solve SAT instances. It is known that in such optimization problems, algorithms using the gradient as a stopping criterion can converge to local optimums; multi-start solving using Latin hypercubes [2] to select starting points could help handle that difficulty. In addition, it would be interesting to combine this reformulation with ideas from other SAT solving techniques, such as backtracking methods. This would help fixing some values of the variables. Combining the reformulation with a complete method could help improve convergence.

References

1. Audet, C., Hare, W.: Derivative-Free and Blackbox Optimization. SSORFE. Springer, Cham (2017). https://doi.org/10.1007/978-3-319-68913-5
2. Chen, J., Qian, P.Z.G.: Latin hypercube designs with controlled correlations and multi-dimensional stratification. Biometrika **101**(2), 319–332 (2014)
3. Cont, R., Heidari, M.: Optimal rounding under integer constraints. CoRR, abs/1501.00014 (2015)
4. Dressler, M., Iliman, S., de Wolff, T.: An approach to constrained polynomial optimization via nonnegative circuit polynomials and geometric programming. J. Symb. Comput. **91**, 149–172 (2019)
5. Duda, J.: P =? NP as minimization of degree 4 polynomial, or Grassmann number problem. CoRR, abs/1703.04456 (2017)
6. Fang, C., Liu, A.: A linear algebra formulation for boolean satisfiability testing. CoRR, abs/1701.02401 (2017)
7. Gu, J.: Global optimization for satisfiability (SAT) problem. IEEE Trans. Knowl. Data Eng. **6**(3), 361–381 (1994)
8. Inala, J.P., Gao, S., Kong, S., Solar-Lezama, A.: REAS: combining numerical optimization with SAT solving. CoRR, abs/1802.04408 (2018)
9. R. M. Karp. Reducibility among Combinatorial Problems, pages 85–103. Springer, US, Boston, MA, 1972
10. Li, Z.: Polynomial optimization problems. PhD thesis, The Chinese University of Hong Kong (2011)
11. Nelder, J.A., Mead, R.: A simplex method for function minimization. Comput. J. **7**(4), 308–313 (1965)
12. Ruder, S.: An overview of gradient descent optimization algorithms. CoRR, abs/1609.04747 (2016)
13. Thengade, A., Dondal, R.: Genetic algorithm - survey paper. In: IJCA Proceeding National Conference on Recent Trends in Computing, NCRTC, 5, January 2012

Algebraic Techniques

PALM: A Technique for Process ALgebraic Specification Mining

Sara Belluccini[1][✉], Rocco De Nicola[1], Barbara Re[2], and Francesco Tiezzi[2]

[1] IMT School for Advanced Studies, Lucca, Italy
`sara.belluccini@imtlucca.it`
[2] University of Camerino, Camerino, Italy

Abstract. We propose a technique to automatically generate a formal specification of the model of a system from a set of observations of its behaviour. We aim to free systems modellers from the burden of explicitly formalising the behaviour of an existing system to analyse it. We take advantage of an algorithm introduced by the process mining community, which takes as input an event log and generates a formal specification that can be combined with other specifications to obtain a global model of the overall behaviour of a system. Specifically, we have adapted a known process discovery algorithm to produce a specification in mCRL2, a formal specification language based on process algebras. The availability of mCRL2 specifications enables us to take advantage of its rich toolset for verifying systems properties and for effectively reasoning over distributed scenarios where multiple organizations interact to reach common goals. This is an aspect that is not supported by the approaches based on Petri Nets, usually used for process mining. The methodology has been integrated in a stand-alone tool and has been validated using custom-made and real event logs.

1 Introduction

Effective cooperation among organizations requires the compatibility of their software systems. Such cooperation is better supported by the continuous observations of systems' behaviour rather than by sharing documentation that is often incomplete and out of date [13]. At the same time, the use of automatic techniques for checking a priori whether the observed behaviours of the involved software systems are compatible reduces the effort of systems integration.

It is worth noticing that different research communities are working on the definition and implementation of techniques to extract or infer a model from a set of observations of the system behaviour (usually called *log*). In the formal methods community, this task has been carried out mainly by generating finite state machine models (see, e.g., [13,17,32]), while the business process community fosters the use of process mining techniques for generating Petri Nets (see, e.g., [3,35,38]). Our work aims at bridging the gap between these two communities and takes as starting point the techniques developed by the process mining community for the generation of system specifications from logs. However, most

© Springer Nature Switzerland AG 2020
B. Dongol and E. Troubitsyna (Eds.): IFM 2020, LNCS 12546, pp. 397–418, 2020.
https://doi.org/10.1007/978-3-030-63461-2_22

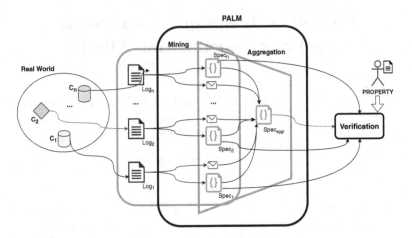

Fig. 1. Overview of the PALM methodology.

of the proposed approaches consider only the point of view of a single organization and do not provide techniques to compositionally derive a specification of a distributed scenario. To overcome this issue, we rely on techniques from the process algebra community, to exploit their inherent compositionality and their large set of analytical tools. This makes it possible to deal with issues of distributed systems that otherwise could not be considered.

We introduce a novel methodology, called PALM - Process ALgebraic Mining, and its related software tool, whose aim is obtaining process algebraic specifications from systems logs via a mining algorithm. The main phases of the methodology are described in Figure 1. The starting point is given by logs taken from components of real world systems; those can be, e.g., logs of an industrial process as well as of a client-server network. In the *mining* step logs are analyzed to generate a formal specification for each of them, together with a mapping associating sending/receiving action and with the exchanged messages. The individual specifications can be exploited for verifying properties of the individual systems, e.g., by means of model checking techniques. But, more importantly, in case the logs originate from components of a distributed system, the individual specifications can be combined, in the *aggregation* step, to obtain a formal model of the global system, which again can be analyzed to consider issues originated by erroneous or unexpected interactions among the components.

Summing up, PALM is a software tool that inputs one or more event logs and outputs the specification for each log. Additionally, in case of multiple logs belonging to a distributed system, PALM also outputs the global specification of the system. We have instantiated the methodology by inputting logs in the standard XES format and outputting mCRL2 specifications. The rich mCRL2 tool-set, providing equivalence and model checking functionalities, can then be used for verification. The methodology has been validated by experiments with both custom-made and real event logs.

2 Background Notions

Process Mining. Process Mining is a discipline combining data mining, computational intelligence and process modeling and analysis [4]. Process mining aims at extracting useful information from event logs for discovering, monitoring and improving real processes [5]. It is an evidence-based approach, and ensures a close correspondence between modeled and observed behavior, being the definition of the model based on real process execution traces. This paper deals exactly with the issue of *process discovery* to produce a model from an event log without using any priori information. An event log is a set of cases, while a case is a sequence of events, that can have attributes to indicate activity name, time, cost, used resource, etc. Event logs are usually formatted using the eXtensible Event Stream (XES) standard format [20]. Process discovery is generally based on an algorithm that produces a model from an event log. Over the years several mining algorithms have been developed [10], which differ for kind and quality of the output. In validating our approach we consider three mining algorithms. The Structured Heuristics Miner [9] first discovers models that are possibly unstructured and unsound, and then transforms them into structured and sound ones. The Inductive Miner [26] extracts block-structured process models, called process trees, by splitting the logs in smaller pieces and combining them with tree operators. Finally, the Split Miner [8] aims at identifying combination of split gateways in order to capture behaviours like concurrency or casual relations, while filtering the graphs derived by the event logs.

mCRL2. mCRL2 is a formal specification language [19], based on ACP [12], that, together with its tool-set [15] can be used to describe and analyze concurrent systems. The subset of mCRL2 processes used in this paper is generated by the following grammar:

$$P::= a \mid \cdot_{i \in I} P_i \mid +_{i \in I} P_i \mid \|_{i \in I} P_i \mid allow(ActSet, P)$$
$$\mid comm(CommSet, P) \mid hide(ActSet, P) \mid K$$

where: a denotes an **action** (including the silent action tau), $ActSet$ denotes a set of actions; and $CommSet$ denotes a set of **communication expressions**, used for renaming of multi-actions (i.e., communicating actions that occur simultaneously) to a single action.

In the syntax, $\cdot_{i \in I} P_i$ denotes a **sequence** of processes, $+_{i \in I} P_i$ denotes a **choice** among processes, $\|_{i \in I} P_i$ denotes the **parallel composition** of processes. $allow(ActSet, P)$ defines the set of actions $ActSet$ that process P can execute; all other actions, except for tau, are blocked. $comm(CommSet, P)$ synchronises actions in P according to the communication expressions $CommSet$; for example, in $comm(\{a|b \rightarrow c\}, (a \| b))$ the parallel actions a and b communicate, yielding action c. $hide(ActSet, P)$ hides those actions produced by P that are in $ActSet$, i.e. it turns these actions into tau actions. K permits to call a process definition of the form $K = P$, where K is a unique process identifier. An mCRL2 **specification** consists of a main process (identified by the keyword *init*) and a collection of process definitions.

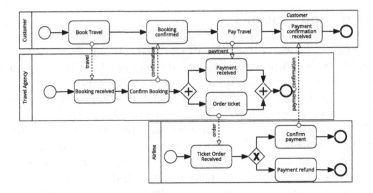

Fig. 2. Running example

Running Example. We illustrate our approach by using, throughout the paper, a simple travel scenario that is graphically represented, in standard BPMN notation, in Fig. 2. The running example includes three participants: the customer, the travel agency and the airline. In the scenario, a customer sends a flight booking to a travel agent and, upon booking confirmation from the agent, pays and waits for payment confirmation. The travel agent manages in parallel reception of the payment and ordering the flight ticket to an airline company. The airline company evaluates the ticket order and either confirms the payment to the customer or refunds him.

3   PALM Methodology

In this section, we illustrate the PALM methodology outlined in Fig. 1. In particular, we describe the mining and the aggregation step.

3.1   Mining

The mining step is the key part of the PALM methodology since it permits passing from raw data stored in a system log to a formal specification suitable for analysis. This step consists of three phases: (1) *Parsing log data*, (2) *Mining tool-independent specification*, and (3) *Transformation into mCRL2 specification*.

Preliminaries. Before going into the details of each phase, we describe the specification language used for describing the intermediate models produced as output in the second phase. Indeed, although we have fully instantiated our proposal for generating mCRL2 specifications, we kept the mining process independent from the final target language, by resorting to a *tool-independent description* of the model's structure. This specification language is based on the typical block structure operators of workflow models, and relies on the operators defined by

G. Schimm [31]. The syntax of the block structure language is defined by the following grammar:

$$B := a \mid S\{B_i\}_{i \in I} \mid P\{B_i\}_{i \in I} \mid C\{B_i\}_{i \in I} \mid L\{B\}$$

A block structure B is built from task actions a by exploiting operators for sequential composition (S), imposing an ordered execution of its arguments; parallel composition (P), imposing an interleaved execution of its arguments; exclusive choice (C), imposing the selection of one block out of its arguments; and loop (L), producing an iterative execution of its argument.

Parsing Log Data. Mining algorithms input an event log and output a model. As already mentioned in Sect. 2, logs are collections of event-based data organized as cases. An event has a name and a lifecycle attribute referring to a state of the transactional lifecycle model of the activity instance producing the event. In this paper, we refer to a simplified version of the lifecycle, indicating when an event started and ended using the values 'start' and 'complete', respectively. We assume that events with the same name and the same attribute of the lifecycle correspond to different executions of the same (unique) system activity.

In the parsing phase of our mining process, each case of the log is transformed into a trace of event names, where the events are ordered according to their completion defined by the 'complete' value of the Lifecycle attribute. In the (excerpt of the) log in Table 1, concerned with the execution of the Travel Agency component of our running example, since the event 'Confirm booking' starts after the event 'Booking received' has completed, the corresponding trace will include the subtrace 'Booking received, Confirm booking'.

Table 1. Excerpt of Travel Agency log

Case	Event name	Lifecycle
75	Booking received	Start
75	Booking received	Complete
75	Confirm Booking	Start
75	Confirm Booking	Complete
75	Payment received	Start
75	Order ticket	Start
75	Payment received	Complete
75	Order ticket	Complete
	....	

Table 2. Excerpt of Airline log

Case	Event name	Lifecycle
93	Ticket Order Received	Start
93	Ticket Order Received	Complete
93	Payment refund	Start
93	Payment refund	Complete
56	Ticket Order Received	Start
56	Ticket Order Received	Complete
56	Confirm payment	Start
56	Confirm payment	Complete
	....	

In this phase, for each trace in the log, we compute a *happened-before relation*, which is used in the next phase. This relation takes into account the chronological order of events and considers only direct dependencies that are given by the lifecycle of the events (and not by the order in the log). This means that an event e is in happened-before relation with an event e' (written $e < e'$) if the completion of e is followed by the starting of e'. In Table 1, the happened-before relation of case 75 is {Booking received < Confirm Booking, Confirm Booking < Payment received, Confirm Booking < Order ticket}. Instead, in Table 2, the happened-before relation of case 93 is {Ticket Order Received < Payment refund}, while for case 56 it is {Ticket Order Received < Confirm payment}.

Mining Tool-Independent Specification. This phase is inspired by the algorithm proposed by Schimm [31]. It consists of seven steps, which manipulate the set of traces in the log to generate the intermediate model described above. Schimm defined his mining algorithm only in a descriptive way, without providing any implementation. We extended his work by filling the gaps left underspecified in the original presentation of the algorithm. In particular, we defined and applied further minimization rules to obtain more compact specifications, and provided a clear definition of what is a loop and how to detect it. In addition, we implemented the algorithm we propose, thus leaving no room for ambiguities.

Definition 1 (Loop). *Let E be an event log, $\rho \in E$ a trace, and hb_ρ the happened-before relation of ρ; every loop in ρ starting from event e is identified by a non-empty set of the form $L_e = \{\rho' \subseteq \rho \mid first(\rho') = e, (last(\rho') < e) \in hb_\rho\}$, where $\subseteq$ denotes the subtrace relation, and $first(\cdot)$ and $last(\cdot)$ denote the first and last event of a trace, respectively.*

According to the above definition, a loop is identified in a trace ρ when this contains at least a subtrace ρ' such that its last event happened before the first one. Notably, more than one subtrace starting with the same event can have this characteristic, depending on the structure of the body of the loop; hence, all these subtraces are collected together in a set, which will be then analysed to define the structure corresponding to the body of the loop.

The steps of our mining algorithm are the following:

1st step - Search for loops *in: traces, out: traces and sets of subtraces.* All traces retrieved from the log file are analyzed in order to identify possible loops. When a subtrace is identified as part of a loop, because its last event is in happened-before relation with the first one (see Definition 1), the subtrace is replaced by a reference to the loop and stored in the loop set (as in Definition 1) to be analysed later. For example, given the log trace $abcdcdf$, after this step we obtain $ab0f$, where 0 is a reference to the loop set $\{cd\}$. From now on, until step 7, we will deal with loop references as events; hence, the happened-before relation of each trace with references will be updated accordingly.

2nd step - Creation of clusters *in: traces, out: traces.* Traces with the same event names and happened-before relations are grouped to form a cluster. This clustering permits reducing the number of traces to process in the following steps, without affecting the structure of the produced model. For example, given the two traces *abcd* and *acbd* with the same happened-before relation $\{a < b, a < c, c < d, b < d\}$, they are unified in the same cluster.

3rd step - Identification and removal of pseudo-dependencies *in: traces and happened-before relation, out: traces.* This step aims at identifying clustered traces that contain pseudo-dependencies, i.e. precedence dependencies between events that are invalidated by other traces. Specifically, given a trace ρ_1 with two events with a dependency of precedence in the happened-before relation of the trace, there should not exist another trace ρ_2 with the same event names in which there is not a relation of precedence between the two events in its happened-before relation. If such other trace ρ_2 exists, then ρ_1 contains a pseudo-dependency and, hence, ρ_1 is removed from the set of trace to be passed to the next step. For example, let us consider a trace corresponding to another case of the log in Table 1 such that its happened-before relation contains the dependency Payment received < Order ticket; this is a pseudo-dependency because the trace corresponding to the case 75 provides the proof that this is not a real dependency; thus it will be discarded.

4th step - Model for each cluster *in: traces, out: set of coarse block structure cluster.* For every cluster of traces we compute the set $\mathcal{P}$ of paths that can be generated by following the happened-before relation. A path is a sequence of events $e_1,\ldots,e_n$, denoted by $e_1 \rightarrow \ldots \rightarrow e_n$. Notably, a path does not represent a trace, but an ordered sequence of events where each event is in happened-before relation with the next one. Now, every event e will correspond to a basic action in our block structure representation. Every path $p \in \mathcal{P}$, with $p = e_1 \rightarrow \ldots \rightarrow e_n$, is rendered as a sequence block $S\{e_1,\ldots,e_n\}$ (denoted by $S\{p\}$ for short). Thus, a set of paths $\{p_1,\ldots,p_n\}$ is rendered as a parallel block that embeds the sequence blocks corresponding to the included paths, i.e. $P\{S\{p_1\},\ldots,S\{p_n\}\}$. For example, from the cluster {Booking received, Confirm Booking, Payment received, Order ticket} obtained by the case 75 in Table 1, with happened-before relation ⟨ Booking received < Confirm Booking, Confirm Booking < Payment received, Confirm Booking < Order ticket⟩, we will obtain the set of paths $\mathcal{P} = \{$Booking received $\rightarrow$ Confirm Booking $\rightarrow$ Payment received, Booking received $\rightarrow$ Confirm Booking $\rightarrow$ Order ticket $\}$. The set $\mathcal{P}$ will result in the following block structure: $P\{S\{$Booking received, Confirm Booking, Payment received$\}$, $S\{$Booking received,Confirm Booking,Order ticket$\}\}$.

5th step - Unify all block structures *in: set of coarse block structures, out: (single) coarse block structure.* All blocks $B_1,\ldots,B_n$ obtained in the previous step are gathered in a single block using the choice operator: $C\{B_1,\ldots,B_n\}$.

6th step - Restructuring the model *input: coarse block structure, output: block structure.* The structure obtained from the previous step does not represent yet a model of the system behaviour; it is still defined in terms of events rather than actions. For example, the same event name may appear many times in the model, since it has been generated starting from different cases in the log, but it has to correspond to a single action of the model; such events should be merged into a single one. To this aim, we apply the following transformation rules (the symbol $\rightsquigarrow$ represents a unidirectional transformation from a block structure term to another) up to commutativity of parallel and choice operators:

$$S\{B\} \rightsquigarrow B \qquad C\{B\} \rightsquigarrow B \qquad P\{B\} \rightsquigarrow B$$
$$P\{S\{e, e_1, \ldots, e_n\}, \ldots, S\{e, e'_1, \ldots, e'_m\}\} \rightsquigarrow S\{e, P\{S\{e_1, \ldots, e_n\}, \ldots, S\{e'_1, \ldots, e'_m\}\}\}$$
$$P\{S\{e_1, \ldots, e_n, e\}, \ldots, S\{e'_1, \ldots, e'_m, e\}\} \rightsquigarrow S\{P\{S\{e_1, \ldots, e_n\}, \ldots, S\{e'_1, \ldots, e'_m\}\}, e\}$$
$$C\{S\{e, e_1, \ldots, e_n\}, \ldots, S\{e, e'_1, \ldots, e'_m\}\} \rightsquigarrow S\{e, C\{S\{e_1, \ldots, e_n\}, \ldots, S\{e'_1, \ldots, e'_m\}\}\}$$
$$C\{S\{e_1, \ldots, e_n, e\}, \ldots, S\{e'_1, \ldots, e'_m, e\}\} \rightsquigarrow S\{C\{S\{e_1, \ldots, e_n\}, \ldots, S\{e'_1, \ldots, e'_m\}\}, e\}$$

The rules are syntax driven; in the implementation the rules are applied from the top block-structure to each child recursively, from left to right. As an example, by applying these rules to the block $C\{P\{S\{$Booking received, Confirm Booking, Payment received$\}, S\{$Booking received,Confirm Booking,Order ticket$\}\}\}$ we obtain the block $S\{$Booking received, Confirm Booking, P$\{$Payment received,Order ticket$\}\}$.

7th step - Replacing loop references *in: loop sets, out: block structure.* In this step, we run the algorithm again over the traces in the loop sets. In this way, we obtain a block structure B for each loop set; the term $L\{B\}$ will then replace all occurrences of the corresponding reference. For example, the trace shown in the first step results in the block $S\{a, b, 0, f\}$, that after this step becomes $S\{a, b, L\{S\{c, d\}\}, f\}$.

Technical details concerning each step of the mining algorithm can be found in the companion technical report [11], which provides comments to the source code of the implementation [2].

Transformation into mCRL2 Specification. The previous phase output is a block structure specification that is independent of a specific analysis tool. This choice makes the mining process flexible to be extended to produce specifications written in different languages, to exploit different process algebras based techniques and tools. Here, to demonstrate feasibility and effectiveness of our proposal, we have targeted the methodology to mCRL2 specifications.

To obtain an mCRL2 specification, we defined a function $\mathcal{T} : \mathbb{B} \rightarrow (\mathbb{P} \times \mathcal{P}(\mathbb{D}))$, where $\mathbb{B}$ is the set of block structures, $\mathbb{P}$ is the set of mCRL2 processes, $\mathbb{D}$ is the set of mCRL2 process definitions, and $\mathcal{P}(\mathbb{D})$ denotes the powerset of $\mathbb{D}$. Intuitively, the transformation function inputs a block structure and outputs a pair composed of a mCRL2 process and a related set of process definitions. The function definition uses auxiliary projection operator $\downarrow_i$, with $i \in \{1, 2\}$, that given a pair $\langle P, D \rangle$, with $P \in \mathbb{P}$ and $D \subseteq \mathbb{D}$, returns the i-th element of the pair, i.e. $\langle P, D \rangle \downarrow_1 = P$ and $\langle P, D \rangle \downarrow_2 = D$. Formally, function $\mathcal{T}$ is defined inductively on the syntax of block structures as follows:

$$\mathcal{T}(a) = \langle a, \emptyset \rangle$$
$$\mathcal{T}(S\{B_i\}_{i \in I}) = \langle \cdot_{i \in I} \mathcal{T}(B_i) \downarrow_1, \bigcup_{i \in I} \mathcal{T}(B_i) \downarrow_2 \rangle$$
$$\mathcal{T}(C\{B_i\}_{i \in I}) = \langle +_{i \in I} \mathcal{T}(B_i) \downarrow_1, \bigcup_{i \in I} \mathcal{T}(B_i) \downarrow_2 \rangle$$
$$\mathcal{T}(P\{B_i\}_{i \in I}) = \langle \|_{i \in I} \mathcal{T}(B_i) \downarrow_1, \bigcup_{i \in I} \mathcal{T}(B_i) \downarrow_2 \rangle$$
$$\mathcal{T}(L\{B\}) = \langle K, \{K = (\mathcal{T}(B) \downarrow_1 . K + \mathcal{T}(B) \downarrow_1)\} \cup \mathcal{T}(B) \downarrow_2 \rangle \text{ with } K \text{ fresh}$$

Actions are straightforwardly transformed into mCRL2 actions, without producing any process definition. Each block-structure operator, except for the loop one, is rendered in terms of the corresponding mCRL2 operator: S as ., C as +, and P as $\|$. Thus, a sequential composition of blocks is transformed into a pair, where the first element is a sequential composition of the processes resulting from the transformation of each inner block, and the second element is the set given by the union of the process definitions resulting from the transformation of each inner block. The transformation of choice and parallel composition is similar. Instead, a loop structure is rendered as a pair whose first element is a process call with a fresh identifier K and second element is the union of the recursive definition of K with the process definitions resulting from the transformation of the inner block. The definition of K is given in terms of the process resulting from the transformation of the block occurring as body of the loop; it ensures the execution of at least one iteration of the body.

A pair $\langle P, \{K_1 = P_1, \ldots, K_n = P_n\} \rangle$ produced by $\mathcal{T}$ corresponds to the following mCRL2 specification (we use notation $act(\cdot)$ to indicate the actions occurring within a term of a specification):

```
act
act(P), act(P₁), ... , act(Pₙ);
proc
K=P; K₁=P₁; ... ; Kₙ=Pₙ;
init K;
```

Example 1. If we apply the $\mathcal{T}$ function to the block structure resulting from the log in Table 1 (since the example does not contain loops, for the sake of readability we omit the second element of the pair generated from $\mathcal{T}$):

$\mathcal{T}(S\{\text{Booking received},\text{Confirm Booking}, P\{\text{Payment received},\text{Order Ticket}\}\})$
$= \text{Booking received}.\text{Confirm Booking}.(\text{Payment received} \| \text{Order Ticket})$

From the block structure resulting from the log in Table 2 we obtain:

$\mathcal{T}(S\{\text{Ticket Order Received},C\{\text{Payment Refund},\text{Confirm payment}\}\})$
$= \text{Ticket Order Received}.(\text{Payment refund} + \text{Confirm payment})$

Using the transformation function $\mathcal{T}$ we have obtained an mCRL2 process specification well defined from the process algebraic point of view, i.e. it respects the syntax of the mCRL2 language given in Sect. 2. However, in this

$$T_p(a) = a$$
$$T_p(\cdot_{i \in I} P_i) = T_{seq}(\cdot_{i \in I} T_p(P_i))$$
$$T_p(+_{i \in I} P_i) = T_{ch}(+_{i \in I} T_p(P_i))$$
$$T_p(\|_{i \in I} P_i) = \|_{i \in I} T_p(P_i)$$
$$T_p(K) = K$$

$$T_{seq}(\cdot_{i \in \{1,\ldots,n\}} P_i) = \begin{cases} \begin{aligned} & T_{seq}\big((\cdot_{i \in \{1,\ldots,j-1\}} P_i).t.Q_1.t.(\cdot_{h \in \{j+1,\ldots,n\}} P_h)\big)\| \\ & \|_{m \in M \setminus \{1\}} t.Q_m.t \\ & \quad \text{with } addComm(t(|t)^{|M|-1} \to t'), \\ & \quad\quad addAllow(t'), addHide(t') \end{aligned} & \begin{aligned} &\text{if } \exists j \in I: \\ & \quad P_j = \|_{m \in M} Q_m \\ & \quad \wedge\ t \text{ and } t' \text{ fresh} \end{aligned} \\[2em] \cdot_{i \in \{1,\ldots,n\}} P_i & \text{otherwise} \end{cases}$$

$$T_{ch}(+_{i \in I} P_i) = \begin{cases} \begin{aligned} & T_{ch}\big((+_{i \in I \setminus \{j\}} t_i.P_i.t_i) + t.Q_1.t\big)\| \\ & \|_{m \in M \setminus \{1\}}\big((+_{h \in I \setminus \{j\}} t_h.t_h) + t.Q_m.t\big) \\ & \text{with } addComm(\{t(|t)^{|M|-1} \to t'\} \\ & \quad\quad \cup \{t_i(|t_i)^{|M|-1} \to t' \mid i \in I \setminus \{j\}\}), \\ & \quad\quad addAllow(t'), addHide(t') \end{aligned} & \begin{aligned} &\text{if } \exists j \in I: \\ & \quad P_j = \|_{m \in M} Q_m \\ & \quad \wedge\ t \text{ fresh} \\ & \quad \wedge\ \forall_{i \in I \setminus \{j\}} t_i \text{ fresh} \end{aligned} \\[2em] +_{i \in I} P_i & \text{otherwise} \end{cases}$$

Fig. 3. Definition of function T_p (and related auxiliary functions).

actual form the specification cannot be used as input for the analysis tools provided by the mCRL2 toolset. Indeed, these tools require the mCRL2 specification to also respect the pCRL format [29], where parallel, communication, renaming and hiding operators must be positioned at top level. Therefore, we have defined another function, T_p, to transform a process specification produced by T (possibly with parallel operator at any level of nesting, and not using communication, renaming and hiding operators) into an equivalent one in the pCRL format. Formally, T_p takes as input a pair $\langle P, D \rangle$ and returns a tuple $\langle P', D', CommSet, AllowSet, HideSet \rangle$, where P' and D' are a process and a set of process definitions where the parallel operator is moved at top level, while $CommSet$, $AllowSet$ and $HideSet$ are sets of communication expressions, allowed actions and hidden actions, respectively. Intuitively, to move nested parallel processes to the top level, the T_p function uses additional synchronization actions that permit to properly activate the moved processes and to signal their termination. These added actions are forced to communicate and the actions resulting from their synchronizations are hidden.

For the sake of presentation, to avoid dealing with projections and other technicalities concerning tuples, we provide in Fig. 3 a simplified definition of T_p in which we do not explicitly represent the sets of communication expressions, allowed actions and hidden actions; such sets are indeed populated (in a programming style) by means of functions $addComm$, $addAllow$ and $addHide$, respectively. The sets $CommSet$ and $HideSet$ are instantiated to $\emptyset$, while the set $AllowSet$ is instantiated to the set of all actions of the process and the process definitions to be transformed. We use t, t_i and t_h to denote the synchronisation actions. In case of process definitions, it is not sufficient to move the parallel operator at top level of the process occurring as body; the operator has to be removed by expanding the term according to the interleaving semantics of the operator (like CCS's expansion law [27, Sect. 3.3]). Specifically, a process definition $K = P$ is transformed into $K = T_d(P)$, where the auxiliary function T_d is defined as follows:

$$T_d(a) = a \qquad T_d(\cdot_{i\in I}P_i) = \cdot_{i\in I}T_d(P_i) \qquad T_d(+_{i\in I}P_i) = +_{i\in I}T_d(P_i)$$
$$T_d(\|_{i\in I}P_i) = +_{s\in(\bigcup_{i\in I} seq(T_d(P_i)))}s \qquad T_d(K) = K$$

with function $seq(P)$ returning the set of all sequences of actions/calls of P.

With T_{seq}, each process in the parallel block is surrounded by a pair of synchronization actions (t and t) that communicate only after the execution of the sequence preceding the parallel process. For example, $a.(b\|c)$ turns into $allow(\{t', a, b, c\}, comm(\{t|t \rightarrow t'\}, a.t.b.t\|t.c.t))$. With T_{ch} we surround each process in the choice with a pair of synchronization actions that are used in the resulting process to preserve the choice in each process inside it. For example, $a + (b\|c)$ turns into $allow(\{t', a, b, c\}, comm(\{t|t \rightarrow t', t1|t1 \rightarrow t'\}, t.a.t + t1.b.t1\|t.t + t1.c.t1))$. Just one between a and $b\|c$ can be executed, thanks to the synchronization actions (t and $t1$).

Example 2. We apply function T_p to $\langle P, \emptyset \rangle$, where P is the first mCRL2 process produced in Example 1 (the second one does not contain the parallel operator). We obtain $T_p(\langle P, \emptyset \rangle) = \langle T_p(P), \emptyset, CommSet, AllowSet, HideSet \rangle$, where:

$$T_p(P) = T_{seq}(T_p(\text{Booking received}).T_p(\text{Confirm Booking}).$$
$$(T_p(\text{Payment received})\|T_p(\text{Order Ticket})))$$
$$= T_{seq}(\text{Booking received.Confirm Booking.(Payment received}\|\text{Order ticket}))$$
$$= \text{Booking received.Confirm Booking.}t.\text{Payment received.}t\|t.\text{Order Ticket.}t$$
$$AllowSet = \{t', \text{Booking received, Confirm Booking, Payment received,}$$
$$\text{Order Ticket}\}$$
$$CommSet = \{t|t \rightarrow t'\} \qquad HideSet = \{t'\}$$

Thus, a tuple $\langle P, \{K_1 = P_1, \ldots, K_n = P_n\}, CommSet, AllowSet, HideSet \rangle$ produced by T_p corresponds to the following mCRL2 specification:

```
act
act(AllowSet), act(CommSet);
proc
K=P;  K₁=P₁;  ...  ;  Kₙ=Pₙ;
init  hide(HideSet, allow(AllowSet, comm(CommSet, K)));
```

3.2   Aggregation

In this step, the specifications obtained from the logs of components of a distributed system can be combined to obtain an aggregate specification of the

overall system. This allows one to focus analysis on the overall behaviour of
a system resulting from the message-based interactions among its components.
This step takes advantage of the parallel composition operators that enable
channel-based communication, to obtain the specification of the full system.

To enable the aggregation step, it is necessary to extract from the logs the
information concerning message exchanges. This information is specified in the
events stored in XES logs by specific attributes indicating input and output
messages. Below, we report the XES code corresponding to an event associated
to the 'Booking received' task, which receives a 'travel' message:

```
<event>
    <string key="concept:name" value="Booking received"/>
    <string key="input_message" value="travel"/>
    <string key="lifecycle:transition" value="start"/>
    <date key="time:timestamp" value="2020-07-01T01:03:10+01:00"/>
</event>
```

Information about message exchanges is extracted from the logs during the
parsing phase, and is made available to the aggregation step in terms of two
partial functions: M_{inp} (resp. M_{out}) takes as input an event name and returns
the name of the received (resp. sent) message, if any.

We define how an aggregate specification is obtained below; we use notation
$cod(\cdot)$ to indicate the codomain of a function.

Definition 2 (Aggregation). *Let $\langle P_i, D_i, CommSet_i, AllowSet_i, HideSet_i\rangle$,
with $i \in I = \{1, \ldots n\}$, be specification tuples obtained at the mining step, and
M_{inp} and M_{out} be input and output message functions; the sets defining their
aggregate specification are as follows:*

- $Act_i = act(P_i) \cup act(D_i)$, *with* $i \in I$;
- $Act_{agg} = \bigcup_{i \in I}(Act_i \cup act(CommSet_i)) \cup cod(M_{inp}) \cup cod(M_{out})$;
- $CommSet_{agg} = \bigcup_{i \in I} CommSet_i \cup$

$$\{a_1|a_2 \to m \mid a_1 \in Act_i, a_2 \in Act_j, i \neq j, M_{inp}(a_1) = M_{out}(a_2) = m\};$$

- $AllowSet_{agg} = \bigcup_{i \in I} AllowSet_i \cup cod(M_{inp}) \cup cod(M_{out}) \setminus$

$$\{a_1, a_2 \mid a_1 \in Act_i, a_2 \in Act_j, i \neq j, M_{inp}(a_1) = M_{out}(a_2)\};$$

- $HideSet_{agg} = \bigcup_{i \in I} HideSet_i$.

Hence, the corresponding aggregate specification is:

```
act
Act_agg
proc
K₁=P₁;  ...;  Kₙ=Pₙ;  D₁;  ...;  Dₙ
init  hide(HideSet_agg,allow(AllowSet_agg,comm(CommSet_agg,K₁||...||Kₙ)));
```

Every time two events correspond to a message exchange between two tasks, the
communication is described as a synchronization of actions, which results in an
action named with the message name.

We conclude with a simple example aiming at clarifying the aggregation step;
a richer example based on the running scenario is provided in the next section.

Example 3. Let us consider a simple collaborating scenario where one participant sends a message m_1 and then waits for a series of messages m_2; on the other side, after receiving m_1, the participant decides either to perform an internal activity and stop, or to perform a different internal activity and send a series of messages m_2. This behaviour is captured by the mining step in terms of the following specification tuples:

$$\langle a.K_1, \{K_1 = (b.K_1 + b)\}, \emptyset, \{a, b\}, \emptyset \rangle$$
$$\langle c.(d + (e.K_2)), \{K_2 = (f.K_2 + f)\}, \emptyset, \{c, d, e, f\}, \emptyset \rangle$$

where the second components of the tuples are sets of process definitions. The functions providing the messages information extracted from the logs are defined by the following cases: $M_{out}(a) = m_1$, $M_{out}(f) = m_2$, $M_{inp}(c) = m_1$, and $M_{inp}(b) = m_2$. Now, the sets defining the corresponding aggregate specification are defined as follows:

$$Act_{agg} = \{a, b\} \cup \{c, d, e, f\} \cup \{m_1, m_2\} \quad CommSet_{agg} = \{a|c \rightarrow m_1, f|b \rightarrow m_2\}$$
$$AllowSet_{agg} = Act_{agg} \setminus \{a, c, f, b\} = \{d, e, m_1, m_2\} \quad HideSet_{agg} = \emptyset$$

The resulting aggregate specification is as follows:

```
act
a, b, c, d, e, f, m_1, m_2
proc
K_3=a.K_1;  K_4=c.(d + (e.K_2));  K_1 = (b.K_1 + b);  K_2 = (f.K_2 + f)
init  allow({d, e, m_1, m_2},comm({a|c → m_1, f|b → m_2},K_3 || K_4));
```

where the hide command is omitted since the hiding set is empty.

4   PALM at Work

The PALM methodology has been implemented as a command-line Java tool, called PALM as well, whose source and binary code is available on GitHub [2].

The tool enables us to analyse both the specification resulting from a single event log and the aggregate specification resulting from multiple logs. It provides the verification of deadlock freedom and of custom formulas and also functionalities to support the validation illustrated in Sect. 5, such as the computation of the fitness measure to analyze the quality of the obtained specifications, and the transformation into the mCRL2 language of the models produced by other process mining algorithms, to compare their outcome with the specifications produced by PALM. In addition, to keep the state space of the produced specifications manageable for the analysis, the tool allows users to set a *loop threshold* parameter, which is used during the generation of the mCRL2 specification to decide whether to unfold a loop or to represent it as a process definition. Such a decision is taken by comparing the value of this parameter with the frequency value computed for each loop in the block structure specification. The loop frequency measures the weight of a loop considering how many times this loop appears in the log and its length. This value ranges between 0 to 100, where 100 means that the loop has high relevance in the log, i.e. every trace in the log is produced by the loop, while 0 means that the loop's events do not appear in the log. Thus, if t is the frequency threshold chosen by the user, the PALM tool will write as recursive processes only those loops that have frequency greater than or equal to t, while all the other loops are unfolded according to their frequency. Loop frequency is computed as follows.

Definition 3 (Loop frequency). *Given a loop l and a set $\{c_i\}_{i\in I}$ of cases of a log, the frequency of the loop is computed as follows:*

$$f_{loop}(l, \{c_i\}_{i\in I}) = \left(\frac{\sum_{i\in I} f_{loop}(l, c_i)}{n_{cases}} + \frac{n_{cases} \times 100}{|I|} \right) / 2$$

where l is the loop, n_{cases} is the number of cases in $\{c_i\}_{i\in I}$ in which l is present. The frequency over a single case is computed as follows:

$$f_{loop}(l, c) = occ(l, c) \times |l| \ / \ |c| \times 100$$

where $occ(l, c)$ returns the number of occurrences of the loop l in c, while $|c|$ (resp. $|l|$) returns the length of c (resp. l).

We conclude the section with the application of the PALM methodology and its tool to our running example.

Example 4. Let us first consider the mCRL2 process specifications obtained (separately) from the event logs corresponding to each participant of our running example (i.e., Customer, Travel agency and Airline). They correspond to processes P0, P1 and P2 in Listing 1.1 (their full mCRL2 specifications are reported in [11]). When these specifications are analysed with mCRL2 tools, the individual process behaves as expected (e.g., no deadlock occurs[1] - all states of the transition system corresponding to the specification have outgoing transitions). However, since they are specifications of components of a single distributed system, it is important to check also their aggregate specification in Listing 1.1.

```
act
Confirmpayment , BookTravel , Bookingreceived , Paymentreceived , Paymentrefund ,
Bookingconfirmed , ConfirmBooking , confirmation , Orderticket ,
TicketOrderReceived , PayTravel , t , Paymentconfirmationreceived , payment ,
payment_confirmation , t0 , order , travel ;
proc
P0=(TicketOrderReceived . ( Paymentrefund+Confirmpayment ) ) ;
P1=(BookTravel . Bookingconfirmed . PayTravel . Paymentconfirmationreceived ) ;
P2=((Bookingreceived . ConfirmBooking . t0 . Paymentreceived . t0 )
    ||(t0 . Orderticket . t0 ) ) ;
init  hide({ t } , allow ({ Paymentrefund , confirmation , t , payment ,
payment_confirmation , order , travel } , comm({ Bookingreceived | BookTravel ->travel ,
Confirmpayment | Paymentconfirmationreceived ->payment_confirmation ,
Orderticket | TicketOrderReceived ->order , PayTravel | Paymentreceived ->payment ,
Bookingconfirmed | ConfirmBooking ->confirmation , t0 | t0 ->t } , P0 | | P1 | | P2 ) ) ) ;
```

Listing 1.1. mCRL2 aggregate specification of the running example.

---

[1] In the deadlock checking, the mCRL2 tool is not able to distinguish between a correct termination and an actual deadlock. Anyway, since the *Terminate* action is appended to each correct termination, we can solve this issue by resorting to the model checking of the logical formula $[!Terminate*] < true > true$.

The fact that the Customer will wait forever to receive the payment confirmation if the Airlane has to refund the payment (see Fig. 2) is observable only having the overall specification, since when analyzed separately there is no communication between the participants. Using one of the mCRL2 checking functionality, we do detect a deadlock. Interestingly, the tool, in case of deadlock, offers a counterexample trace, i.e. the ordered sequence of actions that leads to the deadlocked state. In our example, it reports a trace where the customer has paid for the travel, the order is sent by the travel agency to the airline company, but the latter takes the "Payment refund" choice and the customer process waits forever the "payment_confirmation" message.

5   Validation

In this section, we report the results of the experiments we carried out to validate the PALM methodology and the related tool, considering both logs synthetically generated using PLG2 [16] and logs from a real scenarios [1].

Validation Overview. For validation we compare the results of the experiments conducted with PALM against those obtained by using three well-known process mining discovery algorithms, i.e. Inductive Miner (IM), Structured Heuristic Miner (S-HM), and Split Miner (SM), supported by the TKDE Benchmark tool discussed in [10]. We consider these algorithms since they perform quite well in terms of mining time and, also, perform better than others in terms of quality measures [10]. Our comparison is based on a revised version of the *fitness* quality measure used in process mining to evaluate discovery algorithms [14,30]. Like the original fitness measure, our notion also aims at measuring the proportion of behaviour in the event log that is in accordance with the model but does this differently by taking advantage from the model checking technique enabled by our process algebraic specifications. For this reason, we refer to it as *model checking-based fitness*. In this paper we focus on fitness since it is the measure most considered in the literature; we leave as future investigation the introduction of other quality measures from the process mining field, namely precision and generalization.

Definition 4 (Model Checking-based fitness). *Let C be the set of cases of a log and S be an mCRL2 specification, the Model Checking-based fitness (MC-fitness) measures the ability of the specification S to satisfy the formulas f_c such that $c = [e_1, ..., e_n] \in C$ and $f_c = <tau^*.e_1.tau^*. \cdots .tau^*.e_n.tau^*>true$. The MC-fitness is computed as follows:*

$$MC\text{-}fitness(C, S) = |\{f_c \mid c \in C , S \models f_c\}| \; / \; |C|$$

where $S \models f_c$ indicates that the formula f_c is satisfied by the specification S.

Notably, f_c is a formula describing the case of a log, where each case event is surrounded by an unbounded numbers of silent actions. Formulas are verified

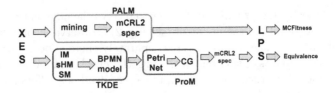

Fig. 4. Transformation steps required by the PALM validation.

using mCRL2 model checker. The values of MC-fitness range from 1 and 0, with 1 meaning that every formula can be satisfied, and 0 that none of them can.

Validation has been also enriched by checking equivalence of process models resulting from the PALM technique and those obtained from the three process mining algorithms. The considered equivalences are those supported by the mCRL2 tool: strong bisimilarity, weak bisimilarity, trace equivalence, weak trace equivalence, branching bisimilarity, strong simulation and divergence preserving branching bisimilarity [24]. This part of the validation is interesting because it permits to detect those situations where two techniques have with similar fitness values but yield different models from the behavioural point of view (i.e., they are not equivalent up to any equivalence relation).

Validation Set-Up. Figure 4 describes the preparatory steps needed for comparing two different kinds of models, i.e. a process algebra specification with a BPMN model. To make such comparison, We resort to a common specification model, that is LPS (Linear Process Specifications) and transform the BPMN models, obtained by executing the three considered process mining algorithms via the TKDE tool [10] according to the following steps. We then use ProM [34], a well-established framework that supports a wide variety of process mining techniques; in particular we use two of its plug-ins, namely "Convert BPMN diagram to Petri net" and "Construct coverability graph of a Petri net". The BPMN models are first transformed into Petri Nets, and then their Coverability Graphs (CGs) is obtained from which it is straightforward to obtain a mCRL2 specifications (Definition 5). mCRL2 specifications are given as input to the appropriate mCRL2 tool to be transformed into LPS, which can be used to calculate the MC-fitness and run conformance checking.

Definition 5 (From Coverability Graph to mCRL2). *Let $\langle E, M \rangle$ be a coverability graph, where E is the set of edges of the form $<v, l, v'>$ with $v, v' \in V$, $l \in L$, while $M \subseteq V$ is the initial marking. V is the set of vertices and L is the set of labels. The corresponding mCRL2 specification is as follows:*

```
act
L
proc
{K_v = l_1.K_{v_1} + ··· + l_k.K_{v_k}  |  < v,l_1,v_1 >,...,< v,l_k,v_k > ∈ E}
∪ {K_v = delta | ∄ < v,l,v' >∈ E}
init  ||{K_v | v ∈ M};
```

where delta *is the special mCRL2 process that cannot perform anything, and* $||\{K_i\}_{i \in \{1,...,n\}}$ *denotes the term* $K_1||\dots||K_n$.

Validation Results. Table 3 summarizes the validation that we ran over three synthetically generated event logs (whose generating models are publicly available in [2]) and six real-life event logs. All the synthetic logs (log1, log2, log3) are built out of 1000 cases that mix parallel and choice behaviours. Specifically, log1 is generated by a BPMN model with two XOR gateways (split and join) and with six tasks, while log2 is generated by a model with four gateways (XOR and AND with split and join) and nine tasks. Differently, log3 is generated by a model with eight gateways (six XOR, two AND split and join), fourteen tasks and also include two loops. The real-life logs (rlog1, rlog2, rlog3, rlog4, rlog5, rlog6) refer to activities of daily living performed by several individuals and collected by using sensors. The logs can be retrieved online [2] as an extraction of what data.4tu makes available[2].

All logs are given as input to PALM and to the other discovery algorithms. For each of them, we register the mining time to generate the specification (in seconds), and the value of the MC-fitness. We also calculate if there exists an equivalence relation between the model generated by PALM and the ones generated by IM, sHM and SM. In the discovery algorithm column, for the rows related to PALM, we also specify the loop frequency values (defined in 3), i.e. 90, 50 and 0. The symbol $-$ used in the Table 3 means that the value of that cell does not need to be computed, while the value $N.C.$ means that we tried to calculate it but a timeout expired.

According to our experimentation, PALM behaves quite well with the synthetic logs. In particular, the application of the PALM methodology to log1 returns an MC-fitness equal to 1. When comparing the three models generated by PALM (with different threshold) and those obtained from the same log by the other algorithms, we can observe that weak-trace equivalence is satisfied. This means that all resulting models can produce the same cases, possibly with a different number of silent actions. Considering log2, the comparison does not change much, apart from the observed equivalence. In this case, even if we obtain the same value for the MC-fitness, the models are not equivalent up to any of the considered relations. This is because the generated models can reproduce cases not included in the current log. For the log3, instead, we do not have a perfect MC-fitness value; this is probably due to the difficulty to properly identify those situations where there is a choice between performing a task and skipping it. For example, let abc and ac be two traces, b can be either performed or skipped.

The experiments with real logs confirm that there is no equivalence relation according to which the four models are equivalent, but we have quite different results for fitness. Since fitness values are so different from each other, it is straightforward that no equivalence exists between the generated models. Hence, let us focus more on the fitness results. PALM generates from logs rlog1 and

---

[2] https://data.4tu.nl/articles/dataset/Activities_of_daily_living_of_several_individuals/12674873.

Table 3. Results of the PALM Validation.

Model Name	Discovery Algorithm	Mining Time (s)	MC Fitness	Equiv.
log1	PALM 90	≤1	1	–
	PALM 50	≤1	1	–
	PALM 0	≤1	1	–
	IM	59,2	1	Weak-trace
	sHM	88,2	1	Weak-trace
	SM	12,4	1	Weak-trace
log2	PALM 90	≤1	1	–
	PALM 50	≤1	1	–
	PALM 0	≤1	1	–
	IM	101,2	1	None
	sHM	163,4	1	None
	SM	24,4	1	None
log3	PALM 90	≤1	0,87	–
	PALM 50	≤1	0,87	–
	PALM 0	≤1	0,87	–
	IM	127,4	0,99	None
	sHM	129	0,99	None
	SM	23,8	1	None

Model Name	Discovery Algorithm	Mining Time (s)	MC Fitness	Equiv.
rlog1	PALM 90	9,5	0,5	-
	PALM 50	4,96	0,5	–
	PALM 0	≤1	0,6	–
	IM	21	1	None
	sHM	73,2	0	None
	SM	42,6	N.C.	N.C.
rlog2	PALM 90	≤1	0,4	–
	PALM 50	≤1	0,4	–
	PALM 0	≤1	0,4	–
	IM	16,4	N.C.	N.C.
	sHM	154	0	None
	SM	59,6	N.C.	N.C.
rlog3	PALM 90	≤1	0,66	–
	PALM 50	≤1	0,66	–
	PALM 0	3	N.C.	–
	IM	23,2	1	None
	sHM	41	0	None
	SM	22,7	N.C.	N.C.
rlog4	PALM 90	≤1	0,85	–
	PALM 50	≤1	0,85	–
	PALM 0	≤1	0,85	–
	IM	6,4	1	None
	sHM	43,8	0,28	None
	SM	53,6	0,57	None
rlog5	PALM 90	≤1	0,71	–
	PALM 50	≤1	0,85	–
	PALM 0	≤1	0,85	–
	IM	6,4	N.C.	N.C.
	sHM	56,4	0,71	None
	SM	23,0	0,42	None
rlog6	PALM 90	≤1	0,77	–
	PALM 50	≤1	0,83	–
	PALM 0	≤1	N.C	–
	IM	27,6	1	None
	sHM	70	0	None
	SM	18,8	0,22	None

rlog2 two specifications with a value of fitness not high, which anyway is in line with the other discovery algorithms (actually, the sHM algorithm generates a model that is not able to reproduce any case in the log). Logs rlog3 and rlog6 show the importance of the loop frequency threshold parameter for real logs, where the number of loops makes the state space to explode. Unfolding the 'less important' loops, i.e. the one with a low loop frequency, allows us to complete the analysis over specifications, which otherwise requires too much time (the timeout to compute the fitness value of rlog3 and rlog6 with 0 as threshold expired). For logs rlog4 and rlog5, our mining tool performs better than the others, as the specifications generated by PALM are able to reproduce most of the cases in the logs, while in rlog1, rlog3 and rlog6 IM outperforms PALM and the other algorithms in terms of MC fitness. In terms of time for generating the models, PALM always outperforms all the other algorithms.

6   Related Works

In the literature, there are other works that pursuit the goal of generating models from a set of observations. Such research topic is investigated by both the process mining community and the engineering and formal method community.

From the process mining perspective, several discovery techniques (see, e.g., [3,8,9,26,37]) use event logs to generate process models with a particular focus on the single organization and with the goal of continuously supporting organizational improvement. Even the used specification languages, i.e. Petri Net or Process Tree, reveal that they do not focus on distribution and communication aspects. Indeed, both these languages have difficulties in composing distributed behaviours. Even when the considered target language is BPMN, which is able to describe distributed scenarios via collaboration diagrams, they still focus on individual processes.

Instead, the engineering and formal method communities focuses on generating finite state machines (FSM) or graph models. They are used to provide program comprehension, test case generation, and model checking. In [13], for example, a communicating FSM is generated from a log of system executions enhanced with time vectors. Although model checking facilities over the models are available via the McScM tool, an automatic way to compose the models generated from different logs is not provided. In [25], message sequence graphs are mined from logs of distributed systems; these models are used for program comprehension, since they provides an higher-level view of the system behavior and no verification technique is mentioned to analyze the obtained models. The authors of [32] exploit an idea close to our work, presenting an algorithm to construct the overall model of a system by composing models of its components. The main difference with respect to our work is that they infer a model by analizying a list of log messages, knowing a priori the architecture dependencies among the components of the distributed system. The output of this inference process is a FSM. The work focusses on the scalability problem of large systems, while no mention to verification techniques is given. Other techniques, like the one proposed in [18], focus on building decision trees from message logs to detect possible failures in the system. Another closely related line of research concerns automata learning; the aim is to construct an automaton by providing inputs to a system and observing the corresponding outputs [33]. In this context, there are two types of learning: active and passive. In the former one (see, e.g., [6,7,23]), experiments are carried out over the system, while the latter one (see, e.g., [21,22,28,36]) is based on generated runs (i.e., logs). Our approach differs from the ones proposed by the automata learning community for the input and the output of the process: we consider as input logs, instead of automaton or traces, and we produce as output a process algebraic specification (in particular, a mCRL2 specification) instead of automata (FSM, state diagrams, I/O automata, etc.). Anyway, tailoring of the automata learning techniques to process algebraic specification mining, and vice versa, certainly deserves an in-depth investigation.

7   Conclusions and Future Work

This work proposes a technique to automatically generate the model of a system behaviour from a set of observations. In particular, being inspired by the results achieved by the process mining community, the proposed technique takes as input the event logs of a distributed system and produces, in a compositional way, a formal specification of the overall behaviour of the system in the mCRL2 language. This enables us to take advantage of the mCRL2 toolset for formal verification, aiming at detecting issues that may arise in a distributed scenario where multiple organizations interact to reach a common goal. The proposed methodology is supported by a software tool and has been validated using custom-made and real event logs.

In the future, we want to investigate how to improve in our mining algorithm the capability of detecting the choice between performing an action and skipping it, and we plan to extend the target language of the PALM methodology with data and time features to generate richer specifications. Of course, these kinds of information must be present in the input logs. Moreover, since the intermediate block structure that is generated in the mining step allows the PALM approach to be extended with other process algebras, we plan to investigate these extensions starting from the CCS and TCCS process algebras and the Caal tool supporting them. In this paper we do not give any correctness criteria with respect to the transformation to pCRL format. In particular, we did not study what properties are preserved by the transformation. In the future, we intend to formally study whether and which behavioural equivalences are preserved. We would also like to extend our work about equivalence checking also to other algorithms, to have a complete scenario about the validation. Finally, we want to improve the replication of the validation experiments, which currently is only partially supported by the application, by integrating the TDKE Benchmark and the ProM plug-ins to generate the BPMN models and consequently the Petri Nets and Coverability graphs.

References

1. 4tu. https://data.4tu.nl/repository/collection:event_logs_real
2. PALM github repository. https://github.com/SaraBellucciniIMT/PALM
3. Van der Aalst, W., Weijters, T., Maruster, L.: Workflow mining: discovering process models from event logs. TKDE **9**, 1128–1142 (2004)
4. Aalst, W.: Data science in action. Process Mining, pp. 3–23. Springer, Heidelberg (2016). https://doi.org/10.1007/978-3-662-49851-4_1
5. van der Aalst, W., et al.: Process mining manifesto. In: Daniel, F., Barkaoui, K., Dustdar, S. (eds.) BPM 2011. LNBIP, vol. 99, pp. 169–194. Springer, Heidelberg (2012). https://doi.org/10.1007/978-3-642-28108-2_19
6. Aarts, F., Vaandrager, F.: Learning I/O automata. In: Gastin, P., Laroussinie, F. (eds.) CONCUR 2010. LNCS, vol. 6269, pp. 71–85. Springer, Heidelberg (2010). https://doi.org/10.1007/978-3-642-15375-4_6
7. Angluin, D.: Learning regular sets from queries and counterexamples. Inf. Comput. **75**(2), 87–106 (1987)
8. Augusto, A., Conforti, R., Dumas, M., La Rosa, M.: Split miner: discovering accurate and simple business process models from event logs (2017)
9. Augusto, A., Conforti, R., Dumas, M., La Rosa, M., Bruno, G.: Automated discovery of structured process models from event logs. DKE **117**, 373–392 (2018)
10. Augusto, A., et al.: Automated discovery of process models from event logs: review and benchmark. TKDE (2018)
11. Belluccini, S., De Nicola, R., Re, B., Tiezzi, F.: PALM: a technique for process algebraic specification mining (technical report). Technical report, IMT. https://github.com/SaraBellucciniIMT/PALM
12. Bergstra, J.A., Klop, J.W.: Process algebra for synchronous communication. Inf. Control **60**(1/3), 109–137 (1984)
13. Beschastnikh, I., et al.: Inferring models of concurrent systems from logs of their behavior with CSight. In: ICSE, pp. 468–479. IEEE (2014)
14. Buijs, J.C.A.M., van Dongen, B.F., van der Aalst, W.M.P.: On the role of fitness, precision, generalization and simplicity in process discovery. In: Meersman, R., et al. (eds.) OTM 2012. LNCS, vol. 7565, pp. 305–322. Springer, Heidelberg (2012). https://doi.org/10.1007/978-3-642-33606-5_19
15. Bunte, O., et al.: The mCRL2 toolset for analysing concurrent systems. In: Vojnar, T., Zhang, L. (eds.) TACAS 2019. LNCS, vol. 11428, pp. 21–39. Springer, Cham (2019). https://doi.org/10.1007/978-3-030-17465-1_2
16. Burattin, A.: PLG2: Multiperspective process randomization with online and offline simulations. In: BPM (Demos), pp. 1–6 (2016)
17. Cook, J.E., Wolf, A.L.: Discovering models of software processes from event-based data. ACM TOSEM **7**(3), 215–249 (1998)
18. Fu, Q., at al.: Contextual analysis of program logs for understanding system behaviors. In: MSR, pp. 397–400. IEEE (2013)
19. Groote, J.F., Mousavi, M.: Modelling and analysis of communicating systems. Technische Universiteit Eindhoven (2013)
20. Günther, C.W., Verbeek, E.: XES standard definition. Fluxicon Lab (2014)
21. Hammerschmidt, C.A., State, R., Verwer, S.: Human in the loop: interactive passive automata learning via evidence-driven state-merging algorithms. arXiv preprint arXiv:1707.09430 (2017)
22. Hammerschmidt, C.A., Verwer, S., Lin, Q., State, R.: Interpreting finite automata for sequential data. arXiv preprint arXiv:1611.07100 (2016)

23. Isberner, M., Howar, F., Steffen, B.: The TTT algorithm: a redundancy-free approach to active automata learning. In: Bonakdarpour, B., Smolka, S.A. (eds.) RV 2014. LNCS, vol. 8734, pp. 307–322. Springer, Cham (2014). https://doi.org/10.1007/978-3-319-11164-3_26

24. Jansen, D.N., Groote, J.F., Keiren, J.J.A., Wijs, A.: An $O(m \log n)$ algorithm for branching bisimilarity on labelled transition systems. TACAS 2020. LNCS, vol. 12079, pp. 3–20. Springer, Cham (2020). https://doi.org/10.1007/978-3-030-45237-7_1

25. Kumar, S., Khoo, S.C., Roychoudhury, A., Lo, D.: Mining message sequence graphs. In: ICSE, pp. 91–100 (2011)

26. Leemans, S.J.J., Fahland, D., van der Aalst, W.M.P.: Discovering block-structured process models from event logs - a constructive approach. In: Colom, J.-M., Desel, J. (eds.) PETRI NETS 2013. LNCS, vol. 7927, pp. 311–329. Springer, Heidelberg (2013). https://doi.org/10.1007/978-3-642-38697-8_17

27. Milner, R.: Communication and Concurrency. Prentice-Hal (1989)

28. Murphy, K.P., et al.: Passively learning finite automata. Santa Fe Institute (1995)

29. Reniers, M., Groote, J.F., van der Zwaag, M.B., van Wamel, J.: Completeness of timed μcrl. Fundamenta Informaticae **50**(3–4), 361–402 (2002)

30. Rozinat, A., et al.: Towards an evaluation framework for process mining algorithms. BPM Center Report BPM-07-06 123, p. 142 (2007)

31. Schimm, G.: Mining exact models of concurrent workflows. Comput. Ind. **53**(3), 265–281 (2004)

32. Shin, D., et al.: Scalable inference of system-level models from component logs. arXiv preprint arXiv:1908.02329 (2019)

33. Vaandrager, F.W.: Model learning. Commun. ACM **60**(2), 86–95 (2017)

34. van Dongen, B.F., de Medeiros, A.K.A., Verbeek, H.M.W., Weijters, A.J.M.M., van der Aalst, W.M.P.: The ProM framework: a new era in process mining tool support. In: Ciardo, G., Darondeau, P. (eds.) ICATPN 2005. LNCS, vol. 3536, pp. 444–454. Springer, Heidelberg (2005). https://doi.org/10.1007/11494744_25

35. Verbeek, H., van der Aalst, W.M., Munoz-Gama, J.: Divide and conquer: a tool framework for supporting decomposed discovery in process mining. Comput. J. **60**(11), 1649–1674 (2017)

36. Verwer, S., Hammerschmidt, C.A.: Flexfringe: a passive automaton learning package. In: ICSME, pp. 638–642. IEEE (2017)

37. Weijters, A., Ribeiro, J.: Flexible heuristics miner. In: CIDM, pp. 310–317. IEEE (2011)

38. van Zelst, S., van Dongen, B., van der Aalst, W., Verbeek, H.: Discovering workflow nets using integer linear programming. Computing **100**(5), 529–556 (2018)

Philosophers May Dine - Definitively!

Safouan Taha[1]([⊠]), Burkhart Wolff[2], and Lina Ye[3]

[1] Université Paris-Saclay, CentraleSupélec, LRI, 91190 Gif-sur-Yvette, France
safouan.taha@lri.fr
[2] Université Paris-Saclay, LRI, 91190 Gif-sur-Yvette, France
wolff@lri.fr
[3] Université Paris-Saclay, CentraleSupélec, LRI, INRIA, 91190 Gif-sur-Yvette, France
lina.ye@lri.fr

Abstract. The theory of Communicating Sequential Processes going back to Hoare and Roscoe is still today one of the reference theories for concurrent specification and computing. In 1997, a first formalization in Isabelle/HOL of the denotational semantics of the Failure/Divergence Model of CSP was undertaken; in particular, this model can cope with infinite alphabets, in contrast to model-checking approaches limited to finite ones. In this paper, we extend this theory to a significant degree by taking advantage of more powerful automation of modern Isabelle version, which came even closer to recent developments in the semantic foundation of CSP.

More importantly, we use this formal development to analyse a family of refinement notions, comprising classic and new ones. This analysis enabled us to derive a number of properties that allow to deepen the understanding of these notions, in particular with respect to specification decomposition principles in the infinite case. Better definitions allow to clarify a number of obscure points in the classical literature, for example concerning the relationship between deadlock- and livelock-freeness. As a result, we have a modern environment for formal proofs of concurrent systems that allow to combine general infinite processes with locally finite ones in a logically safe way. We demonstrate a number of verification-techniques for classical, generalized examples: The Copy-Buffer and Dijkstra's Dining Philosopher Problem of an arbitrary size.

Keywords: Process-algebra · Concurrency · Computational models

1 Introduction

Communicating Sequential Processes (CSP) is a language to specify and verify patterns of interaction of concurrent systems. Together with CCS and LOTOS, it belongs to the family of *process algebras*. CSP's rich theory comprises denotational, operational and algebraic semantic facets and has influenced programming languages such as Limbo, Crystal, Clojure and most notably Golang [15]. CSP has been applied in industry as a tool for specifying and verifying the concurrent aspects of hardware systems, such as the T9000 transputer [6].

© Springer Nature Switzerland AG 2020
B. Dongol and E. Troubitsyna (Eds.): IFM 2020, LNCS 12546, pp. 419–439, 2020.
https://doi.org/10.1007/978-3-030-63461-2_23

The theory of CSP was first described in 1978 in a book by Tony Hoare [20], but has since evolved substantially [9,10,29]. CSP describes the most common communication and synchronization mechanisms with one single language primitive: synchronous communication written -⟦-⟧-. CSP semantics is described by a fully abstract model of behaviour designed to be *compositional*: the denotational semantics of a process P encompasses all possible behaviours of this process in the context of all possible environments $P \, [\![S]\!] \, Env$ (where S is the set of *atomic events* both P and Env must synchronize on). This design objective has the consequence that two kinds of choice have to be distinguished:

1. the *external choice*, written -□-, which forces a process "to follow" whatever the environment offers, and
2. the *internal choice*, written -⊓-, which imposes on the environment of a process "to follow" the non-deterministic choices made.

Generalizations of these two operators $□x \in A. \ P(x)$ and $⊓x \in A. \ P(x)$ allow for modeling the concepts of *input* and *output*: Based on the prefix operator $a{\rightarrow}P$ (event a happens, then the process proceeds with P), receiving input is modeled by $□x \in A. \ x{\rightarrow}P(x)$ while sending output is represented by $⊓x \in A. \ x{\rightarrow}P(x)$. Setting choice in the center of the language semantics implies that deadlock-freeness becomes a vital property for the well-formedness of a process, nearly as vital as type-checking: Consider two events a and b not involved in a process P, then $(a{\rightarrow}P \ □ \ b{\rightarrow}P) \ [\![\{a,b\}]\!] \ (a{\rightarrow}P \ ⊓ \ b{\rightarrow}P)$ is deadlock free provided P is, while $(a{\rightarrow}P \ ⊓ \ b{\rightarrow}P) \ [\![\{a,b\}]\!] \ (a{\rightarrow}P \ ⊓ \ b{\rightarrow}P)$ deadlocks (both processes can make "ruthlessly" an opposite choice, but are required to synchronize).

Verification of CSP properties has been centered around the notion of *process refinement orderings*, most notably -$⊑_{FD}$- and -$⊑$-. The latter turns the denotational domain of CSP into a Scott cpo [33], which yields semantics for the fixed point operator $μx. \ f(x)$ provided that f is continuous with respect to -$⊑$-. Since it is possible to express deadlock-freeness and livelock-freeness as a refinement problem, the verification of properties has been reduced traditionally to a model-checking problem for finite set of events A.

We are interested in verification techniques for arbitrary event sets A or arbitrarily parameterized processes. Such processes can be used to model dense-timed processes, processes with dynamic thread creation, and processes with unbounded thread-local variables and buffers. However, this adds substantial complexity to the process theory: when it comes to study the interplay of different denotational models, refinement-orderings, and side-conditions for continuity, paper-and-pencil proofs easily reach their limits of precision.

Several attempts have been undertaken to develop a formal theory in an interactive proof system, mostly in Isabelle/HOL [12,23,28,37]. This paper is based on [37], which has been the most comprehensive attempt to formalize denotational CSP semantics covering a part of Bill Roscoe's Book [29]. Our contributions are as follows:

- we ported [37] from Isabelle93-7 and ancient ML-written proof scripts to a modern Isabelle/HOL version and structured Isar proofs, and extended it substantially,
- we introduced new refinement notions allowing a deeper understanding of the CSP Failure/Divergence model, providing some meta-theoretic clarifications,
- we used our framework to derive new types of decomposition rules and stronger induction principles based on the new refinement notions, and
- we integrate this machinery into a number of advanced verification techniques, which we apply to two generalized paradigmatic examples in the CSP literature, the CopyBuffer and Dining Philosophers[1].

2   Preliminaries

2.1   Denotational CSP Semantics

The denotational semantics of CSP (following [29]) comes in three layers: the *trace model*, the *(stable) failures model* and the *failure/divergence model*.

In the trace semantics model, a process P is denoted by a set of communication traces, built from atomic events. A trace here represents a partial history of the communication sequence occurring when a process interacts with its environment. For the two basic CSP processes *Skip* (successful termination) and *Stop* (just deadlock), the semantic function $\mathcal{T}$ of the trace model just gives the same denotation, i.e.the empty trace: $\mathcal{T}(Skip) = \mathcal{T}(Stop) = \{[]\}$. Note that the trace sets, representing all *partial* history, is in general prefix closed.

Example 1. Let two processes be defined as follows:

1. $P_{det} = (a \rightarrow Stop) \;\square\; (b \rightarrow Stop)$
2. $P_{ndet} = (a \rightarrow Stop) \;\sqcap\; (b \rightarrow Stop)$

These two processes P_{det} and P_{ndet} cannot be distinguished by using the trace semantics: $\mathcal{T}(P_{det}) = \mathcal{T}(P_{ndet}) = \{[],[a],[b]\}$. To resolve this problem, Brookes [9] proposed the failures model, where communication traces were augmented with the constraint information for further communication that is represented negatively as a refusal set. A failure (t, X) is a pair of a trace t and a set of events X, called refusal set, that a process can refuse if any of the events in X were offered to him by the environment after performing the trace t. The semantic function $\mathcal{F}$ in the failures model maps a process to a set of refusals. Let Σ be the set of events. Then, $\{([],\Sigma)\} \subseteq \mathcal{F} \; Stop$ as the process *Stop* refuses all events. For Example 1, we have $\{([],\Sigma\backslash\{a,b\}),([a],\Sigma),([b],\Sigma)\} \subseteq \mathcal{F} \; P_{det}$, while $\{([],\Sigma\backslash\{a\}),([],\Sigma\backslash\{b\}),([a],\Sigma),([b],\Sigma)\} \subseteq \mathcal{F} \; P_{ndet}$ (the $-\subseteq-$ refers to the fact that the refusals must be downward closed; we show only the maximal refusal

---

[1] All proofs concerning the HOL-CSP 2 core have been published in the Archive of Formal Proofs [36]; all other proofs are available at https://gitlri.lri.fr/burkhart. wolff/hol-csp2.0. In this paper, all Isabelle proofs are omitted.

sets here). Thus, internal and external choice, also called *nondeterministic* and *deterministic* choice, can be distinguished in the failures semantics.

However, it turns out that the failures model suffers from another deficiency with respect to the phenomenon called infinite internal chatter or *divergence*.

Example 2. The following process P_{inf} is an infinite process that performs a infinitely many times. However, using the CSP hiding operator -\\-, this activity is concealed:

1. $P_{inf} = (\mu\, X.\, a \rightarrow X) \setminus \{a\}$

where P_{inf} will correspond to $\bot$ in the process cpo ordering. To distinguish divergences from the deadlock process, Brookes and Roscoe proposed failure/divergence model to incorporate divergence traces [10]. A divergence trace is the one leading to a possible divergent behavior. A well behaved process should be able to respond to its environment in a finite amount of time. Hence, divergences are considered as a kind of a catastrophe in this model. Thus, a process is represented by a failure set $\mathcal{F}$, together with a set of divergence traces $\mathcal{D}$; in our example, the empty trace $[]$ belongs to $\mathcal{D}\, P_{inf}$.

The failure/divergence model has become the standard semantics for an enormous range of CSP research and the implementations of [1,34]. Note, that the work of [23] is restricted to a variant of the failures model only.

2.2   Isabelle/HOL

Nowadays, Isabelle/HOL is one of the major interactive theory development environments [27]. HOL stands for Higher-Order Logic, a logic based on simply-typed λ-calculus extended by parametric polymorphism and Haskell-like type-classes. Besides interactive and integrated automated proof procedures, it offers code and documentation generators. Its structured proof language Isar is intensively used in the plethora of work done and has been a key factor for the success of the Archive of Formal Proofs (https://www.isa-afp.org).

For the work presented here, one relevant construction is:

– **typedef** $(\alpha_1, ..., \alpha_n)t = E$

It creates a fresh type that is isomorphic to a set E involving $\alpha_1, ..., \alpha_n$ types. Isabelle/HOL performs a number of syntactic checks for these constructions that guarantee the logical consistency of the defined constants or types relative to the axiomatic basis of HOL. The system distribution comes with rich libraries comprising Sets, Numbers, Lists, etc. which are built in this "conservative" way.

For this work, a particular library called $HOLCF$ is intensively used. It provides classical domain theory for a particular type-class $\alpha :: pcpo$, i.e. the class of types α for which

1. a complete partial order -$\sqsubseteq$- is defined, and
2. a least element $\bot$ is defined.

For these types, $HOLCF$ provides a fixed-point operator $\mu X.\ f\ X$, fixed-point induction and other (automated) proof infrastructure. Isabelle's type-inference can automatically infer, for example, that if $\alpha :: pcpo$, then $(\beta \Rightarrow \alpha) :: pcpo$.

3 Formalising Denotational CSP Semantics in HOL

3.1 Process Invariant and Process Type

First, we need a slight revision of the concept of *trace*: if Σ is the type of the atomic events (represented by a type variable), then we need to extend this type by a special event $\sqrt{}$ (called "tick") signaling termination. Thus, traces have the type $(\Sigma + \sqrt{})^*$, written $\Sigma^{\sqrt{}*}$; since $\sqrt{}$ may only occur at the end of a trace, we need to define a predicate $front\_tickFree\ t$ that requires from traces that $\sqrt{}$ can only occur at the end.

Second, in the traditional literature, the semantic domain is implicitly described by 9 "axioms" over the three semantic functions $\mathcal{T}$, $\mathcal{F}$ and $\mathcal{D}$. Informally:

- the initial trace of a process must be empty;
- any allowed trace must be $front\_tickFree$;
- traces of a process are *prefix-closed*;
- a process can refuse all subsets of a refusal set;
- any event refused by a process after a trace s must be in a refusal set associated to s;
- the tick accepted after a trace s implies that all other events are refused;
- a divergence trace with any suffix is itself a divergence one
- once a process has diverged, it can engage in or refuse any sequence of events.
- a trace ending with $\sqrt{}$ belonging to divergence set implies that its maximum prefix without $\sqrt{}$ is also a divergent trace.

Formally, a process P of the type $\Sigma\ process$ should have the following properties:

$$([],\{\}) \in \mathcal{F}\ P\ \wedge$$
$$(\forall\ s\ X.\ (s,X) \in \mathcal{F}\ P \longrightarrow front\text{-}tickFree\ s)\ \wedge$$
$$(\forall\ s\ t\ .\ (s@t,\{\}) \in \mathcal{F}\ P \longrightarrow (s,\{\}) \in \mathcal{F}\ P)\ \wedge$$
$$(\forall\ s\ X\ Y.\ (s,Y) \in \mathcal{F}\ P \wedge X \subseteq Y \longrightarrow (s,X) \in \mathcal{F}\ P)\ \wedge$$
$$(\forall\ s\ X\ Y.\ (s,X) \in \mathcal{F}\ P \wedge (\forall c \in Y.\ ((s@[c],\{\}) \notin \mathcal{F}\ P)) \longrightarrow (s,X \cup Y) \in \mathcal{F}\ P)\ \wedge$$
$$(\forall\ s\ X.\ (s@[\sqrt{}],\{\}) \in \mathcal{F}\ P \longrightarrow (s,X-\{\sqrt{}\}) \in \mathcal{F}\ P)\ \wedge$$
$$(\forall\ s\ t.\ s \in \mathcal{D}\ P \wedge tickFree\ s \wedge front\text{-}tickFree\ t \longrightarrow s@t \in \mathcal{D}\ P)\ \wedge$$
$$(\forall\ s\ X.\ s \in \mathcal{D}\ P \longrightarrow (s,X) \in \mathcal{F}\ P)\ \wedge$$
$$(\forall\ s.\ s@[\sqrt{}] \in \mathcal{D}\ P \longrightarrow s \in \mathcal{D}\ P)$$

Our objective is to encapsulate this wishlist into a type constructed as a conservative theory extension in our theory HOL-CSP. Therefore third, we define a pre-type for processes $\Sigma\ process_0$ by $\mathcal{P}(\Sigma^{\sqrt{}*} \times \mathcal{P}(\Sigma^{\sqrt{}})) \times \mathcal{P}(\Sigma^{\sqrt{}*})$. Fourth, we turn our wishlist of "axioms" above into the definition of a predicate *is-process* P of type $\Sigma\ process_0 \Rightarrow bool$ deciding if its conditions are fulfilled. Since P is a pre-process, we replace $\mathcal{F}$ by fst and $\mathcal{D}$ by snd (the HOL projections into a pair). And last not least fifth, we use the following type definition:

– **typedef** $'\alpha\ process = \{P :: '\alpha\ process_0 \,.\, is\text{-}process\ P\}$

Isabelle requires a proof for the existence of a witness for this set, but this can be constructed in a straight-forward manner. Suitable definitions for $\mathcal{T}$, $\mathcal{F}$ and $\mathcal{D}$ lifting fst and snd on the new $'\alpha\ process$-type allows to derive the above properties for any $P :: '\alpha\ process$.

3.2 CSP Operators over the Process Type

Now, the operators of CSP $Skip$, $Stop$, -⊓-, -□-, -→-, -[-]- etc. for internal choice, external choice, prefix and parallel composition, can be defined indirectly on the process-type. For example, for the simple case of the internal choice, we construct it such that -⊓- has type $'\alpha\ process \Rightarrow '\alpha\ process \Rightarrow '\alpha\ process$ and such that its projection laws satisfy the properties $\mathcal{F}\,(P \sqcap Q) = \mathcal{F}\,P \cup \mathcal{F}\,Q$ and $\mathcal{D}\,(P \sqcap Q) = \mathcal{D}\,P \cup \mathcal{D}\,Q$ required from [29]. This boils down to a proof that an equivalent definition on the pre-process type $\Sigma\ process_0$ maintains $is\text{-}process$, i.e. this predicate remains invariant on the elements of the semantic domain. For example, we define -⊓- on the pre-process type as follows:

– **definition** $P \sqcap Q \equiv Abs\text{-}process(\mathcal{F}\,P \cup \mathcal{F}\,Q\,,\mathcal{D}\,P \cup \mathcal{D}\,Q)$

where $\mathcal{F} = fst \circ Rep\text{-}process$ and $\mathcal{D} = snd \circ Rep\text{-}process$ and where $Rep\text{-}process$ and $Abs\text{-}process$ are the representation and abstraction morphisms resulting from the type definition linking $'\alpha\ process$ isomorphically to $'\alpha\ process_0$. Proving the above properties for $\mathcal{F}\,(P \sqcap Q)$ and $\mathcal{D}\,(P \sqcap Q)$ requires a proof that $(\mathcal{F}\,P \cup \mathcal{F}\,Q\,,\mathcal{D}\,P \cup \mathcal{D}\,Q)$ satisfies the 9 "axioms", which is fairly simple in this case.

The definitional presentation of the CSP process operators according to [29] follows always this scheme. This part of the theory comprises around 2000 loc.

3.3 Refinement Orderings

CSP is centered around the idea of process refinement; many critical properties, even ones typically considered as "liveness properties", can be expressed in terms of these, and a conversion of processes in terms of (finite) labelled transition systems leads to effective model-checking techniques based on graph-exploration. Essentially, a process P *refines* another process Q if and only if it is more deterministic and more defined (has less divergences). Consequently, each of the three semantics models (trace, failure and failure/divergence) has its corresponding refinement orderings. What we are interested in this paper is the following refinement orderings for the failure/divergence model.

1. $P \sqsubseteq_{\mathcal{F}\mathcal{D}} Q \equiv \mathcal{F}\,P \supseteq \mathcal{F}\,Q \wedge \mathcal{D}\,P \supseteq \mathcal{D}\,Q$
2. $P \sqsubseteq_{\mathcal{T}\mathcal{D}} Q \equiv \mathcal{T}\,P \supseteq \mathcal{T}\,Q \wedge \mathcal{D}\,P \supseteq \mathcal{D}\,Q$
3. $P \sqsubseteq_{\mathfrak{F}} Q \equiv \mathfrak{F}\,P \supseteq \mathfrak{F}\,Q,\ \mathfrak{F} \in \{\mathcal{T},\mathcal{F},\mathcal{D}\}$

Notice that in the CSP literature, only $\sqsubseteq_{\mathcal{FD}}$ is well studied for failure/divergence model. Our formal analysis of different granularities on the refinement orderings allows deeper understanding of the same semantics model. For example, $\sqsubseteq_{\mathcal{TD}}$ turns out to have in some cases better monotonicity properties and therefore allow for stronger proof principles in CSP. Furthermore, the refinement ordering $\sqsubseteq_{\mathcal{F}}$ analyzed here is different from the classical failure refinement in the literature that is studied for the stable failure model [29], where failures are only defined for stable states, from which no internal progress is possible.

3.4 Process Ordering and HOLCF

For any denotational semantics, the fixed point theory giving semantics to systems of recursive equations is considered as keystone. Its prerequisite is a complete partial ordering $-\sqsubseteq-$. The natural candidate $-\sqsubseteq_{\mathcal{FD}}-$ is unfortunately not complete for infinite Σ for the generalized deterministic choice, and thus for the building block of the read-operations.

Roscoe and Brooks [31] finally proposed another ordering, called the *process ordering*, and restricted the generalized deterministic choice in a particular way such that completeness could at least be assured for read-operations. This more complex ordering is based on the concept *refusals after* a trace s and defined by $\mathcal{R}\ P\ s \equiv \{X \mid (s, X) \in \mathcal{F}\ P\}$.

Definition 1 (process ordering). *We define $P \sqsubseteq Q \equiv \psi_{\mathcal{D}} \wedge \psi_{\mathcal{R}} \wedge \psi_{\mathcal{M}}$, where*

1. $\psi_{\mathcal{D}} = \mathcal{D}\ P \supseteq \mathcal{D}\ Q$
2. $\psi_{\mathcal{R}} = s \notin \mathcal{D}\ P \Rightarrow \mathcal{R}\ P\ s = \mathcal{R}\ Q\ s$
3. $\psi_{\mathcal{M}} = Mins(\mathcal{D}\ P) \subseteq \mathcal{T}\ Q$

Note that the third condition $\psi_{\mathcal{M}}$ implies that the set of minimal divergent traces (ones with no proper prefix that is also a divergence) in P, denoted by $Mins(\mathcal{D}\ P)$, should be a subset of the trace set of Q. It is straight-forward to define the least element $\bot$ in this ordering by $\mathcal{F}(\bot) = \{(s,X).\ front\text{-}tickFree\ s\}$ and $\mathcal{D}(\bot) = \{s.\ front\text{-}tickFree\ s\}$.
While the original work [37] was based on an own—and different—fixed-point theory, we decided to base HOL-CSP 2 on HOLCF (initiated by [26] and substantially extended in [21]). HOLCF is based on parametric polymorphism with type classes. A type class is actually a constraint on a type variable by respecting certain syntactic and semantic requirements. For example, a type class of partial ordering, denoted by $\alpha :: po$, is restricted to all types α possessing a relation $\leq :\alpha \times \alpha \rightarrow bool$ that is reflexive, anti-symmetric, and transitive. Isabelle possesses a construct that allows to establish, that the type nat belongs to this class, with the consequence that all lemmas derived abstractly on $\alpha :: po$ are in particular applicable on nat. The type class of po can be extended to the class of complete partial ordering cpo. A po is said to be complete if all non-empty directed sets have a least upper bound (lub). Finally the class of $pcpo$ (Pointed cpo) is a cpo ordering that has a least element, denoted by $\bot$. For $pcpo$ ordering,

two crucial notions for continuity (*cont*) and fixed-point operator ($\mu X.\ f(X)$) are defined in the usual way. A function from one *cpo* to another one is said to be continuous if it distributes over the *lub* of all directed sets (or chains). One key result of the fixed-point theory is the proof of the fixed-point theorem:

$$cont\ f \implies \mu X.\ f(X) = f(\mu X.\ f(X))$$

For most CSP operators $\otimes$ we derived rules of the form:

$$cont\ P \implies cont\ Q \implies cont(\lambda x.\ (P\ x) \otimes (Q\ x))$$

These rules allow to automatically infer for any process term if it is continuous or not. The port of HOL-CSP 2 on HOLCF implied that the derivation of the entire continuity rules had to be completely re-done (3000 loc).

HOL-CSP provides an important proof principle, the fixed-point induction:

$$cont\ f \implies adm\ Pr \implies Pr\ \bot \implies (\bigwedge X.\ X \implies Pr(f\ X)) \implies Pr(\mu X.\ f\ X)$$

Fixed-point induction requires a small side-calculus for establishing the admissibility of a predicate; basically, predicates are admissible if they are valid for any least upper bound of a chain $x_1 \sqsubseteq x_2 \sqsubseteq x_3 \ldots$ provided that $\forall i.\ Pr(x_i)$. It turns out that -$\sqsubseteq$- and -$\sqsubseteq_{F\ D}$- as well as all other refinement orderings that we introduce in this paper are admissible. Fixed-point inductions are the main proof weapon in verifications, together with monotonicities and the CSP laws. Denotational arguments can be hidden as they are not needed in practical verifications.

3.5   CSP Rules: Improved Proofs and New Results

The CSP operators enjoy a number of algebraic properties: commutativity, associativities, and idempotence in some cases. Moreover, there is a rich body of distribution laws between these operators. Our new version HOL-CSP 2 not only shortens and restructures the proofs of [37]; the code reduces to 8000 loc from 25000 loc. Some illustrative examples of new established rules are:

– $\Box x \in A \cup B \rightarrow P(x) = (\Box x \in A \rightarrow P\ x)\ \Box\ (\Box x \in B \rightarrow P\ x)$
– $A \cup B \subseteq C \implies (\Box x \in A \rightarrow P\ x\ [\![C]\!]\ \Box x \in B \rightarrow Q\ x) = \Box x \in A \cap B \rightarrow (P\ x\ [\![C]\!]\ Q\ x)$
– $A \subseteq C \implies B \cap C = \{\} \implies (\Box x \in A \rightarrow P\ x\ [\![C]\!]\ \Box x \in B \rightarrow Q\ x) = \Box x \in B \rightarrow (\Box x \in A \rightarrow P\ x\ [\![C]\!]\ Q\ x)$
– *finite* $A \implies A \cap C = \{\} \implies ((P\ [\![C]\!]\ Q) \setminus A) = ((P \setminus A)\ [\![C]\!]\ (Q \setminus A)) \ldots$

The continuity proof of the hiding operator is notorious. The proof is known to involve the classical König's lemma stating that every infinite tree with finite branching reference processes are

has an infinite path. We adapt this lemma to our context as follows:

$$infinite\ tr \implies \forall i.\ finite\{t.\ \exists t' \in tr.\ t = take\ i\ t'\}$$
$$\implies \exists\ f.\ strict\text{-}mono\ f \wedge range\ f \subseteq \{t.\ \exists t' \in tr.\ t \le t'\}$$

in order to come up with the continuity rule: $finite\ S \implies cont\ P \implies cont(\lambda X.\ P\ X \setminus S)$. Our current proof was drastically shortened by a factor 10 compared to the original one and important immediate steps generalized: monotonicity, for example, could be generalized to the infinite case.

As for new laws, consider the case of $(P \setminus A) \setminus B = P \setminus (A \cup B)$ which is stated in [30] without proof. In the new version, we managed to establish this law which still need 450 lines of complex Isar code. However, it turned out that the original claim is not fully true: it can only be established again by König's lemma to build a divergent trace of $P \setminus (A \cup B)$ which requires A to be finite (B can be arbitrary) in order to use it from a divergent trace o f $(P \setminus A) \setminus B$ [2]. Again, we want to argue that the intricate number of cases to be considered as well as their complexity makes pen and paper proofs practically infeasible.

4   Theoretical Results on Refinement

4.1   Decomposition Rules

In our framework, we implemented the pcpo process refinement together with the five refinement orderings introduced in Sect. 3.3. To enable fixed-point induction, we first have the admissibility of the refinements.

$$cont\ u \implies mono\ v \implies adm(\lambda x.\ u\ x \sqsubseteq_{\mathfrak{F}} v\ x)\ where\ \mathfrak{F} \in \{\mathcal{T}, \mathcal{F}, \mathcal{D}, \mathcal{TD}, \mathcal{FD}\}$$

Next we analyzed the monotonicity of these refinement orderings, whose results are then used as decomposition rules in our framework. Some CSP operators, such as multi-prefix and non-deterministic choice, are monotonic under all refinement orderings, while others are not.

- External choice is not monotonic only under $\sqsubseteq_{\mathcal{F}}$, with the following monotonicities proved:

$$P \sqsubseteq_{\mathfrak{F}} P' \implies Q \sqsubseteq_{\mathfrak{F}} Q' \implies (P \square Q) \sqsubseteq_{\mathfrak{F}} (P' \square Q')\ where\ \mathfrak{F} \in \{\mathcal{T}, \mathcal{D}, \mathcal{TD}, \mathcal{FD}\}$$

- Sequence operator is not monotonic under $\sqsubseteq_{\mathcal{F}}$, $\sqsubseteq_{\mathcal{D}}$ or $\sqsubseteq_{\mathcal{T}}$:

$$P \sqsubseteq_{\mathfrak{F}} P' \implies Q \sqsubseteq_{\mathfrak{F}} Q' \implies (P\ ;\ Q) \sqsubseteq_{\mathfrak{F}} (P'\ ;\ Q')\ where\ \mathfrak{F} \in \{\mathcal{TD}, \mathcal{FD}\}$$

---

[2] In [30], the authors point out that the laws involving the hiding operator may fail when A is infinite; however, they fail to give the precise conditions for this case.

– Hiding operator is not monotonic under $\sqsubseteq_\mathcal{D}$:

$$P \sqsubseteq_\mathfrak{F} Q \Longrightarrow P \setminus A \sqsubseteq_\mathfrak{F} Q \setminus A \ where\ \mathfrak{F} \in \{\mathcal{T}, \mathcal{F}, \mathcal{T}\mathcal{D}, \mathcal{F}\mathcal{D}\}$$

– Parallel composition is not monotonic under $\sqsubseteq_\mathcal{F}$, $\sqsubseteq_\mathcal{D}$ or $\sqsubseteq_\mathcal{T}$:

$$P \sqsubseteq_\mathfrak{F} P' \Longrightarrow Q \sqsubseteq_\mathfrak{F} Q' \Longrightarrow (P \ [\![A]\!] \ Q) \sqsubseteq_\mathfrak{F} (P' \ [\![A]\!] \ Q') \ where\ \mathfrak{F} \in \{\mathcal{T}\mathcal{D}, \mathcal{F}\mathcal{D}\}$$

4.2   Reference Processes and Their Properties

We now present reference processes that exhibit basic behaviors, introduced in fundamental CSP works [30]. The process $RUN\ A$ always accepts events from A offered by the environment. The process $CHAOS\ A$ can always choose to accept or reject any event of A. The process $DF\ A$ is the most non-deterministic deadlock-free process on A, i.e., it can never refuse all events of A. To handle termination better, we added two new processes $CHAOS_{SKIP}$ and DF_{SKIP}.

Definition 2. $RUN\ A \equiv \mu\ X.\ \square\ x\ \in\ A \rightarrow X$

Definition 3. $CHAOS\ A \equiv \mu\ X.\ (STOP \sqcap (\square\ x \in A \rightarrow X))$

Definition 4. $CHAOS_{SKIP}\ A \equiv \mu\ X.\ (SKIP \sqcap STOP \sqcap (\square\ x \in A \rightarrow X))$

Definition 5. $DF\ A \equiv \mu\ X.\ (\sqcap\ x \in A \rightarrow X)$

Definition 6. $DF_{SKIP}\ A \equiv \mu\ X.\ ((\sqcap\ x \in A \rightarrow X) \sqcap SKIP)$

In the following, we denote $\mathcal{RP} = \{DF_{SKIP}, DF,\ RUN,\ CHAOS,$ $CHAOS_{SKIP}\}$. All five reference processes are divergence-free.

$$D\ (\mathfrak{P}\ UNIV) = \{\} \ where\ \mathfrak{P} \in \mathcal{RP}\ and\ UNIV\ is\ the\ set\ of\ all\ events$$

Regarding the failure refinement ordering, the set of failures $\mathcal{F}\ P$ for any process P is a subset of $\mathcal{F}\ (CHAOS_{SKIP}\ UNIV)$.

$$CHAOS_{SKIP}\ UNIV \sqsubseteq_\mathcal{F} P$$

The following 5 relationships were demonstrated from monotonicity results and a denotational proof. Thanks to transitivity, we can derive other relationships.

1. $CHAOS_{SKIP}\ A \sqsubseteq_\mathcal{F} CHAOS\ A$
2. $CHAOS_{SKIP}\ A \sqsubseteq_\mathcal{F} DF_{SKIP}\ A$
3. $CHAOS\ A \sqsubseteq_\mathcal{F} DF\ A$
4. $DF_{SKIP}\ A \sqsubseteq_\mathcal{F} DF\ A$
5. $DF\ A \sqsubseteq_\mathcal{F} RUN\ A$

Last, regarding trace refinement, for any process P, its set of traces $\mathcal{T}\ P$ is a subset of $\mathcal{T}\ (CHAOS_{SKIP}\ UNIV)$ and of $\mathcal{T}\ (DF_{SKIP}\ UNIV)$ as well.

1. $CHAOS_{SKIP} \ UNIV \sqsubseteq_{\mathcal{T}} P$
2. $DF_{SKIP} \ UNIV \sqsubseteq_{\mathcal{T}} P$

Recall that a concurrent system is considered as being deadlocked if no component can make any progress, caused for example by the competition for resources. In opposition to deadlock, processes can enter infinite loops inside a sub-component without ever interact with their environment again ("infinite internal chatter"); this situation called divergence or livelock. Both properties are not just a sanity condition; in CSP, they play a central role for verification. For example, if one wants to establish that a protocol implementation $IMPL$ satisfies a non-deterministic specification $SPEC$ it suffices to ask if $IMPL \parallel SPEC$ is deadlock-free. In this setting, $SPEC$ becomes a kind of observer that signals non-conformance of $IMPL$ by deadlock.

In the literature, deadlock and livelock are phenomena that are often handled separately. One contribution of our work is establish their precise relationship inside the Failure/Divergence Semantics of CSP.

Definition 7. $deadlock\_free \ P \equiv DF_{SKIP} \ UNIV \sqsubseteq_{\mathcal{F}} P$

A process P is deadlock-free if and only if after any trace s without $\sqrt{}$, the union of $\sqrt{}$ and all events of P can never be a refusal set associated to s, which means that P cannot be deadlocked after any non-terminating trace.

Theorem 1 (DF definition captures deadlock-freeness).
$deadlock\text{-}free P \longleftrightarrow (\forall s \in \mathcal{T} \ P. \ tickFree \ s \longrightarrow (s, \{\sqrt{}\} \cup events\text{-}of \ P) \notin \mathcal{F} \ P)$

Definition 8. $livelock\_free \ P \equiv \mathcal{D} \ P = \{\}$

Recall that all five reference processes are livelock-free. We also have the following lemmas about the livelock-freeness of processes:

1. $livelock\_free \ P \longleftrightarrow \mathfrak{P} \ UNIV \sqsubseteq_{\mathcal{D}} P \ where \ \mathfrak{P} \in \mathcal{RP}$
2. $livelock\_free \ P \longleftrightarrow DF_{SKIP} \ UNIV \sqsubseteq_{\mathcal{TD}} P \longleftrightarrow CHAOS_{SKIP} \ UNIV \sqsubseteq_{\mathcal{TD}} P$
3. $livelock\_free \ P \longleftrightarrow CHAOS_{SKIP} \ UNIV \sqsubseteq_{\mathcal{FD}} P$

Finally, we proved the following theorem.

Theorem 2 (DF implies LF). $deadlock\text{-}free \ P \longrightarrow livelock\text{-}free \ P$

This is totally natural, at a first glance, but surprising as the proof of deadlock-freeness only requires failure refinement $\sqsubseteq_{\mathcal{F}}$ (see Definition 7) where divergence traces are mixed within the failures set. Note that the existing tools in the literature normally detect these two phenomena separately, such as FDR for which checking livelock-freeness is very costly. In our framework, deadlock-freeness of a given system implies its livelock-freeness. However, if a system is not deadlock-free, then it may still be livelock-free.

5   Advanced Verification Techniques

Based on the refinement framework discussed in Sect. 4, we will now turn to some more advanced proof principles, tactics and verification techniques. We will demonstrate them on two paradigmatic examples well-known in the CSP literature: The CopyBuffer and Dijkstra's Dining Philosophers. In both cases, we will exploit the fact that HOL-CSP 2 allows for reasoning over infinite CSP; in the first case, we reason over infinite alphabets approaching an old research objective: exploiting data-independence [2,25] in process verification. In the latter case, we present an approach to a verification of a parameterized architecture, in this case a ring-structure of arbitrary size.

5.1   The General CopyBuffer Example

We consider the paradigmatic copy buffer example [20,30] that is characteristic for a specification of a prototypical process and its implementation. It is used extensively in the CSP literature to illustrate the interplay of communication, component concealment and fixed-point operators. The process $COPY$, defined as follows, is a specification of a one size buffer, that receives elements from the channel $left$ of arbitrary type α ($left?x$) and outputs them on the channel $right$ ($right!x$):

> **datatype** α events $= left\ \alpha \mid right\ \alpha \mid mid\ \alpha \mid ack$
> **definition** $COPY \equiv (\mu\ X.\ left?x \rightarrow (right!x \rightarrow X))$

From our HOL-CSP 2 theory that establishes the continuity of all CSP operators, we deduce that such a fixed-point process $COPY$ exists and follows the unrolling rule below:

> **lemma** $COPY = (left?x \rightarrow (right!x \rightarrow COPY))$

We set $SEND$ and REC in parallel but in a row sharing a middle channel mid and synchronizing with an ack event. Then, we hide all exchanged events between these two processes and we call the resulting process $SYSTEM$:

> **definition** $SEND \equiv (\mu\ X.\ left?x \rightarrow (mid!x \rightarrow (ack \rightarrow X)))$
> **definition** $REC \equiv (\mu\ X.\ mid?x \rightarrow (right!x \rightarrow (ack \rightarrow X)))$
> **definition** $SYN \equiv (range\ mid) \cup \{ack\}$
> **definition** $SYSTEM \equiv (SEND\ [\![SYN]\!]\ REC) \setminus SYN$

We want to verify that $SYSTEM$ implements $COPY$. As shown below, we apply fixed-point induction to prove that $SYSTEM$ refines $COPY$ using the $pcpo$ process ordering $\sqsubseteq$ that implies all other refinement orderings. We state:

> **lemma:** $COPY \sqsubseteq SYSTEM$

and apply fixed-point induction over $COPY$ that generates three subgoals:

1. adm $(\lambda a.\ a \sqsubseteq SYSTEM$
2. $\bot \sqsubseteq SYSTEM$
3. $P \sqsubseteq SYSTEM \implies left?x \to right!x \to P \sqsubseteq SYSTEM$

The first two sub-proofs are automatic simplification proofs; the third requires unfolding $SEND$ and REC one step and applying the algebraic laws. No denotational semantics reasoning is necessary here; it is just an induct-simplify proof consisting of 2 lines proof-script involving the derived algebraic laws of CSP.

After proving that $SYSTEM$ implements $COPY$ for arbitrary alphabets, we aim to profit from this first established result to check which relations $SYSTEM$ has wrt. to the reference processes of Sect. 4.2. Thus, we prove that $COPY$ is deadlock-free which implies livelock-free, (proof by fixed-point induction similar to *lemma*: $COPY \sqsubseteq SYSTEM$), from which we can immediately infer from transitivity that $SYSTEM$ is. Using refinement relations, we killed four birds with one stone as we proved the deadlock-freeness and the livelock-freeness for both $COPY$ and $SYSTEM$ processes. These properties hold for arbitrary alphabets and for infinite ones in particular.

lemma $DF\ UNIV \sqsubseteq COPY$

corollary $deadlock\text{-}free\ COPY$
and $livelock\text{-}free\ COPY$
and $deadlock\text{-}free\ SYSTEM$
and $livelock\text{-}free\ SYSTEM$

5.2   New Fixed-Point Inductions

The copy buffer refinement proof $DF\ UNIV \sqsubseteq COPY$ is a typical one step induction proof with two goals: *base*: $\bot \sqsubseteq Q$ and $1{-}ind$: $X \sqsubseteq Q \implies (\text{-} \to X) \sqsubseteq Q$. Now, if unfolding the fixed-point process Q reveals two steps, the second goal becomes $X \sqsubseteq Q \implies \text{-} \to X \sqsubseteq \text{-} \to \text{-} \to Q$. Unfortunately, this way, it becomes improvable using monotonicities rules. We need here a two-step induction of the form $base0$: $\bot \sqsubseteq Q$, $base1$: $\text{-} \to \bot \sqsubseteq Q$ and $2{-}ind$: $X \sqsubseteq Q \implies \text{-} \to \text{-} \to X \sqsubseteq \text{-} \to \text{-} \to Q$ to have a sufficiently powerful induction scheme.

For this reason, we derived a number of alternative induction schemes (which are not available in the HOLCF library), which are also relevant for our final Dining Philosophers example. These are essentially adaptions of k-induction schemes applied to domain-theoretic setting (so: requiring f continuous and P admissible; these preconditions are skipped here):

- $\dots \implies \forall i{<}k.\ P\ (f^i\ \bot) \implies (\forall X.\ (\forall i{<}k.\ P\ (f^i\ X)) \longrightarrow P\ (f^k\ X)) \implies P\ (\mu X.\ f\ X)$
- $\dots \implies \forall i{<}k.\ P\ (f^i\ \bot) \implies (\forall X.\ P\ X \longrightarrow P\ (f^k\ X)) \implies P\ (\mu X.\ f\ X)$

In the latter variant, the induction hypothesis is weakened to skip k steps. When possible, it reduces the goal size.

Another problem occasionally occurring in refinement proofs happens when the left side term involves more than one fixed-point process (e.g. $P \llbracket \{A\} \rrbracket \, Q \sqsubseteq S$). In this situation, we need parallel fixed-point inductions. The HOLCF library offers only a basic one:

$$- \; \ldots \Longrightarrow P \perp \perp \Longrightarrow (\forall X\, Y.\; P\, X\, Y \Longrightarrow P\, (f\, X)\, (g\, Y)) \Longrightarrow P\, (\mu X.\; f\, X)\, (\mu X.\; g\, X)$$

This form does not help in cases like in $P \llbracket \emptyset \rrbracket \, Q \sqsubseteq S$ with the interleaving operator on the left-hand side. The simplifying law is:

$$(\Box x \in A \to P\, x \; \llbracket \emptyset \rrbracket \; \Box x \in B \to Q\, x) = \quad (\Box x \in A \to (\qquad\qquad P\, x \; \llbracket \emptyset \rrbracket \; \Box x \in B \to Q\, x)$$
$$\Box\, (\Box x \in B \to (\Box x \in A \to P\, x \; \llbracket \emptyset \rrbracket \qquad\quad Q\, x))$$

Here, $(f\, X \; \llbracket \emptyset \rrbracket \; g\, Y)$ does not reduce to the $(X \; \llbracket \emptyset \rrbracket \; Y)$ term but to two terms $(f\, X \; \llbracket \emptyset \rrbracket \; Y)$ and $(X \; \llbracket \emptyset \rrbracket \; g\, Y)$. To handle these cases, we developed an advanced parallel induction scheme and we proved its correctness:

$$\ldots \Longrightarrow (\forall Y.\; P \perp Y) \Longrightarrow (\forall X.\; P\, X \perp)$$
$$- \qquad \Longrightarrow \forall X\, Y.\; (P\, X\, Y \wedge P\, (f\, X)\, Y \wedge P\, X\, (g\, Y)) \longrightarrow P\, (f\, X)\, (g\, Y)$$
$$\Longrightarrow P\, (\mu X.\; f\, X)\, (\mu X.\; g\, X)$$

which allows for a "independent unrolling" of the fixed-points in these proofs. The astute reader may notice here that if the induction step is weakened (having more hypotheses), the base steps require enforcement.

5.3   Normalization

Our framework can reason not only over infinite alphabets, but also over processes parameterized over states with an arbitrarily rich structure. This paves the way for the following technique, that trades potentially complex process structure against equivalent simple processes with potentially rich state.

Roughly similar to labelled transition systems, we provide for deterministic CSP processes a normal form that is based on an explicit state. The general schema of normalized processes is defined as follows:

$$P_{norm}\llbracket \tau, \upsilon \rrbracket \equiv \mu\, X.\; (\lambda \sigma.\; \Box e \in (\tau\, \sigma) \to X\, (\upsilon\, \sigma\, e))$$

where τ is a transition function which returns the set of events that can be triggered from the current state σ given as parameter. The update function υ takes two parameters σ and an event e and returns the new state. This normal form is closed under deterministic and communication operators.

The advantage of this format is that we can mimic the well-known product automata construction for an arbitrary number of synchronized processes under normal form. We only show the case of the synchronous product of two processes:

Theorem 3 (Product Construction). *Parallel composition translates to normal form:*

$$(P_{norm}[\![\tau_1,\upsilon_1]\!] \; \sigma_1) \; || \; (P_{norm}[\![\tau_2,\upsilon_2]\!] \; \sigma_2) =$$
$$P_{norm}[\![\lambda(\sigma_1,\sigma_2). \; \tau_1 \; \sigma_1 \; \cap \; \tau_2 \; \sigma_2 \; , \; \lambda(\sigma_1,\sigma_2).\lambda e.(\upsilon_1 \; \sigma_1 \; e, \; \upsilon_2 \; \sigma_2 \; e)]\!] \; (\sigma_1,\sigma_2)$$

The generalization of this rule for a list of (τ,υ)-pairs is straight-forward, albeit the formal proof is not. The application of the generalized form is a cornerstone of the proof of the general dining philosophers problem illustrated in the subsequent section.

Another advantage of normalized processes is the possibility to argue over the reachability of states via the closure $\Re$, which is defined inductively over:

- $\sigma \in \Re \; \tau \; \upsilon \; \sigma$
- $\sigma \in \Re \; \tau \; \upsilon \; \sigma_0 \Longrightarrow e \in \tau \; \sigma \Longrightarrow \upsilon \; \sigma \; e \in \Re \; \tau \; \upsilon \; \sigma_0$

Thus, normalization leads to a new characterization of deadlock-freeness inspired from automata theory. We formally proved the following theorem:

Theorem 4 (DF vs. Reachability). *If each reachable state $s \in (\Re \; \tau \; \upsilon)$ has outgoing transitions, the CSP process is deadlock-free:*

$$\forall \sigma \in (\Re \; \tau \; \upsilon \; \sigma_0). \; \tau \; \sigma \neq \{\} \Longrightarrow \textit{deadlock-free} \; (P_{norm}[\![\tau,\upsilon]\!] \; \sigma_0)$$

This theorem allows for establishing properties such as deadlock-freeness by completely abstracting from CSP theory; these are arguments that only involve inductive reasoning over the transition function.

Summing up, our method consists of four stages:

1. we construct normalized versions of component processes and prove them equivalent to their counterparts,
2. we state an invariant over the states/variables,
3. we prove by induction over $\Re$ that it holds on all reachable states, and finally
4. we prove that this invariant guarantees the existence of outgoing transitions.

5.4   Generalized Dining Philosophers

The dining philosophers problem is another paradigmatic example in the CSP literature often used to illustrate synchronization problems between an arbitrary number of concurrent systems. It is an example of a process scheme for which general properties such as deadlock-freeness are desirable in order to inherit them for specific instances. The general dining philosopher problem for an arbitrary N is presented in HOL-CSP 2 as follows

datatype *dining-event = picks (phil::nat) (fork::nat)*
                        | putsdown (phil::nat) (fork::nat)
                        | eat (phil::nat)

definition $LPHIL0 \equiv (\mu\ X.\ (picks\ 0\ (N{-}1) \rightarrow (picks\ 0\ 0 \rightarrow eat\ 0 \rightarrow$
$$(putsdown\ 0\ 0 \rightarrow (putsdown\ 0\ (N{-}1) \rightarrow X)))))$$

definition $RPHIL\ i \equiv (\mu\ X.\ (picks\ i\ i \rightarrow (picks\ i\ (i{-}1) \rightarrow eat\ i \rightarrow$
$$(putsdown\ i\ (i{-}1) \rightarrow (putsdown\ i\ i \rightarrow X)))))$$

definition $FORK\ i \equiv (\mu\ X.\quad (picks\ i\ i \rightarrow (putsdown\ i\ i \rightarrow X))$
$$\Box(picks\ (i{+}1)\%N\ i \rightarrow(putsdown\ (i{+}1)\%N\ i \rightarrow X)))$$

definition $PHILs\quad \equiv LPHIL0\ |||\ (|||_{i\,\in\,1..N}\ RPHIL\ i)$

definition $FORKs\quad \equiv |||_{i\,\in\,0..N}\ FORK\ i$

definition $DINING \equiv FORKs\ [picks,\ putsdown]\ PHILs$

Note that both philosophers and forks are pairwise independent but both synchronize on *picks* and *putsdown* events. The philosopher of index 0 is left-handed whereas the other $N{-}1$ philosophers are right-handed. We want to prove that any configuration is deadlock-free for an arbitrary number N.

First, we put the fork process into normal form. It has three states: (0) on the table, (2) picked by the right philosopher or (1) picked by the left one:

definition $trans_f\ i\ \sigma \equiv$ **if**$\quad \sigma = 0\quad$ **then** $\{picks\ i\ i,\ picks\ (i{+}1)\%N\ i\}$
$\qquad\qquad\qquad\qquad$ *else if* $\sigma = 1\quad$ **then** $\{putsdown\ i\ i\}$
$\qquad\qquad\qquad\qquad$ *else if* $\sigma = 2\quad$ **then** $\{putsdown\ (i{+}1)\%N\ i\}$
$\qquad\qquad\qquad\qquad$ *else* $\qquad\qquad\qquad$ $\{\}$

definition $upd_f\ i\ \sigma\ e \equiv$ **if**$\quad e = (picks\ i\ i)\qquad$ **then** *1*
$\qquad\qquad\qquad\qquad$ *else if* $e = (picks\ (i{+}1)\%N\ i)$ **then** *2*
$\qquad\qquad\qquad\qquad$ *else* $\qquad\qquad\qquad\qquad$ *0*

definition $FORK_{norm}\ i \equiv P_{norm}[trans_f\ i,\ upd_f\ i]$

To validate our choice for the states, transition function $trans_f$ and update function upd_f, we prove that they are equivalent to the original process components: $FORK_{norm}\ i = FORK\ i$. The anti-symmetry of refinement breaks this down to the two refinement proofs $FORK_{norm}\ i \sqsubseteq FORK\ i$ and $FORK\ i \sqsubseteq FORK_{norm}\ i$, which are similar to the CopyBuffer example shown in Sect. 5.1. Note, again, that this fairly automatic induct-simplify-proof just involves reasoning on the derived algebraic rules, not any reasoning on the level of the denotational semantics.

From the generalization of "Theorem 3, we obtain normalized processes for $FORKs$, $PHILs$ and $DINING$:

definition $trans_F \equiv \lambda fs.\ (\bigcap_{i<N}.\ trans_f\ i\ (fs!i))$
definition $upd_F\ \equiv \lambda fs\ e.$ **let** $i{=}(fork\ e)$ **in** $fs[i:=(upd_f\ i\ (fs!i)\ e)]$

lemma $FORKs = P_{norm}[\![trans_F,\ upd_F]\!]$ ...
lemma $PHILS = P_{norm}[\![trans_P,\ upd_P]\!]$ ...

definition $trans_D \equiv \lambda(ps,fs).\ (trans_P\ ps) \cap (trans_F\ fs)$
definition $upd_D\ \equiv \lambda(ps,fs)\ e.\ (upd_P\ ps\ e,\ upd_F\ fs\ e)$

lemma $DINING = P_{norm}[\![trans_D,\ upd_D]\!]$

The variable ps stands for the list of philosophers states and fs for the list of forks states, both are of size N. The pair $(ps,\ fs)$ encodes the whole dining table state over which we need to define an invariant to ensure that no blocking state is reachable and thus the dining philosophers problem is deadlock-free. As explained before, the proof is based on abstract reasoning over relations independent from the CSP context.

The last steps towards our goal are the following definitions and lemmas:

definition $INV_{DINING}\ ps\ fs \equiv (\forall i.\ ((fs!i{=}1) \leftrightarrow ps!i \neq 0) \wedge ...\ )$
lemma $(ps,fs) \in \Re\ trans_D\ upd_D \implies INV_{DINING}\ ps\ fs$ ...
lemma $INV_{DINING}\ ps\ fs \implies trans_D\ (ps,\ fs) \neq \{\}$ ...

corollary $deadlock\text{-}free\ DINING$

To sum up, we proved once and for all that the dining philosophers problem is deadlock free for an arbitrary number $N \geq 2$. Common model-checkers like PAT and FDR fail to answer for a dozen of philosophers (on a usual machine) due to the exponential combinatorial explosion. Furthermore, our proof is fairly stable against modifications like adding non synchronized events like thinking or sitting down in contrast to model-checking techniques.

6 Related Work

The theory of CSP has attracted a lot of interest from the eighties on, and is still a fairly active research area, both as a theoretical device as well as a modelling language to analyze complex concurrent systems. It is therefore not surprising that attempts to its formalisation had been undertaken early with the advent of interactive theorem proving systems supporting higher-order logic [12,16,17,22,37], where especially the latter allows for some automated support for refinement proofs based on induction. However, HOL-CSP2 is based on a failure/divergence model, while [22] is based on stable failures, which can infer deadlock-freeness only under the assumption that no livelock occurred; In our view, this is a too strong assumption for both the theory as well as the tool.

In the 90ies, research focused on automated verification tools for CSP, most notably on FDR [1]. It relies on an operational CSP semantics, allowing for a conversion of processes into labelled transition systems, where the states are normalized by the "laws" derived from the denotational semantics. For finite event sets, refinement proofs can be reduced to graph inclusion problems. With efficient compression techniques, such as bisimulation, elimination and factorization by semantic equivalence [32], FDR was used to analyze some industrial applications. However, such a model checker cannot handle infinite cases and does not scale to large systems.

The fundamental limits of automated decision procedures for data and processes has been known very early on: Undecidability of parameterized model checking was proven by reduction to non-halting of Turing machines [35]. However, some forms of well-structured transitions systems, could be demonstrated to be decidable [8,18]. HOL-CSP2 is a fully abstract model for the failure/divergence model; as a HOL theory, it is therefore a "relative complete proof theory" both for infinite data as well as number of components. (see [3] for relative completeness).

Encouraged by the progress of SMT solvers which support some infinite types, notably (fixed arrays of) integers or reals, and limited forms of formulas over these types, SMT-based model-checkers represent the current main-stream to parametric model-checking. This extends both to LTL-style model-checkers for Promela-like languages [14,24] as well as process-algebra alikes [4,5,7]. However, the usual limitations persist: the translation to SMT is hardly certifiable and the solvers are still not able to handle non-linear computations; moreover, they fail to elaborate inductive proofs on data if necessary in refinement proofs.

Some systems involve approximation techniques in order to make the formal verification of concurrent systems scalable; results are sometimes inherently imprecise and require meta-level arguments assuring their truth in a specific application context. For example, in [5], the synchronization analysis techniques try to prove the unreachability of a system state by showing that components cannot agree on the order or on the number of times they participate on system rules. Even with such over-approximation, the finiteness restriction on the number of components persists.

Last but not least, SMT-based tools only focusing on bounded model-checking like [13,19] use k-induction and quite powerful invariant generation techniques but are still far from scalable techniques. While it is difficult to make any precise argument on the scalability for HOL-CSP 2, we argue that we have no data-type restrictions (events may have realvector-, function- or even process type) as well as restrictions on the structure of components. None of our paradigmatic examples can be automatically proven with any of the discussed SMT techniques without restrictions.

7   Conclusion

We presented a formalisation of the most comprehensive semantic model for CSP, a 'classical' language for the specification and analysis of concurrent systems studied in a rich body of literature. For this purpose, we ported [37] to a modern version of Isabelle, restructured the proofs, and extended the resulting theory of the language substantially. The result HOL-CSP 2 has been submitted to the Isabelle AFP [36], thus a fairly sustainable format accessible to other researchers and tools.

We developed a novel set of deadlock - and livelock inference proof principles based on classical and denotational characterizations. In particular, we formally investigated the relations between different refinement notions in the presence of deadlock - and livelock; an area where traditional CSP literature skates over the nitty-gritty details. Finally, we demonstrated how to exploit these results for deadlock/livelock analysis of protocols.

We put a large body of abstract CSP laws and induction principles together to form concrete verification technologies for generalized classical problems, which have been considered so far from the perspective of data-independence or structural parametricity. The underlying novel principle of "trading rich structure against rich state" allows to convert processes into classical transition systems for which established invariant techniques become applicable.

Future applications of HOL-CSP 2 could comprise a combination to model checkers, where our theory with its derived rules is used to certify the output of a model-checker over CSP. In our experience, generated labelled transition systems may be used to steer inductions or to construct the normalized processes $P_{norm}[\![\tau,\upsilon]\!]$ automatically, thus combining efficient finite reasoning over finite sub-systems with globally infinite systems in a logically safe way.

Acknowledgement. This paper has been written with Isabelle/DOF [11].

References

1. FDR4 - The CSP Refinement Checker (2019). https://www.cs.ox.ac.uk/projects/fdr/
2. An, J., Zhang, L., You, C.: The design and implementation of data independence in the CSP model of security protocol. Adv. Mater. Res. **915–916**, 1386–1392 (2014). https://doi.org/10.4028/www.scientific.net/AMR.915-916.1386
3. Andrews, P.: An Introduction to Mathematical Logic and Type Theory. Applied Logic Series. Springer, Netherlands (2002). https://doi.org/10.1007/978-94-015-9934-4
4. Antonino, P., Gibson-Robinson, T., Roscoe, A.W.: Efficient deadlock-freedom checking using local analysis and SAT solving. In: Ábrahám, E., Huisman, M. (eds.) IFM 2016. LNCS, vol. 9681, pp. 345–360. Springer, Cham (2016). https://doi.org/10.1007/978-3-319-33693-0_22
5. Antonino, P., Gibson-Robinson, T., Roscoe, A.W.: Efficient verification of concurrent systems using synchronisation analysis and SAT/SMT solving. ACM Trans. Softw. Eng. Methodol. **28**(3), 18:1–18:43 (2019)
6. Barrett, G.: Model checking in practice: the t9000 virtual channel processor. IEEE Trans. Softw. Eng. **21**(2), 69–78 (1995). https://doi.org/10.1109/32.345823

7. Bensalem, S., Griesmayer, A., Legay, A., Nguyen, T.-H., Sifakis, J., Yan, R.: D-Finder 2: towards efficient correctness of incremental design. In: Bobaru, M., Havelund, K., Holzmann, G.J., Joshi, R. (eds.) NFM 2011. LNCS, vol. 6617, pp. 453–458. Springer, Heidelberg (2011). https://doi.org/10.1007/978-3-642-20398-5_32

8. Bloem, R., et al.: Decidability in parameterized verification. SIGACT News **47**(2), 53–64 (2016)

9. Brookes, S.D., Hoare, C.A.R., Roscoe, A.W.: A theory of communicating sequential processes. J. ACM **31**(3), 560–599 (1984)

10. Brookes, S.D., Roscoe, A.W.: An improved failures model for communicating processes. In: Brookes, S.D., Roscoe, A.W., Winskel, G. (eds.) CONCURRENCY 1984. LNCS, vol. 197, pp. 281–305. Springer, Heidelberg (1985). https://doi.org/10.1007/3-540-15670-4_14

11. Brucker, A.D., Wolff, B.: Isabelle/DOF: design and implementation. In: Ölveczky, P.C., Salaün, G. (eds.) SEFM 2019. LNCS, vol. 11724, pp. 275–292. Springer, Cham (2019). https://doi.org/10.1007/978-3-030-30446-1_15

12. Camilleri, A.J.: A higher order logic mechanization of the CSP failure-divergence semantics. In: Birtwistle, G. (ed.) IV Higher Order Workshop, Banff 1990. WORKSHOPS COMP., pp. 123–150. Springer, London (1991). https://doi.org/10.1007/978-1-4471-3182-3_9

13. Champion, A., Mebsout, A., Sticksel, C., Tinelli, C.: The KIND 2 model checker. In: Chaudhuri, S., Farzan, A. (eds.) CAV 2016. LNCS, vol. 9780, pp. 510–517. Springer, Cham (2016). https://doi.org/10.1007/978-3-319-41540-6_29

14. Conchon, S., Goel, A., Krstić, S., Mebsout, A., Zaïdi, F.: Cubicle: a parallel SMT-based model checker for parameterized systems. In: Madhusudan, P., Seshia, S.A. (eds.) CAV 2012. LNCS, vol. 7358, pp. 718–724. Springer, Heidelberg (2012). https://doi.org/10.1007/978-3-642-31424-7_55

15. Donovan, A., Kernighan, B.: The Go Programming Language. Addison-Wesley Professional Computing Series. Pearson Education, London (2015)

16. Feliachi, A., Gaudel, M.-C., Wolff, B.: Unifying theories in Isabelle/HOL. In: Qin, S. (ed.) UTP 2010. LNCS, vol. 6445, pp. 188–206. Springer, Heidelberg (2010). https://doi.org/10.1007/978-3-642-16690-7_9

17. Feliachi, A., Gaudel, M.-C., Wolff, B.: Isabelle/*Circus*: a process specification and verification environment. In: Joshi, R., Müller, P., Podelski, A. (eds.) VSTTE 2012. LNCS, vol. 7152, pp. 243–260. Springer, Heidelberg (2012). https://doi.org/10.1007/978-3-642-27705-4_20

18. Finkel, A., Schnoebelen, P.: Well-structured transition systems everywhere!. Theor. Comput. Sci. **256**(1–2), 63–92 (2001)

19. Gacek, A., Backes, J., Whalen, M., Wagner, L., Ghassabani, E.: The JKIND model checker. In: Chockler, H., Weissenbacher, G. (eds.) CAV 2018. LNCS, vol. 10982, pp. 20–27. Springer, Cham (2018). https://doi.org/10.1007/978-3-319-96142-2_3

20. Hoare, C.A.R.: Communicating Sequential Processes. Prentice-Hall Inc., Upper Saddle River (1985)

21. Huffman, B., Matthews, J., White, P.: Axiomatic constructor classes in Isabelle/HOLCF. In: Hurd, J., Melham, T. (eds.) TPHOLs 2005. LNCS, vol. 3603, pp. 147–162. Springer, Heidelberg (2005). https://doi.org/10.1007/11541868_10

22. Isobe, Y., Roggenbach, M.: A complete axiomatic semantics for the CSP stable-failures model. In: Baier, C., Hermanns, H. (eds.) CONCUR 2006. LNCS, vol. 4137, pp. 158–172. Springer, Heidelberg (2006). https://doi.org/10.1007/11817949_11

23. Isobe, Y., Roggenbach, M.: CSP-prover: a proof tool for the verification of scalable concurrent systems. Inf. Media Technol. **5**(1), 32–39 (2010). https://doi.org/10.11185/imt.5.32
24. Konnov, I., Widder, J.: ByMC: byzantine model checker. In: Margaria, T., Steffen, B. (eds.) ISoLA 2018. LNCS, vol. 11246, pp. 327–342. Springer, Cham (2018). https://doi.org/10.1007/978-3-030-03424-5_22
25. Lazic, R.S.: A semantic study of data-independence with applications to the mechanical verification of concurrent systems. Ph.D. thesis, University of Oxford (1999)
26. Müller, O., Nipkow, T., von Oheimb, D., Slotosch, O.: HOLCF = HOL + LCF. J-FP **9**(2), 191–223 (1999). https://doi.org/10.1017/S095679689900341X
27. Nipkow, T., Paulson, L.C., Wenzel, M.: Isabelle/HOL—A Proof Assistant for Higher-Order Logic. LNCS, vol. 2283. Springer, Heidelberg (2002). https://doi.org/10.1007/3-540-45949-9
28. Noce, P.: Conservation of CSP noninterference security under sequential composition. Archive of Formal Proofs (2016). https://www.isa-afp.org/entries/Noninterference_Sequential_Composition.shtml
29. Roscoe, A.: Theory and Practice of Concurrency. Prentice Hall, Upper Saddle River (1997)
30. Roscoe, A.: Understanding Concurrent Systems, 1st edn. Springer, Heidelberg (2010). https://doi.org/10.1007/978-1-84882-258-0
31. Roscoe, A.W.: An alternative order for the failures model. J. Logic Comput. **2**, 557–577 (1992)
32. Roscoe, A.W., Gardiner, P.H.B., Goldsmith, M.H., Hulance, J.R., Jackson, D.M., Scattergood, J.B.: Hierarchical compression for model-checking CSP or how to check 10^{20} dining philosophers for deadlock. In: Brinksma, E., Cleaveland, W.R., Larsen, K.G., Margaria, T., Steffen, B. (eds.) TACAS 1995. LNCS, vol. 1019, pp. 133–152. Springer, Heidelberg (1995). https://doi.org/10.1007/3-540-60630-0_7
33. Scott, D.: Continuous lattices. In: Lawvere, F.W. (ed.) Toposes, Algebraic Geometry and Logic. LNM, vol. 274, pp. 97–136. Springer, Heidelberg (1972). https://doi.org/10.1007/BFb0073967
34. Sun, J., Liu, Y., Dong, J.S., Pang, J.: PAT: towards flexible verification under fairness. In: Bouajjani, A., Maler, O. (eds.) CAV 2009. LNCS, vol. 5643, pp. 709–714. Springer, Heidelberg (2009). https://doi.org/10.1007/978-3-642-02658-4_59
35. Suzuki, I.: Proving properties of a ring of finite-state machines. Inf. Process. Lett. **28**(4), 213–214 (1988)
36. Taha, S., Ye, L., Wolff, B.: HOL-CSP Version 2.0. Archive of Formal Proofs (2019). http://isa-afp.org/entries/HOL-CSP.html
37. Tej, H., Wolff, B.: A corrected failure-divergence model for CSP in Isabelle/HOL. In: Fitzgerald, J., Jones, C.B., Lucas, P. (eds.) FME 1997. LNCS, vol. 1313, pp. 318–337. Springer, Heidelberg (1997). https://doi.org/10.1007/3-540-63533-5_17

Algebra-Based Loop Synthesis

Andreas Humenberger[1]([⊠]), Nikolaj Bjørner[2], and Laura Kovács[1]

[1] TU Wien, Vienna, Austria
ahumenbe@forsyte.at
[2] Microsoft Research, Redmond, USA

Abstract. We present a method for synthesizing loops over affine assignments from polynomial invariants. It is complete when the number of auxiliary variables is bounded, thus serving as a foundation for strength reduction optimization that convert polynomial expressions into incremental affine computations. Our work has applications towards synthesizing loops satisfying a given polynomial loop invariant, program verification, as well as generating number sequences from algebraic relations. To understand viability of the methodology and heuristics for synthesizing loops with a large number of auxiliary variables, we implement and evaluate the method using the `Absynth` tool.

1 Introduction

To reduce execution time spent within loops, compiler optimization techniques, such as strength reduction, aim at replacing expensive loop operations with semantically equivalent but less expensive operations [4]. One such optimization within strength reduction replaces "strong" loop multiplications by additions among program variables. The burden of strength reductions comes however with identifying inductive loop variables and invariants to be used for loop optimization.

In this paper we provide an algorithmic solution to the following loop reasoning challenge related to strength reduction: *Given a polynomial $p(\boldsymbol{x})$ over loop variables $\boldsymbol{x}$, how can the entire solution space of $p(\boldsymbol{x}) = 0$ be iteratively computed using only affine operations among $\boldsymbol{x}$?* We refer to this reasoning challenge as *loop synthesis*, which can be considered as the reverse problem of loop invariant generation: rather than generating invariants $p(\boldsymbol{x}) = 0$ summarizing a given loop as in [12,17,22], we synthesize and optimize loops whose functional behavior is captured by a given invariant $p(\boldsymbol{x}) = 0$, such that the synthesized loops use only affine computations among $\boldsymbol{x}$. We believe ours is the first complete approach for synthesizing loops from (non-linear) polynomial invariants. The *inner magic* of our reduction to SMT derives from algebraic insights, allowing us to test existential properties of bounded degree polynomials to derive universal relations.

Motivating Example. Let us first motivate loop synthesis using Fig. 1a. The loop is based on an online tutorial[1] of the Dafny verification framework [18] and can

---

[1] https://rise4fun.com/Dafny/.

© Springer Nature Switzerland AG 2020
B. Dongol and E. Troubitsyna (Eds.): IFM 2020, LNCS 12546, pp. 440–459, 2020.
https://doi.org/10.1007/978-3-030-63461-2_24

be seen as an instance of strength reduction: by maintaining the polynomial loop invariant $n \leq N \wedge c = n^3 \wedge k = 3n^2 + 3n + 1 \wedge m = 6n + 6$, Fig. 1a uses only affine updates among its variables. Yet, Fig. 1a is not partially correct with respect to the precondition $N \geq 0$ and post-condition $c = N^3$ and the task is to revise/repair Fig. 1a into a partially correct program while maintaining the aforementioned invariant.

$(c, k, m, n) \leftarrow (0,0,0,0)$	$(c, k, m, n) \leftarrow (0, \boxed{1}, \boxed{6}, 0)$	$(c, k, m, n) \leftarrow (0, \boxed{1}, \boxed{6}, 0)$
while $n < N$ **do**	**while** $n < N$ **do**	**while** $n < N$ **do**
$\quad c \leftarrow c + k$	$\quad c \leftarrow c + k$	$\quad c \leftarrow c + k$
$\quad k \leftarrow k + m$	$\quad k \leftarrow k + m$	$\quad k \leftarrow k + \boxed{6n + 6}$
$\quad m \leftarrow m + 9$	$\quad m \leftarrow m + \boxed{6}$	$\quad m \leftarrow m + \boxed{6}$
$\quad n \leftarrow n + 1$	$\quad n \leftarrow n + 1$	$\quad n \leftarrow n + 1$
end	**end**	**end**
(a) Faulty loop	(b) Synthesized loop	(c) Synthesized loop

Fig. 1. Strength reduction via loop synthesis. Figures b–c are revised versions of Fig. a such that $c = n^3 \wedge k = 3n^2 + 3n + 1 \wedge m = 6n + 6$ is an invariant of Figs. b–c.

In this paper we introduce an algorithmic approach to loop synthesis by relying on algebraic recurrence equations and constraint solving over polynomials. In particular, we automatically synthesize Figs. 1b–c by using the given non-linear polynomial equalities $c = n^3 \wedge k = 3n^2 + 3n + 1 \wedge m = 6n + 6$ as input invariant to our loop synthesis task. Both synthesized programs, with the loop guard $n < N$ as in Fig. 1a, are partially correct program with respect to the given requirements. Moreover, Fig. 1b–c precisely capture the solution space of $c = n^3 \wedge k = 3n^2 + 3n + 1 \wedge m = 6n + 6$, by implementing only affine operations, solving thus foundational challenges of strength reduction.

Algebra-Based Loop Synthesis. Inspired by syntax-guided synthesis – SyGuS [2], we consider additional requirements on the loop to be synthesized: we impose syntactic requirements on the form of loop expressions and guards to be synthesized. The imposed requirements allow us to *reduce the loop synthesis task to the problem of generating linear/affine recurrences with constant coefficients, called C-finite recurrences* [15]. As such, we formalize *loop synthesis* as follows:

Problem 1 (Loop Synthesis). Given a polynomial $p(\boldsymbol{x})$ over a set $\boldsymbol{x}$ of variables, generate a loop $\mathcal{L}$ with program variables $\boldsymbol{x}$ such that

(i) $p(\boldsymbol{x}) = 0$ is an invariant of $\mathcal{L}$, and
(ii) each program variable in $\mathcal{L}$ induces a C-finite number sequence.

Our approach to synthesis is however conceptually different from other SyGuS-based methods, such as [8,10,20]: rather than iteratively refining both the input and the solution space of synthesized programs, we take polynomial relations describing a potentially infinite set of input values and precisely capture not just one loop, but the *set of all loops* (i) whose invariant is given by our input polynomial and (ii) whose variables induce C-finite number sequences. Any instance of this set therefore yields a loop that is partially correct by construction and only implements affine computations. Figures 1b–c depict two solutions of our loop synthesis task for the invariant $c = n^3 \wedge k = 3n^2 + 3n + 1 \wedge m = 6n + 6$.

The main steps of our approach are as follows. (i) Let $p(\boldsymbol{x})$ be a polynomial over variables $\boldsymbol{x}$ and let $s \geq 0$ be an upper bound on the number of program variables to be used in the loop. If not specified, s is considered to be the number of variables from $\boldsymbol{x}$. (ii) We use syntactic constraints over the loop body to be synthesized and define a loop template, as given by our programming model (5). Our programming model imposes that the functional behavior of the synthesized loops can be modeled by a system of C-finite recurrences (Sect. 3). (iii) By using the invariant property of $p(x) = 0$ for the loops to the synthesized, we construct a polynomial constraint problem (PCP) characterizing the set of all loops satisfying (5) for which $p(x) = 0$ is a loop invariant (Sect. 4). Our approach combines symbolic computation techniques over algebraic recurrence equations with polynomial constraint solving. We prove that our approach to loop synthesis is both *sound* and *complete*. By completeness we mean that if there is a loop $\mathcal{L}$ with at most s variables satisfying the invariant $p(\boldsymbol{x}) = 0$ such that the loop body meets our C-finite/affine syntactic requirements, then $\mathcal{L}$ is synthesized by our method (Theorem 4). Moving beyond s, that is, deriving an upper bound on the number of program variables from the invariant, is interesting further work, with connections to the inverse problem of difference Galois theory [21].

We finally note that our work is not restricted to specifications given by a single polynomial equality invariant. Rather, the invariant given as input to our synthesis approach can be conjunctions of polynomial equalities – as also shown in Fig. 1.

Beyond Loop Synthesis. Our work has applications beyond loop synthesis – such as in generating number sequences from algebraic relations and program optimizations.

- *Generating number sequences.* Our approach provides a partial solution to an open mathematical problem: given a polynomial relation among number sequences, e.g.

$$f(n)^4 + 2f(n)^3 f(n+1) - f(n)^2 f(n+1)^2 - 2f(n)f(n+1)^3 + f(n+1)^4 = 1, \quad (1)$$

synthesize algebraic recurrences defining these sequences. There exists no complete method for solving this challenge, but we give a complete approach in the C-finite setting parameterized by an a priori bound s on the order of the recurrences. For the given relation (1) among $f(n)$ and $f(n+1)$, our work generates the C-finite recurrence equation $f(n + 2) = f(n + 1) + f(n)$ which induces the Fibonacci sequence.

– *Program optimizations.* Given a polynomial invariant, our approach generates a PCP such that any solution to this PCP yields a loop satisfying the given invariant. By using additional constraints encoding a cost function on the loops to be synthesized, our method can be extended to synthesize loops that are optimal with respect to the considered costs, for example synthesizing loops that use only addition in variable updates as a further optimization of strength reduction. Consider for example Figs. 1b–c: the loop body of Fig. 1b uses only addition, whereas Fig. 1c implements also multiplications by constants.

Contributions. This paper brings integrated approaches to formal modelling and analysis of software, by combining symbolic computation, program analysis and SMT reasoning. In summary, we make the following contributions.

– We propose an *automated procedure for synthesizing loops* that are partially correct with respect to a given polynomial loop invariant (Sect. 4). By exploiting properties of C-finite sequences, we construct a PCP which precisely captures *all solutions* of our loop synthesis task. We are not aware of previous approaches synthesizing loops from (non-linear) polynomial invariants.
– We prove that our approach to loop synthesis is sound and complete (Theorem 4). That is, if there is a loop whose invariant is captured by our given specification, our approach synthesizes this loop. To this end, we consider completeness modulo an a priori fixed upper bound s on the number of loop variables.
– We extend our task of loop synthesis with additional constraints, for optimizing the solution space of our PCP (Sect. 5). These optimizations are essential in automating loop synthesis and provide automated approaches for strength reduction.
– We implemented our approach in the new open-source framework `Absynth`. We evaluated our work on a number of academic examples on loop analysis as well as on generating number sequences in algorithmic combinatorics (Sect. 6).

2   Preliminaries

Let $\mathbb{K}$ be a computable field with characteristic zero. We also assume $\mathbb{K}$ to be algebraically closed, that is, every non-constant polynomial in $\mathbb{K}[x]$ has at least one root in $\mathbb{K}$. The algebraic closure $\bar{\mathbb{Q}}$ of the field of rational numbers $\mathbb{Q}$ is such a field; $\bar{\mathbb{Q}}$ is called the field of algebraic numbers.

We denote by $\mathbb{K}[x_1, \ldots, x_n]$ the multivariate polynomial ring with indeterminates $x_1, \ldots, x_n$. For a list $x_1, \ldots, x_n$, we write $\boldsymbol{x}$ if the number of variables is known from the context or irrelevant. As $\mathbb{K}$ is algebraically closed, every polynomial $p \in \mathbb{K}[\boldsymbol{x}]$ of degree r has exactly r roots.

2.1   Polynomial Constraint Problem (PCP)

A *polynomial constraint* F is a constraint of the form $p \bowtie 0$ where p is a polynomial in $\mathbb{K}[\boldsymbol{x}]$ and $\bowtie \in \{<, \leq, =, \neq, \geq, >\}$. A *clause* is then a disjunction $C = F_1 \vee \cdots \vee F_m$ of polynomial constraints. A *unit clause* is a special clause consisting of a single disjunct (i.e. $m = 1$). A *polynomial constraint problem (PCP)* is then given by a set of clauses $\mathcal{C}$. We say that a variable assignment $\sigma : \{x_1, \ldots, x_n\} \rightarrow \mathbb{K}$ satisfies a polynomial constraint $p \bowtie 0$ if $p(\sigma(x_1), \ldots, \sigma(x_n)) \bowtie 0$ holds. Furthermore, σ satisfies a clause $F_1 \vee \cdots \vee F_m$ if for some i, F_i is satisfied by σ. Finally, σ satisfies a clause set – and is therefore a solution of the PCP – if every clause within the set is satisfied by σ. We write $\mathcal{C} \sqsubset \mathbb{K}[x]$ to indicate that all polynomials in the clause set $\mathcal{C}$ are contained in $\mathbb{K}[x]$. For a matrix M with entries $m_1, \ldots, m_s$ we define the clause set $\text{cstr}(M)$ to be $\{m_1 = 0, \ldots, m_s = 0\}$.

2.2   Number Sequences and Recurrence Relations

A sequence $(x(n))_{n=0}^{\infty}$ is called *C-finite* if it satisfies a linear recurrence with constant coefficients, also known as C-finite recurrence [15]. Let $c_0, \ldots, c_{r-1} \in \mathbb{K}$ and $c_0 \neq 0$, then

$$x(n+r) + c_{r-1}x(n+r-1) + \cdots + c_1 x(n+1) + c_0 x(n) = 0 \qquad (2)$$

is a C-finite recurrence of *order* r. The order of a sequence is defined by the order of the recurrence it satisfies. We refer to a recurrence of order r also as an r-order recurrence, for example as a first-order recurrence when $r = 1$ or a second-order recurrence when $r = 2$. A recurrence of order r and r initial values define a sequence, and different initial values lead to different sequences. For simplicity, we write $(x(n))_{n=0}^{\infty} = 0$ for $(x(n))_{n=0}^{\infty} = (0)_{n=0}^{\infty}$.

Example 1. Let $a \in \mathbb{K}$. The constant sequence $(a)_{n=0}^{\infty}$ satisfies a first-order recurrence equation $x(n+1) = x(n)$ with $x(0) = a$. The geometric sequence $(a^n)_{n=0}^{\infty}$ satisfies $x(n+1) = ax(n)$ with $x(0) = 1$. The sequence $(n)_{n=0}^{\infty}$ satisfies a second-order recurrence $x(n+2) = 2x(n+1) - x(n)$ with $x(0) = 0$ and $x(1) = 1$.   □

From the closure properties of C-finite sequences [15], the product and the sum of C-finite sequences are also C-finite. Moreover, we also have the following properties:

Theorem 1 ([15]). *Let* $p = c_0 + c_1 x + \cdots + c_k x^k \in \mathbb{K}[x]$. *Then* $(p(n))_{n=0}^{\infty} = 0$ *if and only if* $c_0 = \cdots = c_k = 0$.   □

Theorem 2 ([15]). *Let* $(u)_{n=0}^{\infty}$ *be a sequence satisfying a C-finite recurrence of order* r. *Then,* $u(n) = 0$ *for all* $n \in \mathbb{N}$ *if and only if* $u(n) = 0$ *for* $n \in \{0, \ldots, r-1\}$.   □

We define a *system of C-finite recurrences* of *order* r and *size* s to be of the form
$$X_{n+r} + C_{r-1}X_{n+r-1} + \cdots + C_1 X_{n+1} + C_0 X_n = 0$$
where $X_n = \big(x_1(n) \cdots x_s(n)\big)^{\mathsf{T}}$ and $C_i \in \mathbb{K}^{s \times s}$. Every C-finite recurrence system can be transformed into a first-order system of recurrences by increasing the size such that we get

$$X_{n+1} = BX_n \qquad \text{where } B \text{ is invertible.} \qquad (3)$$

The closed form solution of a C-finite recurrence system (3) is determined by the roots $\omega_1, \ldots, \omega_t$ of the characteristic polynomial of B, or equivalently by the eigenvalues $\omega_1, \ldots, \omega_t$ of B. We recall that the characteristic polynomial χ_B of the matrix B is defined as $\chi_B(\omega) = \det(\omega I - B)$, where det denotes the (matrix) determinant and I the identity matrix. Let $m_1, \ldots, m_t$ respectively denote the multiplicities of the roots $\omega_1, \ldots, \omega_t$ of χ_B. The closed form of (3) is then given by

$$X_n = \sum_{i=1}^{t} \sum_{j=1}^{m_i} C_{ij} \omega_i^n n^{j-1} \qquad \text{with } C_{ij} \in \mathbb{K}^{s \times 1}. \tag{4}$$

However, not every choice of the C_{ij} gives rise to a solution. For obtaining a solution, we substitute the general form (4) into the original system (3) and compare coefficients.

3   Our Programming Model

Given a polynomial relation $p(x_1, \ldots, x_s) = 0$, our loop synthesis procedure generates a first-order C-finite/affine recurrence system (3) with $X_n = (x_1(n) \cdots x_s(n))^\mathsf{T}$, such that $p(x_1(n), \ldots, x_s(n)) = 0$ holds for all $n \in \mathbb{N}$. It is not hard to argue that every first-order C-finite recurrence system corresponds to a loop with simultaneous variable assignments of the following form

$$
\begin{aligned}
&(x_1, \ldots, x_s) \leftarrow (a_1, \ldots, a_s) \\
&\textbf{while } true \textbf{ do} \\
&\qquad (x_1, \ldots, x_s) \leftarrow (p_1(x_1, \ldots, x_s), \ldots, p_s(x_1, \ldots, x_s)) \\
&\textbf{end}
\end{aligned}
\tag{5}
$$

where the program variables $x_1, \ldots, x_s$ are numeric, $a_1, \ldots, a_s$ are (symbolic) constants in $\mathbb{K}$ and $p_1, \ldots, p_s \in \mathbb{K}[x_1, \ldots, x_s]$. For a loop variable x_i, we denote by $x_i(n)$ the value of x_i at the nth loop iteration. That is, we view loop variables x_i as sequences $(x_i(n))_{n=0}^{\infty}$. We call a loop (5) *parameterized* if at least one of $a_1, \ldots, a_s$ is symbolic, and *non-parameterized* otherwise.

Remark 1. Our synthesized loops (5) are non-deterministic, with loop guards being *true*. We synthesize loops such that the given invariant holds for an arbitrary/unbounded number of loop iterations - for example, also for loop guards $n < N$ as in Fig. 1. □

Remark 2. While the output of our synthesis procedure is basically an affine program, note that C-finite recurrences capture a larger class of programs. E.g. the program:

$$(x, y) \leftarrow (0, 0); \ \textbf{while } true \textbf{ do } (x, y) \leftarrow (x + y^2, y + 1) \textbf{ end}$$

can be modeled by a C-finite recurrence system of order 4, which can be turned into an equivalent first-order system of size 6. Thus, to synthesize loops inducing the sequences $(x(n))_{n=0}^{\infty}$ and $(y(n))_{n=0}^{\infty}$, we have to consider recurrence systems of size 6. □

Algebraic Relations and Loop Invariants. Let p be a polynomial in $\mathbb{K}[z_1, \ldots, z_s]$ and let $(x_1(n))_{n=0}^{\infty}, \ldots, (x_s(n))_{n=0}^{\infty}$ be number sequences. We call p an *algebraic relation* for the given sequences if $p(x_1(n), \ldots, x_s(n)) = 0$ for all $n \in \mathbb{N}$. Moreover, p is an algebraic relation for a system of recurrences if it is an algebraic relation for the corresponding sequences. It is immediate that for every algebraic relation p of a recurrence system, $p = 0$ is a *loop invariant* for the corresponding loop (5); that is, $p = 0$ holds before and after every loop iteration.

4   Algebra-Based Loop Synthesis

We now present our approach for synthesizing loops satisfying a given polynomial property (invariant), by using affine loop assignments. We transform the loop synthesis problem into a PCP as described in Sect. 4.1. In Sect. 4.2, we introduce the clause sets of our PCP which precisely describe the solutions for the synthesis of loops, in particular to non-parameterized loops. Proofs of our results can be found in [13]. We note that our approach can naturally be extended to the synthesis of parameterized loops, as discussed in the extended version [13] of our work.

4.1   Setting and Overview of Our Method

Given a constraint $p = 0$ with $p \in \mathbb{K}[x_1, \ldots, x_s, y_1, \ldots, y_s]$, we aim to synthesize a system of C-finite recurrences such that p is an algebraic relation thereof. Intuitively, the values of loop variables $x_1, \ldots, x_s$ are described by the sequences $x_1(n), \ldots, x_s(n)$ for arbitrary n, and $y_1, \ldots, y_s$ correspond to the initial values $x_1(0), \ldots, x_s(0)$. That is, we have a polynomial relation p among loop variables x_i and their initial values y_i, for which we synthesize a loop (5) such that $p = 0$ is a loop invariant of loop (5).

Remark 3. Our approach is not limited to invariants describing relationship between program variables from a single loop iteration. Instead, it naturally extends to relations among different loop iterations. For instance, by considering the relation in Eq. (1), we synthesize a loop computing the Fibonacci sequence.   □

The key step in our work comes with precisely capturing the solution space for our loop synthesis problem as a PCP. Our PCP is divided into the clause sets $\mathcal{C}_{\text{roots}}, \mathcal{C}_{\text{coeff}}, \mathcal{C}_{\text{init}}$ and $\mathcal{C}_{\text{alg}}$, as illustrated in Fig. 2 and explained next. Our PCP implicitly describes a first-order C-finite recurrence system and its corresponding closed form system. The one-to-one correspondence between these two systems is captured by the clause sets $\mathcal{C}_{\text{roots}}, \mathcal{C}_{\text{coeff}}$ and $\mathcal{C}_{\text{init}}$. Intuitively, these constraints mimic the procedure for computing the closed form of a recurrence system (see [15]). The clause set $\mathcal{C}_{\text{alg}}$ interacts between the closed form system and the polynomial constraint $p = 0$, and ensures that p is an algebraic relation of the system. Furthermore, the recurrence system is represented by the matrix B and the vector A of initial values where both consist of symbolic entries. Then a solution of our PCP – which assigns values to those symbolic entries – yields a desired synthesized loop.

In what follows we only consider a unit constraint $p = 0$ as input to our loop synthesis procedure. However, our approach naturally extends to conjunctions of polynomial equality constraints.

Fig. 2. Overview of the PCP describing loop synthesis

4.2 Synthesizing Non-parameterized Loops

We now present our work for synthesizing loops, in particular non-parameterized loops of the form (5). That is, we aim at computing concrete initial values for all program variables. Our implicit representation of the recurrence system is thus of the form

$$X_{n+1} = BX_n \qquad X_0 = A \tag{6}$$

where $B \in \mathbb{K}^{s \times s}$ is invertible and $A \in \mathbb{K}^{s \times 1}$, both containing symbolic entries.

As described in Sect. 2.2, the closed form of (6) is determined by the eigenvalues ω_i of B which we thus need to synthesize. Note that B may contain both symbolic and concrete values. Let us denote the symbolic entries of B by $\boldsymbol{b}$. Since $\mathbb{K}$ is algebraically closed, we know that B has s (not necessarily distinct) eigenvalues. We therefore fix a set of distinct symbolic eigenvalues $\omega_1, \ldots, \omega_t$ together with their multiplicities $m_1, \ldots, m_t$ with $m_i > 0$ for $i = 1, \ldots, t$ such that $\sum_{i=1}^{t} m_i = s$. We call $m_1, \ldots, m_t$ an *integer partition* of s. We next define the clause sets of our PCP.

Root Constraints $\mathcal{C}_{roots}$. The clause set $\mathcal{C}_{roots}$ ensures that B is invertible and that $\omega_1, \ldots, \omega_t$ are distinct symbolic eigenvalues with multiplicities $m_1, \ldots, m_t$. Note that B is invertible if and only if all eigenvalues ω_i are non-zero. Furthermore, since $\mathbb{K}$ is algebraically closed, every polynomial $f(z)$ can be written as the product of linear factors of the form $z - \omega$, with $\omega \in \mathbb{K}$, such that $f(\omega) = 0$. Therefore, the equation

$$\chi_B(z) = (z - \omega_1)^{m_1} \cdots (z - \omega_t)^{m_t}$$

holds for all $z \in \mathbb{K}$, where $\chi_B(z) \in \mathbb{K}[\boldsymbol{\omega}, \boldsymbol{b}, z]$. Bringing everything to one side, we get

$$q_0 + q_1 z + \cdots + q_d z^d = 0,$$

implying that the $q_i \in \mathbb{K}[\boldsymbol{\omega}, \boldsymbol{b}]$ have to be zero. The clause set characterizing the eigenvalues ω_i of B is then

$$\mathcal{C}_{roots} = \{q_0 = 0, \ldots, q_d = 0\} \cup \bigcup_{\substack{i,j=1,\ldots,t \\ i \neq j}} \{\omega_i \neq \omega_j\} \cup \bigcup_{i=1,\ldots,t} \{\omega_i \neq 0\}.$$

Coefficient Constraints C_{coeff}. The fixed symbolic roots/eigenvalues $\omega_1, \ldots, \omega_t$ with multiplicities $m_1, \ldots, m_t$ induce the general closed form solution

$$X_n = \sum_{i=1}^{t} \sum_{j=1}^{m_i} C_{ij} \omega_i^n n^{j-1} \tag{7}$$

where the $C_{ij} \in \mathbb{K}^{s \times 1}$ are column vectors containing symbolic entries. As stated in Sect. 2.2, not every choice of the C_{ij} gives rise to a valid solution. Instead, C_{ij} have to obey certain conditions which are determined by substituting into the original recurrence system of (6):

$$X_{n+1} = \sum_{i=1}^{t} \sum_{j=1}^{m_i} C_{ij} \omega_i^{n+1} (n+1)^{j-1} = \sum_{i=1}^{t} \sum_{j=1}^{m_i} \left(\sum_{k=j}^{m_i} \binom{k-1}{j-1} C_{ik} \omega_i \right) \omega_i^n n^{j-1}$$

$$= B \left(\sum_{i=1}^{t} \sum_{j=1}^{m_i} C_{ij} \omega_i^n n^{j-1} \right) = B X_n$$

Bringing everything to one side yields $X_{n+1} - B X_n = 0$ and thus

$$\sum_{i=1}^{t} \sum_{j=1}^{m_i} \underbrace{\left(\left(\sum_{k=j}^{m_i} \binom{k-1}{j-1} C_{ik} \omega_i \right) - B C_{ij} \right)}_{D_{ij}} \omega_i^n n^{j-1} = 0. \tag{8}$$

Equation (8) holds for all $n \in \mathbb{N}$. By Theorem 1 we then have $D_{ij} = 0$ for all i, j and define

$$C_{\text{coeff}} = \bigcup_{i=1}^{t} \bigcup_{j=1}^{m_i} \text{cstr}(D_{ij}).$$

Initial Values Constraints C_{init}. The constraints C_{init} describe properties of initial values $x_1(0), \ldots, x_s(0)$. We enforce that (7) equals $B^n X_0$, for $n = 0, \ldots, d-1$, where d is the degree of the characteristic polynomial χ_B of B, by

$$C_{\text{init}} = \text{cstr}(M_0) \cup \cdots \cup \text{cstr}(M_{d-1})$$

where $M_i = X_i - B^i X_0$, with X_0 as in (6) and X_i being the right-hand side of (7) where n is replaced by i.

Algebraic Relation Constraints C_{alg}. The constraints C_{alg} are defined to ensure that p is an algebraic relation among the $x_i(n)$. Using (7), the closed forms of the $x_i(n)$ are expressed as

$$x_i(n) = p_{i,1} \omega_1^n + \cdots + p_{i,t} \omega_t^n$$

where the $p_{i,j}$ are polynomials in $\mathbb{K}[n, c]$. By substituting the closed forms and the initial values into the polynomial p, we get

$$p' = p(x_1(n), \ldots, x_s(n), x_1(0), \ldots, x_s(0)) = q_0 + n q_1 + n^2 q_2 + \cdots + n^k q_k \tag{9}$$

where the q_i are of the form

$$w_{i,1}^n u_{i,1} + \cdots + w_{i,\ell}^n u_{i,\ell} \tag{10}$$

with $u_{i,1}, \ldots, u_{i,\ell} \in \mathbb{K}[\boldsymbol{a}, \boldsymbol{c}]$ and $w_{i,1}, \ldots, w_{i,\ell}$ being monomials in $\mathbb{K}[\boldsymbol{\omega}]$.

Proposition 1. *Let p be of the form (9). Then $(p(n))_{n=0}^\infty = 0$ iff $(q_i(n))_{n=0}^\infty = 0$ for $i = 0, \ldots, k$.* $\qquad\square$

As p is an algebraic relation, we have that p' should be 0 for all $n \in \mathbb{N}$. Proposition 1 then implies that the q_i have to be 0 for all $n \in \mathbb{N}$.

Lemma 1. *Let q be of the form (10). Then $q = 0$ for all $n \in \mathbb{N}$ if and only if $q = 0$ for $n \in \{0, \ldots, \ell - 1\}$.* $\qquad\square$

Even though the q_i contain exponential terms in n, it follows from Lemma 1 that the solutions for the q_i being 0 for all $n \in \mathbb{N}$ can be described as a finite set of polynomial equality constraints: Let Q_i^j be the polynomial constraint $w_{i,1}^j u_{i,1} + \cdots + w_{i,\ell}^j u_{i,\ell} = 0$ for q_i of the form (10), and let $\mathcal{C}_i = \{Q_i^0, \ldots, Q_i^{\ell-1}\}$ be the associated clause set. Then the clause set ensuring that p is indeed an algebraic relation is given by

$$\mathcal{C}_{\mathsf{alg}} = \mathcal{C}_0 \cup \cdots \cup \mathcal{C}_k.$$

Remark 4. Observe that Theorem 2 can be applied to (9) directly, as p' satisfies a C-finite recurrence. Then by the closure properties of C-finite recurrences, the upper bound on the order of the recurrence which p' satisfies is given by $r = \sum_{i=0}^k 2^i \ell$. That is, by Theorem 2, we would need to consider p' with $n = 0, \ldots, r-1$, which yields a non-linear system with a degree of at least $r-1$. Note that r depends on 2^i, which stems from the fact that $(n)_{n=0}^\infty$ satisfies a recurrence of order 2, and n^i satisfies therefore a recurrence of order at most 2^i. Thankfully, Proposition 1 allows us to only consider the coefficients of the n^i and therefore lower the size of our constraints. $\qquad\square$

Having defined the clause sets $\mathcal{C}_{\mathsf{roots}}, \mathcal{C}_{\mathsf{coeff}}, \mathcal{C}_{\mathsf{init}}$ and $\mathcal{C}_{\mathsf{alg}}$, we define our PCP as the union of these four clause sets. Note that the matrix B, the vector A, the polynomial p and the multiplicities of the symbolic roots $\boldsymbol{m} = m_1, \ldots, m_t$ uniquely define the clauses discussed above. We define our PCP to be the clause set $\mathcal{C}_{AB}^p(\boldsymbol{m})$ as follows:

$$\mathcal{C}_{AB}^p(\boldsymbol{m}) = \mathcal{C}_{\mathsf{roots}} \cup \mathcal{C}_{\mathsf{init}} \cup \mathcal{C}_{\mathsf{coeff}} \cup \mathcal{C}_{\mathsf{alg}} \tag{11}$$

Recall that $\boldsymbol{a}$ and $\boldsymbol{b}$ are the symbolic entries in the matrices A and B in (6), $\boldsymbol{c}$ are the symbolic entries in the C_{ij} in (7), and $\boldsymbol{\omega}$ are the symbolic eigenvalues of B. We then have $\mathcal{C}_{AB}^p(\boldsymbol{m}) \sqsubseteq \mathbb{K}[\boldsymbol{\omega}, \boldsymbol{a}, \boldsymbol{b}, \boldsymbol{c}]$.

It is not difficult to see that the constraints in $\mathcal{C}_{\mathsf{alg}}$ determine the size of our PCP. As such, the degree and the number of terms in the invariant have a direct impact on the size and the maximum degree of the polynomials in our PCP. Which might not be obvious is that the number of distinct symbolic roots

Input : A polynomial $p \in \mathbb{K}[x_1, \ldots, x_s, y_1, \ldots, y_s]$.
Output: A vector $A \in \mathbb{K}^{s \times 1}$ and a matrix $B \in \mathbb{K}^{s \times s}$ s.t. p is an algebraic
  relation of $X_{n+1} = B X_n$ and $X_0 = A$, if such A and B exist.

```
1 A ← (aᵢ) ∈ 𝕂ˢˣ¹ // symbolic vector
2 B ← (bᵢⱼ) ∈ 𝕂ˢˣˢ // symbolic matrix
3 for m₁,...,mₜ ∈ IntPartitions(s) do
4 │   sat,σ ← Solve(C^p_AB(m₁,...,mₜ))
5 │   if sat then return σ(A),σ(B)
6 end
```

Algorithm 1: Synthesis of a non-parameterized C-finite recurrence system

influences the size and the maximum degree of our PCP. The more distinct roots are considered the higher is the number of terms in (10), and therefore more instances of (10) have to be added to our PCP.

Let $p \in \mathbb{K}[x_1, \ldots, x_s, y_1, \ldots, y_s]$, $B \in \mathbb{K}^{s \times s}$ and $A \in \mathbb{K}^{s \times 1}$, and let $m_1, \ldots, m_t$ be an integer partition of $\deg_\omega(\chi_B(\omega))$. We then get the following theorem:

Theorem 3. *The mapping* $\sigma : \{\omega, a, b, c\} \to \mathbb{K}$ *is a solution of* $C^p_{AB}(m)$ *if and only if* $p(x, x_1(0), \ldots, x_s(0))$ *is an algebraic relation for* $X_{n+1} = \sigma(B) X_n$ *with* $X_0 = \sigma(A)$, *and the eigenvalues of* $\sigma(B)$ *are* $\sigma(\omega_1), \ldots, \sigma(\omega_t)$ *with multiplicities* $m_1, \ldots, m_t$. □

From Theorem 3, we then get Algorithm 1 for synthesizing the C-finite recurrence representation of a non-parameterized loop of the form (5): IntPartitions(s) returns the set of all integer partitions of an integer s; and Solve(C) returns whether the clause set C is satisfiable and a model σ if so. We note that the growth of the number of integer partitions is subexponential, and so is the complexity Algorithm 1. A more precise complexity analysis of Algorithm 1 is the subject of future investigations.

Finally, based on Theorem 3 and on the property that the number of integer partitions of a given integer is finite, we obtain the following result:

Theorem 4. *Algorithm 1 is sound, and complete w.r.t. recurrence systems of size* s. □

The completeness in Theorem 4 is relative to systems of size s which is a consequence of the fact that we synthesize first-order recurrence systems. That is, there exists a system of recurrence equations of order >1 and size s with an algebraic relation $p \in \mathbb{K}[x_1, \ldots, x_s]$, but there exists no first-order system of size s where p is an algebraic relation.

The precise characterization of non-parameterized loops by non-parameterized C-finite recurrence systems implies soundness and completeness of our approach for non-parameterized loops from Theorem 4.

Example 2. We showcase Algorithm 1 by synthesizing a loop from the loop invariant $x = 2y$. That is, the polynomial is given by $p = x - 2y \in \mathbb{K}[x, y]$, and we want to find a recurrence system of the following form

$$\begin{pmatrix} x(n+1) \\ y(n+1) \end{pmatrix} = \begin{pmatrix} b_{11} & b_{12} \\ b_{21} & b_{22} \end{pmatrix} \begin{pmatrix} x(n) \\ y(n) \end{pmatrix} \qquad \begin{pmatrix} x(0) \\ y(0) \end{pmatrix} = \begin{pmatrix} a_1 \\ a_2 \end{pmatrix} \qquad (12)$$

The characteristic polynomial of B is then given by

$$\chi_B(\omega) = \omega^2 - b_{11}\omega - b_{22}\omega - b_{12}b_{21} + b_{11}b_{22}$$

where its roots define the closed form system. Since we cannot determine the actual roots of $\chi_B(\omega)$, we have to fix a set of symbolic roots. The characteristic polynomial has two – not necessarily distinct – roots: Either $\chi_B(\omega)$ has two distinct roots ω_1, ω_2 with multiplicities $m_1 = m_2 = 1$, or a single root ω_1 with multiplicity $m_1 = 2$. Let us consider the latter case. The first clause set we define is C_{roots} for ensuring that B is invertible (i.e. ω_1 is nonzero), and that ω_1 is indeed a root of the characteristic polynomial with multiplicity 2. That is, $\chi_B(\omega) = (\omega - \omega_1)^2$ has to hold for all $\omega \in \mathbb{K}$, and bringing everything to one side yields

$$(b_{11} + b_{22} - 2\omega_1)\omega + b_{12}b_{21} - b_{11}b_{22} + \omega_1^2 = 0$$

We then get the following clause set:

$$C_{roots} = \{b_{11} + b_{22} - 2\omega_1 = 0, b_{12}b_{21} - b_{11}b_{22} + \omega_1^2 = 0, \omega_1 \neq 0\}$$

As we fixed the symbolic roots, the general closed form system is of the form

$$\begin{pmatrix} x(n) \\ y(n) \end{pmatrix} = \begin{pmatrix} c_1 \\ c_2 \end{pmatrix} \omega_1^n + \begin{pmatrix} d_1 \\ d_2 \end{pmatrix} \omega_1^n n \qquad (13)$$

By substituting into the recurrence system we get:

$$\begin{pmatrix} c_1 \\ c_2 \end{pmatrix} \omega_1^{n+1} + \begin{pmatrix} d_1 \\ d_2 \end{pmatrix} \omega_1^{n+1}(n+1) = \begin{pmatrix} b_{11} & b_{12} \\ b_{21} & b_{22} \end{pmatrix} \left(\begin{pmatrix} c_1 \\ c_2 \end{pmatrix} \omega_1^n + \begin{pmatrix} d_1 \\ d_2 \end{pmatrix} \omega_1^n n \right)$$

By further simplifications and re-ordering of terms we then obtain:

$$0 = \begin{pmatrix} c_1\omega_1 + d_1\omega_1 - b_{11}c_1 - b_{12}c_2 \\ c_2\omega_1 + d_2\omega_1 - b_{21}c_1 - b_{22}c_2 \end{pmatrix} \omega_1^n + \begin{pmatrix} d_1\omega_1 - b_{11}d_1 - b_{12}d_2 \\ d_2\omega_1 - b_{21}d_1 - b_{22}d_2 \end{pmatrix} \omega_1^n n$$

Since this equation has to hold for $n \in \mathbb{N}$ we get the following clause set:

$$C_{coeff} = \{c_1\omega_1 + d_1\omega_1 - b_{11}c_1 - b_{12}c_2 = 0, c_2\omega_1 + d_2\omega_1 - b_{21}c_1 - b_{22}c_2 = 0,$$
$$d_1\omega_1 - b_{11}d_1 - b_{12}d_2 = 0, d_2\omega_1 - b_{21}d_1 - b_{22}d_2 = 0\}$$

For defining the relationship between the closed forms and the initial values, we set (13) with $n = i$ to be equal to the ith unrolling of (12) for $i = 0, 1$:

$$\begin{pmatrix} c_1 \\ c_2 \end{pmatrix} = \begin{pmatrix} a_1 \\ a_2 \end{pmatrix} \qquad \begin{pmatrix} c_1 \\ c_2 \end{pmatrix} \omega_1 + \begin{pmatrix} d_1 \\ d_2 \end{pmatrix} \omega_1 = \begin{pmatrix} b_{11} & b_{12} \\ b_{21} & b_{22} \end{pmatrix} \begin{pmatrix} a_1 \\ a_2 \end{pmatrix}$$

The resulting constraints for defining the initial values are then given by

$$\mathcal{C}_{\text{init}} = \{c_1 - a_1 = 0, c_1\omega_1 + d_1\omega_1 - b_{11}a_1 - b_{12}a_2 = 0,$$
$$c_2 - a_2 = 0, c_2\omega_1 + d_2\omega_1 - b_{21}a_1 - b_{22}a_2 = 0\}.$$

Eventually, we want to restrict the solutions such that $x - 2y = 0$ is an algebraic relation for our recurrence system. That is, by substituting the closed forms into the expression $x(n) - 2y(n) = 0$ we get

$$0 = x(n) - 2y(n) = c_1\omega_1^n + d_1\omega_1^n n - 2(c_2\omega_1^n + d_2\omega_1^n n)$$
$$= \underbrace{(c_1 - 2c_2)\,\omega_1^n}_{q_0} + \underbrace{((d_1 - 2d_2)\,\omega_1^n)\,n}_{q_1}$$

where q_0 and q_1 have to be 0 since the above equation has to hold for all $n \in \mathbb{N}$. Then, by applying Lemma 1 to q_0 and q_1, we get the following clauses:

$$\mathcal{C}_{\text{alg}} = \{c_1 - 2c_2 = 0, d_1 - 2d_2 = 0\}$$

Our PCP is then the union of $\mathcal{C}_{\text{roots}}$, $\mathcal{C}_{\text{coeff}}$, $\mathcal{C}_{\text{init}}$ and $\mathcal{C}_{\text{alg}}$. Two possible solutions for our PCP, and therefore of the synthesis problem, are given by the following loops:

```
(x, y) ← (2, 1)
while true do
    (x, y) ← (x + 2, y + 1)
end
```

```
(x, y) ← (2, 1)
while true do
    (x, y) ← (2x, 2y)
end
```

Note that both loops above have mutually independent affine updates. Yet, the second one induces geometric sequences and requires handling exponentials of 2^n. □

Remark 5. Our approach to synthesis extends to parameterized loops. That is, instead of synthesizing concrete initial values for all program variables, it is possible to keep them symbolic. Hence, the synthesized loops satisfy the given invariant for all possible initial values for those particular variables; Table 2 lists five such synthesized loops. Due to the page limit, we refer to [13] for details on synthesizing parameterized loops.

5   Automating Algebra-Based Loop Synthesis

For automating Algorithm 1 for loop synthesis, the challenging task is to find solutions for our PCPs describing large systems of polynomial constraints with many variables and high polynomial degrees (11). We propose the following (partial) solutions for optimizing and exploring the PCP solution space.

Handling Large Recurrence Templates. It is obvious that the higher the number of program variables in the loop to be synthesized is, the higher is the number of variables in the PCP of Algorithm 1. To face this increase of complexity we implemented an iterative search for PCP solutions in the sense that we preset certain values of the coefficient matrix B in (6). In particular, we start by looking for PCP solutions where the coefficient matrix B is unit upper triangular. If no such solution is found, we consider B to be an upper triangular matrix and further to be full symbolic matrix without preset values. This way we first construct simpler PCPs (in terms of the number of variables) and generalize step by step, if needed. This iterative approach can also be used to the search for only integer PCP solutions by imposing/presetting B to contain only integer-valued.

Synthesizing a (unit) upper triangular coefficient matrix B yields a loop where its loop variables are not mutually dependent on each other. We note that such a pattern is a very common programming paradigm – all benchmarks from Table 1 satisfy such a pattern. Yet, as a consequence of restricting the shape of B, the order of the variables in the recurrence system matters. That is, we have to consider all possible variable permutations for ensuring completeness w.r.t. (unit) upper triangular matrices.

Handling Large Polynomial Degrees. The main source of polynomials with high degrees in the PCP of Algorithm 1 stems from the clause set C_{alg}, i.e. constraints of the form (10) for $n \in \{0, \ldots, \ell-1\}$. For any PCP solution σ in line 4 of Algorithm 1, we have $\sigma(w_1)^n \sigma(u_1) + \cdots + \sigma(w_\ell)^n \sigma(u_\ell) = 0$ for $n \in \{0, \ldots, \ell-1\}$, which yields the following system of linear equations:

$$
\boldsymbol{W u} = \begin{bmatrix}
1 & 1 & 1 & \cdots & 1 \\
\sigma(w_1) & \sigma(w_2) & \sigma(w_3) & \cdots & \sigma(w_\ell) \\
\sigma(w_1)^2 & \sigma(w_2)^2 & \sigma(w_3)^2 & \cdots & \sigma(w_\ell)^2 \\
\vdots & \vdots & \vdots & \ddots & \vdots \\
\sigma(w_1)^{\ell-1} & \sigma(w_2)^{\ell-1} & \sigma(w_3)^{\ell-1} & \cdots & \sigma(w_\ell)^{\ell-1}
\end{bmatrix}
\begin{bmatrix}
\sigma(u_1) \\
\sigma(u_2) \\
\sigma(u_3) \\
\vdots \\
\sigma(u_\ell)
\end{bmatrix} = 0 \qquad (14)
$$

where $W \in \mathbb{K}^{\ell \times \ell}$ is a Vandermonde matrix and $\boldsymbol{u} \in \mathbb{K}^\ell$. Suppose our assignment σ in line 4 of Algorithm 1 is such that $\sigma(w_i) \neq \sigma(w_j)$ for $i \neq j$; if this is not the case we can always create a smaller system of the form (14) by collecting terms. As $\sigma(w_i) \neq \sigma(w_j)$ for $i \neq j$, we derive that W is invertible. Then, it follows by Cramer's rule, that $\sigma(u_i) = 0$ for all $i \in \{1, \ldots, \ell\}$. Based on this observation, we propose Algorithm 2 for solving constraints of the form (10). For simplicity, we only present the case where we have a single constraint of the form (10); Algorithm 2 however naturally extends to multiple such constraints.

Intuitively, Step 1 of Algorithm 2 finds a model σ such that each u_i becomes zero, which makes the values of the w_i irrelevant. To this end, we compute maximum satisfiability of our constraints C using the MaxSAT approach of [19]. If this is not possible, we continue with a partition $\mathcal{I} = \{I_1, \ldots, I_\ell\}$ of the set of indices $\{1, \ldots, \ell\}$. Then $\mathcal{I}$ induces a system of linear equations of the form (14) of size ℓ which is specified in Step 2 of the algorithm. If the PCP is satisfiable (Step 3 of Algorithm 2), then we have found an assignment σ which satisfies $\mathcal{P}$

Input   : An arbitrary satisfiable PCP $\mathcal{P}$ and a constraint C of the form (10).
Output: A model σ for the polynomial constraint problem $\mathcal{P} \cup \{C\}$.

1. Call MaxSAT to compute maximum satisfiability with soft constraints $u_1 = 0, \dots, u_\ell = 0$ and hard constraints from $\mathcal{P}$, and let σ be the resulting assignment. If all soft constraints are satisfied, then **return** σ. Otherwise, let $\mathcal{I}$ be the partition such that for every set of indices $I \in \mathcal{I}$ we have $\sigma(w_i) = \sigma(w_j)$ for $i, j \in I$.
2. Construct a constraint problem $\mathcal{Q}$ as follows:
   (a) For each $I \in \mathcal{I}$, add constraints $w_i = w_j$ for $i, j \in I$.
   (b) For each distinct pair $I, J \in \mathcal{I}$, add a constraint $w_i \neq w_j$ for some $i \in I$ and $j \in J$.
   (c) For each $I \in \mathcal{I}$, add a constraint $\sum_{i \in I} u_i = 0$.
3. If $\mathcal{P} \cup \mathcal{Q}$ is satisfiable with model σ, then **return** σ. Otherwise, learn a new partition $\mathcal{I}$ and go to Step 2.

Algorithm 2: Solving C-finite constraints

and the system of the form (14) for C. If the given PCP is unsatisfiable, then we learn a new partition by making use of the unsatisfiable core and go back to Step 2 of Algorithm 2.

6   Implementation and Experiments

Our approach to algebra-based loop synthesis is implemented in the tool Absynth, which consists of about 1800 lines of Julia code and is available at https://github.com/ahumenberger/Absynth.jl. Inputs to Absynth are conjunctions of polynomial equality constraints, representing a loop invariant. As a default result, Absynth derives a program that is partially correct with respect to the given invariant (Table 1). In addition, Absynth can also be used to derive number sequences for which the given invariant is an algebraic relation (Table 2).

Loop synthesis in Absynth is reduced to solving PCPs. These PCPs are currently expressed in the quantifier-free fragment of non-linear real arithmetic (QF_NRA). We used Absynth in conjunction with the SMT solvers Yices [7] (version 2.6.1) and Z3 [6] (version 4.8.6) for solving the PCPs and therefore synthesizing loops. For instance, Figs. 1b–c and Example 2 are synthesized automatically using Absynth.

As PCPs in Absynth are restricted to QF_NRA, the implementation of Algorithm 1 within Absynth does not yet find solutions containing non-real algebraic numbers. In our loop synthesis experiments we did not encounter instances where non-real algebraic numbers are necessary. The synthesis of recurrences, however, often requires reasoning about non-real algebraic numbers such as the so-called Perrin numbers $p(n)$ defined via $p(n + 3) = p(n + 1) + p(n)$ and satisfying the relation $p(n)^3 - 3p(n)p(2n) + 2p(3n) = 6$. Going beyond the QF_NRA fragment, as well as considering finite domains (bitvectors/bounded integers) within Absynth is a next step to investigate.

Tables 1–2 summarize our experimental results. The experiments were performed on a machine with a 2.9 GHz Intel Core i5 and 16 GB LPDDR3 RAM, and for each instance a timeout of 60 s was set. The results are given in milliseconds, and only include the time needed for solving the constraint problem as the time needed for constructing the constraints is neglectable. In Table 1, the columns `Yices` and `Z3` correspond to the results where the respective solver is called as an external program with and SMTLIB 2.0 file as input; column `Z3*` shows the results where our improved, direct `Absynth` interface (C++ API) was used to call Z3. Finally, column `Z3* + Alg2` depicts the results for Algorithm 2 with `Z3*` as backend solver.

Loop Synthesis. Our benchmark set for loop synthesis (Table 1) consists of invariants for loops from the invariant generation literature. Note that the benchmarks `cubes` and `double2` in Table 1 are those from Fig. 1 and Example 2, respectively. A further presentation of a selected set of our benchmarks can be found in the extended version of our work [13].

The columns UN and UP in Table 1 show the results where the coefficient matrix B is restricted to be unit upper triangular and upper triangular respectively. FU indicates that no restriction on B was set. Note that the running time of Algorithm 1 heavily depends on the order of which the integer partitions and the variable permutations are traversed. Therefore, in order to get comparable results, we fixed the integer partition and the variable permutation. That is, for each instance, we enforced that B in (6) has just a single eigenvalue, and we fixed a variable ordering where we know that there exists a solution with an unitriangular matrix B. Hence, there exists at least one solution which all cases – UN, UP and FU – have in common. Furthermore, for each instance we added constraints for avoiding trivial solutions, i.e. loops inducing constant sequences, and used Algorithm 2 to further reduce our search space.

Recurrence Synthesis. In addition to loop synthesis, we also conducted experiments with respect to synthesizing recurrence equations (Table 2). We took algebraic relations from [16] and synthesized recurrence equations satisfying the given relations. None of the instances could be solved by `Yices` or Z3, but only by `Z3* + Alg2`. In contrast to loop synthesis, the synthesis of recurrence equations often requires reasoning about non-real algebraic numbers which does not fall into the fragment of non-linear real arithmetic. Hence, for synthesizing recurrence equations we plan to integrate a solver which is able to reason about the whole set of algebraic numbers.

7   Related Work

Synthesis. To the best of our knowledge, existing synthesis approaches are restricted to linear invariants, see e.g. [24], whereas our work supports loop synthesis from non-linear polynomial properties. Counterexample-guided synthesis (CEGIS) [3,8,20,23] uses input-output examples satisfying a specification

Table 1. Absynth for loop synthesis (results in milliseconds)

Instance	S	I	D	C	Yices			Z3			Z3*			Z3* + Alg2		
					UN	UP	FU	UN	UP	FU	UN	UP	FU	UN	UP	FU
add1*	5	1	5	173	932	921	-	117	-	-	22	726	-	7	2416	-
add2*	5	1	5	173	959	861	-	115	-	-	22	109	-	7	2323	-
cubes	5	3	6	94	-	-	-	116	114	-	18	496	575	87	-	-
double1	3	1	4	29	114	112	3882	113	111	113	13	21	63	3	5	120
double2	3	1	3	24	110	106	1665	115	106	115	13	18	40	2	5	21
eucliddiv*	5	1	5	185	213	537	-	114	115	-	19	73	-	10	2554	-
intcbrt*	5	2	12	262	-	-	-	117	116	-	22	83	469	89	-	-
intsqrt1	4	2	6	53	-	-	-	113	108	114	15	19	-	35	81	-
intsqrt2*	4	1	6	104	105	1164	-	113	111	115	15	27	37	3	9	-
petter1	3	1	4	29	112	116	-	114	113	113	15	18	32	15	32	3629
square	3	1	4	29	112	112	-	112	114	117	13	17	26	10	29	592
dblsquare	3	1	4	30	109	105	-	105	105	110	12	17	26	14	31	-
sum1	4	2	6	53	617	-	-	108	112	113	17	24	99	39	250	-
sum2	5	3	6	82	-	-	-	220	112	-	20	516	-	60	-	-

S size of the recurrence system
I number of polynomial invariants
D maximum monomial degree of constraints
C number of constraints
* parameterized system
- timeout (60 s)

Table 2. Absynth for recurrence synthesis (results in milliseconds)

Instance	O	Yices	Z3	Z3*	Z3* + Alg2
fibonacci1	2	-	-	-	324
fibonacci2	2	-	-	-	22
example28	2	-	-	-	41
ex1	2	-	-	-	27
ex2	2	-	-	-	20
ex3	2	-	-	-	451

O order of recurrence
- timeout (60 s)

S to synthesize a candidate program P that is consistent with the given inputs. Correctness of the candidate program P with respect to S is then checked using verification approaches, in particular using SMT-based reasoning. If verification fails, a counterexample is generated as an input to P that violates S. This counterexample is then used in conjunction with the previous set of input-outputs to revise synthesis and generate a new candidate program P. Unlike these methods, input specifications to our approach are relational (invariant) properties describing all, potentially infinite input-output examples of interest. Hence, we do not rely on interactive refinement of our input but work with a precise characterization of the set of input-output values of the program to be synthesized. Similarly to sketches [20,23], we consider loop templates restricting the search for solutions to synthesis. Yet, our templates support non-linear arithmetic (and hence multiplication), which is not yet the case in [8,20]. We precisely characterize the set of all programs satisfying our input specification, and as such, our approach does not exploit learning to refine program candidates. On the other hand, our programming model is more restricted than [8,20] in various aspects: we only handle simple loops and only consider numeric data types and operations.

The programming by example approach of [9] learns programs from input-output examples and relies on lightweight interaction to refine the specification of programs to be specified. The approach has further been extended in [14] with machine learning, allowing to learn programs from just one (or even none) input-output example by using a simple supervised learning setup. Program synthesis from input-output examples is shown to be successful for recursive programs [1], yet synthesizing loops and handling non-linear arithmetic is not yet supported by this line of research. Our work does not learn programs from observed input-output examples, but uses loop invariants to fully characterize the intended behavior of the program to be synthesized. We precisely characterize the solution space of loops to be synthesized by a system of algebraic recurrences, without using statistical models supporting machine learning.

A related approach to our work is given in [5], where a fixed-point implementation for an approximated real-valued polynomial specification is presented, by combining genetic programming with abstract interpretation to estimate and refine the (floating-point) error bound of the inferred fixed-point implementation. While the underlying abstract interpreter is precise for linear expressions, precision of the synthesis is lost for non-linear arithmetic. Unlike [5], we consider polynomial specification in the abstract algebra of real-closed fields and do not address challenges rising from machine reals.

Algebraic Reasoning. Compared to works on invariant generation [11,12,17,22], the only common aspect between these works and our synthesis method is the use of linear recurrences to capture the functional behavior of program loops. Yet, our work is conceptually different from [11,12,17,22], as we reverse engineer invariant generation and do not rely on the ideal structure/Zariski closure of polynomial invariants. We do not use ideal theory nor Gröbner bases computation to generate invariants from loops; rather, we generate loops from invariants by formulating and solving PCPs.

8   Conclusions

We proposed a syntax-guided synthesis procedure for synthesizing loops over affine assignments from polynomial invariants. We consider loop templates and use reasoning over recurrence equations modeling the loop behavior. The key ingredient of our work comes with translating the loop synthesis problem into a polynomial constraint problem and showing that this constraint problem precisely captures all solutions to the loop synthesis problem. Additional heuristics for solving our constraints have been also implemented in our new tool `Absynth` for loop synthesis.

Directions for future work include a complexity analysis of our algorithm; further investigating the properties of our constraint problems for improving the scalability of our procedure; generalizing our approach to multi-path loops and inequality invariants; restricting the solution space to integers or bounded domains; extending `Absynth` with reasoning support for arbitrary algebraic numbers; and understanding and encoding the best optimization measures for loop synthesis in the context of strength reduction and other program optimization approaches.

Acknowledgments. We thank Sumit Gulwani and Manuel Kauers for valuable discussions on ideas leading to this work. We acknowledge funding from the ERC Starting Grant SYMCAR 639270, the ERC Proof of Concept Grant SYMELS 842066, the Wallenberg Academy Fellowship TheProSE, and the Austrian FWF research project W1255-N23.

References

1. Albarghouthi, A., Gulwani, S., Kincaid, Z.: Recursive program synthesis. In: Sharygina, N., Veith, H. (eds.) CAV 2013. LNCS, vol. 8044, pp. 934–950. Springer, Heidelberg (2013). https://doi.org/10.1007/978-3-642-39799-8_67
2. Alur, R., et al.: Syntax-guided synthesis. In: Dependable Software Systems Engineering, vol. 40, pp. 1–25. IOS Press (2015)
3. Alur, R., Singh, R., Fisman, D., Solar-Lezama, A.: Search-based program synthesis. Commun. ACM **61**(12), 84–93 (2018)
4. Cooper, K.D., Simpson, L.T., Vick, C.A.: Operator strength reduction. ACM Trans. Program. Lang. Syst. **23**(5), 603–625 (2001)
5. Darulova, E., Kuncak, V., Majumdar, R., Saha, I.: Synthesis of fixed-point programs. In: EMSOFT, pp. 22:1–22:10 (2013)
6. de Moura, L., Bjørner, N.: Z3: an efficient SMT solver. In: Ramakrishnan, C.R., Rehof, J. (eds.) TACAS 2008. LNCS, vol. 4963, pp. 337–340. Springer, Heidelberg (2008). https://doi.org/10.1007/978-3-540-78800-3_24
7. Dutertre, B.: Yices 2.2. In: Biere, A., Bloem, R. (eds.) CAV 2014. LNCS, vol. 8559, pp. 737–744. Springer, Cham (2014). https://doi.org/10.1007/978-3-319-08867-9_49
8. Feng, Y., Martins, R., Bastani, O., Dillig, I.: Program synthesis using conflict-driven learning. In: PLDI, pp. 420–435 (2018)
9. Gulwani, S.: Automating string processing in spreadsheets using input-output examples. In: POPL, pp. 317–330 (2011)
10. Gulwani, S.: Programming by examples: applications, algorithms, and ambiguity resolution. In: IJCAR, pp. 9–14 (2016)
11. Hrushovski, E., Ouaknine, J., Pouly, A., Worrell, J.: Polynomial invariants for affine programs. In: LICS, pp. 530–539. ACM (2018)
12. Humenberger, A., Jaroschek, M., Kovács, L.: Automated generation of non-linear loop invariants utilizing hypergeometric sequences. In: ISSAC, pp. 221–228. ACM (2017)
13. Humenberger, A., Kovács, L.: Algebra-based Loop Synthesis (2020). arXiv:2004.11787

14. Kalyan, A., Mohta, A., Polozov, O., Batra, D., Jain, P., Gulwani, S.: Neural-guided deductive search for real-time program synthesis from examples. In: ICLR (2018)
15. Kauers, M., Paule, P.: The Concrete Tetrahedron - Symbolic Sums, Recurrence Equations, Generating Functions, Asymptotic Estimates. Texts & Monographs in Symbolic Computation. Springer, Vienna (2011). https://doi.org/10.1007/978-3-7091-0445-3
16. Kauers, M., Zimmermann, B.: Computing the algebraic relations of C-finite sequences and multisequences. J. Symb. Comput. **43**(11), 787–803 (2008)
17. Kincaid, Z., Cyphert, J., Breck, J., Reps, T.W.: Non-linear reasoning for invariant synthesis. PACMPL **2**(POPL), 541–5433 (2018)
18. Leino, K.R.M.: Accessible software verification with Dafny. IEEE Softw. **34**(6), 94–97 (2017)
19. Narodytska, N., Bacchus, F.: Maximum satisfiability using core-guided MaxSat resolution. In: AAAI, pp. 2717–2723 (2014)
20. Nye, M., Hewitt, L., Tenenbaum, J., Solar-Lezama, A.: Learning to infer program sketches. In: ICML, pp. 4861–4870 (2019). http://proceedings.mlr.press/v97/nye19a.html
21. van der Put, M., Singer, M.F.: Galois Theory of Difference Equations. LNM, vol. 1666. Springer, Heidelberg (1997). https://doi.org/10.1007/BFb0096118
22. Rodríguez-Carbonell, E., Kapur, D.: Generating all polynomial invariants in simple loops. J. Symb. Comput. **42**(4), 443–476 (2007)
23. Solar-Lezama, A.: The sketching approach to program synthesis. In: Hu, Z. (ed.) APLAS 2009. LNCS, vol. 5904, pp. 4–13. Springer, Heidelberg (2009). https://doi.org/10.1007/978-3-642-10672-9_3
24. Srivastava, S., Gulwani, S., Foster, J.S.: From program verification to program synthesis. In: POPL, pp. 313–326 (2010)

Author Index

Printed in the United States
By Bookmasters